What Is E

PHILOSOPHICAL TRADITIONS

General Editor
Amélie Oksenberg Rorty

1. John M. Rist (editor), *The Stoics*
2. Amélie Oksenberg Rorty (editor), *Essays on Aristotle's Ethics*
3. Myles Burnyeat (editor), *The Skeptical Tradition*
4. Amélie Oksenberg Rorty (editor), *Essays on Descartes's* Meditations
5. Richard Schacht (editor), *Nietzsche, Genealogy, Morality: Essays on Nietzsche's* Genealogy of Morals
6. Amélie Oksenberg Rorty (editor), *Essays on Aristotle's* Rhetoric
7. James Schmidt (editor), *What Is Enlightenment? Eighteenth-Century Answers and Twentieth-Century Questions*
8. Gareth Matthews (editor), *The Augustinian Tradition*

What Is Enlightenment?

Eighteenth-Century Answers and Twentieth-Century Questions

EDITED BY
James Schmidt

UNIVERSITY OF CALIFORNIA PRESS
Berkeley Los Angeles London

University of California Press
Berkeley and Los Angeles, California

University of California Press
London, England

Library of Congress Cataloging-in-Publication Data

What is Enlightenment? : eighteenth-century answers and twentieth-century questions / edited by James Schmidt.
p. cm. — (Philosophical traditions ; 7)
Includes bibliographical references and index.
ISBN 0-520-20226-0 (pbk. : alk. paper)
1. Enlightenment. I. Schmidt, James. II. Series.
B802.W47 1996
190—dc20 95-46975
CIP

Printed in the United States of America

11 10 09 08 07 06 05 04
12 11 10 9 8 7 6 5 4 3

The paper used in this publication meets the minimum requirements of ANSI/NISO Z39.48-1992 (R 1997) (*Permanence of Paper*). ♾

CONTENTS

PREFACE / *ix*

Introduction: What Is Enlightenment?
A Question, Its Context, and Some Consequences / *1*
James Schmidt

Part I. THE EIGHTEENTH-CENTURY DEBATE / *45*

1. The Question and Some Answers / *47*

What Is to Be Done toward the Enlightenment of the Citizenry? (1783) / *49*
Johann Karl Möhsen

On the Question: What Is Enlightenment? (1784) / *53*
Moses Mendelssohn

An Answer to the Question: What Is Enlightenment? (1784) / *58*
Immanuel Kant

Thoughts on Enlightenment (1784) / *65*
Karl Leonhard Reinhold

A Couple of Gold Nuggets, from the . . . Wastepaper,
or Six Answers to Six Questions (1789) / *78*
Christoph Martin Wieland

2. The Public Use of Reason / *85*

On Freedom of Thought and of the Press: For Princes,
Ministers, and Writers (1784) / *87*
Ernst Ferdinand Klein

On Freedom of the Press and Its Limits: For Consideration by Rulers, Censors, and Writers (1787) / *97*
Carl Friedrich Bahrdt

Publicity (1792) / *114*
Friedrich Karl von Moser

Reclamation of the Freedom of Thought from the Princes of Europe, Who Have Oppressed It Until Now (1793) / *119*
Johann Gottlieb Fichte

3. Faith and Enlightenment / *143*

Letter to Christian Jacob Kraus (18 December 1784) / *145*
Johann Georg Hamann

Metacritique on the Purism of Reason (1784) / *154*
Johann Georg Hamann

On Enlightenment: Is It and Could It Be Dangerous to the State, to Religion, or Dangerous in General? A Word to Be Heeded by Princes, Statesmen, and Clergy (1788) / *168*
Andreas Riem

4. The Politics of Enlightenment / *189*

Something Lessing Said: A Commentary on *Journeys of the Popes* (1782) / *191*
Friedrich Heinrich Jacobi

True and False Political Enlightenment (1792) / *212*
Friedrich Karl von Moser

On the Influence of Enlightenment on Revolutions (1794) / *217*
Johann Heinrich Tieftrunk

Does Enlightenment Cause Revolutions? (1795) / *225*
Johann Adam Bergk

Part II. HISTORICAL REFLECTIONS / *233*

The Berlin Wednesday Society / *235*
Günter Birtsch

The Subversive Kant: The Vocabulary of "Public" and "Publicity" / *253*
John Christian Laursen

On Enlightenment for the Common Man / *270*
Jonathan B. Knudsen

Modern Culture Comes of Age: Hamann versus Kant on the Root Metaphor of Enlightenment / *291*
Garrett Green

Jacobi's Critique of the Enlightenment / *306*
Dale E. Snow

Early Romanticism and the *Aufklärung* / *317*
Frederick C. Beiser

Progress: Ideas, Skepticism, and Critique—The Heritage of the Enlightenment / *330*
Rudolph Vierhaus

Part III. TWENTIETH-CENTURY QUESTIONS / *343*

What Is Enlightenment? / *345*
Rüdiger Bittner

Reason Against Itself: Some Remarks on Enlightenment / *359*
Max Horkheimer

What Is Enlightened Thinking? / *368*
Georg Picht

What Is Critique? / *382*
Michel Foucault

The Unity of Reason in the Diversity of Its Voices / *399*
Jürgen Habermas

The Battle of Reason with the Imagination / *426*
Hartmut Böhme and Gernot Böhme

The Failure of Kant's Imagination / *453*
Jane Kneller

The Gender of Enlightenment / *471*
Robin May Schott

Autonomy, Individuality, and Self-Determination / *488*
Lewis Hinchman

Enlightened Cosmopolitanism: The Political Perspective of the Kantian "Sublime" / *517*
Kevin Paul Geiman

CONTRIBUTORS TO PARTS II AND III / *533*

SELECT BIBLIOGRAPHY / *537*

INDEX / *555*

PREFACE

Late in 1783 an article that appeared in a Berlin journal asked, almost in passing, "What is enlightenment?" For the next decade a debate on the nature and limits of enlightenment raged in pamphlets and journals. In the process, the ideals and aspirations of the Enlightenment were subjected to a scrutiny so thorough it is only a slight exaggeration to suggest that subsequent critics have raised few points that were not already considered in the 1780s.

Only one of these essays—Immanuel Kant's "An Answer to the Question: What Is Enlightenment?"—is well known in the English-speaking world. This book begins the long-overdue task of acquainting readers with some of the others. Part I provides a selection of some of the more important contributions to the eighteenth-century German discussion of the question "What is enlightenment?" Part II brings together a number of recent essays on the historical context in which this discussion took place and on those who participated in the debate. The essays gathered in Part III reflect on the significance of these eighteenth-century answers for our own time. In this prefatory note, I would like to sketch the general rationale behind the selection, editing, and translation of the essays that constitute this volume and to offer some thanks to those who aided in bringing this book to completion.

While the Enlightenment was a European event, the debate on the question "What is enlightenment?" was uniquely German. For reasons that defy easy explanation, neither French *philosophes* nor Scottish moralists (to name only the two most likely parties) were as concerned as their German-speaking colleagues with the question of what enlightenment was. In selecting essays from the German discussion of the question, I have been guided both by my own sense of what the debate was about (a subject I discuss at some length in the introduction) and by the choices of those who have gone before me. Norbert Hinske and Michael Albrecht's *Was ist Aufklärung? Beiträge aus der Berlinischen Monatsschrift* (Darmstadt: Wissenschaftliche Buchgesellschaft, 1973) reprinted a wide-ranging selection of articles from the journal that first launched the discussion of the question "What is enlightenment?" It was quickly followed by Ehrard Bahr's *Was ist Aufklärung? Thesen und Definitionen* (Stuttgart: Reclam, 1974), which brought together a few of the more important contributions from other journals, and by Zwi Batscha's selection of essays on the subsequent discussion of freedom of the press, *Aufklärung und Gedankenfreiheit* (Frankfurt: Suhrkamp, 1977). Mention should also be made of French and Spanish translations of some of these essays—Jean Mondot, *Qu'est-ce que les Lumières?* (Saint-Étienne: Publications de l'Université de Saint-Étienne, 1991) and Agapito Maestre and Jose Romagosa, *¿Qué es Ilustración?* (Madrid: Technos, 1988). While these collections differ in their choices and focus, there are a few common points of contact.

Since many of the leading intellectuals in Germany participated in the discussion of the question "What is enlightenment?" it is difficult for any collection to ignore the contributions of Kant, Moses Mendelssohn, Johann Georg Hamann, Friedrich Heinrich Jacobi, and Christoph Martin Wieland. The debate was also joined by writers such as Friedrich Karl von Moser, Carl Bahrdt, and Karl Leonhard Reinhold who, while well known in eighteenth-century Germany, may not be familiar to present-day readers. Andreas Riem presents a unique case: the notoriety he gained in the late eighteenth century rests largely on his pamphlet *Über Aufklärung*, one of the most widely read contributions to the debate. Other contributions merit inclusion because of their historical importance; for example, Johann Karl Möhsen's lecture was instrumental in launching the debate in the first place. Certain essays by obscure authors who remained obscure (such as Johann Heinrich Tieftrunk and Adam Bergk) are included because they develop lines of argument that help us to see the broader implications of the question. Finally, Johann Gottlieb Fichte's essay on freedom of thought, while not directly addressing the question "What is enlightenment?" is a major contribution to discussion of freedom of the press to which the debate on enlightenment led.

Despite the labors of German historians over the last several decades, the German Enlightenment remains, at best, a rumor in much of the English-speaking world. It is worth remembering that Berlin was one of the more important intellectual centers in eighteenth-century Europe and that the debate on the nature of enlightenment was born out of the sense that it was time to take stock of what had been accomplished in the way of enlightenment in Prussia and what the prospects might be for a further enlightenment, both in Prussia and beyond. The essays in the second part of this book explore the historical context that gave rise to this stock taking. Günter Birtsch provides an account of the Berlin Wednesday Society, that remarkable group of civil servants and men of letters who inaugurated discussion of the question; Jonathan Knudsen examines discussions of the notion of "popular enlightenment"; Frederick C. Beiser traces the relationship between the Enlightenment and romanticism; and Rudolph Vierhaus analyzes the Enlightenment's faith in, and skepticism about, progress. John Christian Laursen's account of Kant's notion of publicity, Dale Snow's discussion of Jacobi's political thought, and Garrett Green's examination of Hamann's critique of the Enlightenment reflect on the positions of some of the more important participants in the debate.

The answers that the eighteenth century gave to the question "What is enlightenment?" are not, however, of historical interest only. The Enlightenment stands at the threshold of the modern age, and these answers inevitably tell us a good deal about how we make sense of our own situation. The essays in the last part of this book attempt, from a variety of perspectives, to raise questions about the eighteenth century's answers. Emphasis here has been placed on essays that are either unpublished, untranslated, or otherwise not readily available. Rüdiger Bittner, Max Horkheimer, Michel Foucault, and Jürgen Habermas pose some general questions about the current status of the "project of enlightenment." Georg Picht explores the theological ramifications of enlightened thinking. Hartmut and Gernot Böhme and Jane Kneller investigate the tension between reason and imagination in Kant's thought. Robin May Schott and Lewis Hinchman scrutinize the Enlightenment's ideal of "autonomy." Finally, Kevin Paul Geiman offers some reflections on the cosmopolitan hopes that informed Kant's writings on politics.

The problem of the relationship of historical texts to present-day concerns comes to the fore in a particularly forceful way in the act of translation. This is not the place for an extended consideration of the hermeneutic questions that surround every attempt to move texts from one language and one age into another. It may suffice to lay out a few of the general considerations that guided this work. Ideally (and, of course, in translation more than in any other human endeavor, things will never be ideal) there should be a way of translating these eighteenth-century German texts that respects both the historical distance that separates us from the Enlightenment and the ties of tradition and usage that still bind us to it. In striking this balance between anachronism and archaism, it helps to remember that the writers of the German Enlightenment read English books and shared a certain terminology with their counterparts in other parts of Europe. Hence, on encountering the term *moralische Gefühle* it might be worth remembering that the writer was likely thinking of what Scottish moralists called "moral sentiments"—not "moral feelings"—or that, in the eighteenth century, a *Menschenrecht* was a "Right of Man," not a "human right." But other terms that eighteenth-century German and English once shared are now lost to translators. At the close of the eighteenth century, when John Richardson translated Kant's famous definition of Enlightenment—"der Ausgang des Menschen aus seiner selbstverschuldeten Unmündigkeit"—the English "nonage" provided him with the perfect term for capturing what Kant meant by *Unmündigkeit.* While we have kept "dotage," we no longer have "nonage," so the translator must beat a retreat to "immaturity." But other, less opaque archaisms are worth preserving, if only to drive home that these are not texts from our own time. Thus in eighteenth-century English as in eighteenth-century German, one could render a superior "eye service" as well as "lip service," and there is a whole lexicon of now-forgotten terms for insulting clergy that freethinking English shared with freethinking Germans. It is probably worth a few footnotes to remind readers of what our language once could do.

Eighteenth-century German was still, in many ways, in flux, and philosophical and political terminology was by no means settled. Vocabularies differ radically from author to author. Bergk, Tieftrunk, and Fichte made extensive use of the terminology of Kant's critical philosophy, and conventions for translating that terminology are reasonably well established. But Mendelssohn and Reinhold drew heavily on the vocabulary of Christian Wolff, and since so little Wolff has been translated into English the translator must take a detour from Wolff's German writings to his Latin writings and from there try to find a way back to English. In dealing with Hamann, who once wrote that "to speak is to translate—from the tongue of angels into the tongue of men," it is never clear what language he is speaking. Writers' styles differ, as do their intended audiences. Wieland tried to be witty (and, at times, naughty), Bahrdt's discussion of freedom of the press drew on the vocabulary of natural law theories, the essays by Riem and Jacobi seethe with anger, and Ernst Ferdinand Klein's essay takes the form of an extended impersonation of Frederick the Great. These differences in terminology and style are worth preserving since they drive home rather powerfully the differences in voices that were a central part of that great cosmopolitan argument that was the Enlightenment.

Since the editor and translators worked from eighteenth-century originals, there are a few cases where errors that have crept into subsequent German reprints have been corrected. These are, for the most part, minor, but at least now readers will know that the officer who quipped that limiting freedom of the press in order to promote political stability would be like paving the countryside to prevent moles from harming the fields was not—as Zwi Batscha's reprint has it—General von *Ryan* but rather General von

Kyau. Efforts have also been made to let readers know who people like General von Kyau were and to clarify some of the references and allusions that are likely to stymie present-day readers. In the case of that notoriously hermetic writer Hamann, this has resulted in a rather extensive body of notes.

All that remains is to offer thanks for money, advice, and assistance. The National Endowment for the Humanities (NEH) has been exceedingly generous in its support of this project. I first came to appreciate the complexity of the eighteenth-century German discussion of the question "What is enlightenment?" as a result of an NEH Fellowship for University Teachers. As the director of three NEH Summer Seminars for College Teachers, I was able to explore these essays with scholars who shared my sense that the questions asked in the eighteenth century still matter. A grant from the NEH Division of Texts and Translations provided the funds necessary to begin work on the translation. I am grateful to Stephen Ross of the NEH and David Berndt of the Office of Sponsored Programs at Boston University for their encouragement and advice in the process of applying for funding and to Susan Tomassetti of the University Professors Program at Boston University for her aid in administering these grants.

Both the translators and the editor have spent the last several years annoying friends, colleagues, and, sometimes, total strangers with pleas for help in translating opaque passages and in identifying obscure allusions. Particular thanks go to Karl Ameriks, James Bernauer, Daniel Breazeale, Walter Felscher, Anke Finger, John Gagliardo, George di Giovanni, Gail Hueting, John S. King, Ramona Naddaff, Kristin Pfefferkorn-Forbath, Sabine Roehr, Alexander von Schoenborn, Steven Scully, and W. Daniel Wilson. Frederick Beiser, Rüdiger Bittner, Kenneth Haynes, Dorothy Rogers, Jonathan Knudsen, and Gitta Schmidt were of enormous help in reviewing the translations and suggesting revisions.

I am greatly indebted to Kevin Geiman, Garrett Green, Lewis Hinchman, Arthur Hirsch, Kenneth Haynes, Jane Kneller, Jonathan Knudsen, John Christian Laursen, Dale Snow, and Thomas Wartenberg for the effort they put into their work on this book and for their friendship. It has been a joy to work with them.

Finally, it is unlikely that I would have embarked on this project had it not been for Amélie Rorty's enthusiasm, and inconceivable that I would have finished it without her continued encouragement, her constant counsel, and her ever-increasing threats.

Introduction

What Is Enlightenment? A Question, Its Context, and Some Consequences

James Schmidt

The Enlightenment has been blamed for many things. It has been held responsible for the French Revolution, for totalitarianism, and for the view that nature is simply an object to be dominated, manipulated, and exploited. It has also been implicated in one way or another in European imperialism and the most aggressive aspects of capitalism. While some have insisted that its skepticism about "absolute values" infects our culture with a "nihilistic sluggishness," others have suggested that liberal societies should divest themselves of the Enlightenment's obsession with "philosophical foundations."[1] It is said that its passion for rights and liberties unleashed a destructive individualism that undermines any sense of community.[2] Yet it has also been argued that its assumption that human nature was infinitely malleable has provided the intellectual inspiration for attempts by totalitarian states to eradicate all traces of individuality from their subjects.[3] It has been criticized for its insensitivity to the tragic character of moral conflicts and for its naive assumption that all dilemmas have simple solutions.[4] It has been argued that its attempt to construct a moral philosophy ended in failure, leaving us with either an impoverished moral vision that suppresses all values that cannot be reduced to instrumental efficiency or a corrupted moral discourse in which ethical evaluations are nothing more than a mask for individual preferences.[5] It has been castigated for its affection for "master metanarratives" and its hostility toward "otherness."[6] Its racism and its sexism have not passed unnoticed.[7]

Looking over this list of charges, one wonders how one period could have been responsible for so much and so many different kinds of harm. Puzzled by the multitude of accusations leveled against it—and astonished at the diversity of its critics—one might well ask, "What *is* enlightenment?" It turns out that the question is not a new one.

EIGHTEENTH-CENTURY ANSWERS

In December 1783, the *Berlinische Monatsschrift* published an article by the theologian and educational reformer Johann Friedrich Zöllner questioning the advisability of purely civil marriage ceremonies. Observing that all too often "under the name of enlightenment the hearts and minds of men are bewildered," he asked in a footnote, "What is enlightenment? This question, which is almost as important as what is truth, should indeed be answered before one begins enlightening! And still I have never found it answered!"[8] He did not have to wait long for an answer. Within a year, the *Berlinische Monatsschrift* published responses from Moses Mendelssohn and Immanuel Kant.[9] Other authors entered the fray, and the debate spread to other journals.[10] By the end of the decade, the discussion had become so pervasive that when Christoph Martin Wieland, alone in his privy, glanced at the piece of wastepaper he had picked up to complete his task, he found himself staring at a list of six questions that began with "What is Enlightenment?"[11]

These attempts at defining enlightenment did little to dispel the confusion that had grown up around the term. Looking back over the literature Zöllner's question had spawned, the author of an anonymous 1790 article in the *Deutsche Monatsschrift* argued that the term had become so divorced from any clear conventions of usage that discussions of it had degenerated into "a war of all against all," between combatants who marshaled their own idiosyncratic definitions.[12] The lack of a clear definition of the term can in part be attributed to the way the grounds of the debate shifted in the course of the discussion. At first, the question "What is enlightenment?" centered on the issue of how much enlightenment of the citizenry was possible or desirable and, more concretely, on whether a further liberalization of censorship regulations was advisable.[13] These questions took on a new urgency in the second phase of the debate, which commenced with Johann Christoph Woellner's Religion and Censorship edicts of 1788. The debate on censorship was now intimately intertwined with the question of the possible tensions between enlightenment and faith.[14] Finally, with the outbreak of the French Revolution—and especially after the execution of Louis XVI in January 1793—the discussion was extended to encompass the question of whether enlightenment necessarily undermined public authority and led to political turmoil.[15] Thus by the close of the eighteenth century, answering the question "What is enlightenment?" meant exploring the relationship between public discussion, religious faith, and political authority.

The Public Use of Reason

It is doubtful that Zöllner was as confused about the meaning of *Aufklärung* as his article implied. Like Mendelssohn, Zöllner was a member of the

Mittwochsgesellschaft, a secret society of "Friends of the Enlightenment" closely linked to the *Berlinische Monatsschrift.*[16] On 17 December 1783—the month of Zöllner's request for a definition—J. K. W. Möhsen read a paper to the society on the question "What is to be done towards the enlightenment of fellow citizens?" which urged members to determine "what is enlightenment."[17] Discussion of the topic continued over the next several months, with Mendelssohn delivering a lecture in May 1784 that served as the basis of his subsequent article in the *Berlinische Monatsschrift.*[18] Zöllner's footnote was thus less a testimony to his ignorance of the term than to the intense interest in the question within the small group of influential men of letters, jurists, and civil servants who made up the Mittwochsgesellschaft.

The Mittwochsgesellschaft was a recent addition to the host of secret societies that flourished in Prussia and the other German states in the last half of the eighteenth century.[19] Such societies satisfied a number of needs. In an age in which many individuals no longer found meaning in the rituals of orthodox religion, the ceremonies associated with some of these societies may well have provided an appealing and powerful substitute.[20] In a political system that offered few opportunities for the exercise of political agency outside of the bureaucratic structure of the monarchical state, many of these societies furnished an arena in which political opinions could be debated and programs for reform articulated.[21] And finally, in a society with a strictly defined social hierarchy, secret societies provided a setting in which members of different religions, professional groups, and social classes could come into contact with one another and find a fellowship and solidarity that was not available in the public realm.[22] As Möhsen noted at the close of his talk, the members of the Mittwochsgesellschaft could carry out their responsibilities as "well-intentioned patriots" only because "the seal of secrecy" protected them from both the fear of offending patrons and the "thirst for honor or praise."[23]

In his lecture to the Mittwochsgesellschaft, Möhsen was far from sanguine about the future prospects for enlightenment in Prussia. While he began by hailing the triumph of enlightenment in Berlin, he rather quickly suggested that one of the most crucial tasks facing the Mittwochsgesellschaft was to determine why the ideals of the Enlightenment had been resisted by much of the public. Behind the question "What is enlightenment?" stood the more troubling question of "why enlightenment has not progressed very far with our public, despite more than forty years of freedom to think, to speak, and also to publish."[24] The "forty years" of which Möhsen speaks refers to the reign of Frederick the Great, who had begun his reign with an easing of censorship laws and a toleration of divergent views on religious questions. Political dissent, however, was less welcome, and, as Gotthold Ephraim Lessing bitterly observed, all that Frederick's reforms ultimately amounted to was the freedom "to make as many idiotic remarks against religion as one wants." Contrasting what could be said in Prussia about political issues with what was being written in Vienna, France, and Denmark, Lessing concluded that Frederick ruled over "the most enslaved land in Europe."[25] By the 1780s, calls for a loosening of censorship had begun to appear in the press, including an anonymous essay (subsequently determined to have been written by the jurist and Mittwochsgesellschaft member Ernst Friedrich Klein) published in the *Berlinische Monatsschrift* in which the author, speaking in words taken from the writings of the young Frederick, implicitly criticized Frederick's current policies by subtly urging the aging monarch to follow the example of his younger self.[26]

Möhsen's lecture launched a debate within the Mittwochsgesellschaft on how far the removal of restrictions on the freedom of press should proceed.[27] At issue was the concern that a free and unrestricted discussion of religious, moral, and political concerns might undermine the conventional mores and beliefs on which society rested. Some members felt that the dangers associated with too rapid an "enlightenment" of the public were overstated. Mendelssohn reminded the fainthearted that "when weighing the advantages and disadvantages brought about by enlightenment and the revolutions which have arisen from it, one should differentiate between the first years of a crisis and the times which follow. The former are sometimes only seemingly dangerous and are the grounds for improvement." Even if one conceded that "certain prejudices, held by the nation, must on account of circumstances be spared by all judicious men," Mendelssohn asked whether this deference to prejudices should "be set through law and censors" or whether, like "the limits of prosperity, gratitude, and sincerity," it should be "left to the discretion of every individual." He closed his rejoinder by noting that recently the Montgolfier brothers had made the first successful hot-air balloon flight. Even though it was uncertain whether the "great upheaval" caused by their achievement would lead to "the betterment of human society," Mendelssohn asked the membership, "Would one on account of this hesitate to promote progress?" Answering his own question he concluded, "The discovery of eternal truths is in and for itself good; their control is a matter for Providence."[28]

While Mendelssohn's arguments were seconded by many in the society,[29] others were more wary. The jurist Klein was willing to concede that, in general, "every truth is useful and every error harmful." But he also insisted that it was necessary to consider the practical impact of enlightenment on different groups within society. Because it is sometimes difficult to assimilate individual, isolated truths, these truths will remain unconvincing and without effect. It is thus possible that "for a certain class of men, a certain error can serve to bring them to a higher concept of things which are worthy of greater attention." In such cases, a "useful error" will do more to promote the public good than the truth.[30] Carl Gottlieb Svarez, Klein's colleague in the Ministry of Justice, agreed, noting that the morality of the general public rests on beliefs that are "uncertain, doubtful, or completely wrong," and suggested that enlightenment is dangerous when it "takes from the people these motives of ethically good behavior and substitutes no other." In such cases, "one advances not enlightenment but rather a corruption of morality."[31]

The tension between the agenda of enlightenment and the exigencies of society lies at the heart of the essays Mendelssohn and Kant wrote in response to Zöllner's question. While Mendelssohn's initial response to Möhsen's lecture betrayed few reservations about the consequences of increased enlightenment, his essay in the *Berlinische Monatsschrift* was less confident. He distinguished "civil enlightenment" (*Bürgeraufklärung*), which must adjust itself according to the ranks of society it addresses, from "human enlightenment" (*Menschenaufklärung*), which, addressing "man as man" and not "man as citizen," paid heed neither to social distinctions nor to the maintenance of social order. Nothing ensures that these two types of enlightenment will complement one another. "Certain truths," he noted, "which are useful to man, as man, can at times be harmful to him as citizen."[32] In a short article published a year later in the *Berlinische Monatsschrift*, he was even more leery of the abusive tone of some of his contemporaries' comments on religion. "Nothing is more opposed to the true good of mankind," he cautioned, "than this sham enlightenment, where everyone mouths a hackneyed wisdom, from which the spirit has already long vanished, where everyone ridicules prejudices, without distinguishing what is true in them from what is false."[33]

In his response to the question, Kant sought to balance the demands of enlightened reason and civil order by distinguishing between "public" and "private" uses of reason—a distinction that has puzzled readers for the last two centuries.[34] By "public" use, Kant meant that "use which anyone makes of it *as a scholar* [*Gelehrter*] before the entire public of the *reading world.*" It is contrasted to that "private" use which individuals make of their reason in those specific civil posts or offices that have been entrusted to them.[35] In one's private use of reason, one behaves "passively," bound by an "artificial unanimity" to advance or to defend certain "public ends." One functions as "part of a machine," and "one is certainly not allowed to argue." In contrast, in one's public use of reason, one acts as "a member of the entire commonwealth [*ganzes gemeinen Wesen*], indeed even of a cosmopolitan society [*Weltbürgergesellschaft*]." Here an individual "can certainly argue, without thereby harming the affairs in which he is engaged in part as a passive member." Restrictions on the private use of reason in no way contradict the goal of enlightenment, but the public use of reason must remain free, since "it alone can bring about enlightenment among men."[36]

While Mendelssohn was willing to concede that there might be certain unhappy circumstances in which philosophy must remain silent lest it pose a threat to public order, Kant was uncompromising in his insistence that the public exercise of reason should never be restricted. Examining the question of whether it might be possible for a "society of clergymen" to commit itself by oath to an unalterable set of doctrines, Kant answered decisively:

> I say that this is completely impossible. Such a contract, concluded for the purpose of closing off forever all further enlightenment of the human race, is utterly null and void even if it should be confirmed by the highest power, by Imperial Diets, and by the most solemn peace treaties.[37]

An attempt to require conformity to a fixed set of doctrines is void because it fails the test that any proposed legislation must pass if it is to be legitimate. Invoking his reformulation of social contract theory, Kant explained, "The touchstone of everything that can be concluded as a law for a people lies in the question: could a people have imposed such a law upon itself?" When we apply this test to the proposal to restrict religious belief to a fixed set of doctrines, we find that while it might be possible for a people to agree to such restrictions on free inquiry for a short period of time, "in order to introduce a certain order, as it were, in expectation of something better" even in this case individuals—"as scholars"—would still retain a right to put forward alternative views in writing.[38] Thus while individual religious confessions might require their members to conform to a fixed set of doctrines, it would be absolutely impermissible for the state to use its coercive power to prevent the criticism of these doctrines in books and articles.

Faith and Reason

These discussions of the question of the limits of enlightenment were only the prelude to the impassioned debate on censorship sparked by an abrupt change in Prussian policy regarding freedom of expression. Frederick II died in August 1786 and was succeeded by his nephew, Frederick William II, whose ascent to the throne prompted considerable anxiety within the Berlin Enlightenment.[39] In the early 1780s, Frederick William had been drawn to Christian mysticism and was increasingly influenced by opponents of the Enlightenment such as his most trusted adviser, Johann Christoph Woellner.[40] The year before Frederick William became king, Woellner sent him a treatise on religion that stressed the importance of Christian faith for supporting the Prussian state, denounced the malevolent influence of such "apostles of unbelief" as Friedrich Gedike and Johann Erich Biester, the publishers of the *Berlinische Monatsschrift*, and called for the replacement of K. A. Zedlitz, the enlightened head of the Prussian Ecclesiastical Department.[41] Woellner did not shrink from criticizing Frederick himself, charging that Frederick's public display of his lack of religious faith was the chief cause of the irreligion and unbelief that was rife in Berlin.[42]

The first Sunday after his ascent to the throne, Frederick William made it clear that he intended to set a different example from that of his predecessor. He attended services at the Marienkirche, from whose pulpit Zöllner delivered one of his typically unorthodox and enlightened sermons. It is unlikely that Frederick William was pleased by what he heard, nor could subsequent visits to the churches where Johann Joachim Spalding and Friedrich Samuel Gottfried Sack preached have made him any more comfortable with the religious teaching that had flourished during Frederick's reign.[43] Zöllner, Spalding, Sack, and other enlightened members of the Berlin clergy embraced an approach to Christian doctrine known as "neology" that combined historical and critical approaches to the interpretation of Scripture with an emphasis on the primacy of the moral and practical dimensions of Christian teaching.[44] While they continued to maintain the importance of revelation as the basis for Christian faith, they assumed that the doctrinal content of this revelation contained nothing beyond the fundamental tenets of "natural religion" and hence was completely accessible to natural human reason. Any part of the Scriptures that presented problems for them—for example, such doctrines as original sin, eternal punishment, or predestination—was shown through historical and philological criticism to be of dubious authenticity and was typically avoided as a subject for sermons.[45] They saw no conflict between enlightened reason and Christian faith: enlightenment battled superstition, fanaticism, and prejudice—and, properly understood, Christianity had nothing to do with superstition, fanaticism, or prejudice. The goal of their preaching and writing was to purge such misconceptions from the minds of the faithful and instill a sense of moral rectitude and social responsibility that often extended to such political matters as the loyalty of subjects to the Crown.[46]

While neologists may have seen no conflict between enlightened reason and Christian faith, when pushed far enough, their attempt to "purify" Christian faith could lead to conclusions that were antithetical to conventional Christian teaching. Few pushed harder than Hermann Samuel Reimarus and Carl Friedrich Bahrdt. Reimarus's massive *Apology for the Rational Worshipers of God*, fragments of which were published by Lessing after Reimarus's death, argued that revelation could add nothing to what was already known through natural human reason.[47] He called into question the historical veracity of the biblical narrative and explored the internal contradictions in the account of Christ's resurrection. Jesus' teaching was distinguished from that of his disciples, who in Reimarus's view transformed what had been an attempt to revitalize Judaism into a new religion centered on the image of Jesus as savior of the entire human race. The result of Reimarus's critique, in Henry E. Allison's pithy summary, was that

"Jesus becomes regarded as a well meaning, but deluded fanatic, the apostles clever and self-seeking deceivers, and the Christian religion a colossal fraud."[48]

In much the same spirit, between 1782 and 1785 Bahrdt published a series of widely read articles recounting the life of Jesus in a thoroughly rationalized fashion.[49] Convinced by Johann August Eberhard that there was nothing in Christ's teaching that was not already present in Socrates and persuaded that a process of mythologization similar to what Gedike found in stories surrounding Socrates' birth must be at work in the New Testament, Bahrdt presented a Jesus whose intentions were confined to removing superstition and prejudice from Judaism. He speculated that as a boy Jesus had been instructed in Socrates' teachings by a group of Alexandrian Jews, from whom he also learned to use medications capable of awakening individuals in deathlike comas—hence the explanation for the "miracles" he allegedly performed. Bahrdt's Christ founded a secret society, which like the Masonic movement was dedicated to the spread of rational faith and brotherhood. Its members nursed him back to health after his near-fatal encounter with the cross. After a few subsequent appearances before his followers, he withdrew to spend the rest of his life in a secret lodge, where from time to time he advised Saint Paul.[50]

In the face of writings such as these, it is little wonder that Woellner regarded enlightenment as a threat to the religious fabric that held Prussian society together. But opposition to Bahrdt could also be found among less reactionary thinkers. For example, the moderate Friedrich Karl von Moser, appalled by Bahrdt's New Testament translation of 1773, succeeded in having him removed from his teaching position at Giessen.[51] Moser was well known as an advocate of enlightened absolutism and constitutionalism, and in his writings he sought to strike a middle course between enlightenment and orthodoxy. At pains to distinguish "true enlightenment" from "false enlightenment," he insisted that "all enlightenment that is not grounded in and supported by religion... is not only the way to destruction, immorality, and depravity, but also to the dissolution and ruin of all civil society, and to a war of the human race within itself, that begins with philosophy and ends with scalping and cannibalism."[52] Moser argued that when enlightenment "takes from man what he requires for comfort, light, support, and peace" or "wishes to give him more than he can use, employ, and manage according to his powers of intellect and understanding," it turns into the very enemies it sought to thwart. It becomes "deception, fraud, fanaticism [*Schwärmerei*], treachery against man."[53]

Despite Woellner's revulsion against the Enlightenment, the first two years of Frederick William's reign were difficult to distinguish from that of his uncle.[54] The break came only after Woellner had consolidated his position within the court, eventually replacing Zedlitz as minister of justice on

3 July 1788 and assuming responsibility over the Ecclesiastical Department. Six days later he issued his Religion Edict, which criticized Protestant clergy for reviving "the miserable, long-refuted errors of the Socinians, deists, naturalists, and other sectarians" and disseminating them among the people in the name of *"Aufklärung."* While allowing clergy to believe privately whatever they wished, the edict required adherence to the Bible and the "symbolic books" in their teaching. Those "so-called enlighteners [*Aufklärer*]" who refused to conform were threatened with dismissal, and future candidates for pastoral and teaching positions were to be carefully scrutinized so that there would be no doubts as to their "internal adherence to the creed they are employed to teach."[55]

The reaction to Woellner's edict was immediate and intense. Prominent members of the Berlin clergy including William Abraham Teller, Sack, Spalding, and Zöllner requested that their preaching responsibilities be terminated, and in September 1789 five of the six clerical members of the Lutheran Upper Consistory resigned their positions in protest.[56] A flood of pamphlets denounced the edict.[57] In one of the most widely read polemics, Andreas Riem, co-editor of the *Berlinisches Journal der Aufklärung* and pastor at the *Friedrichshospital,* launched a passionate attack on the central assumption behind the edict—that restrictions on the spread of enlightenment were necessary in order to prevent an undermining of the customary religious faith that secures public order.[58] Listing the atrocities spawned by religious fanaticism, Riem argued that it was enlightenment rather than religious orthodoxy that provided the most secure foundation for political rule. Riem published his pamphlet anonymously but was soon identified as the author. Stating that he could not abide by the provisions of Woellner's Religion Edict because they would force him to teach doctrines that—since they contradicted what could be known on the basis of pure reason—were contrary to his own convictions, he resigned his position at the *Friedrichshospital.*

To silence critics, Woellner issued the Censorship Edict in December 1788, which stipulated that writings on religious matters had to be submitted to a commission for approval.[59] While this measure did force the *Berlinische Monatsschrift* and Friedrich Nicolai's *Allgemeine Deutsche Bibliothek* to leave Berlin, prosecutions under the edict proved difficult, since most censors were drawn from the same enlightened group of councillors who had opposed Woellner's Religion Edict in the first place.[60] In the hope of securing a more energetic enforcement of the Religion and Censorship edicts, Woellner established the Summary Commission of Inquiry (*Immediat-Examinations-Kommission*) in May 1791, entrusted with the task of examining the fitness of clergy and teachers as well as with the responsibility for censoring theological books. But here too his actions met with considerable and often successful opposition, and whatever hope he might have had for a decisive victory over the partisans of enlightenment remained frustrated.[61] As Moser observed four years later, enlightenment had advanced too far to be turned back. "The times have passed, and it is too late to try to shut out the light. The longer it goes on, the more it comes to this: whether this light should only illuminate and enlighten [*leuchten und erleuchten*] or ignite and inflame?"[62] Attempts to preserve public order by restraining the freedom of expression made as much sense as trying to "pave the meadows, so that moles could not harm them."[63]

Nevertheless, Woellner's efforts were not entirely without consequence. Bahrdt was briefly imprisoned in the fortress at Magdeburg for his satirical farce, *Das Religions-Edikt*; Riem was exiled from Prussia in 1793 for his political criticisms of the regime; and, in probably the most famous case, after the publication of *Religion within the Limits of Reason Alone,* Frederick William threatened Kant with future "unpleasant measures" should he continue to "misuse" his philosophy to "distort and disparage many of the cardinal and basic teachings of the Holy Scriptures and of Christianity."[64] Nor should it be assumed that Woellner's efforts met with universal condemnation, even among enlightened intelligentsia. Shortly before Johann Gottlieb Fichte wrote his "Reclamation of the Freedom of Thought from the Princes of Europe"—an impassioned defense of the freedom of the press—he drafted a short defense of Woellner's edicts, arguing that they were aimed only at abuses of freedom of expression that undermined the faith of the common people.[65] It was only after his own *Critique of All Revelation* was censored in Halle that Fichte revised his views and, drawing on arguments from social contract theory, mounted one of the most theoretically ambitious of eighteenth-century defenses of freedom of expression.

Fichte's vacillation is less puzzling than it may initially appear. It should be remembered that the institution of censorship was by no means anathema to all partisans of enlightenment. There was a widespread recognition that the enlightenment of the citizenry must be sensitive to the particular requirements of the differing estates within society.[66] In his comments on Möhsen's lecture to the Mittwochsgesellschaft, Gedike stressed that enlightenment was a "relative" concept differentiated according to such criteria as "place, time, rank, sex." "Thoroughgoing equality of enlightenment," he assured his fellow members, "is as little desirable as full equality of ranks, and fortunately just as impossible."[67] Because enlightenment is differentiated according to the differing ranks in society, it falls to the censor to determine, in Svarez's words, "the degree of enlightenment of powers of comprehension, of capacities of thought and action, and of expressive capabilities" appropriate to each class.[68] Hence while Svarez expressed an admiration for the efforts of his colleagues to refine and rationalize morality and religion, he nevertheless hoped that they would "not seek to explain away and define away hell and the devil, in the usual sense of these words, from the heart of the common man."[69] The members of the Mittwochsgesellschaft and Woellner agreed on at least this much: customary religious beliefs were an indispensable means of maintaining the coherence of civil society.

The Politics of Enlightenment

After 1789, a new element entered into the discussion of the question "What is enlightenment?"—the problem of the relationship between enlightenment and revolution. The French Revolution marked the culmination of a century of political upheavals that began in England with the "Glorious Revolution" of 1688 and continued with uprisings in Holland (1747 and again in 1787), Corsica (1755 and 1793), Geneva (1768 and 1781–1782), the American colonies (1775–1783), London (1780), Ireland (1780–1785), Bohemia (1783), the Austrian Netherlands (1788–1790), and Poland (1791). Writing in 1794, Kant's disciple, Johann Heinrich Tieftrunk, observed, "We now live in a century of enlightenment. Should this be said to be an honor or a disgrace for our century? We also live in a century of revolutions. Is it enlightenment which currently undermines the peace of states?"[70] The possibility that too much or too rapid an enlightenment of the citizenry might rend the social fabric had haunted considerations of the question "What is enlightenment?" from the outset. But after the summer of 1792, as the news from France became more and more disturbing and with French armies advancing into the Rhineland, it seemed as if the worst fears about enlightenment were being confirmed daily.

Between 1792 and 1793, the Revolution entered its most radical phase. In August 1792, Louis XVI was deposed and a revolutionary republic established. Mass arrests of royalist sympathizers followed, many of whom were among the hundreds of prisoners slaughtered when mobs entered the prisons during the "September Massacres." The newly established National Convention initiated treason proceedings against Louis, and he was executed in January 1793. By the summer of 1793, the Jacobins had crushed the Girondist opposition, and the Committee on Public Safety inaugurated the Reign of Terror against suspected opponents. A notice in an August 1793 issue of the *Oberdeutsche Allgemeine Literaturzeitung*, the most prominent journal of the Catholic enlightenment in Austria, suggests how disturbing this turn of events must have been for those who supported the cause of enlightenment.

> The empire of ignorance and superstition was moving closer and closer towards its collapse, the light of the *Aufklärung* made more and more progress, and the convulsive gestures with which the creatures of the night howled at the dawning day showed clearly enough that they themselves despaired of victory and were only summoning up their reserves for one final demented counterattack. Then the disorders in France erupted: and now they reared again their empty heads and screeched at the tops of their voices: "Look there at

> the shocking results of the *Aufklärung*! Look there at the philosophers, the preachers of sedition!" Everyone seized this magnificent opportunity to spray their poison at the supporters of the *Aufklärung*.[71]

As revolution turned to terror, conservative critics of enlightenment were transformed, in T. C. W. Blanning's words, "from outmoded alarmists into farsighted prophets."[72]

The idea that there is a connection between the Enlightenment and the French Revolution is by now so familiar that it is difficult to imagine how troubling the relation must have seemed in the early 1790s.[73] Because we tend to assume a natural affinity between the Enlightenment and liberal politics, we forget that many *Aufklärers* were not liberals, that some of the more ardent liberals were by no means well disposed toward the Enlightenment, and that it was by no means assumed that political revolution was a means for advancing the cause of enlightened political reforms. In the years immediately following 1789, a good deal needed to be sorted out.

If liberalism is defined as a conception of politics that gives priority to "rights" over the "good" and holds that the chief end of the state is to secure individual liberty rather than to attain public happiness, then few of the leading figures in the Berlin Enlightenment could be classified as liberals.[74] They accepted Christian Wolff's view that it was the duty of the state to undertake measures that would further the common well-being of its citizens and viewed as legitimate the police powers that the state exercised over the material and spiritual lives of its citizens in pursuit of this goal.[75] Kant insisted, in an essay published in the *Berlinische Monatsschrift* in September 1793, that a "paternal government," established on the principle of "benevolence" toward its people, represented "the greatest conceivable *despotism*" and called instead for a "*patriotic* government" in which each citizen was pledged to defend the individual's right to liberty.[76] But his rejection of "public well-being" as the proper goal of politics was as novel as his rejection of happiness as the foundation of moral philosophy. Mendelssohn was closer to the norm. Solidly based on Wolff and hearkening back to Aristotle, he saw the ultimate purpose of political life as residing in the greatest possible expansion of the capacities of its citizenry. Such a conception of politics was willing to accept a degree of state intervention in the lives of its citizenry that Kant would have rejected as "paternalistic."[77]

Just as it was possible in eighteenth-century Prussia to embrace enlightenment but eschew liberalism, so too it was possible to advocate liberalism while attacking enlightenment. No thinker demonstrated this better than Friedrich Heinrich Jacobi. His reading of David Hume and Thomas Reid convinced him that reason cannot attain certainty about the existence of external objects. Our experience of such objects, he argued, takes the form of a revelation that is completely beyond argument, which he described as "faith."[78] Carrying this dichotomy between the spheres of faith and knowledge into the domain of theology, he rejected the neological project of reconciling faith and reason, insisting that reason alone can never lead us to certainty of God's existence. In his famous discussions with Lessing that sparked the "Pantheism Dispute," he argued that Spinoza's philosophy demonstrated that any attempt to proceed on the basis of reason alone inevitably resulted in a completely deterministic and fatalistic system that denied both the possibility of human freedom and the existence of a personal divinity.[79]

Jacobi's disgust with the Berlin Enlightenment—which he dubbed the *"morgue berlinoise"* and whose members' "magisterial, self-satisfied demeanour" he despised[80]—extended to its politics. Appalled by "the stupidity of people who in our century regard superstition as more dangerous than the growing power of unrestrained autocracy," he was one of the earliest and most vigorous advocates of liberalism in Germany.[81] His 1782 essay "Something Lessing Said" argued that civil society was "a mechanism of coercion" whose function should be simply "to secure for every member his inviolable property in his person, the free use of all his powers, and the full enjoyment of the fruits of their employment."[82] Attempts to justify a more extensive state intervention in the lives of its citizens—whether justified by appeals to "interests of state" or the "welfare of the whole"—led only to "the advancement of self-interest, money-grubbing, indolence; of a stupid admiration of wealth, of rank, and of power; a blind unsavory submissiveness; and an anxiety and fear which allows no zeal and tends toward the most servile obedience."[83]

The response of German thinkers to the French Revolution tended to trace a course that ran from early enthusiasm to subsequent disillusionment, although there are enough exceptions to make this a gross generalization at best. It was possible for a supporter of enlightened absolutism such as Ewald Friedrich von Hertzberg, who served in the foreign ministry of both Frederick and his successor in addition to pursuing a career as a man of letters in his role as curator of the Berlin Academy, to welcome the French Revolution while defending the Prussian monarchy. He insisted that while the French monarchy was despotic and ruled without restraint, Prussian monarchs were restrained by ancient rights and corporative privileges.[84] As long as the revolution in France appeared to be nothing more than an attempt to set constitutional limitations on the monarch, it could be viewed as little more than an effort to bring about a state of affairs that had long existed in Prussia. It was only when it became clear that the institution of the monarchy itself was under attack that the Revolution became something more troubling.

For at least some supporters of the Enlightenment, the idea of revolution itself was suspect. Writing a year before the Revolution, Riem viewed the "Patriot Rebellion" in Holland as the work of "unenlightened demagogues" and held that the American Revolution was a misfortune that could have been avoided had there been more enlightened leadership in England and the colonies.[85] Tieftrunk came to much the same conclusion in his 1794 essay, "On the Influence of Enlightenment on Revolutions." Far from promoting violent revolutions, he argued, "true enlightenment... is... the only way to work against them successfully." Enlightenment instructs citizens to obey their princes and teaches princes how to improve their nations. The threat to public order comes from a "pseudoenlightenment" that "mocks, doubts, and speaks with arrogant self-assurance about everything others hold sacred and venerable." It is this "pseudoenlightenment" that must bear the blame for events in France. For if France had been "truly enlightened," it "would either never have begun its revolution or else certainly have carried it out better."[86]

Johann Adam Bergk, a younger and more politically radical follower of Kant than Tieftrunk, came to different conclusions in his 1795 essay, "Does Enlightenment Cause Revolutions?" For Bergk, revolutions—which he distinguished from "insurrections" by isolated individuals and from "rebellions" by a majority—could occur only if the "moral enlightenment" of a people had evolved to the point where they were capable of recognizing rights and duties. Mere "speculative enlightenment" would produce, at best, a "cunning, clever, refined, selfish, and still cowardly" nation that, out of fear of violence, "quietly endures all insults to its inalienable rights." This, Bergk argued, was the state of Europe before the French Revolution. In the French Revolution—and, equally important, in Kant's moral philosophy—Bergk saw evidence of a transition to a new level of moral development.[87] Now it was possible for peoples to demand that material conditions "correspond with the pronouncements of conscience," and "if the nation recognizes or senses the injustices that burden it and mock its humanity, then a revolution is unavoidable." Enlightenment thus stands "justly accused as the cause of revolutions." But there can be no question of restraining enlightenment, since "once enlightenment spreads its roots in a nation, it is easier to exterminate mankind than to exterminate enlightenment."[88] His advice to rulers who sought to avoid revolutions was simple enough: "Do not worry about the welfare of the world; you do not know what you want. One thing is demanded of you: to do what is right."[89] For Bergk, the age of revolutions and the age of enlightenment led to a common goal: a state that rejected the paternalistic concern with improving its citizenry and instead dedicated itself to the preservation of liberty.

Kant's paradoxical stance toward the French Revolution is well known: he opposed revolutions on principle but regarded the French Revolution as evidence of the moral improvement of the human race.[90] His 1793 essay, "On the Common Saying: 'This May Be True in Theory, but It Does Not

Apply in Practice,'" rejected the notion of a "right to revolution" largely on the grounds that such a right is typically established by invoking the principle of happiness as the end for which civil society is founded.[91] Yet in his most extended treatment of the French Revolution—the second part of *The Conflict of the Faculties*—Kant argued that the "wishful participation that borders almost on enthusiasm" that greeted the French Revolution constitutes a "sign" within history that demonstrates the presence of a principle at work that would allow us to have hope for the future progress of the species.[92] What is notable here is that Kant has shifted the grounds of the debate from a consideration of the course of the Revolution to a consideration of the reaction of spectators to the event. With this move, the success or failure of the Revolution becomes irrelevant to the question of moral progress. For Kant, the Revolution marked the moment in history when there was an actual effort to put into practice the goal that nature had dictated to the species: the achievement of a republican form of constitution. What mattered was not the ultimate success or failure of that attempt but rather the fact that it spoke so powerfully to the hopes of those who first beheld it.

With the French Revolution, discussion of the question "What is enlightenment?" came to a close. How one understood the Enlightenment came to be determined by the stance one took toward the Revolution. For critics of the Revolution, enlightenment was a process that undermined the traditional patterns of belief on which political authority rested and thus reduced politics to a brutal battle between despotism and anarchy. For those who remained loyal to what they saw as the ideals of the Revolution, enlightenment embodied the vision of a society governed by law and reason. As the new century dawned, the lines of engagement were clearly drawn. For the Right, enlightenment was a synonym for a political naïveté with murderous consequences.[93] For the Left, it expressed the unfulfilled dream of a just and rational society.[94] With both sides sure that they knew the answer, the question "What is enlightenment?" no longer needed to be asked.

TWENTIETH-CENTURY QUESTIONS

It is only in the last fifty years that the question of enlightenment has been reopened in earnest. Both "the Enlightenment" (spelled with a capital "E" and preceded by the definite article) and "enlightenment" (with neither the capital nor the definite article) have once again intruded into scholarly and political discussions. Historians, sociologists, and political theorists have probed the social roots of the Enlightenment, stressed its relation to eighteenth-century political and social movements, and contrasted its development in differing national contexts. At the same time others have criticized, from a variety of philosophical and political perspectives, the blindness, naïveté, and inconsistencies of what they term "the project of enlightenment." We are thus in the curious position of having gained a greater appreciation of the diversity of opinions and intentions within the Enlightenment while becoming increasingly suspicious of many of the things that we once assumed the Enlightenment represented. "What happened," Jean Améry asked a year before his death,

> that the Enlightenment became a relic of intellectual history, good enough at best for the diligent but sterile exertions of scholars? What sad aberration has brought us to the point where modern thinkers do not dare to employ concepts such as progress, humanization, and reason except within damning quotation marks?[95]

What happened can best be understood by tracing how three broad lines of argument, originating in differing responses to the relationship between the Enlightenment and the French Revolution, have come to dominate recent accounts of the nature and viability of "the project of enlightenment." The first, which is concerned with the relationship between reason, authority, and tradition, takes the form of a deepening of Edmund Burke's misgivings about the Revolution. The second, which focuses on the disturbing affinity between reason, terror, and domination, continues a line of argument inaugurated by G. W. F. Hegel's *Phenomenology of Spirit.* The third, which seeks to liberate the ideal of enlightenment from all association with the French Revolution, finds its origins in the writings of Friedrich Nietzsche. While all three of these lines of criticism sometimes resemble one another, there are important differences that justify their being treated separately. And, conversely, while these criticisms diverge in important ways, they share one important feature. Since they originate after the debate on the question "What is enlightenment?" had been displaced by other concerns, these criticisms of "enlightenment" share an ignorance of the Enlightenment's own efforts at self-definition.

Reason, Authority, and Tradition

In 1781, at the start of the *Critique of Pure Reason,* Kant announced,

> Our age is, in especial degree, the age of criticism, and to criticism everything must submit. Religion through its sanctity and law-giving through its majesty may seek to exempt themselves from it. But they then awaken just suspicion, and cannot claim the sincere respect which reason accords only to that which has been able to sustain the test of free and open examination.[96]

In characterizing his age as "an age of criticism," Kant anticipated the answer he would give three years later to the question of whether his was "an enlightened age." "No," he responded, "but we do live in an age of *enlightenment.*"[97] Church and state have been put on notice that they can no longer count on the deference traditionally accorded them. Nor can the individual simply accept passively whatever tradition teaches or what authority dictates. Enlightenment demands that we "think for ourselves"—that is, one must always "look within oneself... for the supreme touchstone of truth."[98]

For Burke, the notion that tradition could simply be set aside as an unfounded prejudice was a dangerous illusion. In his *Reflections on the Revolution in France,* he wrote,

> In this enlightened age I am bold enough to confess that we are generally men of untaught feelings, that, instead of casting away all our old prejudices, we cherish them to a considerable degree, and, to take more shame upon ourselves, we cherish them because they are prejudices; and the longer they have lasted and the more generally they have prevailed, the more we cherish them. We are afraid to put men to live and trade each on his own private stock of reason; because we suspect that the stock in each man is small, and that the individuals would do better to avail themselves of the general bank and capital of nations and of ages.[99]

Contrasting the attitudes of English "men of speculation" to French "literary men and politicians," he observed that while the French "have no respect for the wisdom of others," those English who are not part of the "clan of the enlightened,"

> instead of exploding general prejudices, employ their sagacity to discover the latent wisdom which prevails in them. If they find what they seek, and they seldom fail, they think it more wise to continue the prejudice, with the reason involved, than to cast away the coat of prejudice and leave nothing but the naked reason; because prejudice, with its reason, has a motive to give action to that reason, and an affection which will give it permanence.[100]

The "naked reason" of enlightenment was politically dangerous because it was incapable of turning virtues into habits or of making one's duty become a part of an individual's nature. Prejudice's reasons, in contrast, could move men to action.

There is, however, at least one problem with Burke's argument. He writes that we "cherish" our prejudices "because they are prejudices"—because they are familiar and well established—but immediately offers a rather different reason for respecting prejudices: they have served us well and thus are, in a sense, "reasonable." Since Burke's central concern was to insist that our familiar and well-established prejudices serve us much better than any of the utopian schemes of the partisans of enlightenment, he avoided both the difficult question of whether we would still cherish a prejudice should we not be successful in finding that "latent wisdom" we are seeking and the even more difficult question of who exactly composes the "we" that finds such wisdom in these well-established prejudices. Certain prejudices that are undoubtedly "cherished" by one group in society might strike others as abhorrent. A defense of enlightenment need not insist that all prejudices be rejected simply *because they are prejudices*. Voltaire, for example, acknowledged that there are "universal and necessary prejudices" that, on reflection, prove to be sound and useful: our idea of virtue, he suggested, is made up of such prejudices.[101] All it needs to suggest is that before we avail ourselves yet again of "the general bank and capital of nations and of ages," we make sure that the account is not bankrupt.[102] Against this line of criticism Burke is faced with the unpleasant alternative of defending prejudices simply *because* they are prejudices or of conceding the Enlightenment's position and granting that we ought to cherish prejudices only insofar as they have proven to be reasonable and thus *deserving* of our affection.

A more successful defense of tradition against enlightenment would involve raising the question of whether "reason" itself does not itself ultimately rest on prejudices. It is this line of argument that lies at the heart of Hans-Georg Gadamer's critique of the Enlightenment.[103] He argues that the Enlightenment itself rests on a "fundamental prejudice"—a "prejudice against prejudice itself."[104] The Enlightenment's tendency to equate "prejudice" with "false," "hasty," or "unfounded" judgments rests on the presupposition that reason, not tradition, constitutes the ultimate ground of authority. But what is this if not a prejudice in favor of reason?

Against the Enlightenment's overly hasty identification of "prejudice" with "false judgment" Gadamer appeals to the literal meaning of the German *Vorurteil*, "prejudgment." He argues that all our efforts to make sense of the world necessarily begin with anticipations and projections of meaning that are rooted in the particular, historical situation of the interpreter. These preliminary judgments are not barriers that must be removed before true understanding begins; they are instead the indispensable conditions for any understanding. Because of its misunderstanding of the role of prejudices, the Enlightenment overlooked what for Gadamer is central to authority, properly understood: "authority has to do not with obedience but rather with knowledge."[105] It involves a recognition that one's own knowledge is limited and that others may well have a better understanding. Nor is tradition, as Gadamer understands it, opposed to reason. Tradition does not persist simply through inertia; it must be "affirmed, embraced, cultivated." It must be preserved, and "preservation is an act of reason, though an inconspicuous one."[106]

The critique of prejudice prevented the Enlightenment from recognizing that individuals can never free themselves completely from the historical tradition in which they are situated.[107]

> In fact, history does not belong to us; we belong to it. Long before we understand ourselves through the process of self-examination, we understand ourselves in a self-evident way in the family, society, and state in which we live.

> The focus of subjectivity is a distorting mirror. The self-awareness of the individual is only a flickering in the closed circuits of historical life. *That is why the prejudices of the individual, far more than his judgments, constitute the historical reality of his being.*[108]

Thus, for Gadamer, Kant's imperative to "think for oneself" is abstract, empty, and ultimately impossible. All thinking is grounded in traditions and prejudices that can never be entirely eliminated.

Gadamer does not deny the possibility of reflection and critique. While Burke attributed to traditions a "wisdom without reflection," Gadamer recognizes that a properly functioning tradition is capable of reflecting on and, to a certain extent, criticizing the presuppositions on which it rests.[109] But though Gadamer recognizes that we are never so bound by a particular historical situation as to be unable to engage in dialogues with other traditions, he nevertheless insists that the attempt to illuminate our own historical situation will always remain incomplete.

> We always find ourselves within a situation, and throwing light on it is a task that is never entirely finished.... All self-knowledge arises from what is historically pregiven, what with Hegel we call "substance," because it underlies all subjective intentions and actions and hence both prescribes and limits every possibility of understanding any tradition whatsoever in its historical alterity.[110]

The task Gadamer assigns to philosophical hermeneutics is thus "to retrace the path of Hegel's phenomenology of spirit until we discover in all that is subjective the substantiality that determines it."[111] Reflection can make us aware of the tradition we inherit, but it can never release us from it.

In his critique of Gadamer's rehabilitation of tradition, Jürgen Habermas has questioned Gadamer's assumption that what has been given historically "does not remain untouched by the fact that it is taken up into reflection."[112] He suggests that Gadamer's "undialectical concept of Enlightenment" has underestimated the ability of reflection to criticize authority and to break the hold of dogma. In the process of questioning tradition, we are forced to take a stand on norms and beliefs that had previously been simply accepted. By reflecting on the reasons that support the claims tradition makes on us, blind acquiescence is transformed into conscious agreement. Viewed this way, enlightenment is opposed, not to authority per se, but rather to those forms of authority that are maintained by force and deception rather than by recognition and consent.[113] Gadamer thus overlooks what Albrecht Wellmer takes to be the Enlightenment's central insight:

> The enlightenment principle of reason can be interpreted as the demand for the abrogation of all repressive conditions that could claim no legitimacy other than their sheer existence.... [T]he "dialogue" which we, according to

> Gadamer, "are," is also a context of domination and as such precisely no dialogue.[114]

For Habermas, it is the emancipatory promise of reflection, which lies at the heart of Kant's notion of enlightenment, that represents "the permanent legacy bequeathed to us by German Idealism from the spirit of the eighteenth century."[115]

What is ultimately at issue in the dispute between Habermas and Gadamer is the nature of the claim this legacy has on us today. Gadamer argues that because Habermas has been misled by the Enlightenment's "abstract antithesis" between an "ongoing, natural tradition" and the "reflective appropriation" of this tradition, he fails to see that "reflection" is itself a part of a particular historical tradition.[116] Far from constituting a break with all tradition, the Enlightenment represented an elaboration of particular elements *within* one tradition. The imperative "think for yourself" makes sense, then, only because those who heed Kant's call are not thinking *by* themselves. They are rather thinking with others, as members of a particular tradition in which activities like "critique" and "reflection" have a meaning. But if reflection has meaning only within a particular tradition, there will be limits on its ability to call this tradition into question. To suppose that it is possible to place ourselves in a position where we could reflect on the validity of the tradition we inhabit is on a par with the assumption that we could somehow step outside of our language and certify that it indeed gives us a true account of the world. For reason to accomplish either, it would be necessary for it to sever its ties to tradition or to language. From Johann Georg Hamann through Gadamer to Alasdair MacIntyre and Richard Rorty, the more persuasive of the Enlightenment's critics have stressed the impossibility of doing this.[117]

Enlightenment, Disenchantment, and Domination

While the question of the relationship of reason and tradition originated among critics of the general program of the Enlightenment, more recently those who share its ideals have been plagued by the sense that something has gone terribly awry. The Enlightenment's attempt to free the world from the domination of mythology and superstition has fallen prey to a fatal dialectic in which enlightenment itself reverts into mythology and fosters new forms of domination that are all the more insidious since they claim to be vindicated by reason itself. This is the argument of Max Horkheimer and Theodor Adorno's *Dialectic of Enlightenment.* Written in 1944 as the Second World War ground to a close, it sought to understand what had brought reason to turn against itself.[118] Much of the force of the book lay in its profound ambivalence. At the outset, Horkheimer and Adorno affirmed their allegiance to the progressive hopes of the Enlightenment. They saw their task as "not the conservation of the past, but the redemption of past hopes" and insisted that "freedom . . . is inseparable from enlightened thought."[119] Yet at the heart of their argument lay a bitter paradox: "Enlightenment has always aimed at liberating men from fear and establishing their sovereignty. Yet the fully enlightened earth radiates disaster triumphant."[120] Enlightenment itself, they argued, "already contains the seed of the regression apparent everywhere today."[121]

In this account of the self-destruction of enlightenment, Horkheimer and Adorno were resuming an analysis of the Enlightenment that, like Gadamer's critique, can be traced to the discussion of the relationship between the Enlightenment and the French Revolution. Their model, however, was not Burke's *Reflections on the Revolution in France* but rather Hegel's *Phenomenology of Spirit.* Hegel's account of the world of the "self-alienated spirit"—a world that, perhaps ironically, he dubs "culture" (*Bildung*)—culminates in a section entitled "Absolute Freedom and Terror."[122] It argues that the Enlightenment's efforts to emancipate mankind result only in "death"—a death "which has no inner significance or feeling," a death that is "the coldest and meanest of all deaths, with no more significance than cutting off a head of cabbage or swallowing a mouthful of water."[123] The Enlightenment, which sought to create a new world in which reason would ascend the throne and in which all institutions would be measured against the standard of utility, turns out to be incapable of building anything. The universal freedom that the Enlightenment brought into the world culminates in a "fury of destruction."[124]

While much of Hegel's language resembles Burke's, his account is, in a fundamental sense, opposed to that of *Reflections on the Revolution in France.*[125] For Burke, the Revolution was a mistake, the consequence of a terrible foolishness that ought, and perhaps could, have been avoided. If the French aristocracy and clergy—on whom Burke lavishes what has struck some later commentators as excessive praise—had somehow been able to hold out, if the legions of politically naive writers and philosophers had somehow been kept out of the National Assembly, perhaps disaster could have been avoided. "Rage and frenzy will pull down more in half an hour," he observed sadly, "than prudence, deliberation, and foresight can build up in a hundred years."[126]

Hegel, however, doubted whether the survival of an institution over time testified to its reasonableness. Writing in 1817 of the demand by the Wurtemberg Estates that their king restore the rights guaranteed to them by their "ancestral constitution," he observed,

> One might say of the Wurtemberg Estates what has been said of the returned French *émigrés*: they have forgotten nothing and learnt nothing. They seem to have slept through the last twenty-five years, possibly the richest that world history has had, and for us the most instructive, because it is to them that our

> world and our ideas belong. There could hardly have been a more frightful pestle for pulverizing false concepts of law and prejudices about political constitutions than these twenty-five years, but these Estates have emerged unscathed and unaltered.[127]

For Hegel, the French Revolution inaugurated a new age in which, in Joachim Ritter's words, "the future has no relation to tradition."[128] While Burke saw the disaster of the Revolution to lie in its forgetting of the lessons of the past, for Hegel, its disaster lay in its failure to find an institutional form adequate to the principles on which the present rests.

As Hegel saw it, the task was to create political institutions that could be reconciled with the principle that, for him, represented the irrevocable achievement of the modern age: the freedom of the individual. This required some way of mediating between the particularity of the individual and the universality of laws. The analysis of "culture" in the *Phenomenology of Spirit* traces a number of failed attempts at finding such a reconciliation. The French Revolution was but the last and greatest of these failures, in which an attempt to measure all things against the standard of the good of the whole ultimately expressed itself in a rage against the individual. Jean-Jacques Rousseau's "General Will" thus leads to Robespierre's Terror, not—as Burke would have argued—because Rousseau had turned his back on the lessons of the past, but rather because the ancient models of democracy that Rousseau invoked were no longer adequate to the modern age.

But what sort of political organization would be adequate? In the *Philosophy of Right*, Hegel thought he found a solution with the development of that uniquely modern domain that he denoted with the venerable term "civil society" (*bürgerliche Gesellschaft*). In civil society individuals meet as free and independent creatures of need and carriers of rights. Here they give free play to their uniqueness and peculiarity while, behind their backs, the universal has its way with them through the system of laws that it is the task of political economy to map. Civil society is the domain in which "particularity is educated up to subjectivity."[129] It is here that the *bourgeois*—the individual who cares only for his own interests—learns to become a *citoyen*—an individual who is capable of willing the general good.[130] Or so Hegel argued in 1820. A decade later, in the wake of the July Revolution in Paris, he observed in letters to friends that everything that had once seemed so "solid and secure" had begun to "totter."[131] As his most famous disciple would later observe, all that was solid was melting into air.

A century after Hegel's death, Horkheimer assumed the directorship of the Institute for Social Research at the University of Frankfurt. The work of Horkheimer and his colleagues in the Frankfurt School represented a concentrated effort at seeing how the relationship between the family, the market, and the state had been transformed in advanced capitalism.[132]

While Hegel had argued that the relative independence of these three spheres allowed for a differentiated articulation of freedom in which one found different sorts of satisfactions in one's roles as family member, as bourgeois, and as citizen, the research of the Frankfurt School argued that the boundaries between these spheres had been effaced. State and market had become intertwined, while the socialization of children within the structure of family—which had allowed for the development of individual autonomy—had been overwhelmed by powerful social forces.[133] Hitler's Germany and Stalin's Russia seemed to them to prefigure a horrifying new world in which all traces of individuality would be extinguished.[134] Against this grim background the *Dialectic of Enlightenment*, that bleakest of books, was written.

Hegel prefaced his account of the dialectic of culture with his famous analysis of Sophocles' *Antigone*. Horkheimer and Adorno went back further, to Homer's Odysseus. Here they found, in one and the same figure, the first Aufklärer and the first bourgeois.[135] The mythic powers Odysseus confronts are locked in a cycle of endless repetition; like blind nature, they do the same thing over and over. He is able to overcome them by mastering the art of appearing to yield to them but always somehow finding an escape clause in the contract. "The formula for the cunning of Odysseus is that the redeemed and instrumental spirit, by resigning itself to yield to nature, renders to nature what is nature's and yet betrays it in the very process."[136] Thus Odysseus, bound to the mast, can listen to the song of the sirens, while his men, their ears stopped, row grimly onward. In this, Horkheimer and Adorno found an apt image for the role of art in modern society: stripped of its mythic powers, it becomes a pastime for those who are freed from labor.

This apparent triumph of enlightenment over mythology, like the triumph of enlightenment over faith in Hegel's *Phenomenology*, turns out to be only a struggle of enlightenment with itself.[137] Mythology, as the authors of the *Dialectic of Enlightenment* understood it, was already a step in the direction of enlightenment.

> Mythology itself set off the unending process of enlightenment in which ever and again, with the inescapable necessity, every specific theoretic view succumbs to the destructive criticism that it is only a belief—until the very notions of spirit, of truth and, indeed, enlightenment itself, have become animistic magic.[138]

Enlightenment, as Hegel recognized, demands that everything be measured against the standard of utility. Reason does not exempt itself from this demand and hence is now defined solely in instrumental terms.

> The more ideas have become automatic, instrumentalized, the less does anybody see in them thoughts with a meaning of their own. They are considered

> things, machines. Language has been reduced to just another tool in the gigantic apparatus of production in modern society.... [J]ustice, equality, happiness, tolerance, all the concepts that...were in preceding centuries supposed to be inherent in or sanctioned by reason, have lost their intellectual roots.[139]

Enlightenment routs superstition and obscurity, but in the process it corrodes the substantive principles that had once served as incentives to progress or—at the very least—as checks on barbarism. Once reason has become a mere instrument, it serves whatever power deploys it. Hegel's account of the self-destruction of the Enlightenment ended with the image of the guillotine, a machine that so rationalized punishment that it needed only to touch the body for a moment to deliver its sentence. Horkheimer and Adorno's *Dialectic of Enlightenment* kept pace with advancements in the technology of rationalized cruelty: it closed with an examination of that rage against all that is different that culminated in the death camps of the Third Reich.

The last sentence of the discussion of anti-Semitism in the *Dialectic of Enlightenment*—added, the preface tells us, three years after the initial "publication" of the book in mimeographed form (the initial form of publication, perhaps, can be viewed as exemplary of the book's thesis, since if its account of the eradication of individuality is correct, this should be a book with very few readers)[140]—strikes a strangely hopeful note: "Enlightenment, in possession of itself and coming to power, can break through the limits of enlightenment."[141] But how?

In a letter Horkheimer wrote to Herbert Marcuse shortly after the completion of the first chapter of the *Dialectic of Enlightenment*—which he characterized, accurately enough, as "the most difficult text I ever wrote"—he admitted that the work "sounds somewhat negativistic." While promising to do something to remedy this, he confessed,

> I am reluctant, however, to simply add a more positive paragraph with the melody, "But after all rationalism and pragmatism are not so bad." The intransigent analysis as accomplished in this first chapter seems in itself to be a better assertion of the positive function of rational intelligence than anything one could say in order to play down the attack.[142]

By the time Horkheimer had completed the excursus entitled "Juliette, or Enlightenment and Morality," he must have concluded that it was only through a mercilessly "negativistic" critique of what enlightenment had become that the "past hopes" of the Enlightenment might be redeemed. He appeared to have found a model for his own work in those "dark writers of the bourgeoisie"—such as Mandeville, de Sade, and Nietzsche—who "have not tried to ward off the consequences of enlightenment with harmonizing doctrines." It was the failure to recognize the ties between formalized morality and evil, between reason and crime, and between civil society and domination that bound enlightenment to that which sought to negate it. In contrast, the dark writers' merciless revelation of the Enlightenment's complicity with domination "frees from its shell the utopia that inheres in the Kantian conception of reason as well as in every great philosophy: that a humanity that no longer distorted itself, would no longer need to distort."[143] Thus, paradoxically, it was only by taking up the arguments of the Enlightenment's most vehement critics that the hopes of enlightenment might be kept alive.

Nietzsche's New Enlightenment

Among the "dark writers" to whom Horkheimer turned for inspiration, none had a more complex relationship with the Enlightenment than Nietzsche. At times, Nietzsche spoke as if his goal was that of disentangling the eighteenth-century Enlightenment from its complicity with democratic revolutions. Thus he labored to finish *Menschliches, Allzumenschliches* so that it might appear in 1878, the hundredth anniversary of the death of Voltaire.[144]

> It is not *Voltaire*'s moderate nature, but *Rousseau*'s passionate follies and half-lies that called forth the optimistic spirit of Revolution against which I cry: *"Ecrasez l'infame!"* It is this spirit that has for a long time banished *the spirit of the Enlightenment and of progressive evolution:* let us see—each of us within himself—whether it is possible to call it back![145]

Enlightenment, as Nietzsche understood it, "addressed itself only to the individual." Its association with revolutionary politics was not the least of the damage done by Rousseau.

> He who grasps this will also know out of . . . what impurity it has to be cleansed: so as then to *continue* the work of the Enlightenment *in himself*, and to strangle the Revolution at birth.[146]

The enlightenment Nietzsche demanded must be clear-sighted enough to see the shallowness and the commonness of the egalitarian dreams of the French Revolution.[147]

One way of furthering the goals of the Enlightenment was to call on the very forces that had opposed it. In a section of *Menschliches, Allzumenschliches* entitled "Reaction as Progress" he argued that apparently reactionary responses to "blunt and forceful spirits" often only prepare the way for further progress. Thus Arthur Schopenhauer had a deeper historical understanding of Christianity than the Enlightenment, but once "the mode of historical interpretation introduced by the Age of Enlightenment" had been corrected, "we may bear the banner of the Enlightenment—the banner bearing the three names Petrarch, Erasmus, Voltaire—further onward."[148]

The same argument is made even more forcefully in *Morgenröte* when Nietzsche suggested that even though German resistance to the Enlightenment had taken the form of a piety toward tradition and a cult of feeling,

> after appearing for a time as ancillaries of the spirit of obscurantism and reaction, the study of history, understanding of origins and evolutions, empathy for the past, newly aroused passion for feeling and knowledge one day assumed a new nature and now fly on the broadest wings above and beyond their former conjurers as new and stronger genii of *that very Enlightenment* against which they were first conjured up. This Enlightenment we must now carry forward: let us not worry about the "great revolution" and the "great reaction" against it which have taken place—they are no more than the sporting of waves in comparison with the truly great flood which bears *us* along![149]

In such passages, Nietzsche—like Karl Leonhard Reinhold before him—outlines what might be characterized as "a dialectic of the counterenlightenment": all attempts to resist enlightenment paradoxically turn out only to serve the cause of further enlightenment.[150]

What is troubling about this secret complicity between enlightenment and counterenlightenment is that the relationship can easily be reversed: while counterenlightenment may serve the cause of enlightenment, it is just as possible that enlightenment will lead to a new obscurantism. In a cryptic note from 1885 Nietzsche observed, "When I believe that I am a few centuries ahead in enlightenment not only of Voltaire but even of Galiani, who was far profounder—how far must I have got in the increase of darkness [*Verdüsterung*]."[151] The idea that a progress in Aufklärung was simultaneously an advance in Verdüsterung finds its most powerful expression in Nietzsche's famous parable of the madman who announces the death of God. Even in "the bright morning hours" he must carry a lantern and asks, "Is not night continually closing in on us? Do we not need to light lanterns in the morning?"[152]

This sense that every advance of enlightenment may well be only a further step into the darkness permeates the work of Nietzsche's most faithful twentieth-century disciple, Michel Foucault. From his very first book—which he described as a part of that "great Nietzschean inquiry" that seeks to confront "the dialectic of history" with the "immobile structures of tragedy"[153]—he sought to demonstrate how every victory of enlightenment was also a triumph of a new and insidious form of domination. Tuke and Pinel arrived in eighteenth-century prisons to separate criminals from the insane—and forced the insane "to enter a kind of endless trial for which the asylum furnished simultaneously police, magistrates, and torturers."[154] Freud shattered the silence surrounding sexuality—and inaugurated the "nearly infinite task of telling—telling oneself and an other, as often as possible" anything that might be linked in the remotest way to the body and its pleasures.[155] In *Birth of the Clinic*, the light that penetrates the dark interior of the body in search of life finds only death, just as in *Discipline and Punish* the prisoners who have been freed from the darkness of the dungeon are captured all the more securely in the light that floods through the Panopticon.[156] Like the "dark writers of the bourgeoisie," everywhere Foucault looked he found a complicity between enlightenment and domination.

But—once again like Nietzsche—at times Foucault took up the banner of the Enlightenment. In the last decade of his life, he reflected again and again on Kant's 1784 essay, "What Is Enlightenment?" and in the end announced that he would like to see his own work understood as a part of the "critical ontology of ourselves" that Kant's work had opened.[157] In the very last of his discussions of Kant's essay, enlightenment marches under a banner on which an even more unlikely set of names is inscribed than Nietzsche's trinity Petrarch, Erasmus, and Voltaire. The enlightenment to which Foucault declared his loyalty somehow manages to embrace both Immanuel Kant and Charles Baudelaire.[158]

Foucault's peculiar coupling of Kant and Baudelaire suggests he was concerned neither with the content of Kant's account of enlightenment nor with its connection to Kant's moral philosophy. His emphasis instead fell on what he understood Kant to be doing in posing the question "What is enlightenment?" in the first place. Just as Constantin Guys—the painter whose work Baudelaire examines in his essay "The Painter of Modern Life"—sought to capture what was eternal in "the ephemeral, the fugitive, the contingent," so Kant—as Foucault read him—attempted to find a philosophical significance in the passing controversies of his age. Like Guys, Kant sought "to distil the eternal from the transitory."[159]

Foucault thus came to see in Kant's essay a way of doing philosophy that could serve as a model for his own efforts. Kant is said to herald a "critical ontology of ourselves" in which "the critique of what we are is at one and the same time the historical analysis of the limits that are imposed on us and an experiment with the possibility of going beyond them."[160] Kant found the "motto of enlightenment" in Horace's *Sapere Aude!*—which he glossed as "Have the courage to use your *own* understanding!" Foucault kept the motto but changed the exegesis: for Foucault, like Nietzsche before him, enlightenment meant above all else having the courage to reinvent oneself.

Reopening the Question of Enlightenment

The Enlightenment's critics are in agreement, then, that there is something sinister about the light it casts. Burke complained that

> all the pleasing illusions which made power gentle and obedience liberal, which harmonized the different shades of life, and which, by a bland assim-

> ilation, incorporated into politics the sentiments which beautify and soften private society, are to be dissolved by this new conquering empire of light and reason.[161]

Hamann dismissed the Enlightenment as "a mere northern light," a "cold, unfruitful moonlight" that served only as a cloak for self-appointed guardians who sought to rule over others.[162] As he explained in a letter to Mendelssohn, "I avoid the light, my dear Moses, perhaps more out of fear than maliciousness."[163] And Horkheimer and Adorno's fears have been echoed in Foucault's famous discussion of that most unsettling of all enlightenment schemes, Jeremy Bentham's *Panopticon.*[164] An untroubled partisan of enlightenment, Bentham sought to replace the dark dungeons of the old regime with buildings composed of cells open on two sides to the light which together would form a large ring of as many stories of cells as were necessary to house the population at hand. In the center of the ring he proposed the construction of a watchtower, from whose shielded windows the activities of the residents of the sunlit cells could be observed. This arrangement gave those in the tower a power far beyond what they normally possessed: since those in the tower see but cannot be seen, it really does not matter who is in the tower (Bentham noted that children might find useful employment here) or even whether, at any given moment, there was anyone in it at all. It was enough that the tower serve as a reminder to the prisoners in their sunlit cells that they can always be watched. Those who watch are hidden and hence omnipresent. Those who are watched are isolated, atomized, and always visible—released from dungeons but held all the more securely by the light that bathes them.[165] Here is a vision worthy of Horkheimer and Adorno's darkest moments: the fully enlightened world has become a massive prison.

It is worth asking, however, whether this portrait of the Enlightenment is at all faithful to its subject. Reservations can be registered on at least two fronts. First, the images of the Enlightenment we have considered here are, at best, caricatures that highlight certain features but miss others. Second, what these caricatures miss may very well be what is of greatest importance in understanding the continuing viability of some version of the hopes of the Enlightenment.

What is striking is how rarely the critique of "enlightenment" ever bothers to engage thinkers who were part of "*the* Enlightenment." Burke goes after Dr. Price but never troubles himself with asking whether French thinkers might not actually have given some thought to the question of whether "prejudices" could ever be completely eradicated.[166] Gadamer, as usual, does better. He acknowledges that the "prejudice against prejudices" never went as far in Germany as it is alleged to have gone in England and France and suggests that the German willingness to recognize "the 'true prejudices' of the Christian religion" in part brought about that "modification and moderation of Enlightenment" that laid the groundwork for the romantic movement. "But," he quickly assures us, "none of this alters the fundamental fact."[167] True prejudices still must be confirmed by reason, even if some Aufklärer were less confident than their French counterparts that reason was up to the task. But more recent and more extended discussions of the history of the concept of prejudice provide a more complex picture in which reason is not quite so imperious and prejudice not quite so despised as one would assume from reading Gadamer.[168]

Similar misgivings may be voiced with regard to the image of enlightenment emerging from Hegel, Horkheimer, and Adorno. The difficulties of deciding to whom Hegel happens to be referring at any given point in the *Phenomenology of Spirit* are formidable enough to have fostered a cottage industry of commentaries ready to make suggestions. And it is even more curious that Hegel, who in his youth was an avid reader of the *Berlinische Monatsschrift* as well as of Mendelssohn and other now-forgotten Aufklärer, could manage to provide an account of something called "Die Aufklärung" without a single recognizable German figure. Horkheimer and Adorno drop some eighteenth-century names—Voltaire, de Sade, and Kant—but far more of the *Dialectic of Enlightenment* is devoted to probing the intricacies of the *Odyssey* or the "culture industry" than to exploring how Hamann's critique of Kant (to suggest only one example) turned on such issues as the relationship between mimesis and conceptualization.[169]

The point here is not simply the somewhat pedantic one (though the virtues of pedantry may be grossly underestimated today) that much which passes as a critique of "enlightenment" does not measure up to current standards for historical accounts of "the Enlightenment." There is, after all, probably little danger that anyone would mistake the *Dialectic of Enlightenment* as a guide to eighteenth-century thought.[170] Rather, the point is that any serious attempt to understand the promise and limits of "enlightenment" might profit from at least a passing acquaintance with the ways in which eighteenth-century thinkers dealt with the question "What is enlightenment?"[171]

When Kant answered the question "What is enlightenment?" in 1784, it is notable that he did not invoke those images of light that have cast such a shadow over recent criticisms of the Enlightenment. He instead talked about speech. For him, enlightenment demanded not a world in which everything stood naked to the light but rather a world in which it was possible to speak without fear. The idea that knowing involves seeing lies so deeply embedded in our tradition that it is little wonder we sometimes speak of thought as if it were an inner light. It was Kant's great achievement to recognize that this metaphor is in many ways misleading, and from this recognition flowed his energetic defense of the right to freedom of expression.

> We do admittedly say that, whereas a higher authority may deprive us of freedom of *speech* or of *writing*, it cannot deprive us of freedom of *thought*. But how much and how accurately would we *think* if we did not think, so to speak, in community with others to whom we *communicate* our thoughts and who communicate their thoughts to us! We may therefore conclude that the same external constraint which deprives people of the freedom to *communicate* their thoughts in public also removes their freedom of *thought*, the one treasure which remains to us amidst all the burdens of civil life, and which alone offers us a means of overcoming all the evils of this condition.[172]

While we can see alone, we think best "in community with others"—and this suggests a rather different way of talking about enlightenment.

In Kant's *Critique of Judgment*, the phrase he had employed as the "motto of enlightenment" serves as the first of his three maxims of understanding: "(1) think for oneself; (2) think from the standpoint of everyone else; and (3) think always consistently. The first is the maxim of an *unprejudiced*, the second of a *broadened*, the third of a *consistent* way of thinking."[173] It is only by becoming skilled at the first two—which he labeled the maxims of "understanding" and of "judgment"—that we become proficient in the third, which he called the "maxim of reason."[174] We become reasonable by thinking for ourselves and by thinking from the standpoint of everyone else. And the way in which we can best do this is by thinking in the company of others, offering our ideas to others, who will take them up and criticize them, and by responding in turn to these criticisms.

There is, of course, at least one thinker who has never lost sight of the peculiar connection between speech and enlightenment. In his first work, *The Structural Transformation of the Public Sphere*, Habermas examined the explosion of new forms of public debate and discussion that for him defined the European Enlightenment.[175] In his subsequent writings he has sought to examine how language brings us together into a community with others. "Our first sentence," he once wrote, "expresses unequivocally the intention of universal and unconstrained consensus."[176] In the act of speaking we enter into an implicit and unavoidable contract with others that commits us to clarifying, to discussing, to reformulating what it is that we have said.[177] Our language is extraordinarily well stocked with devices for initiating further discussion, a fact that Habermas argues is central to the way in which language works to bind us together. For it to work in the way that it does—and this is obviously a very large claim—it must implicitly contain within itself the promise of a community bound together by mutual understanding and agreement.

Were the dream of enlightenment only that of seeing the world without shadows, of bathing everything in the light of reason, then indeed there might be something pathological in that dream: for to want to see everything is to aspire to the standpoint of God or to that of the guardian in the Panopticon's tower. Perhaps the most important thing the Enlightenment taught was that we are neither gods nor guardians who survey the world from outside but rather men and women who speak from within it and must summon the courage to argue about what is true and what is false and what is right and what is wrong. And perhaps a reconsideration of the Enlightenment's own discussion of the question "What is enlightenment?" can enlighten our own understanding of what is still at stake when we argue about "enlightenment."

NOTES

1. Leszek Kolakowski, "The Idolatry of Politics," *Atlantic Community Quarterly* 24 (Fall 1986): 219–230, advances the first of these arguments, insisting that the Enlightenment's skepticism about absolute values "threatens our ability to make the distinction between good and evil altogether" (223), that its belief that human beings are "entirely society-made" leaves us "conceptually defenseless in the face of totalitarian doctrines, ideologies, and institutions" (224), and that its "erosion of historical consciousness" leads to a "progressive decline of awareness that our spiritual life includes the sediment of the historical past" (227). For the argument that liberal societies can dispense with "philosophical foundations," see Richard Rorty, *Contingency, Irony, and Solidarity* (Cambridge, 1989), 52–54.

2. See, for example, James Q. Wilson, *The Moral Sense* (New York, 1993), 244–250, which argues that part of the "ambiguous legacy of the Enlightenment" is the "fatally flawed assumption . . . that autonomous individuals can freely choose, or will, their moral life." Wilson argues that this overemphasis on individual rights leads to a system of laws and institutions "that leave nothing between the state and the individual save choices, contracts, and entitlements."

3. See Richard Pipes, *The Russian Revolution* (New York, 1990), 124–133, 135–138. See also Berel Lang, *Act and Idea in the Nazi Genocide* (Chicago, 1990), 165–206, for a discussion of the "affiliation" between Enlightenment ideals of universality and Nazi genocide.

4. See Isaiah Berlin, *The Crooked Timber of Humanity* (London, 1990), 33–34, 39–40, 51–52, 183.

5. See Charles Taylor, *Sources of the Self: The Making of Modern Identity* (Cambridge, Mass., 1989), 321–340, and Alasdair MacIntyre, *After Virtue* (Notre Dame, 1981), 49–75.

6. See Jean-François Lyotard, *The Postmodern Condition* (Minneapolis, 1984), 31–37, and Michel Foucault, *Madness and Civilization: A History of Insanity in the Age of Reason*, trans. Richard Howard (New York, 1973), 35–36, 107–116. See also Hartmut and Gernot Böhme, *Das Andere der Vernunft* (Frankfurt, 1983).

7. On racism, see Richard H. Popkin, "The Philosophical Bases of Modern Racism" and "Hume's Racism," reprinted in *The High Road to Pyrrhonism* (San Diego, 1980), 79–102 and 267–276; and Cornel West, *Prophesy Deliverance!* (Philadelphia, 1982), 61–65. For a discussion of feminist critiques of the Enlightenment,

see Robin May Schott, "The Gender of Enlightenment," this volume; Sandra Harding, "The Instability of the Analytical Categories of Feminist Theory," *Signs* 11, no. 4 (1986): 645–664, esp. 655–657; and Jane Flax, "Postmodernism and Gender Relations in Feminist Theory," *Signs* 12, no. 4 (1987): 621–643.

8. Johann Friedrich Zöllner, "Ist es rathsam, das Ehebündniß nicht ferner durch die Religion zu sanciren?" *Berlinische Monatsschrift* 2 (1783): 516. Reprinted in *Was ist Aufklärung? Beiträge aus der Berlinischen Monatsschrift*, 2d ed., ed. Norbert Hinske (Darmstadt, 1977), 115.

9. Moses Mendelssohn, "Über die Frage: Was heisst aufklären?" *Berlinische Monatsschrift* 4 (1784): 193–200 (reprinted in Mendelssohn, *Gesammelte Schriften Jubiläumsausgabe* 6/1 [Stuttgart–Bad Cannstatt, 1981], 115–119) (translated below, pp. 53–57); and Immanuel Kant, "Beantwortung der Frage: Was ist Aufklärung?" *Berlinische Monatsschrift* 4 (1784): 494 (reprinted in *Kant's Gesammelte Schriften*, Akademie Ausgabe (hereafter cited as AA) (Berlin, 1923), VIII:33–42) (translated below, pp. 58–64).

10. For an overview of these essays, see H. B. Nisbet, "'Was ist Aufklärung?' The Concept of Enlightenment in Eighteenth-Century Germany," *Journal of European Studies* 12 (1992): 77–95, and Werner Schneiders, *Die wahre Aufklärung* (München, 1974), which includes a comprehensive bibliography.

11. Wieland's essay is translated below, pp. 78–83.

12. The author went on to distinguish twenty-one possible meanings of the concept. See "Kritischer Versuch über das Wort Aufklärung zur endlichen Beilegung der darüber geführten Streitigkeiten," in *Deutsche Monatsschrift* 3 (September–December 1790): 11–43, 205–237. Reprinted in Zwi Batscha, ed., *Aufklärung und Gedankenfreiheit* (Frankfurt, 1977), 45–94.

13. See Eckhart Hellmuth, "Aufklärung und Pressefreiheit: Zur Debatte der Berliner Mittwochsgesellschaft während der Jahre 1783 und 1784," *Zeitschrift für historisches Forschung* 9 (1982): 315–345.

14. For a comprehensive overview of this phase of the discussion, see Steven Lestition, "Kant and the End of the Enlightenment in Prussia," *Journal of Modern History* 65 (March 1993): 57–112. For a collection of essays from this period, see Batscha, *Aufklärung und Gedankenfreiheit.*

15. For a recent discussion of German reactions to the French Revolution, see Frederick C. Beiser, *Enlightenment, Revolution, and Romanticism* (Cambridge, Mass., 1992).

16. For discussions of the Mittwochsgesellschaft and its membership, see Günter Birtsch, "The Berlin Wednesday Society," translated below, pp. 235–252; Ludwig Keller, "Die Berliner Mittwochsgesellschaft," *Monatshefte der Comenius-Gesellschaft*, 5, nos. 3–4 (1896): 70–73, 88–91; Heinrich Meisner, "Die Freunde der Aufklärung: Geschichte der Berliner Mittwochsgesellschaft," *Festschrift zur 50jährigen Doktorjubelfeier Karl Weinholds* (Strasburg, 1896): 43–54; Hinske, *Was ist Aufklärung?* xxiv–xxxi; and Horst Möller, "Enlightened Societies in the Metropolis: The Case of Berlin," in *The Transformation of Political Culture: England and Germany in the Late Eighteenth Century*, ed. Eckhart Hellmuth (London, 1990), 226–232.

17. Möhsen was a prominent Berlin physician with an interest in the history of science. He also served as Frederick the Great's personal doctor. His lecture is trans-

lated below, pp. 49–52; the request for a consideration of the question "What is enlightenment?" occurs on p. 49.

18. Norbert Hinske, "Mendelssohns Beantwortung der Frage: Was ist Aufklärung?" 87–88.

19. For a helpful overview of the literature on Enlightenment societies, see Richard van Dülmen, *The Society of the Enlightenment,* trans. Anthony Williams (New York, 1992), and the brief discussions in Horst Möller, *Vernunft und Kritik: Deutsche Aufklärung im 17. und 18. Jahrhundert* (Frankfurt, 1986), 213–231, and Ulrich Im Hof, "German Associations in the Second Half of the Eighteenth Century," in Hellmuth, *The Transformation of Political Culture,* 207–218. Two influential earlier studies, which situate the proliferation of secret societies in the broader process of the development of modern "civil society" are now available in English: see Reinhart Koselleck, *Critique and Crisis* (Cambridge, Mass., 1988), esp. pp. 62–97, and Jürgen Habermas, *The Structural Transformation of the Public Sphere* (Cambridge, Mass., 1989), esp. pp. 31–43.

20. This was particularly true for the so-called Strict Observance lodges (a branch of the Masonic movement that placed a considerable emphasis on ritual and flirted with mysticism) as well as among the Rosicrucians. For a discussion, see Klaus Epstein, *The Genesis of German Conservatism* (Princeton, 1966), 104–111.

21. The Mittwochsgesellschaft exemplified this function. See van Dülmen's discussion of "Patriotic Societies" (pp. 65–81) and "Political Societies" (pp. 104–127). Among the most famous of the "Political Societies" was the Illuminati, which was founded in 1776 with the goal of transforming the absolutist state by infiltrating its offices with individuals dedicated to the ideals of egalitarianism and enlightenment. It was banned in 1784. For a discussion, see van Dülmen, *Society of the Enlightenment,* 104–118, Epstein, *Genesis of German Conservatism,* 87–95, and Koselleck, *Critique and Crisis,* 90–97, 131–137. For an exploration of the political significance of Masonic lodges in Western Europe, see Margaret C. Jacob, *Living the Enlightenment: Freemasonry and Politics in Eighteenth-Century Europe* (New York, 1991).

22. The initial announcement of the formation of the Mittwochsgesellschaft expressed the hope that within the society "no one would be called by title or rank, but rather simply by his name." See von Irwing's letter of 3 October 1783, reprinted in "Die Gesellschaft der Freunde der Aufklärung in Berlin im Jahre 1783," *Litterarischer Anzeiger für christliche Theologie und Wissenschaft überhaupt* 1, no. 8 (1830): 59. For a brief overview of the new patterns of sociability inaugurated within the Masonic lodges, see Margaret C. Jacob, "The Enlightenment Redefined: The Formation of Modern Civil Society," *Social Research* 58, no. 2 (1991): 475–495, esp. pp. 484–488.

23. Möhsen, below, p. 51. Horst Möller has noted the irony of the fact that a discussion of the ideals of enlightenment could only take place in a secret society. See "Enlightened Societies in the Metropolis," 227.

24. Keller, "Berliner Mittwochsgesellschaft," 74.

25. Lessing to Nicolai, 25 August 1769, in Lessing, *Sämtliche Schriften,* ed. Karl Lachmann and Franz Muncker (Stuttgart, 1904), 17: 298. For a discussion of Frederick's views on censorship, see Franz Schneider, *Pressefreiheit und politische Öffentlichkeit* (Neuwied, 1966), 64–66. For an examination of the rather limited range of public discussion in eighteenth-century Prussia, see Thomas Saine, "Was ist Aufklär-

ung?" in *Aufklärung, Absolutismus und Bürgertum in Deutschland*, ed. Franklin Kopitzsch (München, 1976), 332–338.

26. See Klein, below, pp. 87–96. For a discussion of the agitation for freedom of the press in the 1780s, see Möller, *Vernunft und Kritik*, 281–283.

27. For a discussion of the debate within the Mittwochsgesellschaft, see Hellmuth, "Aufklärung und Pressefreiheit."

28. Keller, "Berliner Mittwochsgesellschaft," 80–81 (also in Mendelssohn, *Gesammelte Schriften* 6, no. 1: 113).

29. See the responses by Dohm, von Irwing, and Nicolai in Keller, "Berliner Mittwochsgesellschaft," 83, 86, and 88.

30. Keller, "Berliner Mittwochsgesellschaft," 77–78.

31. Ibid., 79.

32. Mendelssohn, *Gesammelte Schriften* 6, no. 1: 117 (translated below, p. 55).

33. Mendelssohn, "Soll man der einreissenden Schwärmerey durch Satyre oder durch äussere Verbindung entgegenarbeiten?" *Berlinische Monatsschrift* 5 (February 1785): 133–137 (*Gesammelte Schriften* 6, no. 1: 139).

34. Mendelssohn described the distinction as "somewhat strange" in his notes for a discussion of Kant's essay within the Mittwochsgesellschaft and rephrased it as a contrast between "vocational" and "extravocational" uses of reason; see Mendelssohn, *Gesammelte Schriften* 8: 227–228. For a discussion of the distinction, see John Christian Laursen, "The Subversive Kant: The Vocabulary of 'Public' and 'Publicity,'" *Political Theory* 14, no. 4 (1986) (reprinted below, pp. 253–269); Onora O'Neill, "The Public Use of Reason," in *Constructions of Reason* (Cambridge, 1989), 28–50; Thomas Auxter, "Kant's Conception of the Private Sphere," *Philosophical Forum* (1981): 295–310; and James Schmidt, "What Enlightenment Was: How Moses Mendelssohn and Immanuel Kant Answered the *Berlinische Monatsschrift*," *Journal of the History of Philosophy* 30 (1992): 94–95.

35. AA VIII:37 (translated below, p. 60).

36. AA VIII:37 (translated below, p. 60).

37. AA VIII:38–39 (translated below, p. 61). In taking up this example, Kant was joining an ongoing discussion of the status of the "Symbolic Books" of the Lutheran faith, to which Lutheran clergy were supposed to swear conformity. Mendelssohn had already criticized such oaths in his *Jerusalem* as well as in an earlier article in the *Berlinische Monatsschrift*. See my discussion in "What Enlightenment Was," pp. 95–98.

38. AA VIII:39–40 (translated below, p. 61).

39. Frederick's death had been anticipated for some time. An anonymous article published in the *Berlinische Monatsschrift* a year before Frederick's death suggested that while a great monarch such as Frederick could leave his mark after his death through the laws he gave his people, these laws could be secured against the actions by his successors only if the form of the regime itself was transformed into a republic, with the head of the ruling family serving merely as president. See "Neuer Weg zur Unsterblichkeit für Fürsten," *Berlinische Monatsschrift* 5 (1785): 239–247. Friedrich Nicolai published a number of articles during 1785 warning of the dangers of "crypto-Catholicism"—a conspiracy of former Jesuits who, after the order had been dissolved in 1773, were alleged to have begun infiltrating Masonic lodges and

secret societies with the intent of bringing about a counter-reformation in Germany. See Lestition, "Kant and the End of the Enlightenment," 64–65. Kant's former pupil F. V. L. Plessing reported rumors of forthcoming restrictions on freedom of thought in his letter to Kant of 15 March 1784; see Kant, *Philosophical Correspondence, 1759–99,* trans. Arnulf Zweig (Chicago, 1967), 113–115.

40. For a discussion of Frederick William's religious beliefs and the influence of Woellner, see Epstein, *Genesis of German Conservatism,* 356–372, and Lestition, "Kant and the End of the Enlightenment," 64–66.

41. For an abbreviated version of the essay, see Paul Schwartz, *Der erste Kulturkampf in Preussen um Kirche und Schule, 1778–1798* (Berlin, 1925), 73–92. The comments on Gedike and Beister appear on p. 74, and the attack on Zedlitz—a "freethinker and enemy of the name of Jesus"—may be found on pp. 83–84.

42. Schwartz, *Der erste Kulturkampf,* 81. Frederick and Woellner had been bitter enemies ever since Frederick attempted to prevent Woellner's marriage into an old Junker family. Woellner was the son of a poor clergyman, and while his bride's mother approved of the marriage, other members of the family objected to his crossing of class boundaries. When the messenger Frederick dispatched to forbid the marriage arrived too late, Frederick had the bride arrested for a month while an investigation was conducted to see if the marriage was the result of undue pressure. Though no evidence of any wrongdoing was found, Frederick nevertheless refused to grant Woellner a patent of nobility and placed the administration of the estates of his bride's family under state supervision. See Epstein, *Genesis of German Conservatism,* 357.

43. Schwartz, *Der erste Kulturkampf,* 18.

44. The classic discussion of the various tendencies within eighteenth-century German theology is Karl Aner, *Die Theologie der Lessingzeit* (Halle, 1927). For a very helpful English summary, see Henry E. Allison, *Lessing and the Enlightenment* (Ann Arbor, 1966), 38–49.

45. For a discussion of how this approach is deployed in Johann August Eberhard's *New Apology for Socrates,* see Allison, *Lessing and the Enlightenment,* 40–42.

46. For a discussion of typical themes from their sermons, see Günter Birtsch, "The Christian as Subject," in Hellmuth, ed., *The Transformation of Political Culture,* 317–326.

47. Lessing published the first fragment in 1774. This was followed in 1777 by five more selections, with a concluding fragment published in the next year. For a summary of their contents and a discussion of the controversy they sparked, see Allison, *Lessing and the Enlightenment,* 42–49, and Epstein, *Genesis of German Conservatism,* 129–133.

48. Allison, *Lessing and the Enlightenment,* 48.

49. Bahrdt, *Briefe über die Bibel im Volkston,* 5 vols. (Halle, 1772–1783), and *Ausführung des Plans und Zweckes Jesus,* 10 vols. (Berlin, 1783–1785).

50. For a summary, see S. G. Flygt, *The Notorious Dr. Bahrdt* (Nashville, 1963), 250–267.

51. For the struggle between Moser and Bahrdt, see Flygt, *Dr. Bahrdt,* 71–91, 109–118.

52. Moser, "True and False Political Enlightenment," below, pp. 214–215.

53. Ibid., p. 215.

54. In a 1787 defense of freedom of the press, Bahrdt equated Frederick William's views on the question of freedom of expression with those of his uncle. See Bahrdt, "On the Freedom of the Press and Its Limits," below, p. 106.

55. On the Religion Edict, see Epstein, *Genesis of German Conservatism*, 142–153, and Schwartz, *Der erste Kulturkampf*, 93–106. For a discussion of the literature on the edict, see Fritz Valjavec, "Das Woellnersche Religionsedikt und seine geschichtliche Bedeutung," *Historisches Jahrbuch* 72 (1953): 386–400.

56. See Henri Brunschwig, *Enlightenment and Romanticism in Eighteenth-Century Prussia*, trans. Frank Jellinek (Chicago, 1974), 168. The Upper Consistory (*Oberkonsistorium*) was the chief governing body of the Lutheran Church. Established as a part of the Prussian bureaucracy in 1750, it was responsible for the appointment and supervision of clergy, the instruction of theological students, and the approval of candidates for teaching positions at the Lutheran seminaries (the Reformed Church Directory exercised similar control over the Calvinist Reformed Church). In 1788 the six ecclesiastical members of the consistory were Friedrich Samuel Gottfried Sack (who came to the consistory in 1786 on the death of his father, the enlightened theologian Friedrich William Sack), Johann Joachim Spalding, Anton Friedrich Büsching, Johann Samuel Diterich, William Abraham Teller, and Johann Jesaias Silberschlag. Spalding, Diterich, and Teller were members of the Mittwochsgesellschaft (their colleagues in the Mittwochsgesellschaft, Karl Franz von Irwing and Friedrich Gedike, were lay members). Sack and Büsching shared their commitment to enlightened approaches to theology. The sole ecclesiastical member of the consistory who did not resign was Silberschlag, a Pietist who remained loyal to Christian orthodoxy mainly because his interests lay in the areas of science and engineering and he did not bother to keep up with recent developments in theology. For a discussion of the Oberkonsistorium and its responsibilities, see Günter Birtsch, "The Christian as Subject," 310–317.

57. Nicolai's *Allgemeine Deutsche Bibliothek* devoted an entire volume (114, no. 2) to a review by H. P. C. Henke of forty-eight articles in response to the edict. The review was subsequently republished by Henke as *Beurtheilung aller Schriften, welche durch das Religions-Edikt und andere damit zusammenhängende Verfügungen veranlasst sind* (Hamburg, 1793).

58. The first installment of Riem's essay is translated below, pp. 168–187. For discussions of his essay, see Schneiders, *Wahre Aufklärung*, 95–100; Valjavec, "Das Woellnersche Religionsedikt," 395–396; and Epstein, *Genesis of German Conservatism*, 116–117.

59. On the Censorship Edict, see Schwartz, *Der erste Kulturkampf*, 129–150; Epstein, *Genesis of German Conservatism*, 362–363; and Brunschwig, *Enlightenment*, 167–168 (who mistakenly dates the edict as having been issued in December 1789).

60. Epstein, *Genesis of German Conservatism*, 363.

61. For discussions of the work of the commission and resistance to it, see Brunschwig, *Enlightenment*, 168–170; Epstein, *Genesis of German Conservatism*, 363–369; and Schwartz, *Der erste Kulturkampf*, 172–214.

62. Moser, "Publicity," below, p. 115.

63. Ibid.

64. On the case of Bahrdt, see Flygt, *Dr. Bahrdt*, 297–302, and Epstein, *Genesis of German Conservatism*, 118–120. Kant himself offers an account of his conflict with Woellner in the preface to his *Conflict of the Faculties* and reprints the text of Frederick William's letter of 1 October 1794, from which I have quoted. For discussions of the conflict, see Ernst Cassirer, *Kant's Life and Thought*, trans. James Haden (New Haven, 1981), 376–381 and 391–397, and Wilhelm Dilthey's classic study, "Der Streit Kants mit der Zensur über das Recht freier Religionsforschung," in Dilthey, *Gesammelte Schriften* (Stuttgart, 1959), 4: 285–309. For a comparison of the responses of Kant and Bahrdt, see Ludger Lütkehaus, "Karl Friedrich Bahrdt, Immanuel Kant, und die Gegenaufklärung in Preussen (1788–1798)," *Jahrbuch des Instituts für deutsche Geschichte* 9 (1980): 83–106. For a comprehensive and thoughtful account of the broader implications of Kant's response, see Lestition, "Kant and the End of the Enlightenment."

65. Fichte, "Zuruf an den Bewohner der preussischen Staaten," *Gesamtausgabe* II/2: 184–197. For a discussion, see Beiser, *Enlightenment, Revolution, and Romanticism*, 78. Woellner's edict was also supported by Jakob Friedrich Rönnberg, a professor at Rostock University noted for his opposition to serfdom. See Epstein, *Genesis of German Conservatism*, 146.

66. For a general discussion of the "corporatist" or "estatist" character of the German Enlightenment, see Jonathan Knudsen, *Justus Möser and the German Enlightenment* (Cambridge, 1986), 3–19.

67. Keller, "Berliner Mittwochsgesellschaft," 85. Gedike characterized the enlightenment of a nation as consisting of "the collective summation of the differentiated grades of enlightenment among the different ranks." It begins of necessity with the middle class, and "the rays of enlightenment only *gradually* spread to the two extremes, the upper and the lower ranks."

68. Keller, "Berliner Mittwochsgesellschaft," 79.

69. Ibid.

70. Johann Heinrich Tieftrunk, "On the Influence of Enlightenment on Revolutions," translated below, p. 217.

71. Cited in T. C. W. Blanning, "The Enlightenment in Catholic Germany," in *The Enlightenment in National Context*, ed. Roy Porter and Mikulás Teich (Cambridge, 1981), 126.

72. Ibid.

73. For recent discussion of German reactions to the French Revolution, see Thomas P. Saine, *Black Bread—White Bread: German Intellectuals and the French Revolution* (Columbia, 1988); Wolfgang Albrecht, "Aufklärung, Reform, Revolution oder 'Bewirkt Aufklärung Revolutionen?'" *Lessing Yearbook* 12 (1990): 1–76 (see also the exchange between Saine and Albrecht in ibid., 77–96); and the brief overview by T. C. W. Blanning, "France during the French Revolution through German Eyes," in *The Impact of the French Revolution on European Consciousness*, ed. H. T. Mason and W. Doyle (Gloucester, 1989), 133–145.

74. On the problem of the relationship between liberalism and enlightenment in Germany, see Beiser, *Enlightenment, Revolution, and Romanticism*, 15–26 and 309–317.

75. See Marc Raeff, "The Well-Ordered Police State and the Development of

Modernity in Seventeenth- and Eighteenth-Century Europe: An Attempt at a Comparative Perspective," *American Historical Review* 80 (1975): 1221–1243.

76. Kant, "On the Common Saying: 'This May Be True in Theory but It Does Not Apply in Practice,'" trans. H. B. Nisbet, in Kant, *Political Writings*, 2d ed., ed. Hans Reiss (Cambridge, 1991), 74.

77. For a contrast of Mendelssohn's position with that of Kant, see Alexander Altmann, "Prinzipien politischer Theorie bei Mendelssohn und Kant," in Altmann, *Die trostvolle Aufklärung: Studien zur Metaphysik und politische Theorie Moses Mendelssohns* (Stuttgart–Bad Cannstatt, 1982), 192–216.

78. Jacobi's most extended discussion of Hume is found in his *David Hume über die Glaube, oder Idealismus und Realismus*, in *Jacobis Werke* II:127–288, esp. pp. 152–153 and 156–163. As Philip Merlan has pointed out, this interpretation of Hume is influenced by Jacobi's translation of Hume's "belief" by the German *Glaube* (which carries religious connotations not found, for example, in *Meinung*—a more likely candidate to capture Hume's sense); see "Kant, Hamann-Jacobi, and Schelling on Hume," *Rivista Critica di Storia della Filosofia* 22 (1967): 483–484.

79. For general discussions of the dispute, see Frederich C. Beiser, *The Fate of Reason: German Philosophy from Kant to Fichte* (Cambridge, Mass., 1987), 44–126; Dale Snow, "F. H. Jacobi and the Development of German Idealism," *Journal of the History of Philosophy*, 25, no. 3 (July 1987): 397–416; Lewis White Beck, *Early German Philosophy* (Cambridge, Mass., 1969), 352–374; and Heinrich Scholz, ed., *Die Hauptschriften zum Pantheismusstreit zwischen Jacobi und Mendelssohn* (Berlin, 1916), lix–lxxvii.

80. Jacobi, letter to Elise Reimarus, 4 November 1783, in *Friedrich Heinrich Jacobi Wider Mendelssohns Beschuldigungen Betreffend die Briefe über die Lehre des Spinoza*, reprinted in *Jacobis Spinoza Büchlein*, ed. Fritz Mauthner (München, 1912), 17 (the relevant portion of the letter is not reproduced in the version of Jacobi's reply reprinted in *Jacobis Werke* or in Scholz). Jacobi's disgust with the general tenor of the Berlin Enlightenment did not, however, extend to his views of individual members. He respected Wilhelm Dohm, a member of the Mittwochsgesellschaft known for his energetic support of the civil and political rights of the Berlin Jewish community. Dohm served as an intermediary between Jacobi and Mendelssohn in the Pantheism Dispute.

81. Letter to Gleim of 31 May 1782, *Nachlass* 1:54. For a discussion of Jacobi's early political views, see Karl Homann, *F. H. Jacobis Philosophie der Freiheit* (Freiburg/München, 1973), 38–96. For his place in the liberal tradition, see Dale Snow, "Jacobi's Critique of the Enlightenment," below, pp. 306–316, and Beiser, *Enlightenment, Revolution, and Romanticism*, 24 and 138–149.

82. Jacobi, "Something Lessing Said," translated below, p. 195.

83. Ibid., p. 200.

84. See James van Horn Melton, "From Enlightenment to Revolution: Hertzberg, Schlözer, and the Problem of Despotism in the Late *Aufklärung*," *Central European History* 12, no. 2 (1979): 103–123.

85. Riem, "On Enlightenment," translated below, p. 177.

86. Tieftrunk, "On the Influence of Enlightenment on Revolution," translated below, pp. 217–224.

87. Bergk, translated below, pp. 227–228.

88. Ibid., 230.

89. Ibid., 251.

90. For discussions of Kant's views on the "right to revolution," see Lewis White Beck, "Kant and the Right to Revolution," *Journal of the History of Ideas* 32 (1971): 411–422; Sidney Axinn, "Kant, Authority and the French Revolution," *Journal of the History of Ideas* 32 (1971): 423–432; and Frederick C. Beiser, *Enlightenment, Revolution, and Romanticism*, 44–48.

91. AA VIII:302 (Kant, "Theory and Practice," in *Political Writings*, 82–83). In view of Kant's problems with the censor, it is notable that the *Berlinische Monatsschrift* published this three-part essay, at his request, "all in one piece, in a single issue," presumably to avoid the fate of the essays that later made up *Religion within the Limits of Reason Alone*. See the discussion in the letter from Biester to Kant of 5 October 1793, which summarizes Kant's request regarding the disposition of the essay (*Philosophical Correspondence*, 208).

92. AA VII:79, 85–86 (*The Conflict of the Faculties*, trans. M. J. Gregor [Lincoln, 1992], 141, 153–154).

93. This was the lesson that critics of the Revolution such as A. W. Rehberg and Friedrich Genz took from their reading of Edmund Burke. See Beiser, *Enlightenment, Revolution, and Romanticism*, 302–309 and 317–326.

94. In this regard it is notable that the Left-Hegelian Edgar Bauer edited a collection of essays from Bahrdt, Riem, and others. See Martin von Geismar [pseudonym], *Bibliothek der deutschen Aufklärer des achtzehnten Jahrhunderts* (Leipzig, 1846).

95. Jean Améry, "Enlightenment as Philosophi Perennis," trans. Sidney Rosenfeld and Stella P. Rosenfeld in Améry, *Radical Humanism: Selected Essays* (Bloomington, 1984), 135–141.

96. Kant, *Critique of Pure Reason*, preface to the first edition, A xii.

97. Kant, "What Is Enlightenment?" AA VIII:58.

98. Kant, "What Is Orientation in Thinking?" in *Political Writings*, 249. See also the discussion of the meaning of "enlightenment" in *The Critique of Judgment*, §40.

99. Edmund Burke, *Reflections on the Revolution in France*, ed. J. G. A. Pocock (Indianapolis, 1987), 76.

100. Burke, *Reflections*, 76–77.

101. See Voltaire's article "Préjugés" in his *Dictionnaire philosophique*.

102. For a criticism of Burke along these lines, see Christopher Ricks, *T. S. Eliot and Prejudice* (London, 1994), 84–86.

103. See Hans-Georg Gadamer, *Truth and Method*, 2d rev. ed. (New York, 1989), 265–307. For a helpful examination of Gadamer's account of prejudice and tradition, see Georgia Warnke, *Gadamer: Hermeneutics, Tradition, and Reason* (Stanford, 1987), 75–82. Jürgen Habermas suggests a parallel between the arguments of Gadamer and Burke in his *On the Logic of the Social Sciences*, trans. Shierry Weber Nicholsen and Jerry A. Stark (Cambridge, Mass., 1988), 169. See also Jack Mendelson, "The Habermas-Gadamer Debate," *New German Critique*, no. 18 (1979): 67, and Frederick G. Lawrence's introduction to his translation of Gadamer, *Reason in the Age of Science* (Cambridge, Mass., 1981), xxvi–xxvii, which argues that Gadamer's rehabilitation of prejudice, authority, and tradition owes more to Aristotle than to Burke.

104. Gadamer, *Truth and Method*, 270.

105. Ibid., 279.

106. Ibid., 281.

107. Ibid., 282–283.

108. Ibid., 276–277.

109. Burke, *Reflections*, 29. See Alasdair MacIntyre's discussion in *Whose Justice? Which Rationality?* (Notre Dame, 1988), 353.

110. Gadamer, *Truth and Method*, 301–302.

111. Ibid., 302.

112. Habermas, *Logic of the Social Sciences*, 169.

113. Ibid., 168–170.

114. Albrecht Wellmer, *The Critical Theory of Society*, trans. John Cumming (New York, 1974), 46–47. See Habermas's discussion in "The Hermeneutic Claim to Universality," in *Contemporary Hermeneutics: Method, Philosophy, and Critique*, ed. Josef Bleicher (London, 1980), 204–205.

115. Habermas, *Logic of the Social Sciences*, 170.

116. Gadamer, "Hermeneutik," 68–69, 73 (translated as "On the Scope and Function of Hermeneutical Reflection," in Gadamer, *Philosophical Hermeneutics* [Berkeley, 1976], 28–29, 33).

117. See Hamann, "Metacritique of the Purism of Reason," translated below, pp. 154–167; MacIntyre, *Whose Justice? Which Rationality?* and *Three Rival Versions of Moral Inquiry: Encyclopedia, Genealogy, and Tradition* (Notre Dame, 1990), 170–195; and Richard Rorty, *Philosophy and the Mirror of Nature* (Princeton, 1979), 315–394, and *Contingency, Irony, and Solidarity*, 3–7, 44–45, 52. For a very useful collection of essays exploring the implications of the arguments of Habermas, Gadamer, MacIntyre, Rorty, and others, see Michael Kelly, ed., *Hermeneutics and Critical Theory in Ethics and Politics* (Cambridge, Mass., 1990).

118. Max Horkheimer and Theodor W. Adorno, *Dialektik der Aufklärung* (Amsterdam, 1947) (*Dialectic of Enlightenment*, trans. John Cumming [New York, 1972]).

119. Horkheimer and Adorno, *Dialectic of Enlightenment*, xv, xiii (translation modified).

120. Ibid., 3.

121. Ibid., xiii (translation modified).

122. Hegel, *Phenomenology of Spirit*, trans. A. V. Miller (Oxford, 1977), 355–363.

123. Ibid., 360.

124. Ibid., 359.

125. For a comparison, see J.-F. Suter, "Burke, Hegel, and the French Revolution," in *Hegel's Political Philosophy: Problems and Perspectives*, ed. Z. A. Pelczynski (Cambridge, 1971), 52–72.

126. Burke, *Reflections*, 147.

127. Hegel, "Proceedings of the Estates Assembly in Wurtemberg," in *Political Writings*, 282. See also his critique of historical approaches to the study of law in the *Philosophy of Right*, §3.

128. Joachim Ritter, *Hegel and the French Revolution*, trans. R. D. Winfield (Cambridge, Mass., 1982), 61.

129. Hegel, *Philosophy of Right*, §187.

130. For a discussion, see my article "*Paideia* for the '*Bürger als Bourgeois*': The Concept of 'Civil Society' in Hegel's Political Thought," *History of Political Thought* 2, no. 3 (1982): 469–493.

131. Hegel, letter to Göschel, 13 December 1830, and letter to Christiane Hegel, 18 January 1831, in *Briefe von und an Hegel*, ed. Johannes Hoffmeister (Hamburg, 1954), 321–324, 329 (translated by Clark Butler and Christiane Seiler in *Hegel: The Letters* [Bloomington, 1984], 422, 677).

132. For discussions of the interdisciplinary research program of the Institute for Social Research, see Helmut Dubiel, *Theory and Politics: Studies in the Development of the Frankfurt School*, trans. Benjamin Gregg (Cambridge, Mass., 1985), and Rolf Wiggershaus, *The Frankfurt School: Its History, Theories, and Political Significance*, trans. Michael Robertson (Cambridge, Mass., 1994).

133. On the relationship between state and market, see Frederick Pollock, "State Capitalism: Its Possibilities and Limitations" (1941), reprinted in Andrew Arato and Eike Gebhardt, *The Essential Frankfurt School Reader* (New York, 1978), 71–94. For the transformation of the bourgeois family, see Max Horkheimer, "Authority and Family" (1936), reprinted in Horkheimer, *Critical Theory*, trans. Matthew J. O'Connell (New York, 1972), 47–128.

134. See Horkheimer, "The End of Reason" (1941) and "The Authoritarian State" (1940), both reprinted in *The Essential Frankfurt School Reader*, 26–48 and 95–118.

135. In a letter to Friedrich Pollack written in March 1942, Horkheimer described the *Odyssey* as "the first document on the anthropology of man in the modern sense, that means, in the sense of a rational enlightened being." See Wiggershaus, *Frankfurt School*, 324.

136. Horkheimer and Adorno, *Dialectic of Enlightenment*, 57.

137. See Hegel, *Phenomenology of Spirit*, 333.

138. Horkheimer and Adorno, *Dialectic of Enlightenment*, 11 (translation modified). See also Horkheimer's reiteration of this point in *Dawn and Decline*, trans. Martin Shaw (New York, 1978), 124.

139. Max Horkheimer, *The Eclipse of Reason* (New York, 1947), 22–23.

140. See also Adorno's comment in *Minima Moralia*, trans. E. F. N. Jephcott (London, 1974), 51. "In a world where books have long lost all likeness to books, the real book can no longer be one. If the invention of the printing press inaugurated the bourgeois era, the time is at hand for its repeal by the mimeograph, the only fitting, the unobtrusive means of dissemination."

141. Horkheimer and Adorno, *Dialectic of Enlightenment*, 208 (translation modified).

142. Letter to Herbert Marcuse, 19 December 1942, quoted in Wiggershaus, *Frankfurt School*, 321. For a discussion of the subsequent responses of Horkheimer and Adorno to the position they sketched in *Dialectic of Enlightenment*, see Jürgen Habermas, "Notes on the Developmental History of Horkheimer's Work," trans. Mark Ritter in *Theory, Culture & Society* 10 (1993): 61–77.

143. *Dialectic of Enlightenment*, 117–118.

144. In *Ecce Homo*, reflecting on the dedication of *Menschliches, Allzumenschliches* to Voltaire, Nietzsche wrote, "Voltaire was above all, in contrast to all who wrote after him, a *grandseigneur* of the spirit—like me.—The name of Voltaire on one of my essays—that really meant progress—*toward me*." *Ecce Homo*, trans. Walter Kaufmann (New York, 1969), 283. For a helpful overview, see Peter Heller, "Nietzsche in His Relation to Voltaire and Rousseau," in *Studies in Nietzsche and the Classical Tradition*,

ed. James C. O'Flaherty, Timothy F. Sellner, and Robert M. Helm (Chapel Hill, 1976), 109–133.

145. Nietzsche, *Menschliches, Allzumenschliches*, §463 (*Human, All Too Human*, trans. R. J. Hollingdale [Cambridge, 1986], 169). See also *Götzen-Dämmerung* §48 (*Twilight of the Idols*, trans. R. J. Hollingdale [Harmondsworth, 1968], 101–102).

146. Nietzsche, *Menschliches, Allzumenschliches* pt. II §221 (*Human, All Too Human*, 367).

147. Nietzsche, *Die fröhliche Wissenschaft*, §350 (*The Gay Science*, trans. Walter Kaufmann [New York, 1974], 293).

148. *Menschliches, Allzumenschliches* §26 (*Human, All Too Human*, 25–26). Petrarch and Erasmus appear on Nietzsche's "banner of Enlightenment" insofar as they signify freethinking spirits of earlier ages of enlightenment in which an initial progress of "science" was retarded by a subsequent reaction.

149. Nietzsche, *Morgenröte* §197 (*Daybreak*, trans. R. J. Hollingdale [Cambridge, 1982], 117–118).

150. See Karl Leonhard Reinhold, "Thoughts on Enlightenment," translated below, pp. 73–75.

151. Nietzsche, *Wille zur Macht* §91 (*Will to Power*, trans. Walter Kaufmann and R. J. Hollingdale [New York, 1968], 56).

152. Nietzsche, *Die fröhliche Wissenschaft* §125 (trans. p. 181).

153. Michel Foucault, *Folie et déraison* (Paris: Librairie Plon, 1961), v. This passage is not included in the English translation.

154. Michel Foucault, *Madness and Civilization*, trans. Richard Howard (New York, 1973), 269.

155. Michel Foucault, *The History of Sexuality: Volume 1, An Introduction*, trans. Robert Hurley (New York, 1978), 20.

156. Michel Foucault, *The Birth of the Clinic*, trans. A. M. Sheridan Smith (New York, 1975), 195–197; Foucault, *Discipline and Punish: The Birth of the Prison*, trans. Alan Sheridan (New York, 1979), 200–209.

157. For Foucault's major discussions of Kant's "What Is Enlightenment?" see his "Qu'est-ce que la critique (Critique et *Aufklärung*)," Compte rendu de la séance du 27 Mai 1978, *Bulletin de la Société française de Philosophie* 84 (1990): 35–63 (translated below, pp. 382–398); Foucault, "Un Cours Inedit," *Magazine Littéraire*, no. 207 (1984): 35–39 (translated by Colin Gordon as "Kant on Enlightenment and Revolution," *Economy and Society* 15, no. 1 [1986]: 88–96); and "What Is Enlightenment?" in *The Foucault Reader*, ed. Paul Rabinow (New York, 1984), 32–50. For a discussion of the differences between these essays, see James Schmidt and Thomas E. Wartenberg, "Foucault's Enlightenment," in *Critique and Power: Recasting the Foucault-Habermas Debate*, ed. Michael Kelly (Cambridge, Mass., 1994), 283–314.

158. *The Foucault Reader*, 39–42.

159. Charles Baudelaire, *The Painter of Modern Life and Other Essays*, trans. Jonathan Mayne (London, 1964), 12–13.

160. *The Foucault Reader*, 50.

161. Burke, *Reflections*, 67.

162. Hamann, letter to Christian Jacob Kraus, 18 December 1784, below, p. 147.

163. Johann Georg Hamann, *Briefwechsel*, ed. Walther Ziesemer and Arthur Henkel (Wiesbaden, 1956), 2:129.

164. Foucault, *Discipline and Punish,* 200–209.

165. Beethoven captured a similar ambivalence about enlightenment in Act I of *Fidelio* when the prisoners are briefly released from the dungeons. They hesitantly greet the sunlight, delight in the fresh air, and with ever-growing strength, sing of the salvation they trust will some day be theirs. But as they are carried away into an ecstatic vision of emancipation, there is a darkening of the music and one prisoner warns, "Speak softly! Hold yourselves back! We are overheard and watched." *Fidelio* I:ix.

166. Burke's lack of interest in what the philosophes might actually have written may well be only a small part of a bigger problem. As John Pocock has suggested, both Price and Burke may have been principally concerned with the events of 1789 as a point of departure for reconsidering the significance of the events of 1688. See his introduction to Burke, *Reflections,* xi–xxxvi.

167. Gadamer, *Truth and Method,* 273.

168. See Gehard Sauder, "Aufklärung des Vorurteils—Vorurteile der Aufklärung," *Deutsche Vierteljahresschrift für Literaturwissenschaft und Geisesgeschichte* 57, no. 2 (1983): 259–277, and, especially, Werner Schneiders, *Aufklärung und Vorurteilskritik: Studien zur Geschichte der Vorurteilstheorie* (Stuttgart, 1983).

169. Interestingly, Walter Benjamin, whose work exercised an enormous influence over the authors of *Dialectic of Enlightenment,* was a good deal more explicit in acknowledging his debts to Hamann. See *Reflections,* trans. Edmund Jephcott (New York, 1979), 321. Horkheimer's 1959–1960 lectures on the Enlightenment are more careful in tracing the relationship between "enlightenment" understood as a process of demythologization and the Enlightenment as a historical period. See Horkheimer, *Gesammelte Schriften* 13 (Frankfurt, 1989), 570–645.

170. In this context it might be worth noting that John A. McCarthy's suggestion that Cassirer's *Philosophy of the Enlightenment* provides a more "judicious assessment" of the Enlightenment than that found in Horkheimer and Adorno runs the risk of both overstating the likelihood that readers would assume that the two books were in any sense trying to do the same thing, while also perhaps understating the degree to which Cassirer's classic study is itself now frequently the target of criticisms from historians at least in part because of its oversimplification of Enlightenment thought. See McCarthy, *Crossing Boundaries: A Theory and History of Essay Writing in German, 1680–1815* (Philadelphia, 1989), 70. In this light, it might be worth reconsidering the extent to which Cassirer's defense of "enlightenment" might, in part, be read as a response to Fascism rather than simply as an attempt to make historical sense of the Enlightenment.

171. For a good example of what is possible along these lines, see John A. McCarthy, "*Verständigung* and *Dialektik*: On Consensus Theory and the Dialectic of Enlightenment," in *Impure Reason: Dialectic of Enlightenment in Germany,* ed. W. Daniel Wilson and Robert C. Holub (Detroit, 1993), 13–33. See also Werner Schneiders, *Hoffnung auf Vernunft: Aufklärungsphilosphie in Deutschland* (Hamburg, 1990), 175–186.

172. Kant, "What Is Orientation in Thinking?" in *Political Writings,* 247.

173. Kant, AA V:294 (*Critique of Judgment,* trans. Werner S. Pluhar [Indianapolis, 1987], 160–161).

174. Kant, AA V:294 (*Critique of Judgment,* 162).

175. For a discussion of the relationship of this work to the *Dialectic of Enlighten-*

ment and to Habermas's subsequent critique of Horkheimer and Adorno, see Robert C. Holub, "The Enlightenment Dialectic: Jürgen Habermas's Critique of the Frankfurt School," in Wilson and Holub, *Impure Reason*, 34–86.

176. Jürgen Habermas, *Knowledge and Human Interests*, trans. Jeremy J. Shapiro (Boston, 1971), 314.

177. See Jürgen Habermas, *The Theory of Communicative Action*, 2 vols., trans. Thomas McCarthy (Boston, 1984, 1987); and Habermas, *Moral Consciousness and Communicative Action*, trans. Christian Lenhardt and Shierry Weber Nicholsen (Cambridge, Mass., 1990), 43–194.

PART ONE

The Eighteenth-Century Debate

1. The Question and Some Answers

What Is to Be Done Toward the Enlightenment of the Citizenry?

J. K. W. Möhsen

Translated by James Schmidt

Johann Karl Wilhelm Möhsen (1722–1795) was one of the most esteemed physicians of his day. Born in Berlin, he studied at Halle and Jena, returned to Berlin in 1742, and in 1778 became the personal physician of Frederick the Great. He cultivated an interest in the history of science and was a member of a number of learned societies, including the Berlin Wednesday Society, a secret society of Friends of Enlightenment that played a major role in the discussion of the question "What is enlightenment?" In the lecture translated here, Möhsen posed a series of questions about the nature of enlightenment that sparked intense debates within the Wednesday Society.

Our intent is to enlighten ourselves and our fellow citizens. The enlightenment of as great a city as Berlin has it difficulties, but once they have been overcome, light will spread not only into the provinces, but throughout the entire land, and how fortunate would we not be if only a few sparks, fanned here, came in time to spread a light over all of Germany, our common fatherland.

In order to achieve our goal, let it be proposed

1. that it be determined precisely: What is enlightenment?
2. that we determine the deficiencies and infirmities in the direction of the understanding, in the manner of thinking, in the prejudices and in the ethics of our nation—or at least of our immediate public—and that we investigate how they have been promoted thus far.
3. that we first attack and root out those prejudices and errors that are the most pernicious, and that we nurture and propagate those truths whose general recognition is most necessary.

It also would be worth investigating,

Originally delivered as a lecture before the Berlin Wednesday Society on 17 December 1783. Edited and first published by Ludwig Keller in "Die Berliner Mittwochs-Gesellschaft," Monatshefte der Comenius-Gesellschaft *5, nos. 3–4 (1896): 73–76. Some preliminary and concluding comments, dealing with the immediate circumstances of the delivery of the lecture, have been omitted.*

4. why the enlightenment of our public has as yet not advanced very far, notwithstanding that for more than forty years the freedom to think, to speak, and also to publish would seem to have ruled here more than in other lands,[1] and that the education of our youth has also gradually improved.

It is known that our great monarch has recently taken pains, in his essay on German literature,[2] to point out the deficiencies for which it can be reproached, the reasons for these deficiencies, and the means by which it may be improved. He has, on occasion, blamed the lack of enlightenment on defective instruction in schools and universities, on which a great deal has already been written.[3]

Since, however, he accuses our language of imperfection in expressing intelligibly the most accurate, vigorous, and brilliant ideas,[4] then perhaps it should also be an object of our efforts,

5. to see to the improvement of our language, and to investigate how far these reproaches are deserved.

It is indeed not to be denied that our monarch has taken the enlightenment of the nation more to heart than the enlightenment of German literature. It appears, however, that at present he still has great reservations about this step.

Before the essay on German literature was published, the Academy had posed the Prize Question for 1778: "Is it useful for the common mass of mankind to be deceived, either by being misled into new errors or by being maintained in accustomed errors?"[5] One sees from the distribution of the prize—which was divided, with half awarded to the affirmative prize essay and the other half to the negative essay—that the enlightened Royal Academy chose this expedient in order not to give offense with a definitive judgment. In the 1780 royal essay [*De la littérature allemande*], which appeared shortly after the Academy's question, one notes that the monarch—in spite of the fact that he prescribes the style and order of argument to all the faculties and sciences,[6] and in spite of the fact that it could not have been entirely unknown to him that the learned clergy, through their sermons to their congregations and through their influence on the minds of men, could enlighten many more hundreds of people in a shorter time and uproot many more errors than all the treatises—passed over such matters entirely and excused himself by saying that he "would observe a respectful silence with regard to theology, since one says that it should be a holy science, into whose sacred realm the laity may not venture."[7]

From this arises the proposal:

6. whether or not a closer investigation of the two opposing prize essays, and those which received honorable mention,[8] might be arranged, in

order to contrast the arguments for both sides and to consider if our efforts are useful or harmful, not only for the public, but also for the state and the government.

We can surely decide the last proposal according to our own insights, since we fulfill the duties of well-intentioned patriots under the seal of secrecy, our preeminent commandment. We have no Augustus as protector and no Maecenas and maecenatism among us, whom we might fear to offend with our remarks, we do not await the rewards of a house of Este, or Medici, of Francis I and Louis XIV,[9] whom the monarch mentions, nor can our judgment be led by a thirst for honor or praise, for we remain anonymous, and our preeminent and sole reward is the inner conviction, to promote, as well as we can and without any further intention, the best for our fellow citizens and for posterity.

NOTES

1. Frederick the Great (1712–1786) assumed the Prussian throne in 1740 and began his reign with a general relaxation of censorship regulations. For a discussion of Frederick's stance toward censorship, see the essay by Möhsen's colleague in the Mittwochsgesellschaft, Ernst Ferdinand Klein, "On Freedom of Thought and of the Press," *Berlinische Monatsschrift* 3 (1784): 312–330, translated below, pp. 87–96.—TRANS.

2. Frederick's *De la littérature allemande* was published in Berlin in 1780.—TRANS.

3. Frederick devoted part of *De la littérature allemande* to a discussion of the failings of German schools and universities. See *Oeuvres de Frédéric le Grand*, ed. Johann David Erdmann Preuß, (Berlin, 1846–1857), 7:98–101.—TRANS.

4. Möhsen refers here to Frederick's claim in *De la littérature allemande* that the German language could not do justice to "les pensées les plus justes, les plus fortes, les plus brillantes." See Preuß, *Oeuvres*, 7:97, and the more sustained discussion on pp. 101–108.—TRANS.

5. Frederick proposed this question, which he had previously addressed in chapter 18 of his *Anti-Machiavel*, to the academy in 1777. The prize was divided between the affirmative response by Frédéric de Castillon and the negative response of R. Z. Becker.—TRANS.

6. A reference to Frederick's extended discussion, in *De la littérature allemande*, of the proper language and presentation of arguments within the various academic disciplines.—TRANS.

7. "Je me renferme également dans un respectueux silence à l'égard de la théologie. On dit que c'est une science divine, et qu'il n'est pas permis aux profanes de toucher à l'encensoir." *De la littérature allemande*, in Preuß, *Oeuvres*, 7:100.—TRANS.

8. In addition to the two winning essays, three other essays answering the question in the negative and six answering the question in the affirmative were included in the academy's *Accessit*. Three of these essays were eventually published.—TRANS.

9. Caius Maecenas was a Roman statesman who served as adviser to the emperor Augustus and, on his retirement, a patron of Horace, Virgil, and Propertius—

hence the use of his name as a synonym for a patron of the arts (in German, *Mäzene*) and for patronage of the arts (in German, *Mäzenaten*). The Este were a noble family and patrons of the arts in Renaissance Ferrara and Modena; the Medici played the same role in Florence. Francis I (king of France from 1515 to 1547) was the patron of Rabelais, Marot, and Budé and the founder of the Collège de France, while Louis XIV (who reigned from 1643 to 1715) was the patron of Molière, Racine, La Fontaine, and Le Brun, among others. For Frederick's discussion of the absence of such patrons in Germany, see *De la littérature allemande*, in Preuß, *Oeuvres*, 7:95–96.—TRANS.

On the Question: What Is Enlightenment?

Moses Mendelssohn

Translated by James Schmidt

Moses Mendelssohn (1729–1786) was one of the most important figures in the Berlin Enlightenment. Born in 1729 in the Dessau ghetto, he came to Berlin in 1743, embarked on a study of the works of Gottfried Wilhelm Leibniz and Christian Wolff, published a number of highly regarded works, entered into a lifelong friendship with Lessing, and—at the end of his life—was Jacobi's antagonist in the "Pantheism Controversy."

The essay translated here had its origins in a lecture delivered before the Wednesday Society on 16 May 1784 near the end of the series of discussions sparked by Möhsen's lecture of the previous December. It was the only one of the contributions to the debate to be published in the Berlinische Monatsschrift *and may be regarded as an attempt to summarize the main concerns that arose in the course of those discussions.*

The words *enlightenment, culture,* and *education* are newcomers to our language.[1] They currently belong only to literary discourse. The masses scarcely understand them. Does this prove that these things are also new to us? I believe not. One says of a certain people that they have no specific word for "virtue," or none for "superstition," and yet one may justly attribute a not insignificant measure of both to them.

Linguistic usage, which seems to want to create a distinction between these synonymous words, still has not had the time to establish their boundaries. Education, culture, and enlightenment are modifications of social life, the effects of the industry and efforts of men to better their social conditions.

The more the social conditions of a people are brought, through art and industry, into harmony with the destiny of man,[2] the more education this people has.

Education is composed of culture and enlightenment. Culture appears to be more oriented toward practical matters: (objectively) toward goodness, refinement, and beauty in the arts and social mores; (subjectively) toward

Originally published as "Ueber die Frage: Was heisst aufklären?" Berlinische Monatsschrift *4 (1784): 193–200.*

facility, diligence, and dexterity in the arts and inclinations, dispositions, and habits in social mores. The more these correspond in a people with the destiny of man, the more culture will be attributed to them, just as a piece of land is said to be more cultured and cultivated, the more it is brought, through the industry of men, to the state where it produces things that are useful to men. Enlightenment, in contrast, seems to be more related to theoretical matters: to (objective) rational knowledge and to (subjective) facility in rational reflection about matters of human life, according to their importance and influence on the destiny of man.[3]

I posit, at all times, *the destiny of man as the measure and goal of all our striving and efforts*, as a point on which we must set our eyes, if we do not wish to lose our way.

A language attains enlightenment through the sciences and attains culture through social intercourse, poetry, and eloquence. Through the former it becomes better suited for theoretical usages, through the latter for practical usages. Both together make it an educated language.

Superficial culture is called "polish" [*Politur*]. Hail the nation, whose "polish" is the consequence of culture and enlightenment, whose external splendor and elegance have a foundation of internal, genuine truth!

Enlightenment is related to culture as theory to practice, as knowledge to ethics, as criticism to virtuosity. Regarded (objectively) in and for themselves, they stand in the closest connection, although subjectively they very often are separated.

One can say: Nürnbergers have more culture, Berliners more enlightenment; the French more culture, the English more enlightenment; the Chinese much culture and little enlightenment. The Greeks had both culture and enlightenment. They were an educated nation, just as their language is an educated language. Overall, the language of a people is the best indicator of its education, of culture as well as of enlightenment, in both breadth and intensity.

Further, the destiny of man can be divided into (1) the destiny of man *as man* and (2) the destiny of man *as citizen*.

With regard to culture these two coincide; for all practical perfection has value only in relation to social life and so must correspond only to the destiny of man as a member of society. Man *as man* needs no culture: but he needs enlightenment.

Status and vocation in civil life determine each member's duties and rights, and accordingly require different abilities and skills, different inclinations, dispositions, social mores and customs, a different culture and polish. The more these correspond, throughout all the estates, with their vocations—that is, with their respective destinies as members of society—the more culture the nation possesses.

Each individual also requires, according to his status and vocation, different theoretical insights and different skills to attain them—a different degree of enlightenment. The enlightenment that is concerned with man *as man* is universal, without distinction of status; the enlightenment of man *as citizen* changes according to status and vocation. The destiny of man remains as always the measure and goal of these efforts.

Accordingly, the enlightenment of a nation is proportional to (1) the amount of knowledge, (2) its importance—that is, its relation to the destiny (a) of man and (b) of the citizen, (3) its dissemination through all estates, (4) its accord with their vocations. Thus the degree of a people's enlightenment is determined according to an at least fourfold relationship, whose members are in part once again composed out of simpler relations of members.

The enlightenment of man can come into conflict with the enlightenment of the citizen. Certain truths that are useful to men, as men, can at times be harmful to them as citizens. The following needs to be considered here. The collision can arise between the (1) essential or (2) accidental destinies of man and the (3) essential or (4) accidental destinies of citizens.

In the absence of the essential destiny of man, man sinks to the level of the beast; without the unessential destiny he is no longer good and splendid as a creature.[4] In the absence of the essential destiny of man as citizen, the constitution of the state ceases to exist; without the unessential destiny it no longer remains the same in some ancillary relationships.

Unfortunate is the state that must confess that for it the essential destiny of man is not in harmony with the essential destiny of its citizens, in which the enlightenment that is indispensable to man cannot be disseminated through all the estates of the realm without risking the destruction of the constitution. Here philosophy lays its hand on its mouth! Here necessity may prescribe laws, or rather forge the fetters, that are applied to mankind, to force them down, and hold them under the yoke!

However, if the unessential destiny of man comes into conflict with the essential or unessential destiny of the citizen, rules must be established according to which exceptions are made and cases of collisions decided.

If the essential destiny of man has unfortunately been brought into conflict with his unessential destiny, if certain useful and—for mankind—adorning truths may not be disseminated without destroying prevailing religious and moral tenets, the virtue-loving bearer of enlightenment will proceed with prudence and discretion and endure prejudice rather than drive away the truth that is so closely intertwined with it.[5] Of course, this maxim has become the bulwark of hypocrisy, and we have it to thank for so many centuries of barbarism and superstition. Whenever one has desired to apprehend the crime, it sought refuge in the sanctuary. Nevertheless, the friend of mankind must defer to these considerations, even in the most enlightened times. It is difficult, but not impossible, to find the boundary that separates use from misuse.

The more noble a thing is in its perfection, says a Hebrew writer, the more ghastly it is in its decay.[6] A rotted piece of wood is not as ugly as a decayed flower; and this is not as disgusting as a decomposed animal; and this, again, is not as gruesome as man in his decay. So it is also with culture and enlightenment. The more noble in their bloom, the more hideous in their decay and destruction.

The misuse of enlightenment weakens the moral sentiment and leads to hard-heartedness, egoism, irreligion, and anarchy. Misuse of culture produces luxury, hypocrisy, weakness, superstition, and slavery.

Where enlightenment and culture go forward in step, they are together the best shield against corruption. In their manner of destruction they are directly opposed to one another.

The education of a nation, which according to the foregoing clarification of terms is composed of culture and enlightenment, will therefore be far less subject to corruption.

An educated nation knows of no other danger than an excess of national happiness, which, like the most perfect health of the human body, can in itself be called an illness, or the transition to an illness. A nation that through education has come to the highest peak of national happiness is just for that reason in danger of collapse, because it can climb no higher.—But this leads us too far from the question at hand.

NOTES

1. The three terms Mendelssohn employs create problems for the translator since, as he himself goes on to note, the contemporary reader could well regard them as synonymous. *Bildung* is a particularly difficult term, capable of being translated as "culture," "development," "formation," or "education." I have chosen the latter to preserve the contrast with *Kultur*, but the reader should bear in mind that the term has a wider range of meanings than the English term: to possess "Bildung" is to be educated, cultured, and distinguished by a "proper" upbringing.—TRANS.

2. Mendelssohn appropriated the concept "destiny of man" (*Bestimmung des Menschen*) from a book by Johann Joachim Spalding, a fellow member of the Wednesday Society, *Betrachtung über die Bestimmung des Menschen* (first published in 1748). Mendelssohn's most comprehensive discussion of Spalding's concept is to be found in his *Orakel, die Bestimmung des Menschen betreffende*, an essay he published along with his friend Thomas Abbt's *Zweifel über die Bestimmung des Menschen* in 1763. In notes to this edition, Mendelssohn pointed to an ambiguity in the German *Bestimmung*, noting that the word connotes both "determination" (the "establishment of one predicate from among the many that could belong to a subject") and "destination" ("the establishment of a goal, to which something serves as a means"). Mendelssohn suggested that "Bestimmung" should be reserved for "determination," while the sense of "destination" is better captured by the German *Beruf* ("calling" or "vocation") (Mendelssohn, *Gesammelte Schriften* 6/1:35).—TRANS.

3. Mendelssohn gave an even pithier formulation of the distinction between *Aufklärung* and *Kultur* in his letter to August v. Hennings of 27 November 1784: "*Aufklärung* is concerned only with the theoretical, with knowledge, with the elimination of prejudices; *Kultur* is concerned with morality, sociality, art, with things done and things not done." Mendelssohn, *Gesammelte Schriften* 13:234.—Trans.

4. Mendelssohn's distinction between the "essential" destiny of man and the "unessential" [*außerwesentlichen*] or "accidental" [*zufälligen*] destinies of man is derived from Christian Wolff's ontology. As Mendelssohn explained in his letter to v. Hennings, "The essential destiny of man is a matter of *existence* [*Daseyn*], the unessential destiny is a matter of *improvement* [*Besserseyn*]." Mendelssohn, *Gesammelte Schriften* 13:236.—Trans.

5. This point was further developed by Mendelssohn in a subsequent essay, "Soll man der einreissenden Schwämerey durch Satyre oder durch äussere Verbindung entgegenarbeiten?" *Berlinische Monatsschrift* 5 (February 1785): 133–137 (*Gesammelte Schriften* 6/1:139–141). Here he argued, "Nothing is more opposed to the true good of mankind than this sham enlightenment [*Afteraufklärung*], where everyone mouths a hackneyed wisdom, from which the spirit has already long vanished; where everyone ridicules prejudices, without distinguishing what is true in them from what is false." —Trans.

6. In the notes to the critical edition of Mendelssohn's works, Alexander Altmann suggests that Mendelssohn might be referring to the *tractate Yadayim* (IV.6), one of the parts of the Talmud: "The level of defilement corresponds to the level of esteem." (See Mendelssohn, *Gesammelte Schriften* 6/1:240.)—Trans.

An Answer to the Question: What Is Enlightenment?

Immanuel Kant

Translated by James Schmidt

Immanuel Kant's 1784 essay is by far the most famous of the responses to Zöllner's request for an answer to the question "What is enlightenment?" Dated 30 September 1784, it was written, as Kant explained in a footnote at the close of the essay, without knowledge of the contents of Mendelssohn's response, which appeared in the Berlinische Monatsschrift *as Kant was completing his own answer. The essay was the second of the fifteen articles Kant wrote for the* Berlinische Monatsschrift *in the years between 1784 and 1796.*

Enlightenment is mankind's exit from its self-incurred immaturity.[1] *Immaturity* is the inability to make use of one's own understanding without the guidance of another. *Self-incurred* is this inability if its cause lies not in the lack of understanding but rather in the lack of the resolution and the courage to use it without the guidance of another. *Sapere aude!* Have the courage to use your *own* understanding! is thus the motto of enlightenment.[2]

Laziness and cowardice are the reasons why such a great part of mankind, long after nature has set them free from the guidance of others (*naturaliter majorennes*), still gladly remain immature for life and why it is so easy for others to set themselves up as guardians. It is so easy to be immature. If I have a book that has understanding for me, a pastor who has a conscience for me, a doctor who judges my diet for me, and so forth, surely I do not need to trouble myself. I have no need to think, if only I can pay; others will take over the tedious business for me. Those guardians, who have graciously taken up the oversight of mankind, take care that the far greater part of mankind (including the entire fairer sex) regard the step to maturity as not only difficult but also very dangerous. After they have first made their domestic animals stupid and carefully prevented these placid creatures from daring to take even one step out of the leading strings of the cart to which

Originally published as "Beantwortung der Frage: Was ist Aufklärung?" Berlinische Monatsschrift *4 (1784): 481–494.*

they are tethered,[3] they show them the danger that threatens them if they attempt to proceed on their own. Now this danger is not so great, for by falling a few times they would indeed finally learn to walk; but an example of this sort makes them timid and usually frightens them away from all further attempts.

It is thus difficult for any individual man to work himself out of an immaturity that has become almost natural to him. He has become fond of it and, for the present, is truly incapable of making use of his own reason, because he has never been permitted to make the attempt. Rules and formulas, these mechanical instruments of a rational use (or rather misuse) of his natural gifts, are the fetters of an everlasting immaturity. Whoever casts them off would still take but an uncertain leap over the smallest ditch, because he is not accustomed to such free movement. Hence there are only a few who have managed to free themselves from immaturity through the exercise of their own minds, and yet proceed confidently.

But that a public [*Publikum*] should enlighten itself is more likely; indeed, it is nearly inevitable, if only it is granted freedom. For there will always be found some who think for themselves, even among the established guardians of the masses, and who, after they themselves have thrown off the yoke of immaturity, will spread among the herd the spirit of rational assessment of individual worth and the vocation of each man to think for himself. It is notable that the public, which had earlier been brought under this yoke by their guardians, may compel them to remain under it if they are incited to do so by some of their guardians who are incapable of any enlightenment. So it is harmful to implant prejudices, because they ultimately revenge themselves on those who originated them or on their descendents. Therefore a public can achieve enlightenment only gradually. A revolution may perhaps bring about the fall of an autocratic despotism and of an avaricious or overbearing oppression, but it can never bring about the true reform of a way of thinking. Rather, new prejudices will serve, like the old, as the leading strings of the thoughtless masses.

For this enlightenment, however, nothing more is required than *freedom*; and indeed the most harmless form of all the things that may be called freedom: namely, the freedom to make a *public use* of one's reason in all matters. But I hear from all sides the cry: *don't argue!*[4] The officer says: "Don't argue, but rather march!" The tax collector says: "Don't argue, but rather pay!" The clergyman says: "Don't argue, but rather believe!" (Only one ruler in the world says: "*Argue,* as much as you want and about whatever you want, *but obey!*")[5] Here freedom is restricted everywhere. Which restriction, however, hinders enlightenment? Which does not, but instead even promotes it?—I answer: the *public* use of reason must at all times be free, and it alone can bring about enlightenment among men; the *private* use of reason, however, may often be very narrowly restricted without the progress of enlightenment being particularly hindered. I understand, however, under the public use of his own reason, that use which anyone makes of it *as a scholar* [*Gelehrter*] before the entire public of the *reading world*. The private use I designate as that use which one makes of his reason in a certain *civil post* or office which is entrusted to him. Now a certain mechanism is necessary in many affairs which are run in the interest of the commonwealth by means of which some members of the commonwealth must conduct themselves passively in order that the government may direct them, through an artificial unanimity, to public ends, or at least restrain them from the destruction of these ends. Here one is certainly not allowed to argue; rather, one must obey. But insofar as this part of the machine considers himself at the same time as a member of the entire commonwealth, indeed even of a cosmopolitan society, who in the role of a scholar addresses a public in the proper sense through his writings, he can certainly argue, without thereby harming the affairs in which he is engaged in part as a passive member. So it would be very destructive, if an officer on duty should argue aloud about the suitability or the utility of a command given to him by his superior; he must obey. But he cannot fairly be forbidden as a scholar to make remarks on failings in the military service and to lay them before the public for judgment. The citizen cannot refuse to pay the taxes imposed on him; even an impudent complaint against such levies, when they should be paid by him, is punished as an outrage (which could lead to general insubordination). This same individual nevertheless does not act against the duty of a citizen if he, as a scholar, expresses his thoughts publicly on the inappropriateness or even the injustice of such taxes. In the same way, a clergyman is bound to lecture to his catechism students and his congregation according to the symbol of the church which he serves;[6] for he has been accepted on this condition. But as a scholar he has the complete freedom, indeed it is his calling, to communicate to the public all his carefully tested and well-intentioned thoughts on the imperfections of that symbol and his proposals for a better arrangement of religious and ecclesiastical affairs. There is in this nothing that could burden his conscience. For what he teaches as a consequence of his office as an agent of his church, he presents as something about which he does not have free reign to teach according to his own discretion, but rather is engaged to expound according to another's precept and in another's name. He will say: our church teaches this or that; these are the arguments that it employs. He then draws out all the practical uses for his congregation from rules to which he himself may not subscribe with complete conviction, but to whose exposition he can nevertheless pledge himself, since it is not entirely impossible that truth may lie concealed within them, and, at least, in any case there is nothing in them that is in contradiction with what is intrinsic to religion. For if he believed he found such a contradiction in them, he could not in conscience conduct his office; he would have to resign. Thus the use that an appointed teacher makes of his reason before his congregation is merely a *private* use, because this is only a domestic assembly, no matter how large it is; and in this respect he is not and cannot be free, as a priest, because he conforms to the orders of another. In contrast, as a scholar, who through his writings speaks to his own public, namely the world, the clergyman enjoys, in the *public* use of his reason, an unrestricted freedom to employ his own reason and to speak in his own person. For that the guardian of the people (in spiritual matters) should be himself immature, is an absurdity that leads to the perpetuation of absurdities.

But would not a society of clergymen, such as a church synod or a venerable classis (as they call themselves among the Dutch),[7] be justified in binding one another by oath to a certain unalterable symbol, in order to hold an unremitting superior guardianship over each of their members, and by this means over their people, and even to make this eternal? I say that this is completely impossible. Such a contract, concluded for the purpose of closing off forever all further enlightenment of the human race, is utterly null and void even if it should be confirmed by the highest power, by Imperial Diets, and by the most solemn peace treaties. One age cannot bind itself, and thus conspire, to place the succeeding age in a situation in which it becomes impossible for it to broaden its knowledge (particularly such pressing knowledge), to cleanse itself of errors, and generally to progress in enlightenment. That would be a crime against human nature, whose original destiny consists in this progress; and posterity would be fully justified to reject these resolutions as concluded in an unauthorized and outrageous manner. The touchstone of everything that can be concluded as a law for a people lies in the question: could a people have imposed such a law upon itself? Now this would be possible for a specified brief time period, in order to introduce a certain order, as it were, in expectation of something better. At the same time, all citizens, especially the clergy, would be left free, in their capacities as scholars—that is, through writings—to make remarks on the failings of the current institutions. This provisional order would continue until insight into the nature of these things became so public and so reliable that through uniting their voices (even if not unanimously) they could bring a resolution before the throne, to take those congregations into protection who had united into an altered religious organization according to their conception of better insight, without hindering those who wish to remain with the old. But it is absolutely forbidden to unite, even for the lifetime of a single man, in a permanent religious constitution that no one may publicly doubt, and thereby to negate a period of progress of mankind toward improvement and thus make it fruitless and even detrimental for posterity. One man may indeed postpone, for his own person and even then only for a short time, enlightenment in that which it is incumbent for him to know; but to renounce it, for his own person and even more for posterity, is to violate and to trample on the sacred rights of mankind. What even a people may not decide for itself can even less be decided for it by a monarch; for his lawgiving authority consists in his uniting the collective will of the people in his own. If only he sees to it that all true or alleged improvements are consistent with civil order, he can allow his subjects to do what they find necessary for the well-being of their souls. That does not concern him, though it is his concern to prevent one from forcibly hindering another from laboring with all his capacities to determine and to advance this well-being. It detracts from his own majesty if he meddles in this by finding the writings through which his subjects seek to put their insights into order worthy of governmental oversight. He does so if he acts out of his own exalted insight, where he exposes himself to the reproach *Caesar non est supra Grammaticos*,[8] and does so even more if he degrades his supreme power so far as to support the ecclesiastical despotism of a few tyrants in his state against the rest of his subjects.

If it is asked "Do we now live in an *enlightened* age?" the answer is "No, but we do live in an age of *enlightenment*." As matters now stand, much is still lacking for men to be completely able—or even to be placed in a situation where they would be able—to use their own reason confidently and properly in religious matters without the guidance of another. Yet we have clear indications that the field is now being opened for them to work freely toward this, and the obstacles to general enlightenment or to the exit out of their self-incurred immaturity become ever fewer. In this respect, this age is the age of enlightenment or the century of *Frederick*.[9]

A prince who does not find it unworthy of himself to say that he regards it as a *duty* to prescribe nothing to men regarding religious matters but rather to allow them full freedom in this area—and who thus declines the haughty title of "tolerant"—is himself enlightened and deserves to be esteemed by the grateful world and by posterity as the first, with regard to government, who freed mankind from immaturity and left them free to use of their own reason in everything that is a matter of conscience. Under him venerable clergy, in their role as scholars and irrespective of their official duties, freely and publicly present their judgments and insights—which here or there diverge from the established symbol—to the world for examination. Those who are not restricted by the duties of office are even freer. This spirit of freedom spreads further, even where it must struggle with the external hindrances of a government which misunderstands itself. For it is an illuminating example to such a government that public peace and unity have little to fear from this freedom. Men work their way by themselves bit by bit out of barbarity if one does not intentionally contrive to hold them in it.

I have placed the main point of enlightenment—mankind's exit from its self-imposed immaturity—primarily on religious matters since our rulers have no interest in playing the role of guardian to their subjects with regard to the arts and sciences and because this type of immaturity is the most harmful as well as the most dishonorable. But the manner of thinking of a head of state who favors such enlightenment goes even further and sees that even with regard to his own legislation there is no danger in allowing his subjects to make *public* use of their reason and to lay publicly before the world their thoughts about a better formulation of this legislation as well as a candid criticism of laws already given. We have a shining example of this, in which no monarch has yet surpassed the one we honor.

But only a ruler who, himself enlightened, does not himself fear shadows, and at the same time has at hand a large, well-disciplined army as a guarantee of public peace, can say what a republic cannot dare: *argue, as much as you want and about whatever you want, only obey!* Here is displayed a strange and unexpected tendency in human affairs, so that, generally, when it is considered at large, almost everything in it is almost paradoxical. A high degree of civic freedom appears advantageous to the *spiritual* freedom [*Freiheit des Geistes*] of a people and yet it places before it insuperable restrictions; a lesser degree of civil freedom, in contrast, creates the room for spiritual freedom to spread to its full capacity. When nature has, under this hard shell, developed the seed for which she cares most tenderly—namely, the inclination and the vocation for *free thinking*—this works back upon the character of the people (who thereby become more and more capable of *acting freely*) and finally even on the principles of government, which finds it to its advantage to treat man, who is now *more than a machine*,[10] in accord with his dignity.[11]

NOTES

1. The phrase *selbstverschuldeten Unmündigkeit* is central to Kant's entire argument. As Kant explained in his *Anthropology*, *Unmündigkeit* designates both "minority of age" (*Minderjährigkeit*) and "legal or civil immaturity" (AA VII:208–209 [*Anthropology from a Pragmatic Point of View*, trans. Mary J. Gregor (The Hague, 1974), 79–80]). Those who are legally immature—a group that includes children, so long as they remain "naturally immature," and women, no matter what age—must be represented in legal proceedings by a "curator" (*Kurator*), a "proxy" (*Stellvertreter*), or a "guardian" (*Vormund*). (All of these designations have their origins in Roman law and were given exhaustive definitions in Christian Wolff's *Grundsätze des Natur- und Völckerrechts* §§898–912.) Kant's use of these terms echoes that of Ernst Ferdinand Klein, who in an article on freedom of the press published a few months earlier in the *Berlinische Monatsschrift* had called on those kings and princes who had taken on the role of *Vormüdern* over their *unmündigen Kinder* to follow the example of Frederick the Great and grant them freedom of expression (translated above, pp. 90–91). Enlightened theologians such as Semler and Spalding had also used the term

Unmündigkeit in their criticisms of clergy who kept their congregations in a state of "immaturity" (see Steven Lestition, "Kant and the End of the Enlightenment in Prussia," *Journal of Modern History* 65 [March 1993]: 77–78). *Verschuldeten* carries implications of guilt and blame, hence *selbstverschuldet* designates a guilt that is self-incurred.—TRANS.

2. The Latin phrase *Sapere aude!*—Dare to know!—is taken from Horace's *Epistles* 1.2.40. Franco Venturi has traced the history of the phrase, noting that it was used on a medal struck in Berlin in 1736 for the Société des Aléthophiles—Society of the Friends of Truth—a group of clergy, lawyers, and civil servants dedicated to the spreading of truth in general and the Leibniz-Wolff philosophy in particular. See Venturi, "Was ist Aufklärung? Sapere Aude!" reprinted in Venturi, *Europe des lumières* (Paris, 1971), 39–42. The phrase was widely used in the eighteenth century; for example, Kant's friend Johann Georg Hamann used it to close a 1759 letter to Kant.—TRANS.

3. The phrase "leading strings of the cart" is an attempt to translate Kant's "*Gängelwagen*," a small, bottomless carriage with casters that was used, like our present-day baby-walkers, so that children might move around without the danger of falling. Jean Mondot's French translation of Kant's essay notes that the image of the Gängelwagen was used by Kant, Lessing, Wieland, and Mendelssohn as a metaphor for mankind's immaturity. See *Qu'est-ce que les Lumières?* (Saint-Étienne, 1991), 85. Rousseau may have been a possible inspiration for the metaphor: in *Emile*, he states that Emile will not be tied to "leading strings" (*lisères*).—TRANS.

4. The phrase here is *räsoniert nicht!*—which carries connotations of both "reasoning" and "quibbling."—TRANS.

5. By the end of the essay, it is clear that this "*einziger Herr*" is Frederick the Great.—TRANS.

6. In the months preceding Kant's essay, there had been a heated debate over the propriety of requiring Lutheran clergy to swear oaths of conformity to their confession's "Symbolic Books"—the basic principles or Creed of their faith. Mendelssohn had argued against such oaths in his *Jerusalem* and in the January 1784 issue of the *Berlinische Monatsschrift* had responded to criticism of his argument.—TRANS.

7. The term *classis* was employed by the Dutch Reformed Church to designate a subdivision of a synod.—TRANS.

8. "Caesar is not above the grammarians."—TRANS.

9. A reference to Frederick the Great, king of Prussia from 1740 to 1786.—TRANS.

10. An allusion to Julien Offray La Mettrie's *L'Homme machine* (1747), a book whose materialism and atheism prompted such opposition in Leyden (to which La Mettrie had fled in 1745 after his *Histoire naturelle de l'âme* had caused similar problems for him in Paris) that, at Frederick the Great's invitation, he moved to Berlin, where he was a member of the Royal Academy until his death in 1751.—TRANS.

11. I read today in Büsching's *Wöchentliche Nachrichten* of 13 September a notice for the *Berlinische Monatsschrift* of this month, which cites Mr. Mendelssohn's answer to this same question. I have not received this issue, otherwise I would have held back the present essay, which is now presented only as an attempt to see how far agreement in thought can be brought about by chance.

Thoughts on Enlightenment

Karl Leonhard Reinhold

Translated by Kevin Paul Geiman

Karl Leonhard Reinhold (1758–1823) was born in Vienna. At one time a Jesuit novice, he converted to the cause of enlightenment and was active in the Masonic movement. He left Vienna in 1784, settled in Weimar, and worked with Christoph Martin Wieland on the publication of the Teutscher Merkur. *After first attacking Kant in an anonymous response to Kant's review of Herder's* Ideen zur Philosophie der Geschichte der Menschheit, *Reinhold became a Kantian, and his* Briefe über die kantische Philosophie *(1785) played an important role in the spread of Kant's critical philosophy. His later* Elementarphilosophie, *elaborated in a series of essays published between 1789 and 1794, sought to reformulate the grounds of Kantian epistemology. "Thoughts on Enlightenment" originally appeared in three installments in the* Teutscher Merkur *of July, August, and September 1784. The first installment, which has not been translated here, examines the current status of the Enlightenment in Vienna; the second two parts attempt to provide a more general characterization of the nature of enlightenment.*

I think that enlightenment means, in general, the making of rational men out of men who are capable of rationality. The sum total of all the institutions [*Anstalten*] and means that lead to this great end gives the word *enlightenment* its broadest sphere of meaning.

Man brings with himself into the world the possibility, grounded in his physical disposition, of becoming rational. This is his capacity for reason in the broadest sense. Every sense impression, every pleasant and painful sensation, and, in general, everything that brings forth an idea in the soul, furnishing it with the material of reason and further developing its capacities, belongs to enlightenment in the broadest sense.

The capacity for reason in the narrower sense is that state of the soul in which the disposition to reason has already obtained all the determinations which first make it capable of distinct concepts. Reason itself first begins with distinct concepts. Enlightenment in the narrower sense is thus the ap-

Originally published as "Gedancken über Aufklärung" in Der Teutsche Merkur *(August 1784): 122–133 and (September 1784): 232–245.*

plication of the means that lie in nature to elucidate confused concepts into distinct ones.[1]

If the power of representation has resolved even a single confused concept into its constituents, then the means for this success—enlightenment and, hence, true reason—would be at hand. Yet just as no one individual really has only one distinct concept, so too the name "rational" would hardly befit such a person. To be regarded as rational among men, one must have accumulated a certain number of distinct concepts, and have accumulated concepts with a certain degree of distinctness. The institutions which presuppose this level of rational culture [*Vernunftbildung*], indeed, determine the concept of enlightenment more precisely. Yet the rational culture itself must come under closer scrutiny if it is to deserve the name "enlightenment" in its conventional usage. An enlightened individual is one whose reason is noticeably above the ordinary.

All concepts which admit of distinctness in human modes of representation are objects of reason, and consequently also objects of enlightenment. Yet both the limits of our powers and the short duration of our lives make it impossible for every individual to possess all the distinct concepts that are attainable by mankind in general. The development of any individual's reason must thus be limited to a certain number of concepts. As these concepts are distinguished from one another in importance, so is enlightenment. The shoemaker who knows how to give a clear account of the construction of shoes is, in fact, enlightened about his craft. Yet linguistic usage confers this title only to men who have brought sufficient distinctness to those concepts which have a considerable influence on human happiness. The definition that the concept of enlightenment thereby acquires confines it to the development of important concepts.

A nation which can boast of only a few people who are enlightened in this sense does not deserve to be called an enlightened nation. As long as the institutions for rational culture are so inferior and ineffective that their influence can reach only a few, they remain much too unimportant for linguistic usage to honor them with the name "enlightenment." The enlightener must at least have served a large part of his nation well if he would maintain his claim to this honorable name.

The nation which is the object of this rational culture is either still wild or already cultivated [*gesittet*]. In the first case, its rational ability is still not determinate enough, its institutions are still too little developed, the progress of its spirit is still not perceptible enough for the development of its reason, even if zealously executed, to merit the name "enlightenment" in the previously defined sense. The name can thus be given only to the higher rational culture in cultured nations. Peter the Great turned his subjects into men; Joseph enlightens his.[2] Only in a cultured nation can the process of enlightenment be pursued rapidly enough for it to be noticed by its neighbors. It is precisely this pursuit and this rapid movement that observers hail with the name "enlightenment." Even in Portugal the human mind is always progressing. Yet was there ever talk of an enlightenment in Portugal?

The institutions through which the rational culture in a cultured nation can be effected are innumerable. Everything that makes reflection into a need and facilitates it is an institution of this kind, and belongs among the previously indicated determinants of our concept. Conventional usage, however, selects from all these institutions only those that could be attributed to human intention and that, however diverse they may be, for the most part can be traced back to legislation and education. It especially honors them with the name "enlightenment" as soon as they manifest their salutary effects to a particularly striking degree. Never has the word *enlightenment* been used so often in this sense as it has since Joseph mounted his father's throne.[3] This is indeed the noblest meaning the word can attain. Enlightenment in this sense is a moral action, and a moral action of the noblest kind; perhaps the only action through which man can tolerably justify his proud claim to a likeness with the Author of nature.

Many a reader will perhaps be brought up short by the considerable degree of distinctness I expect from entire nations with regard to important concepts. I hear the objection: distinct concepts are the fruits of the long and laborious contemplations of a sage who, removed from the distracting preoccupations and diversions of the world, in intercourse with books and himself, makes the investigation of the truth the chief business of his life. Distinct concepts are the exclusive prerogative of philosophers. The masses [*Pöbel*][4] that always make up the greater part of every nation would have to stop being masses once they had been brought to think distinctly. I respond: just as there is a natural and an artificial logic, so too there is a natural and an artificial distinctness of concepts. The latter may always remain the prerogative of philosophers, but the former can be denied to the masses only if one would have philosophers alone count as men. Note the difference between the distinct concepts of the masses and those of the philosopher, as I believe to have found it. The capacity of the masses for distinct concepts is more passive than active; that of the philosopher is more active than passive. The philosopher teaches; the masses learn. The philosopher analyzes the concept; the masses apprehend that which has been analyzed. The one overcomes all the difficulties that stand in the way of having a distinct concept; the other has nothing to do but to help themselves to the benefits that distinct concepts offer. The former must always have as many distinct concepts at hand as are required to find new truths; the latter are satisfied with the few required to understand an already discovered truth. The first must be able to think distinctly every concept that can be analyzed into its attributes; the second think only those concepts that another has analyzed and, so to speak, has placed into their hands. The philosopher, finally, understands the art of constructing distinct concepts and can analyze his ideas as far as his purpose demands; he can give an account of the adequacy of the discovered attributes and recall them as often as he finds appropriate. The masses, on the contrary, understand nothing of this art; they have only as many attributes of each concept within their power as the skill of their teachers knew how to convey; they can evoke them only in certain cases, when they are prompted, and in general, they do not easily see any further than they are permitted to see. In short, popular concepts are only distinct insofar as they are correct; while in contrast the philosophical concepts are only correct insofar as they are distinct.

Distinct popular concepts are thus not logical and metaphysical definitions, nor ought they be. However, they deserve the name "distinct concepts," because for the most part they must arise through distinct thinking outside the minds of the masses; because they are taught to the masses through distinct explanations; because in the minds of the masses they are always separate attributes of a single concept, presenting actual institutions of the object in its particular qualities or well-considered truths of reason; and because, despite their incompleteness, they are very different from the sensuous concepts of direct empirical knowledge. Distinct concepts in this sense are not rare even in the lowest classes of the masses in a cultured nation. A skilled catechist brings them forth even in children. Yet they need to be *brought* forth. This is the most general institution under which the masses are capable of them. But can there never be a pure philosophical concept which can be fashioned for the sensibility of the masses without losing, along with its form, all its evidence and usefulness? Of course! And I think it happens in the following way.

There are certain concepts which, I would like to say, set up bridges of communication between science and ignorance; concepts that lie neither too high for the masses nor too low for the philosopher; concepts that both the philosopher and the masses—who, for all their distance, are formed from the same clay—have in common; and concepts that are related not only to the most spiritual and finest notions of the philosopher but also—since everything, different as it may be, is intertwined—to the most sensuous ideas of the common man. In these concepts lies the talisman of popular enlightenment. Chance, or the sage who understands the art of drawing both his distinct notion and the confused idea of the masses close enough to this middle concept, performs the trick. As soon as these concepts come into contact with one another, the popular idea catches the light and becomes as distinct as a popular idea can and should become. I want to offer an example. The philosopher's distinct concept of the justice of God shows him that this justice is a wisely allotted mercy and that consequently God can only punish out of mercy, and the philosopher loves God precisely for the sake of this justice. In contrast, the confused concept that the masses have of this justice (for which they must thank their monkish-Christian teachers) presents this justice as nothing other than an unrelenting strictness, a delight in the suffering of frail creatures and in eternal irreconcilability, and I do not know if they can love God despite this justice. What a disparity between these two concepts! Could it be possible to recast the false, dark, loathsome monkish concept into that of the sage? And how should that come about? Quite naturally. Just look for a concept that the sage and the masses have in common and which is akin to their mutual concepts of God, for example, that of a father. God is a wise father, the philosopher begins, and the masses immediately grant him that. The philosopher proceeds: a wise father punishes only out of mercy; and the masses anticipate him with the inference: God punishes only out of mercy. It now will be easily understood, if the masses are taught that this justice is a quality of God, which is as lovable as mercy itself.

In every cultured nation, which consists of scholars and masses, the means of popular enlightenment are constantly at hand. They lie in the civil and domestic relations through which all the members of a state are attached to one another, or, which is just the same, in the concepts on which they all agree, because they must understand one another. The discovery of a truth that has influence on human well-being may have to be fetched from the remotest regions of human knowledge, and monkish fog may shield the understanding of the masses from all access to light, yet the communication of this discovery to the masses remains possible. For every truth, there are channels of communication always present in the minds of the philosopher and the masses. It can happen that the philosopher never finds them or never wants to use them and that certain truths must therefore remain eternal secrets for the masses; but at least the fault does not lie in the capacity of the masses for reason.

The obscurity of a truth, however elevated it may be above the ordinary, is not a quality of the truth itself but rather of its cloak. Dress it in a garment that is neither too dirty for the sage nor too dazzling for the common man, and you have provided it free access everywhere. Many an invention, which only an extraordinary genius with an equally extraordinary effort could bring into the world, is now found in the hands of the most common craftsman, who would be astonished if he were told that a matter so commonplace to him had cost so much in thought and industry. A schoolboy now demonstrates the most brilliant theorems of Archimedes, and the most ignorant monk now grasps how Galileo, who leaves the sun standing, and the Bible, which lets it run, can both be right, and thus solves a problem that nearly cost the good Galileo his life and that in fact cost the holy congregation of the purpled princes of the Church their honor. For every truth there is a moment in the order of time when it surrenders to anyone who can and will have it. Once this moment and the man who knows how to use it are present, truth descends from the intellectual world into the real world and becomes a common good of mankind. But to make this moment arrive more quickly is perhaps no less the work of the enlightener than that of chance.[5]

The contention that nature abandoned the greater part of mankind, or even only one people under her hands, is a manifest slandering of nature. Although she could not observe a perfect equality in the allocation of her gifts, she was as rarely particularly stingy as she was particularly generous. Exceedingly corrupt organizations are just as rare as exceedingly perfect ones. Besides, a more or less perfect organization confines man's capacity for reason less or more, but never above or below a level where it would be incapable of any development. Nature would otherwise have had to intend to make the greatest part of mankind wretched. The greatest part of mankind, in contrast, actually manifests the capacities that are necessary for a considerable number of distinct concepts, or at least a number commensurate to its vocation [*Bestimmung*]. It has enough attentiveness within its power not only to learn its own mother tongue but also to learn one or more foreign ones. Anyone who knows something of the difficulties that even the most capable mind has to overcome in learning foreign languages will find it comprehensible that those masses who are in a position to learn foreign languages could just as easily grasp a multitude of distinct concepts which a skilled teacher knows how to communicate to them in a lucid order and with all the artifices of method.

Nothing can better justify nature than the history of ignorance and of the errors which some would attribute to her stinginess toward the greatest part of mankind. The disposition to everything that man can become in the world is the direct work of nature. What man has actually become is the result of all the situations, from his cradle onward, through which he had to pass. Stupidity generally stands in an inverse relation with civil rank, and although there are members of the masses in all classes, proper linguistic usage attributed this name only to the lowest class of every nation.[6] But why are the masses so great a part of every nation? Because the possessions and places of honor that rise above the lower classes [*Klassen des Pöbels*] suffice for only a small part of mankind. The deeper one descends into the lowest classes, the more obvious becomes the cause of ignorance and errors, the more salient becomes the lack of opportunity and means, as well as the number and the strength of the obstacles to rational culture. Take fools from the higher classes—for example, the monk who, under the cover of the darkness in which the reason of his fellow citizens lies buried, has made his way into teaching positions in the churches and schools of his nation, or the noble, who earned the right to babble nonsense in the Senate of his fatherland by the sole fact that his mother has a noble lord for a husband.

Go through their lives and deduct from the immense mass of their stupidity all that the one owes to the novice master, lector, guardian, and to the whole blessed cloister, and what the other owes to his most noble parents, to court, language, dance, and fencing masters, and then look at how much still remains that may fairly be credited to the account of the original natural disposition. Precisely the same youth who is given by his mother to Saint Anthony and with heart and soul becomes a Capuchin monk, would have become, given by his father to the fatherland, a good soldier in a military school; and the noble, educated by other hands, would himself be able to render his fatherland the services for which he now must pay his secretary. The ordinary fool is thus not born but bred, and under better circumstances would have become what the happy few are who partake of these circumstances. Thus the greater part of mankind actually brings as many capacities into the world with it as it needs to become wise, that is, to acquire a proportional quantity of distinct concepts concerning the objects that have a substantial influence on its happiness—provided that, once it has left its mother's womb, the necessary precautions are taken.

Yet it is a fact that the greater part of every nation consists of the masses, no matter how they become that. Shouldn't the circumstances in which this greater part is degraded into so abject a class have destroyed the mental powers received from nature to the point where enlightenment can accomplish nothing more? Shouldn't the upbringing and the condition of the great multitude be an insurmountable obstacle to the development of its reason? Every error deviates from truth, further limits the capacity for reason, and serves as a bulwark for ignorance. Shouldn't this bulwark now, through the labors of all the enemies of reason for all the centuries down to the present, have finally become strong enough to defy all the power of truth? Shouldn't, for example, the monks have gotten the better of the understanding of their Catholic contemporaries to a point where it would be impossible, at least as far as this understanding is concerned, for Joseph and his sages to help? A few careful glances at the history of the human understanding will answer this question. One should not forget, though, that we are speaking here of cultured nations.

If, on the one hand, we must be astonished by the magnitude and the harmfulness of the errors with which the human species was afflicted for as far back as we can think, the victories, on the other hand, which truth has wrested from its opponents in all ages are certainly no less admirable. What an infinite amount had to be corrected in men's concepts before many a vice to which whole nations built altars appeared in its true form—before one people recognized theft, another the polygamy of women, one people suicide, the other human sacrifice, for what they actually are! Would the initiates of many ancient mysteries have ever imagined that the masses, the profane masses of their descendants, would in many respects think more correctly about God, morality, and so forth, than their mystagogues? Would Socrates have thought that the same people who believed that the alleged contempt of its gods had to be avenged with death would so soon laugh at just these gods? Would Cicero have imagined that his renown would last longer in posterity than the *Dii immortales* of his contemporaries? And if these men, as great observers of human nature, also have foreseen these rapid and important alterations in the concepts of their nations, they certainly must have credited the people with the capacities which are at issue here.

Socrates, who brought philosophy from heaven down to earth, was of course much too Socratic to aim, in all seriousness, at turning the superstitious, childish, volatile masses of Athens into a nation of philosophers. Yet the goal of his method was nothing less than the development of the concepts of the common man—the enlightenment of the masses. He thus did not regard the masses of his nation as so corrupt as to despair of their betterment. The spiritual and temporal Lord Sycophants[7] were, in this, at one with Socrates. What he hoped for, they feared. Undoubtedly, many a truth had already become a commonplace among the people through this man and his method. It was feared, not without grounds, that the sum of these truths would become greater and greater than these spiritual and temporal lords could allow ex officio, and the man and his method had to be eliminated.

The quantity of distinct concepts which would be sufficient to present the Athenian sycophants to the masses in their true character would have had to be quite considerable. Socrates and his opponents thus had a rather high opinion of the rational ability of the masses. All the founders of nations, all the legislators and sages, who have worked with and without success on human happiness, all the despots, Baal-priests, and bonzees[8] who worked against them, all of them have not thought less of the capacity for reason of their respective masses. If not, the one would have thought it superfluous to risk their leisure, their fortune, their health, and their life for the enlightenment of their fatherland, and the other would have thought it superfluous to struggle against this enlightenment for their comfort, their wealth, their reputation. The astonishing revolutions in the minds of a whole nation, which often only a single man prompted, prepared, and carried out, show conclusively how little both enlighteners and endarkeners [*Verfinstere*] have erred in their good opinion of the capacities of the masses.

What has been said here in favor of these capacities is confirmed most undeniably by a multitude of bulls of the most holy fathers in Rome, statutes of the holy College of Cardinals, and decrees of the Holy Inquisition. Through the united endeavors of these supreme, highest, and high [*allerhöchsten, höchsten, und hohen*] tribunals came that well-known Index which imprinted so many works of the greatest minds of all nations with the stamp of their usefulness for enlightenment.[9] Only graduate ministers, lectors, and clergymen—men whose theological armor and thick helmet of faith sufficiently secured them against all the dangers that their holy ignorance must run with such a reading—even received permission to read these works before they refuted them. All other Christians were kept back by the Vatican's thunderbolts. It was thus feared that lay masses might *understand* these books: a thing, of course, that was not to be feared of the theologians. The Roman *Index of Prohibited Books* is an honorable monument to the people's capacity for truth.

In general, all the precautions that can be taken against the possibility of popular enlightenment are in the end useless and ultimately serve only as proof of the existence of this possibility. In all times and all places the monkish fog could never become so thick that they could hold out against the rays of truth which must sooner or later disperse them. Fog can prevent the eyes of our reason from true vision for a long time, but it can never rob them of sight itself. The deepest degree of ignorance and error among a cultured people is precisely the preparation for and the precursor of its further enlightenment. The bonzees themselves would have too much to lose to wish for a cultured nation to be reduced to the state of a Huronic or Iroquoian savagery; and they would have to bring it that far before they could prevent a nation, even in the deepest degree of ignorance and error, from finally beginning at least to sense the need for enlightenment. Many a tyrant, whose name one never hears mentioned without revulsion, has in truth contributed more to the subsequent freedom of his people than the great and good man whom the people venerates as its liberator. The yoke first had to be made unbearable if one was to resolve to throw it off. The spiritual darkness of a people must often become so thick that the people bumps its head, if it gets the idea to look for the light. The stronger and the more immediate the influence on our well-being of those truths which ignorance does not let us recognize and which error makes us mistake, the less our ignorance and our error can hold out in the long run. The further we go away from truth, the more painful our misery becomes. It must finally become so painful that we cannot bear it, and we become aware of the causes, we long for liberation, and we view everyone who can and will correct us as our liberator. Enlightenment is then a need that must be satisfied, and we are never more teachable than when it comes to a need that has become insuperable for us. There can hardly be a people more stupid than the Kamchatkans,[10] and hardly has a people developed further the skill of making clothes. In this case, the education which the coldness of their winters provides is obvious enough. Monks had to depopulate entire lands, exterminate entire lineages, and acquire so much property that one feared they would soon assume temporal sovereignty over the laity—all this before certain Catholic states could risk passing coercive laws which forced their novices first to come of age before they renounced humanity, and before they could risk forbidding the laity to give their children's inheritance to people who forswore ever becoming parents.[11] Through their unrestrained begging and profiteering from holy relics, these same monks had already expropriated the meat the farmer held back for his holiday table—for their tasty everyday table—and the wine he dared not drink because he had to save it to secure bread in future dearths—for their daily carousing. The cry of the hungry—who thus lost those alms which age and sickness left as their only succor, and which were now taken from their mouths by idle gluttons—had to become loud enough if the poor goodhearted folk were to be set to rest with Joseph's salutary decree freeing them from this incessant extortion. The Holy Inquisition had to perform a multitude of human sacrifices in the interest of the Roman court and its army of monks; it had to have burned and banned the states' most useful citizens; the mass of orphaned children, relatives, and friends, and the fear of the people trembling for its life and property had to become substantial enough, before Spain would become capable of that heartrending joy which resounded for us here, when finally, even there, humanity triumphed for a short time over that fire-breathing, bloodthirsty monster. In brief, the bonzees of all nations had to do just as much as they actually did to darken human understanding before the evil consequences could become conspicuous enough to force men to reflect. The religious phantoms, which they employed to place and maintain the masses under forced levies, had to become horrible enough before they could be frightened back into the arms of truth. Allow us an example from the current history of enlightenment in Vienna. The most conclusive refutations of all the sages of the entire world would hardly have been capable of as rapid and as complete an enlightenment of the masses of Vienna about the true character of the Catholic teaching as it received from its chief clergyman, the infamous Father Fast, on just a single page.[12] As long as this vigorous champion of superstition was content with defending, under the commission and with the permission of his bishop, those errors and misuses which, through tradition and habit, had lost their revolting odiousness for ordinary eyes, he always remained the favorite author of the masses. He could tell them:

> The Viennese Church has remained perfectly homologous down to the smallest and most insignificant ceremonies, so that every reform would be not only superfluous, but utterly impossible.
>
> The saints brought about much greater miracles than God, and must therefore be venerated on their feast days with a much greater number of votive lights.

> The badly painted wooden Madonna of Pötsch has cried abundant tears, and had it not cried, the Emperor Leopold would not have been legitimate.[13]
>
> The rights of man are inviolable only in those cases where they do not run counter to God's arrangements.
>
> Philosophy and reason bring forth only heretics and adventurers, and so on.[14]

He could recklessly write this and even more of the same nonsense without losing favor with his readers. For that, a stupidity was necessary, one which was not only contrary to reason but also horrible enough to revolt even the crude kind of moral feelings which reside in the lowest masses of a cultured nation and distinguish them from Hottentots. As soon as Fast suggested public worship of the well-known *membrum* and imputed to the Church that, "it has decreed the Feast of the Circumcision for the sake of this member," the masses of Vienna, from the ladies of the court and of the town down to the market-women, were shaken. Parents hid Fast's Catholic teachings[15] from their children's eyes, and the name Fast brought about general disgust, indignation, and laughter. In vain his archbishop elevated him to rector of the high Metropolitan Church and to first pastor in Vienna as a reward for his works and as an approval of his teaching. The street ballads in which the masses made fun of Fast were only cried out still louder and bought up more avidly.

Nature has thus, to the benefit of humanity, arranged that the reign of stupidity will destroy itself, and that the darkener of human reason must in the end, against his will, promote enlightenment.

NOTES

1. Reinhold's definition and his subsequent discussion of it draws heavily on the terminology of Christian Wolff (1679–1754), whose work had a pervasive influence within the German Enlightenment. Following Descartes and Leibniz, Wolff saw the goal of philosophy to be the production of "clear and distinct" concepts. He defined a concept (*Begriff*) as the "representation [*Vorstellung*] of objects in our thoughts" (*Vernünftige Gedanken von den Kräften des Menschlichen Verstandes* §4). If our concepts are sufficient to allow us to recognize the object which it denotes, no matter what this object happens to be called or where it happens to be located, then our concepts are "clear" (*klar*) as opposed to "obscure" (*dunkel*) (§9). If our concepts are clear enough to enable us to specify the characteristics which allow us to know a thing, then they are said to be "distinct" (*deutlich*) (§13).—Trans.

2. Peter I, czar of Russia from 1682 to 1725, undertook a series of reforms designed to westernize Russian politics and culture; Joseph II of Austria was co-regent with his mother, Maria Theresa, from 1765 to 1780 and sole ruler from 1780 to 1790.—Trans.

3. On his mother's death in 1780, Joseph began a series of sweeping reforms, to which Reinhold alludes throughout this essay.—Trans.

4. "Masses" here should mean nothing less than the common man.

5. The second installment of the essay, published in the *Teutsche Merkur* of August 1784 ends at this point. The final part of the essay appeared in the September 1784 issue.—TRANS.

6. Here Reinhold alludes to a more recent meaning of the word *Pöbel*: the "rabble," the lowest class in society.—TRANS.

7. Reinhold's use of the term "Herren Sykophanten" alludes to the original Greek meaning—an "informer"—which remained current in the eighteenth century.—TRANS.

8. *Despoten, Baalspfaffen, und Bonzen*—a *Baalspfaff* is literally a worshiper of the Phoenician god Baal and more generally any false priest, especially an idolater. In the eighteenth century, the term was also used to refer derogatorily to Catholics. *Bonzen* is a term taken over from the Japanese *bonzi* (religious person) and *bo-zi* (teacher of the law). Initially used in travel literature to refer to Buddhist priests, in the eighteenth century it had come to be employed as a term of contempt for imperious or bigoted clergy.—TRANS.

9. Reinhold refers here to the *Index librorum prohibitorum*, which in eighteenth-century Vienna included the works of Goethe, Jacobi, and Mendelssohn. Since the reign of Ferdinand II (1619–1637), all books having to do with philosophy or theology were censored by the Jesuits, who directed the philosophical and theological faculties at the University of Vienna. Joseph II's decree of 11 June 1781 annulled the *Index*, placing the responsibility for the administration of liberalized censorship regulations with the newly established state board of censorship.—TRANS.

10. The Kamchatkan Peninsula, first discovered by Russians in 1697, was explored and conquered by Czar Peter I in the early part of the eighteenth century. —TRANS.

11. A reference to Joseph's edicts, which prevented any religious order from admitting a novice of less than twenty-four years of age (the Council of Trent had permitted novices as young as sixteen) and which prohibited mortmain.—TRANS.

12. Patritius Fast was rector and church- and choir-master at the Metropolitankirche in Vienna and a well-known critic of Enlightenment theology in general and Joseph II's reforms in particular. His general position was perhaps best exemplified in a pamphlet on Pope Pius VI's visit to Vienna: "Faith teaches me mysteries, but it does not enlighten me. I believe in a triune God, and I am convinced, as clear as day, that I must believe, but I cannot conceive what I believe. Faith does not drive away the clouds which prevent God from being seen by a mortal eye or from being investigated by earthly understanding. This holy darkness permanently beclouds faith, so that enlightened understanding does not brighten the mysteries; rather, mysteries remain in darkness." *Austellungen über die Vorstellung an Se. pabstliche Heiligkeit Pius VI* (Vienna, 1782), 45–46.—TRANS.

13. Leopold I was Holy Roman Emperor from 1658 to 1705 and throughout his life was an ardent supporter of the cult of Mary.—TRANS.

14. Since, to the honor of Vienna, writings of this kind never come across the border, we have faithfully cited the above sentences from the *Wiener-Realzeitung*, in which all of Fast's products appear under the rubric "archnonsense" (*Erzmakulator*). [The *Wiener-Realzeitung*, edited by Alois Blumauer, was the principal organ of the

Viennese Aufklärung. In addition to critical articles, it published translations of English essays. Reinhold contributed articles to it between 1782 and 1783.—Trans.]

15. Reinhold may intend a pun on Fast's name: *Fastisch-katholischen* may also be translated as "barely Catholic."—Trans.

A Couple of Gold Nuggets, from the . . . Wastepaper, or Six Answers to Six Questions

Christoph Martin Wieland

Translated by Kevin Paul Geiman and James Schmidt

Christoph Martin Wieland (1733–1813), one of the more prolific writers of the German rococo, published prose, poetry, and political essays. He was the editor of the influential journal Der Teutsche Merkur, *which—along with the* Berlinische Monatsschrift *and Nicolai's* Allgemeine deutsche Bibliothek—*was one of the principal organs for the dissemination of enlightened opinion in Germany. This essay was written on the eve of the French Revolution and is thus untroubled by the problem of the relationship between enlightenment and revolution, a question that would dominate subsequent discussions of the Enlightenment's political implications.*

It is known all too well that even good books sometimes become maculature.[1] A chance sheet of maculature, from a book unknown to me, has occasioned this essay, and thus in calling it "maculature" I do not want to demean the honor and worth of the book or its author. The book may be an entirely good, or at least a well-meaning, book. I cannot judge it, since I have read nothing of it except a single sheet of maculature, which served as the wrapper for a small brochure sent to me from Leipzig several days ago. In the current, inconvenient fashion, it had not the slightest typographical markings from which one could see the title of the book to which it belonged.[2] It is enough that the book, or at least the sheet, is now maculature, and since everyone knows what maculature is, for what it is used, and what usually happens to it, if it is printed on good, white, soft paper (which was exactly the case with this paper), the gentle reader only needs to recall the adepts who made the attempt (whether it was successful or not, I do not know) to derive the stone of wisdom from a certain unnamed material in order to find the above title to be as clear as the circumstances will permit.

First published under the pseudonym "Timalethes" as "Ein paar Goldkröner aus—Maculator oder Sechs Antworten auf sechs Fragen," Der Teutsche Merkur *(April 1789): 97–105.*

By the way, whether I have distilled true gold from this page of maculature can be shown if it is brought to the chapel, where everyone should welcome me warmly.

Nothing could be more accidental than the origin of this little essay. I thought indeed, as I was tearing about a page from the maculature, that nothing less than fate had destined it to be honored with an elevated use far above its usual destiny. But enough of this! I cast one glance on page 214 of the sheet that I held between the three first fingers of my right hand, when, on the first half of this page, so weighty in content, I found—not without a slight shudder of astonishment—the following six questions posed:

1. What is enlightenment?
2. Over which objects can and must it extend itself?
3. Where are its limits?
4. What are the safe means through which it is advanced?
5. Who is authorized to enlighten humanity?
6. By what consequences does one recognize its truth?

These questions (in the opinion of the author) were still not resolved in the way they must in order to be content with the *concept of enlightenment* and its *course among us*, and they must be answered purely and simply and unequivocally if we do not wish to roam about in an eternal chaos of arrogance, error, and darkness.

In my humble opinion, his six questions had, for the last thousand years, been no longer in question for all reasonable men, and if, thought I, we roamed about in spite of this in an eternal chaos of arrogance, error, and darkness, this must have an entirely different cause. Nevertheless, because the good man regards the matter as so important, why should the editor of the *Teutsche Merkur* deny me two or three pages on which I may venture to answer these six questions so *"purely and simply"* that with regard to the seventh question—whether I have answered them correctly—there should be but one voice? I thus dedicate myself at this point to this good work, and—so that my preface will not be as long as this essay itself—now proceed immediately to the explanation.

I. "WHAT IS ENLIGHTENMENT?"

Answer: This is known to everyone who, by means of a pair of eyes that see, has learned to recognize the difference between brightness and obscurity, between light and darkness. In the dark one either sees not at all or at least not so clearly that one can correctly recognize objects and distinguish them from one another. As soon as light is brought, things are cleared up [*klären sich die Sache auf*], become visible, and can be distinguished from one another. But in addition two things are necessarily required: (1) that enough light be at hand and (2) that those who ought to see by it are neither blind nor jaundiced, nor through any other cause prevented from being able to see or from wanting to see.

II. "OVER WHICH OBJECTS CAN AND MUST ENLIGHTENMENT EXTEND ITSELF?"

The oddest question! Over what, if not over all visible objects? But certainly that is obvious, I would have thought. Or must it be proven? Now then! In the dark (a single laudable and communally useful activity excepted) there remains nothing for honest people to do but to sleep. In the dark one does not see where one is, nor where one goes, nor what one does, nor what happens around us—particularly at some distance. With every step one runs the danger of bumping one's nose, with every movement of knocking something over, of damaging or touching what one should not touch, in short, one runs the danger at every moment of blundering and misstepping, so that whoever wanted to carry out his usual affairs in the dark would carry them out very badly.[3] The application [of this metaphor] is child's play. The light of the mind of which we speak is the knowledge of true and false, of good and evil. Hopefully everyone will admit that without this knowledge it is just as impossible to carry on mental matters correctly as it is impossible without material light to carry on material matters properly. Enlightenment—that is, as much knowledge as is necessary to be able always and everywhere to distinguish truth and falsehood—must therefore extend itself without exception over all objects over which it *can* extend itself, that is, over all that is visible to the outer and inner eye. But there are people who will be disturbed in their work as soon as light comes; there are people for whom it is impossible to carry out their work other than in the dark or at least in the twilight: for example, whoever wants to give us black for white, or pays with counterfeit money, or wants to let ghosts appear; or also (which is very innocent in itself) whoever likes to seize whims, builds castles in the air, and takes trips to Cockaigne or the happy islands—he can naturally not perform this as well in bright sunshine as at night, or in moonshine, or in an expediently self-arranged twilight. All these brave people are thus natural adversaries of enlightenment, and neither now nor ever will they let themselves be convinced that light *must* be spread over all objects that *can* become visible through it. Obtaining their agreement is therefore a pure impossibility; but fortunately it is also not necessary.

III. "WHERE ARE THE LIMITS OF ENLIGHTENMENT?"

Answer: Where, with all the light possible, there is nothing more to see. The question is exactly of the same kind as "where is the world boarded up?"[4] And this answer is really still too serious for such a question.

IV. "WHAT ARE THE SAFE MEANS THROUGH WHICH IT IS ADVANCED?"

The most infallible means of making it become brighter is to increase the light, to remove as many dark bodies as possible that block its passage, and especially to illuminate painstakingly all the dark corners and caverns into which the light-shy person mentioned in Section II drives himself.

All objects of our knowledge are either events or representations, concepts, judgments, and opinions. Events become enlightened when one investigates, to the satisfaction of every impartial researcher, whether and how they occurred. Representations, concepts, judgments, and opinions of men become enlightened when the true is separated from the false, when the entangled is disentangled, when the complex is dissolved into its simple components, when the simple is pursued to its origin, and, above all, when no representation or claim passed off by men as true is granted a reprieve from unrestricted scrutiny. There is—and can be—no other means than this of diminishing the mass of mistakes and pernicious deceptions that darken human understanding.

The discussion here cannot be one of safety or of danger. No one can have anything to fear when it becomes brighter in the minds of men—except for those whose interest it is that it should be and remain dark. Should, however, no consideration be taken for the safety of these latter in answering the question? Truly, we can be completely silent on their account; they will take care of their own security. In the future, as up until now, they will do everything they can to obstruct, to nail shut, and to stop up all openings, windows, and crevices through which light can come into the world. They will not fail, as soon as they are stronger, to smash the lanterns which provide us and others with some light with which to see; and when they are not strong enough, they will not fail to use every imaginable means to bring enlightenment at least into bad repute. I do not like to think badly of my fellow men, but I must confess the *safeness* of the means of enlightenment, so dear to our enquirer, could make me—against my will—suspicious of his integrity. Does he mean that there are respectable things that cannot endure illumination? No, we do not want to think so ill of his understanding! But perhaps he will say, "There may be cases where too much light is harmful, where one should allow it to shine in only cautiously and gradually." Good! only this cannot be the case, at least in Germany, with the enlightenment produced by the distinction between the true and the false; for our nation is not so blind that she must be handled like a person whose black cataract is operated upon. It would be mockery and shame if, after having for three hundred years little by little gotten used to a certain degree of light, we should not finally be in the position of being able to bear bright sunshine. It is obvious that these are mere evasions by the dear people who have their own reason why it should not be bright around them.

V. "WHO IS AUTHORIZED TO ENLIGHTEN HUMANITY?"

Whoever can!—"But who can?"—I answer with a counterquestion: *"Who can't?"* Well my good man? Do we stand there and stare at one another? Thus, because there is no oracle to render a verdict in ambiguous cases (and if there were one, how would it help us without a second oracle that elucidated the first to us?), and because no human tribunal is authorized to arrogate to itself a decision which would by its discretion let so much or so little light reach us as pleased it, so it must no doubt remain that everyone without exception—from Socrates or Kant to the most obscure of all supernaturally enlightened tailors and shoemakers—is authorized to enlighten humanity however he can, as soon as his good or evil spirit incites him to it. One may consider the matter from whichever side one wants; one will find that human society is infinitely less endangered by this freedom than when the illumination of the minds and the actions and the inactions of men is treated as a monopoly or as an exclusive concern of a guild. Only I would possibly want to advise, *ne quid Res publica detrimenti capiat,*[5] the declaration of a most innocent restriction; and this would be to renew the very wise penal law of the old emperors of the first and second centuries against clandestine conventicles and secret fraternities, and, following this, to allow all who are not called to teach in pulpits and rostrums no means for the enlightenment of humanity other than the printing press. A fool who preaches nonsense in a conventicle can make mischief in civil society; a book, on the other hand, whatever its content might be, can today do no harm that either would be worth mentioning or that would not soon be compensated ten- and hundredfold by others.

VI. "BY WHAT CONSEQUENCES DOES ONE RECOGNIZE THE TRUTH OF ENLIGHTENMENT?"

Answer: When everything becomes brighter; when the number of thinking, inquiring, light-bringing people becomes ever greater, and when, in particular, the mass of prejudices and delusions becomes visibly ever smaller in the class of persons who have the most to gain from nonenlightenment; when the shame for ignorance and unreason, the desire for useful and noble knowledge, and especially when the respect for human nature and its rights in all classes increases unnoticed; and (in what is certainly one of the most unambiguous characteristics) when several freight wagons full of brochures against enlightenment are imported and exported in Leipzig.[6] For the figurative night birds are on this point precisely the opposite of the genuine ones: the former first become audible at night; the latter, in contrast, screech most shrilly when the sun pricks them in the eyes.

> Say, am I right? What do you fancy from the matter, good neighbor with the long ear?

NOTES

1. "Maculature" (*Makulatur*) refers specifically to spoiled pages of a press run and more generally to waste or surplus pages. It is also a German idiom for writing nonsense.—Trans.

2. An editorial note in *Wielands Gesammelte Schriften* (Berlin, 1972), I/23:58A, reports that in 1791 Ernst August Anton v. Goechhausen stated, in the *Neuer Deutsche Merkur* (III:104–105), that the book in question was his anonymously published attack on the Masonic movement, *Enthülung des Systems der Weltbürger-Republik* (Rome [Leipzig], 1787).—Trans.

3. This admits of some exceptions, as I well know; but in most cases, it remains the rule.

4. An allusion to the childish belief that, on traveling to the end of the world, one would find the path on which one had been traveling boarded up, preventing one from going any further.—Trans.

5. Cicero, *Against Lucius Sergius Catilina* 2,1: "that the republic should not suffer."—Trans.

6. Leipzig was a center of the German book trade.—Trans.

2. The Public Use of Reason

On Freedom of Thought and of the Press: For Princes, Ministers, and Writers

Ernst Ferdinand Klein

Translated by John Christian Laursen

Ernst Ferdinand Klein (1744–1810) was a prominent Prussian jurist and member of the Wednesday Society. He studied law with Wolff's follower Daniel Nettelbladt at Halle. Beginning in 1781, he was an adviser to Frederick's High Chancellor von Carmer and co-author with Carl Gottlieb Svarez of the Prussian Civil Code, a major project of enlightened legal reform. His book Freedom and Property *(1790) purported to be a series of dialogues between members of the Wednesday Society.*

In the following essay, which appeared in the Berlinische Monatsschrift *several months before Kant's "What Is Enlightenment?" Klein drew on Frederick the Great's own writings to justify substantial freedom of the press. Much of the essay consists of a paraphrase of Frederick's ideas, supported by quotations from Frederick's writings. The main thrust of the essay is probably more liberal than Frederick may have intended, but the ambivalence of the bureaucrat is evident in the last passages, where Klein justifies censorship in those cases in which writings might stimulate civil disorder and reminds writers that "not every truth is useful alike for all times and all circumstances."*

Complaints about the misuse of freedom of the press, on the one hand, and about its restriction, on the other, have been increasing for some time, so that observations about this matter probably could not come at a better time than now. One would have to reach back rather far if one wanted to derive what must be said about this from its first principles. A writer who undertook this might win the admiration of many readers for his acuteness, but they could still find ways in which each could save his own particular opinions. As far as I am concerned, I wish to make my reader favorably disposed toward an opinion which indeed flows from the first principles of natural law and can be less called into question in theory than be subject to chicanery in practice, but which nevertheless will be secured more through the lively presentation of its results than through the development of its first principles.

"Über Denk- und Drukfreiheit: An Fürsten, Minister, und Schriftsteller" appeared anonymously in the Berlinische Monatsschrift *3 (1784): 312–330. A revised version was published by Klein in his* Kurze Aufsätze über verschiedene Gegenstände *(Halle, 1797).*

Frederick of Prussia has had an influence on his contemporaries for almost half a century by means of his writings and, even more, by his example. I leave it to the historians to report on the influence that his conduct has had and will continue to have on public law, the art of government, philosophy, and the morals of the century. But nothing can be more useful for my purposes, I believe, than to collect what Frederick has thought and said on this matter and lay it before my readers. I cannot boast of having received special revelations from him. I can only extract appropriate materials from his writings, which lie before the eyes of everyone. For that reason I will make connections between passages, and also bring together scattered thoughts, so that I can develop his system from its very roots. I can do so, since I am in a position to confirm everything which I put in his mouth, if not through the words of the writer, then through the acts of the king. However, little as I need to worry about the reproach that I am selling my own thoughts under Frederick's stamp, so much must I fear that my stamp might have made his thoughts unrecognizable. So I ask the reader to use his imagination to make up for what my explanations lack in worthiness and vitality.

Imagine the young monarch, alone in his room at the first moments of taking up his government, collecting his thoughts and expressing himself in the following soliloquy:

> Now I have grasped the reins by which a mass of scattered people are to be led in their tracks. With the whip of a Nero I could drive them on like animals. And yet they are men[1]—men, like me—born to live pleasant days—able to bring forth Leibnizes and Wolffs—destined to feel the dignity of humanity—accustomed to honor power that is based on order—inclined to repay love with love. But am I not the king? Are not kings shepherds of the peoples, and so the peoples their herds? I may praise myself for knowing better their destiny and my own.[2] Have we not all the same right to happiness? Is the surplus of the rich not a necessary sacrifice, which he must offer to fill the needs of the poor? Does not my higher station, my royal office, give me the duty to be gentler, more benevolent, more virtuous, and in a word more humane than they? One says that men are ungrateful beasts, they fawn at our feet, wriggle and twist, lick and flatter; and before one expects it, they snap at the hand of the one who feeds them. And what else can one expect, when one teaches them to forget what they are, when one subdues them like animals, and does not rule them like men? Indeed, the worthless ones in whom the spark of divine origin and the whole feeling of the dignity of mankind has been stifled must be controlled and kept within limits by force. But the prince who intends to reign purely through fear changes his subjects into abject slaves; in vain will he expect noble deeds from them. All of their actions will have the stamp of their low character.[3] In vain will he strive for honor through great actions. For all his efforts he will only win the fame of an able taskmaster, and awaken no

man of genius who would be able to collect the rays of his throne, as in a mirror, and display them to the eyes of posterity. As for me, I want to rule over a noble, brave, freethinking people, a people that has the power and liberty to think and to act, to write and to speak, to win or to die. May they at times misuse the freedom given to them, to diminish my greatest deeds! I am that much safer from the low vermin of flatterers, and I will learn the divine art of pardoning. He who does not possess this is unworthy of a throne.[4]

To make men happy is the happy lot of divinity, and should, as far as humanly possible, also become mine. But how can I make my people happy, my government benevolent, and my name immortal? What forms the true strength of states? Is it the wide expanse of territory, requiring a large army for its protection? Or wealth steadily growing through trade and industry, which is only useful when one knows how to use it well? Or finally the number of subjects, who would perish without a leader? No, all these are only raw materials, as it were, that only gain value and consequence when they are worked by a shrewd and dexterous hand. The true power of a country consists solely in the great men whom nature permits to be born there at the right time.[5]

Thus I must awaken genius, provide nourishment for the spirit of inquiry and free play for talents. My peoples do not even suspect the half of what will become of them. They know well that they do not feel and think only to be able to distinguish white bread from black. They would think freely, if they were permitted. They would have Shaftesburys and Lockes among them if they dared to, perhaps also Montesquieus and Voltaires, if they could go unpunished. They should exist and not think? Breathe, and not share their thoughts? Why do the heirs of the rulers of the world languish in the ruins of their forefathers in infamy and poverty? Is it not because their feeble tyrant seeks to reign without limit over deeds and thoughts, property and opinions, rank and conscience?[6]

Why does that eternally famous people, before whose name, accompanied by the thunder of its cannons, both hemispheres tremble, sink into a deathly powerlessness after the conquest of half a world? Why can the treasures of both Indies, and two seas, from which other people enrich themselves, not remedy its daily growing poverty?—Why the decline of this empire at the extreme points of Europe, washed by the great ocean, and so notorious for the persecution of dissenters?[7] Why also must the few efforts of its idle but orthodox inhabitants enrich those proud heretics, who through the cultivation of their talents made half the world their tributary?[8]—Why do the Protestant provinces of Germany share greater prosperity in spite of less fertility?—Why the superiority in power, influence, and honor which distinguishes France from the other Catholic countries?—All this remains unexplained, if one does not take into account the resistance of the inertia, through which superstition, priestly despotism, and intolerance work against the development of talent and inventiveness and against the natural drive of men to be active; if one forgets with what zeal the French parliaments fought against the hierarchy, and if one does not know how much the freedom to think lifts up spirit and heart, and makes them fit for undertakings both great and well considered.

On the one side I see peoples who dare not see beyond the circle that the magic wand of the priests has drawn around them; they recoil trembling from any thought that has not received the spiritual stamp as current coinage. They dare not ask: What is true? but only: What have our elders held for truth? Men who are so accustomed dare not draw their bow differently than their fathers, or give their household furniture a shape which they have not already had the opportunity to observe in their grandmother's legacy. So they sink into idleness out of stupidity, and hand over their treasures to people whom they hate, only to be despised by them. In vain does one encourage them to industry, or seek to bring able foreigners[9] into the nation. One wants to stretch a hemp thread like a steel spring, and lets the grafted branch wither with the trunk.

I observe on the other side those happy peoples, whose spirit has transcended the prejudices of darker times, who prescribed laws to the stars, explored the birthplace of the winds, weighed the air, mastered nature, and put their stamp on the earth from pole to pole.[10] I also see that with restless activity they always discover new means of livelihood, and the riches of all parts of the world grow under their hands. Good taste doubles the value of their work, and their ideas reign unrestricted both at the glittering court and in the dusty school.

The dawn of philosophy and good taste shall also rise over my subjects. They shall throw off the chains of superstition. Power-hungry priests shall not limit their freedom to think. No religion shall rule. All faiths shall be taught with equal freedom. If there were only one religion in the world, it would rule proudly and without limits. Each clergyman would be a tyrant, and would show as much severity against blameless opinions, as leniency for the crimes of the people. They would trample on all enlightenment as their common enemy, and raise stupidity to honor, under the name of piety.[11]

It shall not come to that in my country and under my government. Even if my subjects disagree among themselves over faith, no party shall succeed in pulling the state into their camp. In vain will the one decry the opinion of the other as dangerous. Only fools among princes let themselves become the tools of private vengeance. Errors, even the most dangerous, will never gain fame through my persecution, but as they deserve, will be detested and forgotten.

By contrast, the beneficial influence of philosophy shall not be limited by any coercive laws. Wolff shall come back to my state,[12] and whatever does not plainly contradict the state, good morals, and the universal religion shall be taught freely and publicly.

So thought and so acted the great monarch, who has since become the model for princes and the object of admiration for all of Europe. Oh you, whom God has made, under the names of "king" and "prince," guardians of his immature children, from whose wisdom the people must ask the preservation of their human rights! When will you begin to be a Frederick to your people, not just to appear to be one? When will you give them the freedom to which they have an inalienable title from birth, the freedom to think and to share their thoughts? You imitate Frederick where you cannot. But the art of turning deserts into gardens, of ruling men in a humane way, and of giving the activities of your subjects a useful field—those are the arts whose exercise you leave to him and a few of his more fortunate imitators. You fear, perhaps, that your people, if it came to speech like Balaam's Ass,[13] might make you see the sad condition they are in. But you need hardly fear that. Oppressed peoples argue against their tyrants as seldom as beasts against their riders. When the miracle happens, however, it is as beneficial for Balaam and his ass as it is for princes and their peoples.

Of course, if you consider your own and your servants' and favorites' high persons to be the state, you are right to reject all writings in which your measures are judged as writings against the state.—Not so Frederick, who pays attention to the ideas of the lowest of his subjects and takes those of Raynal under his wing![14]

And what can be gained by limiting the freedom of the press? What you will not allow to be printed in your land enriches, at your expense, a printer in the next country. If you confiscate the work, it will be sought and read, understood and misunderstood, with redoubled zeal.

This principle is valid even if you have reservations about turning your subjects into men, even if they are in the position of the miserable ones who must call themselves dogs in the presence of the king, so that his majesty may not once be reminded even from afar of the duties of humanity. In this case, however, the fate of your people will also be infinitely different from that of the subjects of Frederick, who are taught at his command that he, as a man, demands from them, as men, only human respect.

Perhaps you think that daylight does not benefit your people, and that they are better off with a lamp that burns just bright enough to allow them to find their bread, without showing its blackness. And you are right, if you intend to steal all the rights of man from your subjects, stifle the impulse to activity in them, turn the cities into hunters' huts and the fields into game-hunting grounds; and if you have a plan to change the rest of your subjects into beggars, in order to protect them against those whom you compelled to become thieves and robbers.

Or do you intend to facilitate the traveling philosopher's inquiries by your decrees? Because as soon as he finds out how freedom of the press stands with you, he can with little trouble draw conclusions about the condition of your people and your government. It is a miserable rider who wishes for a horse without mettle, and a bad ruler who wishes for a people without candor.

Your neighbors will also be glad to see that your board of censors is feared more than your armies. Because candor and courage have always been sisters.

At least you cannot hope to be imitated by the Prussian state. There one fights with the same courage against enemies and against prejudices. The freedom to think out loud is the surest bulwark of the Prussian state. There one is, reasonably enough, more afraid of the fearful quiet before the thunderstorm, than of the sharp north wind that might drive snow flurries into the eye. There freedom serves in place of the checks and balances prized by Montesquieu, which work as often against the useful as against the harmful expression of royal power.[15]

The invincible power of the Prussian army rests on *subordination.* The order that reigns in Prussian civil ranks depends on *subordination. Subordination* is the soul of the whole Prussian state. This subordination, on the one hand so indispensable and on the other so burdensome, is moderated, but not obstructed, by the freedom to think out loud. No superior will be hindered by it from doing what he wants, but only from wanting what he should not. Under such circumstances, fear of the judgment of the public can serve as a substitute for patriotism. It will not release the subordinate person from the duty of obedience, and what should be done, will be done. However, one is only forced to obey the command, not to consent to it; to do, not to judge; to follow, not to agree. The bold reasoner bows ever so deep, and obeys as quickly as the rest; but one fears the audacity of his judgment, and takes care not to give him an opening. Suppose the leader of an army is surrounded by officers who strenuously judge all his measures. What is the effect of their reasoning? Will they hold up the execution of commands? Do they reason first, before obeying? Neither of these! Their reasonings after the event have only the result that the leader, if he recognizes their cleverness, seeks their approval either through asking for advice or by considering carefully all his steps.

It certainly may seem as if such criticism makes governing difficult for princes and their servants; and this is true, if one understands that one must engage in greater efforts to hold important posts with honor. A sluggish, cowardly people tolerate the worst as well as the best government in the same way. They grouse about the good out of ignorance, and about the bad because they feel the results; but in both cases only secretly. Under such circumstances it is certainly easy to do justice to one's title, but hard to do justice to one's office. This is so because the ruler will in one case not be encouraged, and in the other not be warned. He carries on his business like a handicraft worker in a village, who does not consider it worth his trouble to improve his work because his customers are just as happy with poor work.

Thus when Prussia's ruler suppresses writings against the state by censorship, he refers only to those which impugn the state itself, which betray it to its enemies, which loosen the subjects from their duty of obedience, and stimulate civil disorder. He does not censor moderate judgments about measures carried out by the prince or his servants. When he protects religion, he understands by that only universal religion, without care for the special names of which they boast, or by which they become hated. Such freedom of the press is the distinguishing mark of a wise government. Its gentle influence gives to unlimited monarchy all the blessings of political freedom, without exposing it to the destructive storms which so often darken the dawn of republican freedom and disturb its noon.

But if freedom of the press is such an invaluable jewel, we must also take care not to place it in danger by imprudent or ignoble use. We must deprive the great of the excuse for taking it away because of our unworthiness. We must not misuse our freedom, like mischievous boys, to besmirch the passersby. *Writers!* If you would teach mankind, then prove that you deserve this sublime title. Remove all suspicion of low purposes, or hasty passion. Do not touch persons, but strike at things. Show not only wit and boldness, but also deliberation and high-mindedness. Think, when you write, not only of the fame that you will earn, but above all of the utility you will provide. Not every truth is equally useful for all times and all circumstances. What is now to be said or to remain in silence you must consider yourself, because no law or officer of the state determines it. Your writing is an arrow whose influence you cannot stop, once you have sent it on its way. You cannot bow before the public and cover your mouth, once the printer has your manuscript. Appear then with timid respect before the assembly of your judges. And if patriotism or love of humanity inspires you, let wisdom guide your steps. Fight with courage against prejudice of all kinds: not with Alexander's sword, but rather with Minerva's lance.

NOTES

1. Ainsi tous ces humains, dont la terre fourmille,
Sont fils d'un même pere & sont une famille;
Et malgré tout l'orgueil que donne Votre rang
Ils sont nés Vos égaux, ils sont de Votre sang.
Ouvrez toujours le coeur à leur plainte importune,
Et couvrez leur misere avec Votre fortune.
Voulez-Vous en effet parôitre aus dessus d'eux
Montrez Vous plus humains plus doux & vertueux
(*Poesies diverses*)

["Thus all these humans that swarm on the earth, / Are children of the same father and make up one family; / And despite all the pride that your rank gives / They are born your equals, they are of your blood. / Open daily your heart to their importuning plaints, / Protect them from misery with your fortune. / Would you in effect appear above them, / Show yourself more humane, more mild and virtuous" Johann David Erdmann Preuß, ed. *Oeuvres de Frédéric le Grand* (Berlin, 1846–1857), 10:59f.—TRANS.]

2. Mais du pouvoir des Rois connoissons l'origine,
Pensez-Vous qu'élévés par une main divine,
Leur peuple, leur état leur ait été commis,
Comme un troupeau stupide à leurs ordres soumis?

Pour faire des heureux Vous occupez l'empire!
(*Poes. div.*)

[But let us recognize the origin of the power of kings, / Do you think that they are elevated by a divine hand, / Their people, their state, committed to them, / Like a stupid herd submitted to their orders? / You hold dominion in order to make people happy! Preuß, *Oeuvres*, 10:218, 165.—TRANS.]

3. "I do not deny that there are ingrates and hypocrites in the world, I do not deny that severity is sometimes very useful; but I maintain that any king whose policy has no other purpose than to create fear, reigns over lackeys and slaves, and that he should not expect great actions from his subjects. For everything that is done out of fear and timidity carries that character forever." (*Anti-Machiavel*) [Preuß, *Oeuvres*, 8:117.—TRANS.]

4. Quel que soit le pouvoir qui Vous tombe en partage,
Que le bien des humains soit toujours Votre ouvrage;
Et plus ils sont ingrats, plus soyez généreux.
C'est un plaisir divin de faire des heureux.
Surtout n'abusez point d'une vaste puissance,
Et n'écoutez jamais la voix de la vengeance.
Qui ne peut se dompter, qui ne peut pardonner,
Est indigne du rang qui l'apelle à regner.

Quoi! je voudrois devoir mon nom & mon merite
Au caprice inconstant d'une foule séduite,
Et n'être vertueux que pour me voir louer?
Que le monde me blâme ou daigne m'avouer!
Je ris de son encens qui s'envole en fumée,
Et du peuple insensé qui fait la renommée.
(*Poes. div.*)

[Whatever is the power that falls to your share, / May the good of humanity be always your work; / And the more ungrateful they are, the more generous you are. / It is a divine pleasure to do them good. / Above all do not abuse vast power, / And do not listen to the voice of vengeance. / He who cannot overcome his own passions, who cannot pardon, / Is unworthy of the rank that calls him to rule. / What! I should owe my name and my merit / To the inconstant caprice of a seduced mob, / And be virtuous only for the sake of being praised? / Let the world blame me or deign to praise me! / I laugh at its flattery that flies away in smoke, / And at senseless people that make reputations. Preuß, *Oeuvres*, 10:59, 144.—TRANS.]

5. "What gives power to states? Is it the wide boundaries, which must be defended? Is it riches accumulated by commerce and industry, that only become useful when well employed? Is it the large number of people, who will destroy themselves if they lack guides? No, these objects are raw materials that acquire their value and importance only to the degree that wisdom and ability know how to set them in motion. The power of a state consists in the great men that nature brings to birth

there at appropriate times" (*Eloge du Prince Henri*) [Preuß, *Oeuvres*, 7:39. Frederick's work in honor of a Prussian prince was an elegy in the aristocratic "great man" tradition, taking for granted that great men were born princes, while Klein appropriates the idea on behalf of men of talent who may rise up among the people.—Trans.]

6. Probably a reference to ancient Rome and the modern pope.—Trans.

7. Klein is presumably alluding to Spain and the Inquisition. The first two sentences of this paragraph, however, could also be an allusion to Portugal.—Trans.

8. Presumably a reference to the Dutch, who enjoyed considerable commercial success in markets that had been initially opened by the Spanish (*zinsbar*, translated here as "tributary," refers more narrowly to interest gained by trade based on investments). Voltaire made a similar point in the short dialogue "*Liberté de pensée*" in his *Dictionnaire philosophique* when an Englishman asks a Spaniard, "Do you find that the Dutch, who have today robbed you of nearly all your discoveries in the Indies, and today are among your protectors, are cursed by God for having given the press complete freedom and for trading in men's thought?" *Philosophical Dictionary*, trans. Theodore Besterman (Harmondsworth, 1972), 279.—Trans.

9. Probably a reference to the Huguenot refugees and other skilled foreigners whom the Prussians and others invited in as immigrants in the seventeenth and eighteenth centuries.—Trans.

10. Par un dernier effort la raison fit parôitre
Ces sublimes devins des mysteres des Dieux;
C'est par leur soin que l'homme aprend à les connôitre.
Ils éclairent la Terre, ils lisent dans les Cieux;
Les Astres sont décrits dans leurs obliques courses,
Les torrents découverts dans leurs subtiles sources.
Ils ont suivi les vents ils ont pésé les airs;
Ils domptent la nature;
Ils fixent la figure
De ce vaste Univers.
(*Poes. div.*)

[As a highest effort reason makes appear / The sublime augurs of the mysteries of God; / It is by their care that man learns to know them, / They enlighten the earth, they read the heavens; / The stars are described in their oblique courses, / The subtle sources of rivers are discovered. / They follow the winds, they weigh the air; / They master nature; / They fix the shape / Of this vast universe. (Preuß, *Oeuvres*, 10:24). Klein took these stanzas in praise of reason from an ode written by Frederick on the reestablishment of the Prussian Academy. Klein subtly twists Frederick's meaning by applying these stanzas to English liberty. Frederick's poem was first published in 1749, but by the time Klein was writing, Frederick's references surely would have reminded readers of scientists working in England such as Priestley (author of *Experiments and Observations on Different Kinds of Air* [1774–1777]) and the German expatriate Herschel (discoverer of the planet Uranus in 1781).—Trans.]

11. "If there were only one religion in the world, it would become arrogant and despotic without restraint. Clergymen would become tyrants, exercising their severity on the people without indulgence for anything except their crimes.—All sects live here in peace, and contribute equally to the good of the state. There is no religion that steps far aside from the others on the subject of morals; thus they can all be

equal to the government, which consequently leaves to each the liberty to go to heaven by the road that he pleases. That he be a good citizen, that is all that is demanded of him. False zeal is a tyrant that depopulates provinces; tolerance is a tender mother that makes them flourish." (*Mémoires de Brandebourg*) [Preuß, *Oeuvres*, 1:207, 212.]

12. Christian Wolff was dismissed from the University of Halle and exiled from Prussia by Frederick's father, Frederick William I, in 1723. On his ascent to the throne, Frederick invited Wolff back to a permanent fellowship at the Berlin Academy, but Wolff preferred Halle, to which he returned in 1740.—Trans.

13. See Num. 22.—Trans.

14. Guillaume Thomas François Raynal (1713–1796), French historian and political economist whose history of commerce in Asia and the New World was condemned by the Parliament of Paris in 1781 on the grounds of impiety and because of its argument that the people had a right to revolt and to withhold consent to taxation. He fled from France and was given protection by Frederick.—Trans.

15. A reference to Montesquieu's discussion of the way in which the English constitution provided checks on the power of the monarch (*Spirit of the Laws* XI:vi). Klein sees freedom of thought and freedom of the press as more effective checks on royal absolutism than the sort of constitutional arrangements endorsed by Montesquieu.—Trans.

On Freedom of the Press and Its Limits: For Consideration by Rulers, Censors, and Writers

Carl Friedrich Bahrdt

Translated by John Christian Laursen

The career and writings of Carl Friedrich Bahrdt (1740–1792) illustrate the close relationship between radical theology, enlightenment, and politics in the eighteenth century. He began his career as an orthodox theologian, but the study of biblical philology led him step by step toward the radical theology of natural religion. His modernized and naturalized translation of the New Testament (1773) was viciously attacked by the orthodox and eventually banned for heresy by Imperial Decree in 1779. His ten-volume Life of Jesus *(1783–1785), in which Jesus appeared simply as a good man, was both popular and controversial. He was hounded out of teaching posts in Leipzig, Erfurt, Giessen, Marschlins, and Heidesheim, either for his personal behavior or for his ideas.*

Several sections from Bahrdt's 1787 book on freedom of the press are translated here. Shortly after its publication, Bahrdt was imprisoned for a little over a year for his brazen satire of Frederick William entitled The Edict on Religion: A Comedy *(1789). He was released from prison early because Woellner did not want him to become a martyr by dying there. He ended his life as an innkeeper near Halle, in Prussia.*

II. WHAT IS ENLIGHTENMENT?[1]

What is enlightenment? An enlightened man? Enlightened times?

Enlightenment can be found as little in the greatness of the powers of understanding as in the amount of knowledge accumulated. For I have seen geniuses, theologians, lawyers, scientists, and historians with enormous masses of knowledge—right among the fools and fanatics [*Schwärmern*]. And if it is the foundation of happiness, enlightenment must be the goal of all men, as indeed the Founder of Christianity considered it.

If a man had learned a system of knowledge by heart (e.g., law) would he then be called an enlightened jurist? And why not? Whoever answers this question will find that it is intrinsic to enlightenment to possess knowledge of *one's own*, not blindly parroted words. Thus enlightenment includes the following:

First published anonymously as Über Pressfreyheit und deren Gränzen: Zur Beherzigung für Regenten Censoren und Schriftsteller *(Züllichau, 1787).*

A. That one learns *to think for oneself.*[2]
   a. That one has distinct concepts of objects which one has oneself located, abstracted, compared, developed, and examined in the material world.
   b. That one knows the sources and criteria of truth and has used them oneself. That one has judged oneself that "this is true, this false," "this is good, this bad," and has derived these judgments from one's *own* principles or experiences. That one has thought through and examined (and in important matters long, often, and stubbornly examined) the grounds for their truth.
   c. That one thus sees everywhere with *one's own eyes,* not letting oneself be led astray by appearances, not believing or judging something because it is pleasing to the heart, to the appetites, to inclinations, or disinclinations. That one does not blindly follow any authority, but that rather, before believing, one investigates with one's own plain human understanding, and thus sees truth only in the light of God, in the light of reason. In short: that one strives toward the most perfect possible knowledge and toward the highest possible level of certainty.

B. Now since no man in this world can be enlightened in all sciences, it is of the essence of enlightenment (insofar as it is to become a universal good) to determine its object: the truth which grounds universal human happiness. This truth can be divided into two different classes, the first of which is wholly decisive for the happiness of men, such as the truths of religion and morality, and the second of which merely has an influence on the increase or decrease of this happiness. In such truths, especially the first class, each man must use his own reason and see with his own eyes, if he does not want to risk his happiness. If, for example, someone tells me that the earth spins around the sun, I can believe his authority because it does not threaten human happiness if this is wrong. But when someone tells me, "Your honor requires that you duel" or "God is enraged and you must try to make it up through such and such means" or "you must kill your son in order to honor God," and so forth, then I must set aside appearances, obscure feelings, authority, and above all listen to my reason, and believe nothing except that to which reason irresistibly leads me.

Whoever seeks the truth in this way with an honest heart, independent of all other sources of knowledge, is a freethinker in the noblest sense. His reason is unfettered. However little he may know, as long as what he knows has become his own property by thinking for himself, he is an *enlightened* man.

And where reason can work unfettered, where each man is able to think and judge freely for himself about what others assert and may share his judgment, where believing and professing of belief in any doctrine is never coerced (i.e., determined by command or by civil reward or penalty): there are *enlightened times.* Where there is any coercion, there is and there rises that *barbarism* by which in olden times princes and priests supported their rule but which no noble-thinking ruler requires today. Nor does he need it today, given that there are standing armies.[3] . . .

V. FREEDOM TO THINK, A UNIVERSAL RIGHT OF MAN

Men! Freedom to think and to judge independently from authority, independently from the pronouncements of the priests, monks, popes, church councils, the Church—this is the holiest, most important, most inviolable right of man [*Recht der Menschheit*].[4] Men have cause to treasure it more highly than all other liberties and rights, because its loss does not merely reduce their happiness, but completely destroys it; because the absence of this freedom makes the perfection of their immortal souls impossible; because human virtue, peace, and consolation rest on this right; because without this right and its exercise they become miserable slaves, and they risk their souls and salvation when they leave it to those to whom they renounced their reason in blind imitation, whether they want to lead them to truth or falsehood, to heaven or to hell.

I call this freedom a right, and indeed an inviolable right, that God has given you, and that no man can or should take from you. Other rights, such as the right to do business in a country, to own houses, and so forth, are given by princes, and they can take them back from you. But this right is given to you by God.

You ask, how do I know this? Learn, men, the unmistakable sign of all God-given rights. It lies in nature and requires no subtle demonstration. Where there is power, drive, and need, bestowed by God, implanted by the Creator, there is right. Animals, for example, have the power, the drive, and the need to reproduce; thus they have a right. And whoever denies them this right fights against nature, that is, against God; he rebels against a God-given right. Men have the power, the drive, and the need to eat, to drink, to breathe; thus they have the right to do so.

Or do rights have other signs? Do you know a better proof of a right? You subjects of Prussia, how do you know that Frederick William[5] has a right to rule you? You lucky children of Joseph,[6] how do you recognize his right to be the father of his people? Do you want to read an abstract deduction in order to understand this right? Go and pay Mr. Pütter a hundred Louis d'or and he will make an artful deduction of the right of the Prussian monarch to Silesia.[7] And when you have read the deduction and now are a believer in this right, pay him another hundred Louis d'or and he will make you just as stringent a deduction of Joseph's right to Silesia. And what have you learned? How much more clever are you now? Oh, you fools, who seek in the minds of learned men the truth that nature teaches you! Believe me, the jurists' right is a wax nose;[8] the right of nature is alone solid, eternal, and unmistakable. Don't ask priests and prophets. God speaks to you more clearly in nature. Only pay attention to His signs. He to whom God gave the power, also has the right. Without God's will, he would not have the power. If God wills that he have the power, that power is a sign of His will and thus the basis of a God-given right. This holds for princes who inherit thrones as well as for princes who steal them. No philosophizing is valid here. Man cannot see God from the front, as Moses said so rightly.[9] One must see Him from behind. That is, one must not determine a priori what God wants. One must judge that a posteriori. One must wait for evidence of God's Providence. What He does, is His will. Whoever He gives the power should use it; he has the right, the duty, to use it. And that is God's right. And thus the right to think and to judge for oneself is a God-given right; because God has given the power, the drive, and the need for it. And because He gave this power to all men, the right to think and judge for oneself is a universal right of man, a right that is holier than all the rights of princes, and thus, just because it is a *universal* right of man, it is above the *particular* rights of princes.

VI. THE FREEDOM TO SPEAK AND TO WRITE IS NO LESS A UNIVERSAL RIGHT OF MAN

And should there still be another question: whether establishing the freedom to think also establishes the freedom to speak. Should one acknowledge the former right as sacred, and believe oneself authorized to snatch the latter away from mankind?

Oh, you tyrants of humanity, who keep the iron scepter of coercing conscience! Step forward and, if you won't listen to the voice of virtue, at least hear the judgment of healthy human reason. Read and examine me. I will make things so clear to you that only an extreme level of stupidity or the blindest dependence on prejudices will be able to keep you from being persuaded. It is true, your minds are armored with bronze and your backs covered with Russia leather, but I will smash the bronze and tear the skin: so that you will feel my blows and at least scream, if your senses are no longer receptive to the harmonious consonance of truth.

The freedom to share one's insights and judgments verbally or in writing is, just like the freedom to think, a holy and inviolable right of man that, as a universal right of man, is above all the rights of princes. And the regent who says that he leaves it to each to hold his own opinion and to believe what he wants, but that he may not speak or write what he wants, plays with human understanding and takes mankind for fools. Because basically that is saying no more and no less than: "I will permit you to do what I cannot prevent, but I will take away this facetious permission by preventing you and the rest of mankind from enjoying it." Judge impartially and tell me if this is the case. Can a prince, if he has half a million soldiers standing ready to execute his orders, coerce my understanding? Can he influence the inner workings of my soul? Can he prevent me from thinking, judging, or believing something? Oh, proud impotence! And still he will take the liberty to say, "I permit my subjects to believe what they will." Is it not foolish to reckon as a favor what is a necessity? And is not this gracious permission as curious as if a master wished to pay his servants with the seven days of the week and, indeed, free light during daytime? No, dear rulers, you must not toy with men who are only different from you by accident; since it is true after all what the wise Frederick said: *"d'etre Roi c'est un hazard."*[10] You must remember that the right to think (thank God!) is not within your jurisdiction; that you are not permitting anything if you rob us of the right to speak, and that you trample underfoot all the rights of mankind if one of them is not sacred to you. Hear my reasons:

1. The freedom to communicate one's knowledge and judgments is, first, a universal right of man, because and insofar as all men have received the power to do so from the Creator. For it was God who gave us reason and speech. Princes can only bestow houses and estates. But these universal goods come directly from God. Since God gave all men reason, it is a right and a duty [*Beruf*] for all to use it and through one's own free reflection to seek the truth. In the same way, since God gave all men speech, it is a right and a duty for all to speak, and to communicate the truth they have found. Therefore, whoever takes away the right to speak rebels against the Creator as much as does he who wants to take away the right to think. For both rights rest on a common foundation which none of the philosophical and theological faculties can invalidate.

2. The second reason is just as important and irreversible. Both rights are so inseparably bound together in their employment that whoever takes away the right to speak also deprives me of the right to think. I ask my reader to heed this quite carefully. What I say here is true from more than one point of view.

a. First: whenever men may not freely communicate the knowledge and insights they have achieved, the purpose for which one collects knowledge is lost—unless one would want to establish the most horrible egoism. After all it is not for myself that I have thought so much and searched for truth in the world. If I were alone in the world, very few concepts and judgments would be sufficient. That I try to collect much knowledge, that I strive daily to rectify, expand, and perfect my insight through experience, observation, reading, etc., happens simply because I live among men, where it is honorable to be an insightful man, and where it brings mutual benefits to communicate one's insight. Thus, who would take the trouble to think and to seek truth, if he must not speak and communicate it? Wouldn't taking away the freedom to speak be the same thing as destroying the use of the right to think? When I rob a thing of its purpose, I might as well destroy it itself.

And whoever tells me that he does not forbid thought when he forbids speech, mocks me just as much as he who allows me to heat my room in the winter, but does not permit me to close the windows and doors. For as it helps little to heat, without the goal of keeping warmth in the room, so it helps little to think, without the goal of being able to communicate it.

b. But communication is not only the principal goal of thought, it is also a universal need the satisfaction of which only makes the right to think enjoyable. Each one need only attend to what it is like when he has heard or learned something new, in history or science. Does he not feel the urge to communicate it? It is as if the newly acquired truth or story were a weight on our heart suppressing its beat. We cannot rest until we have brought our treasure to other men. And this drive is already present in children. The least thing that they have heard for the first time from their teacher becomes important through novelty, and one can see when a child coming home from school has something in his heart, and his parents or servants or playmates must lend him an ear to let him teach them the new, important truth. And in fact it is one of the loveliest and noblest drives of nature implanted in us by the Creator, that it is a necessity for us to communicate. By virtue of this drive, nothing in the world has its full savour for us, if we enjoy it alone. The best Rhine wine only tastes half as good when I sit alone at the table as it tastes when one or two friends are drinking it with me. Mutual enjoyment is the spice of all human joy. No happiness among men is possible without communication and sharing. And it is obvious that the Creator sought in this way to bind together human society and heighten and multiply its happiness, by implanting in each man the drive to communicate and by making him capable of fully tasting each good only when letting others enjoy it with him. And you, fathers of nations, princes! You will rob humanity of this divine joy? You wish to restrain them from satisfying this need? You wish to hinder them from communicating the highest good of humanity, I mean insight and knowledge? Is it not obvious that to prohibit the right to speak is to prohibit the right to think, and to make it unusable and unenjoyable for mankind?

c. I maintain even more. The right to speak is itself the only means, the only way of using the right to think. For one need only consider what would happen if all men were obliged to use their reason for themselves alone, to observe, to ponder, and to collect the knowledge required for their happiness in silence. Could indeed anything other than barbarism arise? Could one man, even if he were the greatest genius, possibly make discoveries, all alone, in any area of knowledge? Does history not teach that all knowledge was at first in its infancy and only grew in a number of centuries to the perfection in which we now find it by researchers communicating their discoveries and insights to one another, talking about them, disputing, examining, and so forth? It is indeed as clear as daylight that all human knowledge rests on the right to speak, and that whoever would not grant the freedom to communicate would hinder all common instruction and thus all knowledge and its spread, growth, and perfection.

3. Here is a third proof: upon the right to communicate one's insights and judgments rests the whole peace of mankind as far as his beliefs are concerned and, hence, as far as all his activity is concerned, as much in civil life as for the sake of virtue. For man cannot strive toward something with energy if he is not firmly convinced that the knowledge on which he acts is true and secure against error. Thus whoever impairs the right to speak and to write takes the great happiness of firm conviction away from men and thus destroys industry and virtue. The rightness of this conclusion is clear, for one only has to consider the sources of human conviction. Experience shows that there are only two means by which one can arrive at certainty in one's perceptions, experiences, judgments, and knowledge.

The first is (a) *self-verification* [*Selbstprüfung*]. I must think over for myself each truth according to which I am supposed to act, whether it be as a citizen or as a Christian. I must verify their proofs, ponder the reasons for and against them, and thus seek to convince myself to affirm or deny them. Suppose now that men would not have the right to communicate their thoughts and ideas, that, for example, in medicine, history, religion no one may raise his voice to express himself openly about the truth that I want to examine. Would I really have an object of my examination? Could I really weigh the reasons pro and con if the latter never allowed themselves to be examined? Or will you say that this examination, this weighing of reasons and objections, is not necessary? Truly, whoever maintains that, whoever considers examining the truth dispensable for his peace of mind, cannot have realized what conviction is and what influence it has on men. Certainly, in things that do not interest men, that have no essential connection with their happiness, one cannot only dispense with examination, one *must* dispense with it, because it is a useless waste of time. If, for example, I tried to verify every report in the newspapers about the manning of a flotilla, the flooding of a province, and so forth, and would travel there myself to see if all is as it is reported, I would act absurdly, wasting too much time and effort on things that are unimportant for me. But when we are talking about truths that affect my civil welfare or decide the salvation of my soul, that is quite a different case. There I must examine the truth with the greatest obstinacy if I do not wish to gamble foolishly with my well-being. There I must listen to doubts, demurrals, counterarguments, and not decide to take anything as solid truth until I have finished this examination. Whoever does not strive after such a conviction, which is bound up with the highest peace of the soul, will never learn to act with warmth and energy according to the truths he recognizes. He will remain a slacker, as most of our Christians are, because their belief is not based on their own reflection and on the firm conviction that grows from such careful examination, and thus cannot lead to an energetic virtue. So it is clear that the right of men to judge freely and to communicate to one another their reasons for and against everything that is the object of thinking, is indispensable for a conviction about truth which gives peace of mind.

But self-verification is not the only path to quiet conviction. Especially in moral matters, we cannot dispense with (b) *authority*, if we wish to arrive at a satisfying certainty in our judgments. This important ground for achieving peace is taken from us if we may not freely exercise the right to write and to speak. I will make myself clearer on this point.

First of all, I must tell my readers what I understand by authority so they will not think that I myself put blinders on reason here. Authority is merely an additional weight on the balance scale of truth. It should give new strength to convictions which are one's own and are based on reflection and examination. It arises when all those whom I recognize as knowledgeable agree among themselves and with me in believing something to be true.

It is self-evident that such an agreement of insightful men gives a high degree of assurance. For a natural feeling of modesty provides that in important matters we do not gladly judge alone, but rather listen to others who understand the matter. Despite the most sincere striving to find the truth, we regard it as all too possible that we err for us to trust our own examination and decision. By contrast, error seems much less likely if others thought about the same point, investigated, weighed arguments and counterarguments, and arrived at the same decision as we did. We feel then much assured by such agreement, and our belief in such a truth found in common becomes firmer and more effective. Thus, when one has a difficult and lengthy accounting before him concerning property, one would not want to trust one's own calculation, no matter how carefully it was done and how many times it was repeated, but would let others recalculate it, to be more certain. And if we generally feel this need for the agreement of knowledgeable people, or authority, how much stronger must it be in matters of religion? There, absolutely no firm belief is possible, if *besides* one's own conviction based on reflection and examination (this must be done, of course, before any authority is consulted), one does not *also* have the agreement of the wise men of all times and nations. For this agreement alone gives human reason infallibility.

And what now, if rulers want to take away from us the right to speak and to write? Where then should authority be derived? How should we find out whether or not others agree with our convictions, and who they are, and whether or not we should rely on their judgment? Truly, without this right, the beliefs of men would be terrified, as if lost in a wilderness. No man would know what others think. No man could compare his truth with the truth of another. No man could gain the invigorating thought that men whom he recognizes as wise think like him and confirm his judgments.

And one should not imagine that a ruler leaves this need of mankind unimpaired, if he gives the right to speak only to a few (e.g., to the priests).

If *all* do not have this right and cannot freely use it, then the *few* cannot assure us through their agreement, because *only* the free judgments of other men can have weight for us. Now were this right given only to a few, one would have to fear that these few would have an agreement or common laws which would enforce the coincidence of their judgments. So their judgment would not be a free judgment. Rather, those who hold a monopoly on the right to speak would use it collectively for their own benefit, to lead by the nose the others to whom this right was denied.

4. Speaking of the monopolists, I recall a fourth major proof of the universality of the right to speak and to write. It is this: if the right to communicate is not a universal right of man, there will arise monopolists of the truth who will enslave the intelligence of all the rest of mankind and rob them of their freedom to think. Examine the elaboration of this proof. I assume what has already been said above, that no man can make discoveries by himself in any of the areas of the sciences. Whoever wants to learn a science fully must already have predecessors who have reflected, observed, and communicated their ideas concerning it. From that point he can think further, make new observations, and broaden the science. Thus, if I am to use my freedom to think, I must have an *object*, that is, there must already be teachings which I now consider and examine. And there must also be other men in the same area of science who work and think with me. For without the contributions of many thinking men no science will arise. Now assume that a monopoly arises in a science and that the monopolists could pull out bits of knowledge as if from a warehouse and could declare anything contraband that did not come from their warehouse. Assume further what follows immediately from this: that the monopolists would hold in their hands all the means by which one can communicate one's knowledge to others, for example, that no other man is permitted to teach the science publicly, that no one else is permitted to write books, and so forth. Wouldn't other men now be forced to think and to judge like them? Only recall that no man *creates* a science, but that he usually can only think what he *finds before him.* If now the rest of men only find the same thing, if they only find what the monopolists give out as truth, then that is also the only thing they can think. It is obvious, after all, that if a prince makes me such a monopolist, and gives me the privilege of all means of communicating knowledge, for example, all the printing presses, so that his subjects come to see nothing but what I print and let them read, that I would have the understanding of the subjects wholly in my power. And can a more horrible tyranny be conceived?

XVII. RIGHTS OF THE AUTHOR WITH RESPECT TO RULERS

...I revere the wisdom and greatness of the monarch who in the decree mentioned above extends the free right to make thoughts and judgments known to thoughts and judgments about rulers, and consequently to thoughts and judgments about himself.[11] That was also the judgment of Frederick II, and certainly the judgment of his worthy successor. Only men as enlightened as Joseph, Frederick, and Frederick William could make such a judgment.[12]

For the sake of the less subtle of my readers, I will give the reasons why it is good if this right of man may also extend to judgments about the ruler.

1. The exercise of this right is useful for the ruler himself. Favorable judgments will encourage him, and unfavorable ones may instruct and warn him. Experience has taught me countless times that my enemy, judging me boldly, was my best teacher. I learned from him what I have not been able to learn from my friends. For my friends flatter me, praise only my good side and cover up my weak side. But my enemy does not flatter me. Only when he is forced does he recognize my good side, and give me my due; and then I have the assurance that the good quality which he recognized must be found in me. His praise delights me all the more, because it will be less suspect to the world than the praise of my friends. He censures my failings all the more sharply, and he reveals to me the weaknesses and flaws in my basic principles, in my actions, and so forth, weaknesses and flaws that I perhaps would never have seen because of self-love and that my friends would never have shown me, at least not in their true light. And because my enemy observes everything about me, and takes every opportunity he can to make my character suspect, to disparage my merit, or to expose my mistakes, he makes me clever and cautious. He warns me in a timely manner about things that I might perhaps have never noticed without him. Considering now that a ruler needs self-knowledge far more than any other man—and that, because of the large number of flatterers that surround him, it is much harder for him to achieve it—it must be recognized as the highest wisdom of a ruler when he himself permits candid judgments to be made about him.

2. But this permitting of candor, this right to praise or to criticize even princes, also makes the nation itself noble.

Men who live under such a ruler feel that they are men, they feel free, and they learn to value and honor the rights of man. And this feeling of freedom ennobles their spirit, makes it brave, courageous, generous. Ultimately, virtue itself gains in this way. For man learns to disdain foolishness more intensely, if he sees that it dishonors even the prince. Where this freedom does not exist, vice and shameful deeds are often respected because the example of the prince gives them a good reputation and there is no patriot who punishes them and tells the truth about them. And the subject, because he must approve everything the ruler does, becomes a flatterer, a lowly servile soul, who learns to deny his moral sensibility.

3. Further, the state gains as a state by granting this right. For no impostor can establish himself, no flatterer can take in the prince, no evil minister can defend himself through trickery, no authority can exploit the subjects and trample on justice, no priest can tyrannize over consciences, because all of these sorts of shameful men must tremble before the writer's candor.

4. Finally, what a glorious prospect for wounded innocence! For those innocents who (as sometimes happens even in the best states) are persecuted, accused, judged, and unhappy, how refreshing the thought must be that some friend will take up the pen and, if he cannot take away the suffering they have endured, will at least vindicate their innocence before the eyes of the world. Truly, that is an inexpressible gain. It is the highest tonic for suffering. It is compensation for the most wrongful treatment.

However, if it is intrinsically great and noble that a prince subjects himself to the rights of man and allows himself to be judged freely and openly, I still believe that here the manner of exercising this right needs restriction in individual cases.

The first restriction concerns the *object* of this freedom of speech and of writing concerning rulers. Things that are public need to be distinguished here from all those things that are not public and should not be publicized. Things that are already publicly known, for example, the person of the prince, his talents, qualities, principles, actions, judgments, edicts, and so forth, can be judged freely by anyone, because the state and the prince lose nothing by it, and often even gain. For every prince is too high above miserable smearers and their twaddle to suffer in his true dignity. I regard it just as foolish to punish a calumniator of princes as it is to punish a calumniator of God. I would much rather regard both as lunatics who only shame themselves and arouse pity. And well-founded reproaches from noble-thinking and insightful men will always contain something the prince can use, without making him blush. On the other hand, things that are not public matters, for example, rights and claims of princes to lands, secret correspondence of the prince, cabinet business, and such, must remain absolutely excluded from the domain of freedom of the press. For if writers were to begin to venture into things of this kind and speak about them before the public, this could become a danger to the state and undermine the respect of foreigners for the prince. And this remains the one sure determination of the limit of all freedom of the press: namely, the relationship of the content of a piece of writing to the well-being and honor of the state and its rulers. Everything that does not harm the state must be able to be freely spoken and written. But whatever directly and effectively harms the state, for example, whatever betrays its secrets to an enemy, provokes rebellion, destroys industry, population, supplies, and so forth, must be forbidden.

A second limitation concerns the *manner* in which a writer judges the state and rulers. And here there are two reasonable demands that can and should be made upon every writer who wishes to exercise his right. The first is a demand of morality, that he speak modestly with and about rulers. I am saying that this is a moral demand, and distinguish it from a demand of the state. For the *legislator* and the *moralist* need to be properly distinguished. Morality guides only the moral actions of men through motivations, that is, through ideas of the benefit for which a man hopes or the harm he fears as a natural result of his actions. But the legislator guides the civil actions of men through the threat of the legal sanctions he will impose on account of the benefit that the state has to lose or the damage it has to fear. Whoever accepts this point of view will find that modesty is only a demand of the moralist. In contrast, the demand of the state would be *truth* in the subject matter about which the writer expresses himself. That means this much: the writer may not send lies and slander into the world through his writing. That of which he speaks, for example, the edict, the sentence handed down, the actions of the ruler, and so forth, must really have happened. In this sense I demand truth *in subject matter* and distinguish from it the truth of *the judgment* which he passes on it. Although others may consider this judgment true or false, this cannot make the writer culpable, because to him it is true, that is, it conforms to his conviction. But the legislator must demand truth of *subject matter,* because otherwise the honor of the ruler would be surrendered without cause by permitting lies and false disseminations.

XVIII. RIGHTS OF THE AUTHOR WITH RESPECT TO FELLOW CITIZENS

And now I still have an important matter that indeed has not, until now, been put in order: the rights of writers vis-à-vis private persons.

It is undeniable that the universal right of man to make known his thoughts and judgments must extend also to judgments about the qualities, opinions, actions, and circumstances of our neighbors. And just as no man would willingly allow the right to judge others to be stolen from him, so he must allow each of the others to exercise and assert the same right against himself.

It is just as clear that the free exercise of this right is very useful for mankind.

1. It provides useful knowledge about capable people in all areas of the arts and sciences as well as about their works, products, manufactured goods, writings, and so forth; it also warns us of bunglers and of bad work. How much would the world lose if we could not read reports and evaluations of all of these things in political and scholarly newspapers, journals, literary reviews, and pamphlets?

2. It enriches our knowledge of men. In part it helps us better to judge men in general, and, by comparing the many characters and actions that we come to know, it enables us to observe human nature with a philosophical eye. In part it helps us to form concepts of national character and peculiarities. In part we come to know individual men, and learn to decide if and how far we should or should not enter into contact with them.

3. Through the exercise of this right many good, wise, and admirable men are shown right next to many fools and rogues. This warns, inhibits, and compels the latter to improve themselves; it encourages, rewards, and

compensates the former, and it gives readers and observers a thousand varieties of instruction, warning, and consolation.

4. The exercise of this right is thus the only means to bring the all-too-great inequality of men, created by status and wealth, back into some sort of equality. At least in this aspect men become equal to each other and feel that they are men, in that they all have the same right to judge candidly and publicly about all other men and to compensate for the privileges of status and wealth.

5. Finally, the exercise of this right is a great support for virtue and a dike against the torrent of vices, in that it makes it possible to unmask the hypocrite; to uncover, humble, and punish the vicious; to honor, vindicate, and protect virtue against denigration; to teach the thoughtless and the reckless to be prudent, and not to make unnecessary enemies through their behavior.

Nevertheless, if on the one hand free judgment about all men is beneficial, one must not forget that on the other hand manifold and great damage can arise if the legislator does not *limit* in some measure *the manner of using* this right.

I will not dwell here on the fact that often all of a man's happiness can be destroyed if others are allowed to dig out and publish his secrets. I will not dwell on the fact that it would be a very hard burden if every man had the right to make known and to subject to scorn other people's innocent infirmities. I will not dwell on the fact that making the thoughts, judgments, and plans of others known in public writings often begets terrible animosities. For against all this it can justly be objected that such injuries arising from the right to speak and to write can be prevented. If, for example, you do not want to see your secrets betrayed, learn to keep them to yourself and be silent, or if you have been imprudent, endure the natural consequences of your loquacity. If you do not want to fall into animosities through betrayals, follow this rule: do not speak critically or express evil thoughts against any man behind his back or into the ears of strangers; or you must endure your betrayer's never sleeping and his dragging your enemy toward you by the neck. Finally, if you do not want your failings to be revealed and subjected to scorn, either strive for such merits as conceal your failings and make it necessary for your neighbors to overlook your weak aspects because of the preponderance of your merits or try, through modesty, kindness, goodness, and noble conduct, to make all men your friends as much as possible, so they will have no incentive to be annoyed at you.

I will restrict myself to the main point, that it is all too easy to disparage completely the good name of a man if everyone, without limits, is allowed to speak and to write in public whatever he wishes about the actions, work, intentions, mistakes, and so forth, of others. I say, to disparage completely, because single insults or offenses cannot be considered here. But what destroys the good name of a man is certainly of the utmost importance and not an easy matter.

After all, the greatest part of human peace of mind rests on a good name. For what can I have that is of more importance, except the approval of God, than the approval and respect of my neighbors? What compensates more in suffering, what gives more courage in dangers, what gives more joyful hours than the thought that I have a certain and definitive worth in the eyes of my neighbors? Further, the credit of the merchant, the confidence of the public that the writer desires, the clientele of the artisan, in short, the chief support each needs for his business and his livelihood, depends on a good name. Finally, a good name is the chief means of keeping friends, supporters, and patrons, and of achieving earthly happiness. It may be observed here, incidentally, that the prince is never in this situation: his throne and his happiness stand, however men may judge him.

And now consider especially that a good name, since it is a good so important and so indispensable to happiness, belongs to the highest needs, and the claim to this good belongs to the universal rights of man. For in this case the principle established above[13] is obviously applicable: "where the manner in which a right of man is exercised comes into collision with either the state or with other rights of man, that is the only certain case where the ruler (who should not concern himself with anything except promoting the flourishing of the state and protecting the full rights, innate as well as acquired, of his subjects) is authorized and obligated to limit the exercise of a right of man (here, for example, the right to free and public judgment) in order to support another right (here, the right to a good name)."

But now the very difficult question arises: when and how should the ruler limit the right of writers in such cases of collision? Should he forbid every free judgment regarding men about which one could cry, "My good name!"? Then he would have to forbid all writing about others, all criticism. Should he only forbid cases in which a good name is completely destroyed? Then, first, he would have to protect every scoundrel from having his bad actions discovered. And second, who should be the judge of whether a public judgment would completely destroy the good name of another? The prince, the censor, or who? I think that with all of this we do not reach a secure position.

The true rule for decisions is this: the legislator should forbid criticism where the person who is judged has not given up his rights. He should permit criticism where the person who is judged has *himself* surrendered his good name. This is the only sure principle to observe, if we want to find a feasible determination of the limits of freedom of the press. I will explain myself further.

A man who speaks or acts publicly—whether within earshot and under the eyes of his own narrow circle, his servants, his companions, and so forth, or before the whole public—himself gives up his right, his claim to a good name, if he speaks or acts foolishly or viciously. He must and can be judged freely by anyone.

However, a man does not surrender his good name if, when alone in his room or with his most trusted friend (e.g., his wife), he says something or talks about something that is in itself not praiseworthy. Thus if a rascal stands and listens at his keyhole, should such a rogue have the right publicly to place the individual he has overheard on the pillory?

Notice the difference. The former gave up his right; the latter did not. The former is not in danger of suffering innocently; the latter can be overheard incorrectly and accused although he is guiltless. The former went willingly into the public sphere; the latter was dragged into it by force. Whoever is convinced by this will agree with me that the ruler must limit the freedom of judging other men in public with the following laws.

1. The person judged must have done things or said things in public. If, for example, a private person who has no wealth, and even has debts, employs two cooks and holds a dinner party, for which the food alone, without the wine, costs 150 Reichsthaler,[14] or if a professor misbehaves in a pub and offers a lady a box on the ears, but then receives one himself, and so forth, anyone must have the right to speak about and to reprimand such public deeds.

2. One must speak or write about things which actually happened, and it must be provable that they happened.

3. What the critic says or writes may be strong or weak, flat or witty, gentle or bitter, only it should not be said in the ill-bred tone of the rabble. Obscenities and insults from the mouth of the rascal pack should not be tolerated from writers in any state. They are not good for anything and are harmful to the good manners that are indispensable to the civilizing [*Bildung*] of humanity.

4. The critic, finally, must never have the right to make himself wholly undiscoverable. I say, "wholly," for it can and should not at all be demanded that a writer who judges with stringency and reprimands publicly the writings or actions of others must always give his name. Otherwise the great and mighty with all their silliness and mischief would escape, because only a few would have the courage to expose their foolishness while providing their names. On the other hand, however, it is quite wrong if the writer is wholly undiscoverable, because then any miserable churl can shame the most honorable and meritorious man and rob him of his good name. Thus a conscientious ruler must have the printer swear that he will not take anything without knowing from whom it comes. But he must strenuously prevent any printer from being forced to betray any author who wants to remain unknown, as long as his work does not contain accusations of actions known to be false. And because of the importance of the matter, he must give public permission to the printer, in case of wrongful coercion ordered by a lower official, to approach the prince directly to seek protection against such chicanery.

5. Lampoons [*Pasquille*], in the strict sense of the word, must not be tol-

erated at all.[15] However, I must say here what is to be understood as a lampoon, in order to prevent every aggrieved author from decrying his reviewers as lampooners. Namely, if in a *publicly readable writing*, brought forth by the pen or the press, anyone makes accusations (a) about *deeds*, for which punishment has already been decreed by a judge, or (b) about *disgraceful things*, which are not, however, punishable, for example, that one has ringworm, or has secret relations with a servant girl, and so forth, and (c) insults *anonymously*, that is the true *Pasquillant.*

6. Finally the ruler who would support the candor of writers subject to these limits must allow whoever is publicly attacked to vindicate himself, just as publicly, against his attackers, even if they are the first minister or the archbishop. And whoever has human sentiments will see without further proof that this is an inviolable demand, and that it is based, like all of the foregoing, on the holy rights of mankind.

And this is what the ruler has to do concerning freedom of the press and its limits. These are the limits on the writer, as far as he is an object of the legislator, who, as explained, has only two considerations from which all of his obligations and powers flow: the well-being of the state and the protection of the full rights of the subjects. And I repeat this once more to ask my reader by all means not to forget what so many people do not yet want to know, that the ruler and the moralist are very different people and that the ruler must never pretend to be a moralist and make prescriptions of virtue effective by physical force.

The moralist, it is true, subjects the writer's freedom, which the state supports, to certain limits which do not concern the ruler but rather must be left to the consciences of men. The moralist, for example, tells us that one should (a) never use one's right as a writer to expose human follies without intending a preponderant good through the publication and public rebuke of these follies and without foreseeing the probability that his well-intentioned goal will be achieved. It follows, (b) that no man should cause an avoidable harm or offense by his candid judgment, (c) that no one should nourish his pleasure in others' suffering [*Schadenfreude*], or satisfy his vengeance, and especially (d) that we should be indulgent toward men of worth and of decided merit, even when they show the most obvious weakness out of human frailty, and injure them least of all by rebuking their failings.

He who has ears to hear, let him hear!

NOTES

1. Only numbers appear in the text at the beginning of Bahrdt's sections. The translator has inserted the section titles from Bahrdt's table of contents.—Trans.

2. See Kant, "An Answer to the Question: 'What Is Enlightenment?'" AA VIII: 35 (translated above, p. 58).—Trans.

3. See Kant, "An Answer to the Question: What Is Enlightenment?" AA VIII:41 (translated above, p. 63).—Trans.

4. I have translated both *Recht der Menschheit* and *Menschenrecht* as "right of man." Bahrdt uses them interchangeably, apparently for stylistic variety. Alternative translations such as "right of mankind" and "human right" have an anachronistic ring.—TRANS.

5. Frederick William II (1744–1797), king of Prussia, 1786–1797.—TRANS.

6. Joseph II (1741–1790), co-regent of the Habsburg Empire from 1765 to 1780, emperor from 1780 to 1790.—TRANS.

7. Johann Stephan Pütter (1725–1807) was professor of law at the University of Göttingen and championed the historical approach to public law. Silesia had long been the subject of disputes between Austria and Prussia.—TRANS.

8. The phrase *ein wächserne Nase*, an idiom for unreliability or too-easy malleability, had a long history in theological writing, appearing most recently in Lessing's *Anti-Goeze*, "The inner truth is no wax nose that every rascal can shape in conformity to his own face as he wishes" (*Lessing Saemtliche Schriften* 13:128). Peter C. Hodgson traces the phrase back to the twelfth century; see his edition of Hegel's *Lectures on the Philosophy of Religion* (Berkeley, Los Angeles, and London, 1984), 1:123.—TRANS.

9. Presumably a reference to Exod. 33:23, where God tells Moses, "You shall see my back, but my face shall not be seen."—TRANS.

10. "Being king is a matter of chance."—TRANS.

11. In Section VII of this book, Bahrdt quoted at length from Frederick II's Edict on Censorship of 11 June 1781 and, in a variation on Klein's strategy of appropriating Frederick for his own purposes, cast the following sections as a commentary on and explication of that edict.—TRANS.

12. The rather surprising presentation of Frederick William II as an enlightened ruler may be attributed to the fact that Bahrdt's book appeared in 1787, within the first year of Frederick William's reign and thus a year before Woellner's edicts. Shortly after Frederick William took the throne, Bahrdt went so far as to send some of his writings to the new monarch, who responded that while he disagreed with Bahrdt's views, as a scholar, Bahrdt was free to pursue his research. See Paul Schwartz, *Der erste Kulturkampf in Preußen um Kirche und Schule (1788–1798)* (Berlin, 1925), 93.—TRANS.

13. Bahrdt first spells out this principle in Section VIII (p. 80) of his book.—TRANS.

14. As an aid in understanding the sum Bahrdt chooses for the cost of this dinner party, it might be noted that the yearly salary of most Prussian educators fell either into a lower income bracket of less than 150 Reichsthaler or a middle bracket of 150 to 600 Reichsthaler. See Anthony J. La Vopa, "The Politics of Enlightenment: Friedrich Gedike and German Professional Ideology," *Journal of Modern History* 62, no. 1 (1990): 38–39.—TRANS.

15. The term "pasquil" derives from the Pasquino or Pasquillo, the name for an ancient statue disinterred in Rome in 1301 which, during the Renaissance, was dressed up on St. Mark's Day to represent a historical or mythological figure. Professors and students enamored of ancient learning posted Latin verses on the statue, verses that in time became satirical. The authors of these ecclesiastical, political, or personal lampoons masked their identity under the name of the statue, hence the term "pasquil" came to denote anonymous lampoons posted in a public place. In emphasizing the "strict sense" of the term, Bahrdt returns to the original meaning of the word: to qualify as a pasquil, a lampoon must be both public and anonymous.—TRANS.

Publicity

Friedrich Karl von Moser

Translated by John Christian Laursen

Friedrich Karl von Moser (1723–1798) served as a civil servant in several of the smaller German courts for many years. He became acquainted with the enlightened reformer Joseph II of Austria and was made an Imperial adviser. His Pietism, his experiences in small courts, and his admiration for Joseph made him a critic of arbitrary absolutism, his views informed by the backward-looking perspective of the seventeenth-century ideal of the patrimonial state.

Moser gained fame for Lord and Servant: Described with Patriotic Freedom *(1759) and was the editor of the* Patriotic Archive for Germany *(1784–1790) and the* New Patriotic Archive *(1792–1794). In spite of his publishing activities, by the time of the French Revolution, Moser had become ambivalent about* Publizität. *This term, which translates literally as "publicity," referred to the explosion of printed matter in periodicals, pamphlets, and books in late eighteenth-century Germany.*

The essay translated here was written as a guide to the myriad books and pamphlets that appeared in German in response to the French Revolution. Moser regarded most of this literature as either flattery of princes or incitement to rebellion, and he sought to identify writings that argued for a middle way.

The torrent of publicity, in the good and bad senses, can no longer be stopped. It has been allowed to go too far. It should have been dammed up long ago and diverted onto another course. No one took the embers seriously because they were covered with ashes. The inner fire was disregarded because no one saw flames, or everyone thought they could be extinguished easily. All the lamentations, all the settlements of terms[1] and committee resolutions with their demands, promises, and threats, come much, much too late. Given the entire constitution of the disharmonious system of the empire, given the laziness, selfishness, and powerlessness of so many greater and lesser estates, each so different in respect to abilities and intentions, given the whole character, politics, and independence of the book trade, the liberty and insolence of so many writers, and the insatiable lust to read

First published as "Publizität" in Neues Patriotisches Archiv für Deutschland *(Mannheim and Leipzig, 1792), 1:519–527. "Written in December, 1791" appeared in parentheses after the title of this piece.*

of all estates, such lamentations and demands do exactly as much good as the well-known proposal of General von Kyau: that one should pave the meadows, so that moles could not harm them.[2]

The times have passed, and it is too late to try to shut out the light. The longer it goes on, the more it comes to this: whether this light should only illuminate and enlighten [*leuchten und erleuchten*] or ignite and inflame?

It is no longer a question of whether the citizen and the peasant should be allowed to know that which, according to God and to law, they ought to know. They know, in any event, how to find what they need, and they do find it. Rather, the question is whether the shepherds and fathers of the people can be and may be indifferent as to whether the people rightly know what they are allowed and entitled to know, or whether they weave what they know into a knot of superstition, that leads them out of truth into error, out of what appears in the beginning to be harmless error into an error with dangerous consequences, from the right way to the wrong way and to the abyss, in the end leading shepherds and herds to a common ruin.

Therefore it is strange enough that writings provoking uprisings are forbidden by imperial and district resolutions, and nothing better is provided in response. Surely, no blaze can be extinguished by mere commands, and just as little can subsequent cleverness make up for neglect. Certainly rulers would prefer that no fire ever burned in the first place or, if it did, that it suffocated itself. Since, however, this expectation is against experience and the nature of things, those at least who know that they are not safe in their houses and that they already have flammable materials around and near them, should possess enough love for themselves not to leave it to pure chance whether sparks will actually burst into flame. In such cases small homemade remedies generally work more safely, more rapidly, more certainly, than the most tumultuous counterforce.

It is precisely these apparently modest and inconspicuous homemade remedies that have been ignored, undervalued, and, indeed, despised by the rulers. They raise up and reward flatterers, yes-men, day laborers, and eye servers [*Augendiener*].[3] Wise men who in seclusion lament the harm to their fatherland, who investigate the causes of decay, ponder them, and finally, out of the passion of their hearts, lift their voice of warning, are not called on, nor is their counsel solicited and encouraged. Rather, they are all the more despised, derided, and mocked as visionaries and dreamers. One can well say of them that the world does not deserve them. They certainly do not push themselves forward, but hold themselves back, find themselves happy in their seclusion, and are satisfied with quietly doing as much good as they can. One does not find them in the waiting rooms of courts, but they let themselves be sought and wait to be found. When they open their mouths, however, they do not have words of revolt, but of warning wisdom and love for humanity.

It is a blessing of the Almighty that such noble men, inflamed by the holy fire of patriotism, can still be found, men who raise their voices out of the purest and most disinterested desire to testify, whether or not they will be heard by those who should be most concerned with listening. As courageous volunteers, with disdain for their own dangers and hardships, they placed themselves before the rift in the sinking fatherland, for it they even sacrifice themselves, like the hero Curtius,[4] to ingratitude, misunderstanding, and scorn.

How different is the worthy tone of such friends of humanity from the babble of political frogs, the chatter of wandering charlatans, disguised in the garb of patriots, whose scribbling one reads with disgust and throws away with ill humor?[5] When there is a fire, the fire horn has only one sound, the alarm bell only one ring. This constant, unchanging repetition makes for a general attention and a greater agitation than all the tinkling of vacuous and spiritless declamations.

"The writer's public," said Ewald so rightly, "is by no means the whole public."[6] It is true that it takes two to communicate, one who says something and one who understands and believes it. These words are especially applicable to those works, regardless of their difference in spirit, in plan, and in purpose, which appear from time to time for the instruction and warning of regents and for the reassurance and informing of the people.

Some of them are so abstractly philosophical that not only can the common man never understand them but also the higher classes will have trouble arriving at their deeper meaning, let alone be able to appreciate their full inner worth. This kind of writing might be called "little treasures" [*Kleinodien*], and be compared with a nest egg, on which one draws in times of need.[7]

Other writings take the middle road between a scholarly investigation and a practical treatment of their materials. They incline, however, more to the first category and are, to be sure, always valuable and useful. However, the too-strong mixture of theories and problems with practical truths diminishes the impression they would create if they were directed less to the understanding and more warmly to the heart, and if their authors had more living knowledge of the world and of humanity and knew the manifold needs and hardship of the lower classes more from their own experience.[8]

Still others are thoroughly practical, attack the evil at its root, call the sickness by its name, neither deceive the princes nor flatter the people. Everywhere they manifest impartiality, righteousness, love for humanity, a sensitive, compassionate heart, a thinking through and comprehending of their object. Dry, but true, in their presentation, they have little concern about embellishments, they call a spade a spade, and their words speak the language of felt conviction. Because they always preach the truth, that is, always give offense, they expect and receive no other reward than the awareness that they have been physicians, helpers, and saviors of the fatherland. They are satisfied to be recognized by Him, who will one day judge each according to his works.[9]

In the last, but certainly not the least, class belong those smaller pieces that are easily understood and which distinguish themselves by their popularity and sincerity. They truly are written for the instruction, reassurance, and correction of the so-called common man, to be distributed among the people at the lowest possible price and, if possible, to be given away. The shorter, the simpler, and the plainer they are, the better. They should all be cheap, as Luther, in his day, demanded of sermons, so that the man in the street gets the message.[10]

These so-called fliers[11] cannot be forbidden, precisely because they are fliers. They might well be shot down in flight (to continue with this simile), but that is all, and then the shot might strike an innocent pigeon just as well as a bird of prey, if the censor executes it as frivolously and injudiciously as is actually the practice in many places.

NOTES

1. The German term is *Wahlkapitulationen*, the name for the terms that were imposed on the emperors of the Holy Roman Empire upon their assumption of office. —TRANS.

2. Friedrich Wilhelm Freiherr von Kyau (1654–1723) was a general in the service of Augustus the Strong, Elector of Saxony, and was renowned for his rough jokes. See A. Wilhelm, *Kyau's Leben und Schwänke* (1800).—TRANS.

3. "Eye server" is the now archaic cousin of "lip server": one who provides only the appearance of service to another.—TRANS.

4. Marcus Curtius was a legendary Roman soldier who supposedly sacrificed himself by riding fully armed into a cleft that had opened in front of the Forum; an oracle had stated that "the chief strength of Rome" must be thrown into the chasm before it would close.—TRANS.

5. To such impostors, one would like to apply the story of the possessed man (Acts of the Apostles, 19:13–16), who answered his exorcists: "Jesus I know, and Paul I know; but who are you?" threw them to the floor, and drove them away wounded and mangled.

6. Johann Ludwig Ewald (1748–1822), *Über Volksaufklärung, ihre Grenzen und Vorteile: Den menschlichen Fürsten gewidmet* (Berlin, 1790), 2.—TRANS.

7. The rich work, *Über das Verhältnis der tätigen und leidenden Kraft im Staat zu der Aufklärung: Bei Veranlassung der neuesten Unruhen* [On the Relation between the Active and Passive Powers in the State to Enlightenment: On the Occasion of the Latest Unrest] (Frankfurt, 1790), especially belongs in this group.

8. I believe that I can, without injustice, count in this class the otherwise excellent work *Über den Freiheitssinn unserer Zeit* [On the Taste for Freedom of our Times] (Altona, 1791), by J. L. Callisen [1738–1806], minister in Oldesloe.

9. I count here, ignoring some prolixity and some silliness, the following work,

written with solid sense for truth and noble simplicity: *Patrioten-Stimme eines freimütigen Deutschen über die damaligen Empörungen, Unruhen und Gärungen in- und außerhalb des Deutschen Reichs. Zur warnenden Beherzigung der Regenten und ihrer Untertanen* [The Patriotic Voice of a Candid German on the Present Rebellions, Unrest, and Ferment Inside and Outside of the German Empire: For the Admonishment of Rulers and their Subjects], printed in the critical year 1790, quarto.

10. In this class is a small piece, one sheet long, but written with great simplicity, that appeared in the time of social unrest in the electorate of Saxony: *Eines Sächsischen Patrioten Gedanken über das Verhältnis der Untertanen zu ihren Obrigkeiten* [Thoughts of a Patriotic Saxon on the Relationship of Subjects to their Rulers], 1790, octavo. I cite only one example for each kind of writing, more to point out its particular character than as an ideal. [Note that when Moser refers to one sheet, this was folded over into eighths (octavo) and thus could have contained up to 16 pages.—Trans.]

11. *Flugschriften,* literally "flying writings," close to the English "fugitive pieces" and usually translated as "pamphlets."—Trans.

Reclamation of the Freedom of Thought from the Princes of Europe, Who Have Oppressed It Until Now

Johann Gottlieb Fichte

Translated by Thomas E. Wartenberg

Johann Gottlieb Fichte (1762–1814) was educated at the universities of Jena, Wittenberg, and Leipzig and first gained fame for his Attempt at a Critique of All Revelation *(1792), an anonymous work that was at first assumed to be Kant's long-awaited treatise on religion. Kant disavowed authorship and praised its previously unknown author. Championed by Goethe, Fichte settled in Jena, where in 1794 he attained a teaching position at the university. His lectures were extraordinarily popular, but his fierce support of republican politics and his religious heterodoxy prompted charges of atheism that resulted in his removal in 1799. After brief tenures at Erlangen and Königsberg, he was called to the newly established University of Berlin in 1810 as dean of the philosophical faculty.*

The pamphlet translated here—which Fichte once called "the most beloved" of his writings—was the first of his political essays, appearing shortly before his more famous Contribution to the Rectification of the Public's Judgment of the French Revolution. *Written in response to Woellner's Censorship Edict, the essay is notable for its attempt to analyze the question of freedom of thought and freedom of the press using the methods of social contract theory.*

Noctem peccatis, et fraudibus objice nubem.[1]

PREFACE

There are learned gentlemen who suppose they can convince us not to have a low opinion of their own profundity when they dismiss as a "declamation" everything written with a certain amount of liveliness.[2] Should the present pages accidentally come into the hands of one of these profound gentlemen, I admit in advance that they were not intended to exhaust such a rich subject. They were only intended to place, with some fervor, a few of

Originally published anonymously in Danzig in the spring of 1793. The place and date of publication were given as "Heliopolis in the last year of the old darkness."

the relevant ideas before the uninformed public, which has at least some influence on public opinion through its critical position and its strong voice. Profundity does not ordinarily reach this public. But if those more profound people should find in these pages neither a trace of a more solid, more profound system nor any hint at all that it is worth further reflection, then the fault might lie in part with them.

It is one of the characteristic peculiarities of our age that one ventures so gladly to place blame on princes and the great. Is it the ease of satirizing princes which is so tempting, or is it believed that one elevates oneself through the apparent stature of one's subject matter? This is doubly striking in an age when most German princes try to distinguish themselves through goodwill and popularity, when they do so much to eliminate the etiquette that once established a monstrous abyss between them and their countrymen, an abyss which became as irksome to the princes as it was injurious to their countrymen, and when, in particular, some princes appear to value both scholars and scholarship. If one cannot bear witness before his own conscience that he is certain about the matter and firm enough to endure, with that same dignity with which he spoke the truth, all the consequences which the spread of acknowledged and useful truth could have for us, then one relies either on the goodwill of these harshly accused princes or on his own insignificant and inconsequential obscurity. The author of these pages does not believe himself to be giving offense to any of the world's princes either by his assertions or by his tone, but rather to be obliged to them all. It could certainly not remain hidden from the author that some believe that, in a certain large state, the propositions which he attempts to prove here are plainly contravened.[3] But he knew as well that in neighboring Protestant states more is happening without anyone becoming especially excited, since that is what they have always been accustomed to there. He knew that it is easier to examine what *should* or *should not* be done than to judge impartially what actually *is* being done, and his position denied him the data for a well-founded judgment of the latter sort. He knew that, even if not all the individual facts as such could be defended, nonetheless the general motives could be very noble. And in our case he would admire the ingenious kindness which, through the pretended attempt to rob us of a good whose protracted enjoyment had made us insensitive, sought to awaken us more strongly to a warmer estimation and more zealous use of it. He could be astounded by the rare magnanimity of deliberately exposing oneself and one's dearest friends to the danger of being misjudged, slandered, hated, just in order to promote and increase enlightenment. Finally, he knew that through these pages he would give each state a desired opportunity to prove the purity of its intentions *by permitting them to be printed and sold in public, by distributing them to the clergy,* and so forth. No state in which these pages are printed and publicly sold seeks to suppress enlightenment. If the author has erred, the truth-loving Mr. Cranz[4] will not hesitate to refute him. Thus it is not for political, but for literary reasons that the author has not signed his name. He will reveal himself without inhibition to whomever has a right to ask for it, and asks in a rightful manner; and in his own time he will name himself without being asked, for he thinks with Rousseau *"chaque honnête homme doit avouer, ce qu'il a écrit."*[5]

We do not wish to examine here how much less misery mankind suffers under most of its present political constitutions than it would suffer under conditions of their total dissolution. It is enough that it suffers—and it should suffer: the land of our political constitutions is the land of toil and trouble; the land of pleasure does not lie on this earth. But this very suffering should be an impetus for mankind to exercise its powers in a battle against it, and, in hard-won victories, to steel itself for future pleasure. Mankind should be miserable, but it should not remain miserable. Its political constitutions, which are the sources of its common misery, admittedly could until now not have been better—or else they would be better—but they should continually improve. This has happened, as far as we are able to trace previous human history, and will happen, for as long as there is human history, in two ways: either through powerful leaps or through gradual, slow but steady steps forward. A people is able to make more progress in half a century through leaps, through powerful convulsions of state and revolutions, than it did in the ten previous centuries—but this half century is also full of misery and trouble. It can also, however, regress just as far and be thrown back into the barbarism of the previous millennium. World history provides evidence of both. Powerful revolutions are always a daring risk for mankind; if they succeed, the victory that is achieved is well worth the adversity that has been endured; if they fail, they force their way through misery to greater misery. Gradual steps forward are a more certain path to greater enlightenment, and with it to the improvement of the political constitution. The progress they make is less noticeable when it occurs, but when you look back, you see a path on which a large distance has been traversed. Thus in our century mankind has come a long way, especially in Germany, without attracting attention. It is true that the Gothic plan of the building is still visible almost everywhere; the adjacent new buildings are still far from being unified into a secure whole; but they are there and are beginning to be occupied, and the castles of the old robber barons fall to ruin. If no one disturbs us, they will be increasingly abandoned and left as dwelling places for the light-shy owls and field mice. The new buildings will spread and gradually unite into an ever more orderly whole.

These were our prospects, and someone wanted to rob us of them through the suppression of our freedom of thought?—And could we allow ourselves to be robbed of them? If the progress of the human spirit is blocked, there are only two possible outcomes: the first and more unlikely—we remain standing where we were, we give up all pretensions of a reduction of our misery and an increase in our happiness, we allow the limits beyond which we will not step to be set for us; or the second, far more likely—the progress of the human spirit destroys everything that stands in its way, mankind revenges itself in the most cruel way against its oppressors, revolutions become necessary. One still must make the true accounting of a dreadful spectacle of this type which happened in our day.[6] I fear there is no more time, or it is high time, to open the dams, which, in light of this spectacle, elsewhere were set against the course of the human spirit, so that the waters do not forcefully break through and horribly ravage the fields.

No, you peoples, surrender everything, everything, only not freedom of thought. Offer your sons to the wild battle in which they struggle with men who never offended them, in which they are either consumed by plagues or bring these plagues back to your peaceful homes as booty. Snatch your last morsel of bread from your hungry children and give it to the minion's dogs. Surrender, surrender everything. Only this heaven-born Palladium[7] of mankind, this pledge that a lot other than suffering, enduring, and contrition stands before us—defend this alone. Future generations may reclaim from you with terror that which your fathers bequeathed to you to pass on to them. Had your fathers been as cowardly as you, wouldn't you still stand under the degrading spiritual and corporeal slavery of a clerical despot? What your fathers won in bloody battles you can defend with only a little steadfastness.

Therefore, do not hate your princes; you should hate yourselves. One of the first sources of your misery is that you have much too high a conception of princes and their accomplices. It is true that they ransack the darkness of half-barbaric centuries with industrious hands, believing that they have discovered a magnificent pearl whenever they come upon the trace of a maxim from one of these centuries. They imagine themselves very wise when they have forced upon their memories these meager maxims exactly as they found them. But you can be sure of this: these princes know less than the most uneducated among you about that which they should know, about their own true vocation, about human worth and the rights of man. Indeed, how should they ever have known such a thing?—they, for whom there is a peculiar truth, which is determined not by the principles on which universal human truth is grounded, but rather by the political constitution, circumstances, the political system of their land—they, whose heads from childhood onward have been laboriously deprived of the universal human form and have been pressed into a form in which alone such a truth fits—they into whose tender hearts from childhood onward the maxim has been impressed: "All the men, Sire, whom you see there, are there for you, are your property."[8] How should they, even if they were to find it out, ever have the power to grasp it?—they whose spirit has been artfully robbed of vitality by an enervating morality, by an early voluptuousness, and, once they are disinclined toward that, by late superstition. When one encounters in history so many more weak princes than evil ones, one is tempted to suppose a continuous miracle of Providence. And I, at least, attribute to the princes as virtues all the vices that they do *not* have, and thank them for all the evil that they do *not* do to me.

And such princes are being persuaded to suppress the freedom of thought—not exactly for your sake. You may think and investigate what you please and preach from the rooftops what you will; despotism's minions pay you no heed. Their power is much too secure. You may or may not be convinced of the legitimacy of their demands, what does that matter to them? They know how to compel you through disgrace or hunger, through imprisonment or execution. But if you make a great clamor during your inquiries—to be sure, they will spare no diligent effort to guard the ear of the prince—it nevertheless still could be possible, it might be possible, that at one time or another an unhappy word would reach him, that he would examine it further, that he would finally become wiser and recognize what would serve his peace and yours. From that alone they want to hinder you; and from that, you peoples, you must not let them hinder you.

Shout it! Shout it in every tone in the ears of your princes until they hear that you will not allow the freedom of thought to be taken away, and show them through your conduct that what you say is to be believed. Be undeterred by the fear of being reproached for immodesty. Toward what could you be immodest? Toward the gold and diamonds of the crown? Toward the purple robes of your prince? Not toward him. It requires little self-confidence to believe that one can tell princes things they do not know.

And, in particular, all of you who have the strength for it: declare the most unforgiving war against that first prejudice from which all our evils result, that poisonous source of all our misery, the proposition that it is the vocation of the prince to care for our *happiness*. Pursue it into all the recesses of the entire system of our knowledge, where it has concealed itself, until it is eradicated from the earth and returns to the hell from which it came. We do not know what promotes our happiness. If the prince knows it and is to guide us to it, then we must follow our leader with closed eyes. He does with us what he wishes and, when we ask him, he gives us his word that it is necessary for our happiness. He places the rope around mankind's neck and cries: "Silence, silence! Everything happens for your own good."[9]

No, prince, you are not our *God*. From *Him* we expect happiness; from *you* the protection of our rights. You should not be *kind* to us; you should be *just*.

DISCOURSE

The times of barbarism are gone, you people, when one dared to proclaim to you in God's name that you were a herd of cattle placed on earth by

God to serve a dozen sons of God as bearers of their burdens, as servants and handmaidens of their comfort, and ultimately as cannon fodder; that God had transferred to them His indubitable right of ownership over you, and that, by virtue of a divine right and as the deputy of God, they torment you for your sins. You know—or can convince yourself if you do not already know—that you are not even God's property, but that He has impressed deep in your breast, along with freedom, his divine seal, to belong to no one but yourself. They also no longer dare say to you: "We are stronger than you, we could have killed you long ago. We have been so charitable as not to do it. Therefore the life that you live is our gift. We have not given it to you freely, but merely as a loan. Thus our demand is just that you use it to our advantage, and that we still take it from you if we no longer can use it." You have learned that, if such reasoning is valid, *you* are the stronger ones, and *they* the weaker; that their strength is in your arms, and that they will stand miserable and helpless if you drop them. They have learned this from examples which still make them tremble. Just as little will you continue to believe that you are all blind, helpless, and ignorant, and that you do not know what to do if they do not lead you, like immature children, with their paternal hands. Only lately have they shown, by making false inferences that the simplest among you would not have made, that they know no more than you and that they plunge themselves and you into misery because they believe they know more. You do not listen to such pretenses any more; you dare to ask the prince who wishes to rule you *by what right* he rules you.

Through the *right of inheritance*, say some hirelings of despotism, who are not, however, its most sagacious defenders. For assuming that your current prince could have inherited such a right from his father, and he again from his father, and so on, from whence did he who was the first receive it? Or, if he had no right, how could he transmit a right that he did not have? And then, you sly sophists, do you believe that one can inherit men like a herd of cattle or its pasture? The truth cannot be skimmed from the surface as you think; it lies deeper, and I ask you to take a little trouble for yourselves by seeking after it with me.[10]

Man can be neither inherited, nor sold, nor given; he can be no one's property, since he is and must remain his own property. He bears deep in his breast a godly spark—his conscience—which raises him above the animals and makes him into a fellow citizen of a world whose first member is God. It commands him absolutely and unconditionally to will this and not to will that; and it commands *freely* and *autonomously*, without any external compulsion. If he is to follow this inner voice—and it commands this absolutely—then he must also not be compelled externally; he must be free of all alien influences. No stranger may rule over him; he must himself act according to the law in him: he is free and must remain free. Nothing other than this law in himself may order him, for it is his only law, and he contradicts this law if he allows another law to be forced upon him—the humanity in him is destroyed and he is degraded to the class of animals.

If this law is his only law, then he may do as he wishes wherever this law does not speak; he has *a right* to all that is *not prohibited* by this exclusive law. Now, under that which is *not prohibited*, there belongs not only that which is *commanded* by the law but also that without which no law is possible at all: *freedom* and *personality*. One can say therefore that man has a right to the conditions under which alone he is able to act according to duty, and to the actions that his duty demands. Such rights can never be given up; they are *inalienable*. We have no right to alienate them.

I have a right to the actions that the law merely allows: but I can also not avail myself of this permission. Then I do not avail myself of my right; I surrender it. Rights of this second type are therefore *alienable*; however, man must surrender them *voluntarily*, he must never *have* to surrender them. Otherwise he would be compelled by a law other than the law in him, and this is unjust for the one who does it, and for the one who endures it when he can change it.

If I may surrender my *alienable* rights unconditionally, if I may *give* them to others, then I may also surrender them conditionally, I may *exchange* them for those rights which others alienate. From such an exchange of alienable rights for alienable rights arises the contract. I renounce the exercise of one of my rights on the condition that the other equally renounces the exercise of one of his. Such rights as are alienated in contracts can only be rights of *external actions*, not of *inner principles*; for in the latter case, no party can convince himself whether or not the other has fulfilled the stipulations. *Inner* principles, truthfulness, respect, friendship, gratitude, and love are freely given; they are not acquired as rights.

Civil society is grounded on such a contract of all members with one, or of one with all, and can be grounded on nothing else, since it is absolutely illegitimate to allow it to be established through any other law. Civil legislation becomes valid for me only by my freely accepting it—how this is indicated is not the issue here—and thereby giving the law to myself. I can allow no law to be forced upon me without thereby renouncing humanity, personality, and freedom. In this social contract, each member gives up some of his alienable rights on the condition that other members also give up some of theirs.

If a member does not honor his contract and takes back his alienable right, society thereby obtains the right to compel his conformity to the contract by infringing the rights which society assured him. Through the contract he has voluntarily subjected himself to this infringement. This is the origin of *executive power*.

This executive power cannot be exercised by the entire society without detriment; it is therefore transferred to one or more members. The one to whom it is transferred is called the *prince.*

The prince thus obtains his right by a transfer from society; society cannot transfer to him any right that it did not itself possess. Hence the question that we wish to investigate here—whether the prince has a right to limit our freedom of thought—rests on this: whether the state could have such a right.

To be able to think *freely* is the most notable distinction between human understanding and animal understanding. There are representations [*Vorstellungen*] in the latter too, but they follow one another necessarily, they produce one another just as one movement in a machine necessarily produces another movement. To resist actively this blind mechanism of the association of ideas, in which spirit is merely passive; to give a specific direction to the sequence of one's ideas according to one's own free will with one's own power; this is the privilege of man, and the more he maintains this privilege, the more of a man he is. The faculty in man through which he is capable of this superiority is also the faculty through which he freely *wills.* The expression of freedom in thought is just as much an internal constituent of his personality as the expression of freedom in volition. It is the necessary condition under which alone he can say: I *am,* I am an independent being. The expression of freedom in both thought and volition assures him of his connection with the spiritual world and brings him into agreement with it; for not only unanimity in volition, but also unanimity in thought, shall rule in this invisible kingdom of God. Indeed, the expression of freedom of thought prepares us for the more continuous and stronger expression of freedom of the will. By the free subjugation of our prejudices and our opinions to the law of truth we first learn to bow down and grow mute before the idea of law in general. This law first tames our selfishness, which the moral law seeks to rule. Free and unselfish love of theoretical truth, *because* it is truth, is the most fruitful preparation for the moral purity of principles. This right, so intimately related to our personality and to our morality—this path to moral improvement, expressly laid out for us by the creating Wisdom—could we have surrendered it in the social contract? We would have had the right to alienate an inalienable right. Would our promise to surrender have meant anything other than: "We promise through entry into your civil society to become irrational creatures, we promise to become animals, so that it will be less work for you to subdue us"? And would such a contract be legitimate and valid?

But, indeed, they cry out to us, "Does anybody want this? Haven't we clearly and solemnly enough given you permission to think freely?" And let us grant this; let us forget their anxious attempts to rob us of our best remedies—forget with what diligence they sought to stain each new light with the old darkness[11]—let us not argue about words. Yes, you allow us to *think*, since you cannot prevent it. But you forbid us to communicate our thoughts. You do not challenge our inalienable right to free thought, but only our right to communicate what we freely thought.

Let us be sure that we do not quarrel with you over nothing: do we originally have such a right? Can we prove it? If we have a right to all that is not forbidden by the moral law, who could show that it is a violation of the moral law to communicate one's convictions? Who could show the right of another to forbid such communication, to regard it as an offense to his property? You tell me that the other can be disturbed in the enjoyment of his happiness based on his previous convictions, in his pleasant deceptions, in his sweet dreams. But how can he be disturbed as a result of merely my action, without listening to me, without paying attention to my speech, without comprehending it in his own form of thought. If he is disturbed, he disturbs himself; I do not disturb him. It is wholly the relation of giving to taking. Don't I have a right to share my bread with him, to let him warm himself at my fire, to let him kindle from my light? If the other doesn't want my bread, he should not stretch out his hand to receive it; if he doesn't want my warmth, he should not stand before my fire. I certainly do not have the right to force my presents on him.

This right of free communication is based, however, not on a command, but only on a permission of the moral law. As a result, it is not in itself considered inalienable, and, further, the consent of the other, his acceptance of my gifts, is required for the possibility of its exercise. Thus, it is certainly in itself conceivable that society could have abrogated such consent for everyone, that it could have made every one of its members, on entrance into society, promise to make his convictions known to no one. Yet such a general renunciation, which does not take individual persons into consideration, cannot be meant that seriously. For do not others distribute the contents of their state-approved cornucopia with the greatest possible generosity, and isn't it merely on account of our stubborn insubordination that they have, until now, withheld the rarest of its treasures from us?[12] But let us grant what we may not want to grant so unconditionally, that at the entrance into society we had a right to surrender our right to communication: then this right of free giving has the right of *free taking* as a counterpart. The first cannot be alienated without, at the same time, alienating the second. Granted, you had a right to make me promise that I will share my bread with no one; did you then also have the right to compel poor starving people either to eat your wretched porridge or to die? Do you wish to cut the loveliest tie that links man to man, that makes spirits flow over into spirits? Do you want to destroy the sweetest commerce of mankind, the free and happy giving and taking of the noblest things they have? Oh, why do I speak with feeling to your dried-out hearts? A cut and dried reasoning, which you cannot get around with all of your sophistries, shall prove to you the illegitimacy of your demand. The right to take freely all that is useful for us is a constituent of our personality. It belongs to our destiny [*Bestimmung*] to make free use of all that lies open to us for our spiritual and moral development. Without this prerequisite, freedom and morality would be a useless gift for us. One of the richest sources of our instruction and education is the communication of mind to mind. We cannot give up the right to draw from this source without giving up our spirituality, our freedom and personality. Consequently, we *may* not give it up; nor may the other give up *his* right to let us draw from it. Through the inalienability of our right *to take*, his right *to give* also becomes inalienable. You yourselves know whether we *impose* our gifts. You know whether we confer offices and positions of honor on those who pretend to have been convinced by us; whether we exclude from offices and honors those who are not able to hear our lectures and read our writings; whether we publicly insult and turn away those who write against our principles. That nevertheless your writings are used to wrap up ours;[13] that nevertheless we have the brighter heads and the better hearts of the nations on our side, and you have the stupid ones, the hypocrites, the mercenary writers on yours—explain that to yourselves as well as you can.

But, you cry to me, "We don't forbid you from handing out bread; only that you should not give poison." But if what you call poison is my daily bread and makes me healthy and strong, how should I foresee that it would not agree with the other's weak stomach? Did he die from my *giving* or did he die from his *eating*? If he can't digest it, then he should not eat it: I haven't stuffed[14] him, only you have that privilege. Or even assume that I had really believed that I gave the other poison—that I gave it to him with the intent of poisoning him. How do you prove that to me? Who, other than my conscience, can be my judge on this?

You say that I may disseminate *truth*, but not *error*.

Oh! What might you who say this call *truth*?—what might you call *error*? Without a doubt, not what we others think it is. Otherwise you would have understood that your restriction cancels the entire permission; that you take from us with the left hand what you gave with the right; that it is absolutely impossible to communicate truth when it is not also permitted to spread errors. Yet I will make myself more comprehensible to you.

Without doubt, you do not speak here of *subjective* truth; for you do not wish to say that I may disseminate what *I* hold as true according to my best knowledge and conscience, but may disseminate nothing which *I myself* acknowledge as erroneous and false. Without a contract between you and me, you have no legally enforceable claim on my truthfulness, for this is merely an inner, not an outer, duty. You obtained no such claim through the social contract, for you can never assure the fulfillment of my promise since you cannot read my heart. Had I promised you truthfulness and had you accepted the promise, then admittedly you would have been deceived, but through your own fault. I would have promised you nothing since by my promise you would have received a right whose exercise is physically impossible. To be sure, if I deliberately tell you a lie, if I knowingly and consciously give you error instead of truth, I am a despicable person; but I thereby injure only myself, not you. I have to settle this with my conscience alone.

You speak, therefore, of *objective* truth; and what is that? O you wise sophists of despotism, who are never at a loss for a definition of it, truth is the correspondence of our representations of things with the things in themselves.[15] The meaning of your demand is therefore *this* (I blush in your name, as I say it): if my representation actually corresponds to the thing in itself, I may disseminate it; if, however, it does not actually correspond to it, then I should keep it to myself.

Correspondence of our representations of things with things in themselves could only be possible in two ways: namely, when either the things in themselves were actually produced by our representations or our representations were produced by the things in themselves. Since both cases are to be encountered in the human faculty of knowledge, but so entangled with one another that we cannot clearly separate them from one another, it is immediately clear that objective truth, in the strongest sense of the word, contradicts the understanding of man and every finite being, and that consequently our representations never do correspond to things in themselves, nor can they ever correspond to things in themselves.[16] You cannot possibly wish to demand that we disseminate the truth, in this sense of the word.

Nevertheless, there is a certain necessary way in which things must appear to us all, according to the organization of our nature, and insofar as our representations correspond with this necessary form of cognizability, we can also call them objectively true. The object in that case should not be called the thing in itself, but rather a thing that is necessarily determined by the laws of our faculty of knowledge and by the laws of intuition (appearance). In this sense, everything that is brought about in conformity with a correct perception through the necessary laws of our faculty of knowledge is objective truth. Besides this truth, which is applicable to the sensible world, there is another truth in an infinitely higher meaning of the word: where we do not first know the given characteristics of things through perception, but instead should *create* them by means of the purest, freest self-activity, according to the original concepts of right and wrong.[17] That which is in accord with these concepts is true for all spirits and for the Father of spirits, and truths of this type are for the most part known very easily and very certainly: our conscience proclaims them to us. So, for example, it is an eternal, human, and divine truth that there are inalienable rights of man, that the freedom of thought is one of them, and that he into whose hands we give our power in order to secure our rights acts most unjustly when he uses this very power to suppress these rights, especially the freedom of thought. There are no exceptions to such moral truths; they can never be problematic, but can always be deduced from the necessarily valid concept of right. Therefore, you do not speak about truth of this latter type—to you they are anyhow of little concern and are often most repugnant—for they are never in dispute. You speak about the first type, about human truth. You command that *we should not assert anything that is not derived from correct perceptions according to the necessary laws of thought.* You are generous, wise, kind fathers of mankind. You order us always to observe correctly, and always to infer correctly. You forbid us to err so that we do not disseminate errors. Noble guardians, we too dislike this; we are just as opposed to it as you. The problem is only that we do not know when we err. So that your fatherly advice might prove useful to us, could you give us a certain, always applicable, infallible criterion of truth?

You have already thought of that. You say, for example, that we should not disseminate old, refuted errors. *Refuted* errors? For whom are they refuted? Do you believe that we would still maintain these errors if these refutations were evident *to us,* if they convinced *us*? Do you believe that we would rather be mistaken than think correctly, would rather rave than be wise; that we might recognize an error as an error and right away accept it? Do you think that we write down and publish things which we ourselves know to be wrong out of a genial mischievousness, in order to tease and anger our good guardians?

You tell us, on your honor, that these errors are long refuted. Then *you* must at least consider them refuted, since you will surely deal with us honestly. Would you not tell us, illustrious sons of the earth, how many nights spent awake in serious contemplation it has taken you to discover what so many men, free of your additional cares of rule, who dedicate their entire lives to such investigations, have not yet been able to discover? Or tell us if you found it without any reflection and without any instruction, but merely with the aid of your divine genius? Yes, we understand you, and we should long ago have presented your true thoughts instead of these investigations, which strike you and your minions as rather dry. You do not speak at all about what we others call truth or error—what do you care about this? Who would have wished to ruin the hope of the country through such melancholy speculations, in the very years when you were bracing yourself for the future cares of ruling? You have divided up human mental powers with your subjects. To them you have left *thinking*—surely, not to think for you, nor for themselves, for in your government that is not necessary. They may do it for their own amusement, if they wish, but without further consequences. You will *will* for them. This collective will that lives in you also determines the truth. Hence that which you want to be true is true; that which you want to be false is false. *Why* you want this is not our question, nor is it yours. Your will, as such, is the only criterion of truth. Just as our gold and silver have value only by your mark, so it is with our concepts.

If a profane eye is permitted a glance into the mysteries of the administration of the state—which must require a deep wisdom since, as is well known, the best and the brightest of men are always raised to its helm—then allow me some timid remarks. If I do not flatter myself too much, I see some of the advantages you intend. Subjugating the bodies of men is an easy task for you. You can place feet in stocks, hands in chains. If necessary, you can, through the fear of hunger or of death, keep them from saying that which should not be said. But, after all, you cannot always be present with stocks or with chains or with torturers—even your spies cannot be everywhere—and such a wearisome regime would leave you no time for humane amusements. You must therefore think of a means to subjugate men more securely and reliably, so that even outside the stock and the chain they will breathe only when you signal them. Paralyze the first principle of spontaneity in them, their thoughts, so that they no longer dare to think otherwise than you order them to, directly or indirectly, through their father confessor or through your religious edicts. Then they are completely the machine that you desire to have, and you can now use them as you please. In history, your favorite subject, I admire the wisdom of a number of the first Christian emperors. The truth changed with each new regime. During even *one* regime, if it lasted for a while, the truth had to be changed once or twice. You have grasped the spirit of these maxims, but you have not—forgive the beginner in your art if he should err—plumbed their depths. You allow one and the same truth to remain the truth for too long; this has been the mistake of more recent statesmanship. The people finally become accustomed to it and regard their habit of believing it as proof of its truth—whereas they should believe it purely and simply because of your authority. Therefore, imitate your worthy exemplars fully, you princes. Condemn today what yesterday you ordered believed, and authorize today what you yesterday condemned, so that the people never wean themselves from the thought that your will alone is the source of the truth. For example, too long have you willed one to equal three.[18] They have believed you, and unfortunately have accustomed themselves to it to such an extent that they refuse you the gratitude you deserve and believe that they discovered it themselves. Avenge your authority! Order for once that one is equal to one—of course, not because the opposite contradicts itself, but because you will it.

I understand you, as you see, but I am dealing with an obstreperous people who ask not about your intentions, but rather about your rights. What should I answer?

It is an irksome question, this question of rights. I am sorry that here I must separate myself from you, with whom I have come this far so amicably.

If you had the right to determine what we should accept as truth, you would have had to receive it from society, and society would have had to receive it through a contract. Is such a contract possible? Can society make it a condition that its members outwardly acknowledge certain propositions?—not that they *believe* them, for society can never be certain of an inner conviction such as this, but only that they say, write, and teach nothing *against* it, which is to express the proposition as mildly as possible.

Such a contract would be physically possible. If only those unimpeachable doctrines were specified firmly and sharply enough that it could be demonstrated incontrovertibly to anyone that he said something against them—and you realize, this is to demand quite a bit—then one could indeed punish him for it as an external action.

But is it morally possible? That is, does society have a right to demand such a promise, and does the member have a right to make it? Wouldn't the inalienable rights of man be alienated in such a contract—something which must not happen in any contract and which makes the contract null and void? Free investigation of every possible object of reflection, in every possible direction and without limitation is, without a doubt, a human right. No one but the individual himself may determine his choice, his direction, his limits. We have proven this above. The only question here is whether the individual might not himself set such limits through a contract. He was permitted to set such limits on his rights to external actions, which are not commanded but only permitted by the moral law. Here nothing impels him to act but, at most, an inclination. Where moral law does not limit it, he can limit this inclination through a law that he imposes voluntarily. When, however, he arrives at the limits of reflection, something impels him to act, to overstep them, and to move beyond them, namely, the essence of his reason, which strives for the Unlimited.[19] It is a characteristic of reason to recognize no absolute limit; and through this it first becomes reason, and the individual first becomes a rational, free, independent being. As a result, unlimited investigation is an *inalienable* right of man.

A contract through which one were to set such a limit on oneself would not immediately mean the same thing as: I want to be an animal. But (given that the propositions privileged by the state were actually universally valid for human reason—which we have granted you, along with a host of other difficulties) it would mean this much: I want to be a rational being only up to a certain point. Once at this point, however, I want to be an irrational animal.

If an inalienable right *to investigate* beyond those fixed conclusions is now proven, the inalienability of the right to investigate beyond them *collectively* is proven as well. For he who has the right to the end also has a right to the means if no other right stands in the way. Now one of the most excellent means of making progress is for one to be taught by others; therefore each has an inalienable right *to accept* freely given instruction without limit. If this right is not to be suspended, then the right of the other *to give* such instruction must also be inalienable.

As a result, society has no right to demand or accept such a promise, for it contradicts an inalienable right of man. No member has a right to give such a promise, for it contradicts the personality of the other and the possibility that he will act morally. Each who gives it acts contrary to duty and, as soon as he recognizes this, it becomes a duty to revoke his promise.

You are shocked by the boldness of my conclusions, friends and servants of the old obscurity, for people of your type are easy to shock. You hoped that I had at least reserved myself a discreet "but only to the extent, of course that...," that I had left open a small back door for your religious oath, for your symbolic books, and so on.[20] And if I had it, I would not broach it to please you. You now raise a cry only because you were always pampered so carefully, were allowed to haggle too much, because one carefully avoided the abscesses that hurt you the most, and scrubbed your blackness without wanting to dampen your skin. From now on you will gradually have to get used to seeing the truth without a veil. Yet even I do not want to let you go without consolation. What do you fear from those unknown lands beyond your horizons, into which you will never pass? Just ask the people who frequent them whether the danger of being eaten by moral giants or of being swallowed by skeptical sea monsters is that great? Just look at these bold circumnavigators of the globe walking among you and see that they are at least as morally healthy as you. Why do you shrink so much from the suddenly breaking illumination that would arise if each were allowed to enlighten as much as he could? The human spirit only advances step by step from clarity to clarity. You will still crawl along in your age. You will still retain your small, select clique and the self-certainty of your great worth. And if the human spirit occasionally makes a powerful advance through a revolution in the sciences—don't worry about that either. Even if the daylight will break around you for others, you and your pupils who lie so close to your heart will preserve your dim eyes in a cozy twilight. Indeed, for your consolation, it will become still darker around you. You must know this from experience. Didn't you, after the strong illumination that fell on the sciences especially for the last decade, become even more confused in your head than before?

And now allow me to turn once again to *you*, you princes. You prophesy unspeakable suffering for us from an unrestrained freedom of thought. It is merely for our own benefit that you pick up freedom of thought and take it away from us, like a harmful toy is kept away from children. You have journalists standing under your supervision who paint in flaming colors the disorders wrought by divided minds and feverishly opinionated minds.[21] You point to a gentle people, reduced to the rage of cannibals; to how they thirst after blood not water; to how they surge more avidly toward executions than toward the theater; to how they display the torn body parts of their fellow citizens, still dripping and steaming, while singing in jubilation; to how their children spin bleeding heads instead of tops. We do not want to remind you of the bloodier festivals that despotism and fanaticism in their usual alliance gave to this very people; we do not want to remind you that this is not the fruit of freedom of thought, but the results of a previous, long slavery of the spirit; we do not want to tell you that it is nowhere quieter than in the grave. We want to grant you everything, we want right away to throw ourselves repentant in your arms and tearfully to ask you to hide us in your fatherly breasts from all the adversity that threatens us, once you have answered only one more respectful question for us.

O you who, as we learn from your mouths, have to watch over the happiness of nations as benevolent guardian spirits; you who—as you have so often assured us—make this alone the highest purpose of your tender concerns, why under your august supervision do floods and tempests still devastate our fields and plantations? Why do conflagrations still break out of the earth and devour us and our houses? Why do swords and epidemics carry off thousands of your beloved children? First order the tempests to be silent; then order the storm of our indignant opinions. Let it rain on our fields when they are parched and give us the invigorating sun when we implore you; then give us the truth that fills us with bliss.[22] You are silent? Can't you do it?

Now indeed! There is one who truly can build a new world from the ruins of devastation, and living bodies from the putrefaction of decay, who lets mountains of blooming grapes flourish on top of collapsed volcanoes, and, above the grave, allows men to dwell, live, and enjoy themselves. Would you be angry if we relinquish to Him as well *that* concern—the smallest of His concerns—to annihilate, to alleviate those evils which we incur through the use of that liberty confirmed by His divine seal or, if we *must* suffer them, to employ them for the higher culture of our spirit through our own power?

Princes, it is good that you do not wish to be our tormentors; it is not good that you wish to be our gods. Why don't you decide to descend among us and be the first among equals? You won't succeed in ruling the world; you know that. I do not want to bring up here—my heart is all too moved—the fallacies you previously advanced day after day, nor the seemingly long-range plans which you altered every three months, nor point out your piles of dead bodies which you confidently reckoned to restore in triumph. One day you will look over a part of the great, certain plan with us and you will be astonished with us that, through your endeavors, you blindly had to support goals of which you never thought.

You are grossly deceived. We do not expect happiness from your hand, we know that you are *men.* We expect the protection and return of our rights, which you surely took from us only in error.

I could prove to you that only freedom of thought—the unhindered, unlimited freedom of thought—founds and strengthens the well-being of states. I could demonstrate it with clear, incontrovertible reasons. I could also show it to you in history. I could indicate to you lands, small and large, that continue to flourish today because of it, lands that blossom before your eyes because of it. But I do not want to do this. I want to commend truth to you in its natural divine beauty and not through the treasures it brings to you as a dowry. I think better of you than all who did this. I have confidence in you. You gladly hear the voice of serious but honest truth:

> *Prince, you have no right to suppress our freedom of thought: and that to which you have no right, you must never do, even if the worlds around you perish and you should be buried in their ruins with your people. He who gave us the rights that you respected will care for the ruins of worlds, for you, and for us among the ruins.*

Even if you could really give us the earthly happiness for which you let us hope, what, after all, would it be? Feel in your breast, you who can enjoy everything, the joys the earth has. Remember the pleasures you have enjoyed. Were they worth your cares, were they worth the loathing and the boredom that follows the pleasure? And would you want to plunge into these cares once again for our sake? Oh, do believe that your pleasure—all the goods you could give us, your treasures, your ribbons of merit, your brilliant circles, or the flourishing of trade, the circulation of money, the abundance of food—qua pleasure is not worth the sweat of nobles, is not worth your concern, is not worth our thanks. Only as instruments of our activity, as a proximate goal that we pursue, does it have some value in the eyes of those who are rational. Our only happiness on this earth—if, indeed, there should be happiness—is free, unhindered self-activity, action from one's own power according to one's own purposes with labor and effort and exertion. You are wont to refer us to another world, whose price, however, you usually set in the suffering virtues of mankind, in passive suffering and enduring. Yes, we glance at this other world, which is not as sharply cut off from the present one as you think, and whose civic right we already hold deep in our breast, and we will not allow you to take it from us. There the fruits of our *actions*, not of our *sufferings*, are even now preserved for us; they are already ripened by a milder sun than this climate's; allow us, through hard labor here, to strengthen ourselves for their enjoyment.

You thus have no *rights* at all over our freedom of thought, you princes; no jurisdiction over that which is true or false; no right to determine the objects of our inquiry or to set limits to it; no right to hinder us from communicating its results, whether they be true or false, *to whomever* or *however* we wish. You also have no *obligations* in this respect; your obligations extend merely to mundane purposes, not to the extramundane one of enlightenment. With regard to enlightenment, you may behave quite passively; *it* does not belong among your concerns. But perhaps you want to do more than you are obliged to do. Well then, let us see what you can do.

It is true that you princes are majestic persons; you are indeed deputies of the godhead, not on account of an inherent majesty of your nature, not as *beneficent* guardian spirits of mankind, but on account of the majestic mandate to protect the God-given rights of mankind, on account of the mass of difficult and unremissible duties that such a mandate places on your shoulders. You think a noble thought: millions of men have said to me, "See, we are descended from the gods, and the seal of our origin is on our brow. *We* do not know how to defend the dignity that this gives us and the rights, which we brought with us from our Father's house to this earth as a dowry, *not we millions:* we place them in *your* hands; be they sacred for you because of their origin; defend them in our names—be our foster father until we return to the house of our true Father."

You confer civil offices and honors; you bestow treasures and tributes; you succor the needy and give bread to the poor. But it is a gross lie if one tells you that these are acts of charity. You cannot be charitable. The office you give is not a gift. It is a portion of your burden that you place on the shoulders of your fellow citizen when you give it to the most worthy. It is a pillaging of society and of the most worthy if it is received by the less worthy. The tributes you bestow are not bestowed by you. Each man's virtue has already awarded it to him and you are only the august interpreter of this virtue to society. The wealth you distribute was never yours; it was a trust that society placed in your hands in order to remedy all their needs, that is, the needs of every single one of them. Society distributes it through your hands. The hungry man to whom you give bread would have had bread if the social compact had not required him to give it up. Through you, society gives back to him that which was his. If you did all of this with unblindable wisdom, with incorruptible conscientiousness, if you never made a mistake, never erred—then you did what you had a duty to do.

You want to do still more. Well then, your fellow citizens are not merely citizens of states, but also of the spiritual world in which you hold a rank no more elevated than theirs. As such, you have no claims to make on them, nor they on you. You can seek the truth for yourself, keep it for yourself, enjoy it with your entire capacity for enjoyment; they have no right to interfere with you. You can let the investigation of truth run its own course without you, without caring in the least about it. You are not at all required to apply the power, the influence, the respect that society placed in your hands to the promotion of enlightenment. For society did not give them to you for that reason. What you do here is done entirely out of goodwill, it is something extra. In this way you cannot really benefit mankind, toward whom you have only compulsory duties.

Personally honor and respect the truth, and let that be noticed. We know, to be sure, that you are our equal in the world of spirits, and that the truth becomes no more holy through the respect of the mightiest ruler than through the homage paid it by the lowliest of the people. We know that you honor not the truth but yourself through your subjection to it. But we are occasionally—and many among us are always—sufficiently influenced by our senses to believe that the truth receives a new luster from the luster of he who honors it. Make this delusion useful, until it disappears. Let your peoples always believe that there is still something more exalted than you and that there are still higher laws than yours. Humble yourselves publicly with them under these *laws*, and they will hold the laws and you in greater respect.

Heed willingly the voice of truth, whatever its object may be, and let it always approach your throne without fear that it will outshine you. Do you wish to hide from it, shunning the light? Why do you fear it if your hearts are pure? Be obedient when it disapproves of your decisions. Take back your errors when it demonstrates them to you. You have nothing to risk in this. We always knew that you are mortal men, that is, that you are not infallible, and we will not learn it first from your confession. Such a subjection does not dishonor you. The more powerful you are, the more it honors you. You could continue to pursue the same measures, who can hinder you from that? You could knowingly and with full conviction continue to be unjust. Who would dare to reproach you to your face about it, to reprimand you for being what you really are? But you choose voluntarily to honor yourselves and to do right—and through a subjection to the rule of justice that makes you equal to the lowliest of your slaves, you promote yourselves at the same time into the rank of the highest finite spirit.

You owe the majesty of your earthly rank and all your external excellences to your birth. If you were born in the hut of a shepherd, the hand that now holds the scepter would hold the shepherd's crook. On account of this scepter, every rational man will honor, in you, the society you represent—but truly not *you*. Do you know to whom we address our deep bows, our respectful decorum, our obedient tone? To the representative of society, not to you. Dress a strawman in your royal robes, put your scepter in his stuffed hand, place him on your throne, and allow us before him. Do you think that we would miss the invisible rays which should stream only out of your divine person; that our backs would be less supple, our decorum less respectful, our words less timid? Has it never occurred to you to investigate how much of this veneration you have yourselves to thank for?—how one would treat you if you were nothing but one of us?

You will not learn it from your courtiers. They will swear mightily to you that they honor and love only you and your person, not the prince in you, once they notice that you like to hear it. You would never even learn it from a wise man—if ever a wise man could survive in the air your courtiers breathe. He would answer the representative of society, not you. To glimpse, as if in a mirror, our personal worth in how our fellow citizens treat us—this is an advantage only available to private persons. One does not openly assess the true worth of kings until they are dead.

If you nonetheless wish an answer to this question, which is truly worthy of a reply, then you must give it yourselves. Your fellow citizens judge you at approximately the same level as you can judge yourselves if you observe yourselves not with the deceptive glass of your own arrogance but in the pure mirror of your conscience. Thus if you want to know whether, once crown and scepter were taken from you, the one who now sings songs of praise to you would compose songs of mockery about you; whether those who now respectfully make way for you would flock to you in order to carry out mischief upon you; whether one would deride you the first day, coldly despise you the second day, and forget your existence the third day; or whether one would even then honor the man in you who did not need to be king in order to be great—then ask yourselves. If you wish not for the former, but for the latter, if you want us to honor you for yourselves, then you must become worthy of honor. Nothing, however, makes a man worthy of honor but free subjection to truth and justice.

You must not interrupt free inquiry. You may protect it, and you can protect it in almost no other manner than by the interest that you yourselves show in it, by the obedience with which you hear its results. The tributes you can give to the truth-loving investigators are seldom required for others, and are never required by the investigators themselves. Their honor does not depend on your signature and seal. It lives in the hearts of their contemporaries, who became more enlightened through them, in the book of posterity, which will light its torches from their lamps, and in the spiritual world, where the titles you give are not valid. The rewards—why do I still say rewards?—the compensations for their time lost in service to others, are the paltry fulfillment of the obligations of society toward them. Their true rewards are much nobler. They are freer activity and greater diffusion of their spirit. These they create themselves without your cooperation. But even those compensations—give them in such a way that they honor you and do not dishonor those to whom you give them; give them freely to the free, so that they may also reject them. Never give them in order to purchase those to whom you give them—for then you do not buy a servant of truth; they are never for sale.

Direct the investigations of the inquiring spirit into the most current, most pressing needs of mankind, but do so with a light, wise hand, never as a ruler, but as a free co-worker, never as a master of the spirit, but as a happy fellow recipient of its fruits. Force is contrary to truth; only in the freedom of its birthplace, the spiritual world, can it prosper.

And in particular—finally learn to know your true enemies, the only traitors, the only defamers of your hallowed rights and your person. Your enemies are those who advise you to leave your peoples in blindness and ignorance, to spread new errors among them and to preserve the old ones, to hinder and prohibit free investigation of all types. They consider your kingdom to be a kingdom of darkness that absolutely cannot exist in the light. They believe that your claims may only be exercised under the cover of the night, and that you can rule only among the blinded and the deluded. He who would advise a prince to block the progress of enlightenment among his people, says to his face: "Your demands are of a type that shocks the healthy human understanding; you must suppress it. Your principles and actions stand no light; do not allow your subject to become more enlightened, or else he will curse you. Your intellectual powers are weak; do not let the people become smarter, or else they will ignore you. Darkness and night are your element, you should seek to spread them around you; you must flee the day."

Only those around you who advise you to advance enlightenment have true confidence in you and true respect for you. They consider your claims to be so well founded that no illumination can damage them, your intentions to be so good that they must only look better in any light, your heart to be so noble that you could even bear the sight of your lapses in this light and would want to behold them in order to better them. They demand from you that you should, like the Deity, live in the light, in order to invite all human beings to your reverence and love. Hear only them, and they will give you their advice without being praised or paid.

NOTES

1. This motto is drawn from Horace's *Epistles* 1.16.62: "The 'good man,' whom the whole forum and the whole court watch respectfully whenever he appeases the gods with a pig or a bull, once he has called out aloud upon 'Father Janus,' called upon 'Apollo,' whispers, fearing to be overheard, 'Lovely Laverna, grant me the power to cheat! Grant me to seem just and holy! Cast darkness over my sins and a cloud over my deceits!'" Laverna is the goddess of gain and hence the patron goddess of rogues and thieves.—TRANS.

2. A "declamation" is defined by the *Oxford English Dictionary* as "a speech of a rhetorical kind expressing strong feeling and addressed to the passions of the hearers." Playing on the term, Fichte calls his own essay a "reclamation" (*Zurückforderung*).—TRANS.

3. Fichte is referring to Prussia.—TRANS.

4. August Friedrich Cranz (1737–1801) was the author of a pamphlet defending Woellner's Religions Edict.—TRANS.

5. "Every honest man has to acknowledge what he has written." In the preface to *Julie, La Nouvelle Héloïse*, Rousseau wrote,"Tout honnête homme doit avoir les livres qu'il publie." *Oeuvres Complètes* (Paris, 1964), II:5.—TRANS.

6. The "spectacle" to which Fichte refers is the French Revolution. His own attempt at a "true accounting" of the spectacle, his long tract *Beitrag zur Berichtigung der Urtheile des Publikums über die französische Revolution*, appeared a few weeks after the publication of this pamphlet.—TRANS.

7. The Palladium was a statue of Pallas Athena whose preservation was held to ensure the safety of Troy.—TRANS.

8. Words that the mentor of King Louis XV said to the royal child during a large public gathering.

9. So said the hangman of the Inquisition to Don Carlos during such an undertaking. Isn't it amazing how people from different trades run into one another!

10. I request that you not skip over this short deduction of rights, of the inalienable and alienable rights of contract, of society, of the rights of princes, but that you read it carefully and preserve it in a fine and good heart, since otherwise the remainder is unintelligible and without demonstrative force. For other uses it is not bad once to acquire determinate ideas about these matters, for example, in order not to talk nonsense in the company of more clever people.

11. Thus one employed a doctrine which appears to be constructed precisely in order to release us from the curse of law, and to bring us under the law of freedom, to support scholastic theology and more recently to support despotism. It is indecent for thinking men to creep to the foot of thrones in order to beg for permission to be footstools for kings.

12. Fichte's point here appears to be that those who advocate restrictions on freedom of the press on the basis of an argument that there could have been a general agreement, on entry into civil society, not to communicate the results of free thought cannot be serious, since in fact the state does sanction the circulation of some ideas by granting rights to publish to certain state-approved journals.—TRANS.

13. A reference to the practice of shipping books wrapped in surplus sheets from the press runs of other books.—TRANS.

14. Pushing well-chewed porridge into the mouths of children is called "stuffing" [*stopfen*] in the provinces, where this is still done.—One also stuffs geese with noodles.

15. Cf. Kant's definition of truth in the *Critique of Pure Reason* A 58/B 82ff.—TRANS.

16. Cf. Kant, *Critique of Pure Reason* B 146–148.—TRANS.

17. Cf. Kant, *Critique of Practical Reason* AA V:42–50.—TRANS.

18. Presumably a reference to the doctrine of the Trinity.—TRANS.

19. Cf. Kant, *Critique of Pure Reason* A 307/B 364ff.—TRANS.

20. Oaths of conformity to the basic religious doctrines as contained in the "symbolic books" had been a long-standing bone of contention among Enlightenment writers. Nicolai had written a novel satirizing them, and Mendelssohn had criticized them in his *Jerusalem.* Woellner's Religion Edict of 1788—the target of Fichte's argument—ordered Protestants to conform to them, and in 1791 the Summary Commission of Inquiry was established to investigate the orthodoxy of prospective candidates for teaching or clerical posts.—TRANS.

21. Fichte is presumably referring to the writings of August Wilhelm Rehberg, who had served as secretary to the Privy Chancellery in Hannover since 1786. In 1789, he was invited by the *Jenaer Allgemeine Literatur-Zeitung* to contribute essays on the French Revolution, and in this capacity he contributed a series of reviews of writings on the Revolution, which were eventually published as *Untersuchungen über die Französische Revolution nebst kritischen Nachrichten von den merkwürdigsten Schriften welche darüber in Frankreich erschienen sind* (Hannover und Osnabrück, 1792–1793). Rehberg's writings, along with Rehberg's friend Ernst Brandes's *Politische Betrachtungen über die französische Revolution, in Rücksicht auf Deutschland* (Hannover, 1792), were criticized in Fichte's *Beitrag zur Berichtigung der Urteile des Publikums über die französische Revolution.*—TRANS.

22. To be sure, your friend, the reviewer in the October issue of the *Allgemeine Literatur-Zeitung* (number 261) does not want one to compare revolutions to natural phenomena. With his permission: as *appearances,* that is, not according to their moral reasons, but their effects in the sensible world, they certainly stand merely under natural laws. *You* won't be able to refer him to the book and the place in it where he can convince himself of this: and *I* may not do it here. You might generally let this friend of yours know privately that he might boldly immerse himself more deeply in the study of philosophy. Then, with his broad knowledge and his manly speech, he would argue your case and, at the same time, the case of humanity, more skillfully than he has done so far.—You never had a better friend than philosophy, if friend and flatterer are not the same for you. Therefore abandon that false friend who since her birth has been at the disposal of the first comer, who let herself be used by everyone, and through whom—it is not so long ago—*you* were subjugated at the hands of a clever person, just as *you* now subjugate *your people* through her. [Fichte refers here to an article by Josephs von Wurmbrand in *Allgemeine Literatur-Zeitung,* 3 October 1792, pp. 17–22, which criticized writings that likened the Revolution to an earthquake or a storm. The book that Fichte cannot cite is presumably Kant's *Critique of Pure Reason*; see, in particular, the discussion of the Third Antinomy. See also the opening paragraphs of Kant's 1784 essay from the *Berlinische Monatsschrift,* "Idea for a Universal History with a Cosmopolitan Purpose," where Kant entertains the notion that history, like nature, could be understood as a system of laws.—TRANS.]

3. Faith and Enlightenment

Letter to Christian Jacob Kraus

Johann Georg Hamann

Translated and Annotated by Garrett Green

Johann Georg Hamann (1730–1788) was one of the most complex and influential figures in eighteenth-century German thought. Born In Königsberg and, for a time, a student of law and theology at its university, he traveled to London in 1757 on a business trip for the family firm of his friend Johann Christoph Berens. When the negotiations entrusted to him collapsed, he remained in London, falling into what he later characterized as a state of "inner desolation" before a reading of the Bible prompted his famous conversion. When Hamann returned to Germany in 1759, Berens enlisted Immanuel Kant in efforts to return Hamann to Enlightenment ideals, but while Hamann remained on friendly terms with Kant for the rest of his life, he was steadfast in his new convictions. Over the next three decades he produced works on philosophy, religion, aesthetics, and language that are remarkable for both their anticipation of later developments in scholarship and their intensely hermetic style. Hamann's letter to Kraus of 18 December 1784 examines Kant's recently published essay on the question "What is enlightenment?" It reveals Hamann at his most enigmatic and erudite—hence the extensive body of explanatory notes appended to the translation.

CLARISSIME DOMINE POLITICE![1]

Because my stiff old bones are hardly capable any longer of peripatetic philosophy, and my moments for labyrinthine strolls do not always occur *before* meals but also occasionally between courses *ab ovis ad poma*,[2] I must now take refuge in a macaronic quill,[3] in order to convey my thanks to you for the enclosed *Berlinsche Christmonath*[4] in the cant style, which the comic historian of comic literature[5] has rendered as "Kantian style" *per e*,[6] like an *asmus cum puncto*.[7]

To the "Sapere aude!" there belongs also from the very same source the "Noli admirari!"[8] *Clarissime Domine Politice!* You know how much I love our Plato[9] and with what pleasure I read him; I will also gladly yield myself up

Hamann's letter was written in Königsberg on 18 December 1784. It was published in Johann Georg Hamann, Briefwechsel, *vol. 5 (1783–1785), edited by Arthur Henkel (Frankfurt, 1965), 289–292. Some of the notes appended to this translation have been adapted from Ehrhard Bahr's edition of the letter in his* Was ist Aufklärung? Thesen und Definitionen *(Stuttgart, 1974).*

to his guardianship for the guidance of my own *understanding*, though *cum grano salis*,[10] without incurring any guilt[11] through lack of *heart*.

To remind a professor of logic & critic of pure reason of the rules of definition [*Erklärung*] would be virtual high treason; since, moreover, you have taken your Hutchinson away from me without returning his *Morals*,[12] I possess no other organon in my paltry supply of books. I am just as little able to account for [*mir aufzuklären*] the coincidence of Jewish and Christian agreement[13] in guardianlike [*vormundschaftliche*] freedom of thought, because the royal librarian in a most merciless manner has refused me the second volume;[14] irrespective of how much I have contributed with all my powers to assisting at the birth of the cosmopoliticoplatonic chiliasm[15] by means of wishes, reminders, intercession, and thanksgiving.

Therefore I can gladly tolerate seeing enlightenment, if not defined, at least elucidated and expanded more aesthetically than dialectically, through the analogy of immaturity and guardianship. Except that for me the *proton pseudos*[16] (a very significant coinage that can hardly be translated unclumsily[17] into our German mother tongue) lies in that accursed adjective *self-incurred.*[18]

Inability is really no fault, as our Plato himself recognizes; and it only becomes a fault through the *will* and its lack of *resolution* and *courage*—or as a *consequence* of pretended faults.[19]

But who is the indeterminate *other*, who twice appears anonymously?[20] Observe, *Domine Politice*, how the metaphysicians hate to call their persons by their right names, and prowl like cats around the hot broth.[21] I, however, see the enlightenment of our century not with cats' eyes but with pure & healthy human eyes, which to be sure have become somewhat dull through years and lucubrations[22] and sweets, but which I find ten times preferable to the moonlight-enlightened eyes of an *Αθηνη γλαυκωπις*.[23]

I ask, therefore, yet a second time with catechetical freedom: who is the *other* of whom the cosmopolitical chiliast prophesies? Who is the other layabout[24] or guide that the author has in mind but has not the heart to utter? Answer: the tiresome guardian who must be implicitly understood as the correlate of those who are immature. This is the man of death.[25] The self-incurred guardianship and not immaturity—

Why does the chiliast deal so fastidiously with this lad Absalom?[26] Because he reckons himself to the class of guardians and wishes thereby to attain a high reputation before immature readers.—The immaturity is thus self-incurred only insofar as it surrenders to the guidance of a blind or *invisible* (as that Pomeranian catechism pupil bellowed at his country pastor)[27] guardian and leader. This is the true man of death—

So wherein lies the *inability* or *fault* of the falsely accused immature one? In his own laziness and cowardice? No, it lies in the blindness of his guardian, who purports to be able to see, and for that very reason must bear the whole responsibility for the fault.

With what kind of conscience can a reasoner [*Raisonneur*] & speculator by the stove and in a nightcap[28] accuse the immature ones of *cowardice*, when their blind guardian has a large, well-disciplined army[29] to guarantee his infallibility and orthodoxy? How can one mock the *laziness* of such immature persons, when their enlightened and self-thinking guardian—as the emancipated gaper[30] at the whole spectacle declares him to be—sees them not even as machines but as mere shadows of his grandeur,[31] of which he need have no fear at all, since they are his ministering *spirits* and the only ones in whose existence he believes?[32]

So doesn't it all come to the same thing?—believe, march, pay,[33] if the d[evil] is not to take you. Is it not *sottise des trois parts*?[34] And which is the greatest and most difficult? An army of priests [*Pfaffen*] or of thugs, henchmen, and purse snatchers? According to the strange, unexpected pattern in human affairs in which on the whole nearly everything is paradoxical,[35] believing seems harder for me than moving mountains,[36] doing tactical exercises[37]—and the financial exploitation of immature persons, *donec reddant novissimum quadrantem*[38]—

The enlightenment of our century is therefore a mere northern light, from which can be prophesied no cosmopolitical chiliasm except in a nightcap & by the stove. All prattle and reasoning [*Raisonniren*] of the emancipated immature ones, who set themselves up as guardians of those who are themselves immature, but guardians equipped with *couteaux de chasse*[39] and daggers—all this is a cold, unfruitful moonlight without enlightenment for the lazy understanding and without warmth for the cowardly will—and the entire response to the question which has been posed is a blind illumination for every immature one who walks at *noon*.[40]

Written on the holy evening of the fourth and final Sunday of Advent '84 *entre chien et loup*.[41]

By the *Magus in telonio*,[42]
bound to *Clarissimi Domini Politici* and Morczinimastix,[43]
and *released* from his ex- and esoteric freedom,
misunderstood by poets and statisticians.
Even in the darkness there are divinely beautiful duties
And doing them unnoticed———[44]

Matt. 11:11[45]

P.S.

My transfiguration [*Verklärung*] of the Kantian definition [*Erklärung*], therefore, comes to this: *true enlightenment* [*Aufklärung*] consists in an emergence of the immature person from a supremely *self-incurred guardianship*. The fear of the Lord is the beginning of wisdom[46]—and this wisdom makes us *cowardly* at lying and *lazy* at inventing—but all the more courageous against guardians who at most can kill the body and suck the purse empty—all the more merciful to our immature brethren and more fruitful in good works of immortality. The distinction between the public and private service of reason is as comical as Flögel's being worthy of laughing at and laughing about.[47] It is a matter, to be sure, of unifying the two natures of an *immature person & guardian*, but making both into self-contradictory hypocrites is no *arcanum* that needs first to be preached; rather, here lies precisely the nub of the whole political problem. What good to me is the *festive garment* of freedom when I am in a slave's smock at home?[48] Does Plato too belong to the *fair sex?*—which he slanders like an old bachelor.[49] Women should *keep silent in the congregation*[50]—and *si tacuissent, philosophi mansissent.*[51] At home (i.e., at the lectern and on the stage and in the pulpit) they may chatter to their hearts' content. There they speak as guardians and must forget everything & contradict everything as soon as, in their own self-incurred immaturity, they are to do indentured labor for the state. Thus the public use of reason & freedom is nothing but a dessert, a sumptuous dessert. The private use is the *daily bread* that we should give up for its sake. The *self-incurred immaturity is* just such a sneer as he makes at the whole fair sex, and which my three daughters will not put up with. *Anch'io sono tutore!*[52] and no lip- or wage-servant [*Maul- noch Lohndiener*] of an overseer—but prefer immature innocence. Amen!

NOTES

1. A Latin address: "Most Revered Master Politician (*or* Statesman)!" Christian Jacob Kraus (1753–1807) was professor of practical philosophy and political science at the University of Königsberg, as well as a student and friend of Kant.—TRANS.

2. Latin aphorism "from eggs to apples" (i.e., from soup to nuts), normally used for long-winded introductions that take forever to get to the point.—TRANS.

3. A pen for writing in macaronic style. The *Oxford English Dictionary* defines *macaronic* as "a burlesque form of verse in which vernacular words are introduced into a Latin context with Latin terminations and in Latin constructions." The Italian Tifi degli Odasi (d. 1488), author of *Carmen Macaronicum,* is credited as its originator. In addition to the mixing of languages, the satirical-comical style is typical of macaronic literature.—TRANS.

4. A reference to the December 1784 issue of the *Berlinische Monatsschrift,* in which Kant's essay "An Answer to the Question: What Is Enlightenment?" appeared on the first page.—TRANS.

5. Carl Friedrich Flögel, in the first volume of his *Geschichte der komischen Litteratur* (1784), characterized the "cant style" as follows: "The low speech (which in England is sometimes called *the cant style*) was dominant in England at the end of the last

century and was introduced by the courtiers of Charles II, who, to express their contempt for the ceremony that had characterized the preceding age, succumbed to the opposite extreme and affected a liveliness of manners and conversation as well as a loose, ungrammatical vulgarity of expression.... *Richard Steele* says that this *Kantischer Styl* is derived from a certain *Andreas Cant,* who was a Presbyterian clergyman in an uneducated part of Scotland, and had obtained through practice the gift of speaking from the pulpit in such a dialect that he was understood only by his own congregation and not even by all of them" (pp. 174f.; cited in Bahr, *Was ist Aufklärung?*, 60–61). Notice that Flögel renders the English "cant style" as *Kantischer Styl,* which Hamann exploits as a pun on Kant's name.—Trans.

6. According to a note in Bahr (p. 61) *per e* means "through (the omission of the terminal letter) 'e.'" In this way English "cant style" becomes German "Kant-Stil," which Hamann writes as "Kantschen Styl."—Trans.

7. According to a note in the Bahr edition (p. 61, attributing the insight to Arthur Henkel), Latin *asmus* becomes *asinus* (ass) *cum puncto* (with a dot)—i.e., when one puts a dot over the first upright of the "m," thus turning it into "in." *Asmus,* a shortened form of "Erasmus," was used as a pen name by Matthias Claudius, with whom Hamann corresponded. The phrase *cum puncto* derives from Hebrew grammar, where it refers to the addition of vowel points. Why one would turn *Asmus* into *asinus* in this way remains unexplained, as does Hamann's reason for referring to it.—Trans.

8. Kant's "*Sapere aude!*" (Dare to Know!)—his "motto" of the Enlightenment—comes from the *Epistles* of Horace (1.2.40); the phrase *"Nil admirari"* (to marvel at nothing), which Hamann has altered to *"Noli admirari!"* (Marvel not!), is found in *Epistles* 1.6.1.—Trans.

9. A reference to Kant; see Oswald Bayer, "Selbstverschuldete Vormundschaft: Hamanns Kontroverse mit Kant um wahre Aufklärung," in *Der Wirklichkeitsanspruch von Theologie und Religion,* ed. Dieter Henke et al. (Tübingen, 1976, 19). It may also be relevant that Kraus lectured on Plato.—Trans.

10. Latin, "with a grain of salt."—Trans.

11. *"ohne eine Selbstverschuldung ... zu besorgen"*—the first of Hamann's many ironical allusions to Kant's definition of enlightenment as "self-incurred [*selbstverschuldet*] immaturity" (see Kant, "Answer to the Question: What Is Enlightenment?" translated above, p. 58). Hamann plays on the root term *Schuld,* which can mean "guilt," "fault," or "debt"—nuances that are lost in translation.—Trans.

12. "Hutchinson" is presumably a reference to the Scottish moral philosopher Francis Hutcheson (1694–1746). The book in question may be Hutcheson's *System of Moral Philosophy,* published posthumously in 1755. Hamann frequently complains in his letters about unreturned books he has loaned.—Trans.

13. An allusion to the footnote at the end of Kant's essay (translated above, p. 64). Kant states that while he knew of the publication of Mendelssohn's essay on the same question in the *Berlinische Monatsschrift,* he had been unable to obtain a copy of the journal and so sent his own essay off to Berlin "as an attempt to see how far agreement in thought can be brought about by chance." Hamann had apparently also been unable to obtain the issue of the *Berlinische Monatsschrift* containing Mendelssohn's essay and knew of Kant's contribution only because Kraus had sent him a copy of the journal.—Trans.

14. The "royal librarian" is Johann Erich Biester (1749–1816), editor of the

Berlinische Monatsschrift and royal librarian in Berlin. The essays by Mendelssohn and Kant appeared in the second volume of the journal.—TRANS.

15. Chiliasm (from the Greek word for "thousand") is the doctrine that the millennium, a thousand-year reign of Christ on earth, will be inaugurated at the Second Coming (see Rev. 20:4). Hamann alludes here to Kant's use of the term in "Idea for a Universal History with a Cosmopolitan Purpose," which had appeared in the November 1784 issue of the *Berlinische Monatsschrift.* Kant had commented that "philosophy too may have its *chiliastic* expectations [*ihren Chiliasmus*]" (AA 8:27 [translated by H. B. Nisbet in Kant, *Political Writings*, 2d ed., ed. Hans Reiss (Cambridge, 1991], 50). Later, in *The Contest of the Faculties*, Kant uses the term to designate one of the three possible futures of historical humanity, namely, the conception that the human race will continually progress, for which his preferred term is "eudaemonism" (AA 7:81 [Kant, *Political Writings*, 178]).—TRANS.

16. Greek, "the first lie," i.e., the basic error from which all further errors follow.—TRANS.

17. Hamann's use of the word *unflegelhaft* may be a pun on Flögel's name and an allusion to his skill as translator (see note 5 above).—TRANS.

18. A reference to the term *selbstverschuldet* in the opening line of Kant's essay: *"Enlightenment is man's exit from his self-incurred immaturity."* (See note 11 above.)—TRANS.

19. The root of Kant's term *selbstverschuldet* (self-incurred) is *Schuld* (fault). In the opening paragraph of his essay, Kant says that immaturity is self-incurred when it results from "the lack of the resolution and the courage" to use one's own reason.

20. Kant twice uses the phrase "without the guidance of another" in the opening paragraph of his essay.—TRANS.

21. The German idiom means "to beat around the bush"; the translator has rendered it literally because of Hamann's reference to "cats' eyes" in the next sentence.—TRANS.

22. *Lucubration* is hard work or study, especially at night (from Latin *lucubrare*, to work by artificial light)—possibly another in Hamann's ongoing series of wordplays on en*light*enment.—TRANS.

23. "Owl-eyed Athena," epithet for the Greek goddess, referring not only to her holiness but also to her flashing eyes, which penetrated the dark of night, and to her gift of vision to human beings.—TRANS.

24. The reference of *Bärenheuter* (layabout, lazybones, idler) remains obscure. It could conceivably be a pun on the name of Johann Christoph *Berens*, Hamann's friend, who along with Kant had tried to reconvert him to Enlightenment ideals after his London conversion to Christianity in 1758.—TRANS.

25. Possibly an allusion to 2 Sam. 12:5, where David, after hearing Nathan's parable of the poor man's ewe lamb, unknowingly passes judgment on himself: "As the Lord lives, the man who has done this deserves to die." The German is closer to Hamann's diction: "So wahr der Herr lebt, der Mann ist ein Kind des Todes, der das getan hat."—TRANS.

26. A reference to the biblical story of the son of David who rebelled and was killed in battle against his father's army. Here, "Absalom" presumably refers to Frederick the Great, who as a young man also rebelled against his father. The

"chiliast" is, of course, Kant, whose deferential stance toward Frederick the Great is criticized by Hamann.—TRANS.

27. The anecdote referred to here is obscure. Pomeranians were sometimes regarded as country bumpkins, hence Hamann has the Pomeranian catechism pupil, presumably reciting the Nicene Creed, mispronounce the German *"unsichtbar"* by placing emphasis on the wrong syllable. Pronounced this way, *unsichtbar* can mean "blind" and possibly "obscene."—TRANS.

28. The idiom *hinter dem Ofen hocken* means to be a stay-at-home, never to stir from one's fireplace. Besides its literal meaning, *Schlafmütze* also implies a dull or sleepy person. Hamann is accusing Kant of being an armchair philosopher, one who sits comfortably at home by the hearth while accusing others of laziness and cowardice.—TRANS.

29. Cf. the concluding paragraph of "What Is Enlightenment?" where Kant's enlightened ruler "has at hand a large, well-disciplined army as a guarantee of public peace" (translated above, p. 63).—TRANS.

30. "To describe as 'enlightened' and to glorify a man who deals with human beings as this king does—that could be done only by an 'emancipated gaper [*eximirter Maulaffe*],' an existentially uninvolved spectator" (E. Büchsel, "Aufklärung und christliche Freiheit: J. G. Hamann contra I. Kant," *Neue Zeitschrift für systematische Theologie* 4 [1962]:151).—TRANS.

31. In the last paragraph of his essay Kant says that "man . . . is *more than a machine*" and that his enlightened ruler does not "fear shadows" (translated above, p. 63). The reference to his "grandeur" (*Riesengröße*) may contain a pun on Frederick the *Great*.—TRANS.

32. Hamann implies that Frederick believes not in God but only in his subjects as "his ministering spirits."—TRANS.

33. "The officer says: 'Don't argue, but rather march!' The tax collector says: 'Don't argue, but rather pay!' The clergyman says: 'Don't argue, but rather believe!'" (Kant, "What Is Enlightenment?" translated above, p. 63).—TRANS.

34. French, "stupidity on three sides," adapted by Hamann from the title of an article by Voltaire, *Sottise des deux parts* (1728).—TRANS.

35. Hamann takes this language nearly verbatim from the last paragraph of Kant's essay.

36. Cf. Matt. 17:20; 1 Cor. 13:2.—TRANS.

37. Hamann's phrase *Evolutionen u Exercitia machen* is presumably technical terminology derived from French military usage (*évolutions tactiques*, "tactical exercises"). French was the official language of Frederick's Prussian government, including the customs office where Hamann was employed.—TRANS.

38. "Till they have paid the last penny" (see Matt. 5:26; Luke 12:59).—TRANS.

39. French, "hunting knives." Frederick the Great hired French tax collectors for service in Prussia.—TRANS.

40. Perhaps an allusion to the riddle of the Sphinx: "What is it that walks on four legs in the morning, on two at noon, and on three in the evening?" Oedipus gave the correct answer: "Man, who first crawls on all fours, then walks upright, and in old age needs a stick as a third leg." Thus the "one who walks at noon" would be the adult, the "mature" one. Büchsel suggests an allusion to Isa. 58:10: "If you pour

yourself out for the hungry and satisfy the desire of the afflicted, then shall your light rise in the darkness and your gloom be as the noonday" ("Aufklärung und christliche Freiheit: J. G. Hamann contra I. Kant," 153n.52). Another possibility is 1 Thess. 5:12: "For you are all sons of light and sons of the day; we are not of the night or of darkness"—a passage that contains all the right metaphors for Hamann's case against Kant.—TRANS.

41. The French expression ("between dog and wolf") refers to twilight, when one cannot distinguish dog from wolf.—TRANS.

42. "Wise Man of the Customs House" (from the Latin, *telonium*, "customshouse"). Hamann, widely known as "Magus in Norden," worked as a civil servant in the customs office in Königsberg.—TRANS.

43. This term is coined on the analogy of Greek *Homeromastix* (hostage of Homer), used of grammarians who searched for errors in Homer. Hamann calls Kraus "Morczinimastix" because in 1784 he had published an exposé of the confidence man Johann Gottlieb Hermann, alias Friedrich Joseph Freiherr von Mortczinni.—TRANS.

44. These two lines are cited from a source that Hamann had long ago forgotten. He had quoted them more than two decades earlier in a letter to Moses Mendelssohn (Johann Georg Hamann, *Briefwechsel*, ed. Walther Ziesemer and Arthur Henkel [Wiesbaden, 1956], 2:129). There, too, Hamann identifies himself as one who prefers darkness: "I avoid the light, my dear Moses, perhaps more out of fear than maliciousness."—TRANS.

45. "Truly, I say to you, among those born of women there has risen no one greater than John the Baptist; yet he who is least in the kingdom of heaven is greater than he."—TRANS.

46. Prov. 9:10.—TRANS.

47. Hamann refers here to Kant's distinction between the "public" and "private" uses of reason (see "On the Question: What Is Enlightenment?" translated above, pp. 59–60). For Flögel, see note 5 above.—TRANS.

48. Possibly an allusion to the parable of the king's wedding feast (Matt. 22:1–14). Hamann is questioning Kant's argument that while the "public" use of reason to write and criticize must remain free, the "private" use of reason may be limited by the terms of the contracts into which one enters (e.g., the clergyman may write critical articles about church doctrine, but his sermons must conform to the teachings of his church).—TRANS.

49. Presumably an allusion to Kant's comment, "Those guardians, who have graciously taken up the oversight of mankind, take care that the far greater part of mankind (including the entire fairer sex) regard the step to maturity as not only difficult but also very dangerous." (see "On the Question: What Is Enlightenment?" translated above, p. 58).—TRANS.

50. Hamann is citing Paul's dictum that "women should keep silence in the churches" (1 Cor. 14:35). In the following verse the apostle continues, "If there is anything they desire to know, let them ask their husbands at home." Hamann takes up this contrast between silence "in the congregation" and speaking "at home."—TRANS.

51. The Latin phrase ("if they had kept silent, they would have remained philosophers") is presumably adapted by Hamann from the story told by Boethius in

book 7 of *The Consolation of Philosophy*. A "certain fellow who had falsely taken upon him the name of a philosopher, not for the use of virtue but for vainglory" was put to the test by another, who berated him in order to determine "whether he were a philosopher or no by his gentle and patient bearing of injuries." The would-be philosopher "took all patiently for a while, and having borne his contumely, as it were, triumphing, said: 'Dost thou now at length think me a philosopher?' To which he bitingly replied: 'I would have thought thee one if thou hadst holden thy peace [*si tacuisses*].' " Boethius, *The Theological Tractates* (Cambridge, Mass., 1936), 216–217.—Trans.

52. Italian, "I, too, am a guardian!"—an ironic variation of the exclamation *"Anch'io sono pittore!"* (I, too, am a painter!), allegedly uttered by Correggio before a picture of Raphael.—Trans.

Metacritique on the Purism of Reason

Johann Georg Hamann

Translated and Annotated by Kenneth Haynes

Hamann wrote this short critique of Kant's philosophy in January 1784 but was never satisfied with it. He sent a copy to Johann Gottfried von Herder, who in turn passed it on to Friedrich Heinrich Jacobi, and the work enjoyed a considerable underground reputation prior to its posthumous publication in 1800. In his oblique and allusive manner, Hamann posed objections to Kant by means of parody, reductio ad absurdum, and polemic. His criticism of Kant for failing to recognize the place of language in the genesis and application of reason has subsequently been of great importance.

Sunt lacrimae rerum—o quantum est in rebus inane![1]

A great philosopher has asserted that "all general ideas are nothing but particular ones, annexed to a certain term, which gives them a more extensive signification, and makes them recall upon occasion other individuals, which are similar to them."[2] Hume[3] declares this assertion of the Eleatic, mystic, and enthusiast Bishop of Cloyne to be one of the *greatest* and *most valuable discoveries* that has been made of late years in the republic of letters.

It seems to me first that the new skepticism owes infinitely more to the old idealism than this chance, fleeting, and particular occasion would give us to understand and that without Berkeley, Hume would hardly have become the *great philosopher* that criticism in unanimous gratitude declares him to be.[4] But as for the *important discovery* itself: the same without any special profundity lies open and bare in the very use of language in the most common perception and observation of the *sensus communis*.[5]

To the *hidden mysteries*, the task of which (let alone their solution) still has not come into a philosopher's heart, belongs the possibility of human knowledge of objects *without* and *before* any experience and thus the possibility of a sensible intuition *before* any sensation of an object.[6] The matter and form of

This essay was first published in Mancherley zur Geschichte der metakritschen Invasion, *ed. F. T. Rink (Königsberg, 1800), 120–134. The translation is based on the text in Hamann's* Sämtliche Werke, *ed. Josef Nadler (Vienna, 1949–1957), 3:281–289. There is another version in the letter to Herder of 15 September 1784, which is printed in Hamann's* Briefwechsel, *ed. Walther Ziesemer and Arthur Henkel (Wiesbaden and Frankfurt, 1955–1979), 5: 210–216.*

a Transcendental Doctrine of Elements and Method[7] is grounded on this double *im*-possibility and on the *mighty distinction* of analytic and synthetic judgments.[8] For besides the particular distinction of reason as *object* or *source of knowledge* or else as *kind of knowledge*,[9] there is a still more general, sharper, and purer distinction which enables reason to ground all objects, sources, and kinds of knowledge. Itself none of the three, reason consequently needs neither an empirical or aesthetic nor a logical or discursive concept; rather it consists solely in the subjective conditions whereby *Everything*, *Something*, and *Nothing* can be thought as object, source, or kind of knowledge. Like an infinite maximum or minimum,[10] it can be *given* (and if necessary *taken*) for direct intuition.

The *first* purification of reason consisted in the partly misunderstood, partly failed attempt to make reason independent of all tradition and custom and belief in them. The second is even more transcendent[11] and comes to nothing less than independence from experience and its everyday induction. After a search of two thousand years for who knows what *beyond* experience, reason not only suddenly despairs of the progressive course of its predecessors but also *defiantly* promises impatient contemporaries delivery, and this in a short time, of that general and infallible *philosopher's stone*, indispensable for Catholicism and despotism.[12] *Religion* will submit its *sanctity* to it right away, and *lawgiving* its *majesty*, especially at the final close of a critical century[13] when empiricism on both sides,[14] struck blind, makes its own nakedness daily more suspect and ridiculous.

The *third*, highest, and, as it were, *empirical* purism thus still concerns *language*, the only, first, and last organon and criterion of reason,[15] with no credentials[16] but *tradition* and *usage*. But it is almost the same with this *idol*[17] as it was with the *ideal* of reason[18] for that ancient.[19] The longer one deliberates, the more deeply and inwardly one is struck dumb and loses all desire to speak. "Woe to the oppressors when *God* troubles himself about them! why then do they seek after Him? Mene, mene, tekel to the sophists![20] Your base coin[21] is found wanting and your banks are broken!"[22]

Receptivity of *language* and *spontaneity* of *concepts*![23] From this double source of ambiguity pure reason draws all the elements of its doctrinairism, doubt, and appraisal.[24] Through an analysis just as arbitrary as the synthesis of the thrice old leaven,[25] it brings forth new phenomena and meteors[26] on the inconstant horizon, creates signs and wonders[27] with its all-creating and destroying mercurial[28] caduceus of a mouth or with the split goose quill between the three syllogistic writing fingers of its herculean fist[29]—

The hereditary defect and leprosy of ambiguity sticks to the very name "metaphysics." It is not lifted up, still less illumined, by going back to its origin in the accidental synthesis of a Greek *prefix*.[30] But granted that in the transcendental topic[31] it would depend less on the empirical distinction of *behind* and *beyond* than with an a priori and a posteriori on a *hysteron-*

proteron:[32] nonetheless the birthmark of its name spreads from its brow to the bowels of the whole science, and its terminology is related to every other language of art, pastures, mountains, and schools as quicksilver to other metals.[33]

A good many *analytic* judgments indeed imply a *gnostic* hatred of matter or else a *mystic* love of form. Yet the synthesis of predicate with subject (the proper object of pure reason) has for its middle term nothing more than an old, cold prejudice for mathematics before and behind it. The apodeictic certainty of mathematics[34] depends mainly on a curiological,[35] so to speak, portrayal of the simplest, most sensible intuition and thus on the ease of proving and representing its synthesis and the possibility of its synthesis in obvious constructions or symbolic formulas and equations, by whose sensibility all *misunderstanding* is excluded of itself. Geometry meanwhile fixes even the *ideality* of its points without parts,[36] of lines and surfaces even in ideally divided dimensions, through empirical signs and figures; metaphysics abuses the word-signs and figures of speech of our empirical knowledge by treating them as nothing but hieroglyphs and types of ideal relations. Through this learned troublemaking it turns the *honest decency* of language into such a meaningless, rutting, unstable, indefinite something = X[37] that nothing is left but a windy sough, a magic shadow play, at most, as the wise Helvétius says,[38] the talisman and rosary of a transcendental superstitious belief in *entia rationis*,[39] their empty sacks[40] and droppings.[41] It is finally understood, by the way, that if mathematics lays claim to the privilege of nobility because of its general and necessary reliability, even human reason itself would have to be inferior to the infallible and certain *instinct* of insects.

If it is still a chief question *how the faculty of thought is possible*[42]—the faculty to think *right* and *left*, *before* and *without*, *with* and *beyond* experience—then no deduction[43] is needed to demonstrate the genealogical superiority of *language*, and its heraldry, over the *seven* holy functions of logical propositions and inferences.[44] Not only is the entire faculty of thought founded on language, according to the unrecognized predictions and derided merit of the miracle worker Samuel Heinicke,[45] but language is *also the center of reason's misunderstanding with itself*,[46] partly because of the *coincidence*[47] of the greatest and smallest concepts, of their vacuity and fullness in ideal propositions, partly because of the infinite advantage of figures of speech over figures of inference and conclusion, and much more of the same.

Sounds and *letters* are then pure forms a priori, in which nothing having to do with the sensation or concept of an object is found; they are the true, aesthetic elements of human knowledge and reason. The oldest language was music, and next to the palpable rhythm of the pulse and of the breath in the nostrils, it was the original bodily image of all *temporal measurements* and ratios. The oldest writing was *painting* and *drawing*, and therefore was occupied even so early with *spatial economy*, the delimiting and determining of space through figures.[48] From them through the exuberant constant influence of the two noblest senses, sight and hearing, the concepts of *space* and *time* have made themselves so universal and necessary in the whole sphere of the understanding, like light and air for the eye, ear, and voice, that space and time, if not *ideae innatae*,[49] seem to be at least matrices of all intuitive knowledge.

But *sensibility* and *understanding* spring as two stems of human knowledge from *One* common root, so that through the former objects are *given* and through the latter *thought*:[50] what is the purpose of such a violent, unjustified, arbitrary divorce of that which nature has joined together![51] Will not both branches wither and dry up through a dichotomy and split of their common root? Would not one single stem with two roots be an apter image of our knowledge, one root *above* in the air and one *below* in the earth? The first is exposed to our sensibility whereas the latter is invisible and must be thought by the *understanding*, which accords with the priority of the *thought* and the posteriority of the *given* or taken, as well as with the favorite inversion of pure reason in its theories.

Perhaps there is as yet a *chemical tree of Diana*[52] not only for the knowledge of sensibility and understanding but also for the explanation and enlargement of both domains and their boundaries. These have been made so dark, confused, and desolate by a pure reason, christened by antiphrasis,[53] and its metaphysics, drudging for the prevailing indifferentism (that ancient mother of chaos and night in all sciences of morals, religion, and law-giving!),[54] that the dew of a pure natural language[55] can be born only from the *dawn*[56] of the promised near regeneration and enlightenment.

Without, however, my waiting for the visit of a new Lucifer[57] rising from on high nor violating the fig tree of the *great goddess Diana!*[58] the evil snake[59] in the bosom of the common, popular language gives us the finest parable of the hypostatic union[60] of the sensible and intelligible natures, the mutual idiomatic exchange of their powers, the synthetic mysteries of both the forms a priori and a posteriori corresponding and contradicting themselves, along with the transubstantiation of subjective conditions and the subsumptions into objective predicates and attributes through the copula[61] of an authoritative or expletive word for cutting short dull whiles and filling out empty space in periodic galimatias[62] by thesis and antithesis.[63]—

O for the *action* of a Demosthenes and his triune energy of eloquence[64] or the mimic art said to be coming, without the panegyric tinkling of an angel's tongue![65] Then I would open the eyes of the reader that he might perhaps see—hosts of intuitions ascend to the firmament of pure understanding and hosts of concepts descend to the depths of the most perceptible sensibility, on a ladder which no sleeper dreams[66]—and the dance of the Mahanaim[67] or two hosts of reason[68]—the secret and maddening chronicle of their courtship and ravishing—and the whole theogony of all the giant and heroic forms of the Shulamite and muse,[69] in the mythology of light and darkness—to the play in forms of an old *Baubo with herself—inaudita specie solaminis*, as Saint Arnobius says,[70] and of a new *immaculate virgin*, who may not however be *Mother of God*, as Saint Anselm[71] considered her—

Words then have an *aesthetic* and *logical* faculty. As visible and audible objects they belong with their elements to the *sensibility* and *intuition*; however, by the spirit of their *institution* and *meaning*, they belong to the *understanding* and *concepts*. Consequently words are pure as well as empirical *intuitions* and therefore also pure and empirical *concepts*. *Empirical* because the sensation of vision or hearing is effected through them; *pure* inasmuch as their meaning is not determined by anything having to do with those sensations. Words as the undetermined objects of empirical intuitions are entitled, in the fundamental text of pure reason, aesthetic *appearances*;[72] therefore by the eternal harping on antithetical parallelism, words, as undetermined objects of empirical concepts, are entitled critical *appearances*, specters, nonwords or unwords, and become determinate objects for the understanding only through their institution and meaning in usage. This meaning and its determination arises, as the whole world knows,[73] from the combination of a word-sign, which is a priori arbitrary and indifferent and a posteriori necessary and indispensable, with the intuition of the word itself; through this reiterated bond by means of the word-sign as by means of the intuition itself, the concept is communicated, imprinted, and embodied in the understanding.

Now is it possible, *idealism* asks, on the one hand, to discover the concept from its mere intuition? Is it possible from the *matter* of the word "reason" [*Vernunft*], from its seven letters[74] or two syllables—is it possible from its *form* which determines the order of those letters and syllables—to draw out something of the *concept* of the word "reason"? Here the Critique answers with both scales even. In some languages there are indeed logogriphs,[75] *charades*,[76] and witty *rebuses* which can be constructed through an analysis and syllables of letters or of syllables in new forms. However, these are then new intuitions and appearances of words which correspond to the given word as little as do the different intuitions themselves.

Is it furthermore possible, *idealism* asks, on the other hand, to find the empirical intuition of a word from the understanding? Is it possible to find from the *concept* of reason [*Vernunft*] the matter of its name, that is, the seven letters or two syllables in German, or in any other language? Here one scale of the Critique indicates a decided *No!* But should it not be possible to derive from the concept the *form* of its empirical intuition in the word, by virtue of which form one of the two syllables stands a priori and the other a posteriori, or could it not be derived that the seven letters are intuited in a definite relation? Here the Homer of pure reason snores[77] as loud a Yes! as Jack and Jill at the altar, presumably because he has dreamed that the *universal character*[78] *of a philosophical language*, hitherto sought, is already found.

Now this last possibility of obtaining the form of an empirical intuition, without an object or sign of the intuition, from the pure and empty quality of our outward and inward sense[79] is the very Δός μοι ποῦ στῶ[80] and πρῶτον ψεῦδος,[81] the whole cornerstone of critical idealism and its tower and lodge of pure reason.[82] The given or taken materials belong to the categorical or idealist woods,[83] the peripatetic and academic[84] storerooms. Analysis is nothing more than the latest fashionable cut, and synthesis nothing more than the artful seam of a professional leather- or cloth-cutter. I have, for the sake of weak readers, explained what transcendental philosophy metagrobolizes,[85] by pointing to the sacrament of language, the letter of its elements, the spirit of its institution,[86] and I leave it to each one to unfold the clenched fist into an open hand.[87]—

But perhaps a similar idealism is the whole partition between Judaism and heathendom.[88] The Jew has the word and the signs; the heathen, reason and its wisdom[89]—(What followed was a μετάβασις εἰς ἄλλο γένος,[90] the finest of which has been transplanted into the little Golgotha.)[91]

NOTES

1. "There are tears for things—o how empty are things!" From Virgil, *Aeneid* 1.417, and Persius, *Satires* 1.1, respectively. The compound quotation is given in Hamann's brief, unpublished 1781 review of Kant's *Critique* (*Werke* 3.280) and in his letter to Herder of 26 January 1784 (*Briefe* 5.120). For the quotation from Persius, see the epigraph to *Socratic Memorabilia* (*Werke* 2.57).—Trans.

2. Hamann translates Hume's account of Berkeley's discovery freely. (From *A Treatise on Human Nature* 1.7.)—Trans.

3. See *A Treatise of Human Nature: Being an Attempt to Introduce the Experimental Method of Reasoning into Moral Subjects*, vol. 1: *Of the Understanding* (London, 1739), 38. To my knowledge, this first masterpiece of the famous David Hume has been translated into French but not, like his last, into German. Also, the translation of the sharp-sighted Berkeley's philosophical works has unfortunately come out badly. The first part appeared in Leipzig in 1781 and contained only the *Dialogues between Hylas and Philonous*, which is already in the *Eschenbach Collection of Idealists* (Rostock, 1756).

4. See the letter to Herder, 20–22 April 1782 (*Briefe* 4.376): "This much is certain that without Berkeley, there would have been no Hume, as without Hume, no Kant. It all comes down to tradition in the end, as all abstractions come down to sensory impressions."—Trans.

5. On the usage and language of the *sensus communis*, see the letters to Jacobi of 2 November 1783 (*Briefe* 5.95) and 1 December 1784 (*Briefe* 5.272).—Trans.

6. See, for example, the *Critique of Pure Reason* (A 20): "The pure form of sensible intuitions in general... must be found in the mind a priori." Translations of Kant's *Critique of Pure Reason* are taken from Norman Kemp Smith's version (London, 1950).—Trans.

7. Kant's *Critique* is divided into the Transcendental Doctrine of Elements and the Transcendental Doctrine of Method. The Doctrine of Elements provides the

materials for the "edifice" of pure reason and the Doctrine of Method provides the plan (A 707).—Trans.

8. A 6–10.—Trans.

9. Kant's *Prolegomena to Any Future Metaphysics* (AA 4.265): "If we wish to present knowledge as a science, we must first determine exactly its differentia.... The particular characteristic of a science may consist in a simple distinction of object, or of the sources of knowledge, or of the kind of knowledge."—Trans.

10. Perhaps the infinite or infinitesimal limits of differential calculus. See *Philological Ideas and Doubts* (*Werke* 3.51n.34) and *Prolegomena* (*Werke* 3.129).—Trans.

11. Kant distinguishes between "transcendent" and "transcendental." A 296: "The principles of pure understanding... allow only of empirical and not of transcendental employment, that is, employment extending beyond the limits of experience. A principle, on the other hand, which takes away these limits, or even commands us actually to transgress them, is called *transcendent.*"—Trans.

12. A xx: "Metaphysics... is the only one of all the sciences which dare promise that through a small but concentrated effort it will attain, and this in a short time, such completion as will leave no task to our successors."—Trans.

13. A xii: "Our age is, in especial degree, the age of criticism, and to criticism everything must submit. Religion through its sanctity, and law-giving through its majesty, may seek to exempt themselves from it. But they then awaken just suspicion, and cannot claim the sincere respect which reason accords only to that which has been able to sustain the test of free and open examination."—Trans.

14. Hamann may be alluding to the phrase "sottise de deux parts," which he takes from Voltaire's title "Sottise des deux parts" (1728), quotes in *Doubts and Ideas* (*Werke* 3.190) and *Golgotha and Scheblimini!* (*Werke* 3.319), and adapts in the letter to Kraus of 18 December 1784 (*Briefe* 5.290).—Trans.

15. Hamann attributes this phrase to Edward Young in the letter to Herder of 8 December 1783 (*Briefe* 5.108) and the letter to Scheffner of 1 February 1785 (*Briefe* 5.360). Also quoted in the letter to Jacobi, 2 November 1783 (*Briefe* 5.95) and in *Crusades of the Philologist* (*Werke* 2.129). Young's *Night Thoughts* 2.469: "Speech, Thought's Canal! Speech, Thought's Criterion too!"—Trans.

16. *Prolegomena to Any Future Metaphysics* (AA 4.278) states that credentials of pure reason consist only in its answer to the question "How is synthetic knowledge a priori possible?"—Trans.

17. For pure reason as "fantasy and idol," see the letter to Herder of 14 April 1785 (*Briefe* 5.418). On philosophical idolatry, see the *New Apology of the Letter h* (*Werke* 3:106–107). For abstractions as idols, Hamann quotes Bacon in *Aesthetica in Nuce* (*Werke* 2.207n.40). Recall also Bacon's discussion of the idols that beset men's minds in the *Novum Organon.*—Trans.

18. God; see the letter to Jacobi of 2–22 November 1783 (*Briefe* 5.94–95) and Kant's chapter "The Ideal of Pure Reason."—Trans.

19. Simonides; see the letter to Kant at the end of December 1759 (*Briefe* 1.452) and the letter to Jacobi of 2 November 1783 (*Briefe* 5.94). Cicero records that after Hiero asked Simonides about the being and nature of god, Simonides continually delayed giving an answer because, he said, "the longer I deliberate, the more obscure the question seems to me." *De natura deorum*, 1.22.—Trans.

20. By Hamann's metaschematism, the Sophists are identified with eighteenth-century enlighteners.—TRANS.

21. Newton was warder and then master of the Mint; Hamann attributes this ambition to Kant in the *Socratic Memorabilia* (*Werke* 3.146). On philosophers as fiscal charlatans, see *Hierophantic Letters* (*Werke* 3.146). On language and money, see *Crusades of the Philologist* (*Werke* 2.129).—TRANS.

22. "Mene, mene, tekel" is the writing on the wall that Daniel interprets for Belshazzar, in Dan. 5. "Tekel" means "Thou art weighed in the balances, and art found wanting" (Dan. 5:27). Jesus overthrows the tables of the money changers, in the temple in Mark 11:15.—TRANS.

23. Contrast Kant's "receptivity for impressions" and "spontaneity of concepts," in both A 50 and A 68.—TRANS.

24. Kant's dogmatism, skepticism, and criticism, A viii and A ix.—TRANS.

25. Matt. 13:33: "Another parable spake he [Jesus] unto them; The kingdom of heaven is like unto leaven, which a woman took, and hid in three measures of meal, till the whole was leavened." Also Luke 13:21.

1 Cor. 5:7 and 8: "Purge out therefore the old leaven, that ye may be a new lump. . . . Therefore let us keep the feast, not with old leaven."

See the letter to Jacobi of 27 April–2 May 1787 (*Briefe* 7.166).—TRANS.

26. Meteors, that is, any atmospheric phenomena or, more specifically, any luminous atmospheric phenomena, are common in Hamann. See the "vain phantom or meteor of reason and virtue" in *Supplement to the Memorabilia* (*Werke* 3.117) and also *A Flying Letter* (*Werke* 3.402).—TRANS.

27. Rom. 15:18–19: "For I will not dare to speak of any of those things which Christ hath not wrought by me, to make the Gentiles obedient, by word and deed, through mighty signs and wonders, by the power of the Spirit of God."—TRANS.

28. Besides "quicksilvery," perhaps a reference to the *Teutscher Merkur*. See the letter to Herder of 17–18 November 1782 (*Briefe* 4.458).—TRANS.

29. Compare *A Flying Letter* (*Werke* 3.401), "these three fingers are dried up, more like their goose quill than a human hand." Here perhaps a reference to Kant. Hamann refers to the syllogism of the *Critique* in his 1781 review (*Werke* 3.278). Kant discusses the three kinds of dialectical syllogisms at A 339–340. There are three parts of a syllogism and three fingers necessary to write.—TRANS.

30. "Metaphysics" is the name applied at least from the first century C.E. to Aristotle's work on first philosophy. It derives from the older "the works after [Hamann has 'behind'] the Physics." The *Oxford English Dictionary* describes the ambiguity of the coinage: "This title doubtless originally referred (as some of the early commentaries state) to the position which the books so designated occupied in the received arrangement of Aristotle's writings. . . . It was, however, from an early period used as a name for the branch of study treated in these books, and hence came to be misinterpreted as meaning 'the science of things transcending what is physical or natural.' This misinterpretation is found, though rarely, in Greek writers, notwithstanding the fact that *μετά* does not admit of any such sense as 'beyond' or 'transcending.' In scholastic Latin writers the error was general (being helped, perhaps, by the known equivalence of the prefixes *meta-* and *trans-* in various compounds)."—TRANS.

31. A 268: "Let me call the place which we assign to a concept, either in sensibility or in pure understanding, its *transcendental location.* Thus the decision as to the place which belongs to every concept according to difference in the use to which it is put, and the directions for determining this place for all concepts according to rules, is a *transcendental topic.*"—TRANS.

32. "The latter first"; glossed as "ass backwards" [ä-ling zu Werk geht] in the 1781 review (*Werke* 3.288). See the letter to Herder, 19 May 1781 (*Briefe* 4.292–293). Kant has *ὕστερον πρότερον* (perversa ratio) at A 692. Aristotle discusses it in the *Prior Analytics* 2.16.—TRANS.

33. "Court, school, professions, closed guilds, troops, and sects have their own dictionaries," from *Crusades of the Philologist* (*Werke* 2.172). For metaphysics as a misuse of language, see the letter to Herder of 1 December 1784 (*Briefe* 5.272).—TRANS.

34. E.g., A 46: "the propositions of geometry are synthetic *a priori,* and are known with apodictic certainty."—TRANS.

35. Hieroglyphs of simple pictures (not in symbolic characters). In *Aesthetica in Nuce* (*Werke* 2.199), Hamann alludes to Johann Georg Wachter's theory (in *Naturae & Scripturae Concordia,* 1752) of the three stages in the development of language: curiological, symbolic or hieroglyphic, and characteristic.—TRANS.

36. Euclid's *Elements* begins, "A point is that which has no part."—TRANS.

37. A 250: "All our representations are, it is true, referred by the understanding to some object; and since appearances are nothing but representations, the understanding refers them to a *something,* as the object of sensible intuition. But this something, thus conceived [*in so fern*], is only the transcendental object; and by that is meant a something = X, of which we know, and with the present constitution of our understanding can know, nothing whatsoever."—TRANS.

38. Claude-Adrien Helvétius (1715–1771). *De l'homme* (1773), 1.2.19: "When one attaches precise ideas to each expression, the scholastic who has so often confounded the world will be nothing but an impotent magician. The talisman which was the source of his power will be broken. Then all those fools who, under the name of metaphysician, have wandered such a long time in the land of chimeras and who in the windy beyond cross in every sense the depths of the infinite will no longer say that they see what they do not see and that they know what they do not know." See the note to the 1781 review of Kant (*Werke* 3.277).—TRANS.

39. "Logical beings": a term originally from scholastic philosophy designating a being that can exist only as an object of thought but that lacks potency for real existence. Kant defines the *ens rationis* as an "empty concept without object" (A 292).—TRANS.

40. See the letter to Jacobi of 27–29 April 1787 (*Briefe* 7.172): "A universal word is an empty sack."—TRANS.

41. Or possibly "rubbish heap"; see *Werke* 6.231.—TRANS.

42. A xvii: "For the chief question is always simply this:—what and how much can the understanding and reason know apart from experience? not:—how is the faculty of thought itself possible?"—TRANS.

43. Probably a reference to Kant's transcendental deduction.—TRANS.

44. Kant has twelve categories of logical functions in judgment [A 80]. Nadler

(*Werke* 6.354) believes Hamann has in mind the seven tables of Kant's *Critique*: A 70, 80, 161, 292, 344, 404, 415.—TRANS.

45. Samuel Heinicke (1727–1790) founded the first school for the deaf and dumb in Germany, in 1778. In his 1780 *Über die Denkart der Taubstummen*, he argued that the uninstructed deaf-mute thinks in gestures and cannot reason abstractly. This view formed the basis for his criticism of previous methods of education and gave rise to the quarrel between Heinicke and the Abbé de l'Epée.—TRANS.

46. For Kant, it is the errors in the nonempirical deployment of reason that set reason "at variance with itself" [A xii].—TRANS.

47. In a letter to Herder of 17 November 1782 (*Briefe* 4.462), Hamann writes, "Giordano Bruno's principium coincidentiae oppositorum is worth more in my view than all of Kant's Critique." (Hamann attributes this principle to Bruno rather than to Nicholas of Cusa.) See also the letter to Herder of 27 April 1781 (*Briefe* 4.287) and *New Apology of the Letter h* (*Werke* 2.107). He elsewhere uses the word in a broader sense (*Konxompax*, *Werke* 3.224).—TRANS.

48. On the priority of painting and song, see *Aesthetica in Nuce* (*Werke* 2.197).—TRANS.

49. On innate ideas, see the letter to Herder of 10 May 1781 (*Briefe* 4.293–294): "[Kant] indeed deserves the title of a Prussian Hume. I think that his whole transcendental theology comes down to an ideal of entity.... Here language and technology are really the deipara [mother of God] of pure scholastic reason, and a new leap from Locke's tabula rasa to formas and matrices innatas." See also the 1781 review (*Werke* 3.278): "Are not ideae matrices and ideae innatae children of one spirit?" On the concept of matrices, important for Jakob Boehme and Paracelsus, see *Historisches Wörterbuch der Philosophie* (1980), 5.940. The concept was also important for German theosophists (such as Johann Georg Gichtel; see *Konxompax*, *Werke* 3.224) and Pietists.—TRANS.

50. A 15: "there are two stems of human knowledge, namely, *sensibility* and *understanding*, which perhaps spring from a common, but to us unknown, root. Through the former, objects are given to us; through the latter, they are thought."—TRANS.

51. Matt. 19:6: "What therefore God has joined together, let no man put asunder." On philosophy's dividing what nature has joined together, see *Philological Ideas and Doubts* (*Werke* 3.40), the 1781 review (*Werke* 3.278), and *Golgotha and Scheblimini!* (*Werke* 3.300).—TRANS.

52. An amalgam resembling a tree, produced by mercury from a solution of silver nitrate. In his 1784 *Reflections of the Philosophy on the History of Mankind*, Herder is impressed with the tree of Diana and by the mineral imitation of vegetable form. Goethe writes to Jacobi on 11 January 1785 that he has a tree of Diana and other metallic vegetation in his room.

G. W. F. Hegel believes Hamann's tree of Diana refers to developed knowledge and science (*Werke in zwanzig Bänden* 11.328). We may also be meant to recall the tree of knowledge in paradise. See the letter to Jacobi of 21 April–2 May 1787 (*Briefe* 7.172): "[Reason] is the tree of knowledge of good and evil."—TRANS.

53. That is, its name is the opposite of its real meaning.—TRANS.

54. A x: "And now, after all methods, so it is believed, have been tried and found wanting, the prevailing mood is that of weariness and complete *indifferentism*—

the mother of chaos and night in all sciences, but happily in this case the source, or at least the prelude, of their approaching reform and restoration. For it at least puts an end to that ill-applied industry which has rendered them thus dark, confused and unserviceable" (translation slightly revised).—TRANS.

55. On natural language (analogous to natural religion) as an *ens rationis*, see the letter to Herder of 11–25 June 1780 (*Briefe* 4.195).—TRANS.

56. Alludes to Ps. 110:3 in Luther's translation.—TRANS.

57. Lucifer, as "bringer of light," is an enlightener.—TRANS.

58. The "all-enlightening Luna-Diana" is associated with the *Berlinische Monatsscrift* in *A Flying Letter* (*Werke* 3.359). For sacral associations of the fig tree in classical antiquity, see the *Real-Encyclopädie der Classischen Altertumswissenschaft* 6.2148–2149. We may be meant to recall the fig tree whose leaves clothed Adam and Eve after they ate the fruit of the tree of knowledge.—TRANS.

59. Perhaps a double reference, both to the serpent of Gen. 3 and the snake of Aesop's fable (*Aesopica*, ed. Ben Edwin Perry, "Fabulae Graecae," 51). In the fable, a farmer's son warms a frozen snake on his breast. The snake recovers, then bites and kills him. (Nadler suggests the Aesopian allusion at *Werke* 6.34.) See too the "serpent deception of language" in *Golgotha and Scheblimini!* (*Werke* 3.298).—TRANS.

60. In theology, the "hypostatic union" can refer to the union of the divine and human natures of Christ.—TRANS.

61. Nadler (*Werke* 6.84) believes that the passage refers to the creation of the word *metaphysics*. By the linking together of "meta" and "physics" a diversion was created for passing the time and filling out space (hence "expletive").—TRANS.

62. Galimatia is confused or nonsensical talk, words placed together without order.—TRANS.

63. Kant's antinomies.—TRANS.

64. By "action," Hamann means Latin *actio* or Greek ὑπόκρισις: the orator's delivery, elocution. See *Crusades of the Philologist* (*Werke* 2.116): "Action [ὑπόκρισις], Demosthenes said, is the soul of eloquence." See also the letter to Scheffner of 11 February 1785 (*Briefe* 5.359): "What Demosthenes calls actio, and [Johann Jakob] Engel the mimic art, and [Charles] Batteux imitation of beautiful nature is for me language—the organon and criterion of reason, as Young says." "Energy" refers to the force or vigor of expression and derives from the traditional confusion of ἐνέργεια and ἐνάργεια. Hamann has "enargy and energy" in *A Flying Letter* (*Werke* 3.364, 365).

"Triune" because of Demosthenes' triple repetition of a key word or phrase. See the letter to Johann Michael Hamann (*Briefe* 5.88) and also the letter to Herder, 6–8 August 1784 (*Briefe* 5.177): "Even if I were as eloquent as Demosthenes, I would not need to do more than repeat three times a single phrase: reason is language, λόγος."—TRANS.

65. The mimic art is a reference to Johann Jakob Engel (1741–1802), whose 1785 *Ideen zu einer Mimik* described appropriate gestures and expressions for actors on stage. "Said to be coming" (*der noch kommen soll*) is Hamann's usual expression for the advent of a queen (*Golgotha and Scheblimini! Werke* 3.315, referring to Kant's metaphysics of nature), a paraclete (*Golgotha and Scheblimini! Werke* 3.317—the "adventitious instructor" at the end of Hume's *Dialogues Concerning Natural Religion*),

or prophet (letter to Herder, 10 May 1781, *Briefe* 4.294, also with reference to the adventitious instructor).

"Panegyric" because of Engel's 1781 panegyric to Frederick II.

Engel in German means "angel"; hence the allusion to 1 Cor. 13:1: "Though I speak with the tongues of men and of angels, and have not charity, I am become as sounding brass, or a tinkling cymbal."—TRANS.

66. Unlike Jacob's ladder, in Gen. 28:12: "And he dreamed, and behold a ladder set up on the earth, and the top of it reached to heaven: and behold the angels of God ascending and descending on it."—TRANS.

67. Mahanaim is taken to mean "two camps" or "two hosts." Gen. 32:1, 2: "And Jacob went on his way, and the angels of God met him. And when Jacob saw them, he said, This is God's host: and he called the name of that place Mahanaim." Song of Sol. 6:13: "Return, return, O Shulamite; return, return, that we may look upon thee. What will ye see in the Shulamite? As it were the company of two armies." (Luther has "the dance of the Mahanaim.")

See also the letter to Bucholtz of 9 March 1785 (*Briefe* 5.395).—TRANS.

68. Hamann is parodying what he believes to be the mysticism of Kant's *Critique*, a parody that culminates in a view of Kant's work as a masturbating Baubo and as an immaculate virgin who will not conceive. The two hosts of reason (i.e., sensibility and the understanding) are described as distinct but interdependent in A 51.—TRANS.

69. The Shulamite is the beloved of the Song of Solomon. Hamann refers to Greek (muse) and Hebrew (Shulamite) sources of inspiration.—TRANS.

70. Arnobius, in *Adversus nationes* 5.25, recounts the story of Ceres, who after the abduction of her daughter wanders disconsolately until she reaches Eleusis, where the dwarf Baubo does what she can to comfort the goddess. Unsuccessful, Baubo changes tactics and tells crude jokes. She then exposes her genitals, causing Ceres to laugh and providing an "unheard of kind of solace" for the goddess. (Arnobius has "inauditi specie solaminis.") Baubo also appears in *A Sibyl on Marriage* (*Werke* 3.201).—TRANS.

71. Presumably a reference to Anselm's argument (in "The Virgin Conception and Original Sin") that the Virgin need not have been immaculately conceived.—TRANS.

72. A 20: "The undetermined object of an empirical intuition is entitled *appearance*."—TRANS.

73. C. M. Wieland's phrase, from *Der Teutsche Merkur*, August 1776, 3.132. (Identified by Nadler, *Werke* 6.406.) Also quoted in *Aprons of Fig-Leaves* (*Werke* 3.211).—TRANS.

74. Hamann refers to the seven different letters of the word *Vernunft*.—TRANS.

75. *Oxford English Dictionary*: "A kind of enigma in which a certain word, and other words that can be formed out of all or any of its letters, are to be guessed from synonyms introduced into a set of verses. Occasionally used for: Any anagram or puzzle involving anagrams."—TRANS.

76. Only in more recent times have charades been dramatically represented and performed. Previously each syllable of the word to be guessed was obliquely described.—TRANS.

77. Horace's *Ars Poetica* 359: "I resent whenever Homer dozes off; however it is allowable that sleep creeps up on a long work." Hamann describes the rational man as a dreamer who snores, sleepwalks, and argues until an authoritative word awakens him, in the letter to Lindner, 16–20 July 1759 (*Briefe* 1.369–370).—TRANS.

78. That is, *character universalis*: Zedler's *Großes vollständiges Universallexicon* (1733) refers to the attempt to invent a writing whose characters would be immediately intelligible to everyone without interpretation. Recall too Leibniz's *characteristica universalis.*—TRANS.

79. A 22. In Kant, by the outer sense we represent objects as outside us in space. By the inner sense, the mind intuits itself in time.—TRANS.

80. "Give me a place to stand"; from Archimedes' claim that with a place to stand outside of the world, he would move the world. See the letter to Jacobi of 14 November 1784 (*Briefe* 5.266).—TRANS.

81. The first falsehood; that is, the initial false premise invalidating the later deductions. Frequent in Hamann, the term derives from Aristotle's *Prior Analytics* 2.18. See the letter to Herder of 8 December 1783 (*Briefe* 5.107).—TRANS.

82. On the edifice of pure reason, see A 707.—TRANS.

83. Wood, Greek ὕλη and Latin *silva,* refers to raw material of any kind, matter. —TRANS.

84. That is, Aristotelian and Platonic.—TRANS.

85. Coined by Rabelais (*Gargantua and Pantagruel* 1.19) and glossed by an early English translator of Rabelais as "to dunce upon, to puzzle, or (too much) beate the braines about." The word also appears in *Lettre perdue* (*Werke* 2.301) and *Knight of the Rose-Cross* (*Werke* 3.32).—TRANS.

86. The language alludes to the sacraments instituted by Christ: baptism and Holy Communion. Their institution (in the words spoken by Christ) and their elements (water, bread and wine) form a unity. In the *Large Catechism* (1529), Luther quotes Augustine for both sacraments: "accedat verbum ad elementum et fit sacramentum, which means that when the Word is joined to the element, or earthly constituent, the result is a sacrament, that is, a holy, divine thing and sign" (*Weimar Ausgabe* 30.1.214) and "Let the Word be joined to the element, and it becomes a sacrament.... The Word must make the element a sacrament, otherwise it remains a mere element" (*Weimar Ausgabe* 30.1.223). "Element" forms a complex pun, invoking the letters of the alphabet and the materials of a sacrament, in contrast to the elements of mathematics or of Kant's *Critique,* to which the Word has not been joined.—TRANS.

87. Cicero's *Orator* 32.113: "debate and dispute are the function of the logicians; the orator's function is to speak ornately. Zeno, the founder of the Stoic school, used to give an object lesson of the difference between the two arts; clenching his fist he said logic was like that; relaxing and extending his hand, he said eloquence was like an open palm" (trans. H. M. Hubbell).—TRANS.

88. See J. A. Starck's *Freymüthige Betrachtungen über das Christentum* (1780) 59: "As there is only one God, who is the Creator, Father, and Ruler of the entire world; as we are all equally children, who all descend from the One, have equally valid claims to God, and are destined for a single end; so the partition between Jews and heathens, all divisions, and all particularism had to be lifted as soon as the true God was

proclaimed." Identified by Oswald Bayer in *Hamann, Kant, Herder*, ed. Bernhard Gajek, (New York, 1987), 13–14.—TRANS.

89. The immediate reference is to Mendelssohn's *Jerusalem* (1783) and Kant's *Critique*. Hamann refers elsewhere to Kant as a Greek; recall above, "the Homer of pure reason."

For Hamann's treatment of Jews and Greeks, recall his interpretation of Hume's *Dialogues* (see the letter to Herder, 10 May 1781, *Briefe* 4.294: "[Hume's] Dialogues end with the Jewish and Platonic hope of a prophet still to come"), and see *Golgotha und Scheblimini!* annotated by Lothar Schreiner (1956), 155–158.—TRANS.

90. A change into another form. See the letter to Jacobi, 14–15 November 1784 (*Briefe* 5.267). Aristotle, *On the Heavens* 268b1, uses the phrase to indicate a leap from one level to another (lines to surfaces to bodies). Kant, A 459, uses the phrase in apposition to *Absprung*, a leap of logic. In rhetoric, *μετάβασις* refers to a transition. Nadler (*Werke* 6.154) reads *γένος* as race. On his reading, the same partition of critical idealism (between word and reason) divides Judaism (word) and paganism (reason). Therefore a transition to a new (theme) race was necessary. The finest of the new race [Christ, the only-begotten, *μονογενής*] was transplanted into Golgotha.—TRANS.

91. The last paragraph is not in Rink, and the last parenthesis is omitted in the version of the *Metacritique* in the letter to Herder (15 September 1784). However, just after the *Metacritique* in the letter to Herder, Hamann writes (*Briefe* 5.217): "What followed was a *μετάβασις εἰς ἄλλο γένος*, for the dear Jerusalem lay next to the Critique in my head, and one idea spoiled the other. So I transplanted the finest into the little Golgotha." Golgotha refers to *Golgotha and Scheblimini!* (1784), Hamann's response to Mendelssohn's *Jerusalem*.—TRANS.

On Enlightenment: Is It and Could It Be Dangerous to the State, to Religion, or Dangerous in General? A Word to Be Heeded by Princes, Statesmen, and Clergy

Andreas Riem

Translated by Jane Kneller

Andreas Riem (1749–1807) came to Berlin in 1782 after studies in theology to serve as pastor at the Friedrichshospital. He published widely on religious and political questions and, with Gottlob Nathanael Fischer, was co-editor of the Berlinisches Journal der Aufklärung, *which appeared in eight volumes between 1788 and 1790. His anonymous pamphlet,* Über Aufklärung, *published early in 1788, had an enormous impact. It appeared in four editions within a few weeks' time and was eventually supplemented by a second volume that elaborated on points raised in the initial pamphlet. After Riem's authorship became known, he was forced to resign his position at the Friedrichshospital, stating that he could not abide by the provisions of Woellner's Religion Edict because they would force him to teach doctrines that—since they contradicted what could be known on the basis of pure reason—were contrary to his own convictions. He maintained his appointment as secretary to the Berlin Academy of Arts and Mechanical Sciences until 1793 when he was exiled from Prussia because of his political writings. He settled in Homburg, where he lived under the name "Dr. Freund," and traveled extensively in Germany, Holland, England, and France. He published eight volumes of reflections on his travels—with special attention to political questions—between 1795 and 1801.*

INTRODUCTION

I have read so much about this important issue and have heard even more; but I freely confess that I do not completely approve of either the writings

First published in Berlin in 1788 as an anonymous pamphlet entitled Über Aufklärung. Ob sie dem Staate—der Religion—oder überhaupt gefährlich sei und sein könne? Ein Wort zur Beherzigung für Regenten, Staatsmänner und Priester.

or the arguments. Let critics and the public judge to what extent my own deserve approval.

Most of those who wrote about enlightenment have not determined, or have incorrectly determined, the concepts this word comprises. What conclusions were to be expected, given that these concepts were not established? And how manifold and various must be the resulting judgments when everyone could substitute his own concepts.

And still nothing is so clear and simple as the idea presented in the mere word *enlightenment.* "It is nothing more than the effort of the human spirit to bring to light, according to principles of a pure doctrine of reason and for the promotion of utility, all the objects of the world of ideas, all human opinions and their consequences, and everything that has influence on humanity." Is it still necessary even for the most mediocre intelligence to ask whether these efforts are beneficial or damaging? Perhaps they would be harmful for someone steeped in prejudice, and who, in the habit of seeing things askew, loves these prejudices dearly and possesses an inordinate abundance of obstinacy that prevents him from giving them up.

Many people blindfold the truth, so that it cannot see their follies. More people, whose spirits are incapable of any noble greatness, wish to banish it from their fellow humans, in order to have no judge of their follies and no critic of their nonsense. And most people have a genuine interest in fostering prejudices, because there is no field of speculation more productive for important financial operations than the stupidity of a class of men which cunning and deceit is ready to bleed dry. I flatter no man, least of all the foolish. Stupid approval is insufferable to me. Just as little do I sacrifice the truth to falsehood for the sake of temporal reward. I can err, but I will guard against doing so; and if this common lot of humanity should fall to me, then I have learned through enlightenment that to allow oneself to be corrected is honorable. I believe, with Solomon, that truth can demand to be proclaimed on every corner, and that stifling it is more damaging than Jesuitism. Proud frivolity may always clothe the truth in hieroglyphs like the Egyptian priests; I prefer its naked beauty to the baroque ornamentation of prejudice's fashion. The reader can reflect on what I am about to say and decide if I am right.

1. ENLIGHTENMENT IS A REQUIREMENT OF HUMAN UNDERSTANDING

If you found yourself in the middle of a barbarous tribe of Negroes on the coast of Africa and saw how they wildly dishonored human rights; if you saw a Xinga[1] dance around the sacrificial victims of a bloodthirsty religion, crushing their skulls with a battle-ax so that the brains sprayed around, and drinking the blood of these unfortunates with fiery thirst—compassionate European!—would you not wish that Xinga might be more enlightened?

When an English barbarian hangs a black slave up in an iron cage in the deepest forest, so that for days birds of prey eat him alive piece by piece, turning his torment into infernal torture—would it not be better for humanity if Carolina, where this occurred, were more enlightened and would learn to honor the rights of humanity?

When the Iroquois roast the Hurons on a spit over a slow fire, the women slowly cutting strips of flesh lengthwise from the body, pulling the nails from the hands and feet in slow torture, and, after having tormented him for days, blame themselves for letting him succumb to their tortures too soon—what better could one wish for this wild barbaric people than enlightenment?

The child on its mother's breast feels the impulse toward it. It looks out at strange objects and its restless spirit tirelessly pursues its efforts toward instruction and truth, until death gives its noble strivings an end. If there can be any duty in the world to stifle or hinder the impulses of the soul toward proper knowledge, then, you enemies of truth, why not raise your children like animals? Yes, you say, but one must allow this impulse to develop only to a certain degree, mix in prejudice instead of truth, and block it where wisdom could be harmful. But who of you has ever demonstrated that prejudice, this shameful synonym of falsehood, is more useful than enlightenment, which is the result of truth? Who has shown the overly wise fools the boundaries of how far they must go to fill the understanding with errors and spoil it for truth? And who can prove the slander which claims that truth can be harmful? Why did God share such a rich measure of understanding if it causes unhappiness? Why give it at all, if one is not permitted to use all of it?

From the wild, uncultured man who locks up the powers of his spirit inside himself and who, tyrannized by the prejudice of eternal rituals, does not develop them, to the European who in dumb obstinacy persists in his prejudices—have not all the smarter, more enlightened peoples and human beings reached a higher level than they, a level envied by short-sightedness and prejudice? If your understanding remains within the borders of custom you will become as laughable to the more enlightened people as the miserable Chinese, who gaze astonished at the works of enlightenment, without assimilating them into their arts and sciences, and who for thousands of years had astronomical calculations which they needed the insights of other peoples to correct, but who have not improved them, because they inherited them from their forefathers.

Have not all arts and sciences had their lamentable epochs, in which even philosophy was nonsense? The Sorbonne was in an uproar and ferment in the days when the entire scholarly community of Paris divided over Aristotle, when Galileo dared to say that the earth was round. What if, in those days, prejudice in the service of stupidity had triumphed over enlightened reason? What would have become of philosophy and natural science? If France had had no Richelieus, no Colberts, if Europe had had no incomparable Frederick, what would European civics and prosperity be now?[2] When our immortal king, this king of all kings, accumulated treasure, the short-sighted cried out about greed. However, when he carried on his magnificent wars without burdening his own land with new taxes while Austria and France strained their nations to the maximum and weighted them with monstrous debts whose interest alone cost millions, repaid by their subjects' sweat, then prejudice was silent and all of Europe followed the rules of his statecraft and thrift.

Should religion alone be excluded from the great privileges of enlightenment? That is of course what monastic stupidity maintained, during Luther's time as well as the time of the abominable Athanasius and of the persecutors of heretics from the Dominican order.[3] And this principle of the most miserable priestly stupidity is supposed to be protected in my time among Protestants? If enlightenment is not necessary, then you Protestants, why not deliver yourselves into the nets of secretive Jesuitism and return to the mother church out of which enlightenment led you? Or, you priests who struggle for prejudices and against enlightenment, name me the man from your midst who would have completely cleansed religion from the nonsense that foolishness, obstinacy, and the miserable opinions of the Roman court had woven into it. Is it Luther or Calvin? Or what is the name of the great mortal who grasped the fullness of all truth, who separated the kernel from the hull and impressed upon religion the stamp of infallible truth? If religion does not need it, why do your theologians scuffle, why do your exegetes battle; why does your De Marees cry out as if human understanding held a knife to the throat of religion?[4] Why is it that unity is everywhere more simple and nowhere more difficult to bring about than among you? If you value understanding, why do you brand its friends with the name of guardians of Zion, a name before which your orthodox used to turn their eyes and bow their heads to the earth? When an unclean spirit arises from an intolerant idol, why must it immediately become a superintendent, distressing the world and harassing the realm of pure understanding with its nonsense?

"Yes," you respond, "but someone must guard the purity of doctrine, and who is better suited to do that than a servant of its views?" So your doctrine is pure, and in order to remain so it must oppose the principles of pure reason? It is true, and must protect prejudices? Perfect, and must avoid the light of judgment? A strange philosophy, that not even Duns Scotus could have concocted so perversely! Religion is pure, true, and perfect, but the understanding may never dare to test and judge this! Mohammed proved the truth of his religion on the same grounds; so did Moses. A fool in Berlin, whose name is not worth mentioning, proved the truth of his nonsense in the same way.[5] So, too, Rosenberg proved his worthiness as Messiah.[6] Enthusiasts of all periods forbid the free use of the understanding because they must fear it. You men with the zeal of Elijah, why do you insult a good religion such as Christianity with such absurd demands?

You will say further "But don't the enlighteners go too far, and what will become of religion in the end?" Where you are right, I grant it. Your complaints are in part justified, in part, however, not. There are false enlighteners, hotheads who pass their notions off as philosophy, and their mistakes as truth. Just like you, and just as intolerantly, they want to set their opinions—which usually begin where they should stop—on the throne in order to reign over those of their fellow men. They destroy systems before they have built better ones. They are brilliant meteors who shine for a moment only to be forever extinguished in darkness. But do you not go too far in generalizing what is true only of *individual cases*, in taking the field against *enlightenment* in general when you should fight the mistakes that individual powerful geniuses [*Kraftgenies*] have promulgated? A man without subtle knowledge of human nature, who thinks himself to be an enlightener but who is not supported by reason, whose teachings betray the stamp of an unpracticed understanding, does not deserve the name "enlightener."

You will not lose the religion of your fathers; don't worry about that. Pure reason does not undermine religion, but rather its aberrations. You will lose prejudices and retain religion. The closer you bring religion to the light of reason, the more securely and durably it will be established for the future. Religion will not have to fear any attack by the understanding because the understanding approves of it, and if the understanding is its support, religion will become necessary and holy to the human race. However, if you oppose reason, a wiser posterity by virtue of its gradual progress which you, with all your usurpatory power, are unable to hinder, will look back on your names with the contempt with which they brand the names of Torquemada, Emser, and all the priests who once played the role you do.[7]

Was enlightenment necessary, when universal stupidity lay upon Europe, when its people were barbarians and its kings were executioners? When the fathers of the fatherland roasted their children to a delicious aroma for the idol of the papacy, the orthodoxy of the Roman court, the devil of superstition and prejudice? When crusades were undertaken against provinces and kingdoms of another faith? When royal envoys in Rome received blows of penance in the name of their kings? When the head of the Roman Empire begged forgiveness in bare feet in the snow at Hildebrand's window?[8] Or was enlightenment not necessary? Oh you kings of the earth—who ally yourselves with priests and associate with the intolerance of unworthy men, who side with intolerance against understanding and enlightenment, which compassionately removed the shameful shackles of priestly despotism from the feet of your ancestors—you have enlightenment to thank for your greatness, the understanding to thank for your security and the purified principles that are the pillars of your throne. What was it but enlightenment that made you into real rulers? It was enlightenment that wrested the anathemas from the hand of the holy sinner in Rome so that they couldn't reach you. It was enlightenment that fought fearlessly for the security of your lives and your honor, which had been undermined by religious prejudices that freed peoples from the oath of loyalty they had sworn to you. It protected you from your own children, whom false religious zeal had turned into your persecutors. It burned the priest defiant in his garb of holiness, who as your subject pushed his way to your throne, raised the disloyal right against you, and, in the midst of your palaces and heroes, cursed you; who robbed your subjects of an honorable burial, of the practice of religion and of everything by virtue of which the state's happiness flourishes. Why do you want to persecute your benefactor? Why do you want to be forced by the obstinacy of your father confessors or insipid advisers into a constraint on your own conscience that you put on more easily than strip off? Why do you who are born to rule want to be slaves to spiritual scandalmongers, who certainly do not seek your welfare, but rather seek their hieratic pride through all sorts of the most cunning deceptions. Go on and believe, in spite of it all, that forgiveness of sins lies within the power of a priest; but then renounce also the privilege of noble freedom: to be accountable only to God and to the reckoning of your conscience! Be slaves on the throne, wear the chains of superstition and prejudice; but thereby renounce forever the respect of the noble men of your nation and of posterity. The future does not flatter sovereigns. Thus it justly condemned Charles IX as an assassin of his subjects.[9] Thus posterity wisely judges Louis the persecutor whom some have called "the Great"[10]—and speaks of his conversions by dragoons, gallows and galleys, as the bloodthirsty man deserves. Weak sovereigns shine only in the circle of their flatterers. When the hand of death snatches the diadem from their head, posterity speaks their name with contempt. Philip II and the accomplice to his intolerance, a devil in the form of a duke from Alba, slaughter hundreds of thousands.[11] What else are they doing but engraving the stamp with which posterity brands their memory and laying the foundation for their eternal shame, as long as history remembers their names? Happy the country that has a king who loves religion but persecutes no one who is a good citizen of the state, who allows his court preachers to hold their own opinions and also protects those who think differently from them, who loves enlightenment and does not hamper it, who would rather rule over reasonable people than over stupid blockheads, who are often more dangerous than rapacious animals. Happy is the land that has enlightenment to thank for its Joseph II, and happy every kingdom that believes it is indebted to enlightenment for the good sovereigns, just laws, noble actions, and all good fortunes that it produces.

Human understanding also needs enlightenment. Every development of its powers, every correction of its ideas, every refinement of its knowledge, and every perfection of its abilities is enlightenment. Without enlightenment there are no corrected principles of human thought, no truth in sensations, no correctness in judgment, no improvement in speculation, and no perfection of the principles of philosophy. It has worked wonders in the realm of nature and in the realm of wisdom. Because of enlightenment we can calmly listen to the thunder roll. Indeed, it has shown us how to harness lightning. Through it the great spectacles of nature received a majesty that without it, in the hands of superstition, were tools of divine vengeance. It showed men the means to navigate, safely and securely, in the most harrowing ocean storm through waves tamed by their inventions. It taught us how to increase the fruitfulness of the earth and showed the farmer how to maintain himself more easily. It encountered resistance in prejudices, but conquered them—only gradually, indeed, but all the more powerfully.

2. HOW FAR DOES ENLIGHTENMENT EXTEND? DOES IT HAVE LIMITS OR NOT?

This question is important. The verdict on whether enlightenment is useful or damaging, and whether enlightenment or deception is better, depends on its consideration.

If enlightenment consists in the justification of concepts in accordance with principles of pure truth, then whoever sets limits on it commits a crime. The further it extends its rule, the happier it makes the state and its rulers. We will consider this with respect to the administration of the state and with respect to religion and then pass judgment.

Does the state lose or gain through enlightenment? Does religion lose or gain through enlightenment? Is deception at all necessary and useful?

3. DOES THE STATE LOSE OR GAIN THROUGH ENLIGHTENMENT?

Enlightenment takes the field against deception and prejudice. What, then, does the state in which enlightenment is victorious lose? Deception and prejudice.

This inquiry proceeds from the ruler, whom enlightenment makes into the father of his land, to the least of his subjects, whom enlightenment would make virtuous.

The ruler who demands mere obedience is a despot. For him, everything—his entire state—is his property. He tyrannizes the thoughts of his subjects, which he must fear. In Siam the despot asserts a claim to everything. When the servants of his tyranny see a tree with lovely fruit they tell the person who planted and cared for it that the fruits are for the emperor. If the Ottoman emperor has a wealthy minister whose treasure he craves, he sends mutes with the cord, and the minister obediently proffers his neck. If he hears of a beauty who is the only daughter of a Muslim, he tears her from the arms of her father and mother for his own desires. The emperor of China sets his mandarins on jackasses; the ruler of Japan commands them to cut open their stomachs; the king of Spain hands his subjects over to the Inquisition; and petty despots usurp rights over one's own conscience. Is the monarch who behaves thus enlightened and happy by virtue of his prejudices and deception? Were not the emperors of Siam, the Ottoman Empire, China, and Japan, and almost all the rulers of the Greek empire either murdered, maimed, blinded, or slaughtered in some other way? All this was the result of despotism, which—after religion—is the most atrocious of deceptions.

Sovereigns who ruled their states as fathers—were their people less subjects to them than in the states of the despots? Did their enlightened principles of statecraft not earn them the love of their subjects and did they not secure the loyalty of their people? Did their subjects not take it to be their duty to die for them? And when virtuous rulers fell, when Ravaillac murdered Henry IV, was it due to enlightenment or the lack of an enlightened religion and its servants?[12] Which of Prussia's monarchs needed a bodyguard to protect him from his subjects, or which could walk freely among them, like a father among his children? And Prussia is indisputably the most enlightened state in the world. In the capital of enlightenment the life of the monarch is secure, and the welfare of the subjects is most firmly grounded in the wisest civil code of all nations, as is—so far—their right of conscience and civil freedom; would God that it were forever. Science and the arts flourish. Its rulers, who did not affect the air of arbitration over Europe's princes, rule with Prussia's usual resolution. Other kings and their ministers speak in their cabinets about influencing Europe. Prussia's rulers, and Hertzberg, and Finckenstein, did not talk, but they acted.[13] They move like a storm high and holy through a land, and evil people are terrified by their thunder. They move through, and the storm was a blessing to the land. Prussia! You shine like a sun before the world. Idolized by his people, your king was the terror and wonder of the nation. Your ministers, just and enlightened, took the rights of peoples into account, and did not, out of pride, fail to recognize the merit of good and wise fellow citizens of lower position. Under their king your people was the freest on earth, because every reasonable, enlightened, and unenlightened person could think and act as he wanted as long as he did not encroach on human rights. You are the living proof that enlightenment makes the state in which it dwells happy. Oh never let priestly cunning and dullness spread their dark hellish wings over you, and never let stupidity eclipse your great name and your honor! Never let it knock the heavenly crown of universal tolerance from your head, lofty Prussia!

There are opponents of enlightenment who maintain the lie that it demands unbounded freedom. Only miserable prejudice and stupid frailty can do this. The introduction of property among people made laws necessary and the requirements of societies necessitated leaders. Call them what you will—emperors, kings, aristocrats, democrats—the name makes no difference here. In short, every society needs a leader, a power to make laws and to execute them. What would the laws be without warders, or the security of the state without an adept helmsman at the rudder? And is there a nobler freedom than this: to want to do nothing against the law? The upright citizen does not even consider overstepping penal law. The laws are not tyrants that shackle his freedom, because he wants nothing that is harmful to the state. Enlightenment accepts the unconditioned necessity of reining in excessive, deliberate, and damaging folly. Only a shallow determinist can defend rancor against laws. But is a determinist an enlightener or a creator of darkness? Once again: for the person who wants to do no evil there is no law that threatens his freedom.

But do not public taxes encroach on human freedom? What does enlightenment say about this? This is its answer: Citizens of the state! Can you protect your property against domestic and foreign enemies by yourselves, if your plunderers are stronger than you? Without laws, what would become of the security of your property? Where there are laws, there must be men who make and administer them. There must be a sovereign who puts these men into action and keeps them active. Isn't it fitting that you contribute your share to the support of your sovereign and his officials, who are there not for his sake but for the sake of the state? And what would your sovereign be without majesty?—like you, and with no competence to maintain the obedience of the rebellious and the respect of all. Your property requires an army against your neighbor's envy and thirst for conquest. Who will sustain them if not the whole of the state on whose account—and for whom alone—they exist?

Detractors of enlightenment allege that it is dangerous and fosters principles of freedom that would be dangerous to the state. The more it spreads, the more clearly it spells out the duties of the monarch to his subjects and of the subject to his monarch, and the more willing it makes both to act in noble consent for the good of the whole. To be sure, it does not laud tyrants or flatter weak minors [*Unmündigen*] because they sit on the throne. But even in weak rulers it honors the blessings of hereditary succession to the throne. And without insulting (for true enlightenment never insults majesty) it becomes adviser to the sovereign and benefactor of the state.

It is shameful when a would-be enlightener publicly and without discretion rises up against monarchs and their servants and maliciously characterizes their intentions. Even when the sovereign and his ministers err, enlightenment says: spare the man for the sake of the monarch, on account of his majesty, which even in tyrants deserves respect, because the laws and the public good require it. The inconsiderate voice of an undeserved reproach sows the seeds of dissatisfaction, discord, and rebellion. The voice of wise reproach is often a useful evil for the state, if only it does not pave the way to tumult. The voice of enlightenment does indeed dare to pass judgment on political errors, but only when they are generally pernicious and the voice of the truth can approach the throne in no other way. But its tone is that of the most ardent goodwill for what is best for the majesty and its subjects. The language to use before majesty is not that of Orbilius but of the fine statesman who clothes his truths in pleasing garments and presents them with the reverence that is owed to the throne.[14] Deception and conceited arrogance, however, throw the slightest error of the ruler and his civil servants onto the scale, and, unmoved by the many other good deeds effected by the active life of kings and their ministers, these armchair politicians criticize them for small failings. But deception never lays the quantity of good brought about by the assiduous efforts of the public administrators on the other side of the scale—otherwise it would be silenced by its conscience.

Further: Did destructive political revolutions arise out of enlightenment or out of deception? What brought about the free state of the United Colonies?[15] Deception of the English government and deception of the colonies. If the ministers of Great Britain had known the truth about the situation in its colonies, they would indisputably have acted differently. If the colonies had acted without deception, they would not now be a sort of anarchic state that maintains itself through weak bonds without any majesty, a state whose constitution is without true inner greatness and without the force that a well-ordered state ruled by a sovereign must have. Every province is sovereign, and so every province is by itself powerless! There is no spirit of harmonious unity, and everywhere there are false concepts of freedom!

How happy was Holland under its old constitution? Was it truth and enlightenment or foolishness and deception that made this land an object of intrigue, a theater of riot, rebellion, and civil war? Did not its unenlightened demagogues lead it to the brink of the abyss, where it would have toppled into the depths of the most frenzied anarchy had not the more enlightened genius of Prussia rushed to save it?[16]

What were the Netherlands when the deception and the prejudices of Philip II made it into a theater for every abomination? Compare Spain with Prussia. The former, however much enlightenment seeks to make progress, still lies very much under the yoke of prejudice and deception. Where is the financial situation, the entire national economy, and political constitution more orderly—in the unenlightened or in the enlightened land? Was it not deception and lack of enlightenment about these matters that devoured the enormous treasures of the New World—all the gold and silver from Peru and Mexico? The mines of Potosi are exhausted and where is their gold?[17] The more enlightened nations have divided among themselves the booty that they earned. Is a proof still necessary of whether enlightenment or deception is advantageous or detrimental to the state?

What may a state expect when its ministers are enlightened men, and what may it expect when they are prejudiced, deceptive, or deceived civil servants? In which court is it more probable that its plans and their execution are good? In the former or the latter? Consider how much devastation and unhappiness is wrought by unenlightened ministers who hold the king's heart in their hands! The reputation of the monarch, whom they make act as they see fit, is at stake. The decrees that brought prejudice and a dearth of enlightenment to the public are eternal documents of shame for those in whose name they were issued. Are there not courts where the priestly spirit, where secret Jesuitism, rules through sovereigns and their ministers? Where reasonable people are persecuted and banished openly? Where rulers are led to renounce their sovereign rights and subject themselves to the pride of a clerical grandee? Where, instead of cultivating right and justice, the placating of the lower courts of law is carelessly connived? Where money can even purchase verdicts? Where the avarice of civil servants exploits the official positions of the land and transfers them, not to the most worthy, but to the highest bidder? Where spiritual office is allotted not to the worthiest but to the most stupid, if only in the fullness of his stupidity he is properly orthodox? Are these consequences of enlightenment or of deception? Where ministers rule like sovereigns, where they closely surround the person of the sovereign so that no plea, no indictment, can come near the throne of the ruler, where the minister flatters the weaknesses of the monarch, admires his mistakes, murders the last kernel of virtue and greatness of soul, and makes him, who would have become a father to his people, into the greatest despot—is it better to be an enlightened or a prejudiced minister?

Will the men employed in any branch of public administration be more useful to the state as deceived or as enlightened men? Enlightenment is opposed to all considerations of self-interest obtained at the expense of official duties and the state. The enlightened person sees himself as the servant of the general interest and not merely of his own. He serves only the law, and pays no attention to the person. Thus Prussian officials in the epoch of Frederick II served the lowliest farmer as well as the most preeminent prince with unflinching impartiality. Our courts of law dispensed justice to those with whom justice sided. No rank confused the calm investigative spirit of the enlightened judge, who, without letting himself be diverted, always focused on the pure goal of his inquiry, namely, truth, justice, and laws.

When deception obscures the gaze of the judge or intrigue is on the lips of the lawyers; when the most well spoken, the most persuasive, carries away the judge's verdict through flowery language and declamation; where rank and position are considered; where innocence is oppressed out of fear of insulting the great and distinguished; where the jurist can be bribed and his verdicts are for sale; where connections bend the law and favors pervert it—where is it better? In the state of deception or the state of enlightenment?

The scholar is, needless to say, a scholar only in proportion to his enlightenment. The more he is ruled by preconceived opinions, false premises, and deceptions, the less he is a scholar. Was Wolff greater, or his persecutor?[18] Galileo, or the priests who made him miserable? If philosophy had remained an eternal, fatuous Aristotelian dialectic, how could the branches of scholarship ever have developed through enlightenment to the high level at which they now stand? Is a Duns Scotus just as good as a Kant? Or is a scholastic Jesuit as good as Leibniz, Lessing, and Mendelssohn? In general, what would have become of philosophy, physics, astronomy, and all types of science, if no men like Locke, Newton, Leibniz, Kant, Bode, Herschel, Euler, and so forth, had enlightened these sciences and enriched them with new discoveries?[19]

The theologian—my heart pounds anxiously when I think of this—what is he without enlightenment? A miserable priest [*Pfaffe*]—a reason-renouncing fool, a persecutor of enlightenment. He and his companions are a gang of conspirators against the rights of human understanding, and when he combines power with his abundant stupid prejudice, he is a bloodthirsty wolf in sheep's clothing—a pestilence on humanity and the corrupter of all good taste. Judge, impartial world, whether these accusations are too strong or too mild! Was it enlightenment or deception that exterminated at least 80 million people by the sword, the pestilence of war, and the glowing flames of the pyre? The stupid theologians, from the earliest times onward, what tyrants of humanity were they? The priests with those sundry Egyptiac labels: the bonzees, talapoins, and priests of all names, what devastation have they not wrought through their influence on the state![20] The demon of rage has infiltrated even you, Christianity, most holy of all religions. You, who fight so nobly against the spirit of persecution and human hatred; you, who with your Founder, shine with greater brilliance with every new light of enlightenment. But what am I saying, that it infiltrated *you*? No, it penetrated your teachers. Through them it usurped the conscience of rulers and bathed itself in the blood of citizens and the so-called unbelievers, or through them it triumphed over the rights of reason and humanity.

From the time of Constantine to the present, how many countless victims, slaughtered by priestly rage, has history produced? In the time of the church's vigorous *coups de main* against heretics, was it thanks to the theologians that even one individual escaped death? Had it been able to annihilate *every heathen on earth*, would the priestly spirit of the unenlightened era of the crusades have spared a single victim from religious frenzy? How many millions does a single enlightened Las Casas reckon to have fallen at the hands of the frenzy of unenlightened religion in America?[21] Who can hear the name of Cajamarca without sympathy, or mention the name of Atahualpa, who was burned as a heretic, without tears?[22] Who can think, without being moved, of orthodox Spaniards hunting irreligious Americans to their death with dogs, then feeding the dogs with their flesh, dismembering and publicly selling the limbs of these unfortunate ones for dog food? What else was Bartholomew's night, but a monument to the unenlightened priestly spirit? The massacres in Ireland, the ubiquitous smouldering pyres of all nations that herald the intolerance of the priests, the courts of the inquisition, the autos-da-fé—do they not all originate in Rome, the seat of unenlightened priestly despotism?[23] I throw up my hands in despair at the countless number of horrifying scenes with which the deceptive priests have ravaged the globe. And Rome would still exterminate all Protestants and subjugate all peoples, its Jesuits would perform the roles of executioners and hangmen while the rest of the priests serve as their lackeys, if enlightenment did not hold its mighty aegis over the peoples.

By enlightening religion, Luther gave it a loftier purview. Burning a Servetus in Geneva and preaching Christian love, Calvin only made use of the weapons of a purer understanding that disciplined much folly in his time.[24] Zwingli was incontestably the best of his time. His enlightenment did not breathe the spirit of exaggerated hate against those who think differently, as did Luther's and Calvin's, but rather displayed the calm seriousness of the thinker and the steadfast but tolerant courage of a reformer. The ardor of the religious reformers was partly inherited by the clergy of their denominations. Lutherans and members of the Reformed church persecuted, reviled, abused, and hated each other, so that their zeal brought Crell to the scaffold because he appeared suspicious to the Lutherans.[25] In England this zeal also produced rebellions and for similar reasons brought Charles I to the scaffold.[26] Enthusiastic Puritans were victorious over their opponents and spattered the earth with the blood of their fellow citizens. What would not a Goeze still have done for a long time, if enlightenment had not removed his sting?[27] And what would so many Protestant priests still do each day, if the dangerous power had not been snatched from them? Deception and prejudice lurk in their lair, surrounded by tools formerly used by the priests to persecute heretics. But thanks be to Providence that enlightenment guards the entrance with the cherub's sword, so that these monstrosities can do no damage. The investigator sees smouldering in the ashes a wildfire that would consume everything if enlightenment did not hinder its explosion. The more the clergyman defends the deceptions with which he cheats and deceives the world, the more he abandons himself to the sophisms that flow from his deception and that gently bolster unscrupulousness. The lower enlightenment sinks, the stronger the head of prejudice, and the higher prejudice climbs, the easier the passage to active persecutions becomes. Give them time to develop without opposition, and they will deliver up enlightened persons, first to hunger and finally to the green wood of the pyre.

No class of men on earth was more destructive than the priesthood. If I am wrong, then name the class which was. There were always laws against murderers and bandits, but not against the treacherous assassins in priestly garb. War was answered with war and it came to an end; but for thousands of years the priesthood's war against reason was protected, and it continues unabated.

All the worthy men who belong to this profession are so many shining proofs that only enlightenment produces genuine dignity. What would Jerusalem, Spalding, Teller, Döderlein, Eichhorn, and all the men of all denominations who are like them and whose numbers, thank heavens, are already great, what would they be if they had not been brought forth by enlightenment?[28] Would not a deserved obscurity brood over the memory of their names, if they had not sought and disseminated the enlightenment of religion, according to their talents and each in his own way? Such men deserve the highest respect, since they could not have soared so high without fighting great obstacles. How long did the intolerant hounds run barking behind many of these men, until enlightenment, taking the upper hand, commanded: "Silence!"? Now they are safe. If here and there a de Marees[29] chafes at the corner of their garment, they can put up with it calmly, because the enemy of reason has lost his teeth.

All that I mentioned above were consequences of deception and prejudice. If the earth could give back the blood of those murdered by religious hatred and collect it in one place, how monstrously large would the dimensions of this sea be? Ha! How triumphantly the orthodox would sail it, build palaces on its islands and pleasure domes on its banks! The religious hatred of all peoples would see to it that its sources never dried up, and its borders would be widened by rivers and streams of blood from all lands, including you, Prussia. In your midst, religious hatred would raise high the purple flag and would curse the world from the pinnacles of your temples, as the powerless ruler in the Vatican now does.

This will seem exaggerated only to him who does not know the spirit of the Roman church and of all intolerant priests, who all along have trampled the rights of majesty and the state, and who refrain from doing so now only because they are not able. And who secures the rulers and their states? Deception or enlightenment?

But a step closer to our Protestant clergy: Do the state, the laws, and more lowly folk stand to gain more from enlightened minds, or from minds full of old rubbish and rigid religious doctrine? The enlightened doctrines of religion's pure truths, and the great central point of their instruction, are that their principal commandment is the sincere fulfillment of duties to others and that the true consolation in life and death springs from the testimony of a good conscience. Later, the blind adherents of a confused and obscure system deceive their numerous followers (since the name of simpletons is legion everywhere) into seeking a good conscience through faith. They undermine civic virtues by placing them far below faith and representing them as imperfect and stained with sin. Pride and ignorance are companions; stupidity and the spirit of persecution are no less so. I know clergy who, in the fire of their billingsgate eloquence,[30] cry out at every opportunity against scoffers at religion where there are none. They set forth the *utility* of the incomprehensible mystery of the Trinity without understanding the principle from which it is supposed to originate. Their lungs are truly their best aid in stigmatizing reason and enlightenment, and their obstinacy and their stupid, eager stubbornness are their only means of supplementing their impoverished nonsense. As much as he may struggle, it is still true that a fool remains a fool, even if ground in a mortar. Was it these sorts of stupid monks who incited congregations against enlightenment—or the intelligent ones? Was it these sorts who incited the dizzy spirit of revolt against the most salutary organizations and fanned the flames of rebellion—or was it the enlightened ones?

And now to the people: Do they gain by deception or by enlightenment? It is a basic tenet of the Roman church that the people be kept stupid, and so it withheld the Bible from them. It is a basic tenet of the Protestant orthodoxy as well, and so it denies the people the right to a true interpretation of the Bible. What do the people gain from religion and the Bible when it is falsely interpreted to them, and when deceiving them is a duty? Is it not a proof of the poverty of the orthodox system itself and the danger of its doctrines that they must be kept secret? Then for whom, gentlemen, was it the truth? Only for the clergy? Go ahead and take the honor for this claim. The rest of us heartily renounce it. So religion contains dangerous, useless truths that are injurious to citizens and the state? So, my lord-defenders of deception in religious matters, this is how you yourselves would describe the religion of Satan, if there were one. And this dangerous, injurious religion would be the true Christian religion, which the common man is not permitted to know. Deceptions—for example, that man is saved by grace alone and not through his works; or that the blood of Jesus Christ makes the most horrible, foul deeds pardonable if only one believes; or that through Christ a sinner in the hour of his death becomes as blessed as if he had never committed a sin; or that all good works do no good without belief in miserable human statutes, and so forth—all of this would be better than convictions grounded in the religion of Christ.[31] The religion of Christ teaches that virtue and good works must unfailingly make blessed even him who cannot believe *everything indiscriminately,* that through nothing other than virtue and a change of heart, all vices can lose their corruptive influence temporally and eternally, without the blood of Christ contributing anything further; that without the testimony of a clean conscience in the hour of death no consolation or happiness is to be expected because the wicked have cultivated no virtues in their hearts that will be carried on in a state of future blessedness; and so forth. Suppose we were to teach that adherence to Christ's pure doctrine of virtue, and not belief in the Trinity, can be advantageous to you. Should not these and similar precepts—the daylight of reasonable Christian religion as opposed to the darkness and midnight of the dogma that you spread—be more advantageous to the people than the lies and deceptions with which you drive the common people like oxen to the slaughterhouse of continuing corruption? Tell me, what harm can the teachings of enlightenment do them? And of what use to them are your doctrines of the necessity of belief in deceptions before good works? And tell me, I ask you, before God and your conscience, what are the deceptions of religion that are supposed to be useful to the people and which are in conflict with reason and better than her truths? If you can answer this, then speak! But if you cannot, then it is best to be silent. Finally, show that these doctrines and those that accord with principles of a pure understanding, or the religion of enlightenment, are not the doctrines of the One whom you falsely claim to be the Founder of your doctrines and who, through the light of nature, has restored divine religion!

Was the Reformation not enlightenment? What would have become of our religion if in those days the priestly clamor that this enlightenment be proclaimed heretical and injurious had been honored? If you speak well of this enlightenment and thank God for it, why do you chastise and groan over its progress? Because perhaps it is going too far? But can the truth become too clear, and would it be more useful if it were obscured? Or, in the event that it is disguised in hieroglyphs, is it not as good as nonexistent for the people? Do the people have a true or a false religion when its truths are withheld from them and in their place they are given deception or falsehood? Do they then have a Christian religion, or one that is false and filled with prejudice and deception? And can I not ask, as Christ once did: "Can one also pick grapes from the thorns, or figs from thistles?"[32] The propagators of error, the guardians of religious deception and those who defend hiding the truth, do they not belong to those of whom Christ said: "They are ravenous wolves in priestly garb"?[33] Does not the claim that the people must not be enlightened presuppose that you are teaching them a false religion?

It is a detestable principle that where such important matters as religion are concerned, lies are more useful than truth. Are not you who know the truth and who spread prejudice, this enemy of truth, willfully perverting the truth? Where did Christ ever teach: Keep quiet about the truth that I teach and encourage the teaching of error? Where did He ever say that the people should be kept superstitious and deceived? Was it not precisely the common people to whom He taught the truths of His Father in heaven, which are the same as the truths of reason? Are you His followers, who do the opposite of what you were sent to do, to waken the spirit of truth that leads to all truths, and not just to some? Did the apostles also lead these people by the nose with errors and deceptions? Or did they set to work honestly and in an upright manner? In Christ's times the miserable Pharisees and the arrogant scriptural authorities sought to preserve the deception of the people and against the wise enlightener and enlightenment cried out: "Crucify, crucify!" Do you do anything different against those who restore his teaching? Like the senseless Jew who cried, "His teaching is not from God, but from the devil,"[34] do you not call out in the same tone: "Their teaching is not Christian because it is the teaching of reason and not of faith"? So, the Christian religion was a doctrine that is against reason and not compatible with reason? A doctrine of prejudice and irrationality?

NOTES

1. Xinga was the sister of the king of Angola who fought against the Portuguese in the seventeenth century.—Trans.

2. Cardinal Richelieu (1585–1642), French prelate and statesman, minister to Louis XIII; Jean Baptiste Colbert (1619–1683), French statesman and adviser to Louis XIV, famous for his fiscal policies.—Trans.

3. Saint Athanasius (ca. 297–373), patriarch of Alexandria, was a champion of Nicene orthodoxy against Arianism, a widespread heresy that argued that Jesus Christ was created by God prior to everything else and hence was neither equal to nor eternal with God. The Dominicans, founded by Saint Dominic in 1216 as a monastic order dedicated to preaching and study, were assigned the task of administering the Inquisition in 1233.—Trans.

4. Simon Ludwig Eberhard de Marees (1717–1802) was a Protestant theologian in Dessau and the author of polemics and theological works that argued strenuously for orthodoxy in matters of faith.—Trans.

5. Possibly a reference to Johann Christian Woellner, Frederick William II's minister who, on gaining control of the Central Consistory and the Higher Board of Education, issued his Censorship and Religion edicts.—Trans.

6. Riem is presumably referring to Johann Paul Philip Rosen*feld*, who was well known in the 1780s for his claim to be the true Messiah and who promised to break the seven seals on the Book of Life if he was provided with the requisite seven virgins. His attempts to recruit the daughters of peasants into his service led to clashes with public authorities, and in 1784, after the death of two of the young women he recruited, he received a life sentence in the fortress at Spandau, where he died in

1788. See Paul Schwartz, "Philipp Rosenfeld (1731–1788) ein neuer Messias in der Mark," *Jahrbuch für brandenburgische Kirchengeschichte* 11/12 (1914): 113–159.—TRANS.

7. Tomás de Torquemada (1420–1498) was notorious for his role as director of the Spanish Inquisition; Hieronymus Emser was a Catholic theologian who engaged in bitter polemics with Luther over Luther's translation of the New Testament.—TRANS.

8. A reference to Henry IV's humbling of himself before Pope Gregory VII (Hildebrand) after his excommunication during the Investiture Controversy.—TRANS.

9. Charles IX (1550–1574), king of France from 1560 under the regency of his mother, Catherine de' Medici. He approved the St. Bartholomew's Day massacre (1570) at which thousands of Huguenots were murdered.—TRANS.

10. Jean Mondot, in the French translation of passages from Riem's essay (*Qu'est-ce que les Lumières?* [Saint-Étienne, 1991]) suggests that this is a reference to Louis XIV.—TRANS.

11. Philip II (1527–1598) was king of Spain during the Inquisition. In 1567, he appointed Fernando Alvarez de Toledo, duque de Alba, as governor of the Netherlands, where rebels were seeking religious toleration and self-government. Alba established a special court in Brussels, the infamous "Court of Blood," and executed about 18,000 people.—TRANS.

12. Henry IV (1553–1610), king of France from 1589, was responsible for issuing the Edict of Nantes, which established political rights and religious liberty for the Huguenots. He was assassinated by François Ravaillac, a religious fanatic.—TRANS.

13. Ewald Friedrich von Hertzberg and Karl Wilhelm Finck von Finckenstein directed the Prussian Department of State under the reign of Frederick the Great and Frederick William II. Both played an active role in the negotiations with England during the Patriot Revolution in the United Provinces between 1781 and 1787 that eventually resulted in the dispatching of 20,000 Prussian troops to put down the rebellion of the Dutch Patriots, supported by France, against the pro-English Orange party.—TRANS.

14. Orbilius Pupillus, a Roman grammarian and schoolmaster, was Horace's teacher. He was famous for the severity of the discipline he imposed on his pupils.—TRANS.

15. A reference to the United States, which at the time of the publication of Riem's pamphlet was governed by the Articles of Confederation, whose weakness Riem proceeds to discuss.—TRANS.

16. A reference to Prussia's intervention in the Patriot Revolution in support of a coalition of patricians and monarchists loyal to the prince of Orange.—TRANS.

17. Potosí, in southern Bolivia, was founded in 1545 and was a rich source of silver (not, as Riem has it, gold) in the second half of the sixteenth century. During the seventeenth century, however, it was unable to compete with mines in Peru and Mexico.—TRANS.

18. Bowing to opposition from the theological faculty, Frederick William I dismissed Christian Wolff from the University of Halle and exiled him from Prussia in 1723.—TRANS.

19. Johann Elert Bode (1747–1826) was director of the Berlin Observatory and

founder of the *Berliner Astronomisches Jahrbuch*. In 1772, he published a paper generating a mathematical series that correlated with the empirical distances between the planets that were known at the time ("Bode's law," as it came to be known, has not held true for Neptune and Pluto). Friedrich Wilhelm Herschel (1738–1822) attained fame as a conductor and astronomer in England where he became Sir William Herschel, private astronomer to the king, after discovering Uranus in 1781 (which did agree with "Bode's law"). Leonhard Euler (1703–1783), the Swiss mathematician, who in addition to his work in calculus also computed the motion of the moon, was invited to Berlin by Frederick the Great in 1741 and lived there until 1766.—TRANS.

20. *Bonzen* from the Japanese *bonzi* (religious person) and *bo-zi* (teacher of the law) and *Talapoinen*, from Peguan *tala pôi* (my lord), were used in eighteenth-century Europe as terms (usually disparaging) for Buddhist monks or priests.—TRANS.

21. Bartolomé de Las Casas (1474–1566) was a Spanish missionary who campaigned against slavery and working conditions among the native population of the Spanish colonies in the New World.—TRANS.

22. Atahualpa was the last Inca chief of Peru. Pizarro imprisoned him after inviting him into the city of Cajamarca. He was executed in 1533.—TRANS.

23. "Massacres in Ireland" is probably a reference to the massacre of Protestants in Ulster in 1641 at the start of a rebellion against the rule of Thomas Wentworth, Charles I's deputy. The revolt was put down in 1649–1650 by Oliver Cromwell with losses in the hundreds of thousands.—TRANS.

24. Michael Servetus (1511–1553) was a Spanish theologian, acquainted with many Swiss and German reformers, whose views on the Trinity were condemned by both Catholic and Protestant theologians. Under an assumed name, he served as physician to the archbishop of Vienne, where he became known for his skill at dissection and for his discoveries about the circulation of blood. He continued to publish his theological writings in secret. Condemned by the Inquisition, he was imprisoned but escaped. He was seized in Geneva by order of Calvin, tried, and burned at the stake.—TRANS.

25. Nikolaus Crell (1550–1601), a Saxon theologian who was viewed by orthodox Lutherans as having led the Saxon ruler, Christian I, away from Lutheran orthodoxy toward the teachings of Melanchthon and Calvin. He lost influence after the death of Christian I and was executed in 1601.—TRANS.

26. Charles I (1600–1649), king of England from 1625, waged a harsh campaign against religious nonconformists in the years leading up to the English Civil War.—TRANS.

27. Johan Melchior Goeze (1717–1786), the well-known orthodox Lutheran theologian who launched a bitter attack on Reimarus's and Lessing's rather unorthodox theological writings.—TRANS.

28. Johann Friedrich Wilhelm Jerusalem, Johann Joachim Spalding, Wilhelm Abraham Teller, and Christian Albrecht Döderlin were prominent Enlightenment theologians. Johann Gottfried Eichhorn was trained as a philologist, Orientalist, and theologian. He taught Oriental languages at Jena between 1775 and 1787 and became a professor of philosophy at Göttingen in 1788.—TRANS.

29. See note 4.—TRANS.

30. The term, which refers to abusive language, appears in English in Riem's pamphlet.—TRANS.

31. Lessing made a similar distinction between "Christianity" and the "religion of Christ" in a posthumously published fragment contained in his *Theologischen Nachlass,* a volume edited by his brother, Karl Lessing, and published in 1784. See *Lessings Werke,* ed. Karl Lachmann and Franz Muncker (Stuttgart, 1904), XVI:518–519 (translated by Henry Chadwick as "The Religion of Christ" in *Lessing's Theological Writings* [Stanford, 1956], 106).—TRANS.

32. Matt. 7:16.—TRANS.

33. See Matt. 7:15: "Beware of false prophets, who come to you in sheep's clothing but inwardly are ravenous wolves."—TRANS.

34. See Matt. 9:32: "He casts out demons by the prince of demons."—TRANS.

4. The Politics of Enlightenment

Something Lessing Said: A Commentary on *Journeys of the Popes*

Friedrich Heinrich Jacobi

Translated by Dale E. Snow

Friedrich Heinrich Jacobi (1743–1819) first came to public notice with his philosophical novels, Allwills Briefsammlung *(1774) and* Woldemar *(1779), and secured his reputation as a leading critic of the Enlightenment with his* Briefe über die Lehre von Spinoza *(1785), the book that launched the Pantheism Controversy. Jacobi criticized the Enlightenment for what he regarded as its exaggerated claims for the primacy of reason and argued that a completely consistent rationalism—exemplified for him by Spinoza—would necessarily culminate in atheism, determinism, and nihilism. From his reading of David Hume, Jacobi concluded that reason could not even attain certainty about the existence of external objects and hence that our experience of the world ultimately rests on a revelation that is completely beyond argument, which he termed "faith."*

It is often assumed that those who, like Jacobi or Hamann, questioned the philosophical foundations of the Enlightenment were reactionaries in their political thinking. Jacobi's 1782 essay "Something Lessing Said" demonstrates how his skepticism about the powers of reason, when coupled with the arguments of such representatives of the civic republican tradition in politics as Machiavelli and Ferguson, could produce a spirited articulation of the principles of political liberalism.

> Dic cur hic? respice finem!
> *Which Leibniz translated as:*
> Où en sommes nous? venons au fait!
> NOUVEAUX ESSAIS, P. 155[1]

This I heard Lessing say: the statements of Febronius and his followers were a shameless flattery of the princes; for all their arguments against the privileges of the pope were either groundless or applied with double and triple force to the princes themselves.[2] Everyone was capable of grasping this; and the fact that no one among the many whose urgent business it would be to

Originally published as Etwas das Lessing gesagt hat: Ein Commentar zu den Reisen der Päpste *(Berlin, 1782). This translation is based on the version Jacobi edited for the second volume of his collected works, which shortens some of the notes and moves some material originally found in footnotes to the text itself.*

point this out has yet said so publicly, with all the incisiveness and precision such a subject permitted and deserved, was odd enough and an extremely bad sign.

Someone finally said it, and loudly enough to be heard by everyone, although not in so many words. For this reason, many may not have been able to extract the larger meaning from his work (I mean the *Journeys of the Popes*),[3] since it appears that we Germans are generally too wrapped up in our profundity to listen nimbly and swiftly. Others will take pains not to grasp its true spirit, but will rather fasten onto the outer husk, in order—with an outcry—to pillory it, and let their hordes drag it through the mud.

Germans will do this to a man who spoke out for German freedom—for humanity's most priceless privilege—without being a German.[4] Yet he does not stand alone. There are still men among us who are fighting for the same cause. Who would not name as first among them our Justus Möser,[5] *advocatum patriae*, who alone in all Germany spoke an emphatic word, when everywhere only jubilation resounded because of the great deed involving the miller Arnold.[6] The passage, in the essay "On German Language and Literature," is well known.[7] Less known is an earlier article, occasioned by just this incident, with the title "On the Important Difference between Real and Formal Law." It says, among other things:

> All men may err, a king just as much as a philosopher, and the latter perhaps first, since they both stand too high, and cannot calmly and precisely observe any one of the many things which pass before their eyes. For this reason all nations have made it the foundation of their freedom and property, that what a person recognizes as law or truth shall never be permitted to be law until it has received the seal of formalism.
>
> It belongs to the form of law that it be pronounced by a legitimate judge, and that it be in force. This is a fundamental law on which all European nations are in agreement as well, and the monarch who bids compliance to a *real* truth just as he does to a *formal* one overthrows this first and fundamental law, holy to every state, without which there is no more security. Even the wisdom of Solomon cannot excuse such an undertaking, since all the wisdom in the world leads only to real (natural, substantial, internal) truth, not to formal (positive, established, external) truth.[8]

The great mass of our thinkers are least able to think this, because they want to see the essentially true and the essentially good spread *by power* [*Gewalt*], and want to see every error suppressed *by power*. They would like to help promote an enlightenment—elsewhere than in the understanding, because that takes too long. They put out the lights, filled with childish impatience for it to be day. Oh hope-filled darkness, in which we hurriedly totter our way toward the goal of our wishes, toward the greatest good on earth; forward, on the path of violence and subjugation!

But power, wherever it was in the world, whether apportioned among several or vested only in one—reigning power, whether established or arbitrary, predetermines and restricts every other cognition on the path to insight as well as every drive [*Trieb*] on the path to happiness—such a power, which only gives laws and itself has none, and which may violate the holiest laws with holiness, has never brought forth *real truth and genuine well-being* anywhere among men. However, much good has originated from the *resistance against it,* out of the original spirit of freedom, out of the externally active drive of reason to enlarge itself and spread its insight over everything. Where there is history, there is also testimony that when great deeds, inclinations, and thoughts, the works of noble men, and noble men themselves did not arise directly out of the kernel of freedom, they at least drew sap from its trunk, like a grafted branch—or stood forlorn like second growth from the roots of the fallen tree. And where there is history, there is also testimony that unrestricted arbitrary power has produced only stupidity and vice, everything that is despicable, unworthy, and small, and that it is incapable of achieving even its own foolish ends.

However, it is obvious that power (and especially a power that is omnipresent and ubiquitous), that a certain compulsion, and certain means to enforce it are absolutely necessary among men. For if the lack of restraint of only a few has already such a deleterious effect on the species, what would happen if all were unrestrained? The extent to which such institutions are truly necessary for humanity, the causes of this necessity and its necessary object, what these institutions ought and ought not to do, what they are and are not capable of doing: this important knowledge can only be drawn from knowledge of man's innermost nature. A close examination of what is peculiar to this nature may help us to form fruitful conclusions.

What distinguishes man from animals and shapes his particular species is the capacity to see a relationship among ends and to guide his conduct by this insight.

Out of this source of humanity flows, in all its tributaries, the same reason [*Vernunft*], only overflowing beds and between banks of immense diversity and size and hiding its efflux from all eyes. These beds, these banks are the passions. Many have wanted to see it differently, and—against all appearances and arguments—have taken reason for the banks and the passions for the stream.

Insofar as man is determined in and by himself—that is, insofar as he is capable of acting freely—to that extent he is motivated by reason, and to that extent he is fully human. Where there is no freedom, no *self-determination,* there is no humanity.

Insofar as man is affected by things outside him and he views them in such a way that his awareness of himself disappears—to that extent he is acting according to a foreign drive and not according to his own. He allows himself to be determined, and he does not determine himself. He does what is demanded by other things and not what his own nature requires. And to that extent we say he is moved by *passion* and that he is only an animal.

A civil society is a human society and not an animal one. It is an institution of reason and not of the passions, a means of freedom and not of slavery, constituted for beings who by nature stand in the middle between the two.

For itself, reason never has need of the passions, which only darken and restrict it. It can thus never command a passion as such, nor make the stimulation of a passion an immediate goal for itself. However, the circumstances of human nature can well force reason to attempt to inhibit or stop one passion by means of another. Since it is incapable of controlling every external impression, it must, in defense of its freedom, set external power against external power.

If reason can never have the promotion of a passion for an immediate goal, and a civil compact arises only through reason—although not without taking the passions into account but *absolutely in relation to them*—then those societies among men which are based on the promotion of passions cannot, *to that extent*, be seen as rational institutions, or as civil societies, or as truly *human* societies.

We also see animals, united by common drives, living with one another in society; yet even this is not a product of passion, for in animals, as in men, passions are far more likely to set the individual members against one another than to bind them to one another, and thus must necessarily produce the opposite of society, that is, that state *in quo vis et dolus sunt virtutes cardinales*.[9] That which unites social animals is *instinct* [*Instinct*], which is clearly distinguished from the nature of the passions [*Leidenschaften*]. And by means of this wonderful agency these animal societies receive a much higher degree of perfection than those human ones which rest more on the basis of passion than reason. For instinct is unalterable and sure and is quite similar to reason in that it demands nothing other than what is obviously the best for one and all, who are bound to one another in pursuit of a common goal.

Now the question arises: Is there a means of reason which, like instinct among social animals, can lead men securely, unalterably, and manifestly to the point where the good of all and the good of each individual are incontrovertibly joined: is there such a means, and what is its name?

Let us examine the matter more closely and the means will be found, along with its name.

Obviously reason is the proper, true life of our nature, the soul of the spirit, the cord which binds together all our powers, an image of the eternal unalterable source of all truth, of all being that perceives itself and takes pleasure in itself. Without reason, it would be impossible for us to do other than to act at odds with ourselves; we would belong more to external things than to ourselves. In reason, we are at one with ourselves, in that among all our *desires*[10] a contract arises, in harmony with the eternal laws of what is advantageous to our enduring nature. Each of our desires has the most legitimate claim to be satisfied, so that virtue consists in the greatest possible unification of all our desires, and true happiness consists in the greatest possible satisfaction of all of them—whereby both become the same thing. The longing for happiness is no more common than the conviction that it can only be found on the path of reason, because reason always reliably commands that which is good for the whole man, that is, that which is truly best for all his parts.

That it is good for the whole man to bind himself to others like himself is a truth obvious to everyone since, on the one hand, nothing in the entire realm of nature can be as useful to him and, on the other, nothing in the entire realm of nature can harm him to so high a degree as another person.

Men who act under the impetus of reason are never harmful to one another, for from this impetus no action can arise which would be in opposition to the action of anyone else who acts according to this very impetus. Rather, every individual, in that he promotes his own true best interest, also necessarily promotes the best interest of all others, and is full of love for them.

Men are thus in a position to cause mutual harm only to the extent that they are motivated by passions, from which develop all conflicts, the entire horde of vices, and not a single real virtue.

If, in every case, the impetus of passion is stronger in men, and for this reason—as two of the greatest scholars have maintained (Hobbes and Spinoza)—man can be seen as the natural and worst enemy of other men, man nevertheless strives solely toward the good with all his *particular*, *innermost* capacities, so that man everywhere follows the laws of the love of humanity, of justice, of honor, and of religion with unabated zeal, insofar as he is determined *solely* by his *own* nature.

It follows from this, as from what has been pointed out above, that it would be impossible for *formal legislation*, or a *system of coercion*, to apply to man insofar as he has the gift of reason and is already determined through this reason to promote his well-being and that of his fellow men. Rather, it applies only to the extent that he is in the grip of the passions and therefore inclined to injustice, inclined to break with others and with himself, unstable, unfaithful, eager for discord and quarrel.

Thus society, insofar as it rests on *external form* and is a *mechanism of coercion*, has *protection* as its one and only object, that is, to ward off from every member of the society every harm that might arise out of injustice; or, in the same way, to secure for every member his inviolable property in his person, the free use of all his powers, and the full enjoyment of the fruits of their employment.

Accordingly, the means by which man could be securely, unalterably, and manifestly led—just as the social animals are led by instinct—to the point where the good of all and the good of each individual are incontrovertibly joined would be security of property in the broadest sense and absolutely in the highest degree, for all as for one, and for one as for all, *inviolable universal justice, without any compulsion to any other end.*

Should anyone argue against us that these means would not lead to the highest goal of the civil condition, but rather that there are other ends whose means, in cases of conflict, should supersede the means of inviolable, universal justice, let him dare to name, in clear words, these ends and means. He will not know of any which do not obviously arise from the passions: lust for land, lust for money—vanity, concupiscence, and pride. And then he would have to maintain that the promotion of these passions—ambition, greed, all the sensual desires—is more appropriate to the vocation and happiness of man than the promotion of reason and its consequences: true insight, moderation, justice, health of the soul, enduring satisfaction, and virtue itself.

There are many other things he would also have to claim, which are not things anyone would want to claim in so many words, and which cannot even be clearly conceived. It is certainly well enough meant by most, when they allow themselves to dream of a certain *interest of the state*, of a certain welfare of the *whole*, which is not the welfare of all its parts, but rather is distinguished from this in that a disproportionate sacrifice from the parts for the sake of the whole can be reasonably conceived and justly demanded from them. However, should these gentlemen scrutinize matters, even if only from a distance, they would discover without much effort that this effusive interest, suspended dimly before them, resolves itself into a purely geographical interest, namely, this one: *that a certain number of square feet of land should be found together under a certain name.* And they would find, these good men—doubtless to their hearty satisfaction!—that for the sake of such a geographical interest, in order to preserve it or increase it, and for no other end, they would give up some of their property, any part of their external freedom, yes, by hundreds and thousands, even life itself. They would find that there are no such parts of a whole which have the ground of their union in itself, a whole, whose unity resides within itself. Rather they would find that they are parts which are together only for the sake of another, parts of a thing whose unity is found outside of it—parts of a blind instrument, of an artificial but unreasoning body, *without a soul of its own.*

In no area of human knowledge does there reign greater confusion and contradiction than in this one. It is acknowledged that every commonwealth must be administered in accordance with the laws of justice; and at the same time it is claimed that these laws cannot be determined, that they are arbitrary, obedient to chance, and need not shrink from injustice. But since by nature it is impossible to be fully justified in coercing what one may be fully justified in refusing, a supreme unrestricted authority must step in, to turn the natural laws around as required—*by force.*

Indeed, the prevailing concept of authority [*Obrigkeit*] is that it is in and of itself the source of justice and property—not the source of the *secure possession* of property, but rather the source of property *itself.* Hence it has to determine the extent and the limit of all the varieties of property, and all of its uses according to indeterminable principles, at most according to a certain indeterminate general good, which authority, quite indeterminately again, is found to know and to strive for.

Who would care to untangle all that is nonsensical in these ideas, and who wants to see it merely untangled? It is better that I hasten to add a few brief points for the clarification and confirmation of my own thoughts.

This was my point of departure: that power must only be countered by power, crime by coercion. The essence of both is not to give rise to actions, but rather to eliminate and to hinder them. They are not in the position to awaken powers, or to create anything that is good in itself. That which is good in itself can only spring from itself, and its original source is always *the unbidden inner movement of a free spirit.*

Without power and coercion men first became brothers and formed societies, where the absence of faulty arrangements gave them more security than many artificial institutions, which often cause more and worse crimes than they prevent. Man is active out of sheer inclination [*Triebe*], and he must be just because he wants to be happy. Kindness and love, discernment, fairness, generosity, courage, and loyalty, these qualities, which constitute the bond and the strength of societies, are original qualities of his nature, immediately bestowed by God. True, the arts of government have exercised the minds of men and, giving rise to all kinds of efforts, inquiries, goals, wishes, and thoughts, enriched their spirit; but they have often also degraded and worsened it. For they have promoted every sort of inequality, privilege, division, and vanity, and, by overburdening the individual with ever new objects of care for himself, they have replaced the trust and goodwill one ought to feel toward one's fellow creatures with an anxious effort to be concerned only with one's own person. However, the happiest men are those whose hearts stand in connection to a community which shares all their wishes and from which they can separate none of their wishes, with a community in which they find every object of magnanimity and ardor and find an end for every talent and virtuous inclination. Animals have sagacity enough to procure their food, and to find the means of their solitary pleasures; but it is reserved for man to advise, to persuade, to oppose, to wax enthusiastic in the society of his fellow creatures, and to lose the sense of his personal interest or safety, in the ardor of his friendships and his oppositions.

Ferguson, in whose words I was just speaking,[11] warns very much of the political refinements of ordinary men who have only repose or inactivity as their objects and which are intended to destroy the noblest activity by means of restrictions aimed at the prevention of bad action—as if the common man had no right to act or even to think. He mentions in this connection the quip of a great prince who sought to make ridiculous the concern that judges in a free country be held to an exact interpretation of the law and then tries as much as possible to alleviate the anxiety of certain people when they find, instead of unbounded submissiveness, indignant demands for rights, as well as failings of policy [*Polizey*]. He tries to do it by asking them to contemplate how a Chinaman might think that the freedom men have in Europe to wander here and there in the streets and fields at will is a sure sign of coming confusion and anarchy: "Can men behold their superior and not tremble? Can they converse without a precise and written ceremonial? What hopes of peace, if the streets are not barricaded at an hour? What wild disorder, if men are permitted in anything to do what they please?"[12]

"Certainly," he says further, "the viper must be held at a distance, and the tyger chained. But if a rigorous policy, applied to enslave, not to restrain from crimes, has an actual tendency to corrupt the manners, and to extinguish the spirit of nations; if its severities be applied to terminate the agitations of a free people, not to remedy their corruptions; if forms be often applauded as salutary, because they tend merely to silence the voice of mankind, or be condemned as pernicious, because they allow this voice to be heard; we may expect that many of the boasted improvements of civil society will be mere devices to lay the political spirit at rest, and will chain up the active virtues more than the restless disorders of men."[13]

What is noble has always been placed in opposition to the mechanical, not just where art is distinguished from handicraft, but rather in all things, and in the following way: one thinks of spiritual activity in the one case, and of mere physical activity in the other; of nobility of sense and ability in the one, and of selfishness and external need in the other; of freedom and self-determination in the one, and of slavery and alien motivation in the other. To confuse and gradually to eliminate these differences could be called the great mission of our time. Gladly would we see all self-determination, all unmediated original power of movement eliminated from nature; gladly would we create life only out of things which have no life, and generate fresh action from pure suffering. Gladly would we renounce all that is spiritual, all that is original, all that exists and acts through itself—in order to introduce in their place gears, weights, and levers. Of our political condition in particular, a wise man still living says:[14] "If men had expressly undertaken to form a society in which as little religion and as little virtue as possible were to be found, they could not possibly have done any better than has in fact happened here. What we have left of virtue and religion," he continues, "we have thanks to the circumstance that lawmakers, in the building of their machine, found that they could not do without this power for movement of one of the main wheels. However, the nature of this religion and virtue do not matter any further to them, if only it does not interfere with the uniform movement of their great clockwork."[15]

Where virtue and religion are no longer felt, or are even denied, there remains no other means to secure the general welfare than to bring the self-seeking partisan tendencies of the members of the society—that is, their passions—into equilibrium. This can only be effected by the utmost power, and even then in an extremely inadequate manner. Since the passions by their nature are lawless, changeable, and of endlessly variable effect, so too the means which serve to hold the self-seeking and personal tendencies in check only through themselves—without awakening any noble sentiments—must be unrestricted and left to *arbitrary choice* [*Willkür*] in response to the indeterminate events of the moment. But arbitrary choice leaves room for error, and unrestricted power allows the suppression of all rights, so that it is precisely the defect requiring such aid that renders its misuse unavoidable. We also see, from one end of history to the other, among such peoples—where out of a combination of mere passions all the virtues were supposed to arise, virtues in the service of these passions, or rather *unpunished vices*—that it is precisely through these means, intended as they were to deal with misdeeds, the outbreak of general adversity, and total ruin, that all these evils were always only made greater and finally driver to the highest pitch. We see incontrovertibly that men who are not themselves in the position to know what is good for them and to strive for it are even less able to owe their well-being to the virtue of a guardian who is without a judge and who will never allow them to achieve maturity.[16] We see that to prevent peoples by force from acting to their own detriment, or really to force them into what is best for them, a god would have to descend, a perfect individual who would never die.

Imperfect creatures like ourselves, only even more strongly tempted by all things evil, among whom a conceit, which drives all wisdom away, and an arrogance, which wishes to rule over justice and truth itself and to elevate itself above all duties, fill the whole soul and make tyranny, for them, the greatest of the goddesses[17]—such creatures are indeed often powerful enough to thwart the satisfaction of our passions, but not for our own best interests, but instead so that we might serve *their* passions instead of our own. If they have wisdom, they can also justly claim the title of *shepherd of their people;* for they provide them with good pastures, growth, and prosperity; they protect them within a secure enclosure; they chain up guard dogs for them, and gird themselves for the watch, like Eumaeus in Homer.[18] Only the herd must not wish to belong to itself, nor must any part of it go beyond its boundaries, or the whip sings and stings and the guard dog is unleashed.—But the advancement of humanity, of its highest joys, its sublimest pleasures, its power and dignity, are never to be expected from one of us who wishes to rule autocratically. Rather one should expect the advancement of all those tendencies that destroy the strength of the soul, the grandeur of the spirit, the nobility of the mind, and all true inner superiority and glory. One should expect the advancement of self-interest, money-grubbing, indolence; of a stupid admiration of wealth, of rank, and of power; a blind unsavory submissiveness; and an anxiety and fear which allows no zeal and tends toward the most servile obedience. "This is the manner of government," says the great and noble Ferguson, "into which the covetous and the arrogant, to satiate their unhappy desires, would hurry their fellow creatures: it is a manner of government to which the timorous and servile submit at discretion; and when these characters of the rapacious and the timid divide mankind, even the virtues of Antonius or Trajan, can do no more than apply, with candor and with vigor, the whip and the sword; and endeavor, by the hopes of reward, or the fear of punishment, to find a speedy and a temporary cure for the crimes, or the imbecilities of men.—Other states may be more or less corrupted; *this has corruption for its basis.* Here justice may sometimes direct the arm of the despotical sovereign; but the name of justice is most commonly employed to signify the interest, or the caprice, of a reigning power. Human society, susceptible of such a variety of forms, here finds the simplest of all. The toils and possessions of many are destined to aswage the passions of one or a few, and the only parties that remain among mankind, are the oppressor who demands, and the oppressed, who dare not refuse."[19]

If it is true, that despotism (why do we not call things by their right names?) does not only deprive men of their best qualities but also does not even permit them afterwards to fulfill their lower wishes, if this is absolutely grounded in the nature of things, then I would like to hear the name of that evil which must be remedied by *the greatest of all evils*, or the advantage which could balance it. The advantage of a better defense against outside enemies—if it could be maintained against the abundance of contradictory examples—counts for too little, since the inner enemy is the worst. I have no constitution to defend in which I may watch over my own rights and protect them myself: and thus I have no freedom and no *fatherland.* My *place of birth* always remains; and perhaps I will gain more from my new master than I lose; in any case no very great disadvantages can arise for me.

We must not overlook an important observation. Namely this: that despotism is capable of assuming very different forms, and that it can be found in *every* constitution to a greater or lesser extent. Here, observed from inside, at its source, it first arouses the greatest disgust. This inner nature cannot be elaborated from out of itself any more than the inner nature of anything evil, any error or vice can be elaborated out of itself. Rather, it must be observed in its opposite, in that of which it is the deficiency. The opposite of despotism is the rule of freedom. Free, in the highest degree, would be he who is determined in his actions by himself alone, consequently he who himself immediately brought all his objects into being—which can be said of no creature conscious of itself only by means of representations and striving after objects which are not in his power. God alone is free in this absolute sense. But free—in his fashion to the very highest degree—is every person and every citizen, insofar as he is not prevented from furthering his own true advantage in every way in his power. Everyone is a slave, insofar as he is prevented in any way from furthering his own true advantage.

I said every *man* and every *citizen*, because the explanation given here is general, and applies to inner moral freedom as well as to external political freedom.

Both are very closely connected: for it is impossible (as has already frequently been alluded to in this essay) for men who are not already very deeply sunken into moral slavery to fall into political slavery, unless it takes place by a sudden conquest. The political slavery of a people is therefore at the same time a sign of its moral slavery, and just as the latter is exclusively grounded in the animal nature of man, so is the former which arises from it. Both aim at making man ever more of an animal—that is: corrupting him from the ground up.

The same connection holds between the two species of freedom. Where there is a high degree of political freedom in fact, not just in appearance, there must be no less a degree of moral freedom present. Both are grounded exclusively in the rational nature of man, and their power and effect is thus to make men ever more human, ever more capable of self-government, of ruling their passions, of being happy and without fear.

Where there are no laws, there is no commonwealth, thus no civic freedom. Where arbitrary laws take hold, there is, so far as these are in force, again no civic freedom; and every law is arbitrary which is not a necessary consequence of the unalterable eternal laws of nature. The enduring implicit agreement of all members of the society can be maintained only by such formal laws which are manifest consequences of the laws of nature. They alone contain what is to the obvious benefit of each and all, and cannot contain anything from which the least harm for a rational creature might ever arise. Where public certainty of the common advantage ceases, there too ceases the warrant of the laws and the system of freedom.

Most people have taken other points of view in the examination of political freedom, so that usually it comes down only to the question of whether it is more bearable to submit to the arbitrary power of one individual, of a certain number out of the many, or to the many itself—that is, which variety of despotism would be the best. This question is not really worthy of a wise man's attention.

For this reason, however, a great deal of virtue, a great deal of moral freedom must be present where much true political freedom is to be found, because the laws cannot protect themselves, but rather must be maintained in force by a power, always and everywhere present, which steadfastly resists all that would attack the laws. Thus where the true laws of freedom in fact rule, their will must be the living will of the people. Laws of freedom are none other than laws of the strictest justice, that is, of rational equality. Thus, the spirit which gives these laws weight and duration must be just as far removed from the desire for domination that wishes to oppress as from the baseness which allows itself to be oppressed; and this spirit is the best, the noblest and strongest, which can hold sway over men.

Pure transcendental virtue, this rarest heavenly gift, is not our topic here, but rather the amount and strength of the good and great qualities of the understanding and the heart. The former, perhaps, is to be found even more often in an unhappy state, among all the horrors of corruption, than in a happy and virtuous one. One could, perhaps, see some similarity in the proportions between the external and internal goods of two such peoples—a thought that leads to many others, and cannot be developed here.

From this flows a truth of great significance: that the doctrine of happiness, of virtue, and of justice rests entirely on the theory of freedom, or if one prefers, on the theory of human ability. And so the opposite, a theory of slavery, of human inability, or of the power of the passions, would present a doctrine of human misery, of all the vices, of all abandonment of duties, misdeeds, and crimes. True freedom would thus be identical with virtue. Virtue, however, can dwell only in the human being himself, and its power can be replaced by no other power. The aim of formal laws is to substitute externally for the power of virtue and of freedom. Since formal laws are always related to and grounded on the opposite of both virtue and freedom, their history contains a history of human inability, which cannot be pondered enough. Xenophon maintained that the Spartan constitution alone had *virtue itself* as its aim. This much is certain; it was directed entirely at the suppression of those tendencies and the elimination of those objects which made civil laws necessary. It wanted to enforce customs and character, not just physical acts of commission or omission. But this is not to have *virtue itself* as an object, and Sparta was very far from that.[20] No constitution of a state can or should have virtue itself for an immediate object, because virtue never arises out of any particular external form.

This happens incessantly among men: they confuse effects with their causes, external characteristics with internal ones, symptoms are taken for the thing itself and its source. Good political laws are the effects of virtue and wisdom, not their first cause. They are the effects of them only insofar as foolishness and vice are present which set themselves in opposition to virtue and wisdom. When foolishness and vice get the upper hand, the good laws lose their force, and others arise which are often more successful at resisting virtue and wisdom than the good laws were at resisting foolishness and vice. According to a prophet of this age, when madness becomes epidemic, it receives the name of reason. So it is with vice as well: when it becomes common, it steps into virtue's place. And then they both issue laws. The stronger rules everywhere—*but does not rule justly everywhere.*

Were it possible for some form or another to produce virtue and happiness, or even preserve it securely, then this would certainly have been accomplished first of all by the form of the true divine religion. It was, however, so little capable of this, and of resisting its misuse, that it was precisely the era in which this form was dominant—and indeed almost the only form of humanity, devouring all others—which surpassed all other ages in history in its horrors, and in the duration of these horrors. We also see how this happened. In order to secure the greatest imaginable good for man, or merely to prepare the way toward it, no means could be left untried. Hesitation seemed an absurdity and a sin to the pious zealots. It would be better to give way to folly, and make truth itself into foolishness; better to serve all the vices and even become their companion; to call on the aid of every charm, every seduction, every betrayal, and every compulsion. It began with the most honest intention, which only after a time, and never entirely, lowered itself to a mere pretext. And thus the letter of the truth became the letter of the most miserable nonsense, the holiest doctrine became a means of exterminating all virtue and even conscience itself; the guiding principle of happiness became a snare of corruption. What an example full of deep lessons for the inquisitive mind!

If, however, this hideous epoch is almost over, whom ought we to thank? Perhaps some new form, some coercive institution? By no means. Our thanks should be directed alone to that inner, invisible power which, if not in the forefront, was at least lying in wait everywhere in the world where good happened and evil had to make way for it: the ceaseless striving of reason. As incomplete as reason is in men, it is still the best he has, the only thing that truly helps and stands him in good stead. Whatever he should see outside its light, he will never glimpse; whatever he undertakes unguided by its help will never succeed. Can anyone become wise elsewhere than in the understanding [*Verstand*]; in the understanding that he himself has? Can he become happy outside his own heart?

Here the question arises: How can human society be aided, since it can neither exist without such an external form containing the means of coercion nor secure its welfare through this form?

The answer to this question has already been given.

That coercion without which the society cannot exist does not have as its object that which makes man *good,* but rather that which makes him *evil*; it has a *negative* rather than a *positive* purpose. This purpose can be preserved and secured through external form; and everything positive, virtue and happiness, then arise of themselves from their own source.

Therefore, we would be well advised never to attempt to bring about by force what cannot be forced; and, on the other hand, to use our unified strength to bring about what can and should be enforced.

However, this can be enforced among men: that no one shall have to suffer coercion by another, and it is the *only* thing that brings a *certain, universal, and immutable advantage.*

Open all the books of history. Was it a lack of riches, population, military force, and territory, which sank so many countries into the deepest misery, subjecting their members to every species of distress and disgrace?—On the contrary, it was the mad pursuit of these objects; *it was the lack of a strict, universal, unchanging law of justice, which made every other law an abomination.*

What made men so miserable everywhere? Was it ignorance and stupidity in and of itself; was it contrariness and laziness?—Far from it! It was the mistaken conclusions of wisdom, the errors of understanding, the delusions of wit, coupled with the impatience to act, with the violence of pursuing the aim of every passing moment and forcing it on the oppressed masses.

The unending history of all the evil with which the passions of rulers have everywhere poisoned the earth is hardly more horrible than the history of what has arisen from their best intentions. The union of the two presents a painting that could make infidels of weak souls.

The more one reads history, and the more thoroughly one reads it, the firmer the conviction grows that, as Spinoza says, the greatest foolishness is to expect from another what no one can obtain from himself—namely, that he repress his own passions in order to satisfy the passions of others; that he renounce lust, ambition, and greed in order to obtain and secure their objects for others—or to expect that that individual alone will be gripped by no passion, whose whole being is of such a nature that he, surrounded by the greatest temptations, must feel the greatest attraction to all the passions.[21]

Still another great man emphasizes this truth very pointedly in more than one place in his best work[22] and I gladly call on him in particular as a witness, because no one can honorably deny his clear unbiased understanding. "It should be noted," he says among other things (Book I, chapter 42), "how promptly the Decemvir Appius came to lose all his virtue and how little the impression of the best education was preserved among the noble young Romans who were gathered around him. One should observe among the second Decemvirate how Quintus Fabius, blinded by ambition, seduced by Appius, soon changed from the best man to the worst of all. All legislators of republics and of monarchies should consider the number of examples of this sort and learn to restrain by all means the desires of men, so that none may have the slightest hope of sinning with impunity."[23]

However, this same great man maintains (Book I, chapter 9) that good laws could not be preserved under an unlimited government, and the matter is obvious, even without the preceding. Bad and foolish laws will then take their place. Foolish laws, which are not the immediate result of passions, and which often arise with good intentions from a will in error, by themselves give rise to enough bad consequences to be compared to any other plague on humankind, especially with respect to the length and the extent of their influence.

It is disgusting to hear how people sometimes weigh in the balance certain advantages in policy [*Polizei*], or some other minor matter against the dreadful consequences of the exercise of arbitrary power. Certainly here and there some good must arise from the worst things, indeed perhaps good of a *particular* kind. The good brought about by unrestricted domination is twice as noticeable, chiefly because it arises unexpectedly, quickly, and all at once. This charms the empty-headed. They no longer notice the evil which they have long seen daily, with which they were brought up, and from which hardly anything new can happen; they are used to it, but not used to the good. In contrast, where freedom reigns, all things take their time; which is not such a great misfortune. And then—without considering the immeasurable dangers in the moral realm which are bound up with any quick way of achieving results, especially where only one person is making decisions for all, while the cares of all must remain idle and mute; without mentioning the important advantage which, where many are allowed to care, to examine the case, and to make decisions, easily outweighs the disadvantages of slowness—there lies *immediately* in the matter an advantage of the greatest importance. Where power is not at once available for good purposes, other forces must be used and applied on a large scale to reach these goals. Every item that is under consideration is viewed from all sides, developed as far as possible, examined in all its relations, fought over, and rescued. It steps forth at the outset already armed with grounds of reason and persuasion: thereafter it must be able to withstand and repulse every attack, supported by patience, steadfastness, cleverness, and courage, until at last all doubt has been erased, all prejudice overcome, all hindrances of partisanship cleared from the path. Thus reflection is stimulated everywhere, insight communicated and sharpened, the whole person given the fullest education. Still more: in order to be heard and easily followed, everyone who seeks influence must be concerned about his good name; in the absence of any other power, he must seek to earn the reputation for uprightness and intelligence and the majesty of wisdom and virtue. When great qualities of soul and spirit arise more frequently among a people in this way, so that the masses as well do not simply enjoy their fruits, but themselves think en masse, learn to take part in the whole, learn to prize things and to order them according to their worth, acquire generosity, a feeling for the rights of human nature, and heart, joy, and courage for these rights; if this is all tightly bound up with that which brings hesitation with it.... Oh, who would not happily wait then! Who would not happily do without a thousand unimportant things, bear with a thousand discomforts, and if he is a man, gladly encounter even the greatest dangers!

Where many people are directly engaged in the administration of the state, there arises—beyond the superior advantage that the best virtues and the best qualities of spirit are more frequently awakened and become the share of many men—something else, related more closely to the external welfare of a state, something which Machiavelli, who always focused only on this external welfare, placed in the strongest light. He remarks that states for the most part have fallen because the circumstances and the times had changed but their ways of doing things had not been altered accordingly. The autocrat cannot always be in harmony with his time, because this would require a multiplicity of spiritual gifts and mental characteristics that cannot be found in one man, and some of which directly contradict one another. The hesitant Fabius could not, like Scipio, want to rush to Africa, and had he been the ruler of Rome, Hannibal might easily have crushed it in the end.[24] In fact, however, the man required for each time stepped forward. Thus a state supported by many individuals can resist fate longer than a state ruled by the will of only one individual. For it is impossible for a person to renounce his character, to change his opinions and his way of thinking, to deny his principles and his prejudices, to transform his insights and experiences. In short, it is impossible for a person to be not what he is, but rather what the course of events at any time demands from him.

Plato has Socrates put this question to Adeimantus:[25]

> But what in heaven's name about business matters, the deals that men make with one another,... the payment of contracts that buyers and sellers make among themselves, or which concern hand-work; or the payment and exaction of any dues that may be needful in markets or harbors; that is, concerning all commercial laws, whether in the city or the market, can we bring ourselves to legislate about these and similar things, whatever their names may be?
>
> *Adeimantus:* Nay, 'twould not be fitting to dictate to good and honorable men. For most of the enactments that are needed about these things they will easily, I presume, discover.
>
> *Socrates:* Yes, my friend, provided God grants them the preservation of the principles of law that we have already discussed.
>
> *Adeimantus:* Failing that, they will pass their lives multiplying such petty laws and amending them in the expectation of obtaining what is best.
>
> *Socrates:* You mean that the life of such citizens will resemble that of men who

are sick, yet from intemperance are unwilling to abandon their unwholesome regimen.

Adeimantus: Precisely.

Socrates: They make the attempt in a most charming fashion. For with all their doctoring they accomplish nothing except to complicate and augment their maladies. And they are always hoping that someone will recommend a panacea that will restore their health.[26]

I doubt that anything wiser or of greater substance concerning the administration of government can be said than what Socrates and Adeimantus have spoken here. Everywhere vain cares and foolish wishes suppressed wisdom and sought to dominate; but it is only in our time that they have been permitted to construct a formal system for themselves, a system which protects every act of violence with an excuse and even wants to grant a right to dominate all rights and to deprive laws at will of their most unalterable intention. These cares and these wishes dissolve into the desire for luxurious pleasures. But that is the nature of passion, which it is not attached to the things themselves, but only to their image. Therefore it must always deceive itself, never capture what it seeks, and see all its means fail. We eagerly seek, not pleasure, not the true means to achieving it, but rather only their representation: wealth, still more its splendor, its glamour. And the century has, with respect to these things, fallen into a kind of superstition, which of all varieties of superstition is perhaps the worst. Indeed it has come to such a pass among us, with the esteem or the enthusiasm for wealth, that wealth must be feigned even where it does not exist, just as one used to feign virtue. It has come to the point where, just as once virtue, freedom, and honor counted above all else, wealth may demand every sacrifice. And where is justice to be found now? Where is moderation and wisdom? Where, in protection of rights, are spirit and concord? Where is fairness and true welfare?—Where is real abundance and peaceful possession?

No one understood this better than Thomas Hobbes, this serious thinker whom Leibniz himself honored for his profundity. He did not fail to notice that between contradictory immoderate desires no internal peace can ever be established and that passions can no more be integrated into a system of virtue and freedom than errors into a system of truth. Since he himself believed only in passions and physical drives, he could not teach others justice and virtue. He therefore was honest enough to deny justice and virtue, and did not attempt to derive them from things from which they do not follow. He left every nature pure in itself and the truth *undistorted.* He did not seek *to give evil a good reputation.* In this he was like Machiavelli in his *Prince,* which has been unjustly maligned, because he has given the *true* theory of the unrestricted dominance of a single ruler, and not a false and deceptive one. Could I distribute laurels, these are the men I would crown and wrest them from the heads of deceivers, hypocrites, or the shallow.

I hear more than one voice, asking me mockingly whether I believe that, in a state constructed according to my principles, men would no longer pursue the passions, but would rather pursue wisdom alone? And I answer very patiently: No, I do not believe this. But I do believe the following: that there is an infinite difference between not expressly healing men of their foolishness and expressly leading them to it; that there is an infinite difference between not freeing men from all misery and thrusting them into it by force.

Right at the beginning of this work I remarked that, as blind drives dominate men more than reason does, the help of certain passions in combating other passions is indispensable, but no passions are to be aroused for their own sake, in order to make their object the ultimate object of all wishes, to set it up as the goal of personal and public happiness. I have shown that where this occurs, despotism necessarily breaks in from all sides, that it has broken in everywhere and in every time, and that despotism can never give rise to anything good. I have, with respect to the necessity of despotism in this system, in the end referred to Thomas Hobbes who will leave no doubt in the minds of those still doubtful. Previously, however, it was demonstrated that in this system too, where despotism is neither to be avoided nor done without, it must thwart the intentions of all of its subjects to a greater or lesser degree, and the overwhelming majority in the most horrible way. For it is entirely impossible, given the relationship of virtue and truth to vice and error among men, that he who is permitted to use power to coerce others for their own good, will not far more often use that power to their disadvantage, even where, and indeed often in particular when, his intentions are good, since human foolishness far exceeds even human malice.

Therefore in a state established according to the principles of this treatise, even the passions of each individual member would be given much greater freedom than in other states, for here power would prevent nothing except violations of property, and all forces would be directed solely against lawless violence and arbitrary regulations. Reason and wisdom would have free rein here to the highest extent—not just because of the absence of restrictions, but rather because they, as already demonstrated, would be continually challenged by the most important objects to develop themselves in every way. Perfection is nowhere to be hoped for, for out of flawed material something flawless can never arise, and so even a human society such as the one we wish to see established, a society united exclusively *to protect the security of all rights through the fulfillment of all duties, without which these rights could not exist and could not be valid*, even such a society, the most perfect imaginable for men and the only one which is consistent with reason, would continually have to battle with very great evils. To overcome these evils and to perfect the happiness of men some general means would have to be found to improve their nature from the ground up, a means which only a fool would seek to find among the things of this earth. But we would only be infinitely miserable, if we, *created as we are*, could succeed in finding peace and satisfaction here; and he is the greatest enemy of our race who will seduce or impel us into hoping and wishing for this.[27]

> The lot of a good man is to explain his thoughts freely. He who does not dare to keep his eyes on the two poles of human life, religion and government, is only a coward.
>
> Voltaire

NOTES

1. Book II, chap. 21 §47. Jacobi cites Leibniz's *Nouveaux Essais sur l'entendement humain* from Rudolph Eric Raspe's 1765 edition (*Oeuvres Philosophiques* [Amsterdam and Leipzig, 1765]).—Trans.

2. Justinus Febronius was the pseudonym of Johann Nicolaus von Hontheim, auxiliary bishop of Trier, theologian, and historian. He defended the limitation of papal powers in his *De statu ecclesiae et legitima potestate Romani Pontificus* (1763, 1765).—Trans.

3. Jacobi's discussion takes its point of departure from Johannes von Müller's tract *Reisen der Päpste* (1782), which was occasioned by Pius VI's journey to Vienna in the spring of 1782 in response to the Emperor Joseph II's educational and ecclesiastical reforms. Müller sent a copy of the book, which criticized the autocratic character of Joseph's reforms, to Jacobi in May 1782.—Trans.

4. Johannes von Müller was Swiss.—Trans.

5. Justus Möser was a leading conservative critic of enlightened despotism who saw the rationalist ideal of a state organized toward a single end as standing in contradiction to the true, organic character of society.—Trans.

6. In 1779, Frederick the Great intervened in a legal case involving a miller named Arnold, who, in Frederick's judgment, had received unfair treatment at the hands of noble Prussian judges. Arnold maintained that he had been unable to pay rent on his mill to the lord of the manor on which it was situated because the carp pond of a neighboring manor had drawn off the water necessary to operate it. Frederick supported Arnold's efforts to sue his lord—who had seized and auctioned off the mill—and imprisoned not only the judges who had originally decided against Arnold's claim but also seven other judges who, under orders from Frederick, had studied Arnold's case but decided it had been properly settled in the local court.—Trans.

7. Justus Möser, "Über die deutsche Sprache und Literatur" (1781). In the course of this response to Frederick's *De la littérature allemande*, Möser noted that few in Germany had seen the danger posed by Frederick's autocratic intervention into the administration of law in the Arnold case. For the relevant passage, see *Justus Mösers Sämtliche Werke* (Osnabrück, 1986), 3:73–74.—Trans.

8. Justus Möser, "Von dem wichtigen Unterscheide des würklichen und förmlichen Rechts," in *Patriotische Phantasien* IV (*Justus Mösers Sämtliche Werke* VII:99–100). The parenthetical explanations were inserted by Jacobi.—Trans.

9. *Leviathan*, Pt. I, Chap. XIII. [The parallel passage in the English version of Leviathan reads "Force, and fraud, are in warre the two Cardinall vertues."—Trans.]

10. The word "desire" [*Begierde*] is here employed in its original sense, which encompasses the highest and purest strivings of the soul, and in which "desire" stands in opposition to "disgust" [*Abscheu*]. In this sense, there is no desire which is not good in and for itself and in harmony with reason. Among the emotions [*Affecten*] (which must be distinguished from the passions, since not all emotions are passions) there are those that are in themselves evil, such as hate, envy, or arrogance, that also produce desires, but are not *original* desires.

11. *An Essay on the History of Civil Society*. [The preceding sentence is a paraphrase of Pt. V, Sec. III of the *Essay*, edited by Duncan Forbes (Edinburgh, 1966), 218.—Trans.]

12. *Mémoires de Brandenbourg*. [Jacobi's reference to Frederick the Great's *Mémoires de Brandenbourg* is taken verbatim from Ferguson's text (Forbes edition, pp. 220–221).—Trans.]

13. *An Essay on the History of Civil Society*, Pt. V, sec. 3. [Forbes edition, p. 221.—Trans.]

14. Jacobi is referring to the Dutch philosopher Frans Hemsterhuis (1721–1790). Hemsterhuis, in the 1772 work *Lettre sur l'homme et ses rapports*, which Jacobi cites, argued that the Platonic notion of Eros plays an analogous role in relations between human beings to that played by the power of attraction in the physical world. His work was admired by both Herder and Jacobi, who wrote Hemsterhuis a long letter in July 1784 that included a dialogue between Jacobi and Spinoza that was later incorporated into Jacobi's *Spinoza-Büchlein*.—Trans.

15. *Lettre sur l'homme et ses rapports*, p. 157. See, in addition, Montesquieu in *L'esprit des Loix*, III:v, in comparison with the third section of this same book, where it says among other things: "The Greek statesmen [. . .] knew of no other support to rely upon than the support of virtue. Our statesmen talk only of manufacturing, of trade and commerce, of public revenues, of wealth, and even of luxury and pomp." [In the third section of the third book of *L'esprit des Loix*, Montesquieu argues that "virtue" is the principle on which democratic constitutions rest, while in the fifth section of the third book he argues that "honor" rather than "virtue" serves as the principle of monarchical constitutions.—Trans.]

16. The image of a guardian who has not been appointed by a judge and who never allows his ward to come to maturity will later play an important role in Kant's essay "An Answer to the Question: What Is Enlightenment?" But for Jacobi, as for his friend Hamann, what is at issue here is less a matter of "self-incurred immaturity" than of "self-appointed guardianship."—Trans.

17. "Deluded wretch, with never in his life a glimpse of even the shadow of the Good! And he says that he is doing all this for honor's sake! Where is there honor without moral good? And is it good to have an army without public authority, to seize Roman towns by way of opening the road to the mother city, to plan debt cancellations, recall of exiles, and a hundred other villainies 'all for that first of deities, Sole Power'?" Cicero, *Letters to Attitus*, Bk. VII, Letter XI (Bailey translation).

18. Eumaeus was Odysseus' faithful swineherd.—Trans.

19. *An Essay on the History of Civil Society*, Pt. VI, Sec. I. [Forbes edition, p. 241.—Trans.]

20. One can read the judgment of a contemporary of Xenophon's on Sparta in the eighth book of the *Republic* of Plato. [Plato explicitly mentions the Spartan and Cretan constitutions as being those "which the many praise" at 544c; this is followed by a discussion of timocracy, the constitution based on the love of honor, from 545c to 550b. However, Jacobi's comments owe more to Ferguson's views, especially as expressed in the section "Of National Defense and Conquest," in *An Essay on the History of Civil Society*, Forbes ed., pp. 146–147.—Trans.]

21. *Tractatus politici* (not the *Theologico-politici*), Chap. VI §3. ["And it is surely folly to require of another what one can never obtain from one's self; I mean, that he should be more watchful for another's interest than his own, that he should be free from avarice, envy, and ambition, and so on; especially when he is one, who is subject daily to the strongest temptations of every passion." *Tractatus politici* VI:3 (Elwes translation).—Trans.]

22. Machiavelli, *Discorsi sopra la prima Deca di T. Livio.*

23. Jacobi's translation of Machiavelli's *Discourses* I:42 is rather free. In the Leslie Walker translation, the passage in question reads as follows: "It should also be noted too in the affair of the Decemviri how easily men are corrupted and in nature become transformed, however good they may be and however well taught. Consider, for instance, how the young men whom Appius chose as a bodyguard, soon became friends of tyranny for the sake of the small advantages which accrued; and how Quintus Fabius, one of the second Ten, though an excellent fellow, was after a while blinded by a little ambition and, under the evil influence of Appius, changed his good habits for bad and became like him. Due consideration of this will cause all legislators, whether in a republic or a kingdom, to be all the more ready to restrain human appetites and to deprive them of all hope of doing wrong with impunity."—Trans.

24. Jacobi's analysis appears to have been taken from Machiavelli's discussion in the *Discourses* III:9, where he argues that while Fabius's tendency to proceed with caution was advantageous in holding Hannibal at bay after Hannibal's initial victories, "if Fabius had been king of Rome, he might easily have lost this war, since he was incapable of changing his methods according as circumstances changed. Since, however, he was born in a republic where there were diverse citizens with diverse dispositions, it came about that just as it had a Fabius, who was the best man to keep the war going when circumstances required this, so later it had Scipio at a time suited to its victorious consummation" (Walker translation).—Trans.

25. In the fourth book of the *Republic.*

26. *Republic* 425c–426a; adapted from the Paul Shorey translation.—Trans.

27. The first edition closed with a translation and annotated commentary on Bk. I, Chap. LVIII of Machiavelli's *Discourses*, which discusses why the people are wiser and more reliable than princes.—Trans.

True and False Political Enlightenment

Friedrich Karl von Moser

Translated by John Christian Laursen

In this essay, written in the shadow of the French Revolution, Moser argues that too much light in the wrong places can indeed be harmful. Enlightenment without religion would be pernicious, taking away the crutch and comfort that men need. Since the prevailing natural law theories are human inventions, Moser writes, they really leave men to live by their own passions and will end in war and the ruin of society. He also turns the word fanaticism [Schwärmerei], *often used by impious enlighteners to describe pietistic religion, against those enlighteners.*

Moser was less sanguine about the compatibility of religion and radical enlightenment than Bahrdt and Riem but more so than Hamann. He makes it clear that he is seeking a middle way between radical enlightenment and reactionary conservatism. The motto of his journal, New Patriotic Archive, *was "to light up, not to set on fire."*

Written by the emperor of Japan to the *Wandsbeker Bothen*; Asmus, fifth part, p. 95:

> I would like to have an enlightenment, through which father and son, man and wife, lord and servant, etc., would become truer and more honest in themselves and for each other, and all my subjects would become better subjects and I would become a better ruler. And I am very curious to find out how far the European enlighteners have succeeded in these matters, and how they set about it.[1]

There is an *intellectual* [*geistische*] power that progresses in equal proportion to the oppression of a people, which in the growth and dissemination of its invisible power not only provides a strong counterweight to despotism with all its arts of seduction and delusion but, as time passes, also threatens more and more to win superiority and to shake and topple despotism's innermost foundations.

It always desires to do this, even if in this upheaval not only the lord of the house perishes but also the house with its inhabitants; even if because

First published as "Wahre und falsche politische Aufklärung," Neues Patriotisches Archiv für Deutschland *1 (1792): 527–536. "Written in January, 1792" appeared after the title of this piece in the table of contents for the issue.*

of its predominance the equilibrium is lost; even if the ills and evils which were abolished and destroyed are replaced by only a meager good, and empty truth is given instead of error.

Just as every forbidden, pernicious, and arbitrary authority is comprehended under the one word *despotism,* so the intellectual power standing and working against this despotism may be designated by the word *enlightenment.*

One would have liked to use the word *philosophy* instead, if she were still the pure, chaste daughter of the heavens, come from the hand of the Creator through the godly gift of reason. Here, however, there are distinctions, as in the whole empire of the intellect. There is a good and bad, and also (on closer examination this distinction is generally agreed on) a *true* and a *false enlightenment.*

The business of the former is light, truth, the growth and dissemination of both, harmony, order, quiet, and peace in and over the entire human race.

The business of the latter is delusion instead of illumination, deception instead of instruction, disruption and discord instead of harmony, insolence instead of freedom, the malignant confusion of minds and seduction of human hearts.

All times have had true and false prophets side by side. Truth has its followers, wisdom its students, and seducers their seduced and deceived. Likewise there are those who truly are *enlighteners*; and there are those who fancy themselves and pass themselves off as enlighteners.

The usual statement, common to both but uttered with very different intentions and applications, is: *truth must be able to endure the light.* Fine—but all good police regulations prevent and prohibit bringing an open flame into flammable places, into hay and straw lofts, into stables and the like. Because of the mortal danger, taking a candle into a room where gunpowder is stored is permitted nowhere. It would be criminal, on the pretext of providing light, to bring so many candles into a room and to place them in such a way that the whole house would catch fire. It would be foolish to light candles at bright midday, in order to make the sun shine brighter. It would be nonsense to place candles in the churchyard so that the dead could see in their graves. These are the operations of some of our modern enlighteners, candle bearers, and lantern carriers.

Of much the same substance and superficiality in its application is the excuse: only through the riskiest, wickedest teaching will the truth become more visible, more refined, and more secure. Will an honorable family allow their father to be called a swindler, in order to have the opportunity to defend his honesty? Will a subject be allowed to go around freely in a country inciting simple peasants to disobedience and rebellion, and persuading them that their lord is a false prince? Will a forger go unpunished because through his fraud he helps the warden of the mint to distinguish between good and fake coins?

If it were to become generally taken for granted that under the *pretense* of truth and freedom everything must and ought a priori to be investigated, then no king would be safe on his throne and no honest man would be safe in his bed.

Or, to give another example: if an Italian were to present himself in Berlin, or even better, in Sans Souci,[2] and prove through experiments that he could make the true *Aqua Tofana*,[3] and if he sought an exclusive privilege for its sale in return for promising to instruct the court pharmacist, is it to be expected that his request would fare well? Or is it not more plausible that such an enemy of the human race and disturber of the peace and security of the household would be locked up, along with all his skills, in good custody, and thus prevented from causing harm? The latter is not only believable, but is what actually happened. In the 1750s, Count Christian Ernst zu Stollberg-Wernigerode[4] had the good sense to send such a poison maker, who presented himself as an errant knight and proved the effectiveness of his art on an animal, to the late king of Prussia[5] with an appropriate recommendation, and the artist was thrown into *perpetual confinement.* I have this story from the mouth of the honorable old count himself, who told it in public in the year 1756 at the table of Herr von Reineck[6] in Frankfurt am Main. Now ask anyone, from the Prussian chief chancellor [*Großkanzler*] to the lowliest professor of law: Would someone who carries a poison around and offers it for sale go unpunished because he had not made the poison himself and had only intended to give others the opportunity to investigate the nature and power of this poison *through antidotes*?

Healthy minds and pure hearts agree on the essence, elements, application, utility, benefits, and blessings of *true* enlightenment in all areas and estates. The wise and good prince certainly is as delighted by it, and certainly recognizes its value as gratefully as the most enthusiastic friend of the people is able to extol its praise, and the prince does far more to spread its light.

However, day and night have not yet separated themselves to the extent that truth and deceit can be adequately distinguished from one another. Use and misuse, good and false coins, still lie too close together for there not to be suspicion of danger and deception, for there not to be fear where there is nothing to fear, or carelessness and indifference where vigilant wariness would be needed.

My short and candid avowal is this: all enlightenment that is not grounded in and supported by religion, all enlightenment that does not grow out of the dependence of the created on its Creator and on the goodness and care of the Creator for his human creations, all enlightenment that draws back from the duties of love, reverence, gratitude, and obedience to His will, His commandments, and the institutions of His great world government, all enlightenment that leaves man to his own willfulness, vanity, and passions and inspires him with Lucifer's pride to see himself as his sole, independent ruler and to make his own arbitrary natural law—all such enlightenment is not only the way to destruction, immorality, and depravity but also to the dissolution and ruin of all civil society, and to a war of the human race within itself, that begins with philosophy and ends with scalping and cannibalism.

Every enlightenment—theological, philosophical, and political—is suspect which, to say the least, does not go hand in hand with the temporal and eternal happiness of men. Any religious and political enlightenment that takes from man what he requires for comfort, light, support, and peace in the current state of education of this earthly life—or that wishes to give him more than he can use, employ, and manage according to his powers of intellect and understanding—is deception, fraud, fanaticism [*Schwärmerei*], treachery against man. It is surely not the action of a reasonable and righteous man and is just as evil and dangerous as superstition, unbelief, and despotism.

The truth lies in the middle: happy is he who finds this way, blessed is he who truly, rightly, and clearly shows it to him.

There are, in my opinion, rather more *negative* answers about what is not true enlightenment than general positive principles that can be put out as boundary stones as to how far and wide it may become light, where the day should cease and the night might begin and remain. We weak, shortsighted fragments of men! That which fifty, one hundred, two hundred years ago one could hardly suspect, hope for, wish for, hardly dare whisper, is now preached in all pulpits and from all roofs. That for which ten years ago one would have been fined for *lèse majesté,* and which would have forced others to shout "Flee! Flee!" as Hutten commanded Erasmus,[7] is now affirmed from all university lecterns. It is printed under imperial and territorial rulers' privileges, and the heads of peoples themselves recognize, understand, praise, value, and, like it or not, act on it. We can well reckon when, where, how, and through whom light and illumination have begun. When, where, and how it will end we will be able to know only after the general transformation of all things.

Each century has its own wisdom and foolishness, its own truths and errors. One begins sometimes with the sale of a great truth and ends up with an even greater error. Often the converse also occurs: one learns to walk by falling and despite errors and guesses eventually finds the right way. So may it also happen with the pet ideas which clever and foolish humanity currently peddles on the great French national market, and which will be palmed off and pressed on their worshipers and blind adherents as philosophical-political paper money.[8]

NOTES

1. This passage is quoted from Matthias Claudius (1740–1815), *ASMUS omnia sua SECUM portans, oder Sämtliche Werke des Wandsbecker Bothen* (Wandsbeck, 1789), 5th part, p. 59 (Moser reversed the order of the numerals in the page number).—TRANS.

2. Sans Souci was the name of Frederick the Great's palace in Potsdam.—TRANS.

3. A legendary poison.—TRANS.

4. Count Stollberg-Wernigerode (1691–1771) employed Moser's brother, William Gottfried Moser, as a forestry official.—TRANS.

5. Moser refers here to Frederick II (1712–1786), king of Prussia from 1740 to 1786.—TRANS.

6. Friedrich Ludwig von Reineck (1707–1775), wine merchant in Frankfurt and host to Goethe, among others.—TRANS.

7. Ulrich von Hutten (1488–1523) and Desiderius Erasmus (1469–1536). For the relationship between the two figures, see Hajo Holborn, *Ulrich von Hutten and the German Reformation* (New Haven, 1937).—TRANS.

8. The German word, *Assignaten*, refers to the paper money issued by the French revolutionary government, known as *Assignats.*—TRANS.

On the Influence of Enlightenment on Revolutions

Johann Heinrich Tieftrunk

Translated by Arthur Hirsh

Johann Heinrich Tieftrunk (1759–1837), a disciple of Kant and the first editor of his works, was called to the University of Halle in 1792 in the wake of Woellner's edicts. Politically more conservative than Kant's younger follower Adam Bergk, he suggested in his 1791 book, On State-Craft and Legislation, *that German princes might avoid the revolutionary violence that swept France by undertaking a prudent program of reforms. The same conviction that enlightened, cautious reforms were the principal means of thwarting the outbreak of revolution animates the essay translated here.*

We now live in a century of enlightenment. Should this be said to be an honor or a disgrace for our century? We also live in a century of revolutions. Is it enlightenment which currently undermines the peace of states? Men from all social ranks stand opposed to scholars [*Gelehrten*]. It is said that through enlightenment they have misled the sentiments of the people into discontent. They have spread principles among them which are dangerous for the peace of states. They have disparaged the religion of the people, and in this way have caused anarchy and a general corruption of morals. They bear the responsibility for all the maladies which provoked and which daily continue to provoke our age's spirit of rebellion. Enlightenment, it is said, is the source of revolutions.

One seeks to make all the advances of human knowledge suspect, and for this reason one seeks to link the concept of enlightenment to all kinds of hateful accessory concepts. Today heresy, freethinking, Jacobinism, and the rejection of all authority, however respectable, are called enlightenment. Today enlightenment is treason. One must define the concept of enlightenment precisely and then the question can be posed: To what extent is it responsible for the events of our age?

Enlightenment means nothing more than progress in thinking for oneself

First published anonymously as "Über den Einfluß der Aufklärung auf Revolutionen," in Pharos für Äonen *(January 1794): 3–12 and (February 1794): 83–94.*

[*Selbstdenken*], and consequently also progress in morality. This endeavor is an appeal of rational nature and is the highest duty we owe ourselves and humanity. No holy and venerable truth, on which mankind relies and on which the welfare of civil society and the respect for virtue and religion depends, can be harmed by that, because it is, after all, presupposed to be true. The more I practice thinking for myself and the more I endeavor to bring clarity and coherence to my knowledge, the closer I approach my destiny as man and as citizen.[1] Practical reason gives me the supreme moral law, through which I am led to the most important fundamental truths of religion. The more I lose myself in the contemplation of nature, the more there grows in me reverence, love, and deep respect toward its great Creator. A good, well-ordered mind does not have the arrogance to know secrets that lie beyond the bounds of all knowledge. Thus how can one malign enlightenment, or the optimum use of reason, for the unfortunate overthrow of the French state and the destruction of old, well-established rights and titles? How can one regard enlightenment as the cause of the atrocious, disgraceful deeds instigated by this political upheaval? The destruction of old laws is considered an injury to mankind; would one muzzle reason—the source of all laws, without which one cannot even create a concept of law? Whoever wishes to restrict enlightenment out of fear of losing certain truths through it either has no idea what he wants, either betrays a mistrust of the truths for which he crusades, or is a hypocrite.

Enlightenment instills obedience and respect for the rights of the sovereign by providing grounds for these rights. It teaches man that without civil law his life could neither be secured nor enjoyed. Moreover, it teaches man that he has the state to thank for the most important parts of his happiness: peace, the opportunity to earn a living, social pleasures, the abundance of food, and everything which belongs to the cultivation of his spirit and the education of his children. Man would have to do without all this or possess it only in the most miserable and also the most burdensome way if no social contract—and with it relations between sovereigns and their subjects—had been introduced. Thus he recognizes that restrictions on freedom, which must arise from every reasonable regulation and consequently also from the laws of the state, are inevitably required for both the common and individual welfare, and hence that every reasonable person must willingly put up with these restrictions as well as with all the burdens that the state lays on its citizens, because without them the prevailing good that is decisive for the whole society's welfare cannot be obtained, since it is possible only through exact compliance with the laws of the state.

A people who has no enlightenment is the pawn of every hypocritical fanatic who makes into a divine commandment whatever he finds most advantageous for his own purposes: his lust for power, his self-interest, or whatever. As soon as the conduct of the sovereign touches in the least on the hypocrite's self-interest, the latter will immediately move heaven and earth to advance his own interests, which he knows how to make appear as the will of God, even to the point of using force against the decrees of the princes. Now a biblical proverb will suffice to arm the ignorant masses with fire and sword against the monarch. Now for the glory of God one may renounce obedience to a leader who still exercises his law-giving power in the name of this God. Now for the glory of God one may even throttle hundreds of thousands of one's brothers who do not want to betray their legitimate rulers for the sake of the interests of a few greedy individuals. Now no enterprise is so rash, no crime so unnatural, that one should not at every moment be ready to perpetrate it. And so it is precisely a lack of enlightenment that makes even the best monarchs insecure on their throne. Wasn't the Middle Ages—the epoch of ignorance and superstition—a long string of centuries with one uprising following another? What does the history of these times yield other than rebellions of the subjects against their kings, fanatical civil wars, and plunders, murders, and atrocities of every kind? In short, the history of every age gives us examples of revolutions which were made possible only by the lack of enlightenment.[2]

France itself—had it been truly enlightened—would either never have begun its revolution or else certainly have carried it out better. Not the parroting of a single great writer, but rather knowledge acquired through one's own activity, makes one truly enlightened. And for a nation to be called fully enlightened, such knowledge must be possessed not merely by a few individuals, but rather by the majority of the population and especially by those who are entrusted with the education of the nation. However, in France the clergy and the people were far too estranged from one another to be enlightened, and far more divided between superstition and nonbelief. The French farmer was far behind our own peasants in good principles. Among the French bishops there were no longer any Fenelons or Bossuets.[3] In most cases the education of their seminarians was the least of their concerns. They believed they had done enough if they left their teaching posts to hirelings and spent the income of their churches in Paris. Thus the priesthood and the people fell to ruin. Even the gruesome deeds before which mankind shuddered show the corruption of the people as a whole. A cultured people distinguishes itself through gentle mores and good principles.

It is surely true that enlightenment accustoms men to reasonable thinking and, on the whole, also makes them freer and more candid; but to fear popular uprisings from enlightenment would be the greatest folly. For surely, simple reasoning over right and wrong, truth and error, benefit or harm, has yet to cause misery to anyone in the world. Reason and the proper employment of reason have always been recognized as the antidote to violent emotions. Where there is deliberation, passion is nearly impossible, and without passion rebellion is inconceivable. A man who philosophizes by the hearth about the state certainly will not resolve, on the basis of this philosophizing, to start a rebellion. What kind of terrible force must be set in motion before the endurance of a people, who had always been accustomed to servitude and harsh treatment, bursts through its limits? What kind of violent tension and turmoil must overcome men and how universally must this turmoil spread through the entire nation before a rebellion against the monarch can take place? Whoever has even the least bit of human understanding knows that rebellion is not possible without the most fearsome passion, and knows that this oppressive passion, which would outrage an entire nation against its princes, could only arise from two sources: either from fanaticism or from an oppression overwhelming all the endurance of the people.

Never—*never* can or will an enlightened people do something so alarming, so shocking to love of self and to reason, as to rebel against their princes.

But the pseudoenlightenment, which was almost continuously in fashion before the revolutionary era and which did, in part, contribute to the French Revolution, should be opposed by every fair writer who is committed to virtue and to the welfare of mankind, as should that vanity which wishes to call it "enlightened" if one mocks, doubts, and speaks with arrogant self-assurance about everything others hold sacred and venerable. Certainly this may be expected from Germany's writers, if but once their reading public were weaned from the fashionable books which, along with vices and principles of licentious living, were borrowed from prerevolutionary France as the only school of taste.

It is impossible that reason, if practiced at thinking for oneself and inseparable from morality, could be the source of any malady. On the contrary, it is the only thing which gives humanity its dignity. However, if reason is degraded to being a slave of sensuality and deluded into being the servant of vice, it can only put forward fallacies. It says that the end justifies the means, it considers itself alone as an end and considers everything around it, including human dignity in others, as mere means to its goal.

Enlightenment shows the thinking man that social life is not mere license [*Willkür*] and chance agreement but rather that it is a duty, for if man isolates himself from his fellow man, for whatever reason, he robs himself of the opportunity for his own development and moral improvement and hence does not attain the dignity that he must have in his own eyes and in the eyes of the Lord. Enlightenment teaches that the social bond between men opens a theater and sphere of action for virtue and that virtue is the highest goal and the foundation of social relations. The enlightened person is fully convinced that the law of virtue must precede every society, that one must first be a good person in order to be a good citizen. Because virtue would have no sphere of activity if there were no society, the commitment to virtue requires that man enter into society. If no impulse existed in man to express his freedom according to rational laws, and consequently to act according to a conception of general rules, there never would have developed a stable human society, nor could such a society ever develop. Men would gather and disperse like animals, depending on the accidental needs of the moment, and nothing would be known of duty. Reason is at work, however, far earlier and lets the traces of its own power be known before man becomes conscious of it and makes that which reason indicates to him into law.

The enlightened person thus regards the highest possible degree of morality and refinement of the nation as the ultimate goal of the state and thereby blocks the single and exclusive source which makes possible each and every disorder in human society and rebellion against the state: selfishness. It is an almost universal error, strongly active in all hearts, that posits mere happiness as the highest object of our endeavors and which either completely overlooks moral cultivation or wishes to pursue it only for the sake of happiness, that is, in the service of egoism. The result of this is that every calculation of happiness, especially when it is generalized, in the end comes to naught. Nowhere, however, are these maxims of prudence more inappropriate than where the welfare of the whole state is at stake. Here the pursuit of the interest of individuals necessarily leads the whole to disaster. The history of ancient and modern times supplies sufficient testimony to this.

If, however, man views the state as an organization for the promotion of his morality, then with reverence and deep respect he will observe those same laws against which his self-interest so gladly makes objections.

The enlightened person is convinced that no state can be completely perfect. It can only approach that ideal through endless stages of perfection. A state which takes itself as having achieved perfection must be about to fall again. But mankind as well can climb only step-by-step toward its refinement. Therefore, a popular rebellion and insurrection could not possibly be the means to alter even the worst form of government. It takes a long period of preparation before a state can ascend to a notable height and perfection. What was the reason that the immortal emperor Joseph was able to attain so few of his goals despite his excellent intentions?[4] Nobody can dispute his high degree of insight, his quick powers of comprehension, and his noble resolve to improve his state. He also found the right place where the problem lay and the proper means to implement his decision. He wanted to refine his people and make them happy. Thus he directed his attention to the education of the youth and the improvement of finances. He sought to eliminate errors and root out prejudices. But he found out that as noble and generous as his intentions were, his people were not sufficiently prepared. Many still drank milk while he set before them a much stronger brew. Moreover, he proceeded too hastily. He held the light of the midday sun before the eyes of those recovering from a cataract. Is it any wonder they became more blinded than enlightened? He wanted to complete by himself work which was only possible over several generations and therefore he rushed his noble plans.

A government can and should approach the ideal of a perfect national constitution and legislation only gradually, though incessantly. Such a constitution would flow from the original worth and purpose of mankind; it would view every citizen as an end in itself and would enact only laws through which the general welfare is achieved. These laws should be such that everyone who has the desire and ability to fathom them obeys them willingly; they follow morality and natural law, are derived from wisdom, and are administered with justice. The approach to this ideal of a perfected national constitution goes on forever, and all efforts to attain it will always fall short. That is precisely why it would never occur to a reasonable man that the path to it can be stormed by violent revolutions. But neither should man recoil disheartened because this good, determined by his transcendent nature, soars too high for him ever to attain it. Far be it that the immeasurable distance to idealized human greatness and political perfection discourages us or makes us timid; it is precisely the infinity of perfection prescribed to both which must fill the soul with greater courage and loftier plans. It must teach man that his being extends as far as the goal is set for him, and that the state should continue to perfect itself so long as it has not achieved the ideal of its constitution. Both the human race and its earthly constitution must be regarded as destined for all eternity to an infinite process of perfection. The state, just like man, has neither a resting place nor a stopping point. It requires continuous efforts, not only to preserve what is present, but to work toward a higher and higher inner perfection.

One must never forget that mankind is in a state of continual growth and, through rational self-activity, ought always advance to a higher level. Likewise, the state also constantly develops according to its internal vitality and external relations. It can never reach the point where it can look down on itself, as it were, from its summit and smugly do nothing more than be content with itself, admire its strength and solidity, and enjoy what is reached. The vain delusion already to be perfect has brought many a man to his misery and many a state to its downfall. As the old saying goes, "He who stands pat should watch out that he doesn't fall."

That humanity advances only through constant activity, only through keeping up its steady diligence and attentiveness, is a truth that must be taken to heart above all else. Not through passivity and idle consumption, but rather through active progress can mankind achieve its goals.

Man, who finds himself unrelentingly called to strive for morality, has an eternal object of his self-activity in this striving. For its own sake morality requires subjective culture of man, that is, the development and application of all his talents and abilities. The object of that culture is man himself and the nature which surrounds him. Consequently, morality requires an endless, universal, and ever-increasing culture of man and of the nature which concerns him. The sensible world is completely in tune with this rule, which flows from the spiritual nature of man, so that the sensible world is sustained in its mechanism precisely according to that rule by which mankind should advance through self-activity. Rest and inactivity in nature could quite soon lead to a universal decay and pollution and thereby to the destruction of all things. Through activity and constant motion, however, the air and sea clean themselves, multitudes of creatures breathe inside and outside the bowels of the earth, plants grow, man lives, and everything advances and approaches its goal.

Enlightenment shows kings the only possible path by which violent revolutions can be avoided: always to keep pace with *the culture of the nation.* Or what is even more praiseworthy: always to lead the way on the road to perfection. The germ of gradual improvement lies deep and indestructible in all men's souls. No man who has viewed his nature with even half an eye can mistake this destiny. It is rooted in the nature of mankind and assigned by an apodictic law. And what the wise Creator has planted, man should not destroy. It will also certainly be impossible for any human power to thwart the plans of the Creator and to block forever the magnificent works of His power and wisdom. Here and there, one people after another awakens from its slumber and gradually moves beyond the rude barriers of animality. Thrice fortunate are they if a wise government shows them the way and extends a benevolent hand to the weak.

The progress of the nation, however, increases and rushes more quickly to its goal once the active spirit is first awakened in it and culture has won the land. This path of refinement may go through winding labyrinths: one moment interrupted, the next moving forward with renewed vigor. But the goal is and always remains the same: it gradually turns to *morality* and a *common welfare based on it.* The noble germ of human majesty which every now and then has flourished so splendidly in Europe, and borne such brilliant fruits, is certainly going to wake up in the rest of the world as well. Providence will find means and show ways which are now surely still in the wisdom of Him who is unfathomable.

The enlightened monarch will never lose track of the goal of his government: the improvement of the moral character of the nation. Each of his laws will be reasonable and will carry the stamp of inner necessity and universality. He will provide for the general welfare in accord with general maxims. He will cultivate the nation and bring all its powers to activity and circulation. He will promote the sciences and the arts, industry and agriculture. He will bring harmony and proportion to all sections of the citizenry: in all the rights they enjoy, in all the duties they have to perform, and in all the burdens they have to bear.

He will thus unfailingly prevent all violent insurrections and undesirable changes.

True enlightenment is therefore far removed from promoting violent revolutions. It is, on the contrary, the only way to work against them successfully. Enlightened subjects feel bound by their own reason to subject themselves to every proper order, to obey the laws, and to respect the executive power of the state; to remain true to their duties within their professional and business circles and to do everything possible for themselves and their fellow man. Likewise, the enlightened monarch considers it his holy duty to work through public institutions and legislation so that the noble germ of morality grows more and more in his nation. He is the father of his people; goodness rings from his lips and justice strengthens his arm. The most talented are his aides and conscientiousness is their honor.

Thus love becomes the bond which connects the sovereign and his subjects, and obedience is a willing sacrifice to the laws. No offense, no rebellion, no fear, no threats are to be found.—Armed might is used only against crime, and wrath lashes out only against misdeeds.—The wise prince becomes creator and lord of a noble and happy nation.

NOTES

1. Tieftrunk's definition of enlightenment combines Kant's maxim "think for yourself" with Mendelssohn's discussion of the relationship between enlightenment and the "destiny of man." Note, however, that unlike Mendelssohn, Tieftrunk saw no tensions between the destiny of man as man and the destiny of man as citizen.—Trans.

2. The rebellion in the Netherlands—which greeted with so much ingratitude the untiring endeavor for virtue and human happiness of Joseph II, the father of his peoples—serves here as the most recent example. [In 1789, the Estates-General of the Austrian Netherlands (which roughly corresponds to modern-day Belgium and Luxembourg), opposing Joseph II's anticlerical reforms, declared Joseph deposed and proclaimed the republic of the United States of Belgium.—Trans.]

3. François Fénelon (1651–1715), archbishop of Cambrai, was a leading spokesman for the Quietist movement and the author of the widely circulated *Explications des maximes des saints.* His former patron, and eventual critic, Jacques Bossuet (1627–1704), was bishop of Condom, tutor to the dauphin, and author of the *Discourse on Universal History.* Both were men of immense moral and intellectual stature in seventeenth-century France.—Trans.

4. Joseph II of Austria (1780–1790).—Trans.

Does Enlightenment Cause Revolutions?

Johann Adam Bergk

Translated by Thomas E. Wartenberg

Johann Adam Bergk (1769–1834) was a private scholar in Leipzig who published widely, both under his own name and under a variety of pseudonyms, in the areas of psychology, legal philosophy, and philosophy of religion. An energetic popularizer of Kant's work, his subsequent writings included studies of Kant's Doctrine of Right *and* Doctrine of Virtue *as well as a discussion of the new French constitution in which this essay was reprinted with a new title that left no doubt as to Bergk's position: "Enlightenment Is the Source of All Political Revolutions."*

Complaints that enlightenment brings about revolutions are so vehement and so common that it does not seem useless to undertake an investigation of their truth and legitimacy. Some writers absolve the enlightenment of these accusations and believe that they must defend its innocence. Others, on the contrary, attack it more and more angrily, and scream and rage against every use of reason which is characterized by autonomy and independence in knowledge, belief, and opinion. One will see from the outcome which of the two parties is right or if both are wrong in their assertions.

The first thing we must do is to explore and define the concept of enlightenment. Its distinguishing characteristic is autonomy and freedom from every alien opinion. All of our knowledge and belief is our property through our own inquiries and our own efforts and is adapted to the form of our spirit. *Enlightenment* is thus *the free, independent use of all of our predispositions and powers in thought and action.*[1] Since every activity of our spirit expresses itself through representation [*Vorstellen*] as the basis of every thought and action, and since every representation consists of matter and form, there is thus a double enlightenment: a material enlightenment and a formal enlightenment.

Originally published as "Bewirkt die Aufklärung Revolutionen?" Deutsche Monatsschrift *(1795): 268–279. Bergk attached a note to the title characterizing this essay as "a sketch for further contributions of political, legal, and psychological content, which will shortly appear." The essay was republished in his 1796 book* Untersuchungen aus dem Natur-, Staats- und Völkerrecht mit einer Kritik der neuesten Konstitution der französischen Republik.

What, then, is formal enlightenment? It is the fitness and readiness of all powers for every autonomous use *insofar as this has been acquired by means of the development and training of all human predispositions in accordance with their natural ends.* Culture and enlightenment are here equivalent. Enlightenment is as various as the differing original predispositions and differing types of activities of the human spirit. Now, man has three predispositions.[2] The first predisposition is toward animality, which restricts itself to sensory pleasure. What is most enlightened here is the seeking out and enjoyment of the most enduring, most complex, and most agreeable pleasures. At this level of culture, man is totally passive, for he awaits and receives all of the material of pleasure from (inner and outer) nature through involuntary impressions. The second predisposition is toward reason, a predisposition which expresses itself through thought. This predisposition, whose receptivity to materiality sometimes binds it to animality and sometimes gives itself its own material, always produces itself autonomously and freely. Reason is not compelled, nor does it have obscure impressions. Rather, it conducts its affairs with self-consciousness, it commands as a ruler, and it impresses on everything that it touches the character of its own nature—unconditioned unity and completeness. The man who has the courage and the power to use his own understanding everywhere has reached the highest level of enlightenment in this regard. He therefore genuinely thinks for himself: he has liberated himself from every certainty that has not been freely accepted by the form of intellect [*Geist*] peculiar to him. The third predisposition is the predisposition toward personality. It tears man completely away from the realm of natural necessity and places him in the realm of freedom. This predisposition manifests itself in two autonomous acts, first as practical reason, second as free will. Independently of all inner and outer compulsion, it determines itself for itself and through its own pure activity. It gives itself a law, which it follows or transgresses through its own freedom. The most enlightened person in this respect is he who, in all his commissions and omissions, acts with consciousness of the law. Such a person has removed all contingency from his life and no longer relates passively to the play of outer or inner impressions. Rather, he possesses a character, that is, the power and prudence always to take up the same maxim through his free action and to subordinate everything to his own autonomy.

Material enlightenment refers to a *particular* object and is thus as various as the countless objects of sensible and supersensible nature for which men strive and which they can fashion as resting within the boundaries of their knowledge and action. As a result, a man is often reasonable and free of prejudice in one science, yet bigoted and superstitious in others, for example, one who dares to think for himself in everything, only to give up all free use of his reason in theological and religious matters.

Now we can draw closer to our problem of whether enlightenment causes revolutions. By a revolution I understand here neither a sensory (physical) nor an intellectual revolution, but rather a moral one—and indeed not a moral one in the sense of belonging to the domain of the conscience, but a political and legal one, standing under the domain of external laws. I distinguish revolution from insurrection [*Aufruhr*] and rebellion [*Aufstand*]. It is not the resistance of an individual against the authorities, or the disobedience of the majority against sundry powers, but rather a violent and total change in the basic principles of a constitution. What, then, is the cause of such an upheaval? It appears to me to have a double aspect: (1) an *occasioning* (external) cause and (2) a *producing* (internal) cause. The presence of external causes will never bring about a revolution so long as internal causes are not simultaneously present. External causes strike lifeless bodies that, at most, alter their positions but are then left at rest. Every external and internal cause is related to *sensory pleasure* or to *thought* or to *law*.

A nation whose needs reach only to the sensory neither can nor ever will undertake a revolution, no matter how extremely oppressed it is and how spare and miserable its pleasures, no matter how stifled its cogitative powers and how wounded its conscience. Insurrections can break out within it, but as soon as force appears against them, the nation will sink back into its lethargy and dishonorable patience. Its entire existence is limited to mere sensibility: fear and hope are the sole motives that reign supreme over it. It is therefore cowardly, lazy, accustomed to oppression and despotism, and it fears the loss of its life on this earth in every gentle breeze that its guardian angel arouses in it as a resistance against injustice. But since all of its influencing causes are transitory and changeable, it immediately forgets all of its suffering and seeks to stupefy and to stifle present sufferings in indolence and intoxication of the senses. History still gives us examples of peoples who suffer everything so long as they still can live and clothe themselves. The Turks and all Asiatic and African peoples stand on this level of culture, where every offense against the inalienable rights of intelligible nature will be patiently borne so long as their sensory life is not totally endangered and their demise is not at hand. Revolutions in favor of external rights are impossible for them, even though insurrections often break out and one despot can dethrone another with the help of his slaves.

The second inducement to revolution is the suppression of the expression of cogitative powers. Can their repression bring about an upheaval? Since these activities limit themselves to objects of speculation that always operate in the inner life of man and that can elude all force; and since a nation at this level of intellectual enlightenment feels no moral indignation over interference in the external operation of thought; and since it is affected by neither higher moral indignation nor disdain for physical force or even for death, it will—regardless of how unjustly the use of its powers may be oppressed—never rebel on account of duty and right. It is, to be sure, practiced in thinking; however, it does not yet see the commandments of moral nature in their solemn strength, fearful holiness, and judicial seriousness. Nearly all the peoples of Europe stood at this level of enlightenment prior to the French Revolution. However, since this epoch, more peoples have taken powerful strides toward a culture that is of an eternal and unalterable nature, that gives life and courage, that forms greatness of character, and that is sternly bound to right. On every side one asks, "Is this act or that practice just or unjust?" or "What right does this or that one have?" Just as powerful as the French Revolution is the effect in Germany of the great convulsion that a German man brought about in the realms of knowledge, belief, and opinion, and that will cause incalculable alterations for the betterment of humanity in all that people think and do.[3] A nation that possesses merely speculative enlightenment is, at most, cunning, clever, refined, selfish, and still cowardly. Out of a fear of physical violence and the loss of its life, it quietly endures all insults to its inalienable rights and is never in the position to establish a condition of public right [*äussere Recht*] through a rebellion against injustice.

When, however, the third predisposition is finally developed in a nation, and it has won force, strength, and endurance through practice, it declares courageously and undauntedly that every violation of the rights of man is contrary to duty. The life of the senses is only worthwhile for it because it is the condition for fulfilling the duties of men on earth. If the exercise of their perfect rights are still hindered, they sacrifice their lives as a duty. No other limitation of sensory pleasure, no other commands that seek to place limitations on the cogitative power will be tolerated, except for those within the limits of external laws—of independence, freedom, and equality.[4] If a nation stands on the level of moral enlightenment and fearlessly judges right and wrong according to universally valid laws, then continual offenses against human rights will result in a revolution. The nation is acquainted with its duties and rights, it knows what it *should* and *may* demand. And even if the greater part of the nation takes no account of its moral indignation at these illegal infringements and even if its feelings are still not raised into concepts which have been illuminated through reflection, such a nation—whose sensitivity to right and wrong has been sharpened and even enlivened by unjust suffering—will require only a slight offense to be placed in a revolutionary condition.

One sees, therefore, that moral enlightenment must precede every revolution, with all its external sufferings and burdens, in order to make a nation eager, strong, courageous, indefatigable, fearless, and unanimous. In epochs of enjoyment and speculation, courage and intrepidity are lacking, and as great a diversity of opinion rules as there are objects for the sensibility and cogitative power. Thus no unanimity or general cooperation is to be expected when oppression curtails enjoyment and tyranny oppresses thought. From the perspective of right, in contrast, we can expect to find unity (since right is contained in the mere form of reason), strength and courage (since right rises above the world of the senses), and disdain for all dangers (since an infinitely persisting enthusiasm constantly invigorates the intent). The foundation of every revolution is therefore external oppression and moral culture. If the external arrangements do not correspond with the pronouncements of conscience, if the nation recognizes or senses the injustices that burden it and mock its humanity, then a revolution is unavoidable. It can be avoided, however, if the constitution keeps equal pace with moral enlightenment, if the government always respects the general will of the nation and executes it, if it does not insolently and rashly continue its offenses against justice, but rather knows the spirit of the time, and how to guide and use it.

So long as a merely sensible and intellectual culture flourishes in a nation, there will arise no thoughts about an alteration of the principles of the constitution. As soon, however, as moral nature develops through the various relationships of men and their conflict with one another, and thus moral sentiments are sharpened and activated, revolutions can only be hindered by bettering the constitution and by introducing a form that administers external law. *Material* enlightenment has no connection to political transformations. Man is often totally ignored by such enlightened people. What, for example, do our naturalists, astronomers, theologians, jurists, and so forth, care about a just constitution among human beings? Only the impulse toward self-interest is awake and active in them, all their thoughts are either concerned with acquisitiveness or with the improvement of their individual discipline. What does man matter to them? Haven't they repressed or even cut off all the noble activity of humanity in themselves? If one speaks with them about the duties and rights of mankind, they believe that they are listening to a being from another world, our thoughts are strange to them and our demands appear to them to be at best charming fictions and lovable fantasies [*Schwärmereien*]. And why?—because they are not men themselves. For man first cultivates all of his predispositions and, not defying nature, subordinates none of them to any standard other than that of following their worth and thus the goal of nature. To him everything that concerns man is valuable and precious, and he takes an interest in it as his own affair. He sharpens, exercises, and enlivens his moral sentiments not only to comprehend the just [*das Recht*] but also to act in accord with its law [*Gesetz*] and to realize it in the world. With what object, however, are these enlightened ones less acquainted than with themselves? Is not human nature and its effects a totally foreign world to them?

One could now raise the question: *May* such a (formal) enlightenment be prevented? If I am not mistaken, this means the same as: May man be man? The moral law commands that this be without exception, in that man *ought* to develop and make useful all of his predispositions and powers since this eases compliance with the moral commandments and promotes obedience to the conscience.[5] But *can* one hinder this enlightenment? So long as men live next to one another and together with one another, their powers will conflict with one another through the intersection of their interests, and thus they attain facility and obtain an ever greater and persistent skillfulness.[6] Nature compels man to enlighten himself: and once enlightenment spreads its roots in a nation, it is easier to exterminate mankind than to exterminate enlightenment.

But who *now* disseminates the most enlightenment among men? Events of the day that have justice [*Recht*] as their exclusive concern, and the writer. Writers take up this office out of duty, out of a concern for the development of the human species, and for the easing and hastening of its culture. Irrationality, prejudice, lust for power, ignorance, and immorality have risen up against every honest writer, have slandered his intentions, blackened his character, and sought to corrupt his conscientiousness. Writers take up this office out of a duty of conscience, for this reason they are defamed as harmful, and in fact they are. But whom do they threaten with destruction? Not truth or virtue: for the former is what they seek and the latter is what they practice with all their powers so that its dominion may be broadened. Rather, they oppose errors of every sort, they have declared war on all prejudices and vices, and in that they do nothing more or less than a human duty. Hence writers promote revolutions out of a sense of duty: for they *ought* to illuminate the understanding, enliven the moral sentiments, enlighten the human race about its duties and rights, and benevolently nurture and enrich the minds and hearts of their readers. In doing so, they alter and broaden views on things and inscribe in the hearts of men the demands that they *ought* and *may* make. Out of necessity they prepare for revolutions and, when there is a persistence of the tension which consists in citizens' understanding something as unjust since it does not correspond with their claims as men, they cause revolutions. For man has an impulse toward truth and toward justice and concerns himself with making all human arrangements adequate to the laws of truth and justice. Now when one of the representations of that which is subordinated to the free choice of men still bears an alien characteristic, man forces and impels all that is dependent on his freedom to be given a new form, analogous to his insights and his enlightenment. Thus men who hold the arrangement of their state to be unjust or inexpedient can find neither rest nor repose until they have given it a new shape. Why should we therefore falsely absolve writers of the honorable reproach that they cause and promote revolutions? We do not, of course, wish them to act without duty or conscience, to distort the truth, and, timidly and, basely, to leave its service. Is this not to say to them: Depart from human nature and become—Heaven knows what! Each such defense is an insult to reason and a disdain for mankind and can only appeal to the craven, selfish, and immature. Enlightenment is justly accused as the cause of revolutions; and writers, who nurture and bolster culture and contribute to this transformation, share the guilt. But cannot the state prosecute and banish and silence writers if they disturb the peace and bring harm and unhappiness to society? Would you rather perform an injustice than suffer harm, and rather be without conscience than be unhappy? What do you call harm and unhappiness for society? That which conflicts with your prejudices and your self-interest? Your happiness, however, makes for injustice. But what about the whole? Do not worry about the welfare of the world; you do not know what you want. One thing is demanded of you: to do what is right. Let writers make their way, they are the salt of mankind since they guard against stupidity and lethargy. If they act unjustly, they will have to answer to their consciences. As writers, they perform their duty to express their opinion and conviction. If you wish to prevent them from doing this, you overstep your duty, for you injure a right of man in them. Therefore, do you dare to appear before the Holy One with your offering in your heart? Give an account of your actions before Him and be a man!

NOTES

1. Cf. Kant's definition of enlightenment as "the courage to use your own understanding" in "An Answer to the Question: What is Enlightenment?" (translated above, p. 58).

2. The discussion of these three "predispositions" roughly parallels that of Kant's *Religion innerhalb der Grenzen der bloßen Vernunft* AA VI:26–28 (*Religion within the Limits of Reason Alone*, trans. T. M. Greene and H. H. Hudson [New York, 1960], 21–23). The section of the book that elaborates these predispositions was initially published in the *Berlinische Monatsschrift* of April 1792.—TRANS.

3. The "German man" in question is Immanuel Kant.—TRANS.

4. See Kant's discussion of "freedom, equality, and independence" as the a priori principles on which the "civil state" rests, in "On the Common Saying: 'This May Be True in Theory, but It Does Not Apply in Practice'" (AA VIII:290–297), an essay that initially appeared in the *Berlinische Monatsschrift* in September 1793.—TRANS.

5. In lectures on ethics delivered between 1775 and 1780, Kant argued that among the duties to oneself was a "universal duty which devolves upon man of so ordering his life as to be fit for the performance of all moral duties" (*Lectures on Ethics*, trans. Lewis Infield [London, 1979], 125). Kant made the same point in §§19–22 of his *Metaphysik der Sitten*, published two years after Bergk's essay.—TRANS.

6. Cf. the "Fourth Proposition" in Kant's "Idea for a Universal History with a Cosmopolitan Intent," AA VIII:20–22 (Kant, *Political Writings*, pp. 44–45).—TRANS.

PART TWO

Historical Reflections

The Berlin Wednesday Society

Günter Birtsch

Translated by Arthur Hirsh

The Society of Friends of Enlightenment, which existed in Berlin between 1783 and 1798 and was commonly known by the name "Wednesday Society,"[1] was founded at the high point of the "society movement" of the Enlightenment.[2] Organized as a circle of friends, it belonged to a common type of enlightened learned societies and had a special significance because of the official status and intellectual influence of the majority of its members. In his autobiography, the important Prussian jurist Ernst Ferdinand Klein characterized not the Royal Academy of Sciences (of which he was also a member) but rather the Wednesday Society as a society of "insightful men of affairs," which had been and would remain "perhaps incomparable." Klein considered it "the greatest happiness" in his life "to have been a member of this society."[3]

Situated on the border between the private circle and the secret society, the Society required in the first sentence of its founding statute, written at the end of 1783, that "each member... on his honor hold in strict confidence everything discussed in the Society, even speaking little of its existence."[4] Although the maximum number of members was set at twenty-four, the frequent meetings held alternately in the members' homes hardly allowed the pledge of secrecy to be upheld: according to the bylaws the Society was to meet on the first and third Wednesday of each month from Michaelmas (29 September) until Easter; for the rest of the year it was to meet on the first Wednesday. The bylaws also provided the "external" name "Wednesday Society," apparently in imitation of the Berlin Monday Club, a purely social organization that had been established in 1749.[5] The

This essay was originally published as "Die Berliner Mittwochsgesellschaft" in Über den Prozess der Aufklärung in Deutschland im 18. Jahrhundert, *ed. Hans Erich Bödeker and Ulrich Herrmann (Göttingen, 1987), 94–112.*

"internal" name, "Society of Friends of Enlightenment," corresponded to its enlightened program.

The rigorously ordered agenda bore out the educational goal of mutual and societal enlightenment.[6] Meetings were to consist of a brief lecture followed by a disciplined discussion in which participants, whose responses [*Vota*] were to be entered into the minutes according to the founding statutes of 1783, spoke according to the seating arrangement. The meeting began at six o'clock, a dinner shared by all ended it at eight. With the exception of double memberships,[7] this was the sole trait shared in common with the weekly Monday Club. Since the lectures and Vota circulated among the members in a set order—written Vota were soon adopted—there was opportunity for thorough discussion of the subject at hand. The spectrum of topics addressed was as multifaceted as the Enlightenment itself. The bylaws prohibited such narrowly scholarly subjects as "pure theology, jurisprudence, medicine, mathematics, philological criticism, and newspaper reports, but not the conclusions resulting from them for enlightenment and for the good of humanity." Purely academic theorizing as well as entertaining conversation about events was to be avoided in favor of practically oriented enlightened reflection.

Members were bound together by a faith in the beneficial consequences of a correctly understood enlightenment and by a readiness to tear down existing barriers—insofar as this was possible and meaningful within the framework of existing social conditions—and to aid the propagation of the blessings of enlightenment in society and the state. Within their fundamental consensus, they were to voice freely the differing intellectual positions and individual values; further, they were to develop an understanding and a program for enlightenment as shaped by the precept of perfectibility, as well as to discuss freely under the protection of the strictest secrecy the relevant proposals for reform. Accordingly, one of the most active members of the Society, the royal physician Johann Karl Wilhelm Möhsen, in his lecture of 17 December 1783 with reference to the question "What is to be done toward the enlightenment of the citizenry?" made a series of proposals he thought especially appropriate to achieve the goal of the Society "to enlighten us and our fellow citizens." Möhsen regarded as a first task that of "determining precisely" the concept of enlightenment; after that, the Society was to investigate the "deficiencies and infirmities in the direction of the understanding, in the manner of thinking, in the prejudices, and in the ethics of our nation—or at least of our immediate public" and the origins of these deficiencies. Further, "those prejudices and errors which are the most pernicious" were to be attacked and eradicated first, and "those truths, whose general recognition is most necessary," were to be "further" developed and disseminated.[8]

The Vota, recorded in Möhsen's papers, on this and other lectures as well as other literary activities sponsored by the Wednesday Society, give an idea not only of the enlightened self-understanding of the Wednesday Society but also of the differing social and political positions of its members.

Following an overview of the composition of the Society (I), its understanding of enlightenment (II) and its concept of society and political ideals (III) will be sketched.

I. THE COMPOSITION OF THE SOCIETY

The statute establishing the Society contains a first list of members. Article 10 sets forth twelve names in numerical order, with the numbers indicating the order of presentations and Vota.[9]

The first named is Wilhelm Abraham Teller (b. 1734), Upper Consistory councillor [*Oberkonsistorialrat*] in the Berlin Consistory since 1767. Teller, who had previously taught as professor of theology in Helmstedt and had encountered strenuous orthodox opposition in 1764 with his textbook on Christian faith, followed the path of a theological rationalism that reinterpreted and ultimately abandoned revealed beliefs in favor of rational truths. During the era of Frederick the Great's reform absolutism, he displayed an enlightened activism within the Prussian ecclesiastical administration and for this reason came into conflict, under Frederick the Great's successor, Frederick William II, with Woellner's reactionary ecclesiastical policy.[10]

Johann Jacob Engel (b. 1741), professor of moral philosophy and fine arts at the Joachimsthal Gymnasium in Berlin since 1776, was appointed director of the Royal National Theater in Berlin in 1787 by Frederick William II. He served the king as royal tutor, teaching the future King Frederick William III as well as Alexander and Wilhelm von Humboldt. He had become known to a wider public as theater director and erudite writer and, above all, as the editor of the three-volume collection *Philosopher for the World*, appearing from 1775 onward, which included writings by Moses Mendelssohn, Christian Garve, and others.

In the third place was Frederich Nicolai (b. 1733), the renowned publisher and bookseller, energetic writer, and tireless defender of a German enlightenment oriented toward "healthy reason." From 1765 onward he was editor of the *Allgemeine Deutsche Bibliothek*, the most important literary forum of the German Enlightenment.

Following him as number four was the scholar and statesman Christian Wilhelm von Dohm (b. 1751), one of the most important figures among the men of letters in the enlightened Prussian bureaucracy and one of the most influential authors of the Enlightenment. A professor of statistics and cameral and fiscal sciences at the Carolinum at Kassel since 1776 and from 1779 onward a Prussian military councillor, Dohm had made a name for himself above all with his "On the Civil Improvement of the Jews," whose first part appeared in 1781. The work was inspired by Moses Mendelssohn, and in it Dohm stepped forward as advocate of especially the poorer segment of Jews. Dohm was also an active member of the Monday Club but had already left Berlin in 1786 because of his responsibilities in the Prussian foreign service.

The previously mentioned Johann Karl Wilhelm Möhsen (b. 1722), physician to Frederick the Great since 1778 and renowned as one of the most learned doctors of his time, was a member of numerous learned societies, including the Parisian medical society. Möhsen embodied the very model of the polymath. Among other matters he dedicated himself to wide-ranging studies reaching far back into the history of the sciences in the Mark Brandenburg.

Following Möhsen in sixth place was Johann Samuel Diterich (b. 1721), pastor at the Marienkirche, who was appointed to the Upper Consistory [*Oberkonsistorium*] in 1770. Diterich was schooled in Wolff's teachings on natural law at Frankfurt/Oder and at Halle and was without doubt of a deep Christian piety. Nevertheless, his theological rationalism and natural law concept of duty left their mark not only on his *Instruction on Attaining Bliss through Christ's Teachings*, which had appeared in numerous editions since 1772, but also on his activities in the area of Protestant church song, as attested by his revisions and new compositions in the *Hymnal for Use in Worship in the Royal Prussian Lands*, on which he collaborated with Teller and Spalding in 1780.

Following Diterich on the list of members was Ernst Ferdinand Klein (b. 1744), who had been called to Berlin in the winter of 1781 by the chief chancellor [*Großkanzler*], Baron von Carmer, to collaborate on Prussian legal reform. Klein made his name not only through an important contribution to the codification of the *Allgemeines Landrecht für die Preußischen Staaten* (Prussian General Code), especially its penal statutes, but also as a teacher of law on the penal philosophy and jurisprudence of the late Enlightenment. With his essay "Freedom and Property" (1790)—fictitious dialogues concerning the resolutions of the French National Assembly—he presented a lifelike sketch of the dialogues occurring in the Wednesday Society. Klein left Berlin in 1791 after his appointment as director of the University at Halle, returning in 1800 as Upper Court Councillor [*Obertribunalsrat*].

In eighth place on the list of members in the founding statutes appeared Johann Friedrich Zöllner (b. 1748), at first pastor at the Charité,[11] after 1782 deacon at the Marienkirche, and in 1788 Upper Consistory Councillor. As a broadly educated and enlightened writer, Zöllner had made popular education his central concern, as attested by his 1782 *Reader for All Classes*, which included generally accessible essays on various disciplines, as well as his work on national education, which appeared in 1804, one year before his death.

After the theologian Zöllner, Christian Gottlieb Selle (b. 1748), doctor at the Charité, is entered. Selle, the physician of Frederick the Great and Frederick William II, was regarded as an important philosophical thinker and polymath. He had published a series of natural scientific and medical studies, and his 1781 handbook of clinical medicine, *Clinical Medicine, or Handbook of Medical Practice*, which was translated into French and Latin, appeared in not less than eight editions. Selle was director of the philosophical section of the Royal Academy of Sciences from 1797. In addition to his works *Philosophical Discourses* (1780) and *Foundations of Philosophy* (1788), he wrote other philosophical treatises, which appeared in installments in the *Berlinische Monatsschrift* between 1783 and 1790. This journal's editors, Friedrich Gedike and Johann Erich Biester, were entered as numbers ten and eleven in the Society's founding statutes.

Friedrich Gedike (b. 1754), trained in theology and classical philology at the University of Frankfurt/Oder, became director of the Friedrich-Werder Gymnasium at the age of twenty-five. As a writer on education and a leading educator (in 1784 he became Upper Consistory Councillor and in 1787 councillor in the newly founded Upper Education Board [*Oberschulkollegium*]), he exercised a considerable influence on the development of Prussia's educational system. In Berlin he took the initiative of founding a teachers' college for prospective secondary school instructors and played a leading role in the introduction of graduation examinations (the *Abitur*) in 1788.

Johann Erich Biester (b. 1749) had been librarian of the Royal Library in Berlin since 1784. After studying law, literary history, and languages at the University of Göttingen and a brief stint teaching at the now-forgotten University of Bützow where he was awarded his doctorate in law, he became in 1777—through Nicolai's good offices—secretary to Baron von Zedlitz, the minister of justice responsible for the administration of educational affairs and the head of the Department for Ecclesiastical Affairs.[12] Together with Gedike he founded the *Berlinische Monatsschrift* in 1783 and, after 1791, edited it himself. The journal was the organ of the Berlin Enlightenment and, in the narrower sense, the public organ of the Wednesday Society of which Biester functioned as secretary.[13]

The Upper Consistory Councillor Karl Franz von Irwing (b. 1728)—like Gedike a lay member of the Upper Consistory and after 1797 president of the Upper Education Board—stood twelfth on the membership list of the founding statutes. Irwing was a trained jurist, but in the words of Minister von Massow, he was regarded "more as a scholar," as "a practical Consistory councillor [*Konsistorialrat*] and public educator." He published philosophical and psychological studies, among which were his *Thoughts on Teaching Methods in Philosophy* (1773) and *Inquiries and Experiences on Mankind* (published in four volumes between 1772 and 1785). He played a decisive role in the founding of the Society, as the letter of invitation of 3 October 1783 reprinted by Tholuck attests.[14]

Möhsen had entered eight additional names in the margins of the copy of the Society's founding statutes (written in Biester's handwriting) found among Möhsen's papers. Two were clergymen active as scholars and writers: the Lutheran pastor of the Church of the Royal Orphanage and Kalandshof, Gottlieb Ernst Schmid (b. 1727), and the Reformed pastor of the Jerusalem and New Church, Johann Georg Gebhard (b. 1743). Representatives of the enlightened bureaucracy were also listed: J. H. Wlömer (b. 1726), a member of the Jurisdictional Commission [*Jurisdiktionskommission*] in the General Directory, Friedrich Wilhelm von Beneke, Cameral Court Councillor [*Kammergerichtsrat*], and H. C. Siebman, councillor of the War and Territorial Chamber [*Kriegs- und Domänenkammer*].

We also find here the names of two of the more important representatives of Prussian reform absolutism: Privy Justice and Upper Tribunal Councillor [*Geheimer Justiz- und Obertribunalsrat*] Carl Gottlieb Svarez and Privy Finance Councillor [*Geheimer Finanzrat*] (later Minister) Karl August von Struensee. C. G. Svarez (b. 1746), the main author of the Prussian General Code of 1794, was schooled in Wolffian natural law by Darjes at Frankfurt/Oder. From 1780 onward, he played a key role in the Prussian Law Commission under Justice Minister Baron von Carmer. His legislative and reform work along with his literary activities reveal him to have been at the height of the scholarship available in his day. His most important intellectual legacy, his lectures to the Crown Prince, allows us deep insight into the natural right and rational juridical foundations of Prussian reform legislation in the late Enlightenment.[15]

Karl August von Struensee (b. 1735), in addition to studying theology, devoted himself to mathematics and philosophy and at the age of twenty-two was engaged as professor of mathematics and philosophy at the academy for nobles [*Ritterakademie*] in Liegnitz. He made a name for himself with studies in military and fiscal science before entering the service of Denmark (1771–1777). In 1782 he became director of Prussian maritime trade, and in 1791 he succeeded Werder as Minister of Excise, Customs, Commerce, and Manufacturing. Among those of Struensee's writings most valuable for the historian are his periodic discussions in the *Berlinische Monatsschrift* of French fiscal administration in the crisis years of 1788–1790.

Finally, the last name written in the margins of the founding statutes was that of the prince's tutor, Franz von Leuchsenring (b. 1746), an enigmatic personality. For a brief period the teacher of the later Frederick William III and enthusiastic member of the Illuminati—with the Lodge name "Leveller"—he allied himself with the followers of the French Revolution. He was expelled from Berlin in 1792 because of his partisanship for the Revolution. He marked the extreme Left of the Wednesday Society and is possibly depicted as the pro-Republican "Menon" in Ernst Ferdinand Klein's discussion, cast in the form of a Platonic dialogue, of the resolutions of the French National Assembly of 1790. Klein's work has been regarded as a reconstruction of the debates within the Wednesday Society itself.[16]

On a second revised and expanded list of names that Biester dated "end of April 1784," the name of the philosopher Moses Mendelssohn (b. 1729) is entered in the fifth position. He was honorary member of the Society, and important Vota by him from 1783–1784 can be found among Möhsen's papers.[17] On this list is also found the name of Upper Consistory Councillor Johann Joachim Spalding (b. 1714) who adhered to the neological wing within Protestant theology. He had early on turned away from orthodoxy, and his numerous writings, among others, *The Usefulness of the Clergy* (1772), demonstrate that he placed enlightened efforts toward the improvement and perfection of humanity, not the preaching of the Gospel, at the center of his work.

Spalding was the oldest member of the Society. Numerically, the generation born in the 1740s was most strongly represented. It included Biester, Engel, Klein, Svarez, Leuchsenring, and Gebhard as well as some others still to be named who joined the Society later, such as Privy Finance Councillor Leopold Friedrich Günther von Göckingk (b. 1748), to whom we owe, among other writings, a biography of Friedrich Nicolai and Privy Upper Tribunal Councillor [*Geheimer Obertribunalsrat*] Johann Siegfried Mayer (b. 1747). Contrary to the accounts of Heinrich Meisner and Adolf Stölzel, Privy Councillor Johann Christoph Andreas Mayer, a physician and former professor of pharmacology at the University of Frankfurt/Oder, was not a member.[18]

The participants in the Society are thus almost all eminent writers and—with the exception of Nicolai and Mendelssohn—Prussian public servants. Still, we can further distinguish among three groups of participants. One prominent group comes from the higher reaches of the judiciary and the civil service: Svarez and Klein as well as Dohm and Struensee are from the highest level. A second group, including Teller and Spalding, consists of ecclesiastical officeholders and members of the Upper Consistory of the Lutheran church. A third group brings together philosophers, polymaths, and publicists. To this group belongs, above all, Moses Mendelssohn and the physician/scholars Möhsen and Selle. Finally, one can count among this group the publicist Friedrich Nicolai and Biester, the secretary of the Wednesday Society.

II. THE WEDNESDAY SOCIETY'S CONCEPT OF ENLIGHTENMENT

The Society of Friends of Enlightenment met together with the conviction, expressed in Irwing's invitation, that "healthy reason will more and more ascend to the throne of all human affairs and will reign without limit over everything in the domain of human knowledge."[19] This basic consensus could not be equated with the clarification of the notion of enlightenment that was to be achieved through societal give-and-take; similarly, given the range of views among the Friends of Enlightenment, one could not count on homologous views concerning the limits and consequences of the strategies used to begin or accelerate "the process of setting reason free."[20] Conceptions of reason and enlightenment were here, as elsewhere, so bound together with established cultural and social systems that their contents and structures—with varied emphasis—permeated the concepts and strategies of enlightenment, a fact that was not first revealed by modern critics of ideology but was already apparent to the members of the Wednesday Society.

Thus Gedike, in the Society's internal discussion of the concept of enlightenment, not only put forth the common view that "enlightenment may be as relative a concept as truth"[21] but also set enlightenment in relation to diverse geographic, historical, social, and personal conditions: "It varies, and it must vary, according to differences of place, time, social rank, sex, and several other subjective as well as objective relations." Gedike approved of this social differentiation of enlightenment, and he wanted it conceived as the presupposition and foundation for strategies of enlightenment. "Thoroughgoing equality of enlightenment" was to him "just as little desirable as complete equality among the estates, and fortunately just as impossible." As surely as "thc notion of 'enlightenment' seen historically and factually [presupposed] the idea of a 'universal human reason' which [was] distributed among different subjects,"[22] it was equally certain to the Friends of Enlightenment that this reason was very unequally apportioned in human society. The idea of universal human reason was a maxim that must live with the disruptions of the real world. This demonstrates the skeptical assumption that, according to Eckhart Hellmuth, predominated in the Wednesday Society. They believed that "the majority of the members of the political community lack sufficient reason and insight and that they are incapable of acting according to principles of reason."[23] This skepticism with regard to the capacity for enlightenment of their fellow man did not, of course, entail the renunciation of enlightened activities. For Möhsen, who here remained uncontradicted, it was the "intent" of the Society "to enlighten, insofar as it is possible, ourselves and our fellow man, from the highest to the lowest rank." The professed goal here was to reduce the superstitions of the "common man"—and especially the "country folk"—and "to promote in them the capacity of thinking for themselves in their required spheres of activity."[24]

Although Möhsen's call for a consensus on a clear definition of the concept of enlightenment did not bring with it a resolution, the majority of the members indicated in their Vota that enlightenment was a process in which not everyone could be granted the same sort of participation and which could not be driven forward heedlessly and at any cost. Indicative of this attitude is the question posed by Svarez: "What is enlightenment, and what level of it is desirable for each class of the nation?"[25] Svarez thereby avoided answering the question of the essence of enlightenment. "In my opinion," Klein wrote in an earlier Votum, "enlightenment exists in spreading such knowledge which will allow us to assess correctly the true value of things, and, taken in this sense, enlightenment must at all times have virtue and happiness as companions."[26] The uncertainty concerning what in fact enlightenment might be was only heightened by such conceptual circumlocutions. For Gedike, they sufficed to demonstrate his insight into the subjective and objective contingency of a concept of enlightenment that appeared to him to be just as relative as "truth" itself.[27] And Wlömer added ominously in his Votum, "Perhaps truths can even be possible ... whose belief or knowledge must be absolutely disadvantageous for every man in his earthly condition."[28] This was not the view of an enlightened theologian of Spalding's mettle who was "completely of the opinion that *in abstracto* all truth is useful and all error damaging." Truth was, for him, always the other side of the common good. An opinion that brings "all in all more harm than utility" could "indeed not be true."[29] With this dovetailing of enlightenment, truth, happiness, and the public utility, he found himself in agreement with the majority of the Friends of Enlightenment, particularly his fellow clergymen among them. Diterich, without venturing to clarify the concept of enlightenment himself, warned against those "who burn away everything in the kingdom of Truth that does not please them" and seek to justify their demolition work by saying, "they wanted to enlighten the world."[30] He himself had introduced into hymns pleas for "truth," "self-knowledge," and an "active" faith that yields the "fruits of virtue."[31] And in his *Instruction on Attaining Bliss through Christ's Teachings*, he linked the aspiration to happiness with the commandment of brotherly love, which included in the service of our fellow man "responsibilities and duties ... with regard to the social good." If observing the duties required for the good of society demanded of the magistrates that they should "protect their subjects and govern them as fathers," the "subjects are obliged to respect their magistrates, obey their laws, and loyally pay the required taxes."[32]

For such issues as the living conditions in an enlightened state and corporate social order, the many-layered complex of political and social loyalties, educational policy, and questions of censorship, the critical touchstone for truth was the proper understanding of the common good.

Among these ecclesiastical and secular officeholders of the absolutist reform state the eudaemonist topos of an enlightened pursuit and dissemination of a truth that was oriented toward the public good ultimately broke down before the expediency of those prejudices that supported this good. In Svarez's opinion, "Commonly held prejudices may be attacked directly and without mercy only if there is clear evidence that the sum of the damaging consequence arising from them is greater than the sum of the good which would fortuitously arise from them."[33] A patrimonial-elitist concept of enlightenment thus committed itself to a strategy of enlightenment that subordinated claims of truth to public utility and thus, without serious internal resistance, could reconcile itself with the preservation of the censor's office.[34]

Such a multitiered conception of truth could not remain unopposed in an enlightenment society, which had been founded specifically with the goal of allowing "healthy reason" to rule over the entire domain of human knowledge. Thus the philosopher Mendelssohn, with the approval of Nicolai and Dohm as well in fundamental agreement with Irwing, did not wish to sacrifice the enlightened search for the truth to prejudice, even where it seemed necessary for reasons of public welfare and morality, to proceed with caution. Mendelssohn held that guardianship by censors was, in any case, "more harmful than *unrestricted* freedom," and he maintained that balancing truth against the public good was certainly questionable: "Montgolfier's discovery will probably lead to enormous upheavals. Whether this will lead to the improvement of human society no one may venture to decide. Would one for this reason hesitate to promote progress? The discovery of eternal truths is in and for itself good; their dispensation is a matter for Providence."[35] This view was not shared by those members of the Wednesday Society who drew a distinction "between the enlightened elite and the rest who remained in need of guardianship."[36] The majority of the Friends of Enlightenment wished, like Svarez, that enlightenment reach a point of irreversibility through a gradual, state-controlled process of education. Participation in the ideal of a universal enlightened reason of which all men should partake as equally as possible was perhaps a general aim here, but by no means an urgent one. The educator Gedike—even though he, like the rest of the members of the Wednesday Society, was an advocate of freedom of thought[37]—wanted unequivocally to see the process of enlightenment channeled through the traditional corporate, estatist society: "The true point, from which enlightenment must begin, is the middle estate as the center of the nation, from which the rays of enlightenment only *gradually* spread to the two extremes, the upper and lower orders." Gedike saw a limited capacity for enlightenment among both the "higher" and "lower" orders in distinction to the educable "middle estate." Hence he was convinced that there might be truths "which could prove damaging in the hands of not-yet-sufficiently enlightened men or estates."[38] The Wednesday Society's comprehension of enlightenment thus leads to the question of the social and political values of its members.

III. ON THE WEDNESDAY SOCIETY'S VIEW OF STATE AND SOCIETY

Gedike's perspective is clearly determined by the sense of self-worth and consciousness of superiority stemming from the bourgeois intelligentsia, one that saw itself confirmed, not least of all, by its activities in the absolutist reform state. Gedike's standpoint brought to the fore points of tension with the traditional social order based on birth and privilege that were echoed in the broader debate on enlightenment transpiring in public as well as in the Wednesday Society.[39] The interventions of the French Revolution into the legal relations in corporate society soon provided the opportunity of discussing the question of the justification of the nobility's privileges more intensively.

A lecture by Svarez before the Wednesday Society in December 1791, in which he concerned himself with the tax exemptions of the nobility, discussed the problem of tax equity with the clarity and precision of an enlightened officeholder in the Prussian reform judiciary against the backdrop of the experience of the Revolution. It seemed to Svarez that "justice, fairness, and interests of the state together require of a Sovereign that he eliminate all these exemption privileges and that he reestablish the principle of the greatest possible equity in tax contributions, even among the various classes of the state's citizens."[40] Svarez sought out the historical origins and the legitimation of a system experienced as unjust, which, with its preferential treatment of the nobility, made the burden on the lower orders all the heavier. He accurately saw the profounder historical cause to lie in the compensation given to the nobility for its defense burden. Consequently, in the late medieval and early modern corporate state, the possibility arose to shift the burden of tax payments onto those parts of the population who did not represent themselves in the territorial assemblies.

Although, in Svarez's view, the tax exemption was no longer applicable due to the changes in the constitution of the state and the military that occurred with the disappearance of the aristocratic duties of vassalage and the emergence of new aristocratic sources of income in the officer corps, he still insisted on the legal validity of dispensation from these contributions since these privileges were based on specific contracts between the nobles and their princes, contracts to whose integrity the monarch and his other subjects were now obligated: "Inequality of contribution" was to him "inequality of wealth. And inequality of wealth and circumstance," grants "no right to demand the reestablishment of equality at the expense of others and their rights, in whose possession they are once located."[41] The disadvantage of the noble tax exemption for the other subjects of the state does not justify breaking the contract and intervening in the property rights of the nobility. Only in an emergency, "where it is truly necessary for the preservation of the existence of the state,"[42] would an infringement on the privilege of exemption appear to be justified.

It is true that in his recommendations on tax policy Svarez opposed guarantees of further exemption privileges at the expense of the whole public. Instead, he pronounced himself in favor of a tax system graduated according to estates that would take into account proportional, social, and political-economic factors. But the higher goal of a comprehensive public law protecting property, including those rights flowing from the particular characteristics of the differing estates, made him a fierce advocate of the legal protection of existing rights.[43] Svarez's concept of property, which here obviously revealed the traditional values of corporate society, in no way met with the general approval of his enlightened friends.

The royal physician Selle, who was free of the scholarly jurist's familiarity with and commitment to received legal perspectives, correctly recognized that the resolution of the exemption question depended mainly on a more exact determination of the concept of property. On this issue Selle took the side of the disadvantaged orders, and, with a view toward the future, he decided in favor of the state's reform efforts. A contract would be binding only "if those to whose expense it was charged . . . approved and agreed" to it. However, this had not happened "because the Third Estate had never been represented." And even if the Third Estate had "freely entered" such a contract, it could "hold no moral sanction because it was opposed to the fundamental law of all social bonds." "A state would be incapable of any improvements whatsoever, if not a single contract could be revoked."[44]

But even the conservative Biester—who made a resolute declaration of loyalty to the corporate system and shared Justus Möser's view "that in all well-ordered states that we know from history, differences of social rank have always existed" and thought the changes in France should be viewed as a risky experiment—even he could not reconcile himself with Svarez's juridical perspective. He set his hopes on the historical proof of the illegitimate origins of exemptions and the invalidity of the one-sided advantage of the nobility in the territorial assemblies. At the very least, he hoped that current events in France would foster insight among the nobility: "Something should indeed be expected on the nobility's own initiative if one presents the issue to them from the perspective of the justice and the precariousness of their claims, and thus in part their patriotism and in part their fear could be brought into play."[45]

Thus, despite his loyalty to corporate society, Biester stood by his divided assessment of the nobility, and he was not alone, as a series of additional comments from the circle of the Wednesday Society shows. Ernst Ferdinand Klein—who assumed his new office in Halle in 1791 and could no longer participate in the debate on noble tax exemption—took issue in the *Berlinische Monatsschrift* with an essay by the Upper Appeals Court judge von Ramdohr on the claims of the nobility toward the highest offices of the state.[46] Klein resolutely opposed von Ramdohr's case for the "special rights of the hereditary nobility to the highest positions of state service" and cited (albeit with a different emphasis from that of the Prussian General Code,[47] which places the special entitlements of the nobility to honorary positions in the state on their qualifications) "industriousness, skill, and honesty" as virtues of office that qualify one to serve, independent of one's rank in society.[48] Somewhat patronizingly, Klein acknowledged class privileges of the nobility based on "mere custom" and "long possession." He conceded that "the order and happiness of human society could not exist . . . if one did not attribute a certain sacredness to custom and to long possession," but "this certainly did not accrue to them because of pure reason alone."[49] What von Ramdohr praised as the nobility's "esprit de corps,"[50] he saw, in contrast, as an "insidious, slow, deadly sickness of the state." As to von Ramdohr's assumption that public opinion supported the privileges of the nobility, he countered with the sarcastic remark, "An opinion that three-quarters of the nation" opposes "in silence could hardly be called a public opinion."[51]

In these critical attacks by Selle and Klein on the corporate privileges and prerogatives of the nobility, there appear to be indications of an ideal of the state that points beyond the existing unrestricted monarchy buttressed by the corporate social system. If we exclude the different political path of Leuchsenring—one that, however, cannot be traced from the surviving records of the Wednesday Society—nowhere is there to be found an explicit declaration in favor of constitutional monarchy. That goes for Klein's conversations on the resolutions of the French National Assembly themselves. At the conclusion, Klein (Kleon) lets the monarch of a people who have come to maturity through enlightenment say, "My laws should only serve to unite the freedom of all with the freedom of each. Examine them! Not my will but rather yours gives them binding force. And even your will obligates every individual only insofar as it serves to protect the common freedom."[52]

The members of the Wednesday Society declared their support for "freedom of thought." As is made clear in their discussions, they objected to the basic tendency of the Woellner Edict on Religion, which wished to bind the subjects through a restricted understanding of freedom of conscience in the sense of the protection of traditional beliefs. But the declaration of faith in inalienable human rights, as is witnessed by the example of Klein and Svarez, chief architects of the Prussian General Code, was confined within the limits of a loyalty to absolute monarchy. Here the historical experience of reform absolutism under Frederick the Great truly left its mark. Participation in the rational activities of the state, which had become possible for members of the reform bureaucracy, had the consequence of making political freedom appear to these trustees of the commonweal—in light of their conceptions of ethical duty and moral perfection—as if it were insignificant, or even the result of partisanship and self-interest, and thus unwelcome.

The Wednesday Society dissolved itself on the basis of the royal edict of 20 October 1798 "for the prevention and punishment of secret societies which could be detrimental to public security." Although no danger to public security was forthcoming from the Society, the majority of members wanted to comply with the letter of the law, which in paragraph 2, section IV prohibited societies "which demand secrecy of membership or swearing oaths of secrecy." Perhaps for the same reason, the members at this time also destroyed the collected papers and Vota, so that the few records of the Society that survive are due more to chance than to conscious preservation.[53]

On the basis of such meager sources, no final judgment on the impact of the Society can be made. Without a doubt, the Wednesday Society was the clearinghouse of Prussian late Enlightenment thought. A great many publications, which were either enlivened or enriched by the work of the Society, came forth from its members. But the extent to which the Wednesday Society influenced Prussian government policy is difficult to determine. Whether Prussian legislation or, especially, the General Code would have been different without the activity of the Wednesday Society is difficult to say in view of the broader public discussion and the numerous memoranda on the draft of the statute book. It does seem certain, for example, that Svarez was not moved to change his views by the criticism his ideas received within the Society.[54] The exchange of ideas and their reciprocal strengthening in the spirit of enlightened reform remain the essential contribution of the Society.

NOTES

I am grateful to the staff of the German State Library in Berlin for having given me access to the papers of Johann Karl Wilhelm Möhsen, member of the Wednesday Society. For special advice in the interpretation of these papers, I am indebted to Walther Gose and Eckhart Hellmuth. I have dealt with the issue at hand earlier in a lecture delivered at the annual meeting of the Arbeitsgemeinschaft zur Preußischen Geschichte, on 24 September 1984.

1. Among earlier writings on the Wednesday Society are (1) a partial edition of the Möhsen Papers with commentary by L. Keller, "Die Berliner Mittwochs-Gesellschaft. Ein Beitrag zur Geschichte der Geistesentwicklung Preussens am Ausgange des 18. Jahrhunderts," *Monatshefte der Comenius-Gesellschaft* 5 (1896): 67–94; (2) a first article based on the Möhsen Papers by their discoverer, H. Meisner, "Die Freunde der Aufklärung. Geschichte der Berliner Mittwochsgesellschaft," in *Festschrift zur 50jährigen Doktorjubelfeier Karl Weinholds am 14 Januar 1896* (Strasburg, 1896), 43–54;

(3) the announcement of a manuscript from the papers of Nicolai with remarks by the members of the Society in A. Stölzel, "Die Berliner Mittwochsgesellschaft über Aufhebung oder Reform der Universitäten (1795)," *Forschungen zur brandenburgischen und preussischen Geschichte* 2 (1889):201–222. An informative analysis of the discussions of the Wednesday Society on enlightenment and freedom of the press, based on the Möhsen Papers, from the point of view of a social-historically oriented critical history of ideas has been provided by E. Hellmuth, "Aufklärung und Pressefreiheit. Zur Debatte der Berliner Mittwochsgesellschaft während der Jahre 1783 und 1784," *Zeitschrift für historische Forschung* 9 (1982):315–345. Supplementing the understanding of enlightenment of the Wednesday Society from a philosophical point of view, with reservations regarding Hellmuth's conclusions, is B. Nehren, "Selbstdenken und gesunde Vernunft. Über eine wiederentdeckte Quelle zur Mittwochsgesellschaft," *Aufklärung. Interdisziplinäre Halbjahresschrift zur Erforschung des 18. Jahrhunderts und seiner Wirkungsgeschichte* 1 (1986):87–101. The contribution of the author lies in the evaluation of a neglected, but important, article with extracts from original sources on the establishment of the Wednesday Society and its discussion of religious matters: A. Tholuck, "Die Gesellschaft der Freunde der Aufklärung in Berlin im Jahre 1783," *Litterarischer Anzeiger für christliche Theologie und Wissenschaft überhaupt* 1 (1830): cols. 57–64, 86–87 (published anonymously).

2. For an overview of the European "society movement" and its contribution to enlightened reform, see U. Im Hof, *Das gesellige Jahrhundert. Gesellschaft und Gesellschaften im Zeitalter der Aufklärung* (München, 1982); on the nature of associations in enlightened states, see also M. Agethen, *Geheimbund und Utopie. Illuminaten, Freimaurer und deutsche Aufklärung* (*Ancien Régime, Aufklärung und Revolution* II) (München, 1984); with reference to the Wednesday Society, see R. van Dülmen, "Die Aufklärungsgesellschaft in Deutschland als Forschungsproblem," *Francia* 5 (1977):251–275.

3. E. F. Klein, "Autobiographie," in *Bildnisse jetztlebender Berliner Gelehrten mit ihren Selbstbiographien*, ed. M. S. Lowe (Berlin, 1806), 1–93; the citation is from pp. 53–54.

4. Möhsen, *Nachlass*, MS. boruss. fol. 443, sheet 1; for the establishment of the Society, see Nehren, "Selbstdenken und gesunde Vernunft."

5. See "Der Montagsklub in Berlin, 1749–1899," in *Fest-und Gedenkschrift zu seiner 150sten Jahresfeier* (Berlin, 1899).

6. J. C. W. Möhsen, "Was ist zu thun zur Aufklärung der Mitbürger," lecture of 17 December 1783, in Möhsen, *Nachlass*, sheets 117–120, and Keller, "Die Berliner Mittwochs-Gesellschaft," 73–76 (translated above, pp. 49–52).

7. About half of the members of the Wednesday Society were at least temporarily also participants in the older Monday Club, in which Biester and Nicolai played active roles.

8. Möhsen, *Nachlass*, sheet 117, and Keller, "Die Berliner Mittwochs-Gesellschaft," 71.

9. The circle of active members, which was soon expanded by eight participants, will be briefly characterized below. Numerous writings have been consulted but have not been individually listed here. Reference is due, however, to the customary biographical collections, such as the *Allgemeine Deutsche Biographie* (Berlin, 1875) and the *Neue Deutsche Biographie* (Berlin, 1953) as well as older handbooks, among others, C. Ch. Hamberger and J. G. Meusel, *Das gelehrte Teutschland* (Lemgo, 1796–1834) and V. H. Schmidt and D. G. Mehring, *Neuestes gelehrtes Berlin* (Berlin, 1795) and to

the *Handbuch über den Königlich Preussischen Hof und Staat.* Of the more recent literature on the subject, only the reflections on the Wednesday Society in the wide-ranging Nicolai biography of H. Möller, *Aufklärung in Preussen. Der Verleger, Publizist und Geschichtsschreiber Friedrich Nicolai* (*Einzelveröffentlichungen der Historischen Kommission zu Berlin* 15) (Berlin, 1974), 229–238, will be mentioned here.

10. On the conflict over the Woellner Edict on Religion, see G. Birtsch, "Religions- und Gewissensfreiheit in Preussen von 1780 bis 1817," *Zeitschrift für historische Forschung* 11 (1984):177–204, esp. pp. 186–197.

11. The Charité was a famous Berlin hospital.—TRANS.

12. The "geistliche Departement" was a branch of the Prussian bureaucracy responsible for the administration of ecclesiastical and educational institutions. Although nominally independent, it was part of the Justice Department.—TRANS.

13. See U. Schulz, *Die Berlinische Monatsschrift (1783–1786). Eine Bibliographie* (*Bremer Beiträge zur freien Volksbildung* 11) (Bremen, 1968); further, see N. Hinske, ed., *Was ist Aufklärung? Beiträge aus der Berlinischen Monatsschrift* (Darmstadt, 1981), xxff.

14. See Nehren, "Selbstdenken und gesunde Vernunft," and Tholuck, "Gesellschaft der Freunde der Aufklärung."

15. On Svarez, compare my biographical sketch, "C. G. Svarez: Mitbegründer des preussischen Gesetzesstaates," in *Geschichte und politisches Handeln. Studien zum europäischen Denken der Neuzeit. Zum Gedenken an Theodor Schieder, 1908–1984,* ed. P. Alter, W. J. Mommsen, and Th. Nipperdey (Stuttgart, 1985), 85–101.

16. E. F. Klein, *Freyheit und Eigenthum, abgehandelt in acht Gesprächen über die Beschlüsse der Französischen Nationalversamlung* (Berlin/Stettin, 1790). A subsequently discovered copy of the dedication suggests identifying the interlocutors as members of the Wednesday Society without, admittedly, identifying them with certainty. See Stölzel, "Die Berliner Mittwochsgesellschaft," 202, with the incorrect citation of Lichtenberg instead of Leuchsenring for Menon. Klein himself, who provided the basis for this speculation, characterized the discussions as fictitious in both *Freyheit und Eigenthum* (pp. IV ff.) and on p. 55 of his autobiography of 1806 (see note 3, above).

17. See A. Altmann, *Moses Mendelssohn: A Biographical Study* (London, 1973), 653ff.

18. From the Möhsen Papers (see note 1, above).

19. See Tholuck, "Gesellschaft der Freunde der Aufklärung," col. 57.

20. Cf. Hinske, *Was ist Aufklärung?* xix.

21. Gedike, in Keller, "Die Berliner Mittwochs-Gesellschaft," 85.

22. See Hinske, *Was ist Aufklärung?* xviii.

23. Hellmuth, "Aufklärung und Pressefreiheit," 321. Hellmuth overemphasizes this viewpoint, but he does correctly recognize that the "immature" citizens should "approach the state of enlightenment through a long-term educational process" (p. 322).

24. Möhsen, *Nachlass,* sheet 145.

25. Svarez, in Keller, "Die Berliner Mittwochs-Gesellschaft," 78.

26. Klein, in Keller, "Die Berliner Mittwochs-Gesellschaft," 77.

27. Gedike, in Keller, "Die Berliner Mittwochs-Gesellschaft," 85.

28. Wlömer, in Keller, "Die Berliner Mittwochs-Gesellschaft," 87.

29. Spalding, in Keller, "Die Berliner Mittwochs-Gesellschaft," 82.

30. Diterich, in Keller, "Die Berliner Mittwochs-Gesellschaft," 81.

31. *Gesangbuch zum gottesdienstlichen Gebrauch in den Königlich-Preussischen Landen* (Berlin, 1780). See especially song nos. 251 (plea for the love of truth), 250 (plea for self-knowledge and truth: "Grant, that I might speak the truth to myself, in order to see myself as I am"..."Here make me wise to heaven and free from vile self-deception"), 193 ("Grant, that my faith be active and bring forth the fruits of virtue").

32. J. S. Diterich, *Unterweisung zur Glückseligkeit nach der Lehre Jesu* (Berlin, 1782). See nos. 199 and 204; pp. 98ff.

33. Svarez, in Keller, "Die Berliner Mittwochs-Gesellschaft," 79–80.

34. On the question of censorship, see Hellmuth, "Aufklärung und Pressefreiheit," 325ff.

35. Mendelssohn, in Keller, "Die Berliner Mittwochs-Gesellschaft," 81.

36. Hellmuth, "Aufklärung und Pressefreiheit," 322.

37. Friedrich Gedike, "Rede bei der Aufnahme in die Königliche Akademie der Wissenschaften (4 February 1790)," *Berlinische Monatsschrift* 15 (1790):219–230, on p. 228.

38. Gedike, in Keller, "Die Berliner Mittwochs-Gesellschaft," 85.

39. See J. Schultze, "Die Auseinandersetzung zwischen Adel und Bürgertum in den deutschen Zeitschriften der letzten drei Jahrzehnte des 18. Jahrhunderts," *Historische Studien* 163 (1925).

40. C. G. Svarez, "Über die Befreiung von Staats Abgaben insofern dieselbe als ein Privilegium gewisser Stände im Staat betrachtet wird," in Möhsen, *Nachlass*, sheets 41–44; quote is from sheet 41a.

41. Ibid., sheet 42.

42. Ibid., sheet 43.

43. Cf. Birtsch, "Religions- und Gewissensfreiheit," 97–98.

44. Selle, in Möhsen, *Nachlass*, sheet 44^{V}. Selle's critical attitude toward the existing social and "governmental system" becomes clear elsewhere as well. Discussing Möhsen's contribution on the enlightenment of "the man in the street and particularly the country-man," he put the blame for the extant lack of education on the constitutional conditions (ibid., 21 July 1786, sheet 153^{V}).

45. Biester, in Möhsen, *Nachlass*, sheet 45.

46. E. F. Klein, "Anmerkungen eines Bürgerlichen über die Abhandlung des Herrn Oberappelationsrates von Ramdohr, die Ansprüche der Adlichen an die ersten Staatsbedienungen betreffend," *Berlinische Monatsschrift* 17 (1791):460–474.

47. See *Allgemeines Landrecht* II, 9, par. 35: "The noble is preeminently entitled to an honored position in the state for which he has qualified himself."

48. Klein, "Anmerkungen," 467.

49. Ibid., 473.

50. Ibid., 472.

51. Ibid., 463.

52. Klein, *Freyheit und Eigenthum*, 183.

53. The Royal Library possibly acquired Möhsen's Papers after his death in 1795 but before the disbanding of the Wednesday Society in 1798.

54. Characteristic of this is the ongoing agreement between Svarez's views as expressed in the Wednesday Society and to the crown prince. This is certainly true of his reports on the question of the tax exemption for the nobility, which corre-

spond (with only slight variation) to the appropriate passages in his lectures to the crown prince. See note 40, above, and C. G. Svarez, *Vorträge über Recht und Staat*, ed. H. Conrad and G. Kleinheyer [*Wiss. Abhandlungen der Arbeitsgemeinschaft für Forschung des Landes Nordrhein-Westfalen* 10] (Köln/Opladen, 1960), 121ff. Of course, Svarez knew how to use the Wednesday Society as a sounding board for his legislative activity, as he himself hinted in his lectures on the censorship question. See Möhsen, *Nachlass*, sheet 263^{V}. On the whole, it seems to me too optimistic to claim that Svarez "amended many of his ideas" as a result of the judgment of the Wednesday Society. See L. F. G. v. Göckingk, *Friedrich Nicolai's Leben und literarischer Nachlass* (Berlin, 1820), 91.

The Subversive Kant: The Vocabulary of "Public" and "Publicity"

John Christian Laursen

Immanuel Kant is often thought of as a timid philosopher who never dared to defy the political authorities. It is a fact of his career that he apparently meekly submitted to a rebuke from the civil authorities in 1793 and promised never to write on religious matters again. Most of his political works were written in the form of light occasional pieces; none was written as a revolutionary manifesto.

This essay argues, however, that Kant's writings on politics were indeed subversive. There was a thread of common vocabulary that tied many of them together. That vocabulary, in Kant's day, was clearly associated with attacks on the contemporary political system. The vocabulary in question here is a complex of terms associated with "public" political life. The first section of this essay deals with Kant's distinction between "public" and "private," and the second explores what was known as "publicity." A survey of contemporary literature reveals that Kant derived his usage of these terms from the German literary and political writers of his day. He used it against the lawyers to subvert the language of absolutism and to solve problems that the natural lawyers had answered inadequately.

PUBLIC VERSUS PRIVATE

The famous "What Is Enlightenment?" of 1784 was one of Kant's earliest political essays. The key to his message is his stand on the meaning of the terms "public" and "private." The private use of reason "is that which a person may make of it in a particular civil post or office with which he is entrusted," he writes.[1] In contrast, the public use of reason is a matter of

Reprinted from John Christian Laursen, The Politics of Skepticism in the Ancients, Montaigne, and Kant *(Leiden: Brill, 1992), ch. 9.*

writing and publishing. Kant explains: "By the public use of one's reason I mean that use which anyone may make of it as a *Gelehrter* [man of learning or scholar] addressing the entire reading public." This is the "public in the truest sense of the word" (8:37).

Kant's use of "public" to refer exclusively to writers and the reading public is striking today, and it would have been in Kant's day, too. We are accustomed to thinking of a career in civil service as part of our "public life" and any writing that we might do evenings and weekends as our own private affair. As many scholars have noticed, Kant turned this meaning around.[2] I shall explore sources for this alternative usage below.

Public as a noun in German (*Publicum* or *Publikum*) derived its meaning directly from roots in the Latin that already possessed a dual tradition. On the one side, the Latin *publicus* took its earliest meaning from *populus*, or "the state, as far as it rests on a natural community of human beings," as one modern commentator puts it.[3] But it also meant that which was out in the open, not in one's house, or of general effect or use in society. Thus streets, plazas, the theater, and viaducts were called "public."[4] *Public* as an adjective in German (*öffentlich*), which translates more literally as "open," became associated with *Publicum* through this latter meaning.

Cicero was the first of the Roman lawyers to make a consistent distinction between *ius publicum* (public law) and *ius privatum* (private law) such that the former referred to laws handed down by the Senate and the latter to private contracts and wills.[5] Following his lead, in the law of the empire *publicus* often referred to the power of the magistrate, as in *imperium publicum, clementia publica, servus publicus*, and so forth. Magistrates possessed *potestas publica* and were *personae publica*. Ulpian's definition of public law ran: *publicum ius in sacris, in sacerdotibus, in magistratibus consistit*. But *publicus* still could be applied to anything outside of the house, or of general use, such as *lux publica, dies publica*, and *verba publica*.[6]

In the Middle Ages, the wider meaning of "public" as anything out in the open prevailed in Germany. The "fundamental significance of the public element in the legal process was thought to be the bringing of the evil of a misdeed out into the light so that it could be punished," as a modern scholar summarizes it.[7] A trial could be "public" simply because it was out in the open, and it was believed that torture could be relied on to bring secrets out into the open. But increased attention to Roman Law, which had been rediscovered in Italy in the twelfth century and began to receive significant attention in Germany by the fifteenth century, led to a narrowing of the meaning of "public."[8]

In the 1600s, the Germans, especially legal scholars writing in Latin, began a process that has been described as a narrowing of the meaning of *publicus* and *öffentlich* to *staatlich*, or having to do with the state.[9] In 1614, for example, Johannes Althusius referred to state power and the power of officials as branches of *potestas publica.*[10] The wider meaning of *publicus* faded. A "public trial" now only meant a trial in a state court. "Public war" had once meant any openly declared and openly pursued war. Now, following Grotius, it came to mean only war between legal sovereigns, whether openly declared and pursued or not.[11]

By the eighteenth century, the process of reduction of "public" to "pertaining to the state" had reached a high point among legal writers. Schütz's translation of Grotius in 1707 rendered *aut privatis aut publicis personis* as "either private persons or those who hold public offices [*öffentlichem Ämtern*]."[12] Johann Heinrich Zedler's dictionary, in volumes published in the 1740s, defined "public persons" (*öffentliche Personen*) as "in law, the rulers and magistrates, and also others in public offices and public service" and "the public" (*das Publicum*) as "in law, properly what belongs to the prince or the higher authorities and not to mere private persons."[13] For some writers the concept of the public as pertaining to the state followed state power in reaching out to absorb much of the wider meaning that "public" had once had. In 1762 the jurist Georg Wiesand wrote that *res publicae*, including everything from rivers, forests, and salt licks to light and water, belong to the prince.[14] They were "public" not because they were out in the open or of general use but because the prince claimed to own them.

In view of this conceptual history, one modern commentator calls Kant's usage "a provocative change in the current legal terminology."[15] It is true that it amounts to a clear rejection of these jurists' association of public and prince. But the wider meaning of "public" had not died out entirely, and Kant could draw on other conceptual resources than those of the mainstream of jurisprudence. Zedler was careful to note that princely aggrandizement of the word occurred especially "in law," as we have seen. Some of his definitions retained the wider reference: *öffentliche Güter* are defined as "pertaining to the assembled people or to the whole community," and an *öffentliches Gericht* is one that is intended to promote the general welfare.

But rather than a change in the current legal terminology, Kant's usage is better characterized as a wholesale rejection of the lawyers' usage and acceptance of the usage of the growing number of books and literary periodicals written by "general writers" for "the whole nation," as Friedrich Just Riedel put it in *Letters on the Public* of 1768.[16] They had done the most to recover and extend the association between the "public" and the "people" in a wider sense.

When, in 1725, Johann Christoph Gottsched was already appealing to the "public" (*öffentliche*) judgment of his readers in *Die Vernunftigen Tadlerinnen*, he was not appealing to any prince but to women readers.[17] Gotthold Ephraim Lessing wrote of his readers as *das Publiko* in his introduction to the *Briefe, die neueste Literatur betreffend* of 1759.[18] Friedrich Nicolai's introduction to the first volume of the *Allgemeine deutsche Bibliothek* in 1766 was addressed to "lovers of the newest literature . . . in many cities," styled as the German *Publici.*[19]

In 1768, Riedel was already complaining, "the word *Publikum* sounds in my ear from all sides," although some listeners do not know what it is and others doubt if it exists. He analyzed suggested meanings of the word, including "the critics," "other authors," "professionals," and "youths," and concluded that "men and women of taste" made up the real public.[20] Significantly, all of the plausible meanings he examined were elements of the reading public.

The preface to the first issue of Wieland's *Der Teutsche Merkur* in 1773 referred often to the taste and judgment of the entire class of educated men as the *Publikum.*[21] The editors of the *Berlinische Monatsschrift*, the journal that published Kant's "What Is Enlightenment?" had thanked *das Publikum* in anticipation in the introduction to the first issue in January 1783.[22] By November 1784, after Kant had sent his manuscript to the publisher but before it was published, Friedrich Schiller explicitly contrasted the prince with the reading public in the announcement of *Rheinische Thalia*: "I write as a citizen of the world, who serves no prince. . . . The public [*das Publikum*] is everything to me, my education, my sovereign, my confidante."[23]

The public and freedom of the press had already been the subject of journalistic attention by the time Kant was writing in 1784. In April of that year, Wilhelm Wekhrlin's *Das graue Ungeheur* celebrated freedom of the press as "the most beautiful present that heaven in its mercy has made to the human race."[24]

That same month, several months before Kant sent his article off to the journal, an unsigned article on freedom of the press appeared in volume 3 of the *Berlinische Monatsschrift.* It used Frederick's own early writings to support an argument for freedom of the press. Among other points that Kant followed up, it raised the issue of the propriety of an army officer's criticism of his superior's orders. Like the other journals, it appealed to the "judgment of the public."[25]

These authors and journals were only a part, if an influential one, of a developing literary tradition associated with reading societies, the stage, published exchanges of letters, and so forth. Many had no intention of promoting political radicalism through their language. But, as one modern commentator observes, mushrooming literary reading societies "opened and widened the space for a public life free from the control of the state and the family."[26] That could not fail to be subversive of the prevailing absolutism. Kant's language in "What Is Enlightenment?" represents a contribution to this movement and probably would not have been conceivable without it.

Liberty to Publish for All Gelehrten

Kant's terminology served to introduce a subversive doctrine. As a "private" military officer, a man must follow orders, Kant concedes. As a "private" citizen (*Bürger*), he must pay taxes, and as a "private" clergyman, he must teach what his church requires. But "as a member of a complete commonwealth or even of cosmopolitan society," he may publicly criticize these private responsibilities in writing. For example, as a "*Gelehrter* addressing the real public (i.e., the world at large) through his writings, the clergyman making public use of his reason enjoys unlimited freedom to use his own reason and to speak in his own person" (8:37–38). This is a call for full freedom of the press.

Kant's theory is a "two hats" doctrine in which each individual can play two roles in society. It may have been suggested by a letter to him from Freiherr von Zedlitz, the enlightened Prussian minister of education, in 1778. Men "can be judges, advocates, preachers, and physicians only a few hours each day; but in these and all the remainder of the day they are men, and have need of other sciences," he wrote, appealing to Kant to suggest means of bringing this home to university students (10:219). We do not have Kant's answer to von Zedlitz at the time, but "What Is Enlightenment?" can be taken as his answer.[27]

The three examples of men who can wear two hats that Kant gives require some explanation. Clergymen and officers were *Beamten,* or civil servants. Like Kant, who was a professor, they were directly dependent on the prince for their livelihood. *Bürger* translates roughly as "town-dwelling citizen-taxpayer"; the standard example was the merchant. Since there is no good English equivalent, we shall use the German term, which is the same in singular and plural. Unless they lived in one of the free cities, German Bürger also had obligations to their prince. According to cameralist theory, their economic activities were a privilege granted by the state, so they, too, were dependent on the prince. Kant's project was to give all of these dependents a sphere of independence.

Kant's choice of examples reflects a shrewd assessment of the roles and needs of the German Gelehrten. He does not bother with the court writers, who are hopelessly dependent on their Maecenases. The independent writers (*freie Schriftsteller*) who made their living by their pens did not especially need Kant's help: he remarks only that freedom to express their opinions "applies even more to all others who are not restricted by any official duties" (8:41). It was the bulk of German Gelehrten, the middle ground of Beamten and Bürger, who needed Kant's help. These were the men who ran the prince's state and operated his economy. They were undoubtedly the bulk of Kant's own readers. If they were to function as enlighteners, they would need some measure of independence.

Kant was very generous in his definition of Gelehrten. He drew on a respected tradition to the effect that greater liberty could be granted to men of learning as long as their disputes did not seep down to the many. Playing on the prestige and legitimacy of the Gelehrten, he extended their privileges to the widest practical circles. If soldiers, clergymen, and Bürger all qualify as Gelehrten, then hardly any official or male head of an urban household, which is to say hardly any full member of society by eighteenth-century standards, would not qualify. "Everyman a part-time man of learning" would have been a radically leveling slogan in Kant's day.

Most of Kant's discussion in "What Is Enlightenment?" focuses on the clergy and matters of religion. He probably felt that this would meet the least opposition from Frederick the Great's censors, and he was probably right. Kant mentions once that the officer should be free to publish observations "on the errors in the military service" and that the Bürger should be free to publish "his thoughts on the impropriety or even injustice of... fiscal measures" (8:37–38). He even goes so far as to suggest that Frederick "realizes that there is no danger even to his legislation if he allows his subjects... to put before the public their thoughts on better ways of drawing up laws, even if this entails a forthright criticism of the current legislation" (8:41). For the rest, the principles he established in respect to clergymen would carry over, mutatis mutandis, to officers and Bürger. But even Kant's one mention each of criticisms of the army, of taxes, and of legislation probably sounded enormous in some quarters.

"What Is Enlightenment?" was not the only work in which Kant presented this theory. In 1793 he published a long article in the *Berlinische Monatsschrift* under the title "On the Old Saying: That May be True in Theory but It Won't Work in Practice." In that article Kant wrote that subjects of a state had absolutely no right to rebel against their superiors. But the quid pro quo for this passivity was that "the citizen must be free to inform the public of his views on whatever in the sovereign decrees appears to him as a wrong against the community, and he must have this freedom with the sovereign's own approval" (8:304).

"Freedom of the pen—within the bounds of respect and affection for the constitution one lives under... is the sole shield of popular rights," Kant asserts. Such freedom also benefits the sovereign: without it, the sovereign would be deprived "of any knowledge of matters which he himself would change if only he knew them. Hence, to limit this freedom would bring him into contradiction with himself" (8:304). But this appeal to the prince's self-interest hardly disguises what he loses by freedom of the press.

Freedom to Publish for Philosophers

In "What Is Enlightenment?" Kant staked a great deal on the power of a free press to bring about enlightenment. However, things got worse for the reading and writing public. Frederick died in 1786, and with his death came a new king, a religious mystic totally opposed to enlightenment. In 1788, Frederick William II asserted in a cabinet order that "press freedom has degenerated into press impudence, and the book censors have fallen completely asleep." He became convinced that the "licentiousness of the so-called *Aufklärer*, who think themselves superior to everything," was a threat to the state.[28] His new minister, Johann Christoph Woellner, issued an edict on religion in 1788 which guaranteed freedom of conscience for the Prussian subject "so long as he keeps any peculiar opinion to himself and carefully guards himself from spreading it or persuading others," and a new, tougher censorship edict followed.[29]

A few years later, Kant's *Religion within the Limits of Reason Alone* ran afoul of the king and his minister. Kant managed to circumvent the theological censor in Berlin by obtaining approval from the philosophical faculty at Jena; but this ploy was transparent, and Woellner issued a stern warning to Kant, threatening "unpleasant measures" (7:6). Kant wrote to Frederick William promising not to write on religion again. This letter was published in the preface to *The Conflict of the Faculties* of 1798, after Frederick William's death.

In the letter Kant claimed a much narrower privilege for the interchange of ideas than he did in "What Is Enlightenment?" He begins with the classic disclaimer that the argument of *Religion within the Limits of Reason Alone* was "not at all suitable for the public; to them it is an unintelligible, closed book, only a debate among scholars of the faculty [*Facultät-Gelehrten*] of which the people take no notice." It would cause no harm. But the university faculties must remain free "to judge it publicly," Kant asserts, attempting to retain his subversive use of the word *public* (7:8).

The clergymen that Kant had championed as part-time men of learning are now disenfranchised. Those "who are appointed to teach the people (in the schools and from the pulpits) . . . are bound to uphold whatever outcome of the debate the crown sanctions for them to expound publicly; for they cannot think out their own religious belief by themselves, but can only have it handed down to them . . . by the competent faculties (of theology and philosophy)." Already the language is changing: it is not the written product of their evening reflections but their official duties that qualify as "public." The strategy is obviously that of the sacrificial lamb: "Accordingly I censured the temerity of raising objections and doubts, in the schools and the pulpits and in popular writings, about the theoretical teachings of the Bible and the mysteries these contain (for in the faculties this must be permitted)" (7:8–9).

At this point it is clear that Kant is reverting to the narrower definition of Gelehrten as scholars. *The Conflict of the Faculties* begins with a distinction between "scholars proper" and "intelligentsia" (*Litteraten*). The latter "are instruments of the government" who may "be called the men of affairs or technicians of learning. As tools of the government (clergymen, magistrates, and physicians) they . . . are not free to make public use of their learning as they see fit" (7:18). The divorce of prince and public is gone, and in its place there is a distinction between the "civil community," subject to government supervision, and a narrowly construed "learned community." The privileges of free debate are reserved for the latter (7:34).

Kant makes further use of the traditional division of the four faculties of the university into three "higher" faculties (theology, law, and medicine) and one "lower" faculty (philosophy). The "higher" faculties are distinguished from the "lower" by virtue of the government's interest in their teachings. Kant writes, "Now the government is interested primarily in means for securing the strongest and most lasting influence on the people, and the subjects which the higher faculties teach are just such means. Accordingly, the government reserves the right itself to sanction the teachings of the higher faculties, but those of the lower faculty it leaves up to the scholars' reason." Although it sanctions the teachings of the higher faculties, Kant clarifies, the government does not have any interest in intervening in "scholarly discussions" or "the teachings and views that the faculties, as theorists, have to settle with one another" (7:19, 34). A new two hats theory emerges for the scholars of the higher faculties: they have to teach what they are told, but they can debate freely among themselves.

The philosophy faculty, however, can claim full freedom. It has "the public presentation of truth as its function" and "must be conceived as free and subject only to laws given by reason, not by government" (7:33, 27). But lest this sound too ambitious, Kant supplies mitigating considerations. The people as a whole will not pay any attention to the arcana of philosophy, "agreeing that these subtleties are not their affair." The reading public of the philosophers is evidently composed of only the government and the higher faculties, who must "put up with the objections and doubts" that the philosophers bring forward (7:29, 28). The philosophers' communication with the larger public is mediated by the higher faculties. New doctrines will only reach the people as a whole through the higher faculties, with the government's sanction.

Kant appeals directly to the prince's interests for freedom for philosophers. By definition, he argues, the truth cannot be established by command, and the government cannot control the philosophers "without acting against its own proper and essential purpose." Indeed, the government must rely on the philosophy faculty to expose errors espoused by the other faculties. Without the philosophy faculty's "rigorous examinations and objections, the government would not be adequately informed about what could be to its own advantage or detriment" (7:27, 34).

On the one hand, Kant characterizes the higher faculties as potential tyrants. Were it not for philosophers, the other faculties "could rest undisturbed in possession of what they have once occupied, by whatever title, and rule over it despotically." The "businessmen of the higher faculties" will set themselves up as "miracle workers," offering panaceas to the public and obtaining the "passive surrender" of the public, "unless the philosophy faculty is allowed to counteract them publicly" (7:28, 31). This appeal to the public harks back to the theory of "What Is Enlightenment?"

But, on the other hand, in case the princes are not entirely unsympathetic to the potential despotism of the higher faculties as long as they control them, Kant also characterizes the higher faculties as potential Jacobins. The "government cannot be completely indifferent to the truth of" the teachings that it authorizes. The doctrines of the higher faculties can "stir up political struggles" and sow "the seeds of insurrection and factions." Without philosophical oversight, "self-appointed tribunes of the people... can steer the judgment of the people in whatever direction they please... and so win them away from the influence of a legitimate government" (7: 32, 35).

Kant's hopes for the effects of freedom of the press among university scholars and especially philosophers reaffirm his hopes in "What Is Enlightenment?" even if the scale of participation is reduced. Progressive improvement can be expected: "the higher faculties (themselves better instructed [by philosophers]) will lead... government officials more and more onto the way of truth." A "constant progress of both ranks of the faculties toward greater perfection... [will] prepare the way for the government to remove all restrictions that its will has put on freedom of public judgment." Political effects will follow: "the government may find the freedom of the philosophy faculty, and the increased insight gained from this freedom, a better means for achieving its ends than its own absolute authority" (7:29, 35). Political freedom will follow freedom of the press for philosophers.

Philosophers as Advisers to Rulers

Toward Perpetual Peace, which appeared in 1795 after the bulk of part 1 of *Conflict* was written but before it was published, also called for a special public role for philosophers. It consisted of proposed preliminary and definitive "articles for a perpetual peace among nations." In a supplement a "secret article" asserts that "the maxims of the philosophers on the conditions under which public peace is possible shall be consulted by states which are armed for war" (8:368). To put it less awkwardly, rulers should consult philosophers on matters of war and peace.

This is a secret article, Kant writes, because rulers might think it beneath their dignity to consult mere subjects about such important matters. The ironic humor of the need for a "secret" article in the midst of a philosophy of publicness should not be lost on the reader. It is an implicit criticism of princely vanity.

This article can remain "secret," according to Kant, because all that rulers have to do is allow philosophers "to speak freely and publicly... and they will indeed do so of their own accord if no one forbids their discussions" (8:369). The rulers do not have to publicly admit to requesting the philosophers' advice; they can simply overhear—or read—the philosophers' discussions.

The reason the ruler should allow the philosopher to speak publicly is the standard one of self-interest: the philosophers "throw light on their affairs." As in *Conflict*, Kant disparages the tendency of the higher faculties of law, theology, and medicine to use their worldly power to interfere with philosophy. No danger should be expected from allowing the philosophers to speak freely because they are "by nature incapable of forming seditious factions or clubs" (8:369).

GERMAN "PUBLICITY"

Another term that was closely related to "public" was also growing in importance in Germany in the last decades of the eighteenth century. Writers of the *Aufklärung*, enthusiastic about the potential for enlightenment in the process of communication with the literate public, termed that process "publicity" (*Publicität*). This was not what we understand by publicity in the twentieth century; it was concerned only with merchandising ideas. It was closely related to *Publizistik*, another relatively new term that translates best as "political journalism." Publicity was the medium of political journalism.

Zedler's dictionary, published in the 1740s, did not even have an entry for the word; but in April 1784, several months before Kant wrote "What Is Enlightenment?" Wekhrlin was using the term in his periodical, *Das graue Ungeheur*. It was a function of freedom of the press. Wekhrlin wrote,

> What must it have been like in the times before printing presses existed! Tyrants had no bridles, the people no refuge. Vice could grow impudent, without becoming red with shame. Virtue knew no means of sharing its suffering, or gaining the sympathy of society. The laws had no critics, morals had no supervisor, reason was monopolized. Providence spoke: let the human race become free! And "publicity" appeared.[30]

"Publicity" would "bring the abuse of power before the judgment seat of the public," Wekhrlin asserted. Writers are "born advocates for mankind." They are the "natural organ of public righteousness"; one cannot expect *Beamten*, "for whom injustices are profitable, to take great pains against them," he argued. And as for criticism of publicity from the authorities, "it is not books which corrupt human society, but actions." Wekhrlin was proud of the power of publicity: the "so-called writing craze [*Schriftstellerey*] is the reason the judgment of the public has such overwhelming power today," he wrote.[31] He later referred to himself as a "priest of publicity."[32]

Kant's correspondent and friend, Johann Erich Biester, one of the editors of the *Berlinische Monatsschrift*, often wrote of the role of his periodical in publicity. "Candidness was ever its character; the spread of freedom of thought... was its goal; the undoing of the chains of untruth, the recovery of the right to one's own investigations and one's own thinking were often, in different disguises, its object," he wrote. Publicity was its "chief aim."[33]

In 1785, a year after Kant's "What Is Enlightenment?" appeared, August Ludwig von Schlözer's *Letters to Eichstädt in Vindication of Publicity* hailed writers as "unpaid servant[s] of civil society" and "adviser[s] to the nation."[34] A minor poet, Eulogius Schneider, went so far as to write a "Hymn to Publicity."[35] Publicity as a liberating ideal reached a high point in Adolf Freiherr von Knigge's 1792 work, *Josephs von Wurmbrand*, written in the first flush of elation at the success of the French Revolution. Publicity will bring the misuse of power and the subterfuges of the powerful "before the judgment seat of the public, of the whole people," he wrote, echoing Wekhrlin.[36]

Among other probable sources of the term for Kant, Schlözer published *Allgemeine StatsRecht und StatsVerfassungsLere* [General Public Law and Constitutional Law], a textbook on politics, in 1793. In it he argued that reforms in Germany would have to include the legalization of publicity, since without it "no community spirit, and no trust of the people in their representatives, is thinkable." In another connection he described the work of the periodical that he published as "general publicity." Like Kant, Schlözer gave a great deal of credit to the freedom of the press that made publicity—communication with the "public"—possible. Like Kant, he argued that the freedom "to think aloud" benefits the ruler. But, unlike Kant, he approved of a right to resistance against usurpers and tyrants: in such cases "pure appeals to the public seldom help."[37]

The reaction to the French Revolution in Germany was profound and far-reaching, and often enough writers and publicity were blamed for social and political unrest. Johann Georg Heinzmann published his *Appeal to My Nation: Concerning the Pestilence of German Literature* in 1795 and included Kant and Kantianism among the radicals responsible for such unrest. "The truly enlightened public," he wrote, "among whom true virtue, true morals/manners, and high-mindedness reigns, is certainly not the so-called reading public."[38] But Heinzmann was swimming against the stream of belle-lettristic and political writers of his times, while Kant had made their language his own.

Publicity was an important element in Kant's *Toward Perpetual Peace* of 1795. Where the foregoing writers had meant no more than that the term implied communication with the public, Kant supplied a philosophical dimension. Publicity was the "formal attribute" of public right (or public law), he wrote (8:381). Publicity is required by public law for conceptual reasons. Justice "can only be conceived of as publicly knowable." Since law or right "can only come from justice," it must accordingly be publicly knowable. This is a "readily applicable criterion which can be discovered a priori within reason itself" (8:381). Following the pattern of his works on morality, Kant articulated two "transcendental" principles of public right. "All actions affecting the rights of other human beings are wrong if their maxim is not compatible with publicity" is the negative formula. "Like any axiom, it is valid without demonstration," Kant asserts. If public admission of a maxim immediately stirs up opposition, that must be because "it is itself unjust and thus constitutes a threat to everyone." The affirmative formula is that "all maxims which require publicity if they are not to fail in their purpose can be reconciled both with right and with politics" (8:381, 386). Kant is saying that virtually by definition any purposes or actions that can be carried out only with full disclosure and public support are going to be legitimate.

Kant uses the principle of publicity to decide contested issues like the right to rebellion, the binding effect of treaties, the justification of preemptive strikes, and the rights of strong countries. In each of these cases he takes a question that had been debated by natural lawyers in other terms and uses the principle he has borrowed from the language of political writers, "publicity," to resolve it. In each case he believes he is elaborating a systematic politics of reason, in contrast to the undisciplined compromises of the natural lawyers.

Kant's predecessors in the natural law tradition had generally opposed the right of rebellion but recognized a handful of exceptions. Grotius had recognized seven exceptions to the prohibition of rebellion, ranging from cases in which a ruler seeks to destroy his people to cases in which the ruler shares power with a senate and tries to infringe the senate's power.[39] Samuel von Pufendorf admitted five of these cases.[40] Christian Wolff distinguished rebellion from civil war and allowed the latter as just resistance to the ruler of a state.[41] Emer de Vattel, perhaps the most liberal on this issue of the well-known natural lawyers, recognized an open-ended right of a nation to depose a tyrant.[42] None of these writers had established an overarching principle to support their conclusions, and their arguments had something of an ad hoc quality. As Vattel put it, although it is clear that no one should obey commands that are clearly contrary to natural law, "it is a more difficult matter to decide in what cases a subject may not only refuse to obey but even resist the sovereign and meet force with force."[43]

Kant's principle of publicity, in contrast, makes short work of the right of rebellion. If it "were publicly acknowledged, it would defeat its own purpose," he argues. Kant does not mean that it would defeat the purpose of rebellion but that implicit in the purpose of setting up a right of rebellion is that there should be a state in the first place, and the division of authority created by a right of rebellion makes the existence of the state as a state "impossible." In this Kant was evidently following Thomas Hobbes. His point was that a right of rebellion means that there is no final authority short of violence (8:382; see also 6:319ff.).

But, Kant points out, the ruler has no need to keep secret his right to punish rebellion. If he has the power—and he must by definition, or he is not the ruler—then he has nothing to fear from making his intentions public. Therefore, according to Kant, his maxims must be legitimate (8:382–383).

Kant's argument does not entirely deny comfort to the rebellious, however. It is "perfectly consistent with this argument that if the people were to rebel successfully, the head of state would revert to the position of a subject . . . [and] he would not be justified in starting a new rebellion to restore his former position" (8:383). There is no right to rebellion; but, as David Hume had acknowledged, a successful rebellion creates its own rights. The rights of a successful rebellion can be publicly admitted without inordinately encouraging rebellions, Kant thinks, because the rebel still has to acknowledge that what he is doing is not yet right, and only success will save him from punishment.

In matters of international relations, the principle of publicity also provides solutions. The natural lawyers had followed the authority of the Roman lawyers Pedius and Ulpian in elaborating a distinction between personal and real treaties to defeat claims that a king who signs a treaty does not bind his country.[44] Kant simply argued that if a ruler's intention that his signature would not bind his country was made public, other countries would not rely on his engagements (8:383–384).

Grotius had held that a state does not have the right to invade another solely because the other is growing in strength and may some day threaten its neighbors, and Pufendorf agreed.[45] Wolff agreed but added that if any such nation should "manifestly be considering plans for subjecting other nations to itself, these ought to provide for their common security by alliances, and the slightest wrong gives them the right to overthrow the growing power by armed force."[46] Vattel agreed that of itself, the growth of another nation could not justify an invasion, but the responsibility for defense of a country was a heavy one and required extreme caution. One could not afford to wait until it was too late. The "first appearances [of a desire of domineering on the part of a neighboring country] may be taken as a sufficient proof" and justify countermeasures.[47] Obviously, the right to invade in such cases could virtually be taken for granted.

Kant's approach was different. If a right to invade growing countries were to be made public, it would be counterproductive. Countries that were growing would anticipate such measures by alliances with their neighbors in accordance with the principle of "divide and conquer" (8:384). Therefore, no such right could be legitimate.

A third question that Kant raised was the right of a larger state to annex a smaller state to round off its territories. Natural lawyers did not address the issue directly, although it would perhaps fall under their proscriptions of the right to go to war for pure utility or advantage.[48] Grotius specifically criticized the German tribes cited by Tacitus who went to war for better lands.[49] If the justification for such annexation is security, presumably it would have been treated much as the invasion of growing states discussed above. But for Kant, again, the resolution is easy, in accordance with the principle of publicity. If the maxim of annexation of smaller states were made public, smaller states would immediately unite to resist the larger states or ally themselves with other larger states for defense. Such a response would defeat the purpose of the right to annexation, and thus that right cannot be just (8:383).

Publicity, it turns out, is also the key to the rightful organization of the international system. Politics and morality "can only be in agreement within a federal union" of states, Kant wrote. A federation provides a state of lawfulness without which no right can exist, but without stifling freedom, he argued. Again, like all of the conclusions drawn from the principle of publicity, this is "necessary and given a priori through the principles of right" (8:385).

Publicity is explicitly tied in with Kant's theory of the special role of philosophers. The "subterfuge of a secretive system of politics could... easily be defeated if philosophy were to make its maxims public, if only they dared allow the philosopher to expose his maxims through publicity" (8:386). That is, if philosophers are given free rein in their publicity, injustice will not prevail.[50]

When Kant's writings are studied, it is usually from within the discipline of philosophy or natural law. Kant "answers" Hume or improves on Grotius. When political matters are raised, Kant is found to be in dialogue with Rousseau or Hobbes, across the years and linguistic boundaries. In contrast, I have examined contemporary German belles lettres and political journalism as a context for Kant's political vocabulary. Kant turned to the terminology of Riedel, Wekhrlin, and Schlözer in developing a political vocabulary that was subversive for its time.

Kant's "What Is Enlightenment?" reads like an occasional piece, a lighthearted, nontechnical paean to the values of the Aufklärung. On this contextual reading, however, we begin to see that its defense of freedom of expression and the public realm of the Gelehrter implicitly undermined absolutism and the conceptual tools of the lawyers who defended it. Kant's later use of the concept of publicity in *Toward Perpetual Peace* served some of the same subversive purposes, after events had forced him to reduce his reliance on the reading public.

Kant's usage was not a mere uncreative adoption of the usage of the men of letters and journalists of his time. He went beyond them by integrating their vocabulary into his systematic analyses of reason and its rights and giving it the cover of his philosophy. "Public" and "publicity" became such effective weapons for him precisely because he could use them in such a presumptively innocuous and noncontroversial way. Although it appeared on the surface that he was writing unobjectionable occasional pieces or elaborating schemes for perpetual peace based on abstract principles, he was actually subtly appropriating and legitimizing the vocabulary of opposition to the ruling princes.[51]

NOTES

1. Imanuel Kant, "An Answer to the Question: What Is Enlightenment?" in *Kant's Political Writings*, ed. Hans Reiss (Cambridge, 1970), 5. Hereafter, citations to Kant appear in the text with the volume number of the standard Academy edition (*Kants Gesammelte Schriften* ed. Royal Prussian Academy of Sciences and later academies, Berlin, 1902–) followed by a colon and the page number. Translations have been borrowed from the Reiss edition and *The Conflict of the Faculties*, trans. Mary J. Gregor (New York, 1979).

2. Most scholars, however, merely remark on this unusual usage, perhaps with an exclamation point (e.g., Susan Meld Shell, *The Rights of Reason* [Toronto, 1980], 171).

3. Hans Müllejans, *Publicus und Privatus im Romischen Recht und im älteren Kanonischen Recht unter besonderer Berücksichtigung der Unterscheidung ius publicum und ius privatum* (Munich, 1961), 5.

4. Lucian Hölscher, "Öffentlichkeit," in *Geschichtliche Grundbegriffe: Historisches Lexikon zur Politisch-sozialen Sprache in Deutschland*, ed. Otto Brunner, Werner Conze, and Reinhart Koselleck (Stuttgart, 1978), 4:420. See also, of general relevance for this essay, Hölscher's *Öffentlichkeit und Geheimnis* (Stuttgart, 1979), esp. pp. 101ff.

5. Müllejans, *Publicus und Privatus*, 13.

6. Hölscher, "Öffentlichkeit," 427, 420.

7. Ibid., 417.

8. Ibid., 418–419.

9. Ibid., 422–426.

10. Ibid., 424.

11. Ibid., 423.

12. Ibid., 426.

13. Johann Heinrich Zedler, *Grosses Vollständiges Universal-Lexikon* (Leipzig and Halle; reprint Graz, 1961), see under "*Öffentliche Personen*" and "*das Publikum.*"

14. Hölscher, "Öffentlichkeit," 424.

15. Ibid., 445.

16. Friedrich Just Riedel, *Briefe über das Publikum* (1768; reprint Vienna, 1973), 115.

17. Johann Christoph Gottsched, *Die vernunftige Tadlerinnen*, in vol. 1 of *Gesammelte Schriften*, ed. Eugen Reichel (Berlin, 1902), 1.

18. Gotthold Ephraim Lessing, *Werke*, ed. Paul Stapf (Munich, n.d.), 2:7.

19. Friedrich Nicolai, ed., *Allgemeine deutsche Bibliothek* 1 (1766): Preface (no page number).

20. Riedel, *Briefe*, 12, 113–114.

21. Christoph Martin Wieland, ed., *Der Teutsche Merkur* 1 (Frankfurt and Leipzig, 1773): Preface (no page number).

22. Johann Erich Biester and Friedrich Gedike, eds., *Berlinische Monatsschrift* 1 (1783): Preface (no page number).

23. Cited in Paul Hocks and Peter Schmidt, *Literarische und politische Zeitschriften, 1789–1805* (Stuttgart, 1975), 18.

24. Wilhelm Wekhrlin, ed., *Das graue Ungeheur* (1784–1787), 2:196.

25. "Über Denk- und Drukfreiheit. An Fürsten, Minister, und Schriftsteller," *Berlinische Monatsschrift* 3 (1784): 327, 326. We now know that this article was written by Ernst Ferdinand Klein: see Norbert Hinske and Michael Albrecht, eds., *Was ist Aufklärung? Beiträge aus der Berlinischen Monatsschrift*, rev. ed. (Darmstadt, 1981), 517.

26. Rolf Engelsing, *Der Bürger als Leser* (Stuttgart, 1974), 263.

27. Eberhard Günter Schulz cites two edicts from the Prussian Ministry of Education that also may have inspired Kant's distinction ("Kant und die Berliner Aufklärung," in *Akten des 4. Internationalen Kant-Kongresses, Mainz 1974*, Teil II, 1: Sektionen, ed. Gerhard Funke [Berlin, 1974], 69). However, they did not go as far as Kant in characterizing official sermons as "private."

28. Cited in Helmut Kiesel and Paul Münch, *Gesellschaft und Literatur im 18. Jahrhundert* (Munich, 1977), 123.

29. Mary J. Gregor, Translator's Introduction to *The Conflict of the Faculties*, pp. ix–x. This is an appropriate place to point out that many accounts of Kant's attitude toward the public, including Jürgen Habermas's otherwise valuable discussion in *Strukturwandel der Öffentlichkeit* (Berlin and Neuwied, 1962) (*The Structural Transformation of the Public Sphere* [Cambridge, Mass., 1989]), treat "What Is Enlightenment?" and *The Conflict of the Faculties* as if they present the same theory, neglecting the differences between these works and the reasons for them.

30. Wekhrlin, *Ungeheur*, 2:124.

31. Ibid., 195, 190, 192, 195, 123.

32. Cited in Jürgen Wilke, *Literarische Zeitschriften des 18. Jahrhunderts (1688–1789)*, Teil II: Repertorium (Stuttgart, 1978), 156.

33. Hinske and Albrecht, *Was ist Aufklärung?* 318ff.

34. Cited in Hans-Wolf Jäger, *Politische Kategorien in Poetik und Rhetorik der zweiten Hälfte des 18. Jahrhunderts* (Stuttgart, 1970), 19.

35. Jäger, *Politische Kategorien*, 69.

36. Adolf Freiherr von Knigge, *Josephs von Wurmbrand...politisches Glaubenbekenntniss...*, ed. Gerhard Steiner (1792; reprint Frankfurt, 1968), 94. It is worth noting that the entries for the English word *publicist* in the *Oxford English Dictionary* suggest that it was borrowed from the German about this time. The earliest uses noted are from Edmund Burke in 1792 and Henry Crabb Robinson in 1801, both referring explicitly to German affairs.

37. August Ludwig von Schlözer, *Allegemeines StatsRecht und StatsVerfassungsLere* (Göttingen, 1793; reprint 1970), 165, 189, 153–154, 173, 200, 108, 106.

38. Johann Georg Heinzmann, *Appell an meine Nation: Über die Pest der deutschen Literatur* (Bern, 1795; reprint 1977), 53.

39. Hugo Grotius, *Of War and Peace*, trans. Clement Barksdale (London, 1655), Sec. 1.LXXII.

40. Samuel von Pufendorf, *The Law of Nature and Nations*, 3d ed., trans. Basil Kennet (London, 1717), Sec. VII.VIII.

41. Christian Wolff, *Jus Gentium Methodo Scientifica Pertractatum (1764)*, trans. Joseph H. Drake (Oxford, 1934), sec. 1012.

42. Emer de Vattel, *The Law of Nations or the Principles of Natural Law (1758)*, trans. Charles G. Fenwick (Washington, D.C., 1916), 3:23; cf. 3:25.

43. Vattel, *Law of Nations*, 3:26.

44. Grotius, *War and Peace*, Sec. II.LXf.; Vattel, *Law of Nations*, 3:170; Gottfried Achenwall, *Ius Naturalis, Pars Posterior* (Göttingen, 1763) [reprinted in vol. 19 of *Kants Gesammelte Schriften* (Berlin, 1934)], sec. 240.

45. Grotius, *War and Peace*, Sec. II.XIV, II.CXVIII; Pufendorf, *Law of Nature*, Sec. VIII.VI.5.

46. Wolff, *Jus Gentium*, sec. 650.

47. Vattel, *Law of Nations*, 3:249; cf. Achenwall, *Ius Naturalis*, sec. 265.

48. Pufendorf, *Law of Nature*, Sec. VIII.VI.5; Wolff, *Jus Gentium*, sec. 645; Achenwall, *Ius Naturalis*, sec. 264.

49. Grotius, *War and Peace*, Sec. II.CIX.

50. Kant reaffirmed the importance of publicity in "An Old Question Raised Again: Is the Human Race Constantly Progressing?" written two years later. Publicity is the only way in which a people can present its grievances to its rulers. "A ban on publicity will therefore hinder a nation's progress" (7:89). Thus Kant manages to insert the subversive notion of publicity into a doctrine that purports to call for no more than reform from the top down.

51. Since the original appearance of this article, several useful articles and books covering some of the same ground have appeared in German. See Norbert Hinske, "Pluralismus und Publikationsfreiheit im Denken Kants," in *Meinungsfreiheit—Grundgedanken und Geschichte in Europa und USA*, ed. Johannes Schwartländer and Dietmar Willoweit (Kehl am Rhein, 1986), 31–49; Hans Erich Bödeker, "Aufklärung als Kommunikationsprozeß," *Aufklärung* 2, no. 2 (1987):89–111; Klaus Blesenkemper, "*Publice Age*"—*Studien zum Öffentlichkeitsbegriff bei Kant* [*sic*—Kant's mistake] (Frankfurt, 1987). In English, see James Schmidt, "The Question of Enlightenment: Kant, Mendelssohn, and the Mitwochsgesellschaft," *Journal of the History of Ideas* 50, no. 2 (1989):269–292, and T.J. Reed, "Talking to Tyrants: Dialogues with Power in Eighteenth-Century Germany," *Historical Journal* 33, no. 1 (1990):63–79.

On Enlightenment for the Common Man

Jonathan B. Knudsen

In early 1789, months before the meeting of the Estates General in Paris, Christian Daniel Erhard launched a new journal, *Amalthea*, with a lengthy polemic on the state of enlightenment.[1] His use of the term "enlightenment" was not uncommon: enlightenment, he wrote, concerns the abolition of prevailing prejudices and errors among individuals and entire peoples.[2] Erhard's article acquired a certain originality, however, when he differentiated between "true" and "false" and "unlimited" and "limited" enlightenment, in order to examine why enlightenment "collides with the self-interest, craving for power, and arrogance of certain classes."[3] He concluded that these defects were to be found within the historical Enlightenment itself. Indeed, "enlightenment is an often misused name."[4] It may substitute new errors for old; old errors may change their shape and survive in a new guise; false individuals may give their "pranks and vices the hue of the Enlightenment"; and new guardians may emerge to enslave the people.[5] In one place he proclaimed, "Damned be the Enlightenment which exchanges blind trust in itself for blind trust in others."[6] In another: "The *same century*, for which *the task of freeing human reason from all forms of the most vile tyranny* appeared to be reserved, *forges new chains!*"[7]

Erhard's essay was a particularly sustained attack on false guardians of the people, instrumental reason, and the tyranny of social interests. Even the phrase "burgher tyranny" appeared in one place.[8] His views, however, were only a somewhat atypical expression of critical views that had emerged

Certain aspects of this paper were delivered at a session of the German Studies Meeting (1988) sponsored by the German Historical Institute, Washington, D.C., and at Cornell University (1991). I would like to thank Hartmut Lehmann, David Sabean, and colleagues and students in the Cornell History Department for their thoughtful comments. Thanks also to James Schmidt, Reinhard Blänkner, Hans Erich Bödeker, and Etienne François.

in the 1780s from sustained debates over the Enlightenment and its claims.[9] In this sense, Erhard's piece is a reminder that the treatment of enlightenment in Theodor Adorno and Max Horkheimer's *Dialectic of Enlightenment* had critical roots in the historical Enlightenment.[10] It cannot be considered anachronistic or ahistorical, moreover, to adopt a critical perspective close to Erhard's—and thus to intersect with those of Horkheimer and Adorno—since such views, while certainly not those of the majority of enlighteners, were embedded in the late Enlightenment itself.

In this chapter I want to consider in greater detail a set of interrelated themes running through Erhard's essay and the debate over the question "What is enlightenment?" The first section begins with the issue of guardianship as debated in the Berlin Wednesday Society. I start here because the views of the Wednesday Society are central to the concerns of this volume and because they reveal with particular clarity the range of positions in the period before the French Revolution. The second section widens the discussion to the phenomenon of *Volksaufklärung*, or popular enlightenment, to examine how and to what extent the Enlightenment forged "new chains" for those who were to be enlightened. The final section shifts perspective to explore the phenomenon of enlightenment from below.

GUARDIANSHIP AND ENLIGHTENMENT

By the time Erhard wrote his thoughts on enlightenment, there was an established tradition of debate on the topic in the journals. Particularly influential had been the discussions within the Berlin Wednesday Society begun by Johann Karl Wilhelm Möhsen in December 1783 when he placed the question "What is enlightenment?" before his fellow members.[11] The ensuing reflections led to the publication of the more famous essays on enlightenment in the *Berlinische Monatsschrift*, those by Johann Friedrich Zöllner, Moses Mendelssohn, and Immanuel Kant. But as Möhsen told his audience, his remarks were themselves occasioned by two other ongoing disputes: one on reform of the German language that had been revived by Frederick II in his pamphlet, *De la littératur allemande* (1780),[12] the other concerning the right of the state to "deceive" the people, which had been the prize question of the Berlin Academy (1780). It is this latter debate, won by Rudolf Zacharias Becker (1752–1822) and Friedrich von Castillon (1708–1791), whose extended themes on the extension of enlightenment to the common man are key to my concerns here. Thus a number of strands came together to shape the question of enlightenment. In each of these, however, the question of guardianship and access to enlightenment remained central: Who was to reform whom? What were the limits of coercion? How much enlightenment was appropriate?

Möhsen was concerned in his lecture that Frederick's views on the inadequacy of the German language and educational system may indeed have provided a partial explanation for the slow advance of the Enlightenment over the course of the king's long reign.[13] The slow pace of change coupled with the "backwardness" of the population also fueled the debate over "deceiving" the people. In addition, it furnished some justification for state censorship and the emergence of reform-oriented "secret societies." The two debates together thus went to the heart of the Wednesday Society's activities: In what sense were their endeavors useful to the public, in what sense to the monarchy and the government? Did secret societies, such as the Wednesday Society, establish the only forum for the disinterested discussion and resolution of serious issues of reform? That these questions were pressing for functioning autocracies, their administrators, and the disenfranchised public is clear from the lengthy controversy over secret societies that was alive and well at the time of Möhsen's lecture. To replace monarchical-aristocratic authority with secret government by clique, even when reformers and the reading public were increasingly frustrated by the slow rate of reform, seemed to threaten both the monarchical principle and an emerging civil society. This was one reason that the Jesuit order had been banned (1773); similarly, the Illuminati were prohibited in the years immediately following Möhsen's lecture (1784–1785), and, eventually, it also led to the self-dissolution of the Wednesday Society itself (1798).[14]

For Möhsen, as for Erhard in his essay, the key term of enlightenment was "superstition" (*Aberglaube*), and the key issue remained to demystify the forms of superstition spread throughout the population. This was the link between the question "What is enlightenment?" and the endeavors of the reformers promoting popular enlightenment. Why, Möhsen asked, had so little light penetrated the dark of the countryside in the past forty years? In his own answer he did not merely focus on language and the educational system. Instead he attacked religious superstition and even Frederick II for inconsequence in the exercise of absolute authority in religious matters.[15] Möhsen sought to be much more invasive in religious life by enlisting the clergy, instrumentalizing prayer, and politicizing the pulpit.

On scrutiny Möhsen's concern with enlightenment was inseparable from the special sense of calling and status felt by the reformers themselves.[16] Many of the society's members asserted a right of privileged access to sensitive knowledge and thus to the differential exercise of power itself.[17] Participation in the debate over enlightenment, moreover, forced intellectual choices on the participants. They were required to identify with the state and its agents or to express an unwillingness thereto. They were also required to accept or reject the existence of an unbridgeable cultural distance between the state, its agents, and the unenlightened, unenfranchised "people."

With varying degrees of self-awareness, this latter point is amply made in the written comments (*Voten*) to Möhsen's paper. Ernst Friedrich Klein and

Carl Gottlieb Svarez, for instance, accepted official censorship because of inequities between the politically and socially constituted estates and the bureaucratic monarchical state. Klein accepted the state's right to prevent the "people" from reading matters otherwise acceptable in a philosophical treatise.[18] Friedrich Gedike saw enlightenment as reflecting the particular consciousness of educated burghers: "The actual point where the Enlightenment must begin is with the middle estate [*Mittelstand*] as the center of the nation; from there the rays of enlightenment will spread only gradually outward to the two extremes, the higher and the lower estates."[19] Moses Mendelssohn and Christian Wilhelm von Dohm were the two members who most emphatically repudiated guardianship in any form. Just as Becker had argued in his prize essay that deception was always inappropriate, they, too, rejected that enlightenment had ever been damaging to the advancement of humanity. Both asked that historical examples be gathered to show where truth and enlightenment had not led to the happiness of humankind.[20] "Surely one will not be able to cite a single case," wrote Dohm, "where the momentary evil of the crisis (or even the unrest that ensues with the overthrow of despotism and superstition) is not transformed into a greater good."[21]

The exchanges within the Wednesday Society over censorship and guardianship establish the epistemological and ideological field in which the movement for popular education or Volksaufklärung must be placed. The charge of the Enlightenment was to eliminate superstition by transforming belief and the conditions under which it thrived. Yet the extensive program of material and moral improvement for the common man cannot be separated from the special status assumed by reformers. This status was partly confirmed and maintained by a populace, viewed as ignorant and recalcitrant, who, perhaps more than being emancipated from the conditions of servitude, needed to be educated and infused with "new" ideas from above. The discussions within the Wednesday Society already point to the pattern of the Volksaufklärung itself: it functioned to sustain the social distance, even as it developed a particular reform program charged with eliminating its preconditions. The language of demystification and emancipation, of "above" and "below," of guardianship and control, simultaneously propelled and undermined the entire endeavor.

THE CULTURAL EXCHANGE BETWEEN "HIGH" ENLIGHTENMENT AND "POPULAR" ENLIGHTENMENT

There was no movement in France similar in scale or intention to the German Volksaufklärung.[22] Hundreds of articles, brochures, and books were printed from the 1750s onward—all of which bear witness to the widespread rediscovery of the common man. The older humanistic *Hausvater* literature, an established genre from the Renaissance onward, now became more specialized. There was an extended campaign to extend literacy through the establishment of rural schools. Special guidebooks, calendars, almanacs, hymnals, and even novels were composed for the lower orders. Massive efforts were made to transform values: reformers propagated the importance of a rationalized work ethic, thrift, and self-discipline. The churches sought to introduce a more "rational" religious practice: Newtonian science meant that life and death were subject to new laws of interpretation; modern ethical views meant that the blood and gore of pietistic song needed to be elevated to a more abstract plane. Medical doctors and administrators attempted to transform public health and to introduce a better diet. And, of course, there was a flood of stereotypical advice on improving rural agriculture. These ranged from the introduction of beekeeping and new crops (clover, potatoes) to rational husbandry of the forests, the elimination of wastelands, and the enclosure of commons.[23] These efforts to systematize daily life, demystify the world of the supernatural, and increase productivity were thus part and parcel of the expansion of the Enlightenment after midcentury. But popular enlightenment also flowed from the general concern for heightened agricultural productivity in the wake of the Seven Years War and the great dearth of the early 1770s.[24] It also followed from the growing book culture and improved printing techniques that made it possible to sell books cheaply to the lower orders. It stemmed, in addition, from Protestant and Catholic concerns for literacy and Christian improvement that were part of the educational movement of these years.[25]

Certain historians have argued that so much was written by reformers in these years that generalization, especially about motive and intention, is almost impossible.[26] Nonetheless, I do not see how one can argue but that the Volksaufklärung was largely an apolitical movement with substantial political implications. Consider the term "Volksaufklärung." In the sixteenth and seventeenth centuries, use of the terms *gemeiner Mann* (common man) and *Volk* (the people) had marked the revival of a political language of participation. But in the wake of the Peasants War, the religious wars, and especially the Thirty Years War, subject or *Untertan* gradually became synonymous with "common man." Increasingly, historians argue, the phrase "gemeiner Mann" was connected with social and political inferiority.[27] When employed in depoliticized contexts, "gemeiner Mann" essentially distinguished between the cultivated classes, the *gesittete Ständen*, and the rest of the population. Even in this depoliticized sense, the language of "common" and "cultivated" was weighted asymmetrically toward the cultivated classes.[28] The term "gemeiner Mann," connected with the notion of a people, or Volk, included the artisanate and the petit bourgeoisie (*Kleinbürgertum*), but in a society overwhelmingly agrarian it largely referred to the peasantry (*Bauer, Bauernstand, Bauerntum*). In this sense Volksaufklärung meant enlightenment of the peasantry. Like "gemeiner Mann," "Volk" "was not able to acquire a genuine political quality after 1648." It was used in an "unmistakenly pejorative tone" to refer to the common people, who were increasingly perceived as an "object of pedagogy."[29]

The reformers of the people used the term "enlighten" in this apolitical, pedagogical sense. The Volksaufklärung had very little to do, for instance, with the revival of natural rights or estatist political language. Unless we return to Michael Gaismair and the Tyrol at the time of the Peasants War, I know of no drafts of future constitutions before the French Revolution where the peasantry was integrated into the political nation. In most cases the notion of "citizen" was urban and estatist, as were the constitutions.[30] The exceptional treatise on peasant emancipation, such as the early work by Georg Christian Oeder (1769), sought to separate emancipation from political participation.[31] Even Justus Möser, who sought to adapt the Lockean language of the joint stock company to create a constitutional fiction of gentry participation, stopped before peasant leaseholders.[32] In my view the recent literature on "communalism" and "republicanism," the first projected forward in time from the late medieval period and the second projected backward from the nineteenth century, assumes continuities concerning participation that simply do not exist for the period of the later Enlightenment.[33] The literature of the Volksaufklärung reveals the fragmentary nature of the political idea of "commons" and "village." Even where writers made distinctions between wealthy hereditary leaseholders, cottagers, and the propertyless, the peasantry remained in its "estate, without freedom of movement, and weighted down with all the duties proclaimed by law and tradition to its seigneurs and the state."[34] We can argue, consequently, that the Volksaufklärung was apolitical in its contours but politically instrumental in its function, since writers focused simultaneously on the improvement and control of the rural population.[35]

As far as I can discover, the word *Volksaufklärung* also implied a limited enlightenment wherever it was used.[36] Typical was Johann Ludwig Ewald's framework in his *On Popular Enlightenment: Its Limits and Advantages* (1790). In this work popular enlightenment was defined in terms of its boundaries: "It is necessary for all men to understand certain matters; certain only for a particular estate, a particular class of men." What are the limits of a "purposeful enlightenment for the people?" he asked. Enlightenment must halt before an "expanded enlightenment" that leads to a "pretentious erudition" (*Vielwisserei*); an enlightenment that leads to brooding and doubt; an enlightenment that leads to political doubt and questioning of the rights of the sovereign and his subject; an enlightenment that leads to too much cultural refinement.[37]

Where the general Enlightenment spoke of human perfectibility, the writers of the popular Enlightenment spoke, in Ewald's terms, of enlightenment according to one's station. In one author's plans for a rural school (1798), for example, children were to be taught religion, writing, arithmetic, civics (*vaterländische Gesetzkunde*), physical geography, and natural history with technology. However, as in Ewald's work, there were clear educational limits.

> I would be very much misunderstood if one were to believe I intended to acquaint the peasant systematically with the full extent of these sciences. That is neither possible nor useful. The slumbering mental capacities of these crude natural men could not comprehend such matters, and even if one were to do everything to awaken them, such learning would be neither intelligible nor useful to them. Of all these subjects the countryman should only become unsystematically acquainted with those matters that will correct his ideas, give him some knowledge of his country, its constitution and related matters, as well as lead to the improvement of his situation and his domestic environment. For this reason only a small and relatively insignificant part of such sciences is useful.[38]

Adolf Freiherr von Knigge (1752–1796), leader of the "radical" Illuminati and propagator of good taste, stated matters even more directly in his *Über den Umgang mit Menschen* (1788).

> That one now gradually attempts to motivate the peasant to abandon many of his inherited prejudices in the methods of planting and indeed in the management of his household, that one hopes through purposeful schooling to destroy foolish fancies, stupid superstitions, the belief in ghosts, witches and similar matters, and that one now teaches the peasant to read, write, and calculate well—all this is indeed commendable and useful. But to give them all sorts of books, stories, and fables, to accustom them to transporting themselves into a world of ideas, to open their eyes to their own impoverished condition which cannot be improved, to make them discontented with their lot through too much enlightenment, to transform them into philosophers who blather about the uneven division of earthly goods—that is truly worthless.[39]

The literature on Volksaufklärung thus supports Rudolf Schenda's provocative second thesis in *People without Books*: "The bourgeois Enlightenment did not formulate a common, interterritorial, and progressive theory with respect to reading and learning. It tended in individual cases to compromise with the states and was in agreement with their restrictions on education."[40] If we clarify Schenda's point somewhat, it is that the movement of enlightenment for the common man sacrificed universal enlightenment in favor of a theory of modernization that would not disrupt the social order of estates. This was typical of the literature on agricultural improvement, rural educational reform, and the utopias of peasant and village life.[41]

An exception to this account of the popular Enlightenment may have been the popular works on medicine and public health. Of course, the medical reform movement was linked to technological rationalization.[42] But besides articles making particular recommendations—for instance, smallpox inoculation or the proper hygiene for burying the dead—there are numerous works that are strikingly sympathetic toward rural life and protective of peasant laborers. Pivotal in this regard were the views of the Swiss doctor Simon André Tissot and his *Avis au peuple sur sa santé* (Lausanne, 1761), a work that went through numerous editions in the later eighteenth century.[43] Tissot was particularly clear that "the most common cause of illness among the peasantry" was "lengthy and excessive labor."[44] Works such as Tissot's, in other words, established a causality about disease and illness that led directly to an analysis of causes beyond the control of the peasant population. Equally significant were the so-called medical topographies, medical histories of cities that sought to locate and explain disease and mortality rates at the microlevel.[45] These works do not belong in the narrow sense to the popular medical Enlightenment. But they, too, analyzed disease in terms of poverty, overwork, and malnutrition and thereby made recommendations that questioned the legitimacy of the old regime.[46]

Crucial to the Volksaufklärung, then, was the link between knowledge and social interest. The social history of doctors in this period remains largely to be written, but it may be that critically inclined medical doctors such as Tissot were able to retain a far greater independence from the state than were other administrators and officials. Two areas are worthy of more detailed comment in this regard: one concerns the alliance between the state and the Volksaufklärung, the other concerns the ambivalent social position of the popular enlighteners themselves.

It is significant to see how readily princes and their administrators could be enlisted in the cause of popular enlightenment. There are a number of examples where princes, imperial cities, and village communes bought and disseminated books to their communities. Frederick II of Prussia distributed a brochure on the use of clover, and the Hanoverian government gave away some twenty-five thousand copies of the new catechism (1790); but the most notable case resulted from Rudolf Zacharias Becker's campaign to acquire subscriptions for the free distribution of his *Noth- und Hülfsbüchlein für Bauersleute*, his fictitious account of peasant enlightenment in the imaginary village of Mildheim.[47] We have encountered Becker in Möhsen's lecture as the co-winner with Friedrich von Castillon of the prize essay from the Berlin Academy of Sciences. Thereafter Becker gave himself over to the cause of popular enlightenment. Between 1784 and 1788, when Becker first published the *Noth- und Hülfsbüchlein*, he was able to gather more than 30,000 prepaid subscriptions. By 1799, sales had risen to more than 150,000 copies;

by 1813, Becker estimated that more than a million copies, including pirated editions, had been distributed. Reconstruction of the subscription lists shows the extent to which the established authorities purchased quantities of the book for free or low-cost distribution. We can see that no peasants, a handful of artisans, and only one reading society subscribed. In contrast, princes, administrators, rural pastors, and Masonic lodges played a significant role.[48] It has been argued that Becker's *Noth- und Hülfsbüchlein* became the most widely distributed secular book in the period: there may have been one copy for every ten households. The problem is that the peasantry most likely did not read it; rather it became part of the intellectual life of the literate classes.[49]

Similar conclusions can be drawn from the case in Braunschweig-Wolfenbüttel of Pastor Hermann Bräß's newspaper for the peasantry, *Die Rothe Zeitung*, printed from 1786 to 1797 and so named because the phrase "für die lieben Landleute" was printed in bold red type. Duke Karl Wilhelm Ferdinand gave free mailing privileges to the newspaper and exempted it from the censor. Pastor Bräß was also able to enlist numerous sponsors from the ducal administration, but we should note that thirty-eight of the fifty-one sponsors came from the rural pastorate. The recent study of this newspaper is able to draw conclusions similar to the work on Becker. It shows that this peasant newspaper never succeeded in its purpose but became increasingly linked to urban, enlightened readers. As the newspaper focused more exclusively on highly literate readers and landholding peasants, the tone and the topics changed, and it became more and more directly a political newspaper. After the paper reported student unrest in Helmstedt in March 1791, the ducal authorities intervened and the paper began to be censored.[50]

State and administration appear to have been interested in controlling and co-opting the popular Enlightenment from the beginning, because it was largely an invention of state officials—administrators, university professors, local justices of the peace, and rural pastors.[51] The rural pastorate, in particular, had long played an ambivalent role in the life of the countryside. Since the Middle Ages the Church had been an instrument of social discipline, and the efforts to control belief through religious schooling and the pulpit had not actually lessened since the sixteenth century.[52] Since the Reformation, in addition, the pastorate, both urban and rural, had become increasingly a homogeneous and closed caste. Recent studies have shown that more than half of the Protestant pastorate was recruited from among its own; that intermarriage was high; that the rest overwhelmingly came from among the urban elite; and that almost none came from the countryside. The lower Catholic priesthood, although celibate, also displayed a similar tendency to control positions through the extended family; but it recruited in far greater numbers from the peasantry and handicraftsmen.[53]

Rural pastors, and priests to a lesser degree, too, thus lived at an extended social distance from their rural parishioners.[54] They remained agents of the state even when filled with Christian commitment. The Church books, which registered marriages, baptisms, and deaths, were also used to organize the payment of the head tax.[55] They controlled access to the sacraments, they manipulated opinion through their sermons, and they had the power to cause dissent to be punished. In this way they legitimated the forms of knowledge that could be tolerated within the rural community.[56] Möhsen had understood this matter well in his remarks to the Wednesday Society.

This pastorate, itself in the process of being transformed into desacralized agents of a rationalizing state, was crucial, then, in the efforts to reform the common man.[57] A chief aim of the Volksaufklärung was to replace the popular tales, myths, and so-called superstitions of the rural population with useful knowledge about the world, with rational prayer, and with Christian discipline. In his *Development of Modern Conscience*, Heinz Kittsteiner has examined relations between ministers and their rural parishioners by studying sermon literature, visitation reports, manuals of piety and penance, and autobiographical writings in order to place the views of enlightened ministers within the sweep of efforts since the Reformation to control and reshape the beliefs of the rural population.[58] The scope of his work allows him to show that the Volksaufklärung was only one significant episode in this lengthier historical pattern of clerical control and cultural superiority over rural parishioners.

ENLIGHTENMENT FROM BELOW?

The systematic efforts by Enlightenment reformers to reshape the values of the lower classes is not an unfamiliar cultural phenomenon. Antonio Gramsci, Albert Memmi, and Jürgen Habermas are prominent among those authors who have explored a variety of historical situations in which elites have sought to control or replace systems of thought among those orders placed in a state of social, political, economic, and cultural dependence.[59] The various studies of North/South and church/state relations in Italy, Tunisia under colonial rule, and German modernization have given us a rich theoretical language dealing with cultural hegemony, intellectual colonization, and the colonization of life worlds. In recent years, in addition, the historian Gerhard Oestreich had sought to study the early modern absolute state from the perspective of "social discipline." Jean Delumeau has also used the phrase "inner mission" to discuss the role of the Church in shaping and controlling cultural life.[60] Such examples remind us that the Volksaufklärung must be situated within both premodern patterns of cultural control and later movements of secular modernization.

The Enlightenment of the eighteenth century was intimately tied to the prolonged transition (1500–1900) to print culture. The spread of literacy did not simply empower the individual; it remained a double-edged sword. As a cultural process, it became attached to the needs of the early modern state for administrators, lawyers, political economists, accountants, and scribes who could systematize social and institutional life. These agents of the state also used their specialized knowledge to gain access to the social system and enrich themselves. Education and literacy thus created new elites who grafted themselves onto the inherited corporate system. This process long preceded the emergence of the Enlightenment, but the Enlightenment intensified the efforts at systemization, even as it sought to make universal claims for the individual by emancipating him and the state from the arbitrary, charismatic patterns of authority.

These points require us to consider the extent to which the historical Enlightenment was an emancipatory movement and whether and to what degree such emancipation was unleashed by these agents of rationalizing states. This was the classic problem that shaped Tocqueville's late work. The literature on popular enlightenment supports the view that the Enlightenment sought within a long generation systematically to remake the value systems of rural Germany. The matter of system is significant, because these writers also genuinely sought to improve public health and diet and to widen intellectual horizons within peasant society. Yet popular enlighteners were hegemonic in their efforts to rework the structure of belief. At the same time, their writings, with rare exceptions, were committed to the differential access to human self-development and unequal entry into a reconstructed political society.

Arguing that the Volksaufklärung was a form of "inner mission" (Delumeau) or a "colonization of life worlds" (Habermas) creates, nonetheless, only a modest theoretical distance from the language and intentions of the proponents of Volksaufklärung. Notions of a popular or traditional culture that is the object of assault presuppose a theory of elites; they assume and require a view of cultural diffusion; they find it difficult to comprehend that complex, rational, and systematic views could be generated from "below"; they find it difficult to explain change; and they ignore cultural strategies of adaptation, transmutation, and resistance. Still it remains difficult to change the perspective from "above" to "below," for one, because the analytical strategy often shifts from an individualizing perspective to a collective one. Becker is a publicist on peasant enlightenment whose individual ideas can be traced and seen as representative of a particular group of reformers. Peasant culture in the early modern period is often viewed as a chorus from which an individual peasant intellectual emanated as sport or idiot savant. For this reason, among others, the entire subject matter of the popular Enlightenment is fraught with difficulties concerning the reception of ideas, definitions of peasant "common sense," and the structure of rural belief.

How were the knowledge, values, and claims of the Enlightenment embedded within the culture of rural life? The response rests in our understanding of the interaction between oral and written traditions in the later eighteenth century.[61] Estimates of literacy vary depending on the observations of contemporaries, statistical evidence of the ability to sign one's name, and the study of testaments and wills. There were clear differences between men and women, rich and poor, town and country, Protestant and Catholic areas, and the north/south and east/west divides.[62] But surprisingly, a leveling of sorts had begun to occur in the regions of western and northern Germany. The newer studies have allowed historians to alter substantially the older view of overwhelming rural illiteracy: except for the areas of seigneurial latifundia (*Großgrundbesitz*) east of the line from Stralsund to Dresden, rural literacy—conceived as an elementary familiarity with printed matters—appears to have been 70 percent or more in the later eighteenth century.[63] In fact, elementary literacy was relatively further advanced in Germany than in France.[64] We must remember that the beginnings of a rural literacy program had been established during the Reformation and that the struggle for the hearts and minds of commoners had generated a massive pamphlet and broadsheet campaign that must have penetrated the countryside. The Thirty Years War brought with it yet another wave of printed propaganda. In addition, the confessional stalemate, sealed in 1648, proved to be a most decisive factor for the three state religions. It created competition among the confessions that caused the levels of schooling in contiguous areas to increase dramatically.[65] We must also not overlook both that decentralization in Germany and the somewhat fluid continuum between city, town, and countryside may have contributed to sustaining a higher functional literacy in the countryside. A recent investigation of reading societies in the parish of Menslage in northwestern Lower Saxony has shown that around 1800, except for servants, the "entire spectrum of the rural population" was involved.[66] Other local studies have been able to show that literacy and the possession of books were substantial among leaseholders and cottagers in Braunschweig, among artisans in the cities along the Rhine, and among weavers in the small protoindustrial weaving villages in the Swabian Alb.[67]

We must conclude, then, that there was a far greater general literacy in Germany in the period before the French Revolution than previously assumed and that a certain demand for reading and literature had developed within rural society. The pressure to create rural schools often came from the communities themselves, although once again we cannot separate the initiatives of local administrators and pastors from the members of the affected communities.[68] Similarly, the demand for rural newspapers was not simply invented by the purveyors of the Volksaufklärung.[69] There were, in addition, isolated "learned peasants" who demonstrate the spread of secular book culture into rural society. One such figure was Bernhard Mangold, the mayor (*Schultheiß*) of the village of Suppingen in the Swabian Alb, who had memorized the German works of Frederick II of Prussia. Other peasant intellectuals such as Isaak Maus and Ulrich Bräker also come to mind.[70]

Still, the movement by the rural population for greater literacy and assimilation of the printed word into daily life cannot normally be equated with a commitment to enlightenment. The surviving testaments show that reading and the ownership of books was predominantly an extension of a religious culture attacked by enlightened reformers for "enthusiasm" and "superstition." Transforming religious belief was after all the primary meaning of enlightenment as expressed by Erhard, Möhsen, and Kant. The later eighteenth century saw persistent efforts by consistories to reform prayer and song through the introduction of new hymnals and breviaries. These attempts often met with equally persistent opposition from local parishes. Significantly, these parishes were just as often split vertically among rich and poor; and in their resistance to the reformer, they often sought to maintain a united front against forced change from above and outside.[71]

Literacy, like other aspects of the Volksaufklärung, was accepted when it was tied to the material and spiritual interests of rural society. Hence one must argue that rural culture resisted the imposition of ideas when they were presented systematically but was able to accept ideas individually. Particular ideas from the body of enlightenment thought were absorbed, in fact, when it became clear that such ideas were needed to survive in the larger world. The case of the jurist Johann Leonhard Hauschild and his defense of the Saxon peasantry in their struggle against their lords (Latin ed., 1738; German, 1771) has been used to show how natural rights arguments entered the world of the Saxon peasantry in the eighteenth century. Such ideas, however, were also consistent with long-standing efforts by the peasantry to erode the conditions of legal dependence (*Leibeigenschaft*). In this sense the newer form of rational argumentation was consistent with traditional perceptions of justice.[72] Others have shown how German peasants from the Palatinate were readily able to adapt themselves in their German-language press to the political language of colonial America. Here, too, the concern was with understanding local property law.[73] Similarly, agricultural innovations—ranging from new crops to enclosures—were also sometimes accepted in piecemeal fashion by competing groups when the advantages could be demonstrated.[74]

CONCLUSION

To understand the issues surrounding enlightenment from below, we cannot adopt a unilinear theory of growing literacy, religious secularization, or gradual politicization. Nor can we necessarily accept Carlo Ginzburg's belief that there was an autonomous strand of peasant materialism that continuously reproduced certain ideas over time.[75] Rather we need to see that certain ideas were absorbed or were made to fit within the cultural universe of rural society. Individual ideas, innovations, or practices could be assimilated without accepting the entire systematic effort of the Volksaufklärung. The special ideological function of the popular Enlightenment in the prerevolutionary period meant that the concerns of the state and rural reformers most likely did not penetrate deeply into rural life. Instead the peasantry continued to follow that defensive strategy of resistance to the outside that Christian Garve described in his *On the Character of the Peasantry and Their Relations Against Their Lords and the Government* (1786).[76] The reformers, including Garve, viewed such "obstinacy" in the older topos of the stupid and the sly peasant, since it confirmed the procedural interests of the reformers to transform rural life systematically.[77]

In his treatise, Garve stood outside the world of the Silesian peasantry to analyze a society alien and closed to him. Early in his remarks he drew an extended comparison of the condition of the peasantry to that of another closed community, the Jews. "They all are engaged in only one form of work, and they have long been oppressed and despised." He continued,

> The Jew, as the peasant, has become wise and clever—not through teaching and books (those which they have are, with both of them, far more likely to ruin their heads than to improve them), but through their employment in their trade.... With both, the result of this self-acquired cleverness in a single matter and a lack of understanding in all other matters is that they imagine themselves to be more clever than they are.[78]

Once again we are witness to that mixture of moral concern, cultural superiority, and distrust of the Other that characterized the Volksaufklärung. Garve's function as observer and chronicler of peasant life was to make the educated classes aware of their own special status through the study and ultimate manipulation of the lower orders. Such observations occurred simultaneous with the adoption of an emancipatory language to which clear limits were set by the study of those "below" and to the margins of burgher life. The reflection on those limits, the reshaping of values within a framework of conformity and social discipline—all this became central to the literary consumption by the educated classes of the lower orders and their distress. The distrust of difference and the traditional patterns of social solidarity were matched by a willingness of reformers to integrate themselves into a rationalized social order, with themselves placed strategically as cultural mediators. It is this vision of a limited enlightenment linked to a revitalized estatist hierarchy that was transformed in the nineteenth century into the ethos of self-cultivation (*Bildung*) and inegalitarian liberalism.

NOTES

1. Christian Daniel Erhard, "Ideen über die Ursachen und Gefahren einer eingeschränkten und falschen Aufklärung," *Amalthea. Für Wissenschaften und Geschmack* 1 (1789): pt. 1, pp. 1–48; pt. 2, pp. 1–23.

2. Ibid., 4–5.

3. Ibid., 10.

4. Ibid., 13.

5. Ibid.; examples from p. 5, quotation from p. 10.

6. The German original: "Verdammt sey die Aufklärung, die blindes Zutrauen in sich mit dem blinden Zutrauen in andere vertauscht." Ibid., pt. 2, p. 8.

7. The German original: "Das *nämliche Jahrhundert*, dem es vorbehalten schien, *das Werk der Befreyung der menschlichen Vernunft* von allen Arten der schändlichsten Tyranney *zu vollenden, schmiedet ihm neue Fesseln!*" Ibid., 29; see also Werner Schneiders, *Die wahre Aufklärung* (Freiburg, 1974), 133–135.

8. "Und *dieser freye* und weder durch religiöse, noch bürgerliche Tyranney gehinderte Gebrach der gesunden Vernunft, ist das *Wahre*, das *Einzige*, was (ohne schon Aufklärung zu seyn) dennoch die Beförderung und Verbreitung derselben möglich macht." Ibid., pt. 1, p. 9.

9. Much of this material has been discussed in detail in James Schmidt, "Kant, Mendelssohn, and the Question of Enlightenment," *Journal of the History of Ideas* 50, no. 2 (1989): 269–292; Günter Birtsch, "The Berlin Wednesday Society" (translated above, pp. 235–252); and Eckhart Hellmuth, "Aufklärung und Pressefreiheit: Zur Debatte der Berliner Mittwochsgesellschaft während der Jahre 1783 und 1784," *Zeitschrift für historische Forschung* 9 (1982): 315–345. I still find valuable Norbert Hinske's introduction to *Was ist Aufklärung? Beiträge aus der Berlinischen Monatsschrift* (Darmstadt, 1973), xiii–lxix. Hinske establishes a slightly different context for the debate, pp. xxxvii–xlvi. See also Schneiders, *Wahre Aufklärung.* Holger Böning stresses that such critical views can already be found in the late 1760s. See his "Der 'gemeine Mann' als Adressat aufklärerischen Gedankengutes. Ein Forschungsbericht zur Volksaufklärung," *Das achtzehnte Jahrhundert* 12, no. 1 (1988): 59.

10. This is not to deny that Adorno and Horkheimer had a peculiarly ahistorical understanding of the Enlightenment. See Hinske, ed., *Was ist Aufklärung?* xiii–xiv.

11. I follow the version printed in Ludwig Keller, "Die Berliner Mittwochs-Gesellschaft. Ein Beitrag zur Geschichte der Geistesentwicklung Preußens am Ausgang des 18. Jahrhunderts," *Monatshefte der Comenius-Gesellschaft* 5 (1896): 67–94.

12. See the critical edition with bibliography and commentary concerning the debate by Christoph Gutknecht and Peter Kerner, eds., Friedrich der Große, *De la littérature allemande* (Hamburg, 1969).

13. Keller, "Berliner Mittwochs-Gesellschaft," 74.

14. Norbert Schindler, "Der Geheimbund der Illuminaten: Aufklärung, Geheimnis und Politik," *Freimaurer und Geheimbünde im 18. Jahrhundert in Mitteleuropa*, ed. Helmut Reinalter (Frankfurt am Main, 1983), 288–289; Richard van Dülmen, "Antijesuitismus und katholische Aufklärung," *Historisches Jahrbuch* 89 (1969): 54–79; Dülmen, "Der Geheimbund der Illuminaten," *Zeitschrift für Bayrische Landesgeschichte*

36 (1973): 795–796. See also the essays by Peter Ludz, Manfred Agethen, and Otto Dann in *Geheime Gesellschaften*, ed. Peter Schulz [Wolfenbütteler Studien zur Aufklärung, 5:1] (Heidelberg, 1979).

15. "In der bald darauf 1780 herausgekommenen königl. Abhandlung bemerket man, dass der Monarch, ohnerachtet er allen Fakultäten und Wissenschaften, die Art ihres Vortrags und dessen Ordnung vorschreibt, und ohnerachtet ihm gar nicht unbekannt sein konnte, dass durch den Vortrag der Gottesgelehrten an ihre Gemeinden, und durch den Einfluss auf die Gemüter der Menschen, viele Irrtümmer ausgerottet werden, besser als durch alle Schriften, so übergeht er solches gänzlich." In Keller, "Berliner Mittwochs-Gesellschaft," 75.

16. Eckhart Hellmuth, "Aufklärung und Pressefreiheit. Zur Debatte der Berliner Mittwochsgesellschaft während der Jahre 1783 und 1784," *Zeitschrift für historische Forschung* 9 (1982): 322–323.

17. On these issues, see Gerhard Sauder, "Verhältnismäßige Aufklärung. Zur bürgerlichen Ideologie am Ende des 18. Jahrhunderts," *Jahrbuch der Jean-Paul Gesellschaft* 9 (1974): 107.

18. Klein wrote: "Z. B. Wenn ich eine Moral für den gemeinen Mann schreibe, so kann der Censor mein Buch nicht verwerfen, weil ich von der Pflicht, Eidschwüre zu halten, nichts gesagt habe. Wenn ich aber sagte, der Soldat werde durch den Eid zu nichts verpflichtet, wozu er nicht ohnedem als Bürger des Staates oder vermöge des eingegangenen Vertrags verbunden sei: So muss der Censor den Druck des Buches verbieten, wenn er auch selbst dieser Meinung wäre. Ganz etwas anders ist es, wenn ich diesen Satz in einer philosophischen Abhandlung vortrage. Von dergleichen Schriften kann ich voraussetzen, dass Sie nicht in die Hände der Soldaten fallen werden." In Keller, "Berliner Mittwochs-Gesellschaft"; Vota on pp. 77–80, quotation from p. 78.

19. "Der eigentliche Punkt, von wo die Aufklärung anfangen muss, ist der Mittelstand als das Zentrum der Nation, wo die Strahlen der Aufklärung sich nur allmählich zu den beiden Extremen, den höheren und niederen Ständen hin verbreiten." Ibid., 85.

20. Ibid., 81, 86.

21. "Sicher wird man keinen Fall citieren können, wo nicht momentanes Übel der Krisis (oder gar die mit Sturz von Despotismus und Aberglauben verbundenen Unruhen) sich in größeres Gute aufgelöset hätten." Ibid., 86.

22. The view of Jürgen Voss, "Der gemeine Mann und die Volksaufklärung im späten 18. Jahrhundert," in *Vom Elend der Handarbeit. Probleme historischer Unterschichtenforschung*, ed. Hans Mommsen and Winfried Schulze [Bochumer Historische Studien, 24] (Stuttgart, 1981), 211. Brief overview in Wolfgang Rüppert, "Volksaufklärung im späten 18. Jahrhundert," in *Deutsche Aufklärung bis zur Französischen Revolution 1680–1789* [Hansers Sozialgeschichte der deutschen Literatur, 3] (Munich, 1980), 341–361; Reinhart Siegert, *Aufklärung und Volkslektüre. Exemplarisch dargestellt an Rudolf Zacharias Becker und seinem 'Noth- und Hülfsbüchlein.' Mit einer Bibliographie zum Gesamtthema* (Frankfurt am Main, 1979) (cited from the original edition: *Archiv für Geschichte des Buchwesens* 19 (1978): 566–1347, with extensive primary and secondary bibliography); Otto Lichtenberg, *Unterhaltsame Bauernaufklärung. Ein Kapitel der Volksbildungsgeschichte* (Tübingen, 1970); Holger Böning, "Das Intelligenzblatt als Medium

praktischer Aufklärung," *Internationales Archiv für Sozialgeschichte der deutschen Literatur* 12 (1987): 107–133; Kai Detlev Sievers, *Volkskultur und Aufklärung im Spiegel der Schleswig-Holsteinischen Provinzialberichte* (Neumünster, 1970). The most analytically critical works remain those by Reinhard Wittmann, "Der lesende Landmann. Zur Rezeption aufklärerischer Bemühungen durch die bäuerliche Bevölkerung im 18. Jahrhundert," in *Der Bauer Mittel- und Osteuropas im sozio-ökonomischen Wandel des 18. und 19. Jahrhunderts*, ed. Dan Berindei (Cologne, 1973), 142–196; and Heinz D. Kittsteiner, *Die Entstehung des modernen Gewissens* (Frankfurt am Main, 1991), 293–411.

23. With Reinhard Siegert, Holger Böning has been constructing a multivolume bibliography of writings on the Volksaufklärung. See their *Volksaufklärung. Bibliographisches Handbuch zur Popularisierung aufklärerischen Denkens im deutschen Sprachraum von den Anfängen bis 1850*. To date, 1: *Die Genese der Aufklärung und ihre Entwicklung bis 1780* (Stuttgart-Bad Cannstatt, 1990). Böning's recent essays show that the subject matter of the Volksaufklärung was certainly present from the early eighteenth century onward and was linked to early work in the humanist tradition but that the sheer number of articles grew rapidly after midcentury. See Böning, "Der Wandel des gelehrten Selbstverständnisses und die Popularisierung aufklärerisches Gedankengutes. Der Philosoph Christian Wolff und der Beginn der Volksaufklärung," in *Vom Wert der Arbeit*, ed. Harro Segeberg (Tübingen, 1991), 93.

24. Christof Dipper, "Volksaufklärung und Landwirtschaft—ein wirtschafts- und sozialgeschichtlicher Kommentar," in *Vom Wert der Arbeit*, 145–155.

25. Helmut König, *Zur Geschichte der Nationalerziehung in Deutschland im letzen Drittel des 18. Jahrhunderts* [Monumenta Paedagogica, 1] (Berlin, 1960), 61–69.

26. Böning, "Der 'gemeine Mann' als Adressat," 59, 61.

27. See, e.g., Peter Blickle, *Deutsche Untertanen. Ein Widerspruch* (Munich, 1981), esp. pp. 15–19, 133–136; and the critique by Norbert Schindler in the introduction to Richard van Dülmen and Norbert Schindler, *Volkskultur. Zur Wiederentdeckung des vergessenen Alltags (16.–20. Jahrhundert)* (Munich, 1981), 50–52, 390.

28. I do not want to exaggerate the uniqueness of the German case, since, for instance, a similar pejorative meaning for the words *popular* and *common* also exists in English. See Schindler, "Spuren in die Geschichte der 'anderen' Zivilisation. Probleme und Perspektiven einer historischen Volkskulturforschung," *Volkskultur*, 23–26.

29. Bernd Schönemann, "Volk, Nation, Nationalismus, Masse," in *Geschichtliche Grundbegriffe*, ed. Otto Brunner et. al. (Stuttgart, 1992), 7:314–315.

30. Jörn Garber, "Politisch-soziale Partizipationstheorien im Übergang vom Ancien régime zur bürgerlichen Gesellschaft (1750–1800)," in *Probleme politischer Partizipation im Modernisierungsprozeß*, ed. Peter Steinbach (Stuttgart, 1982), 27–28; Horst Dippel, ed., *Die Anfänge des Konstitutionalismus in Deutschland* (Frankfurt am Main, 1991), 21–22.

31. See the chapter entitled "Möglichkeit der Zergliederung der Haupthöfe ohne Verlust der Gutsherren an Herrlichkeiten und Sicherheit fürs künftige," in Georg Christian Oeder, *Bedenken über die Frage: Wie dem Bauernstande Freyheit und Eigenthum in den Ländern, wo ihm beydes fehlt, verschaffet werden könne* (Frankfurt and Leipzig, 1769), 46–51. On this general problem, see Jonathan Knudsen, *Justus Möser and the German Enlightenment* (Cambridge, 1986), 132–133, 136–138.

32. Knudsen, *Möser*, 159–161.

33. From the perspective of the medieval experience, see Peter Blickle, "Der Kommunalismus als Gestaltungsprinzip zwischen Mittelalter und Moderne," in *Gesellschaft und Gesellschaften*, ed. Nicolai Bernard and Quirinus Reichen (Bern, 1982), 98–100; and his "Kommunalismus und Republikanismus in Oberdeutschland," *Republiken und Republikanismus im Europa der Frühen Neuzeit*, ed. Helmut G. Koenigsberger (Munich, 1988), esp. p. 74. It is characteristic that no examples from the eighteenth century appear in these articles, except for Jean-Jacques Rousseau and his *Social Contract*. From the perspective of the nineteenth century, see Rainer Koch, "Staat oder Gemeinde? Zu einem politischen Zielkonflikt in der bürgerlichen Bewegung des 19. Jahrhunderts," *Historische Zeitschrift* 236 (1983): 80–85. See the critique in the spirit of my comments by Paul Nolte, "Der südwestdeutsche Frühliberalismus in der Kontinuität der Frühen Neuzeit," *Geschichte in Wissenschaft und Unterricht* 43 (1992): 744–745. Even Nolte cites almost no examples from the eighteenth century.

34. Werner Conze, "Bauer, Bauernstand, Bauerntum," *Geschichtliche Grundbegriffe* (Stuttgart, 1972), 1:414.

35. Siegert, *Aufklärung und Volkslektüre*, cols. 586–587.

36. See the numerous examples in Sauder, "Verhältnismäßige Aufklärung," 109–126; also Dieter Narr, "Fragen der Volksbildung in der späteren Aufklärung," *Studien zur Spätaufklärung im deutschen Südwesten* [Veröffentlichungen der Kommission für Geschichtliche Landeskunde in Baden-Württemberg, Series B, vol. 93] (Stuttgart, 1979), 194–195.

37. Johann Ludwig Ewald, *Über Volksaufklärung; Ihre Gränzen und Vortheile* (Berlin, 1790), quotation from p. 14, examples from pp. 18–22. For other examples, see Schneiders, *Wahre Aufklärung*, 70–80, 133–137.

38. Th. Heinsius, *Ideen und Vorschläge zu der höchstnötigen Verbesserrung des Landschulwesens in der Mark Brandenburg* (Leipzig, 1798), as quoted in König, *Nationalerziehung*, 64.

39. Adolf Freiherr von Knigge, *Über den Umgang mit Menschen* (Essen, 1987), 387; see also Wittmann, "Der lesende Landmann," 158.

40. Rudolf Schenda, *Volk ohne Buch. Studien zur Sozialgeschichte der populären Lesestoffe 1770–1910* (Munich, 1977), 87.

41. Clemens Zimmermann, "Entwicklungshemmnisse im bäuerlichen Milieu: die Individualisierung der Allmenden und Gemeinheiten um 1780, *Landwirtschaft und industrielle Entwicklung*, ed. Toni Pierenkemper (Stuttgart, 1989), 102; Werner Troßbach, *Bauern 1648–1806* [Enzyklopädie deutscher Geschichte, 19] (Munich, 1993), 44–50; Udo Köster, "Modelle der bäuerlichen Arbeit in Texten der Volksaufklärung (1780–1798)," in *Wert der Arbeit*, 116.

42. These reservations are made with hesitation: see Ute Frevert, *Krankheit als politisches Problem 1770–1880: Soziale Unterschichten in Preußen zwischen medizinischer Polizei und staatlicher Sozialversicherung* [Kritische Studien zur Geschichtswissenschaft, vol. 62] (Göttingen, 1984), 46–59.

43. Holger Böning, "Medizinische Volksaufklärung und Öffentlichkeit," *Internationales Archiv für Sozialgeschichte der deutschen Literatur* 15 (1990): 1–92; to this point, pp. 8, 23–29.

44. Quoted in Böning, "Medizinische Volksaufklärung," 25.

45. The numerous medical topographies are collected in the Göttingen Uni-

versity library under Med. pract. 3722. See, e.g., Johann Ludwig Formey, *Versuch einer medicinischen Topographie von Berlin* (Berlin, 1796).

46. Frevert, *Krankheit als politisches Problem*, 84–85, 100–108.

47. See Reinhard Siegert's reprint with afterword of the first edition from 1788: Rudolf Zacharias Becker, *Noth- und Hülfs- Büchlein für Bauersleute oder lehrreiche Freuden- und Trauer- Geschichte des Dorfes Mildheim* (Dortmund, 1980). Also valuable is Siegert's *Aufklärung und Volkslektüre*.

48. Siegert, *Aufklärung und Volkslektüre*, cols. 683–684, 715–717, 1108–1112.

49. Ibid., cols. 1109 and 1015, respectively.

50. Christiane Josch, *Die 'Rothe Zeitung' (1786/87–1797). Ein Organ der späten Aufklärung für die Landbevölkerung im Herzogtum Braunschweig-Wolfenbüttel*, unpublished Staatsexam (Göttingen, 1988), 3–7, 78–80.

51. See, e.g., Holger Böning, "Intelligenzblatt als Medium," 107–133, esp. pp. 126–127.

52. See the discussion of Speyer in Etienne François, "Buch, Konfession und städtische Gesellschaft im 18. Jahrhundert. Das Beispiel Speyers," in *Mentalitäten und Lebensverhältnisse. Beispiele aus der Sozialgeschichte der Neuzeit* (Göttingen, 1982), 38; and James Van Horn Melton, "From Image to Word: Cultural Reform and the Rise of Literate Culture in Eighteenth-Century Austria," *Journal of Modern History* 58 (1986): 95, 97–102.

53. Luise Schorn-Schütte, "Die Geistlichen vor der Revolution," in *Deutschland und Frankreich im Zeitalter der Französischen Revolution*, ed. Helmut Berding, Etienne François, and Hans-Peter Ullmann (Frankfurt am Main, 1989), 216–244, esp. 220–221.

54. The rural pastorate, however, did continue to remain dependent on their parishes for a portion of their salary in kind—as meat, produce, and firewood. Thus a certain amount of negotiation with the community was clearly necessary, for they often lived in relative poverty themselves. Martin Hasselhorn, *Der altwürttembergische Pfarrstand im 18. Jahrhundert* [Veröffentlichungen der Kommission für Geschichtliche Landeskunde in Baden-Württemberg, Ser. B, vol. 6] (Stuttgart, 1958), 3–23; Schorn-Schütte, "Die Geistlichen vor der Revolution," 226–230.

55. Gerd Spittler, "Abstraktes Wissen als Herschaftsbasis. Zur Entstehungsgeschichte bürokratischer Herrschaft im Bauernstaat Preußen." *Kölner Zeitschrift für Soziologie und Sozialpsychologie* 32 (1980): 597, 602n.30.

56. Heide Wunder, "Sozialer und kultureller Wandel in der ländlichen Welt des 18. Jahrhunderts," in *Sozialer und kultureller Wandel in der ländlichen Welt des 18. Jahrhunderts*, ed. Ernst Hinrichs and Günter Wiegelmann [Wolfenbüttler Forschungen, vol. 19] (Wolfenbüttel, 1982), 43–63, esp. pp. 56–59.

57. See the valuable argument, with examples of resistance, in Schorn-Schütte, "Die Geistlichen vor der Revolution," 231–234.

58. Kittsteiner, *Entstehung des modernen Gewissens*, esp. pp. 293–331.

59. Antonio Gramsci, *Prison Notebooks*, ed. Joseph A. Buttigieg, vol. 1 (New York, 1992); Albert Memmi, *The Colonizer and the Colonized*, trans. Henry Greenfeld (Boston, 1965); Jürgen Habermas, *Theorie des kommunikativen Handelns*, 2 vols. (Frankfurt am Main, 1981), 2:489–547.

60. Gerhard Oestreich, "Strukturprobleme des europäischen Absolutismus,"

Vierteljahrsschrift für Sozial- und Wirtschaftsgeschichte 55 (1959): 329–347. In English, see his *Neostoicism and the Early Modern State*, ed. Brigitta Oestreich and H. G. Koenigsberger, trans. David McLintock (Cambridge, 1982). On this problem, see Winfried Schulze, "Gerhard Oestreichs Begriff 'Sozialdisziplinierung in der frühen Neuzeit,'" *Zeitschrift für historische Forschung* 14 (1987): 265–302; Jean Delumeau, *La Peur en Occident (XIVe–XVIIIe siècles): Un cité assiégée* (Paris, 1978); the same author's *Sin and Fear: The Emergence of a Western Guilt Culture 13th–18th Centuries*, trans. Eric Nicholson (New York, 1990). Cf. Kittsteiner, *Entstehung modernen des Gewissen*, 293–295.

61. See the reflections by Rudolf Schenda, "Alphabetisierung und Literarisierungsprozesse in Westeuropen im 18. und 19. Jahrhundert," in *Sozialer und kultureller Wandel*, 1–21.

62. Etienne François, "Regionale Unterschiede der Lese- und Schreibfähigkeit in Deutschland im 18. und 19. Jahrhundert," *Jahrbuch für Regionalgeschichte und Landeskunde* 17 (1990): 154–156, 164, 169; the same author's "Alphabetisierung und Lesefähigkeit in Frankreich und Deutschland um 1800," in *Deutschland und Frankreich*, 408–409.

63. François, "Regionale Unterschiede der Lese- und Schreibfähigkeit," 156–158, with literature, pp. 160–162, Troßbach, *Bauern*, 44–47. See the discussion of Schenda's conclusions in Siegert, *Aufklärung und Volkslektüre*, cols. 591–598; Wittman, "Der lesende Landmann," 145–149.

64. The reasoned argument of François, "Alphabetisierung und Lesefähigkeit in Frankreich und Deutschland," 416–417.

65. This point has been argued persuasively by Etienne François in numerous essays. Most recently in François, "Alphabetisierung und Lesefähigkeit," 417.

66. Karl-Heinz Ziessow, *Ländliche Lesekultur im 18. und 19. Jahrhundert. Das Kirchspiel Menslage und seine Lesegesellschaften*, 2 vols. (Cloppenburg, 1988), 1:88–89.

67. Mechthild Wiswe, "Bücherbesitz und Leseinteresse Braunschweiger Bauern im 18. Jahrhundert," *Zeitschrift für Agrargeschichte und Agrarsoziologie* 23 (1975): 214; Hans Medick, "Ein Volk 'mit' Büchern. Buchbesitz und Buchkultur auf dem Lande am Ende der Frühen Neuzeit: Laichingen 1748–1820," *Aufklärung* 6 (1991): 59–94; Etienne François, "Die Volksbildung am Mittelrhein im ausgehenden 18. Jahrhundert," *Jahrbuch für westdeutsche Landesgeschichte* 3 (1977): 277–304, and his "Buch, Konfession und städtische Gesellschaft im 18. Jahrhundert. Das Beispiel Speyers," in *Mentalitäten und Lebensverhältnisse. Beispiele aus der Sozialgeschichte der Neuzeit* (Göttingen, 1982), 34–54.

68. Wolfgang Neugebauer, *Absolutistischer Staat und Schulwirklichkeit in Brandenburg-Preußen* [Veröffentlichungen der Historischen Kommission zu Berlin, vol. 62] (Berlin, 1985), 632–634.

69. Holger Böning, "Zeitungen für das 'Volk.' Ein Beitrag zur Entstehung periodischer Schriften für einfache Leser und zur Politisierung der deutschen Öffentlichkeit nach der Französischen Revolution, in *Französische Revolution und deutsche Öffentlichkeit. Wandlungen in Presse und Alltagskultur am Ende des 18. Jahrhunderts*, ed. Holger Böning (Munich, 1992), 466–526, esp. pp. 467–468.

70. Medick, "Buchkultur," 52; Holger Böning, "Gelehrte Bauern in der deutschen Aufklärung," *Buchhandelsgeschichte* (1987): 259–285; Reinhart Siegert, "Isaak Maus, der 'Bauersmann in Badenheim.' Ein bäuerlicher Intellektueller der Goethe-

zeit und sein soziales Umfeld," *Internationales Archiv für Sozialgeschichte der deutschen Literatur* 10 (1985): 23–93; Ulrich Bräker, *Der arme Mann im Tockenburg* (1789; reprint Munich, 1965).

71. Of this literature, Hartmut Lehmann, "Der politische Widerstand gegen die Einführung des neuen Gesangbuches von 1791 in Württemberg. Ein Beitrag zum Verhältnis von Kirchen- und Sozialgeschichte," *Blätter für württembergische Kirchengeschichte* 66/67 (1966–1967): 247–293; Heinrich Schmidt, "'Aufgeklärte' Gesangbuch-Reform und ländliche Gemeinde," in *Sozialer und kultureller Wandel*, 85–115, esp. pp. 98–103.

72. Johann Leonhard Hauschild, *Juristische Abhandlungen von Bauern und deren Frondiensten, auch der in Rechten gegründeten Vermuthung ihrer natürlichen Freyheit*... (Dresden, 1771). Hauschild argued, however, that such rights were part of an original freedom: see pp. 3–16, 30–44. See also Peter Blickle, "Von der Leibeigenschaft in die Freiheit," 25–40, and Winfried Schultze, "Der bäuerliche Widerstand und die 'Rechte der Menschheit,'" 54–56, both in *Grund- und Freiheitsrechte im Wandel von Gesellschaft und Geschichte*, vol. 1, ed. Günter Birtsch [Veröffentlichungen zur Geschichte der Grund- und Freiheitsrechte, 1] (Göttingen, 1981).

73. Bernard Bailyn, "From Protestant Peasants to Jewish Intellectuals: The Germans in the Peopling of America," *Annual Lecture Series 1, German Historical Institute, Washington* (Oxford, 1988), 6–7.

74. Zimmermann, "Entwicklungshemmnisse im bäuerlichen Milieu," 106, 111–112.

75. Carlo Ginzburg, *The Cheese and the Worms*, trans. John and Anne Tedeschi (Baltimore, 1980), xix, 112, 154–155.

76. Christian Garve, *Über den Charakter der Bauern und ihr Verhältniß gegen die Gutsherrn und gegen die Regierung* (Breslau, 1786); reprinted in *Popularphilosophische Schriften*, ed. Kurt Wölfel, 2 vols. (Stuttgart, 1974), 2:799–1026. On this problem, see Jan Peters, "Eigensinn und Widerstand im Alltag. Abwehrverhalten ostelbischer Bauern unter Refeudalisierungsdruck," *Jahrbuch für Wirtschaftsgeschichte* (1991–1992): 85–103; Spittler, "Abstraktes Wissen," 586–589.

77. Heide Wunder, "Der dumme und der schlaue Bauer," in *Mentalität und Alltag im Spätmittelalter*, ed. Cord Meckseper and Elisabeth Schraut (Göttingen, 1985), 34–52.

78. I quote from the translation by Robert Berdahl, "Christian Garve on the German Peasantry," *Peasant Studies* 8 (1979): 90. The German original is in Garve, *Popularphilosophische Schriften* 2:808–809.

Modern Culture Comes of Age: Hamann versus Kant on the Root Metaphor of Enlightenment

Garrett Green

When Immanuel Kant announced his famous definition of enlightenment in 1784, he enshrined a metaphor that had long been a favorite self-definition of European modernity and was destined—in large part as a result of Kant's essay—to become the quasi-official criterion of what it means to be modern. Kant defines *Aufklärung*, as virtually every textbook tells us, as "man's emergence from his self-incurred immaturity" and goes on to explain immaturity as "the inability to use one's own understanding without the guidance of another."[1] At the heart of Kant's definition is a metaphor—or, as we shall see, a combination of two interrelated metaphors. Enlightenment, Kant is saying, is analogous to the passage from the status of minor child to the status of adult. Enlightened modernity is the adulthood of the human race.

When Johann Georg Hamann, in the same month that Kant's essay on enlightenment appeared, wrote a thank-you note to a friend for sending it to him, he raised profound questions about the assumptions of the *Aufklärer*, and he did so precisely in terms of Kant's central metaphor of the passage from childhood to adulthood. Hamann's remarks in this remarkable letter[2] exemplify what has often been said about him: that he anticipated, in sometimes uncanny ways, criticisms of the Enlightenment that were not generally recognized until long after his lifetime.[3] Indeed, as I hope to demonstrate, Hamann's letter of December 1784 adumbrates several themes that have been elaborated by leading theorists of the twentieth century. Without the benefit of historical hindsight, Hamann recognized the limitations and dangers lurking in Kant's optimistic endorsement of enlightenment, especially as embodied in his focal metaphor. Hamann's own term for that image—*Gleichnis*, a word that entered the German language as the translation of Latin *parabola* and has never lost its biblical associations—already sets him apart from Kant, who surely did not understand himself to be speaking in parables but rather in clear philosophical concepts. Acknowledging his willingness to be guided by Kant in matters of the understanding (though, significantly, "with a grain of salt"), Hamann identifies the metaphor as the focus of his disagreement with Kant. He can "tolerate gladly," Hamann writes, "seeing enlightenment, if not explained, at least elucidated and expanded more aesthetically than dialectically, through the analogy [*Gleichnis*] of immaturity and guardianship." Before examining Hamann's own "aesthetic" reading of the analogy, we need to attend to the imagery it employs.

Readers of Kant in English translation are likely to misconstrue the controversial metaphor, or even to overlook it entirely. The crucial concept, *Unmündigkeit*, is generally rendered in English as "immaturity." The trouble with that translation is that it subtly shifts the underlying analogy from a legal[4] to a psychological context. Likewise unavailable to the English reader is the common image linking the correlative terms *Vormund* ("guardian" or "tutor" in most English translations) and *Unmündige* (immature ones). Their common root—*Mund* (mouth)—indicates that the underlying meaning of *unmündig* is being unable to *speak* on one's own behalf. For that purpose one has need of a *Vormund*, a legally sanctioned "mouthpiece" to stand *in front of* (*vor*) him—or her—as official spokesman. The closest equivalent in English is the status of being a "minor," a term with the appropriate legal connotations and for which "guardian" is indeed the correlative term. Not only minor children, however, are unmündig. A senile old person might also be assigned a legal guardian. Even more important, *Unmündigkeit* (unlike minority) is tied not only to age but also to gender. As both Kant and Hamann make explicit in their comments on the "fair sex," women were considered unmündig and therefore (in Kant's view) prime candidates for enlightenment. Hamann's intriguing (if cryptic) comments about Kant, women, and his own daughters suggest that one of the later theoretical perspectives he anticipates is feminism.

A major drawback of translating *Unmündigkeit* as "immaturity" is its pejorative implication of childish demeanor. It may be the case that persons deprived of the legal right to speak for themselves suffer the psychological consequence of immature behavior, but the German term emphasizes the legal rather than the psychological or behavioral nuances of immaturity. The absence of adequate English equivalents also obscures the persistence of the metaphor in modern thought and culture. Few English speakers, for example, would suspect a connection between Kant's definition of enlightenment and Dietrich Bonhoeffer's reflections from a Nazi prison about the "world come of age." Yet Bonhoeffer's language is the same as Kant's: he speaks of *die mündiggewordene Welt* in which we moderns live, a world that has exchanged its minority status for responsible adulthood.[5]

WHO SPEAKS FOR THE IMMATURE?

Hamann's letter of 18 December 1784 to his friend Christian Jacob Kraus,[6] professor of practical philosophy and political science in Königsberg, contains an indictment of the basic Enlightenment program expressed in terms of Kant's own metaphor. Hamann finds the key to the root metaphor of immaturity and guardianship (*Unmündigkeit* and *Vormundschaft*) in a second, unacknowledged metaphor with which it is associated. Kant's essay on enlightenment identifies the problem as "*self-incurred* immaturity." Here, too, significant connotations of Kant's language disappear in English translation. The root of what Hamann calls "that accursed adjective *selbstverschuldet*"—*Schuld*—can mean "guilt," "debt," or "fault." Kant is saying that those in need of enlightenment are immature, deprived of the right to speak for themselves, through their own fault; and it is this claim that most arouses Hamann's ire. He returns to the issue repeatedly in the letter, and his language is peppered with allusions to Schuld in its various connotations. Employing one of his favorite Greek phrases, he finds the *proton pseudos*, the basic or original error of Kant's program for enlightenment, in that "accursed adjective."

Never questioning the claim that immaturity is the fundamental issue, Hamann presses the question of who is to blame for it. He uncovers a contradiction in Kant's opening words. No sooner has Kant defined immaturity as the inability to reason on one's own than he calls it self-incurred. But, Hamann points out, "inability is really no fault [*Schuld*]," as even Kant will acknowledge. Kant makes it into a fault, Hamann notes, by introducing categories of the will in his next sentence. Immaturity, Kant writes, "is *self-incurred* if its cause is not lack of understanding, but lack of resolution and courage to use it without the guidance of another. . . . Laziness and cowardice are the reasons why such a large proportion of men . . . gladly remain immature for life." Hamann seizes on the two terms of Kant's indictment of the immature, their lack of resolution (laziness) and their lack of courage (cowardice), and turns them against the accuser.

Those whose wills in fact lack resolution and courage—the truly lazy and cowardly ones—turn out to be not the immature ones but their "enlightened" guardians, among whom is Kant himself. Hamann arrives at this conclusion by pursuing the identity of the one he calls the "indeterminate other" in Kant's essay. If, as Kant had written, "immaturity is the inability to use one's own understanding without the guidance of *another*," this "other" is by definition the guardian, the Vormund who speaks for the immature. Hamann's suspicions are aroused by the fact that this significant figure appears *anonymously* in Kant's account, evidence for the fact that "the metaphysicians hate to call their persons by their right names." The reason for Kant's reluctance to identify the anonymous "other," Hamann surmises, is that "he reckons himself to the class of guardians," thereby exalting himself above the immature candidates for enlightenment.

Hamann now attacks the project of enlightenment head-on, calling into question the image contained in the term itself, through a series of ironic allusions to darkness and light, blindness and sight, night and day. He contrasts his own "pure & healthy human eyes" to the "moonlight-enlightened eyes of an *Athene glaukopis*," owl-eyed Athena who sees in the dark. The "*inability* or *fault* of the falsely accused immature one" comes not from his own laziness or cowardice but rather from the "blindness of his guardian, who purports to be able to see, and for that very reason must bear the whole responsibility for the fault." Immaturity only becomes culpable, "self-incurred," when "it surrenders to the guidance of a blind . . . guardian and leader"—in other words, to an "enlightened" guardian like Kant. Hamann closes his letter with a volley of ironic plays on "en*light*enment": he calls the Enlightenment of his century "a mere northern light," suggesting that the rationalists' program, like the aurora borealis, is both frigid and illusory—"a cold, unfruitful moonlight without enlightenment for the lazy understanding and without warmth for the cowardly will." Such nocturnal enlightenment is a "blind illumination" for the everyday citizen deprived of legal maturity, "who walks at *noon*." In closing Hamann notes that he is writing at dusk ("*entre chien et loup*"), the liminal state between light and darkness. The French phrase was a favorite of Hamann's, for whom the "realm between day and night became a symbol of his eschatological existence between the times."[7]

THE POLITICS OF MATURITY

Recovering the legal context of the metaphor of maturity and immaturity provides a clue to the important political dimensions of the controversy between Hamann and Kant. Both would agree that the enlightenment of individuals is inevitably implicated in a network of social and political forces. Kant's essay defining enlightenment puts the whole question quite explicitly in political terms, most pointedly in his announcement that "our age is the age of enlightenment, the century of *Frederick*."[8] Hamann, writing to a political scientist whom he addresses as *Domine Politice*,[9] does not overlook the implications of Kant's testimonial to their common monarch, toward whom their attitudes could hardly stand in sharper contrast. Elfriede Büchsel notes that the importance of Frederick the Great as opponent in Hamann's writings has won increasing acknowledgment by scholars.[10] When Frederick assumed the throne from his father in 1740, no less an authority than Voltaire had pronounced him "Le Salomon du Nord," appointed to enlighten the eyes of the Prussian *barbares*. Voltaire's epithet, identifying the king with the Old Testament paradigm of the wise man, places Frederick in symbolic rivalry with Hamann, whom Karl von Moser had dubbed "Magus in Norden" after those other biblical wise men, the New Testament magi.[11] Hamann, who accepted the epithet gracefully, signs the letter containing his critique of Kant with the variant "Magus in telonio," which calls attention to his own position as Frederick's unwilling civil servant in the Königsberg customhouse.

Hamann's political critique of Kantian enlightenment goes directly to the issue of power. Kant's flattering description of Frederick as "the man who first liberated mankind from immaturity"[12] betrays the proton pseudos, the root error of the enlighteners, and it has to do with the question of culpability introduced by Kant's "accursed adjective" *self-incurred.* The telling phrase occurs in Kant's almost incidental remark that the enlightened ruler "has at hand a well-disciplined and numerous army to guarantee public security."[13] In Hamann's sarcastic paraphrase, the purpose of the guardian's army is "to guarantee his infallibility and orthodoxy." As the "anonymous other," Hamann fingers the guardian implied by the very existence of the immature, the Vormund whose job it is to speak for the Unmündige, and singles him out for the severest censure: he twice calls him "the man of death." Without ever naming the king directly, Hamann lets Kraus know exactly whom he has in mind. The first clue, not decisive by itself, is the epithet "man of death," which apparently alludes to King David's encounter with the prophet Nathan in 2 Samuel 12. This supposition becomes more likely in light of Hamann's predilection for parables as the most appropriate genre for telling the truth. In the same paragraph Hamann casts Kant in the ironic role of prophet: "who is the *other*, of whom the cosmopolitical chiliast prophesies?" But it is surely Hamann himself who intends to play Nathan to Frederick's David, prophesying in parable, allusion, and "macaronic style" in an effort to catch the conscience of the king—or, if that is expecting too much, at least to warn the consciences of his immature compatriots against the wiles of the "man of death" who has appointed himself their guardian. Such *political* pretension—backed up by "a large well-disciplined army"—is the real fault: "the self-incurred guardianship and not immaturity." A more direct clue to the identity of the "other" is Hamann's allusion to him as "this lad Absalom," another figure in the Davidic royal history, who leads an unsuccessful rebellion against his father. Hamann is surely speaking parabolically about Frederick, who as crown prince had (like Absalom) plotted against his own father, King Frederick William, and (again like Absalom) had failed. In one regard, however, Frederick fared better than his biblical prototype: although he spent some time in prison, he—unlike Absalom—survived to become king in the more conventional manner, by waiting out his father's death.

Hamann's political critique takes special aim at Kant's distinction between public and private discourse. Kant had defined their relative spheres in such a way as virtually to reverse their meaning as ordinarily understood. In Hamann's view, Kant's distinction amounts to taking away with the left hand the freedom that he has just granted with the right. "The *public* use of man's reason must always be free, and it alone can bring about enlightenment among men," Kant argues; "the *private* use of reason may quite often be very narrowly restricted, however, without undue hindrance to the progress of enlightenment."[14] Kant's odd use of these terms is governed not by the size of one's audience but rather by one's employer. Reason is used publicly, he writes, by "*a man of learning* addressing the entire *reading public*"—that is, by the self-employed intellectual. It is used privately, however, by someone performing "in a particular *civil* post or office with which he is entrusted"—that is, by an employee of the political establishment. Kant's three examples of such civil offices—the military officer, the tax collector, and the clergyman—become grist for the mill of Hamann's irony. Kant affirms the right to "argue" (*räsonniern*) to one's heart's content so long as one obeys one's political masters: "The officer says: Don't argue, get on parade! The tax official: Don't argue, pay! The clergyman: Don't argue, believe!" The parenthetical tribute to Frederick that Kant appends is hardly calculated to reassure Hamann: "Only one ruler in the world says: *Argue* as much as you like and about whatever you like, *but obey!*"[15] Hamann's sarcastic rejoinder in the letter to Kraus goes right to the underlying political and economic relations.

> So doesn't it all come to the same thing?—believe, get on parade, pay, if the d[evil] is not to take you. Is it not *sottise des trois parts*? And which is the greatest and most difficult? An army of priests [*Pfaffen*] or of thugs, henchmen, and purse snatchers?

For Hamann, here speaking in his proto-Marxist voice, it all comes down in the end to "the financial exploitation of immature persons" by their self-appointed political guardians. This "enlightened" political arrangement is what Hamann, in the phrase that pithily sums up his whole critique of Kant, calls "a supremely *self-incurred guardianship*." The guilt, in other words, has been attributed to the wrong party; Kant is blaming the victims. The onus of guilt should be removed from the oppressed and imputed to the oppressors—including their philosophical apologists.

Hamann's extended commentary on public and private comes in a postscript that is at once the most trenchant and the most difficult passage in the letter. He calls Kant's distinction "comical," but he doesn't appear to be laughing. He sees it as a distinction without a difference, but one that is nevertheless politically dangerous because it gives aid and comfort to "enlightened" tyrants. In language suggestive of the Chalcedonian definition of Christ's "two natures in one person," Hamann identifies the problem as that of "unifying the two natures of an *immature person & guard-*

ian," though not in the way Kant wants to do it. "Here," he says, "lies precisely the nub of the whole political problem." What follows, however, is a characteristically "macaronic" barrage of metaphor and allusion, involving a New Testament parable and passages from Saint Paul, Boethius, and Kant. Apparently borrowing imagery from Jesus' parable of the king's wedding feast in Matthew 22, Hamann first asks rhetorically: "What good to me is the *festive garment* of freedom when I am in a slave's smock at home?" Kantian "public" freedom is of little use to a civil servant like Hamann, who is "privately" enslaved in the king's service.

There follows the most arcane passage in the letter, in which Hamann's proto-Marxian political critique in terms of money and power appears to take on a feminist coloration as well: "Does Plato [i.e., Kant] too belong to the *fair sex*[?]—which he slanders like an old bachelor." The interpretive puzzle here is why Hamann would infer a similarity between Kant and women. Has he not already demonstrated that Kant wants to set himself up as the enlightened guardian of women and other immature persons? The key lies in Hamann's allusion to the passage in First Corinthians where Paul argues that "women should keep silence in the churches" (1 Cor. 14:35). It is essential to bear in mind that Hamann, unlike many feminists today, acknowledges the authority even of scriptural passages that seem to oppose his own opinions. So the Pauline passage is presumably cited in earnest. Hamann appears, in fact, to remove any suggestion that the apostle is deprecating women by juxtaposing Boethius's association between keeping silent and being a philosopher. The implication would seem to be that women, by remaining silent in accordance with the biblical precept, behave more like philosophers than those (like Kant?) who are full of words.

Even harder to explain, however, is the apparent contradiction in the passage that immediately follows. Still speaking of women, Hamann writes,

> At home (i.e., at the lectern and on the stage and in the pulpit) they may chatter to their hearts' content. There they speak as guardians and must forget everything & contradict everything as soon as, in their own self-incurred immaturity, they are to do indentured labor for the state.

According to Kant's classification, the professional activities of teachers ("at the lectern"), actors ("on the stage"), and preachers ("in the pulpit") are *private,* since they involve performance "in a particular *civil* post or office" entrusted to them. But that would imply that they are *not* free to "chatter to their hearts' content" in those situations. The key to the apparent contradiction lies in the phrase "at home" (*daheim*), which Hamann has used twice already in the postscript. Kant, speaking specifically of religion, had written that the ecclesiastical teacher's use of reason is private, "since a congregation, however large it is, is never any more than a domestic [*häusliche*] gathering."[16] This identification of the congregation as domestic makes clear how Hamann could use *daheim* to refer to activities such as those "in the pulpit." Applying Kant's logic to the Pauline passage, Hamann shows the absurdity of Kant's position by drawing the conclusion that women should be able to chatter away in such "domestic" (private) places as the lectern, the stage, and the pulpit. But in those very roles, according to Kant, people speak as guardians and thus have to give up their freedom of speech as good, "private" servants of the state—thereby becoming immature through their own fault. This bizarre reversal comes about by superimposing the Pauline distinction between congregation and home on the Kantian one between public and private. Paul says that women must remain silent in the congregation but may speak at home; on Hamann's reading, Kant, by making the congregation "domestic," identifies it with the Pauline realm of free speech. The contradiction at the heart of Kant's distinction thus stands exposed, for rather than allow freedom of speech in the congregation, he subjects it to the constraints of "private" reasoning. Hamann has thus demonstrated not only the absurdity of Kant's distinction between public and private but also his violation of scriptural authority. Kantian sleight of hand has turned the "public" free use of reason into a mere "sumptuous dessert," while enslaving the "private" use, which is "the *daily bread* that we should give up for its sake." This phrase resonates with the language of the Lord's Prayer, which includes both a petition for "our daily bread" and a plea to "forgive us our debts [*Schuld*]," by which allusion Hamann returns to the underlying issue of culpability.

The feminist twist comes just at this point: "The *self-incurred immaturity* is just such a sneer as he makes at the whole fair sex, and which my three daughters will not put up with." Hamann has shown that Kant's linkage of guilt with the social status of immaturity amounts to a slander against women, who thus come to stand for all those deprived of a political voice. By falsely blaming these victims for their Unmündigkeit, Kant implicitly makes himself their Vormund, thus acquiring the actual guilt of the "self-incurred" guardian. Hamann's transfiguration of Kant's enlightenment—his *Verklärung* of Aufklärung, as he puts it—leads to his radically different definition of "*true enlightenment*" as the "emergence of the immature person from a supremely *self-incurred guardianship*." Kant is right that the problem is the liberation of the immature, but he chooses the wrong target for his critique. It is not the women and other voiceless groups who incur guilt but rather the "enlightened" monarchs and their court philosophers.

HAMANN'S CRITIQUE OF KANTIAN PURISM

For all its immediacy and the specificity of the issues it handles, Hamann's letter to Kraus is also a key to more general and fundamental differences between these two contemporaries. One significant clue appears near the beginning of the letter, when Hamann first speaks of Kant. In calling attention to the Gleichnis, the parable or metaphor at the heart of Kant's definition of enlightenment, Hamann is at the same time demonstrating his own critical method, which he calls "aesthetic,"[17] in contrast to the "dialectical" method preferred by Kant. Oswald Bayer notes the irony in this situation: "The strict 'dialectician' Kant, 'professor of logic and critic of pure reason,' employs a metaphor [*Gleichnis*] without being aware of it, thus explaining the 'Enlightenment' aesthetically."[18] No better example could be found to illustrate Hamann's relationship to Kantian philosophy, the relationship expressed technically in the title of Hamann's best-known treatment of Kant, the "Metacritique on the Purism of Reason."[19]

Hamann composed this brief but trenchant analysis of Kant's *Critique of Pure Reason* in 1784, the same year as the letter to Kraus, but did not publish it during his lifetime because of his friendship with Kant. Largely on the basis of Hamann's "Metacritique," Frederick C. Beiser calls him "the most original, powerful, and influential critic" of Kant's attempt to vindicate the "Enlightenment faith in the universality and impartiality of reason."[20] The radicalness of Hamann's critique of the Kantian critical philosophy is concentrated in the prefix *meta,* which Rudolf Unger credits him with introducing into German philosophical discussion.[21] For that tiny prefix does to Kant's project the one thing it cannot tolerate: it relativizes the critical philosophy by placing it within a more basic context of interpretation. As Beiser puts it, "The tribunal of critique spoke with such awesome authority not only because its principles were self-evident, but also because they were universal and impartial."[22] If a *meta*critique is possible, the critique loses its claim to these qualities, and thus to its foundational status.

Hamann's principal objection to Kant's philosophy, expressed in the title he chose for his treatment of it, is its "purism"—that is, its attempt to rid knowledge of any intrinsic connection with tradition, experience, or language. Here Hamann foreshadows a broad range of twentieth-century thinkers who have found in language the key to philosophical conundrums. An example would be Ludwig Wittgenstein's insistence that the "meaning" of words is rooted in their actual use in ordinary language and its associated forms of life rather than in some "essence" to be abstracted from it. Hamann's stress on tradition likewise presages the attention of later thinkers to the cultural location of ideas and systems of thought. Hamann calls language "the only, the first and the last instrument and criterion of reason" and affirms its "genealogical priority... over the seven holy functions of logical propositions and inferences."[23] Kant's wish to "purify" philosophy of its dependence on language rests, according to Hamann, on "nothing more than an old and cold prejudice for mathematics."[24] Hamann expresses with particular clarity the antithesis between the foundational roles of language in his own thought and reason in Kant's in a letter to

Friedrich Heinrich Jacobi written in 1784, the same year as both the "Metacritique" and the letter to Kraus.

> For me the question is not so much What is reason? as What is language? It is here I suspect the basis of all paralogisms and antinomies can be found which are ascribed to reason: it comes from words being held to be concepts, and concepts to be the things themselves.[25]

Hamann's appeal to language and experience as the ground of reason rests on a still more basic disagreement with Kant. For if one asks why language should be the criterion of reason, Hamann appeals to the priority of the sensual over the intellectual, which amounts to an appeal to the bodily—and even sexual—basis of human language, experience, and thought. Here we encounter the most surprising of Hamann's anticipations of later thinkers. A century before Sigmund Freud, the pivotal importance of sexuality was acknowledged by a thinker whose life, values, and philosophical principles are about as far from Freud's as one could possibly imagine.

Hamann's emphasis on sexuality follows from his insistence on the priority of sense over intellect.[26] Language, rather than "pure" reason, has philosophical priority because "the whole ability to think rest[s] upon language"; but language in turn depends on the body. "Sounds and letters are therefore pure forms a priori," he says in contrast to Kant. "Music was the oldest language, and next to the palpable rhythm of the pulse and the breath in the nostril was the original bodily image of all measurement of time and its numerical relations."[27] Hamann's point in stressing the bodily foundation of thought is not, however, to exalt sense over reason; he intends, rather, to restore the original integrity that Kant's purism threatens. Since "sensibility and understanding spring as two branches of human knowledge from one common root," he writes, Kant errs by perpetrating "an arbitrary, improper and self-willed divorce of that which nature has joined together."

Hamann's treatment of sexuality differs from other writers who use sexual imagery and analogies because, as James C. O'Flaherty points out, "his allusions stem from an epistemological principle."[28] That principle is rooted in Hamann's holistic conception of human nature, which, W. M. Alexander argues, has been "secularized in Romanticism and distorted in Kierkegaard and existentialism."[29] Hamann's point is not to exalt will over intellect or emotions over reason but rather to respect the integrity of what nature—and God—has joined together. The error of Kantian purism is that it violates the bodily basis of that integrity: "*Sensus* is the principle of all *intellectus*;"[30] "the *heart* beats before the *head* thinks."[31] But Hamann is also capable of making the point in explicitly sexual terms. "The *pudenda* of our nature," he wrote to Johann Friedrich Hartknoch (once again in 1784), "are so closely connected with the chambers of the heart and the brain that too strict an abstraction of such a natural bond is impossible."[32] Some years earlier he had confessed to Johann Gottfried von Herder that "my crude imagination has never been able to picture a creative spirit without genitalia."[33] Hamann's unflinching insistence on the importance of sexuality—its *epistemological* importance, in particular—sets him apart from all the major voices of his time, whether those of Enlightenment rationalism, theological orthodoxy, or the "neologians," the theological progressives of his day.

THE THEOLOGICAL FOUNDATION OF HAMANN'S CRITIQUE

Hamann's unfashionable attention to sex turns out to provide an unexpected clue to the underlying motive of his attack on Kant and the Enlightenment. At the root of his philosophical and political critique is a theological commitment to biblical revelation. The earthiness of his view of human nature and human knowledge probably owes more to his immersion in the Bible and the writings of Martin Luther than to any contemporary influences. Hamann's break with the Enlightenment had come, after all, as a direct result of his own dramatic, if rather mysterious, conversion in London in 1758. From the day he arrived back in Königsberg to the end of his life, he demonstrated an unflagging tenacity in his adherence to a Christian sensibility that left him immune to the endeavors of his enlightened friends, including Kant, to win him back to the cause and made him remarkably independent of the spirit of the age.

Hamann liked to describe his own vocation as "spermalogian," a term whose ambiguity links the theological and sexual themes in his thought. It is first of all a biblical term (Acts 17:18), whose literal meaning ("picking up seeds," used of birds) had come to be used metaphorically of persons to mean "gossip," "chatterer," or "babbler."[34] Interpreters of Hamann are in general agreement, however, that he intends the sexual implications of the word as well. In his biblical commentary written shortly after his conversion in London, Hamann comments that "our reason should be impregnated by the seed of the divine word . . . and live as man and wife under one roof." The devil endeavors, he says, to disrupt this marital bliss, seeking not only "to put asunder what God has joined together" but "in our times to institute a formal divorce between them, and to titillate the reason through systems, dreams, etc."[35] The Bible should be our criterion, "our dictionary, our linguistics, on which all the concepts and speech of the Christian are founded."[36] Reason, however, plays a role for the Christian analogous to that of the law for the apostle Paul. Hamann put it this way in 1759:

> the commandment of reason is holy, just, and good. But is it given to us—to make us wise? No more than the law of the Jews was given to justify them, but rather to convince us of the opposite: how unreasonable our reason is; that

> our errors are to be increased by it, just as sin was increased by the law. If everywhere Paul speaks of the law one puts *reason*—the law of our century and the watchword of our wise men and scribes—then Paul will speak to our contemporaries.[37]

Twenty-four years later he used the same analogy in a letter to Jacobi: "You know that I think of reason as St. Paul does of the whole law and its righteousness—that I expect of it nothing but the recognition of error, and do not regard it as a way to truth and life."[38] Human reason unfertilized by the Word of God, concludes the self-professed "spermalogian," is like the law without the gospel, like the letter without the life-giving spirit: while retaining its formal validity, it nevertheless kills.

Given the vast difference between Hamann's theologically grounded "linguistics" and Kant's philosophical commitment to a critical "purism," their disagreement about the Enlightenment quest for maturity was inevitable. The gulf separating Hamann from Kant and his contemporaries has not always been sufficiently taken into account by his interpreters. Even Bayer, who as a theologian himself is aware of the theological basis of Hamann's critique, tries to portray him as a radical Aufklärer, one in whom "the Enlightenment is driven further, radicalized."[39] But when a position is so radicalized that its basic premise and criterion of truth is called into question, that amounts to a new position, not an extension of the old. This becomes even clearer in Hamann's attack on the ideal of "purism," so fundamental to the whole project of critical philosophy. Such a position is not just a correction of Kant but a fundamental rejection in favor of another and more adequate criterion. Hamann's method is more like G. W. F. Hegel's practice of showing how the dialectical tensions within a position finally cause it to collapse into its opposite. A more contemporary comparison might be deconstruction, which tries to subvert the text by turning its own unacknowledged premises against it. As Bayer himself repeatedly emphasizes, Hamann's objective is not to reform Kant but to *convert* him. It is a battle between advocates of rival absolutes, not a disagreement among fellow Aufklärer. Bayer is right in rejecting the interpretation of Hamann as an "irrationalist." But he apparently assumes that the only alternative to enlightenment is "irrationality." Since this term does not adequately describe Hamann's position, Bayer is forced to see him as some kind of enlightener. But Hamann speaks on behalf of a radically *different* concept of reason from that of the Aufklärer—one based not on human autonomy but on the "fear of the Lord."

On one point Hamann and Kant agree: the root of the issue is religious. In his essay on enlightenment, Kant explicitly identifies "*matters of religion* as the focal point of enlightenment" and argues accordingly that "religious immaturity is the most pernicious and dishonourable variety of all."[40] Their basic difference, not surprisingly, is also religious, and it is epitomized in the root metaphor of *Mündigkeit.* Just as Kant's commitment to the purism of reason led him to the metaphor of adult maturity, so Hamann's allegiance to the Bible suggested a different image: "Truly, I say to you, unless you turn and become like children, you will never enter the kingdom of heaven" (Mt 18:3). When Hamann died in Münster in 1788, the Dutch philosopher Franz Hemsterhuis chose as the inscription for his tombstone a passage from the apostle Paul—one that Hamann himself was fond of citing, and one that epitomizes his Christian critique of the Enlightenment:

> To the Jews an offense
> to the Greeks foolishness,
> but God elected the foolish things
> of the world to confound the wise,
> and God elected the weak things of
> the world to confound the strong.[41]

As the Magus himself might well have added, "and God elected the immature of the world to confound the guardians."

NOTES

1. Immanuel Kant, "An Answer to the Question: What Is Enlightenment?" (AA 8:35) (translated by H. B. Nisbet in *Kant's Political Writings,* ed. Hans Reiss, 2d ed. [Cambridge, 1991], 54).

2. An annotated translation of Hamann's letter appears elsewhere in this volume.

3. The comment of Frederick C. Beiser is representative: "Judged by twentieth-century standards, Hamann's thought is often striking for its modernity, its foreshadowing of contemporary themes." *The Fate of Reason: German Philosophy from Kant to Fichte* (Cambridge, Mass., 1987), 17.

4. Elfriede Büchsel notes that "*Mündigkeit* and *Unmündigkeit* are primarily concepts from the legal world." "Aufklärung und christliche Freiheit: J. G. Hamann contra I. Kant," *Neue Zeitschrift für systematische Theologie* 4 (1962): 141.

5. See, e.g., Bonhoeffer's comments in his letter to Eberhard Bethge of 8 June 1944 from Tegel prison. Dietrich Bonhoeffer, *Letters and Papers from Prison,* ed. Eberhard Bethge, enl. ed. (New York, 1972), 324–329.

6. According to James C. O'Flaherty, "An especially warm friendship obtained between Hamann and Christian Jakob Kraus, who became professor of practical philosophy and of economics at the University of Königsberg, and who was, next to Kant, the most brilliant docent there. Although much younger than Hamann, Kraus was probably closer to him in his later life than anyone except Herder." *Johann Georg Hamann* (Boston, 1979), 33.

7. Oswald Bayer, "Selbstverschuldete Vormundschaft: Hamanns Kontroverse mit Kant um *wahre* Aufklärung," in *Der Wirklichkeitsanspruch von Theologie und Religion,* ed. Dieter Henke et al. (Tübingen, 1976), 27–28.

8. Kant, "What Is Enlightenment?" (AA 8:40; Reiss 58).

9. Büchsel interprets this form of address to mean that Hamann sees Kraus as one "qualified and authorized to judge political problems." "Aufklärung und christliche Freiheit," 145.

10. Büchsel, "Aufklärung und christliche Freiheit," 234n.4.

11. See the references cited by O'Flaherty, *Johann Georg Hamann*, 25.

12. Kant, "What Is Enlightenment?" (AA 8:40; Reiss 58).

13. Ibid. (AA 8:41; Reiss 59).

14. Ibid. (AA 8:37; Reiss 55).

15. Ibid. (AA 8:37; Reiss 55).

16. Ibid. (AA 8:38; Reiss 57).

17. "Poetry is the mother-tongue of the human race," Hamann writes in his *Aesthetica in nuce*; and "parables [*Gleichnisse*] [are] older than reasoning." Hamann, *Sämtliche Werke*, ed. Josef Nadler (Vienna, 1949–1957), 2:197; trans. in *German Aesthetic and Literary Criticism: Winckelmann, Lessing, Hamann, Herder, Schiller, Goethe*, ed. H. B. Nisbet (New York, 1985), 141.

18. Bayer, "Selbstverschuldete Vormundschaft," 17–18.

19. Hamann, "Metakritik über den Purismum der Vernunft," in *Sämtliche Werke*, 3:281–289 (translated above, pp. 154–167).

20. Beiser, *Fate of Reason*, 8–9.

21. Rudolf Unger, *Hamann und die Aufklärung: Studien zur Vorgeschichte des romantischen Geistes im 18. Jahrhundert* (Jena, 1911), 1:526. It should be noticed, however, that Hamann himself is ironic in his use of "meta-," calling it "the casual synthesis of a Greek prefix." "Metacritique" (Nadler 3:285; translated above).

22. Beiser, *Fate of Reason*, 8.

23. Hamann, "Metacritique" (Nadler 3:284, 286; translated above).

24. Ibid. (Nadler 3:285; translated above).

25. Johann Georg Hamann, *Briefwechsel*, ed. Arthur Henkel (Frankfurt, 1965), 5:264–265. I have revised the translation in Smith, *J. G. Hamann 1730–1788: A Study in Christian Existence* (New York, 1960), 249.

26. For an instructive treatment of the theme of sexuality in Hamann, see O'Flaherty, *Johann Georg Hamann*, chap. 2, esp. pp. 38–42.

27. Hamann, "Metacritique" (Nadler 3:286; translated above, p. 156).

28. O'Flaherty, *Johann Georg Hamann*, 40.

29. W. M. Alexander, *Johann Georg Hamann: Philosophy and Faith* (The Hague, 1966), 177.

30. Letter to Jacobi, 14 November 1784, in *Briefwechsel*, 6:27.

31. Letter to Hans Jacob von Auerswald, 28 July 1785, in *Briefwechsel*, 6:27; trans. from Alexander, *Johann Georg Hamann*, 177.

32. *Briefwechsel*, 4:167; I have revised the translation in Alexander, *Johann Georg Hamann*, 177–178.

33. Letter of 23 May 1768, in *Briefwechsel*, 2:415.

34. William F. Arndt and F. Wilbur Gingrich, *A Greek-English Lexicon of the New Testament and Other Early Christian Literature* (Chicago, 1957), 769.

35. *Sämtliche Werke*, 1:52–53.

36. Ibid., 1:243.

37. Letter to Johann Gotthelf Lindner, 3 July 1759, in *Briefwechsel*, 1:355–356. I have revised the translation in Alexander, *Johann Georg Hamann*, 153.

38. Letter of 2 November 1783, in *Briefwechsel,* 5:95, following the translation in Smith, *J. G. Hamann,* 248.

39. Bayer, *Zeitgenosse im Widerspruch: Johann Georg Hamann als radikaler Aufklärer* (Munich, 1988), 145.

40. Kant, "What Is Enlightenment?" (AA 8:41; Reiss 59).

41. 1 Cor. 1:23, 27, cited according to the translation in Alexander, *Johann Georg Hamann,* 13. The original Latin (from the Vulgate) can be found in Sven-Aage Jørgensen, *Johann Georg Hamann* (Stuttgart, 1976), 95.

Jacobi's Critique of the Enlightenment

Dale E. Snow

If Friedrich Heinrich Jacobi is remembered at all today, it is probably as the instigator of the pantheism controversy, in the context of which he presented the first formulation of an exceedingly fruitful criticism of Kant: that one cannot get into the *Critique of Pure Reason* without the concept of the thing in itself, and one cannot remain in the *Critique* with it.[1] Richard Kroner calls this discovery "the starting point of German idealism,"[2] and I have discussed the implications of this claim elsewhere.[3] However, it will be my thesis in this essay that Jacobi is both misunderstood and diminished if he is seen only as a perceptive though unsystematic critic of Kant, one who only pointed in the direction German idealism would later go. A closer look at his work reveals a two-pronged critique of the Enlightenment that shares with his *Kantkritik* his trademark style of slicing through a dizzying array of detail to point out significant problems in blunt, homely language. Jacobi's role in the intellectual conflagration that later became known by the name of the *Pantheismusstreit* has long been the object of scholarly attention.[4] This controversy of 1785–1787, however, is only the second prong of Jacobi's critique of the Enlightenment; there is an earlier part of the story.

In his brief treatment of Jacobi's 1782 tract, *Something Lessing Said*, Alexander Altmann describes it as "a minor literary skirmish that in a way foreshadowed the real fight,"[5] and it is with the desire to discover what light this earlier work may shed on Jacobi's critique of the Enlightenment that I turn to consideration of this frequently misunderstood work. In the *Vorerrinerung*, or "reminder," that prefaces the work, Jacobi tells us that it was the effort to gain a wider audience for the historian Johannes von Muller's *Journeys of the Popes* which led him to attempt to publish a favorable review of it in the *Hamburger Correspondenten*; when it was rejected on the grounds that the editors were "unwilling to permit the printing of an essay praising a work likely to displease Kaiser Joseph" (*Werke*, II:325), he took it back and added to it, finally publishing an expanded version of it in Berlin, where he encountered no difficulty with the censors. Thus by the time it appeared, the reference to von Muller's work had been relegated to the subtitle: *Etwas das Lessing gesagt hat: Eine Commentar zu den* Reisen der Päpste *nebst Betrachtungen von einem Dritten.*

What was it Jacobi wished to praise in von Muller's tract, indeed, as he says, to compare favorably with a remark he once heard Gotthold Lessing make? The reader may be forgiven for being unsure, for no less a critical intelligence than Moses Mendelssohn, who criticized the author for abandoning his first argument and wavering in his train of thought,[6] was vociferously castigated by Jacobi for missing his point. Indeed, when Jacobi realized how widely he had been misunderstood, he actually found it necessary to attack his own views anonymously to create an opportunity for him to make clearer what his original point had been! He was fortunate that the editor of the *Deutsches Museum*, Wilhelm Christian von Dohm, was a close personal friend, so that Jacobi could appeal to him: "the article that I am sending you is directed against my own person. That this makes me in a way a traitor to myself is something that should remain between us.... I still cannot grasp that some [readers] are stumped by the title of the *Something* and a certain incoherence in the first part."[7]

The article Jacobi enclosed with his letter, entitled "The Thoughts of Various Persons on the Occasion of a Noteworthy Essay," appeared in the January issue of the *Deutsches Museum*. It was intended to establish once and for all Jacobi's anticlerical and antiauthoritarian position and also included anonymous comments from Mendelssohn and von Dohm. Jacobi, having orchestrated the publication of these objections to *Something Lessing Said*, then proceeded to respond to them in the February *Deutsches Museum*.[8] Tempting though it may be to conclude from all this that *Something Lessing Said* is simply hopelessly poorly written, there is another reason for the bewilderment felt by its first readers: most of them were unaware that it was the continuation of an argument that had begun several years earlier.

The clue to the substance of that earlier argument is in the odd turn the essay takes at the very beginning. Its ostensible topic is the merits of von Muller's claim in *Journeys of the Popes* that force was not the most efficient means of achieving political change—but neither von Muller, who was inspired by the famous journey of Pope Pius VI to Kaiser Joseph in Vienna which had taken place in the spring of 1782, nor any of the variety of historical examples he uses to illustrate how the popes had achieved their desired ends are ever mentioned again. Jacobi's tract begins with a comment on the exercise of papal power. He quotes Lessing as saying that the arguments of Febronius (an advocate of the limitation of papal power) were equally applicable to secular authority figures. With this awkward and transparent ruse, Jacobi then shifts the discussion to one of his own favorite themes: the proper extent of the powers of government.

How Jacobi arrived at his political views is difficult to ascertain. What is certain is that since 1777 he had been embroiled in a quarrel with Christoph Martin Wieland, his former friend and with him the co-founder of the literary journal *Der Teutsche Merkur* in 1773, in imitation of the *Mercure de France.* It was here that Jacobi published a number of translations and reviews as well as his philosophical novels, *Allwills Briefsammlung* and *Woldemar.* His falling-out with Wieland, who had become an ardent defender of enlightened despotism, was but an early instance of a lifelong pattern, according to Kurt Christ.

> It is to be observed throughout Jacobi's biography the peculiarity that his character tended toward an overly strong identification with and reliance on his mentor to the point of self-abnegation—this went so far as an imitation of the speech of the other—but that at the same time, as he became strengthened in his sense of self, he began to assert himself in opposition to this mentor, to separate, to distance himself, to set himself up in opposition to the point of an enthusiastic defense of a contrary point of view.[9]

In 1777, Wieland had published an essay entitled "On the Divine Right of Authority,"[10] which argued that since it was a law of nature that the strongest should always prevail, this principle of the dominance of the more powerful should also be applied to the political sphere. Jacobi replied with a first installment of an essay entitled "On Law and Right, or a Philosophical Evaluation of an Essay of Herr Councillor Wieland on the Divine Right of Authority."[11] However, he never published the second installment, as his literary executor Friedrich Roth observes in his preface to the sixth and final volume of the *Werke* (Jacobi had died as the fourth volume was at the press): "The treatise on Law and Power directed against Wieland is indeed incomplete—Jacobi was so enraged over the gross disfigurement it suffered in the extremely negligent version published in the *Deutsches Museum* in 1781 that he refused to submit the continuation—however, its completion is contained in the work: *Something Lessing Said* (*Werke,* VI:vi).

Understanding the circumstances of its genesis goes a long way toward explaining why *Something Lessing Said* appears to begin in the middle; it was conceived and carried out, not for the purpose of gaining a wider audience for von Muller, but as a more effective means of having the last word in the quarrel with Wieland. Under the pretext of using Lessing's authority to defend the embattled von Muller, Jacobi was also claiming a weighty ally for his own attacks on absolutistic political authorities.

What views was Jacobi defending in "On Law and Power" and in *Something Lessing Said*? In his introductory remarks to "On Law and Power," Jacobi expresses his surprise that in the three years since Wieland's essay had appeared, only one objection had been raised to its alarming claims; therefore he feels that he must speak out (*Werke*, VI:424). The essence of Wieland's pernicious doctrine, says Jacobi, is summed up in the claim that "the right of the stronger is, *jure divino*, the true source of all the power of authority" (*Werke*, VI:425). Wieland does not shrink from the consequences of the highest possible application of this idea: on this view, even God's power over us derives, in the final analysis, not from his love or omniscience but from his omnipotence, Jacobi notes indignantly. Thus when in the state of nature the will of the stronger prevails over the will of the weaker, this is but the unimpeded operation of the law of nature. Wieland calls it the "same law of necessity according to which the sun controls the planets" (*Werke*, VI:426).

Jacobi can hardly control his irritation at this conflation of natural with moral necessity. He compares Wieland's pretension to explain all power relations by means of this argument to "a wild whirlpool, sucking in and turning faster and faster, to the point where one feels overcome, unwell, and dizzy" (*Werke*, VI:437). Noting that Wieland himself employs the example of Charles the First, who was king of England by divine right until his formerly loyal subject Cromwell overthrew him, which was also right, since Cromwell was then the stronger, Jacobi asks sarcastically if then regicide is a great crime only up to the point when it is successful (*Werke*, VI:427)?

However, the worst consequence of the acceptance of the doctrine "might makes right" is that it relegates the citizens to a sort of permanent immaturity (*Unmündigkeit*) and therein lies its danger, Jacobi claims: "for what do we silly children know about whether we are being dealt with too strictly or too leniently? He who has the power, also has the right. . . . [W]e are and remain as citizens eternal children" (*Werke*, VI:428). This may also be a reference to the quotation from Paul, recommending the unconditional submission of subjects to authority, with which Wieland ends his essay.[12]

The main body of "On Law and Power" is devoted to a comparison of Wieland's views with those of Spinoza in the *Tractatus Politicus*. Jacobi's basic point is that although the two share an initial agreement that one's rights are coextensive with one's power, they arrive at very different conclusions: Wieland celebrates a despotism that presumes to call itself enlightened; Spinoza proves the superiority of the rule of law over the rule of men. Jacobi asks, "From the same presuppositions, such opposed conclusions? But it is no wonder! Herr Wieland knows of no rule other than one arising through usurpation, and takes the voluntary adoption of a civil constitution by a group of men to be total nonsense[;] therefore he also spurns, with highly expressive gestures of fear and disgust, anything which appears headed in that direction, as for example the republics of the ancients or the constitution of England. In contrast, Spinoza holds such a civil constitution not just as possible, but as the only true one and the best" (*Werke*, VI:444–445). This is roughly the point at which *Something Lessing Said* begins.

Clearly Jacobi understands himself, in his attack on Wieland's rejection of any form of social contract theory and praise of enlightened despotism, to be attacking a dangerous mutation in the political views of the Enlightenment. After the initial mention of the problem of the abuse of power by religious authorities, Jacobi quotes a lengthy passage he attributes to a little-known work by Justus Möser, who argues that since all men are subject to error, the rule of law is vastly preferable to the rule of any one person, no matter how enlightened. It is indeed regrettable, says Jacobi, that even those who are reflective [*denkende Köpfe*]

> want to see the essentially true and the essentially good spread *by power* [*Gewalt*], and want to see every error suppressed *by power*. They would like to help promote an enlightenment—elsewhere than in the understanding, because that takes too long. They put out the lights, filled with childish impatience for it to be day. Oh hope-filled darkness, in which we hurriedly totter our way toward the goal of our wishes, toward the greatest good on earth; forward, on the path of violence and subjugation![13]

This rather elliptical utterance of Jacobi contains the seeds of what would become a criticism of the Enlightenment so trenchant that even Hegel would take notice of it: even faith in reason *is* faith. Reason can become a religion, that is, institutionalized and imposed willy-nilly from without, on those who neither desire it nor are in a position to benefit from it. The import of Jacobi's heavy reliance on ideas and quotations from Adam Ferguson's *An Essay on the History of Civil Society* seems to be to secure a slightly more respectable authority than Spinoza to back up his insistence that no governmental structure is capable of forcing men into virtue; this is and must remain the responsibility of the individual. However, this does not prevent Jacobi from borrowing arguments from Spinoza's political works with a free hand; indeed, what may seem to be an imprudently free hand, until one recalls the bibliographical rarity of Spinoza's works in Germany at that time.[14]

The guiding vision behind both the political polemics and the better-known pantheism controversy is Jacobi's almost mystical faith in the potential of the power of the individual to self-determination; at least one writer has traced this strain in Jacobi's thought to his strict Pietist upbringing and noted the parallels to Kant,[15] but its closeness to Spinoza is also unmistakable.[16] Those who think of Jacobi as the apostle of irrationalism would doubtless be surprised to encounter Jacobi's argument that the way to self-mastery is through the use of reason: "Insofar as man is determined in and by himself—that is, insofar as he is capable of acting freely—to that extent he is motivated by reason, and to that extent he is fully human. Where there is no freedom, no *self-determination*, there is no humanity. Insofar as man is affected by things outside him . . . he does not determine himself" (*Werke*, II:340).[17]

Jacobi also agrees with Spinoza that chief among these intrusive external determinants were oppressive political arrangements. Unhappily, in Jacobi's view, most thinkers are not even asking the right questions with respect to the problem of political freedom. All their deliberations amount to at bottom is one form or another of the question "whether it is more bearable to submit to the arbitrary power of one individual, of a certain number out of the many, or to the many itself—that is, which variety of despotism would be the best." This question, he sniffs, is "not really worthy of a wise man's attention."[18]

That this is an idiosyncratic version of the political views of most Enlightenment thinkers is indisputable,[19] and if all that were at issue here was the outcome of Jacobi and Wieland's quarrel, it would be of limited interest indeed. Yet behind the sprawling and disorganized argumentation of *Something Lessing Said* lies a single political vision, that of Spinoza; it is explicit in "On Law and Power," much of which reads like a paraphrase of the *Tractatus Politicus*, and implicit but still evident in *Something Lessing Said*. This may seem both ironic and inexplicable in view of Jacobi's later reputation as a bitter opponent of Spinoza, but a careful consideration of what Jacobi found valuable in Spinoza may dispel much of the air of paradox.

MODEL OF SOCIAL CONTRACT

Jacobi has a view very similar to Kant's with respect to the role of reason in conduct: instinct is the shortest and surest guide to happiness, as we see in the case of animals, who are subject to it alone; however, human beings cannot rely on instinct and must use reason instead. What reason can serve to do is create a contract that imposes harmony where conflict had previously reigned, and it is characteristic of Jacobi that he first discusses how the individual achieves that harmony within himself; only then does he proceed to draw a conclusion about political harmony. "In reason, we are at one with ourselves, in that among all our *desires* a contract arises, in harmony with the eternal laws of what is advantageous to our enduring nature. . . . Men who act under the impetus of reason are never harmful to one another."[20] Jacobi is well aware that this is true only for exceptional men and exceptional states. Still he calls on the authority of Hobbes and Spinoza to argue that even though the majority of men are more readily moved by passion than by reason, they still desire the protection of the state, for only with that protection can every member of society be assured of "his inviolable property in his person, the free use of all his powers, and the full enjoyment of the fruits of their employment."[21]

The heart of Jacobi's literary efforts had been the celebration of personality and individuality; in his political polemics, inspired as he was by the radical individualism of Spinoza's moral ideal of self-mastery, he is attempting to define and defend the form of the state most conducive to the flourishing of individuality. Since neither virtue nor brotherhood can be legislated, at best government can remove obstacles to their growth. Jacobi's later defense of the importance of individual lived experience in the context of the pantheism controversy, and by contrast, the impoverishment and abstraction of "rational religion," is only the best-known expression of his insistence on the significance of individual experience, which cannot be grasped, much less superseded, by philosophy.

Indeed, in a reflection on his literary and philosophical writing, which took the form of letters and dialogues far more frequently than that of unadorned systematic argument, Jacobi concludes: "The form of my presentation is always the form of my reception. I try to produce an effect such that the reader will have the same experience that I had. My talent, my individuality, and my originality consist in the fact that I have occasionally been highly successful in this."[22] Thus what some readers, notably Hegel, have seen as a total incapacity for systematic thinking is really a deliberate strategy on Jacobi's part, as he hints in a late reflection on his entire intellectual career, the "Introduction to the Author's Complete Philosophical Writings": "After all, the aphoristic presentation . . . is often closer to the target than the most artificially correct lecture" (*Werke*, II:107).[23]

Thus wherever system or prescribed rules may be appealed to—in writing, in religion, or in government—Jacobi is concerned to argue against them. His interest in the Spinozistic model of a social contract that is in accordance with reason but also appeals to the interest in self-preservation that all, even those ruled by passion, can be expected to share, arises out of the overriding need to protect the freedom of the individual. Animals must be content with solitary pleasure, but human beings only thrive in a community in which they "find an end for every talent and virtuous inclination."[24]

MINIMALIST STATE

Jacobi is in firm agreement with Ferguson that more government is almost inevitably worse government, for government's sole legitimate function is the protection of citizens from fear, whether of one another or of external enemies. When it attempts to extend itself beyond this sphere, it errs. It cannot create good men, for virtue can be neither forced nor enforced; it is always and only the product of freedom. The only legitimate use of force is to counter force or deter crime. Jacobi uses Ferguson's words: "we may expect that many of the boasted improvements of civil society will be mere devices to lay the political spirit at rest, and will chain up the active virtues more than the restless disorders of men."[25] Thus we see that Jacobi is far from simply rejecting the values of the Enlightenment in favor of private irrationalism; he rather believes that government has only a negative role to play in the cultivation of those, or indeed any, values.

Jacobi was convinced that social existence is both man's fate and his glory, as he states most directly in the *Spinoza-Buchlein*: "we are all born into society and must remain in society... for without you, no I is possible" (*Werke*, IV:1, 210–211).[26] The self is the foundation of everything, but there is no self in the singular. However, just as nothing is so useful to us as other human beings, nothing can be so dangerous. *Something Lessing Said* is a warning about the dangers posed to the individual by a despotic political regime; perhaps the greatest danger of all is that it may destroy the conditions of the possibility of his existence.

He points out that history teaches us that those men, and by extension, those societies, who are not capable of recognizing their own good are still less capable of gratitude toward those who would attempt to correct them. More important, they are being prevented by this well-intentioned interference from achieving maturity on their own. Jacobi concludes that "to prevent peoples by force from acting to their own detriment, or really to force them into what is best for them, a god would have to descend, a perfect individual who would never die."[27] In other words, even an enlightened despotism could only work with someone genuinely, and as it were, permanently, enlightened at the helm. Jacobi may also be alluding here to Spinoza's discussion of theocracy in chapters 17 and 18 of the *Theological-Political Tractatus*, especially the claim that theocracy was both impossible and undesirable after the death of Moses.

MORAL AND POLITICAL SLAVERY

If, Jacobi asks rhetorically, despotism is so frequently the death of the virtues and the scourge of the individual, what advantages does it have? The common claim that it provides the best defense against the incursion of enemies "counts for too little, since the inner enemy is the worst."[28] Despotism is the opposite of freedom, and freedom is the precondition for every individual excellence. We have already encountered Jacobi's Spinozistic understanding of freedom: to be free is to be determined to action only through oneself. Here the argument takes a Schopenhauerian twist: Jacobi claims that no one can truly be thought of as free who is conscious of himself "by means of representations" and who strives "after objects which are not in his power."[29] This reference to one's awareness of being in some sense closest to reality in that wellspring of the sense of self which is prior to all representation is certainly tied to Jacobi's later attempts to formulate a theory of *Glaube* that is immediately certain and known to us.

In the most general sense, unfreedom is the condition of being prevented from pursuing one's own advantage. Jacobi's entire argument rests on the assertion that there is a connection between moral and political freedom, a connection that Enlightenment thinkers have failed to explore carefully enough. The question then arises of whether Jacobi is claiming that political freedom is a necessary or a sufficient condition for moral freedom, when he says, "Where there is a high degree of political freedom in fact, not just in appearance, there must be no less a degree of moral freedom present."[30]

It is clear that since he holds law to be a record of human frailty, for there are no laws against things people are not tempted to or cannot do, law is always grounded on the desire for prevention. The example of the constitution of Sparta, of which Xenophon maintained that it had as its object virtue itself, shows the impotence of law directed at ends other than prevention.[31] Thus political freedom is at least a necessary condition for the best society: "That coercion without which the society cannot exist does not have as its object that which makes man *good*, but rather that which makes him *evil*; it has a *negative* rather than a *positive* purpose. This purpose can be preserved and secured through external form; and everything positive, virtue and happiness, then arise of themselves from their own source."[32]

Jacobi argues in support of this, his most cherished political insight, in the words of Spinoza, of Plato, of Machiavelli, and of Ferguson. Yet he speaks in his own voice too when, near the conclusion of *Something Lessing Said*, he anticipates the question put to every political visionary, and perhaps especially frequently to those who argue that reason ought to guide our political lives:

> I hear more than one voice, asking me mockingly whether I believe that, in a state constructed according to my principles, men would no longer pursue the passions, but would rather pursue wisdom alone? And I answer very patiently: No, I do not believe this. But I do believe the following: that there is an infinite difference between not expressly healing men of their foolishness and expressly leading them to it; that there is an infinite difference between not freeing men from all misery and thrusting them into it by force.[33]

This is the message Jacobi is sending to Wieland above all but also to the direction of political thought of the Enlightenment of which he was but one representative: enlightenment always and only the product of freedom and thus the province of the individual.

NOTES

1. *Friedrich Heinrich Jacobi's Werke* (Leipzig, 1812–1825), II:304; hereafter *Werke.*
2. Richard Kroner, *Von Kant bis Hegel* (Tübingen, 1924), I:304.
3. Dale Snow, "F. H. Jacobi and the Development of German Idealism," *Journal of the History of Philosophy* 25, no. 3 (July 1987): 397–416.

4. For a recent discussion, see Frederick Beiser, *The Fate of Reason* (Cambridge, Mass., 1987); see esp. chap. 2, "Jacobi and the Pantheism Controversy," 44–91.

5. Alexander Altmann, *Moses Mendelssohn* (1973), 598.

6. Mendelssohn's comments are reprinted in the "Anhang: Gedanken Verschiedener bey Gelegenheit einer merkwürdigen Schrift," in *Werke*, II:396–398.

7. Letter of 3 December 1782, in *Friedrich Heinrich Jacobi's Auserlesener Briefwechsel*, ed. Friedrich Roth (Leipzig, 1825–1827), I:350.

8. This article, originally entitled "Erinnerungen gegen die in den Januar des Museums eingeruckte Gedanken über eine merkwürdige Schrift," is reprinted in *Werke*, II:401–411.

9. Kurt Christ, *Jacobi und Mendelssohn: Eine Analyse des Spinozastreits* (Wurzburg, 1988), 42.

10. "Über das göttliche Recht der Obrigkeit, oder Über den Lehrsatz 'Dass die höchste Gewalt in einem Staat durch das Volk geschaffen sey'," *Der Teutsche Merkur* (November 1777).

11. "Über Recht und Gewalt oder philosophische Erwagung eines Aufsatzes von dem Herrn Hofrath Wieland, über das göttliche Recht der Obrigkeit," *Deutsches Museum*, 6 Stuck, 1781; reprinted in *Werke*, VI:419–464.

12. "*Children*, obey your parents in *all* things, *for this is pleasing to God*! *Fathers*, do not *embitter* your children, that they may not become *resentful*!" *Christoph Martin Wieland, Politische Schriften*, ed. Jan Philip Reemtsma (Nordlingen, 1988), Bd. 1, 112. However, the analogy between the people (*das Volk*) and children had long been a favorite of Wieland's, as Friedrich Sengle points out in *Wieland* (Stuttgart, 1949), 445–446.

13. *Werke*, II:337 (translated above, p. 192).

14. N. Altwicker, *Texte zur Geschichte des Spinozismus* (Darmstadt, 1971), 30.

15. Norman Wilde, "A Study in the Origins of German Realism," Ph.D. dissertation, Columbia University, 1984, 9–16.

16. Lewis Feuer describes Spinoza's thought as "a landmark in man's achievement of self-understanding" because it provides a blueprint for the individual to find freedom and self-mastery through knowing causes, most directly through knowing his own nature. *Spinoza and the Rise of Liberalism* (Boston, 1958), 210.

17. Compare with Part I, Def. VII of Spinoza's *Ethics*: "That thing is called free, which exists solely by the necessity of its own nature, and of which the action is determined by itself alone. On the other hand, that thing is necessary, or rather constrained, which is determined by something external to itself."

18. *Werke*, II:367 (translated above, pp. 201–202).

19. It could also be argued that it is an idiosyncratic and partial view even of Wieland himself; Sengle argues that Wieland did not take "Über das göttliche Recht der Obrigkeit" very seriously himself and did not include it in his *Samtliche Werke*; see *Wieland*, 441. Wieland's political views are discussed in depth most recently in Irmtraut Sahmland, *Christoph Martin Wieland und die deutsche Nation: Zwischen Patriotismus, Kosmopolitanismus und Griechentum* (Tübingen, 1990).

20. *Werke*, II:344–345 (translated above, p. 195).

21. *Werke*, II:347 (translated above, p. 195).

22. *Friedrich Heinrich Jacobi's Auserlesener Briefwechsel*, 2:433.

23. Jacobi has been hailed as a forerunner of *Lebensphilosophie* because of his

stress on lived experience as the only touchstone of truth. His claim that one's character and individual mode of life determines one's choice of philosophical system found an echo in both Schelling and Fichte, especially the former, who in the "Philosophical Letters on Dogmatism and Criticism" of 1795 goes so far as to say "every *system* bears the stamp of individuality on the face of it, because no system can be completed other than *practically*, that is, subjectively." *Schellings Werke*, ed. Manfred Schroter (Munich, 1979), I:304.

24. *Werke*, II:353 (translated above, p. 197).

25. *Werke*, II:355 (translated above, p. 198).

26. "*denn ohne Du ist das Ich unmöglich.*"

27. *Werke*, II:359 (translated above, p. 199).

28. *Werke*, II:363 (translated above, p. 200). "Necessity is often the mother of invention, but she has never yet succeeded in framing a dominion that was in less danger from its own citizens than from open enemies, of whose rulers did not fear the latter more than the former." *Theological-Political Tractatus*, Chap. XVII.

29. *Werke*, II:364 (translated above, p. 201).

30. *Werke*, II:365 (translated above, p. 201).

31. *Werke*, II:369–370 (translated above, p. 202).

32. *Werke*, II:373 (translated above, p. 204).

33. *Werke*, II:385 (translated above, p. 208).

Early Romanticism and the *Aufklärung*

Frederick C. Beiser

I

It is a commonplace of intellectual history to regard the birth of German romanticism at the end of the eighteenth century as the death of the *Aufklärung*.[1] Supposedly, romanticism was the reaction against the Aufklärung, its self-conscious opposition and antithesis. Hence the growing popularity of romanticism in the early 1800s spelled the end of the Aufklärung, which accordingly should be relegated to the eighteenth century.

If we carefully examine the secondary literature, we find that at least three reasons are given why romanticism broke with the Aufklärung. First, it attempted to replace the rationalism of the Aufklärung with aestheticism. Rather than make reason their highest authority, the romantics gave primacy to the imagination and intuition of art. Hence romanticism is often accused of "antirationalism."[2] Second, romanticism criticized the "individualism" of the Aufklärung and advocated instead an ideal of community, in which the individual was subordinated to the group.[3] While the *Aufklärer* tended to see society only as an instrument to ensure the happiness or protect the rights of the individual, romanticism insisted that communal life was an end in itself to which every individual was obliged to contribute. Third, romanticism was an essentially conservative ideology, breaking with the liberal values of the Aufklärung, such as the separation of church and state, religious tolerance, and freedom of the individual.[4] Hence romantic thinkers like Friedrich Schlegel, Ludwig Tieck, and Novalis either sympathized with or converted to the Roman Catholic church and eventually sided with the Restoration. In sum, then, we are told to contrast the antirationalism, communitarianism, and conservatism of romanticism with the rationalism, individualism, and liberalism of the Aufklärung.

But, like so many generalizations in the history of ideas, this commonplace view is a very misleading oversimplification. It is misleading, first of all, because romanticism was a very protean movement, undergoing many transformations and passing through several phases. It is commonly divided into three periods: *Frühromantik*, from 1797 to 1802; *Hochromantik*, to 1815; and *Spätromantik*, to 1830.[5] Accordingly, the relationship of romanticism to the Aufklärung also underwent change. It is generally true that romanticism became more conservative, collectivist, and antirationalist and hence increasingly more hostile to some of the values of the Aufklärung. But even this is an oversimplification, which holds at best for Spätromantik. Second, this generalization grossly distorts the romantic attitude toward the Aufklärung. In each phase or period, the response of the romantics to the Aufklärung was never a simple and straightforward rejection but a much subtler and more complex ambivalence. If the romantics were critics of the Aufklärung, they were also its disciples. The problem is then to determine, for each period, in what respects the romantics accepted and rejected the Aufklärung.

The task of this essay is to address this problem, though only in a preliminary and partial manner. I will examine the complex relationship between romanticism and the Aufklärung in the early formative years of romanticism from 1797 to 1802, the period known as Frühromantik. This is the most interesting and revealing period for an understanding of the romantics' relationship to the Aufklärung. For it was during this early period that most of the young romantics took issue with, and developed their attitudes toward, the Aufklärung, which was still the reigning ideology in late eighteenth-century Berlin. Although conclusions about Frühromantik do not necessarily apply to the later stages of romanticism, they will suffice for our purposes here: to determine whether the beginnings of romanticism were a reaction to the Aufklärung and whether its origins should be regarded as a complete break with it.

If we closely consider the young romantics' relationship to the Aufklärung, it immediately becomes clear that early romanticism cannot be described merely as the antithesis of the Aufklärung. This is for the simple but important reason that the young romantics never put themselves in self-conscious opposition against the Aufklärung as a whole. If they strongly criticized it in some respects, they also firmly identified themselves with it in others. They were loyal to two of the most fundamental ideals of the Aufklärung: radical criticism and *Bildung*, the education of the public. Rather than combat the Aufklärung, their aim was to resolve its crisis at the close of the eighteenth century.

By the late 1780s it had become clear that the Aufklärung was in danger, not so much from its external enemies as from its own internal tensions. The most significant of these inner conflicts was that the radical criticism of the Aufklärung jeopardized its ideal of Bildung. While its criticism seemed to end *per necessitatum* in skepticism or nihilism, its ideal of Bildung presupposed a commitment to some definite moral, political, and aesthetic principles. How is it possible to educate the public about the principles of morality, politics, and art when reason casts nothing but doubt on them? The challenge facing the young romantics in the 1790s was therefore clear: to achieve Bildung without compromising the rights of radical criticism. In attempting to resolve this problem, though, the romantics not only rescued the Aufklärung, they also transformed it. Rather than regard early romanticism as the antithesis of the Aufklärung, then, it would be more accurate to regard it as its transformation.

II

To understand the relationship between Frühromantik and the Aufklärung, it is first necessary to have some basic idea of the beginnings, ideals, and members of the early romantic circle.

If we are to assign an official date for the beginning of German romanticism, then we would do well to take the year 1797. It was in this year that some young poets, philosophers, and literary critics began to meet in the salons of Henriette Herz and Rahel Levin in Berlin. Later, and until 1802, they would meet at the house of A. W. Schlegel in Jena. The purpose of their meetings was to hold frank and free discussions about philosophy, poetry, politics, and religion. They would read one another their latest work, criticize one another openly, and collaborate on literary projects. This circle was called by contemporaries "the new sect," "the new school," or, as it later became known to history, "the romantic school."

The members of this circle later became famous in German intellectual history. They were the brothers August Wilhelm (1767–1845) and Friedrich Schlegel (1772–1829), the novelist Ludwig Tieck (1773–1853), the natural philosopher Friedrich Wilhelm Joseph Schelling (1775–1854), the theologian Ernst Daniel Schleiermacher (1768–1834), the art historian Wilhelm Heinrich Wackenroder (1773–1801), and the poet and political philosopher Friedrich von Hardenberg (1772–1801), who called himself "Novalis." On the fringes of this circle, though sharing many views with it, was the tragic and lonely figure Friedrich Hölderlin (1774–1843).[6] The leading figure of the romantic circle was undoubtedly Friedrich Schlegel. It was he who formulated the group's aesthetic ideals and who founded and edited its common journal, the *Athenäum*.

In its early formative years from 1797 to 1802, German romanticism was primarily an aesthetic movement. Its chief aim was the rebirth of German art, its liberation from the stranglehold of the sterile and artificial classicism of the eighteenth century. The early romantics gave enormous importance to art, which they saw as the key to the rebirth of German cultural and political life. If the powers of art were only fully developed and recognized, the young romantics fervently believed, then religion, science, and politics would undergo nothing less than a renaissance. Thus, in his *Reden über die Religion*, Schleiermacher saw art as central to religion, as the chief means of attaining its characteristic "intuition of the universe."[7] In his *System des transcendentalen Idealismus*, Schelling proclaimed art the organon of his new *Naturphilosophie*, the criterion of the intellectual intuition of the universe as a whole.[8] And in his *Blütenstaub* and *Glauben und Liebe*, Novalis viewed art as the very foundation of the state, as the most effective means of ensuring political stability and allegiance.[9] We can put the young romantics' emphasis on art in its proper historical perspective by seeing it as the reversal of Plato's infamous doctrine in the *Republic*. While Plato wanted to banish the artists, the romantics wanted to enthrone them. What is the best prince, the young Novalis asked,[10] but the artist of artists, the director of a vast drama whose stage is the state?

Why, though, did the young romantics give such great importance to art? Why did they regard it as the key to social, political, and cultural revival? The answer to this question is crucial for an understanding of the young romantics' relationship to the Aufklärung. For their aestheticism was their means of executing the ideals, and resolving the outstanding problems, of the Aufklärung.

The aestheticism of the young romantics is comprehensible only in the context of their reaction to the French Revolution. The Revolution had a profound impact on the early romantics. It gave birth to their political consciousness, and it set much of the problematic of their early social, political, and aesthetic thought. With the exception of A. W. Schlegel, who was skeptical from the beginning, the young romantics greeted the French Revolution as the dawn of a new age. They were delighted by the collapse of the ancien régime, and they looked forward to an era free of its privilege, oppression, and injustice. Novalis, Schelling, Schleiermacher, and Friedrich Schlegel affirmed the ideals of liberty, equality, and fraternity, and they insisted that true humanity could be realized only in a republic. What is most striking about their reaction to the Revolution is how long they retained their sympathies. Unlike so many of their compatriots, their loyalties were not affected by the September massacres, the execution of the king, the invasion of the Rhineland, or even by the Terror.[11] Novalis, Schelling, Schleiermacher, and Schlegel became critical of the Revolution only around 1798. They then began to attack the egoism, materialism, and utilitarianism of modern civil society, which they believed had been encouraged by the Revolution.[12] They also expressed their fears of ochlocracy and insisted on some measure of elite rule. The true republic, they believed,[13] should be a mixture of aristocracy, monarchy, and democracy, because in any true state the educated must have power over the uneducated. Such cautious and moderate doctrines were not, however, peculiar to the romantics. Rather, they were typical of the late 1790s, mirroring the trend of opinion in France itself, where the elections held in March 1797 resulted in the return of royalist majorities in the two legislative councils. Despite their increasing moderation and caution, the romantics did not abandon their republicanism, which they hoped to incorporate within a constitutional monarchy. As late as the early 1800s, we find Novalis, Schlegel, Schelling, and Schleiermacher reaffirming the ideals of liberty, equality, and fraternity.[14] If, then, we confine ourselves to the early romantics, it becomes absurd to speak of a "romantic conservatism." The young romantics were more loyal to liberal and progressive ideals than many of the Aufklärer, who still clung to their faith in enlightened monarchy.[15]

Although the romantics were republicans in the 1790s, they were not revolutionaries. Though they endorsed the ideas of the Revolution, they renounced its practice. With the possible exception of Hölderlin,[16] they did not believe that insurrection was feasible, or even desirable, in their native land. The events in France made them fear that a revolution would result in incurable anarchy and strife, and hence they insisted on the need for gradual, evolutionary change from above. Like so many of the Aufklärer, the romantics held that the main danger in radical political change lay with the people themselves, who were not ready for the high moral ideals of a republic. A republic demanded wisdom and virtue, just as Montesquieu and Jean-Jacques Rousseau had always taught; but it was not possible to expect these in Germany, given the low level of education and the slow progress of enlightenment in most territories of the empire. The fundamental political problem facing the young romantics was therefore plain: to prepare the German people for the high ideals of a republic by giving them a moral, political, and aesthetic education. Their task as intellectuals in the Germany of the 1790s was to define the standards of morality, taste, and religion, so that the public would have some ideal of culture and some model of virtue. Thus, in their crucial formative years from 1797 to 1800, the romantics were neither revolutionaries nor reactionaries. Rather, they were simply reformers, moderates in the classical tradition of Schiller, Herder, Humboldt, Wieland, and a whole host of Aufklärer.

It is in the context of this reformism that we must place the young romantics' aestheticism. They gave such enormous importance to art mainly because they saw it as the chief instrument of Bildung, and hence as the key to social and political reform. If the people were to be prepared for the high moral ideals of a republic, then it would be through an aesthetic education. An aesthetic education then would be the spearhead of the new social and political order. In this regard the young romantics proved themselves to be the disciples of Schiller, who had put forward this very thesis in his famous *Aesthetische Briefe* of 1793.[17] The young romantics agreed with Schiller's analysis of the political problem, that Bildung was the precondition of social and political change, the only basis for a lasting republican constitution; and they accepted no less his solution to this problem, that an aesthetic education should be the core of Bildung. According to Schiller, it was art, and art alone, that could unify the divided powers of humanity, provide it with a model of virtue, and inspire people to action. In no respect did the young romantics demur.

If, then, we place the young romantics' aestheticism in its original historical context, it turns out to be nothing less than their strategy for social and political reform. This reveals, however, how their main goals were continuous with the Aufklärung. The young romantics remained loyal to one of the fundamental goals of the Aufklärung: the education of the public, the perfection and development of its moral, intellectual, and aesthetic powers.[18] Such, indeed, was the aim of the journal *Athenäum*, which was explicitly devoted to the goal of Bildung, like so many of the *Zeitschriften* of the Aufklärung.[19] The young romantics' insistence on further education and enlightenment as the precondition for fundamental social and political change only reiterated a point frequently made by the Aufklärer in the 1790s. Indeed, in their attempt to make enlightenment serve the growing demands for social and political change, the young romantics seem to be nothing less than the Aufklärer of the 1790s. They seem to differ from the earlier generation of Aufklärer only in their disillusionment with enlightened absolutism and in their readiness to embrace republican ideals. So it is tempting to conclude that the romantics were the Aufklärer of the postrevolutionary age. But, as we shall soon see, the truth is much more complicated than that.

III

If the young romantics were loyal to the Aufklärung's ideal of Bildung, they were no less faithful to its ideal of radical criticism. The Aufklärung had proclaimed the absolute right of criticism, the right of reason to criticize everything on heaven and earth. Neither religion in its holiness nor the state in its majesty, as Kant put it,[20] could escape the tribunal of critique. The young romantics did not dispute this principle but enthusiastically endorsed it. Novalis, Hölderlin, Schlegel, and Schleiermacher all greatly valued the power of criticism, which they regarded as indispensable to all philosophy, art, and science.[21] Indeed, if they had any complaint against the Aufklärer, it was that they were guilty of betraying their cause by not taking their reason far enough and compromising with the status quo.[22] The value of radical criticism, of a thoroughgoing critique of religion, morals, and social conventions, was one of the guiding motifs of the *Athenäum*. "One cannot be critical enough," Friedrich Schlegel wrote, summing up the general attitude of the group.[23] It is indeed striking how the young Schlegel admired Gotthold Lessing for his daring and uncompromising criticism of the moral conventions and religious beliefs of his day.[24] His ambition was to become nothing less than the Lessing of the 1790s.

The young romantics' attitude toward criticism becomes especially apparent from their reaction toward the pantheism controversy, the true acid test for someone's loyalty to reason in late eighteenth-century Germany. During this controversy, which began in 1786, F. H. Jacobi argued that a consistent rationalism must end in the atheism and fatalism of Spinozism and that the only way to rescue one's moral and religious beliefs was through a *salto mortale*, a leap of faith. Schlegel, Novalis, Hölderlin, Schelling, and Schleiermacher were, however, all critical of Jacobi's salto mortale.[25] In their view, Jacobi's great sin was that he had turned his back on reason when he saw that it threatened his cherished beliefs. It would have been better and more honest, they thought, for him to renounce his beliefs rather than his reason. Although the romantics themselves were not immune to the attractions of mysticism, they never approved of leaps of faith that were contrary to reason. If it was permissible to hold beliefs for which one did not have evidence, it was forbidden even to entertain those that were contrary to it.

The young romantics greatly valued criticism because they saw it as the instrument by which the individual could liberate himself from the oppressive social norms and conventions of his day. Rather than wish to subordinate the individual to the ends of the group, the young romantics developed an ethic of individualism, of "divine egoism," according to which the end of life should be the development of every individual's moral, intellectual, and aesthetic powers as a whole.[26] They stressed, however, that for such development to take place the individual would have to engage in fearless and uncompromising criticism. The sovereign rights of criticism were for the romantics confirmation of the sovereign rights of the individual.

Yet, for all their belief in the value of criticism, the romantics were also aware of its dangers. It was high time, the young Schlegel believed, that philosophers began to ask themselves where their reason was taking them. If reason could criticize everything on heaven and earth, should it not also criticize itself?[27]

By the late 1790s, some of the more troubling consequences of radical criticism had become clear. First of all, it seemed as if criticism, if it were only consistent and thorough, would end in the abyss of skepticism. All moral, religious, political, and commonsense beliefs had been examined; but rather than reveal their underlying foundation, criticism had shown them to be nothing better than "prejudices." In the late 1790s the danger of skepticism seemed more acute than ever. Philosophers such as Solomon Maimon, J. G. Hamann, Thomas Wizenmann, A. W. Rehberg, H. A. Pistorius, G. E. Schulze, and Ernst Platner had criticized Kant's last-ditch effort to rescue belief through an appeal to practical faith; and to counter Kant's philosophy they developed a new form of Humean skepticism. In a similar vein, in his famous *Brief an Fichte,* Jacobi had argued that the fundamental principles of Kant's philosophy ultimately result in "nihilism" (*Nihilismus*), the doctrine that nothing exists except one's passing sensations.[28]

Another disturbing consequence of radical criticism, the young romantics believed,[29] was that it had alienated modern man from nature. Now that nature had been subjected to rational examination, it had lost its beauty, mystery, and magic. It was no longer to be admired or contemplated but analyzed and conquered. Rather than a work of art, it was only an annoying obstacle in the path of moral progress. But if nature was ugly, lifeless, and subjugated to human purposes, how would it be possible to feel at home in the world?

The most problematic result of radical criticism, the young romantics contended,[30] was that modern man had lost his sense of community, his feeling of belonging to a group. For all their insistence on the value of individualism, the young romantics also stressed the value of participating in, and identifying with, the community. For they argued that human beings were essentially social animals and that they could realize their characteristic powers only within the group. But radical criticism seemed to undermine the possibility of self-realization within the community. By bringing all forms of social and political life under criticism, the individual began to regard them as a form of irrational authority, as a threat to his individual autonomy. If the individual should accept no belief or law until it agrees with the critical exercise of his own reason, then there will be as many sources of authority as there are individuals. Thus radical criticism seemed to lead not only to skepticism but also to anarchism.

The consequences of radical criticism raised some very serious questions, however, about the very coherence of the Aufklärung. For it seemed as if two of its most basic ideals—radical criticism and Bildung—were in conflict with one another. For if criticism ends in complete skepticism, then according to what moral, political, and religious principles should we educate the people? If it destroys all the beauty of nature, then how can we develop or cultivate our sensibility, which is an essential part of our humanity? And if it results in complete anarchism, how can we educate people so that they play a responsible and productive role in society? Thus the moral idealism behind the Aufklärung's program of Bildung was undermined by its commitment to radical criticism.

The general problem facing the romantics in the 1790s should now be clear. How is it possible to fill the vacuum left by the Aufklärung without betraying reason? How is it possible to restore our beliefs, our unity with nature and society, without forfeiting our individual autonomy? Or, in short, how is it possible to reconcile the Aufklärung's ideal of Bildung with its demand for radical criticism? The young romantics knew that they could not escape this problem by simply reaffirming the value of "prejudice" in the manner of Edmund Burke and Joseph de Maistre. For that reactionary strategy simply failed to recognize that the powers of criticism were as inescapable as they were invaluable.

IV

What was the romantics' path out of this dilemma? It lay with their faith in art. It was art, and art alone, they believed, that could restore man's beliefs and his unity with nature and society. Only it could fill the vacuum left by the deadly powers of criticism. While reason was an essentially negative and destructive power, art was a positive and productive one. It had the power to create an entire world through the imagination. What had been *given* to early man on a naive level—moral and religious belief, unity with nature and society—had been destroyed by the corrosive powers of criticism; the task now was *to re-create* it on a self-conscious level through the powers of art. Art could restore man's moral and religious beliefs through the creation of a new mythology.[31] It could regenerate our unity with nature by "romanticizing" it, that is, by restoring its old mystery, magic, and beauty.[32] And it could reestablish this unity with society by expressing and arousing the feeling of love, which is the basis of every true community, the natural feeling found between all free and equal persons.[33]

It was this aesthetic credo, then, that served as the romantics' response to the crisis of the Aufklärung at the close of the eighteenth century. The ideals of Bildung and radical criticism could coexist, the young romantics believed, provided that the task of Bildung was left to the creative powers of art. A conflict arose only when reason presumed to play a more positive role in Bildung; for such a presumption did not square with the essentially destructive powers of criticism. Like many critics of reason at the close of the eighteenth century, the young romantics tended to limit reason to a strictly negative role: its task was merely to combat prejudice, dogmatism, and superstition. They seem to agree with one of the fundamental points behind Kant's and Jacobi's critiques of reason: reason does not have the power to create facts, but only the power to relate them to one another through inference; the facts themselves must be given to reason from some other source. For the romantics, this source could be only the productive imagination.

There was, however, a deep ambivalence at the bottom of the romantics' program of aesthetic education, an ambiguity reflecting their own uncertainty about the powers of reason. It was unclear whether they intended their program of aesthetic education to replace or support the authority of reason. Was its task *to create* the moral, religious, and political principles that reason seemed only to destroy? Or was its aim only to provide a stimulus or incentive for the moral, religious, and political principles that reason could create but merely not bring into practice? Although the romantics usually seem to think that reason does not have the power to produce substantive principles, at times they also appear to hold that it does have the power to justify at least the basic principles of morality and politics. Thus the young romantics were ardent students of Johann Gottlieb Fichte's *Grundlage des Naturrechts*, in which these principles were demonstrated to be universal and necessary truths.[34] They seemed to concur with Kant and Fichte that, though reason could not demonstrate the *theoretical* principles of metaphysics, it could justify at least the *practical* principles of morality and politics.[35]

This ambivalence, though, is of the first importance in determining the romantics' relationship to the Aufklärung. For if the young romantics intended art to replace reason, then they were indeed going beyond the confines of the Aufklärung by attempting to supplant rational authority with the power of art. If, however, they intended art only to support reason, to provide its principles only with an incentive or stimulus, then they were still within the limits of the Aufklärung. Like the Aufklärer, they were simply attempting to overcome the gap between thought and action, theory and practice, and to realize the principles of reason in public life. In the end, then, the problem of determining the young romantics' relationship to the Aufklärung depends on precisely ascertaining their attitude toward reason. But it is just here that the texts of the young romantics prove to be very elusive, vague, and, at best, ambivalent.

Whatever the young romantics' attitude toward the powers of reason, it is still difficult to regard them *simply* as the Aufklärer of the postrevolutionary age. For this rides roughshod over their own concern with the crisis of the Aufklärung at the end of the 1790s. While the older generation of Aufklärer attempted to refute the criticisms of Kant and Jacobi,[36] the young romantics felt that they had no choice but to build on them. If the aesthetic program of the young romantics was their solution to the crisis of the Aufklärung, then we have no choice but to view early romanticism as *both* the affirmation and negation of the Aufklärung. Like a phoenix, the Aufklärung was consumed by its own flames. From its ashes arose romanticism.

NOTES

1. See, e.g., Hermann Hettner, *Geschichte der deutschen Literatur im Achtzehnten Jahrhundert* (Berlin, 1979), II:634–654, and Walter Linden, "Umwertung der deutschen Romantik," in *Begriffsbestimmung der Romantik*, ed. Helmut Prang (Darmstadt, 1968), 243–275, and, more recently, Robert C. Solomon, *Continental Philosophy since 1750*

(Oxford, 1988), 12–15. Fortunately, the tendency of much new scholarship has been to question this commonplace view. See, e.g., Helmut Schanze, *Romantik und Aufklärung. Untersuchungen zu Friedrich Schlegel und Novalis* (Nuremberg, 1976); Wolgang Mederer, *Romantik als Aufklärung der Aufklärung* (Frankfurt, 1987); and Lothar Pikulik, *Frühromantik: Epoche-Werke-Wirkung* (Munich, 1992), 20–25. All these authors see a much more complicated and ambivalent relationship between early romanticism and the Aufklärung.

2. See, e.g., Carl Schmitt, *Politische Romantik* (Munich, 1925), 79–84; Jacques Droz, *Le romantisme allemand et l'état* (Paris, 1966), 19–49; Reinhold Aris, *A History of Political Thought in Germany* (London, 1936), 272; and Hans Reiss, *Political Thought of the German Romantics* (Oxford, 1955), 3.

3. See especially Walter Linden, "Umwertung der deutschen Romantik," 243–275.

4. See, e.g., Heinrich Heine, *Romantische Schule, Kritische Ausgabe* (Stuttgart, 1976), 30–31; Arnold Ruge, "Plan der Deutsch-Französische Jahrbücher," in *Werke* (Mannheim, 1848), IX:145–160, esp. pp. 151–152; and Hettner, *Geschichte*, II:653.

5. This is the typology of Paul Kluckhohn, *Das Ideengut der deutschen Romantik*, 3d ed. (Tübingen, 1953), 8–9.

6. Hölderlin's membership in the romantic circle has been subject to dispute. His affinities with and departures from the circle are explained by Rudolf Haym, *Die romantische Schule* (Berlin, 1870), 289–324.

7. Friedrich Schleiermacher, *Kritische Gesamtausgabe*, ed. G. Meckenstock et al. (Berlin, 1984f), II/I:262–263.

8. See F.W.J. Schelling, *Ausgewählte Schriften*, ed. Manfred Frank (Frankfurt, 1985), I:680–697.

9. See Novalis, *Blütenstaub*, no. 122, and *Glauben und Liebe*, no. 39, in *Schriften*, ed. Richard Samuel et al. (Stuttgart, 1975), II:468, 498.

10. *Glauben und Liebe*, no. 39, in *Schriften*, II:498.

11. The general view that the romantics became disillusioned with the Revolution after the execution of the king and the onset of the Terror is untenable. On the reaction of the romantics to the Revolution, see my *Enlightenment, Revolution and Romanticism* (Cambridge, MA: 1992), 228–229, 241–244, 250–253, 266–267.

12. See, e.g., Schlegel's *Ideen*, no. 41, in *Kritische Ausgabe*, ed. Ernst Behler et al. (Stuttgart, 1956), II:259; Novalis, *Glauben und Liebe*, no. 36, in *Schriften*, II:495; and Schleiermacher's *Reden*, in *Gesamtausgabe*, II/1:196.

13. See, e.g., *Athenäums Fragmente*, no. 81, 212–214, 369–370; and Novalis, *Glauben und Liebe*, nos. 22, 37, in *Schriften*, II:490, 496.

14. See, e.g., Novalis, *Schriften*, II:518, 522; Schlegel, *Vorlesungen über Transcendentalphilosophie, Kritische Ausgabe*, XII, 44, 47, 56–57, 88.

15. Thus in the 1790s, Aufklärer like C. Garve, J. A. Eberhard, and C. G. Svarez continued to defend absolute monarchy against the ideas of the Revolution. On the attitude of the Aufklärer toward the Revolution, see Zwi Batscha, *Despotismus von jeder Art reizt zur Widersetzlichkeit: Die Französische Revolution in der deutschen Popularphilosophie* (Frankfurt, 1989).

16. In his *Hölderlin und die Französische Revolution* (Frankfurt, 1969), 85–113, Pierre Bertaux has assembled evidence that Hölderlin was involved in a plot to establish a

Swabian republic. On the whole, however, Hölderlin insisted on the value of gradual, evolutionary change and the need for Bildung. See, for example, his 10 January 1797 letter to J. G. Ebel, and his 1 January 1799 letter to his brother, in *Grosse Stuttgarter Hölderlin Ausgabe*, ed. Friedrich Beissner et al. (Stuttgart, 1954), VI/1:229–230, 303–305.

17. On the young romantics' relationship to Schiller, see Arthur O. Lovejoy, "Schiller and the Genesis of German Romanticism," in Lovejoy, *Essays in the History of Ideas* (Baltimore, 1948), 207–227; and Josef Körner, *Romantiker und Klassiker* (Berlin, 1924), 11–56.

18. On the importance of the ideal of Bildung for the Aufklärung, see Moses Mendelssohn's famous essay "Ueber die Frage: was heisst aufklären?" *Berlinische Monatsschrift* 4 (1784):193–200.

19. See the Vorerinnerung to the *Athenäum*, Bd. I, 1798. In a manifesto for the contributors to his journal, Schlegel wrote that their aim should be "Der Bildung Strahlen All in Eins zu fassen, / Vom Kranken ganz zu scheiden das Gesunde, / Bestreben wir uns treu in freien Bunde."

20. Kant, *Kritik der reinen Vernunft*, A xii.

21. See Novalis, *Heinrich von Ofterdingen*, in *Schriften*, I:280–283; Hölderlin, *Hyperion*, *Grosse Stuttgarter Ausgabe*, III:93, and his 2 June 1796 letter to his brother, ibid., VI/1:208–209. On Schlegel and Schleiermacher, see below, note 25.

22. This is especially apparent from Schlegel's critical remarks about the Berlin Aufklärer C. F. Reichhardt. See Schlegel's letter to his brother, 31 October 1797, in *Kritische Ausgabe*, XXIII:30.

23. Schlegel, *Fragmente*, no. 281, in *Kritische Ausgabe*, II:213. See also *Fragmente*, nos. 1, 47, 48, 56, 89, 96.

24. On the young Schlegel's relationship to Lessing, see Johanna Kruger, *Friedrich Schlegels Bekehrung zu Lessing* (Weimar, 1913).

25. See Schlegel's review of Jacobi's *Woldemar*, in *Kritische Ausgabe*, II:57–77, esp. pp. 69–72; Novalis, *Schriften*, III:572, no. 121; and Schleiermacher, *Gesamtausgabe*, I/1:513–597.

26. On the romantic ethic of individualism, see Schlegel, *Fragmente*, no. 16, in *Kritische Ausgabe*, II:167, and *Ideen*, no. 60, II:262; and Schleiermacher, *Reden*, in *Gesamtausgabe*, II/1:229–230, and *Monologen*, III/1:17–18.

27. See Schlegel, *Fragmente*, nos. 1, 47, 48, 56, 89, 96, 281.

28. See F. H. Jacobi, *Werke* (Leipzig, 1816), III:1–57.

29. See, e.g., Novalis, *Lehrling zu Sais*, in *Schriften*, I:84, 89–90, and *Christenheit oder Europa*, in *Schriften*, III:515–516. See also *Schriften*, II:45, no. 105.

30. This criticism is most apparent in Novalis's *Glauben und Liebe*, no. 36, in *Schriften*, II:495. It also appears in some of Schlegel's early classical essays, especially "Ueber die Grenzen des Schönen," in *Kritische Ausgabe*, I:19–33, esp. pp. 23. See also Schlegel's *Lucinde*, in *Kritische Ausgabe*, V:25–29.

31. On the romantic program for a new mythology, see "Systemprogramm des deutschen Idealismus," in *Materialien zu Schellings philosophischen Anfänge*, ed. Manfred Frank (Frankfurt, 1975), 110–113; and Schlegel's *Gespräch über die Poesie*, in *Kritische Ausgabe*, II:311–328.

32. See Novalis, *Schriften*, II:545, no. 105.

33. See Schlegel, *Brief über den Roman, Kritische Ausgabe,* II:333–334. This essay should be compared with Schlegel's earlier essay, "Ueber die Grenzen des Schönen," where he argues that the highest form of aesthetic enjoyment is love, which can only be found in a community of free and equal persons. See *Kritische Ausgabe,* I: 34–44, esp. p. 42.

34. See, e.g., Schelling's *Neue Deduktion des Naturrechts,* in *Werke,* ed. Manfred Schröter (Munich, 1927), I:169–204; and Schlegel's, "Versuch über den Begriff des Republikanismus," in *Kritische Ausgabe,* VII:11–25.

35. As the heirs of Kant, the young romantics rejected the old metaphysics of the Leibnizian-Wolffian school. They were also critical of attempts to vindicate this metaphysics through appeals to the practical interests of reason. On this theme, see Schelling's early essay, "Briefe über Dogmatismus und Kriticismus," in *Werke,* I: 205–266.

36. Thus Eberhard, Garve, and Feder all attempted to thwart Kant's critique of metaphysics and the natural law tradition. Concerning their reply to Kant, see my *The Fate of Reason: German Philosophy from Kant to Fichte* (Cambridge, Mass., 1987), 165–225.

Progress: Ideas, Skepticism, and Critique—The Heritage of the Enlightenment

Rudolph Vierhaus

Translated by Jonathan B. Knudsen

I

A return to the eighteenth-century Enlightenment movement and to the French Revolution requires no particular justification, for it is suggested by the very theme of "Progress: Ideas, Skepticism, and Critique." Still one must be warned from the start of potential misinterpretations. An incontrovertible relationship most certainly existed between the French Revolution and the European Enlightenment; yet the Revolution cannot be understood as the result of the Enlightenment, and the Enlightenment cannot be understood as the legacy or burden of the Revolution. Both views are true only in a very limited sense. Even linking the idea of progress to the Enlightenment and the Revolution must be questioned critically: this idea is older, and the Revolution, which in France was followed by the military dictatorship of Napoleon and the restoration of the monarchy, bequeathed not only the idea of a better political system and a more just social order but also the counterexperience of *dérapage* once it attempted to accelerate progress in a revolutionary manner. The revolutionary outbreak disintegrated into the Terror and the sovereign nation *une et indivisible* fell under the rule of a caesar. Since then the idea of social progress and the belief in its feasibility have been accompanied by doubt and critique. The course of the Revolution itself, driven forward as it was by a faith in progress, gave food to the doubters and critics: it provided the most important and successful argument against the Enlightenment. Those who had fol-

Originally published as "Fortschrittsidee, Forschrittsskepsis, Fortschrittskritik. Das Erbe der Aufklärung," in Das Andere Wahrnehmen. Beiträge zur europäischen Geschichte [August Nitschke zum 65. Geburtstag gewidmet], *ed. M. Kintzinger, W. Stümer, and J. Zahlten (Köln, Weimar, and Wien: Böhlau Verlag, 1991): 533–545.*

lowed the Enlightenment from the beginning with doubt and rejection saw their views confirmed. Many enlighteners were irritated and repulsed, turning away after they had at first greeted the outbreak of the Revolution as the breakthrough of enlightened ideas. Self-doubt and a self-critical questioning of the meaning of enlightenment had, of course, already begun before 1789.

Therefore one needs to warn against all overly simple historical divisions. The inheritance that the Enlightenment and the French Revolution left to the "modern world" is ambivalent—and for this reason it is left open to ever new interpretation. Such cannot simply be limited to the ideas and intentions of the participants; it also includes the question of the continuance of these ideas until our own day. In the following I will not consider the causes of the Revolution of 1789 in France and its development and expansion into Germany; rather I am concerned with whether and to what extent it changed the world; whether it derived from "enlightened" motives that can be assumed still to be alive today (or should be alive today); whether it adapted goals that had been formulated and propagandized by the Enlightenment and whether these goals are still of value today; whether it unleashed a disaster under which we still suffer; and whether it created an exemplar that still needs to be understood. Did the Revolution discredit the project of "enlightenment"—a project that is often simply equated with the project of "modernity"—or did it not demonstrate the ambivalence of this project at an early historical moment and in a dramatic fashion?

Such questions acquire their actuality from confusingly diverse contemporary phenomena, for which slogans are created and exhausted in rapid succession: dialectic of enlightenment, dialectic of progress, the *neue Unübersichtlichkeit* (new obscurity), deconstructionism, and postmodernism, to name only a few. A critical stance toward science and an animosity toward technology circulate, calls to return and offers of new doctrines of salvation are the order of the day. A sense of helplessness and an anxiety about the future are on the rise; the demand to abandon the increasingly complex and threatening processes constituting the modern world becomes ever stronger, as do the number of those who want to profit from the mood. One speaks of a crisis in social orientation and identity, of a transformation in meaning and values. One might think that an era is coming to a close, a lengthy secular historical process, and with it the belief that this era was meaningful, productive, and legitimated by a ubiquitous progress.

Why this crisis of modernity today, even though the existence of humanity—notwithstanding all Cassandra calls and public self-pity, all fears of catastrophe and the very real suffering—is dependent in numerous areas on further technical, economic, and political progress? Skepticism and criticism of progress are not only to be found among those whom modernization has passed by or who have decided to drop out. Even those who have conceived themselves to be the carriers of progress have been filled with doubt. The suspicion is that progress brings with it immeasurable dangers and that a stage has been reached wherein the social costs have outstripped the gains. Was the trust in the possibility of rational progress a dangerous error? Does it reside in both a naive and an excessive valuation of human nature? Has Pandora's box been opened by theoreticians, who continuously have challenged us to use our reason independently, and practitioners, who have sought to replace—even violently—traditional authority and historically evolved relations with a rationally conceived order?

Much has been said and written about the beginnings and spread of doubt concerning the process of modernity—too little, however, about the fact that this process was accompanied from the beginning by skepticism and critique. The idea of progress and the transformations some viewed as progress generated in others the feeling of loss and barrenness. The dialectic of progress has emerged with ever greater clarity today under the impress of manifest dangers and potential catastrophes, fundamentalist revolts against modernity in technologically developed societies, and the experience that the period of unlimited economic growth, popular participation, and political consensus appears to be coming to an end.

This dialectic was already visible in the French Revolution, that event which, like no other before it, was borne by the assumption that with it would begin a new and better world. As Karl Jaspers formulated it in his famous analysis of 1931, *Die geistige Situation der Zeit*, the Revolution "took the unexpected course of transforming itself into the opposite of its origins. The will to create human freedom changed into the Terror that destroyed all freedom. The reaction against it grew. To destroy the possibility of its return became the ruling principle of the European states. Once it had occurred, however, a sense of unease remained in men with respect to the whole of their existence, one for which they themselves carried the responsibility, since it was to be changed according to plan and hopefully to be constructed for the best." Since then there has been "a specifically new awareness of the epochal meaning of the age"—if indeed one that is bifurcated. "Standing in the way of belief in the dawn of a magnificent future is the horror of the abyss out of which there is no salvation."[1] Even this alternative appears today to be outmoded, for who still believes in the dawn of a magnificent future?

Two hundred years after the revolutionary and dramatic effort of men and women to take their fate into their own hands and construct their social and political world according to principles of reason, it has become inescapable to ask what has gone wrong. Or was the attempt utopian and false from the beginning? Has the idea of progress in its expansion beyond the scientific-technical and economic-material dimensions proven to be a chimera? A glance into the history of the idea of progress may help us come closer to finding an answer to these questions.

II

The modern idea of progress differentiates itself fundamentally from medieval and early modern Christian conceptions of time due to an openness to an unlimited future. Christian thought had indeed reoriented itself to the world in its sinfulness after expectations by the primitive Church of an early return of Christ had not been fulfilled. But it held onto its belief, from the standpoint of salvation history, in the finitude of the world and in the ultimate redemption from sinful temporality. Over time certain changes for the good might indeed occur, but there could be no general progress. A history whose goals and course were set and coordinated by men or an immanent redemption either were unthinkable ideas or remained a utopian sketch. The Renaissance gave rise to the awareness of living in a new age but not to the idea of entering into a better future. The ancient world remained for them the best of all times, a model they sought to repeat and emulate. A new, "progressive" understanding of historical time first occurred with the new rational perception of nature that gradually emancipated itself from the authority of the ancients and the Church and that, so it was thought, would also lead to human betterment. With this method of thought—in the terms of René Descartes in his *Discours de la méthode pour bien conduire sa raison et chercher la vérité dans les sciences* (1637)—nothing will remain undiscovered if one does not accept as true what is not so and if one proceeds strictly from the simple to the complex. Thereby enormous theoretical and practical advances were made in the realm of the natural sciences and technology that continuously reconfirmed the optimism. When the rational principles of the natural sciences were transferred to history, it led to the view that humanity could free itself from the constraints of nature and traditional authority and make itself master over nature and shaper of its own history.

Francis Bacon saw that humankind had such a capacity due to the convergence of its scientific and practical capabilities, which the Creator had invested in it as a particular promise and which realized itself in turn in the progress of humanity itself. For the human spirit had the unlimited capacity to perfection. Gottfried Wilhelm Leibniz conceived of happiness not in terms of "complete possession" but rather in terms of a "continuous and unbroken progress" (*un progrès continué et non interrompu*). The expansion of the idea of progress to the process of the development of humanity was reinforced by the anthropological-ethnographic knowledge gained from contact with the non-European world and by the conviction that the peoples from other parts of the world would be incorporated into a European civilization that was based on the rational mastery and use of nature. In the course of an ever-expanding and unlimited reason, humankind would finally achieve a rational sovereignty over nature and thus freedom itself.

Indeed, in the eighteenth century we can observe numerous successful attempts at legislative and administrative reforms. Fiscal concerns were certainly at their base, but such efforts were legitimated in enlightened and humanitarian terms. The enlightened public was susceptible—perhaps too susceptible—to such explanations, but it saw such measures as proofs of the practicability of rational planning. A progressive historical vision developed: it was not utopian but rather committed to empirical verification. The purest expressions of this vision are to be found in Turgot's *Tableau philosophique des progrès successifs de l'esprit humain* (1750) and in Condorcet's *Esquisse d'un tableau historique des progrès de l'esprit humain.* The latter appeared in 1795 after the Reign of Terror had been overthrown and after Condorcet, a delegate to the Convention, had himself fallen its victim. "Everything now tells us," he wrote at the beginning,

> that we are now close upon one of the great revolutions of the human race. If we wish to learn what to expect from it and to procure a certain guide to lead us in the midst of its vicissitudes, what could be more suitable than to have some picture of the revolutions that have gone before it and prepared its way? The present state of enlightenment assures us that this revolution will have a favorable result, but is not this only on the condition that we know how to employ our knowledge and resources to their fullest extent? And in order that the happiness that promises may be less dearly bought, that it may be diffused more rapidly over a greater area, that it may be more complete in its effects, do we not need to study the history of the human spirit to discover what obstacles we still have to fear and what means are open to us of surmounting them?[2]

This is the creed of an as yet unshattered, optimistic enlightenment. History is conceived as the result of "revolutions" driven by discontent and generating progress. They have created a level of enlightenment that makes it possible for mankind consciously to will progress, control its course, and thereby avoid reversals. One senses a certain concern on Condorcet's part, but the essay is dominated by the conviction that revolution brings with it the "happiness" that can be achieved on the basis of the progress of the human spirit.

It belongs among the emphatic claims of the French Revolution that a new age has dawned and a new sociopolitical order has been created in which the sovereign people reign, human and civil rights are guaranteed inviolable, and governmental authority is divided and controlled by the people's representatives. In this order the prerogatives of birth and estatist privileges have been abolished and merit alone is decisive. In a single stroke of world historical progress, the *volontée générale* of this democratic nation *une et indivisible* has made the principles of liberty, equality, and fraternity the foundation of the state. As is well known, Hegel described these events in his *Philosophie der Weltgeschichte* with the words: "Never since the sun has stood in the firmament and the planets revolved around her, has it been perceived that man's existence centers in his head, i.e., in thought, inspired by which he builds up the world of reality."[3]

The Revolution was doubtless not the transformation of the Enlightenment into political practice, but without the Enlightenment the formulation of the legitimacy of the Revolution and its goals would have been unthinkable, the stirring slogans would have been unavailable, and it would not have been able to speak for humanity and its progress. This is not the place to continue the endless debate on the particular mix of factors—ideational, economic, social, and political—that were responsible for the outbreak, the course, and the "dérapage" of the Revolution. In the context of our questions, it is necessary to reconsider an Enlightenment whose character, not without reason, has often been misunderstood and whose significance has been often over- or undervalued.

The term "enlightenment" is one that, although proclaimed by its own adherents, is often used or even misused in a sweeping and inexact manner. It characterizes in historical terms an intellectual and moral movement with a practical intent. It was not homogeneous, nor did it ever dominate the thought and attitudes of all men and women, not even the stratum of the educated, this is, the writing and reading public. The diffusion and impact of the Enlightenment and those groups attacked in its critique, as well as the real social differentiation—all these depended on the confessional and political relations in the specific lands, the economic life, and the social composition of the particular cities. We are still able to refer to the eighteenth century as the "age of enlightenment" because over its course certain principles and a particular style of thought and argument became a permanent part of European civilization and under this term has remained so up to our own day in spite of all countercurrents.

It is characteristic that the term "enlightenment" was rarely used in England and the Netherlands; in those countries there was apparently no need for programmatic slogans. The language was most charged in those countries where the Enlightenment was able to assert itself against the traditional authorities only with the greatest efforts. There it appeared as especially critical and reformist, filled with the pathos of improvement, modernization, and progress. Even in these countries there were special accents: Whereas the Enlightenment in Catholic countries adopted an anticlerical, antiecclesiastical, and even atheistic stance, in Protestant countries it penetrated into theology itself. Even Pietism, the other significant eighteenth-century intellectual movement in Germany, developed only partially in opposition to the Enlightenment. As the movement of Pietism in Halle reveals, there could be ties between the two. In its social composition and sociopolitical program, the Enlightenment was overwhelmingly a "bourgeois" movement; it directed itself against the estatist, feudal society of privilege as well as monarchical divine right absolutism. But it could also join a reforming absolutism represented by enlightened princes and their administrators. Enlightened governments launched programs for improvement especially in those states burdened with diverse and highly traditional institutions, with little social dynamism, and with underdeveloped economies. There the enlightened public debated and rapidly developed high expectations for change and improvement in the legal and criminal justice system, the struggle against poverty, the promotion of trade and industry, the tax system, and education. The precondition for this public discussion was the growing concentration of the system of communication, the expansion of the book market, journals, and newspapers. Simultaneously there was a loosening of censorship and the emergence of an enlightened discourse that concerned itself with the private ethics of the citizen and basic principles of politics, public education, and social relations. For enlightened writers, general "publicity" was the decisive medium of progress. They were persuaded that publicity would be able to denounce injustice and arbitrary rule, administrative stupidity, and incompetence; and through publicity they would be able to subject their present conditions to critical scrutiny and demand improvements.

Critique of the Bible and secular knowledge, of language and the inherited texts, all in accord with reason, was supposed to illuminate man's consciousness, encourage independent thought, and promote better decision making. If the enlighteners brought traditional patterns of thought and customary relations before the tribunal of critical reason, they presented plans and programs, not without a certain arrogance and self-importance, without realistically comprehending the resistance of tradition. They themselves needed to pass through the learning process they viewed the Enlightenment to be and to submit to the critique they themselves applied to traditional ideas, institutions, and ways of life. It is a credit to the movement that they raised and examined the question of what enlightenment was and what it had achieved—most conspicuously in the famous debate in the *Berlinische Monatsschrift* in 1784. The process of the Enlightenment was seen to have begun but was still in an early phase. The goal of a republican constitution within the individual states and a league of nations that could secure permanent peace was, as they knew, still far away.

Kant was convinced that not simply individuals but "a public" could become enlightened if man were given the freedom "to make public use of his reason in all of its aspects." Nevertheless this could occur only step-by-step. "Revolution might decrease personal despotism and egocentric and tyrannical repression, but it will never bring about a true reform of the mode of thought."[4] For enlighteners, "reform of the mode of thought" was the most important and fundamental reform; without it all political reforms and revolutions appeared useless and even disruptive. As late as 1843, Arnold Ruge, a descendant of the Enlightenment, stated in his "Self-Critique of Liberalism," "The old failure of liberalism is to expect worldly salvation from a reform of the political structures: everything depends on the reform of consciousness. The reform of consciousness is the reform of the world, and no god can hinder it."[5]

There were numerous reasons why in Germany this view was advocated with particular vehemence. Because of the extreme territorial diversity, significant preconditions for political revolution were lacking, and the reform initiatives of enlightened governments had led to the expectation that timely improvements in social and political life could be achieved without revolutionary disruptions. This expectation was particularly held by officials, teachers, pastors, and lawyers who saw themselves as responsible for decisive participation in such improvements, and, like other educated individuals under the influence of the literary-philosophical culture, they were persuaded by the ultimately irresistible power of education and public opinion.

The plea for reform had gradually acquired antirevolutionary and apologetic tones. These were already apparent in the distinction between "true" and "false" enlightenment. But the French Revolution brought with it the first massive and lasting experience of the ambivalence of the Enlightenment. The Revolution generated enthusiasm and horror and kindled wide-ranging expectations, and these turned into deep disappointment. It failed as revolution but still changed men's ideas. It created a new consciousness of time and unleashed an unending debate on the Enlightenment that focused on its responsibility for the Revolution.

III

The presuppositions and conditions for the possibility of this revolution, its ambivalent consequences and historical meaning, are not our concern here. But this much must be stated: Without a doubt the Enlightenment belongs to the Revolution's preconditions, but it was not its cause. The delegates of the Third Estate did not go to the gathering of the Estates General at Versailles in 1789 with the intent of launching a revolution. Much more significant were the mistakes of the monarchy and the various movements in countryside and city spawned by misery and discontent. The Revolution became radicalized through catchwords and slogans that articulated enlightenment ideas simply and effectively, by the pressure of popular demands and mass gatherings, by the speeches of individual agitators, and by the fear of invasion and counterrevolution. It became violent against its real and imagined domestic opponents and militarily aggressive beyond France's borders. What had begun in the name of reason and humanity transformed itself into political terror in the name of bourgeois virtue and into an anarchic struggle among competing groups. In Germany many still held onto the view that the inability of the old regime to reform itself had made the Revolution necessary and that the erstwhile oppressors were accountable for the blood now spilled. But in the face of the radicalization of the Revolution, they saw themselves strengthened in the view that only rational reforms could be successful over the long term and that revolutions only opened the floodgates to disorder and passion. Over the course of the Revolution, the progress achieved at the beginning was thus once again placed at risk.

Friedrich Gentz, Ernst Brandes, August Wilhelm Rehberg, and others emphasized that Germany and Europe had been on the path of progress in the quarter century since the end of the Seven Years War and the outbreak of the Revolution. The Revolution disrupted this progress. The Enlightenment was made directly or indirectly responsible insofar as its abstract ideas of freedom and equality and its naive, ahistorical belief in the capacity of man to create a better society had launched a process that could no longer be controlled. In opposition to them, other, more resolute Enlightenment figures continued to view the French Revolution as the first great experiment in shaping society and the state according to the principles of reason. It was indeed an experiment that, unlike the one in North America, became derailed with horrifying consequences and made Restoration unavoidable, but a level of reform had been attained before which one could not retreat. For the conservatives, in contrast, the Revolution revealed the iniquity and corruption of the secular Enlightenment. Among those accusations that have since continuously been leveled against the Enlightenment and the Revolution are that they undermined a traditional, diverse, and deeply rooted order and replaced it with abstract and general constructs; that they ignored the incomplete nature of man and instead brought forth the seductive chimeras of the autonomous individual and the progressive perfection of the species; and that they delivered us to the new despotism of the ideologues and political theoreticians, the bureaucrats and the pedagogues. Against the Enlightenment and the Revolution, the Restoration and romanticism mobilized the integrative forces of religion, the family, the estates, and the national group. Even this camp did not fail to recognize the need for change and reform, but change and reform should proceed as "organic" developments. Its adherents did not contest the notion of progress in the material world, but certainly in the moral world. Especially in Germany, and even among the moderate liberals, a view of historical development was placed in opposition to rational natural rights theory and idealistic views of history.

In the lectures that Leopold Ranke delivered to King Maximillian II in Berchtesgaden in 1854, he explained: "Insofar as we can trace the course of history, we can assume absolute progress in the area of material interests, wherein no reversal will be able to take place without a totally massive upheaval. In moral terms, however, we cannot trace any progress."[6] At the moment when Ranke expressed himself in this manner, the February Revolution in France, with its signs of social revolution, had failed and the Second Empire had followed. For the first time a political revolution had shaken Germany on the basis of its own internal dynamic, even if it had not indeed achieved its own goal of political unification and had not been able to move the monarchical constitutional form of government in the individual states in a parliamentary-democratic direction. Still, a new phase of German history began with far-reaching economic and social change.

In a few decades sweeping industrialization and growing mobility created a decisive willingness among the bourgeois middle classes to accept a form of modernity that stood in noticeable contradiction to the relatively backward political constitution and the social prestige system that underpinned it. The labor movement was more strongly oriented toward modernity. It linked together progress with a vision of a better and more just social order, a new society that would be the result of a revolutionary transformation of the political relations. With this goal in mind, the labor movement affirmed technical and scientific progress and its political instrumentalization, simultaneous with political struggle against the decisive carriers of this progress, the middle class. Labor understood itself as the legitimate heir of the Enlightenment, accusing the middle class of betraying the ideals of humanity of the "bourgeois" Enlightenment. In labor's view, the bourgeoisie had rigidified into a class, lost the impetus to reform, and under the impress of economic, scientific, and technical progress, had abandoned its earlier social and moral goals. For this reason industrialization based on scientific-technical progress and the modern society based on the division of labor belong in the hands of the one truly progressive class, the proletariat, who does not represent its own interest but that of humanity itself. The proletariat will give to the idea of progress, which has only been used to maximize the profit of capital, true social and humanitarian goals.

IV

It was only over the course of the nineteenth century that technical-economic progress became a practical way of life through the application of scientific knowledge, the deliberate investment of capital, and political support. Progress appeared to be feasible by transforming knowledge into practice. Scientific-technical progress, it was increasingly believed, would also gradually solve the problem of social inequality and transform the political power struggles among nations into a peaceful economic and cultural contest. Increased prosperity would bring with it an increase in social morality; every gain in scientific knowledge and its application would improve society as a whole. There appeared to be no limit to progress, at least in the foreseeable future.

Obvious quantitative and qualitative progress in the production of foodstuffs and industrial goods, in transportation and public hygiene, in the educational system and science, and so forth has not been able to silence worry and doubt completely. The dominant optimistic belief in progress, based on science and technology, growth rates, and the European-North American penetration of the rest of the world, is observable only from the last third of the nineteenth century onward. Simultaneously, however, a broad cultural criticism emerged, a confusing multiplicity of movements among youth groups and others in the counterculture who sought changes in diet, belief, and way of life. Such phenomena were not unique to Germany but were particularly apparent there where economic, social, and political development had been frequently dammed up, had taken a disparate course, and therefore had pressed forward with far greater discontent. In Germany such movements were often deliberately critical of enlightenment and rationality and were hypernationalistic, anti-Western, and antidemocratic. Especially in Germany skeptics and critics of progress have never been silenced. That conservatives used their views as arguments against liberalism and socialism should not allow us to overlook that the ambivalence inherent in progress and its idea intensified toward the end of the nineteenth century. It is an ambivalence that was already inherent in the Enlightenment and that belongs to the modern world itself.

The Enlightenment had formulated principles for a future social and political order before the preconditions for their realization existed and before their consequences could be observed. One had not yet experienced the dynamic of a mass movement that made enlightened ideas into its slogans or the revolutionary, explosive forces released by the calls for freedom, equality, and popular sovereignty. The enlighteners of the eighteenth century had wanted, in the words of Kant, to initiate a process by which man left the state of his self-incurred immaturity, in order to be able to use his own reason without the direction of another. The philosopher from Königsberg had not assumed that this process would be rapid or even revolutionary or that all men would equally be in the position to come of age. Like most of the critical figures of the Enlightenment, he remained skeptical about individuals, even though he was convinced of the progress of man as a species. The "mature" man and citizen, the "republican" constitution that created a legal code that the citizen could ratify freely, the federation of sovereign states that guaranteed the external peace—these were for Kant basic ideas and regulative principles of social practice that were discredited by the Revolution but not disproven.

Since then, however, the costs of progress and its dangers have become generally visible. The problem that Kant had already formulated presents itself in even sharper terms than before: How can rational progress, moral responsibility, and aesthetic need be brought in agreement? That we have not yet been successful does not prove that the problem is unsolvable, but it also does not allow us unbridled optimism, particularly with a view back to the history of the twentieth century.

NOTES

1. Karl Jaspers, *Die geistige Situation der Zeit* [Sammlung Göschen] (1932; reprint 5th ed., Berlin, 1947), 10. In English as *Man in the Modern Age*, trans. Eden and Cedar Paul (London, 1951), 14–15. [I have retranslated the Jaspers quotation.—TRANS.]

2. Condorcet, *Sketch for a Historical Picture of the Progress of the Human Mind* (1793), in Condorcet, *Selected Writings*, ed. Keith Michael Baker (Indianapolis, 1976), 217–218.

3. Georg Wilhelm Friedrich Hegel, *Philosophie der Weltgeschichte*, ed. Georg Lasson (Leipzig, 1944), 926. In English: *The Philosophy of History*, trans. J. Sibree (London, 1900), 447.

4. Immanuel Kant, "Beantwortung der Frage: Was ist Aufklärung?" *Werke in zehn Bänden*, vol. 9, ed. Wilhelm Weischedel (Darmstadt, 1968), 55.

5. Quoted from Hans Fenske, ed., *Vormärz und Revolution 1840–1849 [Quellen zum politischen Denken der Deutschen im 19. und 20. Jahrhundert*, 4] (Darmstadt, 1976), 77.

6. Leopold Ranke, *Die Epochen der neueren Geschichte. Historische-kritische Ausgabe*, ed. Theodor Schieder and Helmut Berding [Aus Werk und Nachlaß, vol. 2] (Munich, 1971), 68.

PART THREE

Twentieth-Century Questions

What Is Enlightenment?

Rüdiger Bittner

"Enlightenment," in the first instance, is something people do. What results from these doings is called enlightenment as well. And a historical epoch for which these doings are said to be characteristic also bears this name. Only the first of these three is the topic of discussion here.

This is in line with the usage of the authors collected in this volume. For the most part they did not investigate the characteristic marks of their own age. They wanted to know what a person does who is doing enlightenment. Admittedly, to use the term in this way allows judgments that will strike many as anachronistic: to say that the Sophists in the fifth century B.C. represent a movement of enlightenment is not a misuse of terms.

Again in line with the authors collected here, this discussion will deal only with what the German term "*Aufklärung*" means. Thus, strictly speaking, "enlightenment" does not stand for enlightenment here. It stands for whatever "Aufklärung" in German stands for.

The discussion has four parts. The first offers a critique of the most widely known conception of enlightenment, Kant's. The second proposes an alternative conception. The third considers the arguments of those who think that enlightenment is a bad thing. The fourth presents arguments for saying that enlightenment is a good thing.

WHAT ENLIGHTENMENT IS NOT: A CRITIQUE OF KANT'S CONCEPTION

With admirable succinctness, Kant expresses his conception in the few opening lines of his article on enlightenment:

> Enlightenment is man's stepping out of an immaturity which is his own fault. Immaturity is the inability to use one's own understanding without guidance

> by another. This immaturity is one's own fault, if it is caused, not by a lack of understanding, but by a lack of resolve and courage to use it without guidance by another. *Sapere aude!* Have the courage to use your own understanding! is thus the motto of enlightenment.[1]

Famous though these sentences are, it is hard to make good sense of them. First, it is hard to make good sense of the idea that the immaturity in question is somebody's own fault. To be sure, immaturity is an inability, as Kant explains, and generally it does make sense to speak of an inability as being one's own fault. For example, it may be one's own fault that through lack of exercise one lost or never acquired competence in a language. The inability to use one's own understanding without guidance by another is a special case, however, for it seems precisely to be a condition of something's being somebody's fault that the person be able at the time to use her own understanding without guidance by another. Thus if a person, failing because of laziness or cowardice to do what will make her able to use her own understanding, does not at that time have the ability to use her own understanding, then the failure is not her fault. However, to suppose that man had the ability to use his own understanding at the time of his failure to do what would let him have this ability at a future time is to tell an improbable story. Nothing supports the idea that at an earlier stage we already had the independence of thought to which enlightenment is supposed to lead us now. Nothing supports the idea that enlightenment is really man's return to his original maturity. It is true, some writers in the epoch called the Enlightenment seem to have thought so, notably Jean-Jacques Rousseau.[2] That, however, is to turn enlightenment itself into mythology. Original maturity, lost through our own fault and regained by the endeavors of enlightenment, is a mere repetition of paradise, lost by our sin and regained through redemption—and no more plausible.

Second, it is hard to make good sense of how the idea of immaturity itself is employed here. "Immaturity" stands for *Unmündigkeit* in German, which means the condition of somebody who cannot himself, for example, for reasons of age, perform actions of legal significance, but for whom others can do so.[3] Kant uses the term metaphorically: immature is he who cannot use his understanding by himself, but only guided by another.

It is not clear, though, what it is to use one's understanding guided by another. A first try could be this: somebody is guided by another if, in thinking about some matter, he takes into account what the other thinks about it. This cannot be right, however. On that understanding, maturity would be neither desirable nor even attainable. We do not wish, nor are we able, to do our thinking alone to the point of not even considering others' views.

Alternatively, the idea may be: somebody is guided by another if he acts on the basis of somebody else's judgment, without checking its accuracy himself. This is the reading Kant suggests when in the second paragraph he has the immature person explain herself thus:

> I do not need to think, if only I can pay. Others will undertake the annoying business for me.

The analogy here is with a person who, unwilling, say, to clean her windows, hires somebody to do the job for her. Just as in this case the person in the end enjoys a clear view without doing a hand's turn, so the immature person, according to Kant, avails herself of the results of another's reflections without going herself through the thoughts leading there. Yet here again maturity seems to be unattractive, if not impossible. I hate to prepare my tax return and get an accountant to do it. Here indeed I do not need to think if only I can pay. I accept the accountant's judgment without checking its accuracy, and yet I act on this basis, since it is still me, not the accountant, who is declaring my income to the tax authority and who is legally responsible for the declaration. However, saving myself some thought by paying does not seem such a terrible thing in this case. So one wonders what should be wrong in principle with immaturity, so understood. Indeed, one wonders whether it is even possible to shun all reliance on somebody else's judgment and to do, in this sense, all one's thinking oneself. Booksellers at any rate would find such a maxim of enlightenment uncongenial.

Someone may defend a third position as follows. Sure, there is nothing wrong in general with relying on another's judgment. There is something wrong with it in particular instances. Sometimes people give more weight to another's judgment than is warranted in the case at hand. It is all well to pay somebody for preparing your tax return. It is a mistake to pay somebody for telling you what to do in every situation of life and always to feel bound to that person's orders. This is the sort of mistake that Kant has in mind when he speaks of somebody being guided by another, and it is the sort of mistake that enlightenment is intended to overcome.

There are two difficulties with this idea. First, the injunction not to let oneself be guided by another becomes useless on this reading. The injunction now means: Do not put too much weight on others' judgments. This, however, while difficult to do, is trivial to say. We would need to know what the right weight is in any particular case in order to use that rule, and this is just what we do not know. Johann Gottlieb Fichte makes fun of those who want to allow only true statements to be printed: if they could provide us with a general criterion of truth, this would be a useful strategy.[4] Those who demand that pronouncements of authorities should be given only the appropriate weight are in no better position.

Second, while people certainly do sometimes give too much weight to the judgment of others, it is misleading to describe this metaphorically as immaturity. True, in the ordinary sense of this word people show their immaturity in judgment when they rely too heavily on the pronouncements of authority figures. However, the word *immaturity* translates "Unmündigkeit" here, and so it means the condition of a person whose actions do not form a part of the relevant "game," the example being a child whose actions do not count in legal terms. In this sense it is not immaturity to rely too heavily on others' judgments. The person who thinks that birth control is wrong on the grounds that the Pope said that it is wrong is mistaken in her reasoning, yet she is reasoning. She does save herself some steps in the reasoning process by relying on the Pope, just as I save myself some steps by relying on the tax accountant. Neither of us is immature in the sense of *unmündig*, however. We are both acting in our "games," she trying to find out whether to use birth control measures, I trying to find out what to declare to the tax office. Presumably she is playing her game badly and mine I am playing all right, because there are reasons against trusting the Pope and reasons for trusting a tax accountant in matters of birth control and tax returns, respectively. Yet players in our own right we both are: reasoners reaching in our particular ways a judgment on the matter in question.

If guidance by another, in the sense of giving another's judgment too much weight, does not count as immaturity in the relevant sense, it is as misleading to describe the person overcoming her excessive reliance on another's judgment as starting to use her own understanding. She did that all along, only she did not do it well. If she trusted the pope, she did not therefore fail to use her own understanding. It takes understanding to accept the pronouncements of an authority.[5] There is, then, no opposition between guidance by another and using one's own understanding. Being guided and not being guided by another are two ways of using one's understanding, one correct, the other incorrect.

So the grand enlightenment gesture "Have the courage to use your own understanding!" falls flat. Whether you give appropriate or inappropriate weight to what others are saying, you cannot fail to obey that injunction: you are in the game of reasoning already. Thinking for oneself, an idea of which Kant, together with many of his contemporaries, tried to make a great deal,[6] is a triviality: to be thinking at all, however excessively relying on others' judgments, is to be thinking for oneself.

With this, talk of resolve and courage goes by the board as well. To use one's own understanding is not an achievement, so it needs no courage, either. Not to put too much weight on what others are saying is admittedly an achievement, but it is not a matter of courage in the sense in which courage goes together with resolve. It is not a matter of courage in the sense in which jumping from the diving board is. Kant's phrase "stepping out of immaturity" suggests that it is a matter of courage precisely in this sense: as if by a simple bold turn we could convert ourselves into reasoners relying just to the right extent on others' judgments. In fact it is a matter of slow learning, at best.

As such it may need courage after all, but in a different sense: the sense in which courage is opposed to discouragement, not to cowardice, the sense in which a courageous person is one who has the force to face the unwelcome news and to keep going under adverse circumstances. This sense is relevant, for giving the right weight to others' judgments may well mean to come to live in a more uncertain world. Yet this is not the sense in which Kant is speaking of courage here. It is not the sort of courage that could be enjoined in an imperative.

"Enlightenment is man's stepping out of an immaturity which is his own fault"—on the present argument, there is no stepping out here, no immaturity, and no fault of his own.

WHAT ENLIGHTENMENT IS

Enlightenment is, basically, to illuminate something, that is, to gain or to communicate an understanding of it. The German verb *aufklären*, unlike its English counterpart *to enlighten*, allows a construction with an impersonal object. Thus in German one can "enlighten" a crime, an obscure passage, or the genesis of the Alps—which is simply to explain them.

The term "enlightenment" is used more specifically in cases where the understanding in question has a particular importance for a person.[7] As Christian Gotthilf Salzmann put it, true enlightenment consists "in improving our understanding primarily of those things to which we are closely connected."[8] Thus it would be odd, or ironic, to speak of enlightening somebody about the square root of 29, whereas one could correctly speak of enlightening him about why a seemingly harmless remark of his drew an angry reaction. The German term for a doctor's obligation to inform the patient, for example, before an operation, is *ärztliche Aufklärungspflicht* (a doctor's enlightenment obligation), which makes good sense given how closely the person is connected to what he learns there. The same explanation holds for the peculiar German usage of calling the sexual education of children "enlightenment": the information provided there is important to the child.

This meaning of enlightenment is still not specific enough. It does not capture the idea conveyed in statements like these: "Lessing's work is carried throughout by an enlightenment impulse," "The sophistic movement was a movement of enlightenment," "Autonomy is the centerpiece of an enlightened morality." In such phrases, enlightenment means more than gaining or communicating important understanding. The word does not refer simply to the historical period here. It refers, rather, to the intellectual endeavor that is supposed to characterize the period. What that endeavor is needs to be explained.

An example from the heartland of Enlightenment thought, from the critique of religion, will help. Thomas Hobbes wrote,

> And they that make little, or no enquiry into the naturall causes of things, yet from the feare that proceeds from the ignorance it selfe, of what it is that hath the power to do them much good or harm, are enclined to suppose, and feign unto themselves, severall kinds of Powers invisible; and to stand in awe of their own imaginations; and in time of distresse to invoke them; as also in the time of an expected good successe, to give them thanks; making the creatures of their own fancy, their Gods. By which means it hath come to passe, that from the innumerable variety of Fancy, men have created in the world innumerable sorts of Gods. And this Feare of things invisible, is the naturall seed of that, which every one in himself calleth Religion; and in them that worship, or feare that Power otherwise than they do, Superstition.[9]

This is a theory of religion, or more precisely, an answer to the question of why there is such a thing as religion among humans. Never mind whether the theory is true. The way the theory is set up is this. There is on one hand the phenomenon we want to understand, religion. There is on the other hand a phenomenon with which we are familiar, human fear. The theory is essentially the claim that the former is produced by the latter. With a bit more detail, people's ignorance of the natural causes of things gives rise to fear and their fear leads them to imagine invisible powers and to believe in them, to honor them, to serve them—which is religion.

This is scientific reasoning first of all; "an attempt to introduce the experimental method of reasoning into moral subjects," to use David Hume's phrase.[10] Ordinary scientific explanation shows of some strange or surprising event that it is after all an instance of something familiar. "What on earth made the radiator break?" "Well, the temperature went way below freezing last night, and frozen water expands."[11] Similarly here: "What is it that leads people to the strange beliefs and practices of religion?" "There is nothing surprising in this. Fear does it, and with fear we are familiar."

Hobbes's theory has another characteristic, however, which it does not share with ordinary scientific reasoning. In analogy to the expression "friendly amendment," one might say that what Hobbes offers is an unfriendly explanation. If this explanation is correct, it shows that religion is wrongly honored. Religion is supposed to teach us true beliefs and appropriate practices with respect to invisible powers, and it is respected for teaching them. If there are no such powers, if the beliefs and practices turn out to be mere products of fantasy and fear, the respect falls to the ground, or at least it should. Religion loses its dignity since it shows itself, with the expression of another Enlightenment author, to be "human, all too human":[12] human, because only our fear, nothing in the nature of things, is grounds for these beliefs and practices; all too human, because the fear that grounds religion is itself an immature reaction, one that will vanish on a clear understanding of things. In one word, Hobbes's theory is a reduction, in the polemical sense of this expression which is only related, not identical, to the sense that is usual in philosophy of science: it attempts to show that what seemed high is only a particular instance of what is low.

This is the mark of Enlightenment thought in general. With Spinoza, an enlightened reading of the Bible subjects the Holy Scripture to the same method of interpretation as the ordinary phenomena of nature.[13] With Hobbes, an enlightened political philosophy describes the state, not as an essential part of human perfection, but as a mere artifact for enhancing the chances of surviving.[14] With Voltaire, an enlightened conception of history dismisses the framework of a sacred history and discovers world history.[15] With Hume, an enlightened theory of knowledge surrenders the claim to give the idea of causality a foundation in reason and settles for deriving it from a mere habit of association.[16] And so on.[17]

Enlightenment, then, gains or communicates an understanding that finds the ordinary in the sublime, reduces the sacred to the profane, or proves the noble unworthy of respect.[18] Don Juan invites the statue of stone of the Commendatore to have dinner with him: this is the image of what enlightenment does in the field of understanding.

Wrongly to believe of something that it is noble, celestial, or sublime may be called superstition, in an extended sense: one can be superstitious not only in matters of religion but in art, politics, and history as well. Thus enlightenment is an understanding that subverts superstition of all kinds. With this Kant agrees after all: "Liberation from superstition is called enlightenment," he wrote a few years later.[19]

This is why enlightenment is primarily critical. Kant speaks in the same passage of "the merely negative, which is what enlightenment proper amounts to":[20] negative it is with respect to whatever purports to be of a higher order. People's tendency to imagine such things that are beyond them gives enlightenment its unending task. Thus one effect that is germane to enlightenment is distrust—distrust of grand speech as mere fantasy. In its tendency the world of enlightenment is, as the romantics correctly noted, a prosaic world, a world of ordinary things: these quiet enlightenment suspicion.

It may seem to be stacking the cards to describe enlightenment in this way as reductive understanding. To call it understanding is to imply that enlightenment is right in what it says, and similarly, to call superstition what enlightenment fights against is to imply that in any case its opponent is wrong. In fact there is no bias here. Yes, enlightenment is always right against its opponent, but of any given consideration or argument it is still the question whether it can rightly be called a piece of Enlightenment thought or merely claims that status. It is the question whether Hobbes's critique of religion, Spinoza's method of interpretation, Voltaire's philosophy of history, or whatever candidates may be put forward, deserve the label "enlightenment." According to the present usage, they only deserve it if they are true.

And how do we find out whether they are? The same way we find out about any statement whether it is true, by considering the arguments that can be advanced in the case at hand. To stay with the example from Hobbes, it is an argument in favor of his account of religion that there are many religions, for we know beforehand of the diversity of human imagination, and if religion grows from imagination, it should show variety, too. It is an argument against his account that sometimes religion stills the anxiety about what may happen, which would mean that religion, improbably, dries up its own source. Every such argument may in turn meet a counterargument, denying the alleged fact or explaining it in a different way, and so on: by discussing views in this way, we find out whether they are true.

Only in such discussion does enlightened thought prove its strength. Enlightenment is not a doctrine, nor is it a particular technique. What enlightened thought has to offer are considerations that are critical in tendency but enter the arena of thought on the same standing as any other. Thus, in particular, enlightenment is not a philosophical task. Perhaps answering the question "What is enlightenment?" is. Enlightenment is not. Enlightenment may be done by anyone anywhere. No particular kind of argument is specific for enlightenment, but its end is—which is desecration.

REASONS AGAINST ENLIGHTENMENT

Given what has been said, it is not a reason against enlightenment that its arguments are poor: only an understanding supported by good, or at any rate the best, arguments is to count as "enlightenment."

Nor do the rigidity and self-righteousness of alleged enlighteners speak against enlightenment. True, these are vices to which they are especially exposed. It is difficult not to pound the truth into a blind world, rather than make it inviting to open one's eyes. Still, this is a different point. Even somebody who offers enlightened thought gently is subject to the question whether enlightenment is a good idea in the first place.

Many think it is not. They do not say it as bluntly, for the term "enlightenment" carries a favorable prejudice, and it is no praise to be called an enemy of enlightenment. Still, what it comes down to is this: enlightenment is bad. It is supposed to be bad, whatever the strength of its arguments. Nor is it untenable right away to say such a thing. Since enlightenment consists in gaining or communicating a certain kind of understanding, such understanding may be correct and well supported, while gaining or communicating it may still be a bad thing. Truth may be harmful, and truth well argued for, too.

The reasons against enlightenment follow one pattern: reducing the high to the low, enlightenment deprives us of something vital. Ideas differ about what that is. Enlightenment is variously said to dissolve our fundamental values; to obliterate any genuine commitment and so to render all action arbitrary; to disorientate our life and turn it into a meaningless jumble. What these things mean and how they are related would certainly need further inquiry, but for now the vague idea may suffice. More urgent is the question, Why should the meaning and purpose of our actions depend on the specious grandeur that enlightenment attacks? Specious it is, since by hypothesis the arguments are sound which enlightenment offers.

One way, not to answer, but to avoid answering this question, is to tinker with the notion of truth: Yes, what enlightenment offers is true and well supported, but only in the enlightenment sense of the terms. There is another, a superior truth inaccessible to these reasonings, and in terms of this truth the higher things attacked by enlightenment are not specious. The mistake of enlightenment consists in confusing its truth with truth in general. This is a way to avoid answering the question, because it really ends the discussion with the enlightener. Once it is not truth in the same sense that the interlocutors are trying to reach, they are no more speaking to each other. It is no wonder that the idea of a superior kind of truth has never been clarified satisfactorily. That idea just indicates that the field of satisfactory clarifications has been left behind.

An answer to the question, if a poor one, is given by those who argue that we are not merely rational but also emotional creatures and that it is only when our emotions find suitable objects that we can experience our lives as substantial and meaningful. Now precisely the higher things that enlightenment disparages are those to which our emotion responds, and this is why the experience of meaning and purpose depends on them. (One could call this the argument for monarchy.) Unfounded here is the assumption that emotionally we starve without the grand things that enlightenment tries to subvert. The romantics indeed claimed that the prosaic world of enlightenment, leaving us nothing to divine, to revere, to adore, is a world of tedium; but there is little reason to accept their charge. Why should not the ordinary things that enlightenment favors fill our hearts as much? Why should only the specious be, literally, specious, that is, pleasing to look at? The fear of boredom from enlightenment appears, rather, to be a mere hangover from intoxication with the higher.

The strongest answer takes its cue from the way Hobbes expresses his critique of religion. Fear, he said, inclines the ignorant "to stand in awe of their own imaginations." This term "awe" is the same that Hobbes uses a number of times to describe the situation of those who, subjects of a sovereign power, are forced to obey its laws: Leviathan is "a common Power to keep them all in awe."[21] Now it may be argued that this coincidence of the words marks an identity in the matter. Hobbes taught in his political philosophy that humans will live together in peace only if they stand in awe of something. That truth has a wider purview than Hobbes thought. Humans will only do what is right and what is good, what is helpful and what is liberating, if they stand in awe, not just of the visible power of Leviathan but of the invisible power of God. Generalized to the other fields of Enlightenment critique, the argument says: only those who know something holy will lead a life worth living, a truly human life; he who recognizes only ordinary things will lack both respect and genuine love, his actions will be heartless, ruthless, and in the end destructive. This is why enlightenment is bad: however good its arguments, by "eradicating any trace of the holy,"[22] it dehumanizes life.

The metaphors commonly employed in such a critique of enlightenment give the idea more relief. It is said that without subordinating itself to something higher, human life loses its moorings, becomes floating, untied, dislocated, uprooted. The striking thing about these metaphors is that they put positive value exclusively on being anchored and tied to a place, whereas one may as well take as desirable being unfettered and afloat. It is similar with "family ties" and "bonds of affection": to be bound seems to be a good thing here, whereas ordinarily no one welcomes it. What makes these expressions nevertheless appear appropriate is the idea just indicated: a good human life depends on some things being, not just unmoved, but unmovable, so that we can be said to be tied to them; a good human life depends on recognizing something different from the ordinary things that may be handled as preferences and circumstances require; a good human life depends on something being holy.

Max Horkheimer and Theodor Adorno used the story of Ulysses and the Sirens to give their critique of enlightenment color: Ulysses is the exemplar of enlightenment since he listens to the Sirens' song and is ravished like anybody else, but by having himself tied to the mast he prevents himself from actually being seduced, thus subjugating nature and reducing the song to a source of ineffective aesthetic pleasure.[23] The story may be used in the opposite direction, too: Ulysses exemplifies the antienlightenment wisdom of the present argument in that he does not leave the decision about what to do to preferences and circumstances but ties himself and excludes some things, like going to the Sirens, once and for all from consideration, thereby saving himself. We will only live and live well, the moral of the story is on this reading, if we treat some things as sacred.

This Ulysses is too fearful a fellow, as is Horkheimer and Adorno's, for that matter. Both readings take for granted that he who listens to the song and is free to use his limbs cannot avoid disaster. Yet this idea itself may be a mere product of fearful imagination, like the ideas Hobbes discovered in religion. (The Sirens are demi-goddesses, after all.) Those who tie themselves to the mast from fear of the seductive women may have originated the false story that yielding to their song leads you inevitably onto the cliffs; and not the other way round, that because of the threatening cliffs they tie themselves to the mast. That is to say, tying himself may not be what saves Ulysses. Tying himself may be what deprives him, say, of a nice chat with these beautiful singers, or whatever else they could be doing together.

In other words, the present argument against enlightenment does not stand up. It is not true that a good human life needs something holy. We may well be doing better without the unmovable. It is not true that respect and love require the mysterious and inaccessible. We can appreciate and enjoy what we encounter in full daylight. It is not true that awe is legitimate in a wider field than Hobbes thought, in religion and elsewhere. On the contrary, it should be eliminated from political philosophy, too. People do not need to stand in awe of the mortal God Leviathan to live in peace together. It suffices that they reckon with being harmed, in case they violate the law, by those who have more power. To live and to live well does not take anything beyond the ordinary things that enlightenment cherishes.

"In what world are you living? Haven't you heard of the destruction of nature and of human things brought about precisely by those who do not recognize anything sacred, anything limiting the ruthless exercise of their technical powers?" It is necessary to distinguish here. Yes, the current destruction of human and nonhuman things is being brought about to a large extent by those who no longer revere what is higher. No, it is not being brought about by them because they no longer revere what is higher. They bring it about, or to speak more honestly, we bring it about, because we are doing things rashly, that is, we overlook side effects, underestimate risks, give misleadingly simple accounts of unfamiliar situations, and so forth, for the sake of a bigger or faster gain. Such rashness has nothing to do with enlightenment. Admittedly, enlightenment in the sense explained does not render agents more considerate. Neither does it foster rashness, however, and caution, prudence, patience, and consideration are not the privilege of those for whom there are higher things.

"Are you not impressed by the fact that for all the efforts of enlightenment, superstition, as it is called, did not perish, but is rising in power these days? All the things are returning that enlightenment has tried to chase, God, myth, nation, witchcraft, and their kin. That shows, doesn't it, that humans by nature need something higher than mere human things and that, consequently, the enterprise of enlightenment is bound to be futile and for that reason already bad?" No, it does not show that. First, we do not know of human nature in these matters, we only know of human history. So far we may have needed stories of higher things, but we may not need them from now on. Second, there is another explanation for the return of superstition: we are slow in learning, and even the best insight we do not easily preserve. Considering how long we have been practicing superstition, and how short enlightenment, it is no wonder that we are not at home with the latter. Finally, even if mankind should stick to superstition for the rest of its time, this shows only that enlightenment failed, for whatever reasons. It does not show that enlightenment, as we put it mythologically, was doomed to failure and therefore not a good idea to begin with.

"Still, even if man does not need to stand in awe of something, some people sometimes do need it. What enlightenment arrogantly calls superstition is sometimes for someone the condition of a tolerable, or even happy, life. So enlightenment, depriving a person of what she needs, is at least in these cases a bad thing." Such cases may well be rare, for we may not be as wedded to our superstitions as is usually supposed. Rare or not, there are such cases; and enlightenment is bad then. If the choice is really between truth and living well, the latter takes precedence: that is what we want above all. Still, it is hard to tell whether this *is* the choice in some particular situation; whether insight may not help in the long run. This is especially hard to tell because the enlightener's own position bears on the question, in this way: what she says may also, by virtue of being said by a trusted and trustworthy human being, help to heal the wound it caused.

In sum, there is no good reason to think that enlightenment as such is a bad thing. It is bad sometimes for some people. Nor should that be surprising. Any piece of insight offered at the wrong time to the wrong person may be harmful.

REASONS FOR ENLIGHTENMENT

Enlightenment is something people do. It is not a reason for doing enlightenment that it is, as such, not a bad thing. A reason for doing enlightenment is only that it is, in some way and to some extent, a good thing. So the question is: What is good about enlightenment? The question is the more urgent if in some cases enlightenment is harmful, for that would suggest to play it safe and to refrain from enlightenment entirely, unless something recommends it. Is there anything that does?

Two things. The first is the advantage promised by any understanding, enlightening or not. It is fun to know about things, and it helps. Just as people know more about the pancreas these days than they did thirty years ago and can better help those who are in trouble there, so people know more about the origin of the biblical writings now than at Spinoza's time and can better help those who have a problem with the meaning of some passage. According to the usage proposed here, the latter change counts as a piece of enlightenment, because applying the tools of philology to the biblical texts involved demoting them from the status of Holy Scriptures to that of any other text. The former change does not count as a piece of enlightenment, since it did not involve such a demotion (though an earlier step of enlightenment was needed to open the path for this kind of medical research). For the point at hand this difference is immaterial: enlightening or not, understanding recommends itself. To be sure, it does not recommend itself to everybody any time; "all humans by nature desire to understand"[24] is false. Still, for quite a number of us understanding is enjoyable or beneficial or both. That recommends it.

What enlightenment in particular promises is an open world: freedom. The ordinary things to which the enlightener reduces the false sublime present no barriers in principle to human action and to human understanding. Here, if anywhere, we are at home, it is our field, and we can move freely. Sacred or sublime things are, just as such, alien, so like in a dark unfamiliar room we hit our heads, or we go through tortuous gestures to avoid hitting them. It is an inconvenience "to take blessed water and to have masses read,"[25] and it is an inconvenience to declare one's allegiance to a national flag. By contrast, the world of enlightenment is like a valley opening before us that is inhabited and cultivated by humans: here there will be paths to go and to go upright.

If this is the fruit of enlightenment, how can anyone fail to be convinced and to join the endeavor? That is because moving freely is appreciated only by those who learned to enjoy their movements, and this joy does not grow well under the shadow of what is above us. In this way superstition even dims the eyes for the promise of enlightenment. Still, that works both ways: enlightenment in turn leads people to see what is enjoyable in it. As with other good things, the appetite for enlightenment comes with the eating.

NOTES

1. Immanuel Kant, "An Answer to the Question: What Is Enlightenment?" (1784) [author's translation].

2. The declaration opening the book *Du contrat social* is a characteristic mark of this way of thinking: "Man is born free, but everywhere he is in chains."

3. See the informative article by Manfred Sommer on *Mündigkeit* in *Historisches Wörterbuch der Philosophie* 6 (Darmstadt [Basel], 1984). In particular, Sommer points out that, contrary to what is widely supposed, *Unmündigkeit* is etymologically unconnected with *Mund*, "mouth." So the idea is not that somebody immature in this sense lacks, metaphorically, a mouth to speak up. "Unmündigkeit" derives from *munt*, a legal term now obsolete, and means the quality of not being one's own master legally, of not being sui juris. Still, as the articles on *mündig* and *unmündig* in Grimm, *Deutsches Wörterbuch*, show, the understanding of the word that follows the

mistaken etymology was already current in Luther and Lessing. Kant, however, does seem to take the word in the basic sense of "legal independence."

4. Johann Gottlieb Fichte, "Reclamation of the Freedom of Thought from the Princes of Europe" (translated above, pp. 128–131).

5. In *What Reason Demands* (Cambridge, 1988), chap. 5, I have argued against a similar mistake in Kant's moral philosophy. It takes autonomy even to submit to somebody's orders; autonomy is a condition of agency, not something that could be morally required of agents. Here is also the source of Kant's difficulty in preserving the concept of an immoral action: often it seems that what violates moral requirements thereby is disqualified for the status of an action too.

6. Kant, "What Is Orientation in Thinking?" (1786), final footnote: "The maxim always to think for oneself is the enlightenment." See Onora O'Neill's discussion of this point in her article "Reason and Politics in the Kantian Enterprise," in *Constructions of Reason* (Cambridge, 1989).

7. See Karl Leonhard Reinhold's essay above, p. 66.

8. "In Verbesserung unserer Einsichten vorzüglich in die Dinge, die mit uns genau verbunden sind." Christian Gotthilf Salzmann, *Carl von Carlsberg, oder über das menschliche Elend* 3 (Karlsruhe, 1787), 100.

9. Thomas Hobbes, *Leviathan*, chap. 11, penultimate paragraph.

10. This is the subtitle of the *Treatise of Human Nature.*

11. Carl Gustav Hempel, "The Function of General Laws in History" (1942), in *Aspects of Scientific Explanation* (New York, 1965), 232.

12. Friedrich Nietzsche, *Human, All Too Human* (*Menschliches, Allzumenschliches*, 1878), trans. R.J. Hollingdale (Cambridge, 1986).

13. Baruch de Spinoza, *Tractatus Theologico-Politicus* (1670), chap. 7.

14. Thomas Hobbes, *Leviathan* (1651), in particular, introduction and chap. 17.

15. Voltaire, *Essai sur l'histoire générale et sur les moeurs et l'esprit des nations* (1756) and *Philosophie de l'histoire* (1765), the latter becoming the introduction to the former in its 1769 edition.

16. David Hume, *A Treatise of Human Nature* (1739), Bk. I, pt. 3.

17. Nietzsche portrays this reductive attitude, though without relating it explicitly to enlightenment, in the opening section of the first part of *Genealogy of Morals*, where he describes the English psychologists of morals in the nineteenth century.

18. A similar conception of enlightenment emerges in G. W. F. Hegel's treatment: *Phenomenology of Spirit* (*Phänomenologie des Geistes*, 1807), trans. A. V. Miller (Oxford, 1977), sections 541–573.

19. Immanuel Kant, *Critique of Judgment* (*Kritik der Urteilskraft*, 1790), trans. J. H. Bernhard (New York, 1951), §40.

20. "das bloß Negative, welches die eigentliche Aufklärung ausmacht."

21. Hobbes, *Leviathan*, chap. 17, fourth paragraph.

22. The phrase is Novalis's: *Die Christenheit oder Europa* (1799), in *Schriften* III, ed. R. Samuel (Stuttgart, 1968), 515.

23. Max Horkheimer and Theodor W. Adorno, *Dialektik der Aufklärung* (Amsterdam, 1947), 76.

24. Aristotle, *Metaphysics*, first sentence.

25. Pascal's recommendation to the infidel, *Pensées* 418 (ed. L. Lafuma).

Reason Against Itself: Some Remarks on Enlightenment

Max Horkheimer

The collapse of a large part of the intellectual foundation of our civilization is to a certain extent the result of technical and scientific progress. Yet this progress is itself an outcome of the fight for the principles which are now in jeopardy, for instance, those of the individual and his happiness. Progress has a tendency to destroy the very ideas it is supposed to realize and unfold. Endangered by the process of technical civilization is the ability of independent thinking itself.

Reason today seems to suffer from a kind of disease. This is true in the life of the individual as well as of society. The individual pays for the tremendous achievements of modern industry, for his increased technical skill and access to goods and services, with a deepening impotence against the concentrated power of the society which he is supposed to control. He is ever engaged in modeling his whole existence, down to the minutest impulse, after prefabricated patterns of behavior and feeling.

These developments in the individual are the by-products of developments in industrial society. By the application of the industrial division of labor to the realm of the spirit, scientific reason has been separated from religious truth. Science, as a well-defined profession, sharply demarcated from philosophy, has almost relinquished its prerogative to tackle the most decisive problems of human existence. It may claim to probe occasionally into the functional significance of values, but their discovery, expression, or

These remarks are based on studies in which Theodor W. Adorno and the author have been engaged for a number of years. Some of the results are contained in two books to be published this year: Eclipse of Reason *(New York: Oxford University Press) and* Philosophische Fragmente *(Amsterdam: Querido). [Originally presented as a lecture at the Twentieth Annual meetings of the American Philosophical Association, Eugene, Oregon, December 28, 1946. Reprinted by permission of S. Fischer Verlag GmbH. Frankfurt am Main.* Philosophische Fragmente *was the original title of* Dialektik der Aufklärung—Ed.*]*

justification rests with other branches of culture. It abandons the definition of human aims to religion, the struggle for such aims to politics, and their dissemination to the mass media of communication. With regard to the blueprint of intellectual activities in our society, scientific thought is at best the supervisor, the architect being anonymous. If the scholar raises his voice against the use to which his findings are put, he speaks as a citizen, not as a scientist. Not only must he step out of his own special province in order to discuss such problems, but in the light of the strict separation of science from any other intellectual endeavor he cannot believe that the idea of truth, as it is implied in his research, might also apply to the ultimate decisions of society or the individual. Science is impartial with regard to what should be. It is devoted to means, whatever end may be served. Religion, in turn, is isolated on its reservation, neutralized and well protected within the modern world of industry. True, it fulfills, together with other culture-forms, important functions of social control. Yet, with the deliverance of Faith from the deadly struggle with secular Reason, much of its original substance seems to have dwindled away. Religion's fight against its enemies on the political scene has almost superseded its fight against the doubts within man's conscience. The emphasis is on its wholesomeness, on its contribution to civilization rather than on the truth of its specific doctrines. Religion is concerned with man's goals and destiny, science with truth alone. It is this division between the search for knowledge, on the one hand, and the evaluation of norms, on the other, which threatens to destroy all meaning.

The decay of independent thought in the individual and the dichotomy between scientific and religious truth in society are only two symptoms of the same dilemma characterizing our era. Philosophy, almost synonymous with Reason, should at least be able to show how the catastrophe came about. As technical civilization has emerged from precisely that undaunted Reason which it now is liquidating, Reason must reconstruct the history of its vicissitudes—try, as it were, to recollect its origins and understand its own inherent self-destructive trends and mechanisms, "for all inquiry and all learning is but recollection."[1] The overwhelming achievements of Reason in the domination of nature, both physical and psychological, have rendered it forgetful of the sacrifices by which these achievements were attained. Therefore today's mentality and wisdom, penetrating as they are, include an element of blindness and fanaticism.[2] Reason's ability to render an account of its transformation from the power by which the meaning of all things is perceived, to a mere instrumentality of self-preservation, is a condition of its recovery.

One specific development in the history of philosophy will exemplify the self-destructive tendency of Reason. The eighteenth century in France has been called the era of Enlightenment. The school of thought to which this term refers includes some of the greatest names of human history. The movement was not limited to a small elite but had a broad base in the French middle class. However, it was in the philosophical works of the *encyclopédistes* that the idea of enlightenment received its classical formulation. We might characterize this movement by two quotations from Voltaire: "Oh, philosopher," he exclaims, "the experiences of physics well observed, professions and industry, there you have the true philosophy."[3] The second quotation, taken from the same work, is: "Superstition sets the whole world in flames; philosophy extinguishes them."[4] The movement of Enlightenment, so typical of Western civilization, expresses the belief that the progress of science will finally do away with idolatry. Indeed, there are good reasons for this prediction.

Men have always been haunted by innumerable fears. In preliterate culture, the world was conceived in terms of evil forces, subject to control through propitiatory acts and magic. The process of emancipation from this conception of the universe is the predominant motive in the history of human culture. Each conquest of science has carried the attack deeper into the realm of fear. Science gives to man the power over that which earlier seemed completely under the control of uncanny forces. The awe of nature as an overwhelming unpredictable Being has been replaced by confidence in abstract formulae.

Thus nature changes its aspects. In the preanimistic age, nature bore the aspect of the terrible overwhelming entity Mana: then it assumed the mask of many spirits and gods who were characteristically vague and undefinable. In the epic poems of humanity such as those of Homer, gods took on clear contours; in classical philosophy as in that of Plato the gods were transformed into eternal concepts and ideas, or as by Empedocles into the elements of all things. Eventually, mythology, as the adequate expression of man's relationship with nature, vanished and mechanics and physics took its place. Nature lost every vestige of vital independent existence, all value of its own. It became dead matter—a heap of things.

Nevertheless, mythology has survived in various spheres of thought and behavior throughout the centuries. Idolatry is present in any absolute devotion to a finite entity, whatever it may be: a human being or a land, nature, or tradition. Thus, in romantic love, the beloved individual is deified; life and death depend on the favor or disfavor received from the adored. The reverence directed toward one's ancestors and the craving for immortality exemplify mythological reactions. In the absence of any residue of mythology, piety toward the dead or any rite becomes an empty mummery which the living enact for each other. The reverence manifests an attitude which no longer exists.

As far as the French Enlightenment is concerned, it tried to attack mythology in all its forms, even when incorporated in the most powerful institutions of the day. However, there were certain points at which they wittingly or unwittingly compromised. Among these were the body of principles believed essential to the functioning of the commonwealth, i.e., ethical and sometimes religious truths. These basic moral laws, according to the great enlighteners, were engraved on the mind of man. As Voltaire said,

> It is proven that nature alone instills in us useful ideas which precede all our reflections. . . . It is the same in morals. . . . God has given us a principle of universal Reason as he has given feathers to the birds or a fur to the bears; and this principle is so persevering that it subsists despite the passions which combat it, despite the tyrants who want to submerge it in blood, despite the imposters who want to destroy it through superstition.[5]

This principle of Reason expressed itself in the sentiments of justice and pity, which were, according to Voltaire, the basis of society.

Voltaire is not aware of the inconsistency between this doctrine and his other philosophical teachings. One does not with impunity embrace Locke's theory of knowledge and at the same time side with Leibniz when it comes to ethical truth. It is impossible to attack for long the awe of gods and demons and yet maintain reverence for the categories and principles of universal morality. This, however, is precisely the path which the philosophical founders of modern society, including Locke himself, tried to follow. Clearly it runs counter to the inner logic of enlightened thought itself. Scientific Reason, which uprooted the ideas of Plato no less efficiently than Plato undermined Homer's gods, is not in harmony with the doctrine of "native ideas" or any natural law or principle demanding respect as an eternal truth.

According to modern thinking, general concepts may figure in theories, providing they help us to predict and influence the course of events. This is how these concepts partake of truth, if such a thing at all exists. Science does not know any other meaning of this word. This also is the verdict of modern "philosophy of science," if we are permitted to speak roughly and without pretending to that precision which we admire in the formulations of this philosophy. The fact that so many thinkers of the last two or three centuries have tried to reconcile scientific thought with some kind of philosophical ethics and with the justification of certain social categories should not deceive us about the divergence of these two different endeavors. Philosophy, in terms of Voltaire's definition, namely as "the experiences of physics well observed, professions and industry," and philosophy in terms of the doctrine of "natural law" or any concepts such as "intuition" or "innate ideas" can only be combined artificially. The inherent tendency of the first conception of philosophy is to attack and destroy the second as being some kind of mythology, known today as metaphysics.

Since the sixteenth and seventeenth centuries metaphysics has been the attempt of representative thinkers to derive from Reason what in earlier days had come from revelation: the meaning and eternal maxims of human life. They tried to integrate theory and practice through intuition or dialectical insight. The more philosophical rationalism later on lost out to a nominalistic and empiricist epistemology, the more apparent became the weakness of the transition from the first to the second concept of philosophy, from the epistemological part of the respective system to the basic concepts of society. As far as Religion was concerned, the Epigoni of Enlightenment made a truce with it. The need for Faith was too imperative. Industrialist society put religion and science in two different drawers of its chromium filing cabinet. Metaphysics, however, during this rearrangement of the office, was thrown into the closet.

This process was not just intellectual. What we have outlined so far is merely one aspect of the economic and social development of this era: the streamlining of social life for the ruthless struggle for power over nature and man. In this fashion we may describe humanity's transition into the epoch of industrialism and mass culture. The consequences can hardly be exaggerated. By no means does industrial progress as expressed in intellectual enlightenment affect only such concepts as man, soul, freedom, justice, and humanity, which have a direct impact on moral and practical problems. It also concerns the meaning of the basic concepts of all philosophy, primarily the notions of concept, idea, judgment, and reason. All these terms are still used in everyday language as well as in scholarly works whether or not those who use them belong to the "philosophy of science" school. But there is no doctrine which would be in line with the modern development in technics and industry, and at the same time be able to supply these culturally decisive concepts with any adequate philosophical foundation or with any of the qualities that could inspire the reverence that was once given them. The respect which these principles today receive in speeches and treatises, and even in the hearts of people, should not lead us to overestimate their impregnability. They are undermined not only in scientific thought but in the public mind as well. Whereas Voltaire thought metaphysics was only for the *honnêtes gens*[6] and too good for shoemakers and housemaids,[7] for whom he wanted to preserve religion, we now see religion preserved for society in but a neutralized form, and metaphysical reason in disrepute even with what he called the "*canaille*".

The dwindling away of the philosophical substance, as it were, of all the decisive ideas in the face of the seemingly victorious Enlightenment, is one of the instances of the self-destructive trends of Reason. It is useless to differentiate here between individual Reason and Reason in social life, since the effects are felt in both of them and are brought about through a continuous and very delicate interaction of the various historical forces. As soon as our culture is put to a crucial test, we shall realize the extent of the destructive process which has taken place.

The concept of the individual, which in the history of Christian society results from the secularization of the idea of the eternal soul, shares the fate of all metaphysical categories. The entities to which these categories once referred lead a shadowy existence in the minds of men who still respond to their names if not to their meaning. However, such categories appear as completely irrational when confronted with the conceptual framework of modern science. The reverence which the modern scientist may exhibit with regard to them when they are used in a context other than that of his specific studies does not change the fact that the inner logic of science itself tends toward the idea of one truth which is completely opposed to the recognition of such entities as the soul and the individual.

The positivistic attempt to take refuge in a new kind of pluralism in order to maintain, in the face of scientific enlightenment, the moral and religious principles so necessary to the functioning of society, betrays the crisis in which society finds itself. Pluralism is the streamlined revival of the doctrine of "double truth" which, from the Averroists to Francis Bacon (that is, during the transition from the religious to the bourgeois idea of the individual), has played such a great role and now, at the decline of bourgeois individualism, is tried out again. Originally, double truth was invoked in order to permit science to emancipate the individual from dogmatic ideologies. Today, philosophy tries to keep science from emancipating society too energetically from even the secularized forms of such dogmas as the absolute value of the individual soul. But in the eager assurance of prominent representatives of science that it does not even so much as touch the conceptual framework of individualism, secular or theological, we notice a sign of bad conscience and despair. The times in which old and intelligent nations could shed their high humanistic culture overnight, as though it had been a dead skin, while science itself was worshiped and applied down to the last details of the murder factories, are still too fresh in our memories. Pluralism is a veil behind which the beliefs of the Western world, separated from the idea of binding truth, are fading away.

With regard to the individual, it is obvious that the ideological decay reflects the shrinkage of his economic and social basis. His rise and fall is deeply interconnected with the fate of middle-class property. The so-called transcendental factors which constitute the ego: memory and foresight, conceptual thinking, the integration of all experiences into one identical conscience knowing itself as the same in past and future, all these elements were tremendously enhanced by the economic situation of the independent producer and businessman. The enterprise, handed down in the family, forced him to think in terms which transcended by far his immediate needs, even his own life span. He thought of himself as an autonomous subject on whom depended not only his own well-being but the prosperity of his family as well as that of his community and state. There was no agency which would tell him what to produce or where and what to buy and sell. He had to plan all by himself, to rely on his own farsighted calculations.

In our days, these operations tend to be taken over more and more by collective agencies. On the one hand, social strata whose members in earlier centuries were never given the opportunity to develop so much as the rudiments of individuality are now being transformed into kinds of miniature economic subjects. They develop an ego whose conscious material interests, despite all the information thrust upon it, does not extend beyond its own life span. As long as prosperity lasts in peace and war they can depend on their skill. The same goes for their children. On the other hand, the independent entrepreneur is supplanted by the director or manager. He acts on objectivized economic and political interests and must conform to powerful groups and collectivities. Thus the structure of the human mind at both poles of society becomes more and more alike. Today the trend is toward increasing adjustment and conformity, toward being a good member of associations, corporations, unions, and teams. As society assumes many of the coordinating functions which had been exercised with so much friction within the human being, man seems more and more able to get along with a shrunken ego and to do without that highly developed inner life which once defined the individual. That is why the concept of the individual itself has become a romanticism. Despite official ideology it seems to yield to the social trends reflected by modern enlightenment.

One might ask whether our thesis of the self-liquidation of reason in recent Western history is not one-sided. Are there not many philosophical and other public currents which are in contradiction to the general development to which we referred? Although there are naturally some important countertendencies, attempting to bolster the collapsing categories, most of the philosophical and religious attempts at artificial respiration of old metaphysical doctrines contribute, against their will, to the pragmatization and dissolution of the concepts they hope to revive. The direct or naive contact with any supposed eternal entities or principles, whether they belong to a pagan or an orthodox philosophy, has been disrupted by technological development. Through being used for the purpose of modern mass manipulation the antiquated dogmas lose, as it were, the last spark of genuine life. There is no intellectual way back. The more strongly the masses feel that the concepts which are to be revitalized have no real basis in today's social reality, the more can they be led to accept these concepts only by mass hypnosis and, once accepted, the more will they adhere to them with fanaticism and not with reason. Mythologies which at one time represented the level of development reached by humanity are now left behind by the social process. Yet these same mythologies are often used by political factions which want to turn back the course of history. If these factions are victorious the masses must embrace their respective ideologies despite their incongruence with man's experience and skill in his industrial existence. The masses must force themselves into believing them. Truth is thus replaced by purpose and naive faith by boisterous allegiance. This is what we have witnessed so often in history and recently in Germany and other Fascist states.

The situation is similar when, instead of antiquated philosophies, new synthetic beliefs are to be instilled in the public mind. As long as they are not enforced by the state, they play the role of "mind cures" and fashions. However, as part of the manipulating machinery of any authoritarian government, they become commands, even more dehumanizing than those requiring abject outward behavior, for they dispossess man of his own conscience and make of him a mere agent of modern social trends. Each change in these synthetic beliefs, as decreed by the small group in power, however trifling in content, is accompanied by purges, by the destruction of human beings, intellectual potentialities, and works of art.

But if neither the revival of old nor the invention of new mythologies can check the course of Enlightenment, are we not thrown into a pessimistic attitude, a state of despair and nihilism? The answer to this critical objection is very simple but so seldom heard nowadays that the Sartrean version of existentialism appears to be quite revolutionary because it has assumed this attitude. The absence of a predetermined way out is certainly no argument against a line of thought. The resolution to follow the intrinsic logic of a subject regardless of the comforting or discomforting outcome is the prime condition of true theoretical thinking. As far as our situation today is concerned, there seems to be a kind of mortgage on any thinking, a self-imposed obligation to arrive at a cheerful conclusion. The compulsive effort to meet this obligation is one of the reasons why a positive conclusion is impossible. To free Reason from the fear of being called nihilistic might be one of the steps in its recovery. This secret fear might be at the bottom of Voltaire's inability to recognize the antagonism between the two concepts of philosophy, an inability contrary to the idea of Enlightenment itself. One might define the self-destructive tendency of Reason in its own conceptual realm as the positivistic dissolution of metaphysical concepts up to the concept of Reason itself. The philosophical task then is to insist on carrying the intellectual effort up to the full realization of the contradictions, resulting from this dissolution, between the various branches of culture and between culture and social reality, rather than to attempt to patch up the cracks in the edifice of our civilization by any falsely optimistic or harmonistic doctrine. Far from engaging in romanticism, as have so many eminent critics of Enlightenment, we should encourage Enlightenment to move forward even in the face of its most paradoxical consequences. Otherwise the intellectual decay of society's most cherished ideals will take place confusedly in the undercurrents of the public mind. The course of history will be hazily experienced as inescapable fate. This experience will provide a new and dangerous myth to lurk behind the external assurances of official ideology. The hope of Reason lies in the emancipation from its own fear of despair.

NOTES

1. Plato, *Meno*, 81.

2. To overcome our blindness in the midst of all the brand-new facts on which we look, modern philosophers of the most antagonistic schools have tried to draft methodologies aimed at obtaining access again to what is undistorted and concrete. Through a conscious and methodical effort they wish to regain the preconceptual sphere of life, the point of departure for any delineating, determining activity of the mind. Reason is supposed to get hold of itself by finding its way back to that point from which it started its triumphal march toward objectivization and quantification. In this respect, Husserl's phenomenology, notwithstanding the discrepancies of the two doctrines, indeed agrees with that of Hegel. Here lies one of the most potent motives for the theory of knowledge as it originated in the later part of the nineteenth century, particularly in neo-Kantianism. Furthermore, Bergson's metaphysical effort to replace "mechanical memory" by what he calls "independent recollections" is aimed at a return from the reified world of science to concrete reality and thus make Mind conscious of itself. In his endeavor to "*briser le cercle du donné*" (*L'Évolution créative* [Paris], 210), to break the circle of the given, Bergson is not so far from Dewey's early effort to break through the walls of static intellectualistic concepts to genuine experience. The recent attempts to lay open the fundamental structure of existence, which, as it were, has been covered by the cloak of business and scientific language and mentality, express the same perplexity. All these philosophers feel that Reason, on the verge of losing itself to its various practical functions, must reflect upon its genesis in order to remain identical with truth.

3. Voltaire, *Dictionnaire philosophique, Oeuvres complètes*, ed. Louis Molland [Paris, 1877–1885], 20:599.

4. Ibid., 20:452.

5. Ibid., 11:22–23.

6. Ibid., 39:167.

7. Ibid., 46:112.

What Is Enlightened Thinking?

Georg Picht

Translated by Garrett Green

"Enlightenment," according to the famous statement by Kant, "is man's emergence from his self-incurred immaturity." Enlightened thinking has always understood itself accordingly as thinking that, in the process of emancipation from guidance [*Bevormundung*] by theology and church, has achieved consciousness of itself and its freedom, hence consciousness of its own maturity [*Mündigkeit*]. Out of this historical process, which finds its first high point in Europe with the Renaissance and then in the seventeenth and eighteenth centuries finds the course on which we are still moving today, there emerged that new form of culture, society, and the state that we are accustomed to designate the "secular world." The secular world is not the natural world that is given to us; it is not the world in whose space the stars move, in which rivers flow, plants grow, in which birth and death occur; it is also not the world of relativity theory and quantum physics. The secular world, rather, is the one that emerged out of the process of secularization, the historical world of nineteenth- and twentieth-century civilization; it is the artificial world of the man of the technological age, produced by science, technology, economics, rational politics, administration, and social planning. As the product of the human will to power, it is in an eminent sense real; but at the same time we know that it arose out of the uncanny

The lecture offered here for discussion was delivered on 4 February 1967 at the Dozententag *of the Theological Faculty of the University of Heidelberg. It contains a few citations from my works "Aufklärung und Offenbarung" (Enlightenment and Revelation) (in* Der Gott der Philosophen und die Wissenschaft der Neuzeit *[Stuttgart, 1966]) and "Das Wesen des Ideals" (The Nature of the Ideal) (in* Festschrift für Professor Hans Bohnenkamp *[Weinheim, 1963]) but shifts the ideas developed there into another context. It lies outside my competence to develop the theological consequences that follow from the considerations presented here. I therefore publish this work as a question for theology that should be understood as an invitation to a conversation. [Originally published in* Zeitschrift für evangelische Ethik *11 (1967): 218–230.]*

marriage of rationality and utopian fantasy, that it is artificial, hence that its reality derives its aggressiveness and its dynamism from the negation of actuality as it is given. Because it is governed by rational thinking, the secular world is a world whose subject is, and wants to be, human reason. It is subjected to rule by human beings; the secular world is thus defined as a world for which man himself bears responsibility. Humanity in the twentieth century became enlightened concerning this responsibility less through its own insight than through historical experiences, in a manner that compels us to repeat Kant's question "What is enlightenment?" on a new level; we must test the Enlightenment itself and the whole sum of its results in the light of those critical principles that we owe to the first phase of the European Enlightenment. The question of the responsibility of thinking *in* the secular world *for* the secular world is not posed to this thinking from without, as an inappropriate demand; rather, in posing it we are following the original intention of this thinking itself. Thinking that achieves its self-consciousness in the emergence from a self-incurred immaturity understands itself as mature thinking. A person becomes mature when he assumes the right and the duty to bear responsibility in the future for himself and his action without oversight, that is, on his own authority. Enlightened thinking is thinking whose maturity shows itself in the fact that it is responsible for itself and its consequences. Thus enlightened thinking reaches its goal in comprehending its responsibility for thinking.

We are therefore allowing the method by which we wish to investigate the historical phenomenon of enlightenment to be sketched out by the intentions of the Enlightenment itself. We are thereby making a preliminary decision about the form in which the conversation between theology and secular science should be conducted. Theology cannot do justice to the phenomenon of enlightenment if it retreats to the very positions from which the Enlightenment has emancipated itself. Theology owes to the Age of Enlightenment the insight that the knowledge entrusted to it is denied when it understands itself as a timeless and ahistorical science and that it is thinking untheologically as long as it keeps chasing after history. Therefore, theology must without reservation join in the process of that enlightenment, which in the age of scientific civilization pervades and dominates the whole course of history. The more theology realizes the newly comprehended historicity of its thinking, hence the more thoroughly it comes to enlightenment itself, the more clearly will it become evident that the object of theology cannot be dissolved in the acid of enlightened thinking, that it cannot be secularized. Enlightened thinking has until now found the criterion of its own maturity in the fact that it recognizes no authority outside of itself from which it would let itself be determined or would let its standards be prescribed. It gives itself its own norms. Here reason is its own court of appeal; its responsibility is interpreted as self-responsibility. If we attempt to ask the question "What is enlightened thinking?" in an enlightened form, we must make ourselves participants in the responsibility of this thinking. For this reason theology too may not attempt to determine the essence of enlightenment from without; rather, it must try to clarify, on the basis of enlightened thinking itself, the meaning of the responsibility claimed by that thinking, which has devolved irrevocably upon it. Theology must thus attempt an enlightenment of the Enlightenment. In this sense we are investigating the implications, the possibilities, and the limits of a thinking that claims its own maturity.

After these preliminary remarks it is necessary for us to secure more precisely the ground on which we—thoughtlessly, perhaps—have placed ourselves. Still determinative for the self-understanding of scientific thinking in the twentieth century, in Germany at least, is the sharp division between the two types of life, the *vita contemplativa* and the *vita activa*, which Max Weber in his lectures on "Science as a Vocation" and "Politics as a Vocation" tried to keep alive in the world of modern industrial society. Science should be borne by an "ethic of conviction," which in the pure unconditionedness of its ascetic attitude refrains from asking after its own meaning and the consequences of its action. It is without responsibility and should be. The opposite type, the "ethic of responsibility," is reckoned exclusively to politics. Through his own thinking and influence Max Weber denied the division of science and politics that he postulated. It also contradicts his sociological argument that modern science based on the division of labor is determined by the structural laws of industrial production and is therefore constituted as an apparatus of power. The ideology of the two lectures by Max Weber nevertheless largely prevailed, at least in Germany, because it corresponds to the situation of interests—actual or alleged—of science. The connection of enlightenment and responsibility has an alienating effect and awakens the suspicion that the concept of responsibility has only been introduced in order to aid theology surreptitiously in a new grounding of its claims and to reestablish the immaturity that has scarcely been overcome. It will therefore be necessary to show that the assumption of real responsibility for this world, that human domination of the world and revolution, have from the beginning been regarded by the enlightened consciousness as the way to the realization of reason.

The concept of enlightenment was understood already by Kant as a concept in the philosophy of history. It intends to bring to expression the fact that according to the self-understanding of the eighteenth century a great turning point in the history of humanity had taken place at that time. That "revolution in the manner of thinking" which, according to Kant, begins in the natural sciences with Bacon and is consummated in metaphysics by the *Critique of Pure Reason* spreads in the process of enlightenment to the area of politics and here too, according to the expectation of the eighteenth century, will bring to an end the period of groping about and wandering astray. To the extent that reason becomes conscious of itself and achieves influence in shaping human relationships—to the extent, therefore, that humanity is able to become the subject of its own history—human history as a whole gains, according to Kant, what only individual sciences had attained in the past: a sense of direction and that secure forward course that has been described as "progress." By contrast, the history of humanity in the condition of its immaturity appears merely as prehistory without direction or goal. Thus it corresponds thoroughly to Kant's own interpretation of his epoch that the French Revolution began with a new reckoning of time. The emergence from self-incurred immaturity is the beginning of true history, determined by the autonomy of reason. Thus in his essay Kant answers the question "What is enlightenment?" not in terms of metaphysics but of politics and philosophy of history; he determines the historical locus of his own philosophy by conceiving his whole age as the Age of Enlightenment. Not the single individual but the whole epoch should free itself through enlightenment from the chains that held all previous history in bondage. The tool of enlightenment is criticism. Therefore Kant writes in a note to the preface to the first edition of the *Critique of Pure Reason* (A xii): "Our age is, in especial degree, the age of criticism, and to criticism everything must submit. Religion through its sanctity, and law-giving through its majesty, may seek to exempt themselves from it. But they then awaken just suspicion, and cannot claim the sincere respect which reason accords only to that which has been able to sustain the test of free and open examination."[1] That means that reason can carry out the enlightenment of itself and its task only by entering into the political struggle with the powers that rule the world and oppose the process of enlightenment. In the struggle for the freedom of public criticism, reason must also realize itself politically. Kant says in the Transcendental Doctrine of Method of the *Critique of Pure Reason* (B 766f.): "Reason depends on this freedom for its very existence. For reason has no dictatorial authority; its verdict is always simply the agreement of free citizens, of whom each one must be permitted to express, without let or hindrance, his objections or even his veto."[2] "On this freedom"—political freedom, as liberalism understood it—"reason depends for its very existence," for the concept of existence signified in Kant actual being in time. Every human being possesses reason as an ability. But the actual exercise of this ability (i.e., rational thought and rational action) is bound to the political freedom to make public use of one's reason in all matters. Thinking is thus enlightened only if it has achieved enlightenment concerning the fact that man can realize his own reasonableness only by simultaneously endeavoring to produce the political prerequisites that determine whether his rational ability will achieve existence.

Because enlightenment can be understood only as historical process and can be carried out only in historical process, it is not possible to confine it to a specific area of private existence, such as, for instance, the relationship of single individuals to religion. To the extent that enlightenment is carried out at all, it is always carried out in all areas at once. In religion it appears as the revolt of conscience and reason against clericalism and orthodoxy, as the struggle for tolerance against superstition and inquisition. In politics it appears as the struggle for freedom of thought, equal rights, and the commonweal against privileged capriciousness and despotism. In natural science it means empiricism and mechanism, technology and scientific expansion. In science generally it means the transference of natural scientific forms of thought and methods to the entire investigation of the knowable world. In philosophy it appears as liberation from the guardianship [*Vormundschaft*] of theology, as struggle against dogmatism and metaphysics, as analysis of consciousness and philosophical anthropology. Out of the ferment of this powerful movement of emancipation, the great ideas have proceeded on which rests the order of the secular world: human rights, separation of powers, toleration, domination of nature and the political world through science and technology—but above all, the great thought of the solidarity of all humanity beyond the borders of cultures and religions. No one can deny that wherever these ideas succeed in being realized human beings achieve a level of maturity that they can give up again only at the price of a relapse into barbarism and inhumanity. That we in Germany, in consciousness of the alleged superiority of German culture, believed ourselves capable of dismissing the naïveté and shallowness of the ideas of the Enlightenment—this fact we have had to pay for with catastrophes that should preserve us for all time from holding enlightened thinking in contempt.

The Enlightenment did not stop with Kant. Precisely in realizing itself it has gone beyond itself. We cannot follow this process here, but we are in need of a few marks of orientation before we are able to formulate the question as it is posed for us in the second half of the twentieth century.

If enlightened thinking posits standards for itself out of itself, if it is supposed to be its own tribunal, then the process of enlightenment itself invites the question who the subject of this thinking, the lawgiver of this tribunal, is supposed to be. The empirical individual cannot lay claim to this legislative role, for he is aware, precisely if he is enlightened, that by his drives and interests he is entangled in the world in manifold ways and subject to dependencies from which he cannot free himself for true autonomy. The liberal faith in the power of criticism and the free agreement of citizens called for by Kant is contradicted by political experience, even in the quiet republic of the sciences. It provides an incomplete answer at best, because it does not say what the free agreement rests on. Therefore the Enlightenment stands in need of a second step, a second-order enlightenment, as it were, able to enlighten us about how the subject of the free agreement of citizens—hence the *transcendental* reason—is constituted, and whence reason derives the ability to be the source of its own truth. The question of the subject of pure reason is inseparably bound up with the question of the possible source of the truth of reason; for reason is only autonomous—it is only mature in the Enlightenment sense—when it not only contains the ability to know but at the same time also contains in itself the light in which the known becomes visible. One and the same reason must be capable of being thought of not only as the power of knowledge but also at the same time as the source of truth; for if the truth had its source in another light, thinking would necessarily be heteronomous; in that case it could never achieve the form of maturity to which it lays claim. The question "What is enlightened thinking?" is therefore not to be separated from the following questions: By what light does thinking enlighten itself? What is the source of the *lumen naturale*? How is the essence of truth itself to be conceived if we are unable to separate reason and freedom, if, in other words, reason determines itself from the knowledge of truth? In this way "second-order enlightenment" leads with strict logical consistency to the question posed by Kant about the self-knowledge of pure reason. Space does not suffice to present the way in which this question, in the double form of the question of the subject of knowledge and of the light of knowledge, determines the course of thought from Kant to Hegel. It leads to the knowledge of God as the ultimate subject of subjectivity and finds its high point in the statement by Hegel: "philosophy has no other object but God and so is essentially rational theology and, as the servant of truth, a continual divine service."[3] This statement does not signify a retreat into the old immaturity; rather, it signifies the high point of the second great act of the Enlightenment: of philosophy from Kant to Hegel, in which reason, achieving enlightenment about its own essence, takes possession of the entire content of theology in order at last truly to become lord over theology, and as "rational theology" realizes absolute enlightenment as continual divine service.

The third act of the Enlightenment begins at the moment in which reason, knowing itself, achieves enlightenment concerning the fact that the historically existing subject of reason cannot postulate its own identity with the absolute subject of transcendental reason. At this point the history of the decline of reason begins. Only in this great world-historical drama—that is, in the history of thought of the last one hundred fifty years—has it become progressively clear which ideas held together the previous heroic phase of the European Enlightenment. If we want to understand the crisis into which reason was driven by the process of enlightenment, we must once again become clear about the simple postulates on which rested the faith in the power of reason at the high point of the European Enlightenment: we can trust that we reach enlightenment through the pure power of thinking, when our thinking produces out of itself the light in which we are enabled to know the facts of the matter to be clarified as they are related according to the laws of nature. The criterion for the truth of our thinking is the free agreement of all thinking human beings. We take a cognition to be true when every other person who is capable of thinking, so far as he is of good will, hence free, must reach the same cognition. Where such is the case, we say a cognition is secured. The subject of the cognition is thus no longer the single thinking individual, but rather the essence of all thinking human beings, who according to the same rules recognize the same thing, or the "transcendental subject"—that identity of the thinking consciousness in all human beings who are capable of thinking, on which rests the agreement by which they measure the truth of our cognition. What the individual thinks counts as true when it agrees with what all are able to think. The criterion of truth is the identity of the empirical with the transcendental consciousness. But enlightenment is not thereby secured, for the agreement might well be an agreement in blindness. The agreement can serve as a criterion of truth only if the ground of the agreement, the transcendental subjectivity, is simultaneously the condition of the possibility of the truth of the cognition, if it contains within itself the lumen naturale—that is, that light in which thought recognizes itself and the world. European thought since Plato gives the name "God" to the source of the light of cognition. The truth of the Enlightenment is therefore secured only if God can be thought of as the ground of the subjectivity of thought, as the absolute subject. The agreement of the rational thought of empirical individuals rests, then, on the agreement, mediated by transcendental subjectivity, of the reason of the empirical subject with the absolute subject—that is, with God—whose light appears in the rational thought of the individual who achieves enlightenment. Empirical thought is enlightened whenever universal and timeless rationality is represented within its temporal limitation. Through the process of enlightenment, temporal thought, that is, existence insofar as it becomes rational, gains the possibility, to cite Hegel, "of being manifested in the restrictedness of its own content as at the same time universality and as the soul which is alone with itself."[4] Absolute Spirit alienates itself in the limitation of the historical figures of reason, impresses on them the stamp of its own infinity, and thus returns to itself in them. God is the source of light and the cohesion of all rational thought in general. Therefore He is the absolute subject of reason.

In order to comprehend how the path that led the Enlightenment to this high point led by its own logic to the crisis of absolute thought, and thus simultaneously to the crisis of the Enlightenment, we must consider how this crisis already breaks out in Hegel's thought itself. Were we to take our orientation from other philosophers, such as Feuerbach or Marx, the suspicion might arise that the crisis is only a product of the decline of that royal road of the Enlightenment that Hegel exhibited and traversed. But if Hegel's thought itself falls into this crisis, the way to the crisis of reason and ultimately to the dissolution of reason is already prefigured by the consummation of the autonomy of reason in its ascent to absolute reason. The following reflections build on the work in which the philosophy of German idealism reflectively comprehends its own end: Hegel's *Aesthetics*. In the epoch from Kant's *Critique of Judgment* to Nietzsche, aesthetics became, for reasons that cannot be developed here, the fundamental metaphysical discipline; accordingly, we can explain the fact—surprising at first glance—that in Kant, in Schelling, in Hegel, and in Nietzsche aesthetics offers the deepest insight into the basic structure of their thought.

If we want to understand the circumstances that led to the failure of absolute thought, we need to recall that the secular world is not the world in itself but rather a product of enlightened thought. Rational thought subjects the world to the rational systems of the state, which it has itself produced, and to the technological economy. It objectivizes itself in these systems; it becomes objective spirit. The secular world is the product of this process. It is objectified—and in the objectification, as it were, congealed—reason; it is reason petrified and robbed of its freedom. The organizational matrix on which this world rests, its substructure, cannot be shaken precisely because it is reason become structure; for that which is organized by reason interlocks, dovetails, establishes functional interdependencies, and consequently cannot be forced apart without resulting in a universal catastrophe. By objectifying itself, reason also objectifies the identity on which the possibility of its truth rests. Therefore the products of reason objectifying itself in the social process always have the character of a system—more precisely, of a system of domination. But reason, as already mentioned, is frozen and petrified in these systems. By the act of objectification it has alienated itself from freedom; it is not autonomous vis-à-vis its own productions but rather heteronomous, and it is thus able to receive its freedom vis-à-vis its own constructions only in the form of negativity as free-floating individuality. Thus the bearers of enlightenment become intellectuals.

We want now to look at how Hegel himself describes this process. In the individual the autonomy of reason emerges as spiritual freedom; in Hegel it bears the name "independence." "True independence consists," as he says, "solely in the unity and interpenetration of individuality and universality. The universal wins concrete reality only through the individual, just as the individual and particular subject finds only in the universal the impregnable basis and genuine content of its actual being."[5] Here there emerges, however—and this is the remarkable aspect of Hegel's doctrine—an inevitable collision of autonomy with the reality of the modern world. Hegel establishes that freedom and independence cannot make their appearance if the conditions and relations of the surrounding world have achieved essential objectivity on their own and independently of that which is subjective and individual. The autonomy of this subjective reason is possible only so long as what is objective does not move and perform on its own, disengaged from the individuality of subjects, "because otherwise the individual retreats, as something purely subordinate, from the world as it exists already independent and cut and dried."[6] But this is precisely what has happened in the life of the modern state, in which particular individuals are "no longer... with their character and heart the sole mode of existence of the ethical powers. On the contrary, as happens in genuine states, the whole details of their mental attitude, their subjective opinions and feelings, have to be ruled by this legislative order and brought into harmony with it."[7] Hegel maintains: "in such a state of affairs the independence we required is not to be found."[8] Nothing less is said thereby than that the objective realization of autonomous reason in state and society severs the authentic nerve of autonomy—namely, the unity of empirical and transcendental reason—that reason, therefore, by realizing itself in the production of the secular world, destroys the condition of its own possibility—namely, the freedom of its rational existence. Reason itself, by objectifying itself in the schematisms of the state, of positive law, and of administration, begets a new and irrevocable heteronomy, and its subordination to its own products limits its freedom far more mercilessly than those old forms of immaturity from which it had freed itself in the process of enlightenment. Autonomy now maintains itself only as delusion or as the mere negativity of the subject that keeps itself free of the universal in its empty particularity, in its invalidated individuality. But that autonomy which plays within itself has lost the truth as well as the freedom of reason; for truth comes to light only where the universal manifests itself in the particular cognition. The consciousness of the intellectuals, thrown back upon separate particularity, *can* no longer be enlightened, for along with true independence it has simultaneously lost the possibility of truth.

The fatality of the situation into which the enlightened consciousness thereby falls—that reason estranges itself irrevocably from itself in its objective realization—shows up in the field of economics. The following citation comes not from Marx but rather from the aesthetics of Hegel.

> In this situation the long and complicated connection between needs and work, interests and their satisfaction, is completely developed in all its ramifications, and every individual, losing his independence, is tied down in an endless series of dependences on others. His own requirements are either not at all, or only to a very small extent, his own work, and, apart from this, every one of his activities proceeds not in an individual living way but more and more purely mechanically according to universal norms. Therefore there now enters into the midst of this industrial civilization, with its mutual exploitation and with people elbowing other people aside, the harshest cruelty of poverty

> on the one hand; on the other hand, if distress is to be removed [i.e., if the standard of living is to be raised], this can only happen by the wealth of individuals who are freed from working to satisfy their needs and can now devote themselves to higher interests. In that event of course, in this superfluity, the constant reflection of endless dependence is removed, and man is all the more withdrawn from all the accidents of business as he is no longer stuck in the sordidness of gain. But for this reason the individual is not at home even in his immediate environment, because it does not appear as his own work. What he surrounds himself with here has not been brought about by himself; it has been taken from the supply of what was already available, produced by others, and indeed in a most mechanical and therefore formal way, and acquired by him only through a long chain of efforts and needs foreign to himself.[9]

In this world substantial freedom and substantial truth are no longer possible. The realm of the absolute spirit now appears, according to Hegel's own word, as a realm of shadows. This recognition underlies the famous statement from the preface to the *Philosophy of Right*: "When philosophy paints its gray in gray, then has a shape of life grown old. By philosophy's gray in gray it cannot be rejuvenated but only understood. The owl of Minerva spreads its wings only with the falling of the dusk."[10]

There is not room here to delineate how the further course of the European Enlightenment led in Marx, in Nietzsche, or in Freud out of the dusk already falling in Hegel's philosophy into an ever deeper night. A single citation may suffice to make visible the terrible consistency that is at work here. It comes from Nietzsche's *Gay Science* and yet reads like a direct continuation of the passage from Hegel's *Philosophy of Right*.

> The greatest recent event—that "God is dead," that the belief in the Christian god has become unbelievable—is already beginning to cast its first shadows over Europe. For the few at least, whose eyes—the *suspicion* in whose eyes is strong and subtle enough for this spectacle, some sun seems to have set and some ancient and profound trust has been turned into doubt; to them our old world must appear daily more like evening, more mistrustful, stranger, "older." But in the main one may say: The event itself is far too great, too distant, too remote from the multitude's capacity for comprehension even for the tidings of it to be thought of as having *arrived* as yet. Much less may one suppose that many people know as yet *what* this event really means—and how much must collapse now that this faith has been undermined because it was built upon this faith, propped up by it, grown into it; for example, the whole of our European morality. This long plenitude and sequence of breakdown, destruction, ruin, and cataclysm that is now impended—who could guess enough of it today to be compelled to play the teacher and advance proclaimer of this monstrous logic of terror, the prophet of a gloom and an eclipse of the sun whose like has probably never yet occurred on earth?[11]

The God whom Nietzsche here says is dead, is, as I tried to show in another place,[12] that God whom Pascal called the God of the philosophers, the God of absolute metaphysics, the sun of the Platonic parable of the cave, which in modern philosophy had transformed itself into that absolute subject which reason must presuppose as ground of its subjectivity when in the sense of autonomy it tries to conceive its own ground as the source of the light in which it recognizes the truth of that which is. As soon as the emancipated—or, in Nietzsche's concept, the free—spirit recognizes that its freedom has dissociated itself irrevocably from the universality of objective spirit, the light of enlightenment is also extinguished. The way of enlightenment appears henceforth as a way of progressive darkening. It leads ever deeper into the shadow of an "eclipse of the sun whose like has probably never yet occurred on earth." The fearlessness of the enlightened spirit proves itself in the resolution not to evade the "shadows that must soon envelope Europe": "At long last the horizon appears free to us again, even if it should not be bright.... [A]ll the daring of the lover of knowledge is permitted again; the sea, *our* sea, lies open again; perhaps there has never been such an 'open sea.'"[13] But the openness of the horizon that is not bright is the openness for the fearless journey into night. The great noonday, toward which the journey aims, proves to be a noonday without sun. The Enlightenment has erred into a course that leads not into the clear but into the darkness.

The process of experience through which thought passed in the epoch of the eclipse of European philosophy has taught us that we can no longer equate the subject of thought with that light in which truth appears to us. The faculty of reason is no longer its own light. Both sides of the classical concept of the subject, which in Hegel were still dialectically mediated—being at once autonomous ego and ground of truth—have broken irrevocably asunder. We are able to ground neither the freedom of man nor the truth of his cognition on the subjectivity of his consciousness. The system of equations on which rested the classical concept of the subject, the classical concept of reason, and the classical concept of freedom was irrevocably burst open by the process of enlightenment itself. The enlightened consciousness saw itself forced to understand itself as historical consciousness; and when thought asks after the conditions of its possibility, it encounters, instead of the absolute, its own history in its relativity and finitude. Thus history becomes, instead of timeless identity, the actual content of philosophy. But history does not beget its own light. The insight into the truth of thought is lost in recalling the historicity of thought. In view of the inadequacy of a consciousness that has succumbed to relativity, thought becomes resigned before the ancient questions of the unity of being, the meaning of truth, and the conditions for the possibility of freedom—that is, the questions of the *unum*, *verum*, or *bonum* of classical metaphysics. One behaves like the fox toward the sour grapes: one declares oneself to be uninterested; and thus is realized in modern consciousness that phase in the history of the secular world that Nietzsche described as the phase of incomplete nihilism. In this phase it has become senseless to talk any longer with Hegel and Marx of alienation; for modern consciousness has discovered that that all-pervasive noncommitment of thought and action, which we attribute to the abdication of the question of truth and the foundation of our freedom, is the last comfort of modern man's intellectuality, absorbed in the enjoyment of its particularity. The Enlightenment has lost its sting; it is released from the duty of maturity and is no longer the foundation for man's responsibility for the system of objective spirit and the history of the secular world. It no longer liberates for political action but rather, like its adversary, religion, has become a private affair. One practices enlightenment no longer in parliament but rather on the psychotherapist's couch, in order that the adjustment of the individual to the mechanisms of society may take place with less friction.

But reason does not renounce with impunity the question of its own essence and of the conditions of its possibility. The abdication of reason's self-knowledge—thus the abdication of philosophy—has brought about a disintegration of reason in the last century, which defines the history of Europe in the period of its self-destruction. Because modern consciousness no longer feels itself bound to ask after the relation of freedom and truth, scientific thought submits to the schematism of those objectifications that at the same time produce and continuously reproduce the secular world. The functional principle to which thought submits is the principle of the mechanized division of labor, to which we owe the expansion of modern science and technology. But division of labor always means heteronomy. The basic principle of the Enlightenment, autonomy, has been so fundamentally abandoned in the system of the modern specialized sciences that thought does not even notice the loss of its enlightened freedom. Division of labor means disintegration. The rationality of the technological world is a disintegrated rationality. But since the reasonableness of reason was grounded in the relation of every individual cognition to the unity of the transcendental consciousness, the disintegrated rationality of the twentieth century has in the true sense of the word lost its reason; it is a reasonless rationality. More precisely: it is a rationality that is indifferent to reason or unreason. That shows itself most plainly at those points where the specific form of the rationality of modern science was carried to the extreme: in nuclear weapons systems and space technology. The instruments fashioned here serve insanity as well as reason. The rationality of their systems behaves in a manner indifferent to the possible consequences of their application. The indifference of modern rationality to reason and unreason is, however, the total negation of the basic principles of the Enlightenment. In the functionally secure systems of mathematicized science, that maturity of human reason for which the Enlightenment wanted to free itself is already excluded at the start. Kant's expression "self-incurred immaturity" applies here with a precision of which the eighteenth century could as yet anticipate nothing.

Simultaneously, however, the might of science and technology forges ahead into dimensions in which the future of all humanity becomes dependent on their commanding power. The *dominium terrae*[14] once promised to human beings has passed against their will, and as it were behind their backs, to a science that has always refused to accept responsibility for its own consequences. It bears responsibility for the future of the world whether it wants to or not. It is therefore condemned to enter into responsibility for its own action—to become enlightened about itself and its consequences, its internal possibilities, and its limits. At the outset I said: enlightened thought is thought whose maturity proves itself in the fact that it is responsible for itself and its results; therefore, enlightened thought reaches its goal in grasping the responsibility of thought. If a science that holds sway over the world does not transform itself in this sense into an enlightened science, if it perseveres in its present blindness and in self-forgetfulness of the reason that rules within it, then the name "secular world" will designate a world that prepares itself for its own end, because it is incapable of carrying out the enlightenment that is its fundamental law. Because rationality holds sway over the world, the enlightenment of reason about itself has become today the condition for the existence of all humanity. But since Nietzsche, reason is enlightened about the fact that the horizon in which it could achieve enlightenment has faded into the empty openness of an unending night. Reason no longer finds within itself the source of its own light; it is not capable any more of tracing out of itself the horizon of its own possibility. It is no longer possible to conceive autonomy as the condition of the possibility of reason; or expressed otherwise: it is not possible any longer to interpret freedom as autonomy. Freedom and truth are moving into a new context, as yet scarcely disclosed. To clarify it [*aufzuklären*] is the task of philosophy, insofar as it is the science of the conditions of the possibility of reason. If philosophy wishes to remain the science of science, for which it was once founded, it will fulfill its meaning in the twentieth century when it becomes the science of a comprehended enlightenment, in which reason discovers its responsibility in history as the ground of its possible freedom. Then philosophy will transform itself into a science of the transcendental and the real conditions for the possibility of human responsibility in history. According to its ancestry, however, the concept of responsibility is, as can be shown, a concept of Christian eschatology. It contains a kernel that is not to be secularized. Does the name "eschatology" perhaps designate that horizon of reason to be disclosed anew, in which thought could again discover its maturity? Does revelation set thought free for enlightenment? May it suffice to have posed these questions; the mere fact alone that it is thinkable to pose them in direct fulfillment of the process of enlightenment indicates an epochal turning point, which is taking place today in the relationship of faith and thought.

NOTES

1. *Immanuel Kant's Critique of Pure Reason,* trans. Norman Kemp Smith (New York, 1968), 9n.

2. Ibid., 593.

3. G. W. F. Hegel, *Aesthetics: Lectures on Fine Art,* trans. T. M. Knox (Oxford, 1975), 101 (Jubiläumsausgabe 12: 145f.). The term *Gottesdienst,* which Picht repeats in the following sentence, is the usual German term for "worship," though its literal meaning is "service of God" (cf. English "worship service"). Thus Hegel could be translated as saying that philosophy is "continual worship of God."—TRANS.

4. Hegel, *Aesthetics,* Knox 155 (JA 12: 215).

5. Hegel, *Aesthetics,* Knox 180 (JA 12: 247).

6. Hegel, *Aesthetics,* Knox 181 (JA 12: 248).

7. Hegel, *Aesthetics,* Knox 182 (JA 12: 250).

8. Hegel, *Aesthetics,* Knox 184 (JA 12: 252).

9. Hegel, *Aesthetics,* Knox 260 (JA 12: 350f.). [The bracketed interpolation is Knox's.]

10. *Hegel's Philosophy of Right,* trans. T. M. Knox (Oxford, 1945), 13 (Jubiläumsausgabe 7: 36f.).

11. Friedrich Nietzsche, *The Gay Science,* trans. Walter Kaufmann (New York, 1974), sec. 343.

12. Georg Picht, *Der Gott der Philosophen und die Wissenschaft der Neuzeit* (Stuttgart, 1966).—TRANS.

13. Nietzche, *The Gay Science,* sec. 343.

14. The "dominion over the earth" that God gave to the newly created human beings according to Gen. 1:26–28.—TRANS.

What Is Critique?

Michel Foucault

Translated by Kevin Paul Geiman

I would like to express my deep gratitude to you for inviting me to this meeting of the society. If I am not mistaken, I spoke here almost ten years ago on the subject "What Is an Author?"[1]

I do not have a title for the question on which I would like to speak today. M. Gouhier was kind enough to say that this was because of my stay in Japan.[2] To tell the truth, that is an amiable mitigation of the truth. Indeed, until the last few days, I could hardly find a title; or rather I had been haunted by one that I would prefer not to use. You will see why: it would have been immodest of me.

The question I want to speak about, one that I have always wanted to speak about, is this: What is critique? It is necessary to try to retain several points about this project that do not cease to take shape, to persist, to be reborn on the frontiers of philosophy—quite close to it, quite against it, at its expense, in the direction of a philosophy yet to come, in the place perhaps of every possible philosophy. And it seems that between the lofty Kantian enterprise and the small polemico-professional activities that bear the name "critique," there was in the modern West (dating, roughly, from the fifteenth to the sixteenth century) a certain manner of thinking, of speaking, likewise of acting, and a certain relation to what exists, to what one knows, to what one does, as well as a relation to society, to culture, to others, and all this one might name the "critical attitude." Of course, you will be surprised to hear that such a thing as a critical attitude exists, one that is specific to modern civilization, when there have been many critiques, polemics, and so forth, and when some of the Kantian problems no doubt

Lecture given at the Sorbonne on 27 May 1978 and first published as "Qu'est-ce que la critique [Critique et Aufklärung*]," *Bulletin de la Société française de Philosophie* 84 (1990): 35–63. A few preliminary remarks and the transcript of the discussion that followed the lecture have not been translated here.*

have origins dating much further back than the fifteenth and sixteenth centuries. It is equally surprising to see that I am trying to find a unity to this critique, even though it appears destined by nature, by function—I was going to say "by profession"—to dispersion, to dependence, to pure heteronomy. After all, critique only exists in relation with something other than itself: it is an instrument, a means for a future or a truth that it will not know and that it will not be; it is a gaze on a domain that it wants very much to police and where it is incapable of laying down the law. All this makes it a function that is subordinated in relation to that which is positively constituted by philosophy, science, politics, morals, law, literature, and so forth. And at the same time, whatever might be the pleasures or the compensations accompanying this curious activity of critique, it seems that it not only bears with it regularly enough—indeed, almost always—a certain inflexibility in its appeals to utility but that it also is undergirded by a more general sort of imperative—more general still than that of warding off errors. There is something in critique that is related to virtue. And in a certain way, what I wanted to speak to you about was the critical attitude as virtue in general.

There are many ways to construct the history of this critical attitude. I would like simply to suggest this one to you, which is—I repeat—*one* possible path, among many others. I will propose the following variation: the Christian pastoral, or the Christian church insofar as it deployed an activity that was precisely and specifically pastoral, developed this idea—unique, I believe, and completely foreign to ancient culture—that every individual, whatever his age or his status, from the beginning to the end of his life and down to the very details of his actions, ought to be governed and ought to let himself be governed, that is to say, be directed toward his salvation, by someone to whom he is bound in a total, and at the same time meticulous and detailed, relation of obedience. And this operation of direction toward salvation in a relation of obedience to someone must be performed in a triple relation to truth: truth understood as dogma; truth also insofar as this direction implies a certain mode of particular and individualizing knowledge of individuals; and finally insofar as this direction is deployed as a reflective technique comprised of general rules, particular kinds of knowledge, precepts, methods of examination, of confessions, of interviews, and so forth. After all one must not forget that what for centuries in the Greek church was called *techné technôn* and in the Roman Catholic church *ars artium* was precisely the direction of conscience; this was the art of governing men. This art of governing, of course, remained for a long time tied to relatively limited practices, tied ultimately, even in medieval society, to monastic existence and practiced above all in relatively restricted spiritual groups. But I believe that from the fifteenth century and right before the Reformation, one can say that there was a veritable explosion of the art of governing men, an explosion understood in two senses. A displacement first in relation to its religious source—let us say, if you will, a laicization—an expansion into civil society of this theme of the art of governing men and the methods for doing it. And then, second, the reduction of this art of governing in its various domains: how to govern children, how to govern the poor and beggars, how to govern a family, a house, how to govern armies, how to govern different groups, cities, states, how to govern one's own body, how to govern one's own mind. *How to govern*: I believe that that was one of the fundamental questions of the fifteenth or sixteenth century. A fundamental question to which the multiplication of all the arts of governing—pedagogical art, political art, economic art, if you will—and of all the institutions of government, in the broad sense that the word government had at this time, responded.

Now this governmentalization, which seems to me characteristic enough of these societies of the European West in the sixteenth century, cannot be dissociated from the question "How not to be governed?" I do not mean by this that governmentalization would be opposed, in a kind of inverted contrary affirmation, to "We do not want to be governed, and we do not want to be governed *at all.*" What I mean is that in the great anxiety surrounding the way to govern and in the inquiries into modes of governing, one detects a perpetual question, which would be: "How not to be governed *like that*, by that, in the name of these principles, in view of such objectives and by the means of such methods, not like that, not for that, not by them?" And if one really gives this simultaneous movement of governmentalization, of society and individuals, what I believe to have been its own historic insertion and fullness, it seems that one could identify in all this something close to what might be called the critical attitude. Against this, and like a counterpoint, or rather as at once partner and adversary of the arts of governing, as a way of suspecting them, of challenging them, of limiting them, of finding their right measure, of transforming them, of seeking to escape these arts of governing or, in any case, to displace them, as an essential reluctance, but also and in that way as a line of development of the arts of governing, there would have been something that would be born in Europe at this time, a kind of general cultural form, at once a moral and political attitude, a way of thinking, and so forth, and which I would simply call the art of not being governed, or the art of not being governed like that and at this price. And I would thus propose this general characterization as a rather preliminary definition of critique: the art of not being governed so much.

You will tell me that this definition is at once quite general, quite vague, quite fuzzy. But of course! Yet I still think that it allows me to locate several precise anchoring points for what I would like to call the critical attitude. Historical anchoring points, of course, which one could delineate in the following way:

1. First anchoring point: at a time when the governing of men was essentially a spiritual art or an essentially religious practice linked to the authority of a church, to the magisterium of Scripture, not wanting to be governed in that way was essentially seeking in Scripture a relationship other than the one that was linked to the operating function of God's teaching. To not want to be governed was a certain way of refusing, challenging, limiting (said as you like) the ecclesiastical magisterium. It was a return to Scripture, it was a question of what is authentic in Scripture, of what was actually written in Scripture, it was a question concerning the kind of truth Scripture tells, how to have access to this truth of Scripture in Scripture and perhaps despite what is written, until one arrives at the ultimately very simple question: Was Scripture true? In short, from Wycliffe to Pierre Bayle, I believe that critique was developed in an important, but of course not exclusive, part in relation to Scripture. Let us say that critique is historically biblical.

2. To not want to be governed—this is the second anchoring point—not wanting to be governed in this way is not to accept these laws because they are unjust, because they are antiquated, or because they hide an essential illegitimacy under the more or less threatening splendor given by their present-day sovereign. From this point of view, critique is thus, in the face of the government and the obedience it demands, to oppose universal and indefeasible rights to which every government—whatever it might be, whether it has to do with the monarch, the magistrate, the educator, or the father of the family—will have to submit. In short, this is where one finds the problem of natural law.

Natural law is certainly not an invention of the Renaissance, but from the sixteenth century on it took on a critical function, one it would always retain. To the question "How not to be governed?" it responds by saying: "What are the limits of the right to govern?" In fact, this is the place where critique is essentially juridical.

3. Finally, and I will note this very briefly, "not wanting to be governed" is, of course, not accepting as true what an authority tells you to be true, or at least it is not accepting it as true because an authority tells you that it is true. Rather, it is to accept it only if one thinks oneself that the reasons for accepting it are good. And this time, critique finds its anchoring point in the problem of certainty in the face of authority.

The Bible, right, science; writing, nature, the relation to self; the magisterium, the law, the authority of dogmatism. One sees how the game of governmentalization and critique, the one in relation to the other, gave rise to phenomena that are, I believe, cardinal in the history of Western culture, whether it is a matter of the development of the philological sciences, or the development of reflection, of juridical analysis, of methodological reflection. But above all, one sees that the focus of critique is essentially the cluster of relations that bind the one to the other, or the one to the two others, power, truth, and the subject. And if governmentalization is really this movement concerned with subjugating individuals in the very reality of a social practice by mechanisms of power that appeal to a truth, I will say that critique is the movement through which the subject gives itself the right to question truth concerning its power effects and to question power about its discourses of truth. Critique will be the art of voluntary inservitude, of reflective indocility. The essential function of critique would be that of desubjectification in the game of what one could call, in a word, the politics of truth.

I am arrogant enough to think that this definition, despite the fact that it is at once empirical, approximate, and deliciously distant in relation to the history it surveys, differs little from the one Kant gave, not of critique, but precisely of something else. Ultimately, it is not very far from the definition he gave of *Aufklärung*. It is indeed telling that in his 1784 text on the question "What is Aufklärung?" he defined Aufklärung in relation to a certain state of immaturity in which humanity would be maintained, and maintained authoritatively. Second, he defined this immaturity, he characterized it by a certain incapacity in which humanity would be held, an incapacity to make use of its own understanding without something that would be precisely the direction of another, and he used the word *leiten* whose religious meaning is historically well defined. Third, I believe that it is characteristic that Kant defined this incapacity by a certain correlation between an authority that is exercised and that maintains humanity in this state of immaturity, a correlation between this excess of authority and something that he considers, which he calls a lack of decision and courage. And so this definition of Aufklärung will not be only a historical or speculative one; in this definition of Aufklärung there will be something that appears a bit ridiculous to call "preaching," but in this description of Aufklärung Kant issues an appeal to courage. We must not forget that this is a newspaper article. A study is yet to be done of the relationship of philosophy to journalism beginning with the end of the eighteenth century—unless it has been done, but I'm not sure about that. It is quite interesting to see at what moment philosophers intervene in newspapers in order to say something that is for them philosophically interesting and that, however, is inscribed in a certain relation to the public with the purpose of an appeal. And finally it is characteristic that in this text on the Aufklärung Kant gives as examples of the maintenance of mankind in immaturity, and consequently as examples of the points on which Aufklärung ought to lift this state of immaturity and turn men in some way into adults, precisely religion, law, and knowledge. What Kant described as Aufklärung is indeed what I tried earlier to describe as critique, as that critical attitude one sees appear as a specific attitude in the West from, I believe, what was historically the great process of the governmentalization of society. And in relation to this Aufklärung (whose motto, you know well and Kant recalls it, is "*Sapere Aude*," but not without another voice, that of Frederick II, saying in counterpoint, "Let them reason as much as they want as long as they obey"), in any case, in relation to this Aufklärung, how is Kant going to define critique? Or in any case, for I do not claim to grasp what the Kantian critical project was in all its philosophical rigor (I would not even attempt this before such an audience of philosophers, for I am not a philosopher myself, being barely critical), how could one situate *critique* itself in relation to this Aufklärung? If, properly speaking, Kant calls critique the critical movement that preceded Aufklärung, how is he going to situate what he himself means by critique? I would say, and it sounds completely puerile, that in relation to Aufklärung, critique for Kant will be that which says to knowledge: Do you really know how far you can know? Reason as much as you like, but do you really know how far you can reason without danger? Critique will say, in sum, that our freedom rides less on what we undertake with more or less courage than in the idea we ourselves have of our knowledge and its limits and that, consequently, instead of allowing another to say "obey," it is at this moment, when one will have made for oneself a sound idea of one's own knowledge, that one will be able to discover the principle of autonomy, and one will no longer hear the "obey"; or rather the "obey" will be founded on autonomy itself.

I am not trying to show the opposition that Kant would make between the analysis of Aufklärung and the critical project. It would be, I believe, easy to show that for Kant himself, this true courage of knowing that was invoked by Aufklärung, this same courage of knowing [*savoir*] consists in recognizing the limits of knowledge [*connaissance*]; and it would be easy to show that for him autonomy is far from being opposed to obedience to sovereigns. But it no less remains that Kant affixed the understanding of knowledge to critique in his enterprise of desubjectification in relation to the game of power and truth, as a primordial task, as a prolegomena to any present and future Aufklärung.

I would not want to dwell further on the implications of this kind of slippage between Aufklärung and critique that Kant wanted to denote. I would simply insist on the historical aspect of the problem that is suggested to us by what happened in the nineteenth century. The history of the nineteenth century has laid itself open to the continuation of the kind of criticism—which Kant had placed somewhat in the background in relation to Aufklärung—with regard to something like Aufklärung itself. Or to phrase it another way, the history of the nineteenth century—and of course, the history of the twentieth century even more—seemed, if not obligated to decide in favor of Kant, at least to give substance to this new critical attitude, to this critical attitude hovering in the background of Aufklärung which Kant had foreseen as a possibility.

This historical foothold that seemed to be offered to Kantian critique much more than to the courage of the Aufklärung consisted quite simply of these three fundamental traits: first, a positivist science, that is, a science fundamentally having confidence in itself, even as it found itself carefully criticized with regard to each of its results; second, the development of a state or a state system that, on the one hand, presented itself as the profound reason and rationality of history and that, on the other, chose as instruments procedures of rationalizing the economy and society; whence the third trait, in the style of this scientific positivism and the development of states, a science of a state or a statism, if you will. A whole fabric of tight relations is woven between them insofar as science will play an increasingly determinate role in the development of productive forces; insofar as, on the other hand, the powers of a statist type will be exercised more and more across sophisticated technical ensembles. From there, the question of 1784, "What is Aufklärung?"—or rather the way in which Kant tried to situate his critical enterprise in relation to this question and to the answer he gave—this interrogation of the relations between Aufklärung and critique will legitimately take the demeanor of a distrustful, or in any case, of a more and more suspicious interrogation: for what excess of power, for what governmentalization (all the more ineluctable as it is justified in reason) is this reason itself historically responsible?

Now this question, I believe, did not turn out entirely the same in Germany and in France, for historical reasons that would be necessary to analyze because they are complex.

One could put it roughly this way: less perhaps because of the recent development of a completely new and rational state in Germany than because of a very old attachment of the universities to *Wissenschaft* and to administrative and state structures, this suspicion that there is something in rationalization and perhaps even in reason itself that is responsible for the excess of power, well, it seems to me that this suspicion was especially developed in Germany and let us say in order to cut this still shorter, that it was especially developed in what one could call a German Left. In any case, from the Hegelian Left to the Frankfurt School there was a whole critique of positivism, of objectivism, of rationalization, of techné and of technicization, a whole critique of the relations between the fundamental project of science and of technique that has as its objective making apparent the ties between a naive presumption of science, on the one hand, and the forms of domination proper to the form of contemporary society, on the other. To take as an example one who no doubt was most distanced from what one could call a critique of the Left, it must not be forgotten that in 1936 Husserl ascribed the contemporary crisis of European humanity to something where the question of the relations of knowledge to technique, of *epistemé* to *techné*, was at stake.

In France, the conditions of the exercise of philosophy and of political reflection were quite different, and because of that the critique of presumptuous reason and its specific effects of power do not seem to have been carried out in the same way. And it would be, I think, from within a certain thought of the Right during the nineteenth and twentieth centuries that one would find this same historical accusation of reason or of rationalization in the name of the effects of power it carries with it. In any case the bloc constituted by the Lumières and the Revolution no doubt hindered in a general way this relation of rationalization and power from being really and profoundly called into question. Perhaps, too, the fact that the Reformation—which I believe to have been, in its very profound roots, the first critical movement in the way of the art of not being governed—did not have in France the fullness and success it knew in Germany no doubt meant that in France this notion of Aufklärung with all the problems it posed did not have as great a significance, and besides it never took hold of a historical reference with as long a range as in Germany. Let us say that in France one was content with a certain political valorization of the eighteenth-century philosophes, at the same time as one downplayed the thought of the Lumières as a minor episode in the history of philosophy. In Germany, on the contrary, that which was understood by Aufklärung was considered, for better or worse, less important, but it was certainly considered an important episode, a kind of vivid manifestation of the profound destiny of Western reason. In the Aufklärung and in this whole period—which, in short, from the sixteenth to the eighteenth century serves as a reference for this notion of Aufklärung—one tried to decipher, to recognize the most prominent line of ascent of Western reason, while it was the politics to which it was tied that became the object of a distrustful examination. Such is, if you will, roughly, the chiasm that characterizes the way in which the problem of Aufklärung was posed during the nineteenth and the whole first half of the twentieth century in France and in Germany.

Now I believe that the situation in France has changed in the course of the last few years. In fact, it seems to me that in France we have come to a time when precisely this problem of Aufklärung (which had been so important for German thought since Mendelssohn, Kant, passing through Hegel, Nietzsche, Husserl, the Frankfurt School, etc.) can be taken up again in a meaningful enough proximity with, let us say, the works of the Frankfurt School. Let us say, I am again being brief, that—and this is not surprising—it is from phenomenology and the problems it raised that the question "What is Aufklärung?" returned to us. It returned to us, in effect, through the question of meaning [*sens*] and of what can constitute meaning. How does meaning arise from nonmeaning [*nonsens*]? How does meaning come to be? One really sees that this question is the complementary of this other one: How is it that the great movement of rationalization led us to so much noise, so much rage, so much silence and dismal mechanism? After all, it must not be forgotten that Sartre's *Nausea* is the contemporary within a few months of Husserl's *Crisis*. And it is through the postwar analysis of this, namely, that meaning is only constituted by systems of constraints characteristic of the signifying machinery, it is, it seems to me, through the analysis of this fact that there is meaning only through effects of coercion proper to structures, that—by a strange shortcut—the problem between *ratio* and *power* was recovered. I think too (and, no doubt, a study should be done of this) that the analyses of the history of the sciences, this whole problematization of the history of the sciences (which, also, is no doubt rooted in phenomenology, whose history in France followed an altogether different path, moving through Cavaillès, Bachelard, to Georges Canguilhem), it seems to me that the historical problem of the historicity of the sciences has some relations and analogies, echoes up to a certain point, with this problem of the constitution of meaning: How is this rationality born, how is it formed, from something that is wholly other? Here is the reciprocal and the inverse of the problem of Aufklärung: How is it that rationalization leads to the rage of power?

Now it seems that either this research on the constitution of meaning with the discovery that meaning is only constituted by the coercive structures of the signifier or the analysis made in the history of scientific rationality with the effects of constraint linked to its institutionalization and to the construction of models, all these historical researches, it seems to me, have only affirmed in a small way and, as it were, through an academic loophole, what was after all the basic movement of our history for the last century. For, by dint of our story that our social or economic organization lacked rationality, we found ourselves before—and I do not know if it is too much or not enough reason—in any case surely before too much power, by dint of hearing ourselves singing the promises of revolution—and I do not know if where revolution did occur it is good or bad—but we found ourselves before the inertia of a power that maintained itself indefinitely; and by dint of hearing ourselves singing of the opposition between the ideologies of violence and the veritable scientific theory of society, of the proletariat and of history, we found ourselves with two forms of power that resembled one another like two brothers: Fascism and Stalinism. Thus the return of the question "What is Aufklärung?" And in this way the series of problems that had distinguished Max Weber's analyses is reactivated: What is it about this rationalization that one agrees characterizes not only Western thought and science since the sixteenth century but also social relations, state organizations, economic practices, and perhaps even the behavior of individuals? What is it about this rationalization in its effects of constraint and perhaps of obfuscation, of a massive and growing and never radically contested implantation of a vast scientific and technical system?

The problem of "What is Aufklärung?" which we are truly obliged in France to take on our shoulders again can be approached by different paths. And I am absolutely not retracing the path by which I would like to approach it—and I would like for you to believe me—in a polemical or critical spirit: two reasons why I am seeking nothing other than to mark differences and in some way to see how far one can multiply, reduce, demarcate some in relation to the others, to dislocate, if you will, the forms of analyses of this problem of Aufklärung, which is perhaps after all the problem of modern philosophy.

I would like right away to note, in approaching this problem which makes us brothers with the Frankfurt School, that to make Aufklärung the central question at once means a number of things. It means first of all that one is engaged in a practice that one could call historicophilosophical, which is nothing like the philosophy of history and the history of philosophy, a certain historicophilosophical practice, and by that I mean that the domain of experience to which this philosophical labor refers does not absolutely exclude any other. This is not interior experience, these are not the fundamental structures of scientific knowledge, but neither is this an ensemble of historical contents elaborated elsewhere, prepared by the historians and received ready-made as facts. In fact, in this historicophilosophical practice it is a matter of making one's own history, of fabricating as through fiction the history that would be traversed by the question of the relations between the structures of rationality that articulate the true discourse and the mechanisms of subjugation that are tied to it. One really sees that this question displaces the historical objects that are habitual and familiar to the historians in the direction of the problems of the subject and of truth with which historians are not concerned. One sees too that this question puts philosophical labor, philosophical thought, philosophical analysis into empirical contents sketched out precisely by it. Thus, if you will, before this historical or philosophical labor, historians are going to say "Yes, yes, of course, perhaps," in any case this is never completely like that, which is the effect of the confusion due to this displacement toward the subject and the truth of which I spoke. And the philosophers, even if they don't get their feathers ruffled, generally think, "Philosophy, despite everything, is something else altogether," this being due to the effect of the fall, due to this return to an empiricity that is not even guaranteed by an interior experience.

On the one hand, let us grant these voices all the importance they have, and this importance is great. They indicate at least negatively that one is on the right track, that is, that across the historical contents one elaborates and to which one is tied because they are true or because they count as true, one asks the question: What am I then, I who belong to this humanity, perhaps to this fringe, to this moment, to this instant of humanity that is subjected to the power of truth in general and of truths in particular? To desubjectify the philosophical question by referring to its historical content, to liberate the historical contents questioning the effects of power from this truth which they are supposed to restore, this is, if you will, the first characteristic of this historicophilosophical practice. On the other hand, this historicophilosophical practice evidently finds itself in a privileged relation to a certain empirically determinable epoch: even if it is relatively and necessarily fuzzy, this epoch is, of course, designated as a moment in the formation of modern humanity, "Aufklärung" in the broad sense of the term to which Kant, Weber, and so forth, referred, a period without a fixed date, with multiple entries because one can define it just as well by the formation of capitalism, the constitution of the bourgeois world, the establishment of the state system, the foundation of modern science with all its correlative techniques, the organization of an opposition between the art of being governed and that of not being governed in such a manner. The relationship of historicophilosophical labor to this period is privileged because it is there that these relations among power, truth, and the subject that it is concerned with analyzing appear in some way, raw and at the surface of visible transformations. But it is privileged too in the sense that it forms from there a matrix for the course of a whole series of other possible domains. Let us say, if you will, that it is not because one privileges the eighteenth century, because one is interested in it, that one encounters the problem of Aufklärung; I would say that it is because one wants to pose fundamentally the problem "What is Aufklärung?" that one encounters the historical scheme of our modernity. It will not be a matter of saying that the fifth-century Greeks are a little like eighteenth-century philosophers or that the twelfth century was already a kind of Renaissance, but rather of trying to see under what conditions, at the price of what modifications or what generalizations, one can apply to any moment of history this question of Aufklärung, the relationship of power, truth, and the subject.

Such is the general framework of this research that I would call historicophilosophical, and here is how one can now carry it out.

I said earlier that I wanted in any case to trace very vaguely other possible paths than those that seem to me until now to have been the most readily trodden. This is in no way to accuse them of leading nowhere or of bearing no valid result. I wanted simply to say and to suggest this: it seems to me that this question of Aufklärung since Kant, because of Kant, and likely because of the slippage between Aufklärung and critique that he introduced, was essentially posed in terms of knowledge, that is to say, in departing from what was the historic destiny of knowledge at the moment of the constitution of modern science; that is also to say, in seeking in this destiny what already marked the undetermined effects of power to which it would necessarily be linked by objectivism, positivism, technology, and so forth, by referring this knowledge to the conditions of constitution and of legitimacy of all possible knowledge, and finally, in seeking how the passage outside of legitimacy had taken place (illusion, error, oversight, recovery, etc.). In a word, it is the procedure of analysis that seems to me at bottom to have been engaged by the slippage of critique in relation to Aufklärung effected by Kant. It seems to me that from there, one has a procedure of analysis that is at bottom that which was followed most often, a procedure of analysis one could call an inquiry into the legitimacy of the historical modes of knowing. It is in any case in this way that a certain number of philosophers of the eighteenth century, it is in this way that Dilthey, Habermas, and so forth, understood it. More simply still: what false idea did knowledge make of itself, and to what excessive use was it found exposed, to what domination consequently was it found tied?

Well, rather than this procedure, which takes the form of an inquiry into the legitimacy of historical modes of knowing, one could perhaps envision a different procedure. It could take as an entry into the question of Aufklärung, not the problem of knowledge, but that of power, it would proceed, not as an inquiry into legitimacy, but as something I would call a test of eventialization [*événementialisation*]. Pardon the horror of the word! And, quickly, what does it mean? What I would mean by procedure of eventialization, may the historians cry horror, would be this: first to take ensembles of elements where one can detect in a first approximation, thus in a completely empirical and provisional way, connections between mechanisms of coercion and contents of knowledge—diverse mechanisms of coercion, perhaps even legislative ensembles, regulations, material devices, phenomena of authority, and so on; contents of knowledge that one will take equally in their diversity and in their heterogeneity, and which one will retain in function of the effects of power of which they are bearers in that they are valid as making part of a system of knowledge. What one seeks then is not to know what is true or false, justified or not justified, real or illusory, scientific or ideological, legitimate or abusive. One seeks to know what are the ties, what are the connections that can be marked between mechanisms of coercion and elements of knowledge, what games of dismissal and support are developed from the one to the others, what it is that enables some element of knowledge to take up effects of power assigned in a similar system to a true or probable or uncertain or false element, and what it is that enables some process of coercion to acquire the form and the justifications proper to a rational, calculated, technically efficient, and so forth, element.

Hence, at this first level, not to work out the distribution of legitimacy, not to fix the point of error and illusion.

And it is why, at this level, it seems to me that one can use two words that do not have the function of designating entities, forces, or such things as transcendentals, but only of effecting, in relation to the domains to which they refer, a systematic reduction of value: let us call it a neutralization of the effects of legitimacy and an illumination of what, at a given moment, makes them acceptable and which allows for their actual acceptance. Thus, the word *knowledge* [*savoir*] is used to refer to all the procedures and all the effects of knowledge [*connaissance*] that are acceptable at a given moment and in a defined domain; and second, the term "power" does nothing other than cover a whole series of particular mechanisms, definable and defined, that seem capable of inducing behaviors or discourses. One sees immediately that these two terms only have a methodological role: it is not a matter of locating across them general principles of reality, but of fixing in some way the frontier of the analysis, the type of element that ought to be pertinent for it. It is a matter in this way of avoiding triggering the entrance of the perspective of legitimation as the terms "knowledge" [*connaissance*] or "domination" do. It is also a matter, at every moment of the analysis, of being able to give them a determinate and precise content, some element of knowledge, some mechanism of power; one ought never consider that there exists *a* knowledge or *a* power, still worse *the* knowledge or *the* power that would be in themselves operative. Knowledge, power, this is only a grid of analysis. One sees also that this grid is not composed of two categories of elements foreign to one another, those of knowledge on one side and those of power on the other—and what I said about them earlier made them exterior to one another. For nothing can appear as an element of knowledge if, on the one hand, it does not conform to an ensemble of rules and constraints characteristic, for example, of some kind of scientific discourse in a given epoch, and if, on the other, it is not endowed with effects of coercion or simply incitation proper to what is valid as scientific or simply rational or simply commonly received, and so on. Inversely, nothing can function as a mechanism of power if it is not exerted according to procedures, instruments, means, or objectives that can be valid in more or less coherent systems of knowledge. Thus it is not a matter of describing what knowledge is and what power is and how the one would repress the other or how the other would abuse the one, but rather it is a matter of describing a nexus of knowledge-power that allows one to grasp what constitutes a system's acceptability, be it the system of mental illness, of punishment, of delinquency, of sexuality, and so on.

In short, it seems to me that the path from the empirical observability for us of an ensemble to its historical acceptability, to the very epoch when it is effectively observable, passes through an analysis of the knowledge-power nexus that supports it, grasps it from the fact that it is accepted, in the direction of what makes it acceptable not, of course, in general, but solely where it is accepted: this is what one could characterize as grasping it in its positivity. Thus one has there a kind of procedure, which, beyond the concerns of legitimation and consequently moving away from the fundamental point of view of law, runs the cycle of positivity in moving from the fact of the acceptance to the system of acceptability analyzed on the basis of the knowledge-power game. Let us say that this approximates the level of archaeology.

Second, one sees immediately that from this type of analysis a certain number of dangers threaten, which can only appear as the negative and costly consequences of similar analysis.

These positivities are ensembles that are not self-evident in the sense that whatever may be the habit or the usage that rendered them familiar to us, whatever may be the blinding force of the mechanisms of power that they put into play or whatever may be the justifications they elaborated, they were not made acceptable by some originary right; and that which it is a matter of making stand out in order to grasp what could make them acceptable is precisely that which is not self-evident, it was inscribed in no a priori, it was contained in no anterior condition. Bringing out the conditions of acceptability of a system and following the lines of rupture that mark its emergence are two correlative operations. It was not at all a matter of course that madness and mental illness be superimposed in the institutional and scientific system of psychiatry; it was no more a matter of course that the punitive processes, imprisonment and the discipline of the penitentiary, came to be articulated in a penal system; it was no more a matter of course that desire, concupiscence, the sexual behavior of individuals ought effectively be articulated by one another in a system of knowledge and normalcy called sexuality. The locating of the acceptability of a system is inseparable from the locating of what made it difficult to accept: its arbitrariness in terms of knowledge, its violence in terms of power, in short, its energy. Thus the necessity of occupying oneself with this structure in order to better follow its artifices.

The second consequence, also costly and negative, is that these ensembles are not analyzed as universals to which history, with its particular circumstances, would bring a certain number of modifications. Of course, many accepted elements, many conditions of acceptability, can have a long career behind them; but what is a matter of grasping in the analysis of these positivities is that they are in some way pure singularities, not the incarnation of an essence, not the individualization of a species: singularity as madness in the modern Western world, singularity absolute as sexuality, singularity absolute as the juridic-moral system of our punishments.

No founding recourse, no escape into a pure form—that is no doubt one of the most important and most contestable points of this historicophilosophical approach: if it does not want to fall either into a philosophy of history or into a historical analysis, it ought to maintain itself in the field of immanence of pure singularities. What then? Rupture, discontinuity, singularity, pure description, immobile tableau, no explanation, no passage, you know all that. It will be said that the analysis of these positivities is not elevated to those procedures called explanatory to which one ascribes a causal value on three conditions: (1) one only grants causal value to the explanations that aim at a last instance valued as profound and unique, economy for some, demography for others; (2) one only grants as having causal value that which obeys a principle of pyramidization pointing toward the cause or the causal source, the unitary origin; and finally (3) one only grants causal value to that which establishes a certain inevitability or at least that which approaches necessity. The analysis of positivities, to the extent that it has to do with pure singularities related not to a species or an essence but to simple conditions of acceptability, supposes the deployment of a causal network that is at once complex and tight, but no doubt of another type, a causal network that would not obey precisely the requirement of saturation by a profound, unitary, pyramidalizing, and necessitating principle. It is a matter of establishing a network that takes account of this singularity as an effect: hence the necessity of the multiplicity of relations, of the differentiation between the different types of relations, of the differentiation between the different forms of necessity of the linkages, of deciphering interactions and circular actions, and of taking into account the intersection of heterogeneous processes. And hence nothing is more foreign to such an analysis than the rejection of causality. But what is important is that it is not a matter in such analyses of reducing an ensemble of derived phenomena to one cause, but of making intelligible a singular positivity in that which is precisely singular.

Let us say roughly that in opposition to a genesis that orients itself toward the unity of a weighty principal cause of a multiple descent, we are concerned here with a *genealogy*, that is, of something that tries to restore the conditions of appearance of a singularity from multiple determining elements, of which it would appear, not as the product, but as the effect. Thus this singularity is made intelligible, but it is not seen as functioning according to a principle of closure. We are not concerned here with a principle of closure for a number of reasons.

The first is that the relations that allow one to take account of this singular effect are, if not in their totality, at least in a considerable part, relations of interactions between individuals or groups, that is, that they imply subjects, types of behaviors, decisions, choices: it is not in the nature of things that one could find the backing, the support of this network of intelligible relations; it is the logic proper to a game of interactions with its always variable margins of noncertitude.

No closure either, because the relations that one tries to establish in order to account for a singularity as effect, this network of relations, ought not constitute a unique plan. These are relations that are perpetually being undone in relation to one another. The logic of interactions at a given level plays between individuals, being able at once to guard its rules and its specificity, its singular effects, all the while constituting interactions with other elements that run at another level in such a way that, in a certain fashion, none of these interactions appears primary or absolutely totalizing. Each one can be replaced in a game that extends beyond it; and inversely none, as local as it may be, is without effect or without risk of effect on that of which it is a part and which envelops it. Thus, if you will and schematically, there is a perpetual mobility, an essential fragility, or rather an intermingling, between that which accompanies the same process and that which transforms it. In short, it would be a matter here of deriving a whole mode of analyses that could be called *strategic*.

In speaking of archaeology, strategy, and genealogy, I am not thinking that it is a matter of marking the three successive levels that would be developed on the basis of one another, but rather of characterizing three necessarily simultaneous dimensions of the same analysis, three dimensions that would allow in their very simultaneity the grasping of what is positive, that is, what the conditions are which make acceptable a singularity whose intelligibility is established by marking the interactions and strategies in which it is integrated. Such research takes into account . . . [several sentences are missing because of the turning over of the cassette] . . . is produced as effect, and finally eventialization in that one has to deal with something whose stability, whose rooting, whose foundation is never such that one cannot in one way or another, if not think its disappearance, at least mark that through which and that from which its disappearance is possible.

I said earlier that, rather than pose the problem in terms of knowledge [*connaissance*] and legitimation, it was a matter of approaching indirectly the question of power and eventialization. But you see, it is not a matter of making power understood as domination or mastery by way of a fundamental given, a unique principle of explanation, or of a law that cannot be gotten around; on the contrary, it is always a matter of considering it as a relation in a field of interactions, it is a matter of thinking it in an inseparable relation with forms of knowledge, and it is always a matter of thinking it in such a way that one sees it associated with a domain of possibility and consequently of reversibility, of possible reversal.

You see that in this way the question is no longer: Through what error, illusion, forgetting, by what lack of legitimacy does knowledge come to induce effects of domination that show the hold of [inaudible word] in the modern world? The question would rather be this: How can the inseparability of knowledge and power in the game of multiple interactions and strategies induce at once singularities that fix themselves on the basis of their conditions of acceptability and a field of possibilities, of openings, of indecisions, of reversals, and of eventual dislocations that make them fragile, that make them impermanent, that make of these effects events—nothing more, nothing less than events? In what way can the effects of the coercion proper to these positivities not be dissipated by a return to the legitimate destination of knowledge and by a reflection on the transcendental or the quasi-transcendental that fixes it, but rather be inverted or undone inside a concrete strategic field, this concrete strategic field that induced them, and from the decision precisely to not be governed?

In sum, would one not now have to try to take the inverse path to the movement that tipped the critical attitude into the question of critique or, rather, to the movement that made the enterprise of Aufklärung again part of the critical project in such a way that knowledge can make a proper idea, would one not now have to try to take the inverse path to this movement of tipping over, to this slippage, to this way of displacing the question of Aufklärung onto critique? Could one not try to take this path, but in the other direction? And if it is necessary to pose the question of knowledge [*connaissance*] in its relation to domination, it would be first and foremost on the basis of a certain decisive will not to be governed, this decisive will, an attitude at once individual and collective of emerging, as Kant said, from one's immaturity. A question of attitude. You see why I was not able to give, to dare to give, a title to my paper which would have been "What Is Aufklärung?"

NOTES

1. Michel Foucault, "What Is an Author?" trans. Donald F. Bouchard and Sherry Simon, in *Language, Counter-Memory, Practice* (Ithaca, 1977), 113–138.—TRANS.

2. Henri Gouhier had opened the meeting of the Société française de philosophie by explaining that Foucault did not submit a title for his talk because of his extended visit to Japan.—TRANS.

The Unity of Reason in the Diversity of Its Voices

Jürgen Habermas

Translated by William Mark Hohengarten

"The One and the Many," unity and plurality, designates the theme that has governed metaphysics from its inception. Metaphysics believes it can trace everything back to one. Since Plato, it has presented itself in its definitive forms as the doctrine of universal unity; theory is directed toward the one as the origin and ground of everything. Prior to Plotinus, this one was called the idea of the good or of the first mover; after him, it was called *summum ens*, the unconditioned, or absolute spirit. During the last decade this theme has taken on renewed relevance. One side bemoans the loss of the unitary thinking of metaphysics and is working either on a rehabilitation of pre-Kantian figures of thought or on a return to metaphysics that goes beyond Kant.[1] Conversely, the other side attributes responsibility for the crises of the present to the metaphysical legacy left by unitary thinking within the philosophy of the subject and the philosophy of history. This side invokes plural histories and forms of life in opposition to a singular world history and lifeworld, the alterity of language games and discourses in opposition to the identity of language and dialogue, and scintillating contexts in opposition to univocally fixed meanings. To be sure, this protest against unity made in the name of a suppressed plurality expresses itself in two opposed versions. In the radical contextualism of a Lyotard or a Rorty, the old intention behind the critique of metaphysics lives on: to rescue the moments that had been sacrificed to idealism—the nonidentical and the nonintegrated, the deviant and the heterogeneous, the contradictory and the conflictual, the transitory and the accidental.[2] In *other* contexts, on the other hand, the apologetics of the accidental and the aban-

Originally published in Postmetaphysical Thinking: Philosophical Essays *(MIT Press: Cambridge, Mass., 1992), 115–148. This edition © 1992 Massachusetts Institute of Technology.*

donment of the principled lose their subversive traits. In these contexts, all that is retained is the functional significance of shielding the powers of tradition, which are no longer rationally defensible, against unseemly critical claims; the point is to provide cultural protection for the flanks of a process of societal modernization that is spinning out of control.[3]

Thus, the nuanced debate surrounding the one and the many cannot be reduced to a simple for or against. The picture is made even more complex by latent elective affinities. The protest against the overpowering one that is made today in the name of an oppressed plurality allows itself at least a sympathetic detachment vis-à-vis the appearance of unitary thinking in renewed metaphysical form. For the fact is that radical contextualism itself thrives on a negative metaphysics, which ceaselessly circles around that which metaphysical idealism had always intended by the unconditioned but which it had always failed to achieve. But, from the functionalist perspective of a compensation for the burdens of societal modernization, the less radical form of contextualism can also get by with metaphysics, even though this contextualism itself no longer believes in the metaphysical claims to truth. The parties for and against the unitary thinking of metaphysics only form a clear constellation in relation to a third party, in which they detect a common opponent. I am referring to the humanism of those who continue the Kantian tradition by seeking to use the philosophy of language to save a concept of reason that is skeptical and postmetaphysical, yet not defeatist.[4] As seen by the unitary thinking of metaphysics, the procedural concept of communicative reason is too weak because it discharges everything that has to do with content into the realm of the contingent and even allows one to think of reason itself as having contingently arisen. Yet, as seen by contextualism, this concept is too strong because even the borders of allegedly incommensurable worlds prove to be penetrable in the empirical medium of mutual understanding. The metaphysical priority of unity above plurality and the contextualistic priority of plurality above unity are secret accomplices. My reflections point toward the thesis that the unity of reason only remains perceptible in the plurality of its voices—as the possibility in principle of passing from one language into another—a passage that, no matter how occasional, is still comprehensible. This possibility of mutual understanding, which is now guaranteed only procedurally and is realized only transitorily, forms the background for the existing diversity of those who encounter one another—even when they fail to understand each other.

I want to begin (I) by recalling the ambiguous significance of the unitary thinking of metaphysics, which, in emancipating itself from mythological thinking that focuses on origins, still remains tied to the latter. Along the way, I will touch on three topics that have sparked the critique of metaphysics within the very framework of metaphysics: the relationship of identity and difference, the problem of what is ineffably individual, and the discontent with affirmative thinking—above all with the merely privative determinations of matter and evil. Then I would like to retrace (II), in the case of Kant, the turn away from a rational unity derived from the objective order of the world and toward a concept of reason as the subjective faculty of idealizing synthesis; admittedly, the old problem of idealism, how *mundus intelligibilis* and *mundus sensibilis* are to be mediated, returns here in a new form. Hegel, Marx, and Kierkegaard attempt, each in his own way, to lay claim to the medium of history in order to conceive of the unity of a historicized world as process—whether it be the unity of the world as a whole, or of the human world, or of the life history of the individual. Positivism and historicism reply to this with a new turn (III), this time toward the theory of science. As we see today, this turn prepared the way for contextualism in one version or another. The objections to this position draw attention in turn to the impossibility of circumventing the symmetrical structure of perspectives built into every special situation, a structure that makes possible the intersubjectivity of reaching understanding in language. Thus (IV), a weak and transitory unity of reason, which does not fall under the idealistic spell of a universality that triumphs over the particular and the singular, asserts itself in the medium of language. The theme of the one and the many arises in different ways in the ontological, the mentalistic, and the linguistic paradigms.

I

"The one and the many" is the central topic in the *Enneads* of Plotinus. That work recapitulates the movement of thought within philosophical idealism that began with Parmenides and that led beyond the cognitive limits of the mythological way of seeing the world. *To hen panta* does not mean that everything is absorbed into one but that the many can be traced back to the one and can thereby be conceived as a whole, as totality. Through this powerful abstraction, the human mind gains an extramundane point of reference, a distancing perspective, from which the agitated in-one-another and against-one-another of concrete events and phenomena are joined together in a stable whole that is itself freed from the mutability of occurrences. This distancing view is then able to differentiate between the totality of what is and individual entities, between the world and what occurs within it. In turn, this distinction makes possible a level of explanation that is remarkably different from mythological narratives. The world in the singular refers to *one* origin, and indeed to one that can no longer be of the same sort as the original powers of mythology, which appear in the plural and compete with one another. The latter remained interwoven with the chain of generations and had their beginning *in* time; but as presuppositionless beginning, the one is a first from which time and the temporal first emerge.

Because every phenomenon in need of explanation must now be related in the last instance to the one and the whole, the necessity of disambiguation asserts itself—everything innerwordly must be made univocal as a being that is identical with itself, that is, as an object that is in each case particular. And the explanation for the phenomena that have become objects cannot be sought at the level of the phenomena themselves but only in something that underlies the phenomena—in essences, ideas, forms, or substances, which, like the one and the whole, are themselves of a conceptual nature or, in the manner of the archetype, at least occupy a middle ground between concepts and images. The one is therefore regarded as the first not only in the sense of the first beginning or origin but also as the first reason or ground, the primordial image, or the concept of the concept. Explanation by principles, which grasps the particular under the universal and derives it from a final axiom, this deductive mode of explanation modeled on geometry, breaks with the concretism of a worldview in which the particular is immediately enmeshed with the particular, one is mirrored in the other, and everything forms an extensive flat weave of oppositions and similarities. One could say, with Nietzsche, that mythology is familiar only with surface, only with appearance and not with essence. In opposition to that, metaphysics delves into the depths.

The world religions, especially the monotheistic ones and Buddhism, attained a conceptual level on a par with philosophical idealism. But when they put the world as a whole at a distance by means of a history of salvation or of a cosmology, the great prophets and founders of religions were led by questions posed *ethically*, whereas the Greek philosophers made the break with the immediacy of the narrative weave of concrete appearances *theoretically*. In this latter case, the advance from mythos to logos had more than sociocognitive potential. Yet even the act of contemplation had an ethicoreligious significance. A manner of living crystallized around the theoretical attitude of one who immerses himself in the intuition of the cosmos. This *bios theoretikos* was laden with expectations similar to those of the privileged paths to salvation of the wandering monk, of the eremite, or of the monastic brother. According to Plotinus, in the medium of thought the soul forms itself into a self, which becomes conscious of itself as a self in the recollective, reflexive intuition of the one. *Henosis*, the uniting of the philosopher with the one, for which discursive thinking prepares the way, is at once ecstatic self-transcendence and reflexive self-reassurance. The dematerializing and dedifferentiating recognition of the one in the many, the concentration upon the one itself, and the identification with the source of the limitless light, with the circle of circles—all this does not extinguish the self but intensifies self-consciousness. Philosophy refers to the conscious life as its telos. The identity of the ego forms itself in the contemplative presentation of the identity of the world. Thus, the thinking of the philosophy of origins did indeed have an emancipatory meaning.

Metaphysics also belongs to the world-historical process described by Max Weber from the perspective of the sociology of religion as rationalization and by Karl Jaspers as the cognitive advance of the "axial period" (extending from Buddha via Socrates and Jesus up to Muhammad).[5] Of course, that was a process of "rationalization" in an entirely different sense as well. From Freud to Horkheimer and Adorno, the dialectic inherent in metaphysical enlightenment has been retraced.[6] The spell of mythological powers and the enchantment of demons, which were supposed to be broken by the abstraction of universal, eternal, and necessary being, still live on in the idealistic triumph of the one over the many. The fear of uncontrolled dangers that displayed itself in myths and magical practices now lodges within the controlling concepts of metaphysics itself. Negation, which opposed the many to the one as Parmenides opposed nonbeing to being, is also negation in the sense of a defense against deep-seated fears of death and frailty, of isolation and separation, of opposition and contradiction, of surprise and novelty.[7] This same defensiveness still betrays itself in the idealist devaluation of the many to mere appearances. As mere *images* of the Ideas, the surging phenomena become univocal, the surveyable parts of a harmonic order.

The history of metaphysical thinking fuels the materialist suspicion that the power of mythological origins, from which no one can distance himself and go unpunished, is merely extended in idealism in a more sublime and less merciful way. Metaphysics labors in vain on certain key problems that seem to result from the rebellion of a disenfranchised plurality against a unity that is compulsory and, to that extent, illusory. From at least three perspectives, the same question is posed again and again: how are the one and the many, the infinite and the finite, related to each other?

First, How can the one, without endangering its unity, be everything (*Alles*), if the universe (*das All*) is indeed composed of many different things? The question of how the identity of identity and difference can be conceived, which was still the concern of Hegel's *Differenzschrift*, emerges out of the problem of *methexis* in the Platonic doctrine of Ideas. Plotinus had already incisively stated this problem with a paradoxical formulation: "The one is everything and yet not even one (among all things)."[8] The one is everything insofar as it resides in every individual being as its origin; yet, at the same time, insofar as it can preserve its unity only through its distinction from the otherness of each individual being, the one is also nothing among them all. In order to be everything, the one is thus in everything; at the same time, in order to remain the one itself, it is above everything—it both lies beyond and underlies everything innerworldly.

Metaphysics entangles itself in such paradoxical formulations because, thinking ontologically, it vainly tries to subsume the one itself under objectifying categories; but as the origin, ground, and totality of all beings, the one is what first constitutes the perspective that allows the many to be objectivated as the plurality of beings. For this reason, it was still necessary for Heidegger to insist upon the ontological difference between Being and beings, which is supposed to guard against the assimilation of the one to the other.

Plotinus transfers this paradox out of the one itself and into *nous*: only within the human faculty of cognition does the gap open up between discursively grasping the many and intuitively melting together with the one; the former process merely moves toward the latter. Of course, this negative ontological concept of the one as something effusive, which refuses all involvement with discursive reasoning, clears the way for a self-referential critique of reason that continues to hold the thinking of Nietzsche, Heidegger, and Derrida under the influence of metaphysics. Whenever the one is thought of as absolute negativity, as withdrawal and absence, as resistance against propositional speech in general, the ground (*Grund*) of rationality reveals itself as an abyss (*Abgrund*) of the irrational.

Second, there arises the question of whether idealism, which traces everything back to one and thereby devalues innerworldly beings to phenomena or images, can do justice to the integrity of the particular entity in its individuality and uniqueness. Metaphysics uses the concepts of genus and specific difference in order to break the universal down into the particular. Following the genealogical model, the family tree of the Ideas or generic concepts branches off from each level of generality into specific differences, each species of which can in turn constitute a *genus proximum* for further specifications. The particular is a particular only relative to a universal. For the individuation of the particular into single entities there are available the nonconceptual media of space, time, and matter, as well as those accidental features through which the individual deviates from what is appropriate to it by virtue of its membership in genera and its specific differences. Thus, the individual remains accessible only in the accidental husk that clings to the core of the generically and specifically determined being, only as something that is external and contingent. Metaphysical concepts break down in the face of the individual. In the end, this motivates John Duns Scotus to extend the essential all the way down to single entities. He coins the paradoxical concept of *haecceitas*, which stamps individuation itself with the seal of the essential, yet which, as something that is itself like an essence, persists in an indifferent universality vis-à-vis what is truly individual.

From its inception, idealism had hidden from itself the fact that the Ideas inconspicuously include within themselves the merely material and accidental moments of individual things, from which they had indeed only been abstracted.[9] Nominalism exposed this contradiction and demoted substances or *formae rerum* to mere names, to *signa rerum* that, as it were, the knowing subject tacks on to things. When the modern philosophy of consciousness finally dissolved even desubstantialized individual things into the material of sensation, from which the subjects themselves first form their objects, the problem of the ineffability of an individuality that withdraws from conceptual subsumption became even more acute. The critique of the understanding (*Verstandesdenken*) is motivated by the murky constellation joining the universal, the particular, and the individual. After Hegel, this is transformed into the critique of a form of reason that controls and identifies; it terminates in Adorno's attempt to rescue the moment of the nonidentical from the assaults of instrumental reason.[10]

From within the movement of metaphysical thought itself there emerges the third theme in the critique of metaphysics—namely, the suspicion that all its contradictions come together in the venerable concept of matter; the latter constitutes the dross, as it were, of affirmative thinking. Should matter, to which innerworldly beings owe their finitude, their concretion in space and time, and their resistance, be determined purely negatively as nonbeing? Must not matter, in which the Ideas are supposed to be deluded and to wane into mere phenomena, be conceived as a principle that not only contrasts with the intelligible but *contradicts* it—not merely as privation, as a residue that is left over after the removal of all determinate being and all good, but as an active power of negation that first generates the world of appearance and evil? This question has been insistently repeated from a genetic perspective. Once the primacy of the one, which precedes and underlies everything, is posited—why then are there any beings at all, rather than nothing? The question of theodicy is simply a moral-practical variant of this: given the primacy of the good, from which everything is derived, how then does anything evil come into the world in the first place? Schelling still labored away on this question in 1804 and again in 1809 (in his treatise on human freedom). He set himself against the Platonic tradition, in which what is material or evil is represented as a mere shading, weakening, or diminishing of the intelligible and the good, and not as the principle of negating and of egoity, of closing off, of actively striving back into the depths. In his remarkable polemic against the bias toward the affirmative, against the purification and the harmonization of the unruly and the negative, of what refuses itself, there also stirs an impulse to resist the danger of idealist apotheosis—the same impulse that directly provides the impetus for the critique of ideology that extends all the way up to the pessimistic materialism of the early Horkheimer and to the optimistic materialism of Bloch.[11]

II

Schelling's reflections already presuppose the premises of a philosophy of consciousness that no longer thinks of the unity of the many as an objective whole prior to the human mind but conceives of it as a result of the synthesis executed by mind itself. Beyond this, Schelling's *System des transzendentalen Idealismus* (1800) already contains a first, partially elaborated construction of world history. Both of these elements—reason as the source of *world-constituting* ideas, and history as the medium through which mind carries out its synthesis—revolutionize the basic concepts of metaphysics and give rise to the resulting problems that, with the Young Hegelians, set postmetaphysical thinking in motion.

It is well known that Kant connected the concept of knowledge with the synthetic accomplishments of the productive imagination and of the understanding, through which the manifold of sensations and representations are organized into a unity of experiences and judgments. Apprehension within intuition, reproduction within imagination, and recognition within the concept are spontaneous actions that run through the manifold, take up its elements, and combine them into a unity. Kant uses the construction of simple geometric forms and number series to elucidate the operation of *producing* unity in a previously unordered multiplicity. In doing this, the independently acting subject proceeds according to fundamental rules, for the representation of unity cannot emerge out of the act of combination itself. And for their part, these synthetic connections in the understanding are unified by the higher-level synthesis of pure apperception. With this title Kant refers to the formal "I think," which must be capable of accompanying all of my representations if the egological unity of a constantly identical self-consciousness is to be preserved in the manifold of representations. If the subject is not to forget itself and submerge in the stream of its lived experiences, it must hold itself fast as the same subject. Only this identity, which is produced in apprehending self-consciousness, and which is by no means empirically given but is instead transcendentally presupposed—only this identity permits the self-attribution of all of my representations. Only through the transcendental unity of apperception does the manifold of my representations take on the general connectedness of representations that are my own, that *belong* precisely to me as the knowing subject.

The *Critique of Pure Reason* thus reaches the point from which, in its own way, it connects with that metaphysical figure of thought, universal unity. That is, the transcendental unity of the knowing subject who relates itself to itself requires, on the side of what is known, a symmetrical concept of everything that stands over and against the subject, a transcendental concept of the world as the totality of all appearances. Kant calls this world concept a cosmological idea, that is, a concept of reason by means of which we make the totality of conditions in the world into an object. A new type of synthesis thereby comes into play. Cosmological ideas generate the "unconditioned synthetic unity of all conditions in general"; by aiming at the whole of possible experience and at the unconditioned, they follow principles of completeness and perfection that transcend all experience. This idealizing surplus distinguishes the *world-constituting* synthesis of reason from the synthetic accomplishments of the understanding, which allow us to know something *in the world.* Because the ideas are concepts that project a world, nothing that looks in any way like an object of experience could correspond to them. In relation to the world of appearances, they are suitable only as principles that regulate the use of the understanding and obligate it to the goal of systematic knowledge, that is, to theory formation that is as unitary and complete as possible. They have heuristic value for the progress of knowledge.

By taking the totality of beings and making it dependent upon the synthetic accomplishments of the subject, Kant downgrades the cosmos into the object domain of the nomological natural sciences. The world of appearances is no longer a "whole organized according to ends." Thus, although the transcendental concept of the world traces everything back to one, it differs from the old metaphysical concept of the world in that it can no longer also satisfy the need for establishing a meaningful organization, an organization that would absorb contingencies, neutralize what is negative, and calm the fear of death, of isolation, and of what is simply new. In exchange, Kant now offers the compensation of another world, namely, the intelligible. True, the latter remains closed off to theoretical knowledge, but its rational core, the moral world, is nonetheless attested to by the fact of the "ought." That is, unlike the cosmological idea, the idea of freedom finds support in the moral law; it not only regulates but determines moral action: "Reason is here, indeed, exercising causality, as actually bringing about that which its concept contains."[12] It is only the affiliated concept of a "world of rational beings" that is regulative, a world in which each acts as if, through his maxims, he were at all times a legislating member in the universal kingdom of ends. In this way like theoretical reason, practical reason also projects an unconditioned unity of all conditions in general—but this time the whole to which it is directed is that of an "ethical-civic" commonwealth. The latter would come about by systematically connecting all humans through shared objective laws. The world-constituting synthesis of reason once again comes into play, but this time its idealizing surplus does not have a merely heuristic meaning that guides cognition but a moral-practical meaning that obligates us.

Through this doubling of the transcendentally redirected concept of the world, Kant solves two of the three problems mentioned above, upon which metaphysics had labored in vain. The question of how the identity of the one and the many is to be conceived was only an unsolvable problem under the constraints imposed by the conceptual strategy of an ontologically objectifying thinking, which mixes up the world and beings in the world. But the transcendental illusion that the one and the whole must correspond to objects vanishes as soon as world-concepts are seen through as ideas of reason, that is, as the result of an idealizing synthesis. The problem of matter, too, is dissolved, because synthetic accomplishments are attributed to a subject that must be *given* its material, both in cognition and in action. Of course, the initial metaphysical question—how the one and the many or the infinite and the finite are related to each other—now reappears in a transcendentally modified form. The murky side-by-side status of the intelligible and the sensible worlds translates the old problem into many new questions, questions about the relationship between practical and pure reason, between the causality of freedom and the causality of nature, between morality and legality, etc. Kant is unable to overcome this dualism of worlds even by introducing a third kind of Idea of Reason, one that places the consideration of nature and history under teleological perspectives. For, without the solid empirical foundation provided by the judgments of the understanding, Ideas of this kind do not have even heuristic significance. Rather, they form the *focus imaginarius* for a way of viewing nature and history that treats them *as if* they *were* capable of constituting a kingdom of ends.

In any case, the inherited problem of the ineffability of the individual remains unsolved.[13] The scientific activity of the understanding subsumes what is particular under universal laws without having to worry about what is individual. No place remains for the ego qua individual person between the ego as something universal and the ego as something particular, that is, between the transcendental ego as one over and against everything and the empirical ego as one among many. To the extent that knowledge of myself is transcendental, it encounters the naked identity of the ego as the formal condition for the connectedness of my representations. To the extent that this self-knowledge is empirical, my inner nature appears as foreign to me as outer nature.

As long as a redemptive significance for the individual soul extended to philosophical theory as a form of life, the subject who devoted himself to theory did not need, *within* theory itself, to reassure himself of his unique existence; he could be satisfied by the promise of the salvation that was to be obtained through participation in the theoretical life. It was secularized confessional literature, for which Rousseau provided the great example, that recalled that the basic concepts of rational psychology had never gotten a hold on the fundamental experience of the Judeo-Christian tradition, despite the kinship of metaphysics with theology. The experience to which I am referring is the individuating gaze of that transcendent God, simultaneously judging and merciful, before whom every individual, alone and irreplaceable, must answer for his life as a whole. This individuating power of the consciousness of sin, which could not be captured by the concepts of philosophy, sought for itself a different, literary form of expression in the autobiographical revelation of one's life story, as the published documentation of an existence that has always to answer for itself. In addition, the theme of ineffable individuality takes on new relevance as historical thinking comes on the scene.

Both romanticism and the cultural sciences that arose in its spirit filled the transcendental concept of the world with new unities in the temporal, social, and spatial dimensions: with (the one) history, (the one) culture, and (the one) language. These new singulars introduced a synthetic unity into the plurality of histories, cultures, and languages, which had until then been seen as products of natural growth. Herder, Humboldt, and Schleiermacher assumed straightaway that this synthetic unity resulted from an underlying mental or spiritual productivity. And yet *this* synthesis must be conceived according to a model *different from* that of the construction of a straight line or of a number series, because in the spheres disclosed by the cultural sciences, the particular can no longer be subsumed under the universal while the individual is disregarded. It is, in an emphatic sense, individuals who are enmeshed in their histories, their forms of life, and their conversations, and who for their part convey something of their individuality to these engulfing, intersubjectively shared, yet concrete contexts. The particular of a specific history, culture, or language stands, as an individual type, between the universal and the singular. It was with groping concepts such as these that the old historical school operated.[14]

It was to this stage of the debate, which had been transformed equally by Kant's critique of metaphysics and by post-Kantian historical consciousness, that Hegel responded. The ambivalence that was only incipient in Kant emerges openly in Hegel's philosophy: by taking up and radically developing the theme of self-critique that had issued from the movement of metaphysical thought, Hegel renews the unitary thinking of metaphysics for the last time. In demolishing Platonic idealism, he adds the last imposing link to the chain of tradition that extended through Plotinus and Augustine, Thomas, Cusanus and Pico, Spinoza and Leibniz; but he does this only by revitalizing the concept of universal unity in a distinctive way. Hegel sees his philosophy of reconciliation as an answer to the historical need for overcoming the diremptions of modernity in modernity's own spirit. The same idealism that had denied any philosophical interest to the merely historical qua nonbeing is thereby placed under the historical conditions of the new era. That explains *first* why Hegel conceives of the one as absolute subject, thereby annexing the metaphysical figures of thought to that concept of autonomously acting subjectivity from which modernity draws its consciousness of freedom and, indeed, the whole of its characteristic normative content consisting of self-consciousness, self-determination, and self-realization. And it explains *second* why he lays claim to history as the only medium for the mediation of the one and the many, the infinite and the finite.[15]

These two aspects of his conceptual strategy compel Hegel to revise a premise that had remained in force from Plotinus to Schelling's *Jenaer Identitätsphilosophie.* Conceived in the terms of first philosophy, the one, as the ground of everything, could not be equated with the totality of beings. And the absolute had been held fast as the one itself, prior to and higher than everything. To this relationship between the one and the many, the infinite and the finite, there corresponded a subordinate position for a human spirit that was reflected into itself and already divided within itself. Characteristically, *nous* formed the first hypostasis in Plotinus: in the discursive mind, the one had already stepped outside itself. In place of this, Hegel now makes reflection itself absolute—reflection as the self-reference of a spirit that works its way up out of its substantiality to self-consciousness and which bears within itself the unity as well as the difference of the finite and the infinite. What had still been true for Schelling is inverted: the absolute subject is precisely not supposed to *precede* the world process. Rather, it exists only in the relationship of the finite and the infinite to each other, in the consuming activity of reflection itself. The absolute is the mediating process of a self-reference that produces itself unconditionally. One and all no longer stand over and against each other as relata; instead, it is now the relation itself, set in motion historically, which establishes the unity of its relata.

With this innovation, Hegel confronts both problems that Kant had bequeathed to his successors. As soon as history is placed on the level of metaphysics and the self-mediation of absolute spirit takes on the grammatical form, so to speak, of the historical progressive, the fractured continuity of a single self-formative process generates itself. This self-formative process sublates the dualisms of the sensible world and the moral world, of the constitutive and the regulative use of the Ideas of Reason, of form and content. Moreover, each particular is granted the solid form of a concrete universal by syntheses that have congealed to shapes of spirit, and for which nothing provides the material other than the preceding shapes of spirit themselves. The concrete universal is supposed to allow each conceptually grasped individual to receive its due in exactly the same way that it allows history to be glimpsed as a self-formative process. Adorno's negative dialectics can only sue for the recovery of the nonidentical from Hegel because the nonidentical was already on Hegel's programme.

But in the present context I am merely interested in the thesis that spirit falls within history. Until Hegel, metaphysical thinking was cosmologically oriented; nature was identical with the totality of beings. Now, the sphere of history is supposed to be integrated into this totality. Moreover, the synthetic labor of spirit is supposed to be performed through the medium of history and assimilated to the progressive form of the latter. Along with history, however, contingencies and uncertainties break into the circular, closed-off structure of unifying reason, and in the end these contingencies and uncertainties cannot be absorbed, even by a supple dialectic of reconciliation. With historical consciousness Hegel brought a force into play whose subversive power also set his own construction teetering. A history that takes the self-formative processes of nature and spirit up into itself, and that has to follow the logical forms of the self-explication of this spirit, becomes sublimated into the opposite of history. To bring it to a simple point that had already irritated Hegel's contemporaries: a history with an established past, a predecided future, and a condemned present, is no longer *history*.

III

Marx and Kierkegaard drew the moral from this. Along with the primacy of practice and of existence, the participant perspective of the "for us" and the "for me" also takes the lead theoretically. Historical consciousness thereby recognizes its provinciality in relation to the future. The synthesis of the process of world history or of a life history, whether it be executed through social labor and revolutionary practice or through Christian consciousness of sin and radical choice, follows the Kantian rather than the Hegelian model. But the stages run through by social formations or by one's own existence still obey a teleology, even if it is only to be carried to its end practically or existentially. A foundationalist residue adheres to Marx's social theory and to Kierkegaard's existential-dialectical writing. Since their day, it has become ever harder to ignore the way in which history intrudes into the structures of unifying reason with the contingencies of what is unforeseeably new and other, and these contingencies belie all rash syntheses and limiting constructions. For the later nineteenth century, this experience made the scientistic renunciation of metaphysics and the withdrawal into the theory of science seem advisable.

With Newton's physics in view, Kant had already set phenomenal (which primarily means scientifically objectified) nature free from metaphysical structures of meaning; he watered the unity of the cosmos down to the heuristic goal of unified theory construction. Why, then, should history not be similarly released from the burden of unitary thinking in the philosophy of history, which was a substitute for metaphysics, and be left to the human sciences that had since been established? Indeed, unlike the nomological sciences, the hermeneutic appropriation and narrative representation of tradition no longer seemed to obey even the heuristic imperative of a unified description of reality. Historicism, in any case, declared the context-dependent knowledge of the interpreter and of the narrator to be the domain of a plurality that escapes the claims of objectivity and unity for knowledge. In dualistic conceptions of science, which arose above all in Germany, the unity of reason was removed not only from the cosmos but from subjectivity as well. Unity evaporates into a methodological ideal that is now supposed to be valid only for the natural sciences, whereas according to historicist self-understanding, a plurality set free from all syntheses makes relativism inevitable in the human sciences. In the latter arena, then, histories triumph over the philosophy of history, cultures and forms of life triumph over culture as such, and the histories of national languages triumph over the rational grammar of language in general. Interpretation and narration supersede argumentation, multivalent (*vieldeutig*) meaning emancipates itself from simple validity, local significance is freed from the universalist claim to truth.

Philosophers have seldom been satisfied with such dichotomies; every dualism prods them to an explanation. Joachim Ritter's compensation theory represents such an attempt to come to terms with the historicist dichotomization of the scientific world.[16] Ritter begins by placing the natural sciences, which are committed to unity and universality, in relation to civil society, and the human sciences, which are committed to plurality and individuality, in relation to personal life. Then, by way of these contexts of employment, he brings the two types of science into a complementary relationship with one another. The natural sciences develop the productive forces of an industrial society undergoing modernization; the human sciences look after the powers of tradition in a lifeworld threatened in its historical substance. The natural world and the historical world are said to form a rational and dynamic whole only as long as the human sciences, which specialize in narrative re-presentation, compensate for those losses in the lifeworld that are unavoidably brought about by the depersonalization and modernization of life conditions induced by the natural sciences.

I refer to this familiar thesis because today it serves to limit the human sciences to the business of narration and, in the name of a culture of multivalence, to release them from cognitive claims of the kind connected with theory construction and, indeed, with argumentation in general. This moderate variety contextualism includes the further thesis that the lifeworld can only be protected from disintegration and civil war, from "hermeneutical manslaughter," when reason, in the sense of an orientation toward agreement based on reasons, is no longer imputed to it.[17] The text of the lifeworld must be made up of contexts alone. I do not want to dwell on the fact that the explanatory social sciences, together with linguistics and other reconstructive human sciences, find no place in the model of science thus established (which, incidentally, Schelsky already noted in his own day).[18] More important in the present context is the fact that the compensation theory itself operates with a concept of reason that it fails to identify. Without saying so, this theory relies on an anthropology that would have to explain why human beings require an equilibrium between modernization and historicization. Such an anthropology would have to indicate *why* a deficit of compensatory enchantment, refamiliarization, and transmission of meaning comes about in the first place; *when* the deficit grows into a "loss unbearable for humans"; and *how* it can be balanced out through the production of narratives by the human sciences.[19] There is no such anthropology. And if one has any idea how difficult it is to come by universal statements about *the* human being, one is almost tempted to consider a theory that is at least available in draft form, one which tries to use the structures of the type of action that is oriented to mutual understanding in order to explain why and when lifeworlds are in danger of becoming deformed under the pressure of system imperatives.

Praising the many, difference, and the other may be able to count on acceptance today, but a mood is no substitute for arguments.[20] Of course, postempirical theory of science has indeed used arguments to change the image we have of the sciences.[21] In the wake of Kuhn, Feyerabend, Elkana, and others, unifying reason has been deprived of its last domain, physics. Richard Rorty[22] had only to draw the consequences from this to deconstruct the picture of the "mirror of nature" that had been derived from the philosophy of the subject and to relieve the natural sciences as well as epistemology from the requirement of unitary theory construction and the need for "some permanent neutral framework of all possible inquiry."[23] Finally, then, even the weakest of the Kantian ideas of reason has been retracted. Without the spur of an idealizing world projection and a transcendent truth claim, objectifying science is swallowed up by its contingent contexts in the very same way as everyday practices are. In the laboratory as in life, the *same* culture of multivalence prevails once all standards of rationality and practices of justification claim to be nothing more than actually exercised conventions—nothing more "than just such practices."[24]

Having arrived at the threshold of the present, I want to end my retrospective in the history of ideas. As it is, the impression of a history of ideas might have been given only because an elaborate development of the arguments wrapped up in the ideas has been unnecessary for an audience of philosophical experts who are informed about the subject. However, in the matter of radical contextualism I have to become explicit. But first, one more comment about the shift in paradigms from the philosophy of consciousness to the philosophy of language.

Of course this linguistic turn had various motives. I will name one: the conviction that language forms the medium for the historical and cultural embodiments of the human mind, and that a methodologically reliable analysis of mental activity must therefore begin with the linguistic expressions of intentional phenomena, instead of immediately with the latter. Now it is not accidental that this realm of objective spirit came into view from two angles, on the one side from the angle of language, culture, and history in general, and on the other side from the angle of individual national languages, cultures, and histories. Hence the old theme of unity and plurality comes up once again in the question of how these two aspects are to be brought into relation to each other. As before, nothing would stand in the way of the concept of *one* reason today if philosophy and science were able to reach through the thicket of natural languages to the logical grammar of a single language that describes the world, or could at least come close to this ideal in a promising way. In contrast, if even the reflexive activity of mind always remained caught in the grammatical limits of various particular worlds that were linguistically constituted, reason would necessarily disintegrate kaleidoscopically into a multiplicity of incommensurable embodiments.

The question of how objective knowledge is possible has been answered by some theorists in an objectivistic and by others in a relativistic sense. Members of the first group reckon on an independent reality, toward which our interpretations finally converge, in the sense intended by a correspondence theory of truth. This group leaves intact the idea of reason that holds that in the long run exactly one true and complete theory would have to correspond to the objective world. On the other hand, the relativists hold a socialization theory of truth. They are of the opinion that every possible description only mirrors a particular construction of reality that inheres grammatically in one of various linguistic worldviews. There are no standards of rationality that point beyond the local commitments of the various universes of discourse. Both these positions are, however, confronted with insurmountable difficulties. The objectivists are faced with the problem of having to take up a standpoint between language and reality in order to defend their thesis; but they can only argue for such a null-context from within the context of the language they themselves use. On the other hand, the relativistic thesis, which concedes a perspectival right to every linguistically constituted view of the world, also cannot be put forth without a performative self-contradiction. So whoever absolutizes one of the two aspects of the linguistic medium of reason, be it its universality or its particularity, gets caught in aporias. Both Richard Rorty and Hilary Putnam want to find a way out of this situation, and I will link up with their discussion here.[25]

Rorty represents a contextualism that avoids the relativistic consequence of equal status for incommensurable standards and perspectives. If he did not, he would have to explain how a kind of truth extending beyond the perspective of our Western traditions could be thought to accrue to the perspectivistic thesis itself. Rorty recognizes that contextualism must be *cautiously* formulated in order to be radical. The contextualist must exercise caution in order not to take that which he may assert as a participant within a specific historical linguistic community and a corresponding cultural form of life and translate it into a statement made from the third-person perspective of an observer. The radical contextualist claims only that it is pointless to uphold the distinction, going back to Plato, between knowledge and opinion. "True" denotes what we hold to be justified according to our standards in a given case. And these standards of rationality are simply not to be distinguished in type from any other standards used in our culture. Practices of justification, like all other social conduct, are dependent upon our language, our traditions, and our form of life. "Truth" does not signify the correspondence between statements and some *X* prior to all interpretations; "truth" is simply an expression of commendation, with which we advise those who speak our language to accept the conceptions that we hold to be justified. Rorty explains the objectivity of knowledge in terms of the intersubjectivity of an agreement based, in good Wittgensteinian manner, on agreement in our language, our factually shared form of life. He replaces the aspiration to objectivity with the aspiration to solidarity within the linguistic community to which he contingently belongs. The cautious contextualist is not going to extend his lifeworld into the abstract; he must not dream of an ideal community of all those who communicate (Apel), freed from their provinciality, as Peirce and Mead dreamed of the ultimate community. He must rigorously avoid every idealization, and it would be for the best if he did without the concept of rationality altogether. For "rationality" is a limit concept with normative content, one which passes beyond the borders of every local community and moves in the direction of a universal one.[26]

An idealization of this sort, which conceives of truth as acceptability grounded in reasons under certain demanding conditions, would constitute a perspective that would in turn point beyond the practices of justification that are contingently established among us, one that would distance us from these practices. According to Rorty, that is not possible without a backslide into objectivism. The contextualist should not let himself be lured out of his participant perspective even when the price he has to pay for this is admitted ethnocentrism. He admits that we have to privilege the interpretive horizon of our own linguistic community, although there can be no noncircular justification for this. But this ethnocentric standpoint only means that we have to test all alien conceptions in light of our own standards.[27] Confronting this position, Hilary Putnam shows that an idealizing concept of truth or of validity in general is both necessary and possible without objectivistic fallacies.

Putnam establishes the unavoidability of an idealizing conceptual construction with the following argument. If the distinction between a conception that is held to be true here and now and a conception that is true, that is, one that is acceptable under idealized conditions, collapses, then we cannot explain why we are able to learn reflexively, that is, are able also to *improve* our own standards of rationality. The dimension in which self-distancing and self-critique are possible, and in which our well-worn practices of justification can thereby be transcended and reformed, is closed off as soon as that which is rationally valid collapses into that which is socially current. To this Rorty would reply that of course someone could at any time come up with new evidence, better ideas, or a novel vocabulary; in order to take that into account, however, we should not hold our conceptions, which are always only locally justified, to be "true" in an objectivistic sense. But the objectivistic alternative invoked by Rorty does not pose itself for Putnam. Rorty once said that for him the aspiration to objectivity is not the desire to flee from one's own linguistic community but simply the desire for as much intersubjective agreement as possible, namely, the desire to expand the referent of "for us" to the greatest possible extent.[28] In light of this intuition, I would reformulate Putnam's objection as follows: can we explain the possibility of the critique and self-critique of established practices of justification at all if we do not take the idea of the expansion of our interpretive horizon seriously *as an idea*, and if we do not connect this idea with the intersubjectivity of an agreement that allows precisely for the distinction between what is current "for us" and what is current "for them"?

Putnam and (in a penetrating contribution to the relativism controversy) Thomas McCarthy rightfully insist upon the existence of a *symmetrical* relationship between "us" and "them" in the exemplary cases of intercultural or historical understanding, in which rival conceptions collide not only with each other but with conflicting standards of rationality as well.[29] The cautious contextualist's ethnocentrism, admitted by Rorty, cannot but fail to capture the symmetry among the claims and perspectives of *all* participants in a dialogue because it describes the process of understanding as an assimilative incorporation of what is alien into our (expanded) interpretive horizon. But in a situation of profound disagreement, it is not only necessary for "them" to try to understand things from "our" perspective, "we" have to try in the same manner to grasp things from "their" perspective. They would never seriously get a chance to learn from us if we did not have the chance to learn from them, and we only become aware of the limits of "our" knowledge through the faltering of "their" learning processes. The merging of interpretive horizons, which according to Gadamer is the goal of every process of reaching understanding, does not signify an assimilation to "us"; rather, it must mean a convergence, steered through learning, of "our" perspective *and* "their" perspective—no matter whether "they" or "we" or both sides have to reformulate established practices of justification to a greater or lesser extent. For learning itself belongs neither to us nor to them; both sides are caught up in it in this same way. Even in the most difficult processes of reaching understanding, all parties appeal to the common reference point of a possible consensus, even if this reference point is projected in each case from within their own contexts. For, although they may be interpreted in various ways and applied according to different criteria, concepts like truth, rationality, or justification play the *same* grammatical role in *every* linguistic community.

Certainly, some cultures have had more practice than others at distancing themselves from themselves.[30] But all languages offer the possibility of distinguishing between what is true and what we hold to be true. The *supposition* of a common objective world is built into the pragmatics of every single linguistic usage. And the dialogue roles of every speech situation enforce a symmetry in participant perspectives. They open up both the possibility for ego to adopt the perspective of alter and vice versa, and the exchangeability of the participant's and the observer's perspectives. By no means do these universal pragmatic presuppositions of communicative action suggest the objectivistic fallacy according to which we could take up the extramundane standpoint of a subject removed from the world, help ourselves to an ideal language that is context-free and appears in the singular, and thereby make infallible, exhaustive, and thus definitive statements which, having neither the capacity nor the need for a commentary, would pull the plug on their own effective history. From the possibility of reaching understanding linguistically, we can read off a concept of situated reason that is given voice in validity claims that are both context-dependent and transcendent: "Reason is, in this sense, both immanent (not to be found outside of concrete language games and institutions) and transcendent (a regulative idea that we use to criticize the conduct of all activities and institutions)."[31] To put it into my own words: the validity claimed for propositions and norms transcends spaces and times, but in each actual case the claim is raised here and now, in a specific context, and accepted or rejected with real implications for social interaction.[32]

IV

The linguistic turn did transform reason and unitary thinking, but it did not drive them out of the philosophical discussion, as is shown by the outcome of the controversy surrounding both versions of contextualism. All the same, contextualism has become a manifestation of the spirit of the times. Transcendental thinking once concerned itself with a stable stock of forms for which there were no recognizable alternatives. Today, in contrast, the experience of contingency is a whirlpool into which everything is pulled: everything could also be otherwise, the categories of the understanding, the principles of socialization and of morals, the constitution of subjectivity, the foundation of rationality itself. There are good reasons for this. Communicative reason, too, treats almost everything as contingent, even the conditions for the emergence of its own linguistic medium. But for everything that claims validity *within* linguistically structured forms of life, the structures of possible mutual understanding in language constitute something that cannot be gotten around.

All the same, the postmodern mood is making its mark, all the way into the detective novel and onto the back-cover blurb. The publisher extols Enzensberger's new book with the notice that he enlists what is irregular against the project of homogenization, the margins against the center of power, living from difference against unity—Derrida's jargon migrates into commodity aesthetics. And a well-known author of detective stories has the thematic thread of his fable unravel in the confusion of a rich variety of contexts, to the extent that the genre-specific distinction between perpetrator and victim becomes unrecognizable in the weave of many small differences—after a sympathetic talk with the likable murderer, who is finally caught, the police neither report him nor prosecute him.[33] Repulsion towards the One and veneration of difference and the Other obscures the dialectical connection between them. For the transitory unity that is generated in the porous and refracted intersubjectivity of a linguistically mediated consensus not only supports but furthers and accelerates the pluralization of forms of life and the individualization of lifestyles. More discourse means more contradiction and difference. The more abstract the agreements become, the more diverse the disagreements with which we can *nonviolently* live. And yet in the consciousness of the public, the idea of unity is still linked to the consequence of a forced integration of the many. Greater universalism is still treated as the enemy of individualism, not as what makes it possible. The attribution of identical meanings is still treated as the injury of metaphorical multivalence, not as its necessary condition. The unity of reason is still treated as repression, not as the source of the diversity of its voices. The background for this anxiety is still formed by the false suggestions of a unitary thinking that was left behind one hundred fifty years ago—just as if it were necessary today, as it was for the first generation of Hegel's students, to defend ourselves against the predominance of the great masters of metaphysics.

The reasons for this attitude appear to reside in society rather than in philosophy itself. For society has indeed become so complex that it can hardly still be made transparent from within as the dynamic whole of a structural organization. The functionally differentiated society is decentered; the state no longer forms the political apex in which the functions relevant to the whole of society could be united; *everything* appears to have become part of the periphery. The economy and public administration have in fact expanded beyond the horizons of the lifeworld. These media-steered subsystems have congealed into a second nature. As depersonalized networks of communication, they recede from the intuitive knowledge of members, who are shunted aside into the environment of these systems. It thus seems plausible to treat society, which can no longer be grasped through narratives, in a way similar to that in which nature has been treated, to entrust it to an objectifying social science—now, of course, with the result that our self-understanding is immediately affected. That is, to the extent that the objectifying descriptions of society migrate into the lifeworld, we become alienated from ourselves as communicatively acting subjects. It is this self-objectification that transforms the perception of heightened societal complexity into the experience of being delivered over to sheer contingencies. All referents for coping with these contingencies have been lost—both the societal subject and transcendental consciousness have long since slipped away from us, the anxious members of the high-risk society.

The resulting discouragement is expressed in the radically contextualist processing of paralyzing experiences with contingency. But this discouragement will shed its character of being unavoidable if it is possible to defend and make fruitful for social theory a concept of reason that attends to the phenomenon of the lifeworld and permits the outmoded concept of the "consciousness of society as a whole" (which comes from the philosophy of the subject and finds no foothold in modern societies) to be reformulated on the basis of a theory of intersubjectivity. Even the decentered society cannot do without the reference point provided by the projected unity of an intersubjectively formed common will. I cannot pursue this thought further here. It signals, however, the practical implications resulting from the transformation of the unitary thinking of metaphysics and from the controversy surrounding contextualism. I have gone into this controversy with the intention of rendering plausible a weak but not defeatistic concept of linguistically embodied reason. I want to close with a few brief theses relating to (1) the transformed status of the debate, and to (2) the question of what still remains of the normative content of metaphysics "at the moment of its downfall" (Adorno).

(1) The concept of reason that is identified in the presuppositions of action oriented toward mutual understanding frees us from the dilemma of having to choose between Kant and Hegel. Communicative reason is neither incorporeal, like the spontaneity of a subjectivity that is world-constituting yet itself without a world (*weltlos*), nor does it twist history into a circular teleology for the sake of the absolute self-mediation of a historicized spirit. The transcendental gap between the intelligible and the empirical worlds no longer has to be overcome through the philosophy of nature and the philosophy of history. It has instead been reduced to a tension transferred into the lifeworld of the communicative actors themselves, a tension be-

tween the unconditional character of context-bursting, transcendent validity claims, on the one hand, and, on the other hand, the factual character of the context-dependent "yes" and "no" positions that create social facts in situ. Kant's irreconcilable worlds, the objective world of appearances and the moral world of autonomous action, shed their transcendental-ontological dignity. Together with the inner world of the empirical subject, they return in everyday communicative practice as more or less trivial suppositions of commonality that make possible the cognitive, the regulative, and the expressive uses of language, and thus the relation to "something in the world."

Yet, beyond this, communicatively acting subjects are freed from the work of world-constituting syntheses. They already find themselves within the context of a lifeworld that makes their communicative actions possible, just as it is in turn maintained through the medium of these processes of reaching understanding. This background, which is presupposed in communicative action, constitutes a totality that is implicit and that comes along prereflexively—one that crumbles the moment it is thematized; it remains a totality only in the form of implicit, intuitively presupposed background knowledge. Taking the unity of the lifeworld, which is only known subconsciously, and projecting it in an objectifying manner onto the level of explicit knowledge is the operation that has been responsible for mythological, religious, and also of course metaphysical worldviews. With criticizable validity claims, and with the ability to orient oneself toward validity claims, everyday practice becomes permeated with idealizations that nevertheless set the stage for social facts. The ideas of meaning-identity, truth, justice, sincerity, and accountability leave their marks here. Yet they retain world-constituting power only as heuristic ideas of reason; they lend unity and organization to the situation interpretations that participants negotiate with each other. A transcendental illusion arises therefrom only when the totality of the lifeworld, presupposed as a background in everyday practice, is hypostatized as the speculative idea of the One and All, or as the transcendental idea of a mental spontaneity that brings everything forth out of itself.

The concept of pragmatic, yet unavoidable and idealizing presuppositions of action oriented toward reaching understanding must be differentiated according to the various burdens it has to bear. Those acting communicatively presuppose the lifeworld behind them in a different manner than the validity basis of their speech. In yet another way, understanding a thematically uttered propositional content presupposes understanding the associated illocutionary act, whose meaning "comes along" unthematically in the performance of the complete speech act.

The philosophical tradition, as we have seen, has always held only privative concepts or negatively encircling formulas ready for what is individual because it has privileged the being of entities, the knowledge of objects, and the assertoric sentence or propositional content and has *equated* these with the comprehensible. But if we assume that the only thing we can understand is the propositional contents of assertions, then the individual essence—the very expression is paradoxical—unavoidably eludes the infinitely many (falsely objectifying) specifications. Since Kierkegaard we have been in a position to know that individuality can only be read from the traces of an authentic life that has been existentially drawn together into some sort of an appropriated totality. The significance of individuality discloses itself from the autobiographical perspective, as it were, of the first-person—I alone can performatively lay claim to being recognized as an individual in my uniqueness. If we liberate this idea from the capsule of absolute inwardness and follow Humboldt and George Herbert Mead in grafting it onto the medium of a language that crosses processes of socialization and individuation with each other, then we will find the key to the solution of this final and most difficult of the problems left behind by metaphysics.[34] The performative attitude we have to take up if we want to reach an understanding with one another about something gives every speaker the possibility (which certainly has not always been put to use) of employing the "I" of the illocutionary act in such a way that it becomes linked to the comprehensible claim that I should be recognized as an individual person who cannot be replaced in taking responsibility for my own life history.

(2) The concept of communicative reason is still accompanied by the shadow of a transcendental illusion. Because the idealizing presuppositions of communicative action must not be hypostatized into the ideal of a future condition in which a definitive understanding has been reached, this concept must be approached in a sufficiently skeptical manner.[35] A theory that leads us to believe in the attainability of a rational ideal would fall back behind the level of argumentation reached by Kant. It would also abandon the materialistic legacy of the critique of metaphysics. The moment of unconditionality that is preserved in the discursive concepts of a fallibilistic truth and morality is not an absolute, or it is at most an absolute that has become fluid as a critical procedure. Only with this residue of metaphysics can we do battle against the transfiguration of the world through metaphysical truths—the last trace of "Nihil contra Deum nisi Deus ipse." Communicative reason is of course a rocking hull—but it does not go under in the sea of contingencies, even if shuddering in high seas is the only mode in which it "copes" with these contingencies.

This foundation is not even stable enough for a negative metaphysics. The latter after all continues to offer an equivalent for the extramundane perspective of a God's-eye view: a perspective radically different from the lines of sight belonging to innerworldly participants and observers. That is, negative metaphysics uses the perspective of the radical outsider, in which one who is mad, existentially isolated, or aesthetically enraptured distances himself from the world, and indeed from the lifeworld as a whole. These outsiders no longer have a language, at least no speech based on reasons, for spreading the message of that which they have seen. Their speechlessness finds words only in the empty negation of everything that metaphysics once affirmed with the concept of the universal One. In contrast, communicative reason cannot withdraw from the determinate negations in language, discursive as linguistic communication in fact is. It must therefore refrain from the paradoxical statements of negative metaphysics: that the whole is the false, that everything is contingent, that there is no consolation whatsoever. Communicative reason does not make its appearance in an aestheticized theory as the colorless negative of a religion that provides consolation. It neither announces the absence of consolation in a world forsaken by God, nor does it take it upon itself to provide any consolation. It does without exclusivity as well. As long as no better words for what religion can say are found in the medium of rational discourse, it will even coexist abstemiously with the former, neither supporting it nor combating it.

There is also something more in being able to do less and in wanting to do less than negative metaphysics entrusts to itself. The analysis of the necessary conditions for mutual understanding in general at least allows us to develop the idea of an intact intersubjectivity, which makes possible both a mutual and constraint-free understanding among individuals in their dealings with one another and the identity of individuals who come to a compulsion-free understanding with themselves. This intact intersubjectivity is a glimmer of symmetrical relations marked by free, reciprocal recognition. But this idea must not be filled in as the totality of a reconciled form of life and projected into the future as a utopia. It contains no more, but also no less, than the formal characterization of the necessary conditions for the unforeseeable forms adopted by a life that is not misspent. No prospect of such forms of life can be given to us, not even in the abstract, this side of prophetic teachings. All we know of them is that if they could be realized at all, they would have to be produced through our own combined effort and be marked by solidarity, though they need not necessarily be free of conflict. Of course, "producing" does not mean manufacturing according to the model of realizing intended ends. Rather, it signifies a type of emergence that cannot be intended, an emergence out of a cooperative endeavor to moderate, abolish, or prevent the suffering of vulnerable creatures. This endeavor is fallible, and it does fail over and over again. This type of producing or self-bringing-forth places the responsibility on our shoulders without making us less dependent on "the luck of the moment." Connected with this is the modern meaning of humanism, long expressed in the ideas of a self-conscious life, of authentic self-realization, and of autonomy—a humanism that is not bent on self-assertion. This project, like the communicative reason that inspires it, is historically situated. It has not been made, it has taken shape—and it can be pursued further, or be abandoned out of discouragement. Above all, the project is not the property of philosophy. Philosophy, working together with the reconstructive sciences, can only throw light on the situations in which we find ourselves. It can contribute to our learning to understand the ambivalences that we come up against as just so many appeals to increasing responsibilities within a diminishing range of options.

NOTES

1. Robert Spaemann, "Natur," in *Philosophische Essays* (Stuttgart, 1983), 19ff.; Spaemann, *Das Natürliche und das Vernünftige* (Munich, 1987); Dieter Henrich, *Fluchtlinien* (Frankfurt, 1982); Henrich, "Dunkelheit und Vergewisserung," in *All-Einheit, Wege eines Gedankens in Ost und West*, ed. D. Henrich (Stuttgart, 1985), 33ff.

2. Jean-François Lyotard, *The Differend*, trans. Georges van den Abbeele (Minneapolis, 1988); and generally, Jonathan Culler, *On Deconstruction* (Ithaca, 1983).

3. Odo Marquard, *Farewell to Matters of Principle*, trans. Robert M. Wallace (Oxford, 1989).

4. Hilary Putnam, *Reason, Truth, and History* (Cambridge, 1981).

5. See Max Weber, *The Sociology of Religion*, trans. Ephraim Fischoff (Boston, 1963); and Karl Jaspers, *The Great Philosophers*, Vol. I, trans. Ralph Manheim (New York, 1962).

6. Max Horkheimer and Theodor Adorno, *The Dialectic of Enlightenment*, trans. John Cumming (New York, 1972).

7. Klaus Heinrich, *Dahlemer Vorlesungen*, Vol. I (Frankfurt, 1981).

8. Werner Beierwaltes, *Denken des Einen* (Frankfurt, 1985), 31ff.

9. Karl Heinz Haag, *Der Fortschritt in der Philosophie* (Frankfurt, 1983), 33.

10. Theodor Adorno, *Negative Dialectics*, trans. E. B. Ashton (New York, 1973).

11. H. Brunkhorst, "Dialektischer Positivismus des Glücks," *Zeitschrift für Philosophische Forschung* 39 (1985): 353ff.; M. Korthals, "Die kritische Gesellschaftstheorie des frühen Horkheimer," *Zeitschrift für Soziologie* 14 (1985): 315ff.

12. Immanuel Kant, *Critique of Pure Reason*, trans. Norman Kemp Smith (New York, 1965), B385.

13. See "Individuation through Socialization," in Jürgen Habermas, *Post-Metaphysical Thinking* (Cambridge, Mass., 1992), 149–204.

14. E. Rothacker, "Die dogmatische Denkform in den Geisteswissenschaften und das Problem des Historismus," *Abhandlungen der Akademie der Wissenschaft und der Literatur* (Mainz, 1954).

15. Jürgen Habermas, *The Philosophical Discourse of Modernity*, trans. Frederick Lawrence (Cambridge, Mass., 1987), 7ff.

16. Joachim Ritter, "Die Aufgabe des Geisteswissenschaften in der modernen Gesellschaft" (1963), in *Subjektivität* (Frankfurt, 1974), 105ff; see my critique in J. Habermas, *On the Logic of the Social Sciences*, trans. Shierry Weber Nicholsen and Jerry Stark (Cambridge, Mass., 1988), 16ff.

17. Odo Marquard, "Über die Unvermeidlichkeit der Geisteswissenschaften," in *Apologie des Zufälligen* (1986), 98ff.; Marquard, "Verspätete Moralistik," *Frankfurter Allgemeine Zeitung*, 18 March 1987.

18. Helmnut Schelsky, *Einsamkeit und Freiheit* (Reinbeck bei Hamburg, 1963), 222ff.

19. Odo Marquard, "In Praise of Polytheism," in *Farewell to Matters of Principle*, 87ff.

20. The compensation theory does not become more plausible when its political meaning is revealed to us. Marquard's "In Praise of Polytheism" is based on the following narrative. There are wholesome myths; they are the ones that we normally call myths and that always appear in the plural. What is harmful is monomythology, because it always lays claim to exclusivity; monomythology first appears in the doctrines of universal unity in monotheism and the philosophy of origins. Due to a paucity of safeguarded non-identity among the circle of their followers, these doctrines generate an unfree ego-identity. In the wake of the disintegration of this religious-metaphysical unitary thinking, a vacuum arises, which in the course of the eighteenth century is filled by the most harmful monomythology of all, namely, that of progress. The absolute autarchic mythology is the philosophy of history, which takes the power of the one over the human many and intensifies it into open terror. The only thing that could help counter this would be a *disenchanted* return of polytheism, in the form of *Geisteswissenschaften* that are no longer bewitched by the universalism of reason. I am amazed by the explanatory burden that this story is expected to bear. Why should the thinking of the philosophy of history, which has always entertained arguments, be vanquished by an anti-philosophy-of-history that is offered narratively, that is, without arguments? I also have no idea who, today, still thinks in terms of the philosophy of history at all, if that means "defining history as the long march into the universal and as the dissolution of the individual in the species." ("Universalgeschichte und Multiversalgeschichte," in *Apologie des Zufälligen*, 70.) Only the political meaning of the whole undertaking is clear: the continuation of a very German tradition, namely, the venerable struggle against the ideas of the French Revolution.

21. Richard Bernstein, *Beyond Objectivism and Relativism* (Philadelphia, 1983).

22. Richard Rorty, *Consequences of Pragmatism* (Minneapolis, 1982).

23. Richard Rorty, *Philosophy and the Mirror of Nature* (Princeton, 1979), 211.

24. Ibid., 390.

25. Richard Rorty, "Solidarity or Objectivity?" in *Post-Analytic Philosophy*, ed. John Rajchman and Cornel West (New York, 1985), 3ff.; Hilary Putnam, "Why Reason Can't Be Naturalized," *Synthese* 52 (1982): 1ff. (Reprinted in *After Philosophy—End or Transformation?*, ed. K. Baynes, J. Bohman, and T. McCarthy [Cambridge, Mass., 1987], 222ff.)

26. Richard Rorty, "Pragmatism, Davidson, and Truth," in *Truth and Interpretation*, ed. E. LePore (Oxford, 1986), 333ff.

27. Richard Rorty, "Solidarity or Objectivity?" 12f.

28. Ibid., 8.

29. Thomas McCarthy, "Contra Relativism: A Thought Experiment," in *Relativism: Interpretation and Confrontation*, ed. Michael Krausz (Notre Dame, 1989), 256–271.

30. Martin Hollis and Steven Lukes, eds., *Rationality and Relativism* (Oxford, 1982).

31. Putnam, "Why Reason Can't Be Naturalized," 228.

32. Jürgen Habermas, *Philosphical Discourse of Modernity*, 322f.

33. Jan van de Wetering, *Rattenfang* (Hamburg, 1986).

34. See "Individuation through Socialization," Sec. IX, in *Postmetaphysical Thinking*, 188–193.

35. Albrecht Wellmer, *The Persistence of Modernity* (Cambridge, Mass., 1991).

The Battle of Reason with the Imagination

Hartmut Böhme and Gernot Böhme

Translated by Jane Kneller

IMAGINATION, DREAM, AND COGNITION

Banishing Fantasy

Just as the fool was driven from his social position,[1] so the Enlightenment also banishes fantasy from philosophy. Although the imagination had always been met with caution, and in philosophy precautions had been taken from the start against its deceptions, even into the seventeenth century it still had its ancestral place among the faculties of knowledge. It lost this position with Kant—once and for all, one might say, if one views the philosophy of the romantics as an intermezzo. Of course, it experienced a rebirth in the manifold relations to the not-yet-conscious in Bloch.

In return for being disqualified as a faculty of knowledge, the imagination was valued more and more highly in aesthetics, which in the course of the eighteenth century emancipated itself from law and order and ended up glorifying creativity as such in the cult of genius.[2] This ambivalent development in the appraisal of imagination suggests a far-reaching process, a change in the human constitution itself. Analyzing the process in philosophy, it appears to be a change in the structure of the faculties of human knowledge. Heidegger[3] carried out this analysis of Kant's theory of knowledge with particular attention to the difference between the two editions of the *Critique of Pure Reason.*

According to Kant, knowledge has, "as is well known," two sources: sensibility and understanding, or receptivity and spontaneity. On the other hand, he speaks of *three* sources in the first edition of the *Critique of Pure Rea-*

Originally published as chapter 4 of Hartmut Böhme and Gernot Böhme, Das Andere der Vernunft: Zur Entwicklung von Rationalitätsstrukturen am Beispiel Kants *(Frankfurt, 1983).*

son: "There are three original sources (capacities or faculties of the soul) which contain the conditions of the possibility of all experience, and cannot themselves be derived from any other faculty of the mind, namely, *sense*, *imagination*, and *apperception*" (A 94).[4] In complete accordance with this, Kant says at A 115: "There are three subjective sources of knowledge upon which rests the possibility of experience in general and of knowledge of its objects—*sense*, *imagination*, and *apperception*." As Heidegger claims, in the second edition of the *Critique of Pure Reason* the imagination is "still there in name only."[5] That is, the imagination lost its position as an independent faculty. "Imagination" appears only as an expression for a particular function of another faculty. This other faculty is the understanding. Kant says that the understanding determines inner sense "under the title of a *transcendental synthesis of imagination*" (B 153).

The function of the imagination is retained. But what was it? Kant holds fast to a characteristic of knowledge that distinguished human beings from gods already in Plato: human knowledge relies on images. In cognition we do not stand in direct relation to objects, but we must "make an image" for ourselves. Our objects must be given to us in intuition.

The fact is, Kant radically subjugates the imaging faculty to the rule of the understanding—so radically that it loses its independence. The understanding itself takes over the function of imagination. It carries it out by regulating sensibility. To say that the understanding determines sensibility means that we take up, or better, must take up, the given in objective experience in a manner that is adequate to the concepts of the understanding. These concepts themselves, understood as rules, regulate the determination of sensibility. Kant gives an empirical example that at least makes plausible how this takes place. In the chapter on the schematism he illustrates the process, also called "figurative synthesis," with the concept "dog." "The concept 'dog' signifies a rule according to which my imagination can delineate the figure of a four-footed animal in a general manner" (*CPR*, A 141/B 180). Seeing a dog, I make myself an image of a dog by organizing my perception to correspond to the schema of a dog. Kant does not illustrate the process any further but characterizes it as the effect of "an art concealed in the depths of the human soul, whose real modes of activity nature is hardly likely ever to allow us to discover, and to have open to our gaze" (B 180ff.).

What is decisive is that in this process all independence and freedom is taken from the imagination and that the understanding alone rules. This is decisive because everything that Kant can prove in his theory of knowledge depends on it: the objective validity of the concepts of the understanding, the principles of pure understanding, the principles of mathematical science. How else is the applicability of the concepts of the understanding and the validity of principles a priori for empirical objects to be shown, if that which is given in experience is not already taken up in accordance with rules of the understanding? The possibility of objective experience depends on the banishing of fantasy from the realm of knowledge and on the understanding's determining sensibility.

That sounds plausible within the frame of the theory of knowledge of the *Critique of Pure Reason.* Wouldn't the free play of the imagination only disturb us, juggling before us its own images? Excluding the imagination from the faculties of knowledge appears to be a purely impartial precaution. But this impression changes immediately upon taking up Kant's anthropological, pedagogical, and medical writings. There are all the signs of a panic fear of imagination. Heidegger, who refused to concede a systematic significance to these writings, nevertheless identified the reason why the imagination was eliminated in the second edition of the *Critique of Pure Reason*: Kant retreated from the imagination "in order to save the rule of reason."[6]

Imagination as an Empirical Faculty

Where Kant speaks as an empiricist, in his observations on medicine, pedagogy, and in the *Anthropology*, the existence of the imagination as a basic power is undisputed. It is part of the human being's equipment as a living being (*Lebewesen*). Animals also have imaginations. Imagination plainly belongs to the bestial part of human beings, as will become even clearer. It is something native to us, closely linked with vital energy (*Lebenskraft*) itself. Thus it is the imagination that prevents us from dying when we sleep. When sleeping, there occurs "an involuntary play of the imagination (which in a healthy condition is dreaming) which through a wonderful feat of animal organization, relaxes the animal movements of the body, but *agitates* its vital inner movements through dreams . . . because otherwise, if these were totally lacking, life could not continue for even a moment" (*Streit der Fakultäten,* VII:105–106).[7] Here Kant formulates the fascinating thought that man does not live by bread alone—but also by images. This alone makes the imagination into a faculty that cannot be dispensed with and relinquished. On the other hand, if it becomes threatening, it can always be disciplined or limited to the realm of the irrelevant. Perhaps to the realm of dreams?

If the imagination is closely paired with vital energy itself, then it is especially suited to find its origins in bodily sensation, to begin with the corporeal. It plainly seems that repressed physicalness forces its way into consciousness again and again through the imagination. As a teacher, and also from his own bodily experiences, Kant knew of this. Sexuality, about which one must not speak and which is only to be lived out within the narrow confines of marriage, is thus nevertheless always present in fantasy. "How much wit has been squandered, from time immemorial, on throwing a flimsy veil over something that, though we delight in it, still shows such a close relationship between man and the lower animals that it calls for modesty; and in polite society we may not speak of it plainly" (*Anthr.*, 17 [VII:136]).[8] Although sexuality may be chastely hidden and hinted at only indirectly in conversation, the imagination keeps the issue alive: "Here imagination likes to stroll in the dark," Kant continues in this passage. Similarly in the battle against onanism: one might check the activity itself, but there remains an even more terrible opponent, one that is more difficult to conquer, namely, fantasy: "Even if the thing remains only in the imagination, it still eats away at [one's] vital energy" (*Über Pädogogik*, IX:497).

The animal in the human being must not be awakened, but one toys with it when the imagination is excited. Kant sees the most well known means to this, drunkenness, as a condition of aroused imagination. And this easy arousal—here Kant is not even thinking of sensory disorientation or hallucination—already means that the rule of reason has been violated. "It is very easy to overlook and cross the bounds of self-control," says Kant (*Anthr.*, 17 [170]). A person is then no longer capable of objective knowledge. To be drunk or intoxicated means "that he is temporarily incapable of ordering his sense repesentations by laws of experience" (*Anthr.*, 46 [170]).

Other bodily stirrings that are weaker and more indeterminate than sexual ones also reach consciousness through the imagination. Kant, plagued by flatulence and constantly bothered by irregularity, could sing a song about this. He cannot forget his body. This inability to forget, this constant reminder of himself, is produced under the condition of the repression of the imagination, which represents in consciousness the repression of bodily motions.

Kant, being even less capable of recognizing the body than the imagination, mistook hypochondria for a product of the latter (*Streit*, VII:103 [187]). He believed that the diffuse anxieties and apprehensions of the hypochondriac are a breakdown of controls on the imagination, although its play only represents a more deep-seated repression in consciousness. The imagination, by way of sexuality, hypochondria, and drunkenness, has already led people into the margins of insanity. And although Kant defines genius as "originality . . . of the imagination when it harmonizes with concepts" (*Anthr.*, 48 [172]), this positive assessment contains at the same time a decisive limitation of the imagination (it must "harmonize with concepts"). For Kant, it is clear "that genius contains a certain dose of madness" (*Anthr.*, 62 [188]). He would thus rather leave open this question:

> Does the world benefit more, on the whole, from great geniuses, who often take new paths and open new prospects, or from mechanical minds, who with their commonplace understanding that advances slowly on the rod and staff of experience have contributed most to the growth of the arts and sciences, even if they make no epochs (and although such a mind arouses no admiration, it also does not cause disorder)? (*Anthr.*, 94 [226])

Kant's own opinion is evident, however. The productive capacity of imagination cannot be given up, but even in genius it is only useful when it is disciplined. "This must be studied in strict academic fashion, and is certainly an imitative process. To free imagination from even this constraint and let individual talent carry on without rules and revel in itself, even against nature, might produce original folly" (*Anthr.*, 93 [225]).

If the imagination is aroused even a little, one is rendered incapable of objective knowledge. Dwelling too much on one's own bodily stimuli in hypochondria is already a harmless form of mental illness. Genius not subjected to strict rules produces an idiot. And finally, if imagination floods intuitions with its images, mental derangement results. Madness (*Verrücktheit*), according to Kant's definitions in "On Mental Illnesses" (1764), is the mental illness that cancels the regular functioning of perception.[9] It consists in mistaking imagination for reality. Already in his 1766 satire of Swedenborg, *Dreams of a Spirit-seer, Illustrated by the Dreams of Metaphysics*, Kant had tried to identify Swedenborg's visionary character as mental illness. This view is also laid down several times in the *Anthropology* (39 [161], 53 [178], 85 [215]). It is thus natural for him that such people "simply be dismissed as candidates for the mental hospital" (*Geisterseher*, II:348). Of course, he means that "although it was once deemed necessary to burn some of these [people], now it is enough that they be purged" (*Geisterseher*, II:348).

If the imagination is such an inescapable but dangerous fellow lodger within ourselves, we would do well to break it in early. Thus Kant also speaks in his *Pedagogy* of a cultivation of the imagination that aims at being used "only to the advantage of the understanding" (*Pädagogik*, IX:472). Children by nature have a very active imagination, since they are of course not yet cultivated humans. It is quite unnecessary to strengthen or excite their imaginations. "They must instead be reined in and brought under rules" (*Pädagogik*, IX:476). Of course, the imagination should not be left unoccupied—and here it is again clear that, nevertheless, we remain dependent on this power—but it must for that very reason be occupied only in the service of the understanding. Thus Kant recommends methods for restraining the enthusiasm of the imagination: One should not prolong the period before going to sleep and after waking up, but much rather see to it that waking and sleeping are abruptly separated. One should remain vigilant in order to be able to put a halt to the imagination's occupation with bodily activities or to stop at any time its associative process, which could lead to dangerous representations. Taming the imagination by going to bed early in order to get up early is a rule that is a very useful psychological regimen (*Anthr.*, 55 [181]).

Considering the devastating tendencies of the imagination, it is understandable that Kant renounced its positive participation in the constitution of cognition and tried to limit it as far as possible to its unavoidable vital function in sleep. And yet in one particular characterization of the imagination, Kant intimates a deeper presentiment: "To all this we can add, further, the effects produced by sympathetic imagination" (*Anthr.*, 54 [179]).

Following this somewhat sibylline pronouncement, Kant portrays phenomena whereby people get involved in the suffering of their fellow human beings merely by watching. He mentions phenomena ranging from such harmless ones as infectious yawning to mass hysteria. Naturally, here again he cautions wariness of the imagination, since this "weakness" of contracting suffering through sympathy is naturally not advisable. In particular, neurasthenics are advised not to visit lunatic asylums. Still, this relationship between imagination and sympathy suggests that the imagination in its original productivity could perhaps be the faculty that expresses the kinship of human beings with nature and with the Other. One is reminded, as without a doubt was Kant, that Rousseau assigned the cause of the possibility of intersubjectivity in general to sympathy. Does the imagination perhaps bear witness to a closer relation of human beings to the object of their cognition than Kant's "theory of alienated knowledge" would allow?

For Kant, the imagination is only fit for knowledge in servile form. On the other hand, he was not averse to letting imagination have its play area where nothing of particular importance was at stake—in the realm of the fine arts. In the *Critique of Judgment* the imagination reappears as an independent faculty, that is as the faculty of intuition opposed to, but as important as, the understanding as the faculty of concepts (*CJ*, 30 [190]).[10] It is generally understood that the imagination brings about intuitions, and that means, of course, the unity of the intuition as well. Everyone knows what Kant is talking about, namely, that we see in images; that the given is given in images. But in the *Critique of Pure Reason*, every unity, including the unity of the intuition, is attributed to the activity of the understanding (cf. *CPR*, B 152). In the *Critique of Judgment* the imagination is now granted its freedom—the freedom to "play."

When this play inadvertently manages to correspond to the lawfulness of the understanding, then, according to Kant, a feeling of pleasure arises, a pleasure in this correspondence between imagination and understanding. This feeling of pleasure, in turn, is the basis of the judgment of taste, that is, of the judgment that the object of the imagination is beautiful. We do not here wish to deal with reduction of the experience of the beautiful to a synchronized team playing of the inner psychic apparatus, or with the bourgeois reduction of the philosophy of art to a theory of taste.

But it can still be established, that also here, where the independence of the imagination is at least accepted as play, the joy taken in this play occurs precisely where it is well mannered, that is, where it conforms to the understanding. Classicism delights in the allegorized and domesticated figures of Greek mythology—figures that once were gripping and overwhelming powers. The imagination itself is turned from Eros into Cupid (Putto), into a child that one delights in because it does of its own accord what one would otherwise ask of it. As Kant means to defend it, here as elsewhere, the freedom of the imagination in art is also only apparent. In the *Anthropology* Kant says, "Moreover, an artist in the political sphere, like one in the aesthetic, knows how to guide and rule the world by dazzling it with images in place of reality [,] . . . for example, the *freedom* of the people . . . or their estates and *equality*. . . . Still, it is better to have even the mere illusion of possessing this good that ennobles humanity than to feel clearly the privation of it" (*Anthr.*, 56 [181–182]).

Dream Is Not Knowledge

"Let us suppose we are dreaming," Descartes says in the first *Meditation*, as if he couldn't care less. Nevertheless, he forges ahead, hunting the certainty that will guarantee that what he sees, feels, and thinks is *not* a dream, but rather reality, and that it is not an evil demon that deceives him in all these things. Why this dread? Why the uncertainty? What destroyed the certainty that we ourselves, and our surroundings, are real and that our senses communicate this reality to us? Simultaneous with the first great successes in the modern sciences toward the end of the seventeenth century, human beings lost their intimacy with their surroundings. Calderon's "Life Is a Dream" appeared in the right moment. Cartesian pride in having recognized oneself as *res cogitans*, as thinking substance, is paired with the horror of no longer being connected to anything, or philosophically speaking, with the embarrassment of placing this thinking substance in some sort of plausible relation to *res extensa*, to the rest of the world. Wilder and wilder constructions are raised to bridge this gulf, along with an idealism that becomes ever stronger and more radical: *esse est percipi*. Here, as usual, Leibniz is the most consistent in formulating, in the *Monadology*, total alienation as the price of progress in knowledge. Everyone is an isolated monad who in the endless sequence of its representations within itself lets the rest of the world pass by without contact.

Kant by no means avoids this fate. It remains the case also for him that knowledge is constantly menaced by the doubt that what we believe we experience is only a dream. To be sure, the worst fear is overcome. Kant proves to himself and against idealism that the existence of the outside world is just as certain as is our own existence. The monads gained windows, but we remain inside them. Signals come in from the outside, and produce images in us, but we don't know what they have in common with the outside world. Empirical images cannot occur without the play of imagination, this constantly active faculty that also produces images when there is no stimulus from outside.

> The soul of every man, even in the healthiest condition, is always busy painting all sorts of images of things that are not present, or it is busy completing some incomplete likeness in the representation of objects that are present, through this or that chimerical trait that the creative talent for invention [*Dichtungsfähigkeit*] sketches into the sensation. ("On Mental Illness," II:264)

Our representations can rest on sensation or on the free play of the imagination, and in the case of the former, participation of the imagination cannot be ruled out; indeed, it is necessary.

The origin of representations cannot be seen by looking at them. "But the difference between truth and dreaming is not ascertained by the nature of the representations which are referred to objects" (*Prol.*, 38 [290]).[11]

From Descartes to Kant, the cost of the elevation of human beings to mental beings and of the establishment of the rule of reason was the dread of being cut off from everything and of being delivered up to the webs of inwardness. For the sober Kant, who on all biographical accounts was far removed from everything mystical, this situation must have become unbearable because he himself had to confront fantasts, mystics, and seers. The appearance of the so-called goat-prophet in Königsberg occasioned the writing of "On Mental Illnesses" in 1764. Kant reacted to the great sensation among the educated world caused by the mystic and prophet Swedenborg with the work *Dreams of a Spirit-seer.*

In this work Kant made it clear to himself and his readers that it is precisely traditional metaphysics that makes space for the spirit-seer. The rationalist position that presents the outer world as merely the sphere of dead matter and reduces knowledge of it to the order of phenomena made space for thinking of arbitrary organic, pneumatic, spiritual substances as the causes behind the phenomena and within matter (*Geisterseher*, II:329f.). Thus Kant's verdict that the spirit-seer should be banished to the mental hospital is at the same time his turn against traditional metaphysics—the *critical turn.*

From now on, knowledge must prove itself by differentiating itself from dreams. That is not easy, since dream representations are not distinguishable from those that rest on sensation. With a firm hand, however, Kant identified characteristics of dreams that rested on the relation of dreams to each other and the relation of dream representations to one another. The fragmented, disconnected, and private nature of dreams allows them to be set off from objective experience. If this were not the case, "if we did not, on awakening, find many gaps in our recollection . . . and if our dream the following night began where it left off the night before, would we not believe that we lived in two different worlds? I do not know" (*Anthr.*, 51 [175]). Several times Kant cites with approval the supposed dictum of Aristotle: "When we are awake we share a common world, when we dream, however, everyone has his own" (*Geisterseher*, II:342). From then on, connection and the possibility of publicity became criteria of truth. Thus in the *Critique of Pure Reason* Kant recommends this rule against dreams and sense deceptions: "Whatever is connected with a perception according to empirical laws, is actual" (A 376). In the passage from the *Prolegomena* cited above, the difference between dream and truth is said to be constituted "by the connection [of representations] according to those rules which determine the coherence of the representations in the concept of an object, and by ascertaining whether they can subsist together in experience or not (*Prol.*, 38 [290–291]). All representations that cannot be brought into a necessary succession, namely, into a succession that (due to publicity) must be able to include not only my own representations but also those of other subjects, "I should have to regard . . . as a merely subjective play of my imagination; and if I still represented it to myself as something objective, I should have to call it a mere dream" (*CPR*, B 247).

The criteria are good. They require that the connection of experience be produced intersubjectively if it is to guarantee truth. They even suffice as the basis for the political demand for a bit of freedom, the freedom of the press (*Anthr.*, 88f. [219f.]). But the veil is flimsy. It might protect against madness (*Verrücktheit*), defined by Kant as that mental illness in which one's own imaginations are taken to be sensations. But it still does not prevent dementia (*Wahnsinn*). It could still be that one could invent for oneself a consistent, connected system. But what is worse, the same verdict is also passed on things other than the waking dream of madness (*Verrücktheit*). According to the *Critique of Pure Reason*, "empirical consciousness is in itself scattered [*zerstreut*]" (B 133). Moreover, the judgment of perception is not intersubjective, but remains private. Securing knowledge by identifying it as an objective connection of experience allows an undifferentiated mix of imagination, dream, subjective experience, and perception to arise outside it. Individual experience counts for nothing, the subjective judgment is insignificant, and personal knowledge loses all worth.

ENLIGHTENERS AND FANTASTS

If the eighteenth century defined itself as the century of enlightenment, philosophy, and criticism, then this was because the enlighteners, philosophers, and literati held the power of definition. Men like Voltaire, d'Alembert, and Kant tried to bind the century to this understanding of itself. Looking back, the historian could just as well designate it as the century of irrationalism. Promies summarizes his history of the citizen and the fool in the eighteenth century, when, after an initial banishment, folly emerges even more powerful and pervasive, as follows: "What finally stamped German cultural history during the course of this century was the battle against reason, against abstract rationalism."[12]

The eighteenth century was full of fantasts, spirit-seers, *Wundermänner*, saints, mystics, and fools, and of movements of the enthusiasts, fanatics, and afflicted folk who followed them. This century produced critical philosophy, but it also produced the literature of sentimentalism (*Empfindsamkeit*), of Storm and Stress and of romanticism. The philosophers of the Enlightenment were not prepared to recognize these contemporaries. What stirred in the name of fantasy, feeling, and piousness, and in the name of immediacy and naturalness, was for them an anachronism—old, dark, and obsolete. They repeatedly reacted with consternation and vehemence to the apparitions of their time as if to ghosts of the past. Friedrich Nicolai, for instance, described the scene as follows:

> Just a few years ago Gaßner was still able to draw thousands of people with the most senseless trickery. Just as many thousands would run to Vienna for the Pope's blessing. The urine-prophet Schuppach gathered together credulous people from all corners of Europe. Mesmer performed the most enormous charlatanry with his magnet cure in Vienna, and then went to Paris where he performed even greater charlatanry with his magnetism that wasn't even magnetic. . . . St. Germain was held up as a god, and aroused the attention of many princes and others who were not at all stupid. Through public spectacles Cagliostro knew how to present himself throughout Europe, and also to Lavater, as the most extraordinary man, and he agitated some of the most important men. . . . The followers of Swedenborg's insane enthusiasm are multiplying daily. Exorcists and spirit-seers are greatly esteemed in many places.[13]

These phenomena forced the enlighteners to formulate their position repeatedly. Indeed, what enlightenment *is* first becomes explicit in the attempt to ward off the fantasts. Looking back it almost seems as if enlighteners and fantasts were bound to each other, alternately calling each other out for repeated appearances on the stage.

Rationalism and irrationalism determine each other, and yet this relationship is still asymmetrical. Reason defines itself—that is the program of critical philosophy—but the Other is only the Other. It is the irrational; a cloudy mixture that at best is reduced in the polemic to a single common denominator: imagination. The enflamed, unbridled, sick imagination is held responsible for everything.

The historian will not accept this abbreviation. The attempt once again to discuss the Other of reason must show precisely that this "Other" is not merely imagination. The historian must also speak of the body, of the vaporous powers of feelings, of social movements, and of nature and the acquisition of nature.

But in what did this interrelation of enlighteners and fantasts consist? What balance was lost, such that the pendulum was set swinging so violently between rationalism and irrationalism? Some historians simply define the Enlightenment as the defense against seers and enthusiasts. Thus Schings, in his book *Melancholie und Aufklärung*, says, "Enlightenment appeared in such a manner quite literally as the dietetics of reason, as a grand therapeutic achievement."[14] He pursues the reductionist tendency of his authors to situate the enemy in the imagination and deeper still in the character and bodily constitution of melancholia.

In fact, many of the writings of the early enlighteners such as More, Casoubon, Locke, and Shaftesbury were elicited by and directed against enthusiasm. It is understandable that the "positive" bourgeoisie, aiming at acquisition and progress, found enthusiasm, depression, lack of resolve, and idleness deeply offensive and dangerous. In short, the enlightened, progressive bourgeoisie had to define melancholic persons as the other of itself. But one may still ask, where did these repeated bouts of melancholia come from in the "Age of Enlightenment"?

The Enlightenment had more stalwart opponents in ecclesiastical and philosophical doctrines, in institutions like the church and the state, the Estates, and authorities everywhere. Could it be that in the process of fighting these opponents, the Enlightenment nurtured an in-house adversary? The bourgeoisie fought the nobility, but insofar as it was itself preparing to dominate, the masses posed a threat. Similarly, reason, which had prevailed over external powers, both natural ones like authority and supernatural ones like ghosts and demons, found itself confronted with a new opponent: imagination and feeling.

Reason, preparing to dominate, grew narrow. Enlightened reason in the eighteenth century is no longer the self-assured and far-reaching reason of a Leibniz, nor is it any more the radical and aggressive critique of a Bayle. The reason that wants to dominate limits itself. It leaves the Other outside and at the same time is codetermined with this Other. From this point on, defense and dread accompany the domination of reason. Enlighteners like Locke, Shaftesbury, and Kant feel themselves directly and personally threatened, or at the very least challenged and irritated, by the appearance of seers, mystics, and Wundermänner. For them the "banding together" of simple folk (a phenomenon that is quite different from the idea of a community of discourse of free citizens), the religious movements, and the massive gatherings in the wake of charismatic figures were sinister. Fascinated as well as repelled, they were forced to deal with these phenomena again and again. Shaftesbury consorted with the followers of Casimard, Kant personally watched the carryings-on of the goat-prophet.

Some enlighteners sensed that here they glimpsed their own Other. Thus d'Alembert writes, after celebrating the progress of his century, "New light that was to be shed over many objects; new darknesses that arose, were the fruits of this universal ferment of spirits."[15] And Kant concluded his classification of the "sicknesses of the head" with the claim: "The ferment for all of this corruption is found in the constitution of the citizen [*Bürger*], so that even if it does not immediately produce corruption, it still serves to entertain and to enlarge it."[16]

What? The Enlightenment produces darkness, and the bourgeois constitution nourishes insanity? How can that be?

The domination of reason produces resistance, and the delimitation of the reasonable dislocates other *humaniora*. The secularization of public life turned prophets like Swedenborg into cranks and committed Christians like Antonia Bourgignon into outcasts. Speculative thinking became "dreamings of metaphysics" just as presentiments and visions became "dreamings of sensibility." Whatever did not fall within the realm of reasonable speech, including speechlessness, became irrational: body, feelings, "metaphysical needs," needs for immediacy, life, and nature. When isolated, these spheres become "crazy"—they take on ludicrous or chaotic traits. The reasonable person unlearns deportment with this Other and instead reacts to it with panic and dread.

Kant's critique of reason is a part of this process. It could be called tragic. His efforts to ensure a secure land of truth and his demarcation of the use of reason contributed to making the rest of the world insecure. Reason withdrew into itself and thereby withdrew from the Other. Traffic over the fortified borders became difficult. The Other became foreign and incomprehensible.

KANT AND SWEDENBORG, OR THE ORIGIN OF THE CRITICAL PHILOSOPHY

Already in the nineteenth century Kuno Fischer called attention to the fact that Kant's plans for a critique of reason were developed during precisely the same time as his dispute with Swedenborg. Nevertheless, it has been maintained that Kant's philosophy issued from a dialectical movement between Leibniz/Wolff-type rationalism and English sensualism. Kant's remark that Hume had awakened him from his dogmatic slumber seemed to legitimize this view. This view fails to notice the disturbance that caused Kant to lose confidence in the cognitive faculties in general, and that forced him to the metalevel in his work. The problems of physics, morality, theology, and logic were no longer treated, but rather, reason itself became the subject. This view also fails to represent the motivation and origin of that unprecedented energy with which Kant for twenty years worked on the project of the critique of reason drafted in 1765. Describing the critical turn as merely cognitive progress is not appropriate to the radical nature of this revolutionary changeover. An attempt must also be made to understand it as a psychodynamic process, and the key to this is Kant's relation to Swedenborg. We presume that in Swedenborg Kant perceived a sort of twin brother, his counterpart, from whom he found it vitally important to distance himself.

To begin with, Swedenborg was for Kant, as for every good enlightener, simply repulsive. In a letter on this matter to Charlotte von Knobloch, Kant writes that it is "always most appropriate to the rule of healthy reason to align oneself (in these matters) on the negative side." But he had to confirm that philosophy supplied no grounds for this decision of enlightened taste. Philosophy left him in the lurch, and furthermore, as he himself demonstrated in the *Dreams of a Spirit-seer*, it could develop options for making spirit-seeing plausible. Finally, in his intensive study of Swedenborg, Kant must have noticed that in his own fantastical excursions in the universe and his speculations on the inhabitants of other worlds and their spiritual abilities as they appear in *Theory of the Heavens*, he was not unlike Swedenborg. This began to appear sinister to him

The text against Swedenborg, *Dreams of a Spirit-seer, Illustrated by the Dreams of Metaphysics*, was published in 1766. In a letter to Lambert from the same year Kant says that his publisher, Kanter, already announced a book of his on "the peculiar methods of metaphysics." Kant, however, was of the opinion that he must first do "the metaphysical elements of natural philosophy" and "the metaphysical elements of practical philosophy." The sequence was eventually reversed, with the *Critique of Pure Reason* appearing in 1781, the *Metaphysical Elements of Natural Science* in 1786, and the *Groundwork of the Metaphysics of Morals* in 1785. But the program was manifestly clear. So also with the principles of the "Peculiar Methods of Metaphysics." They were formulated in the work on the spirit-seer itself. They are the principles of the critique of reason.

Kant's work shows the extent to which spirit-seeing and speculative metaphysics are related. The one makes possible the other, and they have related features. They are only accessible to select people, they do not fit into the connected experiences of everyone, or into a discourse in which every reasonable person can partake. Spirit-seeing as well as metaphysics are thus to be characterized as dreams, although differently than is maintained in the saying (falsely attributed to Aristotle by Kant)[17] that we each have our own world when we dream and only live in a common world when waking. Irreverently referring to Crusius and Wolff, Kant says, "we will put up with the contradictions of their visions, until these gentlemen have finished dreaming." Then, when the philosophers have awakened, they will "inhabit a common world" (*Geisterseher*, II:342). In connection with this he speaks of "certain signs and omens" that herald this period and "that for some time have appeared on the horizon of science." What else is Kant accomplishing here if not heralding himself?!

In his letter to Lambert, Kant mentions the "peculiar methods of metaphysics." Although three years earlier in the prize essay written for the Berlin Academy, *Investigations of the Meaning of the Principles of Natural Theology and Morals* (published in 1764),[18] Kant had already spoken of the "peculiar methods of arriving at the highest possible certainty in metaphysics," one would not want to relate this to the remarks in the letter to Lambert. In the essay Kant simply states that metaphysics, as opposed to mathematics, must proceed analytically. Explication of concepts was, according to the essay, the method of metaphysics. On the other hand, already Borowski, in his biography of Kant published in 1804, indicated that the first formulations of the principles of critical philosophy appeared in the *Spirit-seer*.[19]

The task of critical philosophy was to determine the limits of the true, legitimate use of reason. It fulfilled this task by securing the knowledge of objects by a reflection on the relation of the object to human cognitive faculties, that is, by the so-called transcendental method. This method distinguished things as they may be in themselves from things as they appear to us. There can only be knowledge of the latter, because objects that we want to cognize must be given to us. For cognition, these must always be created from two sources, a priori and a posteriori. Finally, the objectivity of knowledge is guaranteed if it can be fitted into a universal connected experience.

This all occurs in fact in the *Dreams of a Spirit-seer*, and indeed, it occurs there first and with the mark of a discovery. There Kant defined metaphysics, whose themes were by then determined with regard to content to be God, freedom, and immortality, as "a science of the limits of human reason" (II:368). Its method is characterized as "transcendental" in the sense of the *Critique of Pure Reason*. Knowledge is defined as transcendental in the *Critique* as that "which is occupied not so much with objects as with the mode of our knowledge of objects" (B 25). In the *Spirit-seer*, Kant writes,

> When this investigation breaks into philosophy, which judges its own processes and knows not only objects but also their relation to human understanding, then the borders contract and the boundary-stones are set, which prevent the investigation from straying beyond its specific compass. (II:369–370)

That the distinction between appearance and thing-in-itself and the limiting of knowledge to the former is central in the *Spirit-seer* piece will be shown immediately. They appear as the distinction between empirical reality (gravitation, organic being, moral feeling) and the "spirits" that produce it. Moreover, the doctrine of the two sources occurs in this early piece: "Since one must know that all knowledge can be conceived according to its two ends, the one a priori and the other a posteriori" (II:358). Finally, the central concern of the piece against the spirit-seer is naturally to distinguish dreams from knowledge—an effort that later culminated in the concurrence criterion.

It is an undisputed fact among scholars that Kant drew up the program of the critical philosophy in the years 1764–1766. That its principles are sketched out in the *Spirit-seer* has been shown here. But the question still remains, whether the dispute with Swedenborg is related to the conception of the critical philosophy in respect of its content or whether it was even its occasion. After all, perhaps Kant, busy in these years with the plan of critical philosophy, was just giving incidental hints to this plan in a piece that was being written on the side, namely, the *Spirit-seer.*

Let us examine the publications that occupied Kant during the years 1764–1766. Along with the work on Swedenborg, Kant worked through the eight volumes of the *Arcana Coelestica*—already quantitatively no secondary work. He was also occupied with the "goat-prophet" Jan Komarnick, who was the occasion for the piece "On Mental Illnesses" (1764). In addition, he also wrote the *Observations on the Feeling of the Beautiful and the Sublime* (1764) and the work for the Berlin Academy, *Investigations of the Meaning of the Principles of Natural Theology and Morals* (1764). There are then essentially three themes that occupied him: enthusiasm, the feeling of the beautiful and the sublime, and the new method of metaphysics. What goes through the head of a man who is occupied with these three themes at the same time? How do they hang together? Do they perhaps have a common root?

Our goal is to show what the dispute with the enthusiasts and the new critical method of metaphysics have to do with each other. The *Investigations of the Meaning of the Principles of Natural Theology and Morals* show that Kant had been clearly uneasy about the condition of metaphysics for quite a while. But compared to the statements in the *Spirit-seer,* which were written with the sense of a breakthrough, the presentation of the "single method" in metaphysics is so vague that this prize essay is at most meaningful as a *terminus post.* The actual impulse to the "critical turn" was still outstanding.

The *Observations on the Beautiful and the Sublime* appear to be more of a secondary work, originating in Kant's reading of the English theorists of taste and the Common Sense philosophers. But it is important that insofar as he dealt with the sentiments, Kant occupied himself with the "powers that move the human heart," about which he said in the *Spirit-seer* that "some of the mightiest appear to lie outside it" (II:334). Kant does something here that after the critical turn he would no longer permit himself to do: he investigates objective feeling qualities, or characters. He finds the characters of the beautiful and the sublime equally in human beings, animals, landscapes, and nations. The peculiar appearance of such characters in such diverse realms and the possibility that they have an effect on the human heart must have raised questions for Kant whose answers in the writings of Swedenborg, which he was reading simultaneously, shocked him. According to Swedenborg, this possibility was based on the existence of a realm of spiritual beings that merely express their "inclination" in the ordinary world but are in constant direct communication according to their inner relationship. Kant explicitly appropriated this meaning from Swedenborg where he dealt with another one of what the English philosophers called feelings, namely, the moral, the "feeling" for the good. Kant had clearly sensed the danger that is bound up with powers that move the human heart and are so powerful that we are inclined to attribute them to other beings outside us. He had correctly noted that Swedenborg also explained other things that arise in us spontaneously without our will, namely, the irruptions of the imagination, as effects from "outside." That is, they were explained as the way in which the angels speak to us (*Geisterseher*, II:339). What is being threatened here is what Kant later called the "autonomy of reason." Under its rule "heart" gradually disappeared from among the faculties of the mind, and the sublime and beautiful become achievements of judgment. The moral feeling is replaced by the consciousness of the law.

The extraordinary work that Kant invested in the case of Swedenborg cannot be motivated solely by the interests of his acquaintances who had begged him for enlightenment. On the contrary, Kant first called forth this interest in his friends by his *own* intensive occupation with Swedenborg. He wrote to Mendelssohn about it on 4 April 1766:

> By being so inquisitive about Swedenborg's visions with people that had the opportunity to know him personally as well as through letters, and also by obtaining his works, I had at one time given people much to talk about, I thought that I would not put to rest all the inquiries until I discharged all my supposed knowledge about these matters.

The irritation that Kant himself experienced, in particular the light that it cast on the "method of metaphysics," occasioned Kant's intensive work on Swedenborg. Thus it can at least be said that the work on the *Spirit-seer* piece was a detour on the way to the method of metaphysics. That is, it turns out at the end of the work that with respect to Swedenborg, Kant was no wiser than before. His work had led him "to the same point of uncertainty" (II:367). After making this observation, Kant says that in fact he was only concerned with the fate of metaphysics: "But I had in fact one purpose that seemed more important than that which I asserted, and this I believe I have achieved. Metaphysics, of whose fate I am enamored" (II:367). And then he arrives at the definition of the task of metaphysics as determiner of the limits of human reason, which we cited above.

Kant learned something about metaphysics from the case of Swedenborg, and thereby also something about himself. He had uncovered a relationship between enthusiasm and metaphysics that frightened him away. Where he presents the content of Swedenborg's books read by him, he says, "Such a marvelous accord prevails in this work with what the finest subtleties of reason can produce about the self-same object" (II:360).

This accord portrayed the spirit realm from two different sides, namely, to speak with the later Kant, from the side of intuitions and from the side of concepts. In the *Spirit-seer* he opposes the "fanatical intuiting" of Swedenborg to the "perversely subtle reason" (*verkehrt grübelnden Vernunft*) of metaphysics. Prophecy is, as it were, the experiential basis of metaphysics, as metaphysics, for its part, shows that prophecy is possible. In fact, Christian metaphysics has become a theory of the beyond or the spirit world. Kant demonstrated this connection in his work by showing how the possibility of Swedenborgian spirit communication can be proved by metaphysical constructions.

We want now to sketch this proof. Kant indicates that empirical knowledge and thus also science remain responsible for decisive answers in three areas and, indeed, directly provokes speculation. These are the question of the "cause of gravitation," the origin of the organization of matter, and the origin of the moral feeling in human beings.

Kant is clearly aware that Newton said he had provided the law of gravitation but that the "cause of gravitation" was unknown to him. "Yet he had no misgivings about treating this gravitation as a genuine effect of a universal activity of matter on itself" (II:335). Kant said of organic beings that they are not to be understood as mere mechanical effects, "but activate themselves and the dead stuff of nature besides, through inner activity" (II:329). Thus "immaterial beings" are presumed here "whose particular operating laws are called pneumatic, and insofar as physical beings are mediate causes of their effects in the material world, are called organic" (II:329). These are only examples that supply analogies leading to the decisive argument on the basis of moral feeling. This is "perhaps a sensed dependence of our own judgments upon *universal human understanding*..., and a means... of providing a kind of rational unity in the entire thinking being" (II:334). Thus moral feeling forces us into agreement with a general will. What is more obvious than to hypostatize this general will as an effective power that necessitates this agreement in us? "A secret power necessitates us to adjust our own views conjointly with the welfare of others or with others' power of choice" (II:334). Accordingly, spiritual beings are presumed to be causes for the empirical facts of gravitation, for living organization, and for moral feeling. If this is so, nothing stands in the way of postulating a special interaction between these spiritual beings. Then it may be said:

> The human soul would therefore have to be regarded as being conjoined in its present life with two worlds at once. Inasmuch as its personal unity is bound up with a body, it perceives only the material world clearly. But as a member of the spiritual world it receives and imparts the pure influxes of material natures, so that as soon as the accidental bond has ceased, all that remains is that communion that it has with spiritual nature at all times, and that it must present to its consciousness in a clear intuition. (II:332)

That is, Swedenborg is deduced.

Spirit-seeing and metaphysics, enthusiasm and reason prop each other up. That is Kant's experience, and he knows that he himself is affected by this intimate connection—recall Kant's "enthusiasm" in the *Theory of the Heavens*. If in its first phase the Enlightenment defended seers, prophets, and enthusiasts against the institutional calumny and persecution of the Inquisition, it must now find them threatening. His relationship to Swedenborg became clear to Kant, forcing him to critique and limit reason.

Kant's constantly repeated apologies and justifications for his thorough treatment of Swedenborg show how painful this relationship was to him. He sees himself as among those philosophers who, "caught between the assurances of a reasonable and completely convinced eye-witness, and the inner resistance of an insuperable doubt, cut a most foolish figure" (II:317). He feels "somewhat ashamed" (II:367) about his ventures. In the *Spirit-seer*, he therefore vehemently explains "that I do not appreciate the humor" (II:359) were someone henceforth to presume in Kant's work an affinity between spirit-seeing and metaphysics. In a private letter to Mendelssohn from the same year, however, he frankly admits that the cure that he accomplished in his satire of Swedenborg was a kind of self-healing.

> It seemed to me wisest to forestall other people's mockery by first of all mocking myself; and this procedure was actually quite honest, because the condition of my mind was contrary to reason [*wiedersinnisch*] on this matter. Also with regard to the spirit reports, I cannot restrain myself from a small attachment to these sorts of stories, nor can I help nourishing some suspicion of the correctness of their rational basis.[20]

Kant had never before in his life turned to another author with such intensity. How close Swedenborg is to him is shown not only by the fact that he so successfully borrows from his metaphysical understanding but also by the exceptional appreciation he shows for the contents of Swedenborg's doctrine in the section "The ecstatic travels of an enthusiast." And this in spite of his maintaining that the writings of Swedenborg are "confused [*wirr*]." Herder, who attended Kant's lectures at the time, clearly had a sense for this affinity, because he certified of Kant precisely that which Kant criticized in Swedenborg. In his review of Kant's *Spirit-seer*, he wrote, "It can be seen everywhere that the author [Kant] is friends with the genius of philosophy, just as Socrates also spoke with his demon in sacred dreaming."[21]

Kant wanted to have nothing more to do with demons, dreams, and ghosts, however. Although he arrived at his position by a non sequitur, and although he could only say, of all the spiritual things whose possibility for thought he had at first so thoroughly developed, "How many things there are that I do not need" (II:369), he shoved them away with a violent, disgusted gesture. He agreed with the average "enlightened" judgment of his time that it involved "a real illness" (II:340) and that Swedenborg was to be looked on as a "candidate for the mental hospital" (II:348).

Reason retreated to secure terrain. "Ecstatic travels," as well as the imagination, were forbidden it. It was no longer supposed to dream. The advantage is that philosophers, once awakened, "inhabit a common world" (II:342). But how many "dreams" were sent to the mental hospital for this, and how long will it take until the realms that reason's retreat had made irrational are recovered?

THE LANGUAGE OF THE ANGELS

Seers, enthusiasts, and fantasts continue with their mumbling what under the Enlightenment's censorship of reason had to disappear from official discourse. Displaced, it appeared scurrilous and expressed itself in figurative language forms. Moreover, reason produced its own Other, the thorough rationalization of the being of its irrational part, its Arreton. That which was repressed expressed itself in the language of poor lunatics. We want to discuss here only one example of this, namely, how in Swedenborg's vision the wish for immediacy produced by courtly, and later, bourgeois, conventions of human intercourse was expressed in alienated form in the speech of the angels. Other examples could be chosen from Swedenborg's writings, for instance, the return of the microcosm/macrocosm analogy, which was proscribed by modern science, in his doctrine of the "great man," namely, that the universe with its systems and planets forms an organism: the great man; or his doctrine of "correspondences" (*Entsprechungen*), a distant hideaway for the notion that the world is meaningful, which is now, according to modern principles of reality, no longer conceivable. We choose the doctrine of the language of the angels because it directly confronts Kant's instructions for rational conduct in an especially clear way.

Swedenborg's writings are not confused. They do strike the modern reader as scurrilous and unstable, and even, as Kant already said, as born of an unbridled fantasy. They can nevertheless be understood throughout as examples of a particular tradition of speech, namely, as Ernst Benz has shown, that of the prophet.[22] However, this interpretation of Swedenborg serves only the theologian and his audience since, as Benz also knows, Swedenborg opposed his era not only with *what* he said, as did prophets of earlier periods, but also with his very existence as a "prophet" or "seer," with his manner of speaking. But although Swedenborg's existence must be seen in sharp contrast to the ideology of the Enlightenment, the Enlightenment created the historical conditions under which it is even possible to take Swedenborg seriously. To list him in the historical roll of prophets makes him into an anachronism in his own time. We want to show that what he had to say belonged most intimately to his time, and the figurative nature of his speech complements the development of rational discourse.

To begin with, we present a full selection from Swedenborg's "report" on the speech of angels.

> In the entire heaven all have the same language, and they all understand one another, to whatever society, near or remote, they belong. Language there is not learned but is instinctive with every one, for it flows from their very affection and thought, the tones of their speech corresponding to their affections, and the vocal articulations which are words corresponding to the ideas of thought that spring from the affections; and because of this correspondence the speech itself is spiritual, for it is affection sounding and thought speaking.
>
> Anyone who gives any thought to it can see that all thought is from affection which pertains to love, and that the ideas of thought are the various forms into which the general affection is distributed; for no thought or idea is possible apart from affection—the soul and life of thought is from affection. This enables angels to know, merely from another's speech, what he is—from the tone what his affection is, and from the vocal articulations or words what his mind is. The wiser angels know what the ruling affection is from a single series of words, for that affection is what they chiefly attend to.
>
> It is recognized that each individual has a variety of affections, one affection when in joy, another when in grief, another when in truth, another when in love and charity, another when in zeal or in anger, another when in simulation and deceit, another when in quest of honor and glory, and so on. But the ruling affection or love is in all of these; and for this reason the wiser angels, because they perceive that love, know from the speech the whole state of another.
>
> This it has been granted me to know from much experience. I have heard angels disclosing the character of another's life merely from hearing him speak. They also said that from any ideas of another's thought they could know all things of his life, because from those ideas they know his ruling love, in which are all things in their order. They know also that man's book of life is nothing else.[23]

What is peculiar about the language of the angels is above all the immediacy of its mode of expression. Strictly speaking, it is already wrong to speak of expression, because there is no difference between thought and speech, or between feeling and expression. According to Swedenborg, angels are human beings who in the second phase of their postmortal career have given up the "outer man." Thus there is no longer a distinction between inner and outer, and their language is immediate communication, "affection sounding and thought speaking."

The desperate longing that is expressed in such a representation of communicative immediacy must be seen against a background of civil history, just as the form of its expression refers to the condition of enlightenment language theory that makes it impossible to rationally articulate an alternative.

In the eighteenth century the manners and forms of speech of the court, and in imitation of courtly practices, more and more in the bourgeoisie, were subjected to the strictest rules of conduct and of speech [*façon de parler*]. Simple and straightforward behavior was "boorish [*bäurisch*]." A direct expression of feeling or thought was already considered tasteless in itself. If this stylizing of behavior and speech constituted the person, that is, the civilized or "politic" person, then it was also advisable to hide one's true intentions and feelings out of prudence. In the intrigues and plots of court life as well as in bourgeois businesses one wanted to get something from association with other people. If social roles already prescribed a certain behavior that was independent of how one actually felt, then dissimulation in order to achieve one's purposes was also useful. Finally, skeptics were of the opinion that without this civilizing external gloss, human society would not be possible at all, because the ineradicable chaos of vices had to be hidden under it. Kant is to be numbered among these skeptics. "So it already belongs to the basic composition of a human creature and to the concept of his species to explore the thoughts of others but to withhold one's own," he writes in the *Anthropology from a Pragmatic Point of View* (192 [332]).

Thus the difference between thoughts and feelings and outer behavior, the difference between the inner and the outer person, is stylized into a characteristic of the species. In fact, however, this difference is one that is produced by upbringing and discipline, as this century in its sentimental view of children and simple people knew very well. To be human is not given, it must be developed. "The human being can only become human through upbringing [*Erziehung*]," Kant says (*Pädagogik*, IX:443). A cleft in human beings is thereby produced that causes them to suffer and that "does not fail to progress gradually from *dissimulation* to *deception* [*vorsetzlichen Täuschung*] and finally to *lying*" (*Anthr.*, 192 [332]). Skepticism about the human race and the hypostatizing of the civilized condition of his time also led Kant to be able to imagine an alternative only in the phantasm about communicating angels. One can see the effects of working on Swedenborg when Kant writes,

> It could well be that some other planet is inhabited by rational beings who have to think aloud—who, whether awake or dreaming, in company with others or alone, can have no thoughts they do not *utter*. How would their behavior toward one another then differ from that of the human race? Unless they were all as *pure as angels*, we cannot conceive how they could live together peacefully, have any respect at all for one another, and get on well together. (*Anthr.*, 192 [332])

The difference between being and appearance, and the inner and outer human being, is essential for making a *human* society possible. Thus it must be bred through upbringing and discipline. The individual might suffer, but from a moral point of view this human condition is merely a lesser evil. "We live in a period of discipline, culture and civilization, but we are a long way yet from living in a period of moralizing [*Moralisierung*]" (*Pädagogik*, IX:451). Kant designates the semblance concealing the rudeness and animosity of human beings toward each other as a "permissible moral semblance" (*Anthr.*, 30 [151]). It is permissible because of its civilizing effect, but also because the deception bound up with it is mutual. Social manners are a game, though of course a serious one: "One would have to be a child to take [small change] for gold" (*Anthr.*, 32 [151]).

> Men are one and all actors—the more so, the more civilized they are. They put on a show of affection, respect for others, modesty and disinterest without deceiving anyone, since it is generally understood that they are not sincere about it. (*Anthr.*, 30 [151])

Civilized behavior as the art of dissimulation calls forth on the other side the corresponding art of disclosure. For Kant, too, this second art appears along with the first when it is a matter of educating children to prudence. Prudence is the art "of bringing our skill to bear on a man, that is of how one is able to use people for one's own purposes" (*Pädagogik*, IX:486). To be able to sell oneself and manipulate others requires that one be able to see through others.

> If the child is to be taught worldly wisdom, then it must conceal itself and become impenetrable, but be able to examine others thoroughly. Above all it must conceal its character. The art of outward appearance is decorum, and one must possess this art. It is difficult to examine others thoroughly, but one must necessarily understand this art in order to make oneself impenetrable to it. To this art belongs the art of dissimulation. that is, of suppressing one's mistakes, and that outer semblance. (*Pädagogik*, IX:486)

Practical psychology arose in the eighteenth century as such an art of disclosure. This is also the assigned aim of *Anthropology from a Pragmatic Point of View*. The entire second part is dedicated to the art of "How to Discern Man's Inner Self from His Exterior." Lavater's efforts in physiognomy also belong to this context. In 1762, Christian Thomasius extolled the invention of a new science to the elector of Brandenburg: "To be able to recognize in daily conversation what is hidden in other people, even against their will."[24] He unreservedly proffers this science as an instrument of control and even points to the successful espionage techniques of Richelieu and Mazarin as models.[25] There are plenty of people at court, he says, "who practice this science," and it is only a matter of making them principled and teaching them at the universities.

It should not be forgotten, however, that along with this worldly-wise and cynical dealing with the human split into inner and outer came expressions of suffering and desperate longing for closeness. To these belong Rousseau's fantasies of the natural life, Lessing's longing to base society on sympathetic love, as well as the culture of friendship and letter-writing of sentimentalism [*Empfindsamkeit*]. Swedenborg's visions of the angels' relations with each other doubtless originate in the sufferings of civilization. In *Heaven and Hell*, he writes,

> In a civil society you judge others on the basis of what you have heard or learned from rumors and personal acquaintance with them, but in conversation with them you do not let on how you judged them. Even if you judged them to be bad, you behave cordially towards them. . . . All this makes clear that there are two kinds of thinking, external and internal, and these people speak with external thoughts, but internally their thoughts are completely different. (317)

He writes that "due to civil relationships on earth" we live in constant fear "that the thoughts of the will could emerge" (319). There is therefore an inner control that watches over outer thought (i.e., what gets expressed), "to keep him from transgressing the limits of propriety and honor" (ibid.). Self-imposed coercion, the unfamiliarity that everyone must maintain toward every other due to the difference between inner and outer persons, one's own inner turmoil—all will be overcome when after their death human beings develop themselves into angels. Angels see or hear each other's true being and the passion that constitutes them, and that as human beings they already carried inwardly. For this reason the doctrine of "marriages in heaven," along with that of the language of the angels, was of such significance for Swedenborg. In heaven those people come together who really love each other. In bourgeois relations, on the other hand, one marries by convention, out of pride, or for financial reasons.

Now it is natural to wonder why Swedenborg was unable to formulate such a "reasonable" concern in a more reasonable way. What we have already seen in Kant must also be true of Swedenborg, namely, that he esteems civilization's product of an inner world as an inescapable component of human existence. But there is another consideration. If we understand Swedenborg's talk of the communication of angels, it is because ordinary communication always has some features of the communication of angels. These features were not only suppressed by the demands of civilization, but they were not even statable in terms of contemporary eighteenth-century theory of language. This is characteristically conceived in the *Port Royal Logic* as the theory of signs. Linguistic expressions are not—as Herder later wants to counter—actions, but much rather signs whose transmissions are supposed to call forth the representation of something else, of that which is designated. Even the communication of wishes, prayers, and commands occurs by way of signs *for* wishing, praying, and commanding.[26]

In such a theory of language, the possibility of deception is essential to language. In the words of the *Port Royal Logic*, a sign is able "as a thing, to conceal what it, as a sign, reveals." Arnauld illustrates this with an example that is worth citing in relation to Swedenborg's angel theory: "The forms, understood as things, taken on by the angels conceal the angels; understood as signs, they signify them."[27]

This theory of language, like the theory of knowledge, stands in a peculiar relation to the social conditions of the eighteenth century. Language, like knowledge, is representational. Just as the idea is an inner representation of the outer object, so speech is an outer representation of inner thought. Language is by its very nature mediation, and the idea of an unmediated language is an absurdity.

Swedenborg's rudimentary language theory exemplifies this absurdity. Since the difference between the inner and outer person is omitted, it is feeling that connects the angels in communication. Through feeling they experience the harmony or discrepancy between each other's passions. Swedenborg reported that feelings are the sound of the angels' language, let us say, the tone of their communicative relation. Thoughts are then the articulation of this sound and consist in linguistic expression. This possibility does not appear so absurd if thoughts are understood as inner speech or inner discussion. This view differs with Swedenborg's only in that not every thought must be expressed outwardly. But now this theory of linguistic representation does become absurd. How are thoughts to represent speech when they are already themselves speech?

The representational theory of language essentially contains the possibility of deception and falsification. It reflects the reality of culturally determined forms of communication. Thus the "language of the angels" had to have the peculiar form in which Swedenborg formulated his vision of another life.

REASON UNDER STRESS

> Out of the so-called *Baumwalde*, in the domain of Alex, an adventurer, about fifty years old, a new Diogenes and a showpiece of human nature, was brought to Königsberg. There were attempts to cloak the ludicrous and improper aspects of his lifestyle with some biblical fig leaves. Because of this and because up until then, besides an eight-year-old boy, he led around a herd of 14 cows, 20 sheep, and 46 goats, he received the name of a goat-prophet from the gaping crowd.[28]

Kant also went there. Borowksi finishes his report on the event in the province of Königsberg with the remark, "The adventurer, who first occasioned the work 'On Mental Illnesses,' was allowed, together with the young wild boy, across the border."[29]

The institutional reaction to the ridiculous and improper is ostracism. The philosophical reaction is classification. That is the well-known procedure analyzed by Foucault and Dörner, through which the bourgeois Enlightenment tried to have done with insanity. To be more exact, "insanity" was first produced through hospitalization and conceptual definition.

Was the goat-prophet insane? He obviously lived in a completely uncivil way, moved around, wore inappropriate clothing, did not eat like other people. Further, it was said that he suffered from an illness accompanied by stomach cramps and had vowed to make a seven-year pilgrimage. To be sure, he also claimed to have seen Jesus several times, after twenty-day fasts. That was obviously too much for Kant. He went home and wrote a piece on mental illnesses. He strictly distinguished these from illnesses of the heart, and defined them as purely cognitive disorders. They are thus to be classified according to the faculties of knowledge: disorders of perception [*Verrücktheit*], disorders of judgment [*Wahnsinn*], disorders of inference drawing [*Wahnwitz*]. Kant favors somatic explanations of the causes and thus refers the stricken to a doctor, and only occasionally wants to hear of a philosopher being consulted. For Kant, as a true enlightener, Kowarski was not a goat-prophet, as he was for the people, but mentally disturbed.

Kant wrote something else when he got home. He wrote a short notice about the goat-prophet's child. He portrayed the "little wild one" in Rousseauian terms as a "perfect child," gay, carefree, lacking any "stupid embarrassment." He portrayed him as an example of original nature.[30]

On the one hand, the wild child of nature; on the other, the improper and mentally disturbed. In this event Kant must have experienced what he himself was as a civilized man of reason and what marked off the boundaries of his existence.

Human beings are not rational beings from birth. We first become so through upbringing and discipline, and we are never completely rational. Rationality consists much more in the concealing and disciplining of the original wildness that must be renounced in ourselves. Civilization sets itself up as the moral appearance over raw nature. To be rational is strenuous. Rationality's status is constantly threatened by the Other that it constitutes through its domination. It is the body, the feelings, nature, and the imagination (because it represents the Other itself in consciousness). The reason of the Enlightenment, Kantian reason, is marked by strain and fear. It is a spastic reason: rigid and closed.

"It is very easy to overlook and cross the bounds of self-control," Kant writes. Constantly threatened, reason retreats. It fortifies its own territory and widens its borders. What lies beyond the borders is left on its own. No more reason in the senses, no more reason in the body, no more reason in religion, no more reason in nature. Thus reason in retreat produces at the same time its own irrationality. The senses become mere sensibility, the body becomes the bestial part of the human being, religion outside the limits of reason alone becomes enthusiasm, and nature becomes part fearful, part glorified wilderness. From the point of view of the Other of reason, reason proves itself to be a retreat. Reason does indeed determine its legitimate borders and fortifies the land of truth, but this land of truth proves to be an island. Reason isolates itself.

NOTES

1. Wolfgang Promies, *Der Bürger und der Narr* (Munich, 1971).
2. J. Engell, *Creative Imagination: Enlightenment to Romanticism* (Cambridge, Mass., 1981).
3. Martin Heidegger, *Kant und das Problem der Metaphysik*, 2d ed. (Frankfurt, 1951).
4. *Critique of Pure Reason*, trans. Norman Kemp Smith (New York, 1965). References to Kant's other works in this text are to the Prussian Academy edition of Kant's works (*Kants Werke: Akademie Textausgabe* [Berlin, 1968]) and are indicated by volume number and page. Except where noted, translations are my own.—TRANS.
5. Ibid., 149.
6. Ibid., 155.
7. *The Conflict of the Faculties*, trans. Mary J. Gregor (Lincoln, 1992), 191–193.
8. *Anthropology from a Pragmatic Point of View*, trans. Mary J. Gregor (The Hague, 1974). References in the text are to Gregor's translation, with Academy (Vol. VII) pagination in square brackets.—TRANS.
9. "Versuch über die Krankheiten des Kopfes," in *Königsbergsche Gelehrte und Politische Zeitungen* (27 February 1764), 14–30.
10. *Critique of Judgment*, trans. Werner S. Pluhar (Indianapolis, 1987) (Academy Vol. V).
11. *Prolegomena to Any Future Metaphysics*, trans. Lewis White Beck (Indianapolis, 1975) (Academy Vol. IV).
12. Promies, *Der Bürger und der Narr*, 204.
13. Quoted in Hans-Jürgen Schings, *Melancholie und Aufklärung* (Stuttgart, 1977), 144.
14. Ibid., 195.
15. Jean d'Alembert, quoted in Ernst Cassirer, *Die Philosophie der Aufklärung* (Tübingen, 1932), 3.
16. Kant, "Versuch über die Krankheiten des Kopfes," in *Kants Werke* (Ak), II:269.
17. Heraclitus, Fragment 89.
18. Cf. "Nachricht von der Einrichtung seiner Vorlesungen in dem Winterhalbjahre von 1765–1766" (1:910) [Ak].
19. L. E. Borowski, "Darstellung des Lebens und Charakters Immanuel Kants," in *Immanuel Kant. Sein Leben in Darstellungen von Zeitgenossen* (Darmstadt, 1978).
20. 8 April 1766. [English translation adapted from *Kant: Philosophical Correspondence, 1759–88*, trans. Arnulf Zweig (Chicago, 1967), 55.]
21. Herder, *Sämtliche Werke* (Berlin, 1877), I:130.
22. Ernst Benz, *Emanuel Swedenborg: Naturforscher und Seher* (Munich: 1948).

23. Emanuel Swedenborg, *Himmel und Hölle, nach Gehörtem und Gesehenem* (Zurich, 1977), 148ff. [English translation is by J. C. Ager from Swedenborg, *Heaven and Its Wonders and Hell from Things Heard and Seen* (New York, 1900), 134–135. Subsequent page references to Swedenborg are to this translation.]

24. Fritz Brüggemann, ed., *Aus der Frühzeit der deutschen Aufklärung* (Darmstadt, 1974), 69.

25. Ibid., 73.

26. Antoine Arnauld, *The Art of Thinking: Port Royal Logic*, trans. J. Dickoff and P. James (Indianapolis, 1964).

27. Ibid.

28. Hamann, quoted by Borowski, "Darstellung des Lebens," 95.

29. Ibid., 96.

30. Ibid.

The Failure of Kant's Imagination

Jane Kneller

In a well-known account of the role of transcendental imagination in Kant's philosophy, Martin Heidegger practically accused Kant of intellectual cowardice. That is, Heidegger argued that Kant's refusal in the second edition of the *Critique of Pure Reason* to grant that the imagination was a fundamental faculty was a result of Kant's having originally identified the transcendental imagination with the "common root" of sensibility and understanding, and of his subsequently being unwilling to grant such basic status to a faculty whose obscure nature frightened him: "He saw the unknown," Heidegger says, and "he had to draw back."[1]

In what has become a classic critique of Heidegger's Kant interpretation, Dieter Henrich's "On the Unity of Subjectivity"[2] takes up his challenge to the integrity of the Kantian enterprise and defends Kant on the grounds that his refusal to explore the common root of both sensibility and understanding really has nothing to do with Kant's attitude toward the imagination but rather represents his adoption of the view, already promulgated against Christian Wolff by Christian August Crusius, that subjectivity cannot be traced to a single basic faculty or principle. Far from suggesting the need to identify any common root of human subjectivity, Henrich argues, Kant denies outright the possibility of ever knowing such a basic power and is agnostic about the existence of such a power even apart from the conditions of human knowledge.[3] Since Kant ultimately "renounces" a positive answer to the question of what conditions the possibility of human subjectivity, the "unknown" common root that Kant refers to in the introduction to the *Critique of Pure Reason* cannot be *any* known faculty and hence cannot be the imagination.[4] The imagination is not suppressed or "displaced" in Kant's philosophy, but is simply not central.

Historically, the notion that human subjectivity must be unified on the basis of its stemming from a common source in that which mediates sensibility and understanding was a theme worked out in Johann Gottlieb Fichte, F. W. J. Schelling, and G. W. F. Hegel and voiced again, Henrich argues, in Heidegger. But for critical philosophy such unity was unknowable and could only be explained regulatively, in terms of some sort of "intrasubjective" purposiveness.[5]

> The unity of subjectivity, in Kant's final construction of it, is conceived as teleological. Kant feels compelled to look beyond what is immediately given in consciousness, "to look beyond the sensible to the supersensible as the point where all our a priori powers are reconciled, since that is the only alternative left to us for bringing reason into harmony with itself."[6]

But so far as knowledge is concerned, the structural unity of the faculties is contingent. If this is Kant's view, then of course no account could be established for the primacy of imagination as original source of knowledge. The imagination is only one of the faculties of the mind, all of which can only be encountered "derivatively" through experience.[7]

This, Henrich argues, explains Kant's turn away from any attempt to "deduce" the faculties in the first edition of the *Critique* to a "logical analysis" of the conditions of knowledge in the revised second edition. Not a fear of the unknown source of reason, but rather a recognition of its unavailability, led Kant to focus on the conditions of the understanding, whose structures—the logical forms of judgment—unlike imagination or sensibility, he was convinced were available for examination. Hence, according to Henrich, Kant became increasingly cautious about any attempt to explain the exact nature of sensibility or the relationship of the imagination to the understanding. Since the unity of the faculties in any absolute sense is unknown to human beings, the mediating role of the imagination must be understood as merely "the unity of activities that are required in addition to the objective principles of knowledge in order to render intelligible the actuality of knowledge."[8] Conceiving the imagination in this operational sense explains Kant's move, in the second edition of the *Critique*, to assimilate it to the understanding as one of its functions.

Henrich's argument seems historically correct. Few would argue the claim that the idealists' move to extend knowledge to an account of its ultimate origins constituted a decisive break with Kantian philosophy, even if not all its proponents saw it as such at the time. Yet the success of Henrich's "epistemological" approach has had the effect of pushing interesting aspects of Heidegger's reading into a corner to gather dust. In particular, Kant scholars have tended to neglect what Heidegger, on his reading, was able to appreciate, namely, the fact that Kant *was* unusually struck by what he took to be the mysterious nature of the imagination and that, even in the realm of cognition (not to mention human action and motivation) Kant did appear suspicious of the imagination's inscrutability.[9]

Yet a third wrinkle has been added to the fabric of the debate by Gernot Böhme and Hartmut Böhme, in their book *Das Andere der Vernunft.* They agree with Henrich that the critical turn in some sense necessitated Kant's move away from viewing the imagination as a separate faculty but take this shift to be grounds for criticizing the entire Kantian enterprise.[10] They argue that, whatever his philosophical reasons, Kant's unwillingness to grant the imagination any sort of autonomous status was rooted in psychological misapprehensions of phobic proportions. And while subconscious fears of the imagination and its close association with feeling and the body were typical of the Enlightenment psyche, they were by no means "healthy." After some very illuminating and entertaining textual analysis, the Böhmes conclude that the critical turn was an anxiety-driven swerve away from philosophical engagement with creative and enriching aspects of human experience. On a more sinister note, they suggest that Kant's philosophy sealed the fate of any such philosophizing in the future.

> Although the imagination had always been met with caution . . . even into the seventeenth century it still had its ancestral place among the faculties of knowledge. It lost this position with Kant—once and for all, one might say, if one views the philosophy of the romantics as an intermezzo.[11]

The Böhmes see the critical turn as symptomatic not simply of Kant's "angst" as a typical eighteenth-century man of reason but of much that ails contemporary "modern" thought generally.

In what follows I would like to make an initial attempt at adjudicating the debate between those who, like the Böhmes,[12] believe critical philosophy's antipathy to imagination and sensibility in general ought to undermine its significance and those (typically Kant scholars) who view such critiques as misplaced psychologizing that misses the point of the critical enterprise.[13]

Henrich argues that the unity of the faculties for Kant can only be understood "teleologically," hence the move to the imagination as transcendental *origin* is ruled out, and any attempts to rewrite Kant's account of subjectivity in terms of the imagination could only be misguided. The Böhmes argue that Kant was pathologically averse to giving the imagination any genuine status next to the understanding and reason and hence could not find a proper place for it in his account of knowledge. Henrich's account is a methodological explanation of the "displacement" of imagination in Kant's critical philosophy, the Böhmes' is a psycho-social one. Both may contain elements of truth—and they are by no means mutually exclusive—but, I believe, neither view can be the last word on the subject. For, as I will argue in what follows, it is not clear that, in the final analysis, the imagination was entirely displaced in Kant's philosophy, nor is it clear that he continued to hold that all functioning of imagination a priori must be subsumed under the understanding.

Two considerations support the view that the role of imagination was not displaced in Kant's overall theory. First, the role of teleological judgment came to have significance as a transcendental condition of human judgment for Kant, and his concern with it eventually resulted in the capstone of critical philosophy with the publication of the *Critique of Judgment*. Here, in the final phases of his mature philosophy, the imagination plays a pivotal role in Kant's account of the nature of human experience reflectively (teleologically) organized. Second, Kant was not *uniformly* negative in his view of the imagination, even of what he perceived to be its excesses. And at least one of these excesses, "enthusiasm," plays an important role in his later social theory.

A third consideration is also important in evaluating the extent to which Kant's philosophy was tainted by problematic motivations. Scholars have recently argued that a crucial motivating force behind Kant's "rejection" of metaphysics was his reading of Rousseau and his consequent radical revision of the prevailing instrumentalist conception of reason.[14] To the extent that this interpretation of the critical turn rests on Kant's deeply felt conviction that metaphysical speculation led to an "elitist" picture of morality, it clearly represents an additional element for consideration in any complete analysis of the psychology that drove critical philosophy. I look at each of these considerations in turn and conclude with an assessment of the Böhmes' contribution to Kant's interpretation in light of them.

IMAGINATION AND REFLECTION

The Böhmes' claim that the imagination lost its place as one of the faculties of knowledge in Kant's philosophy is relatively uncontroversial, if one considers the fate of the imagination in the *Critique of Pure Reason*. In the second edition of the *Critique*, Kant defines the imagination as "the faculty of presenting [*vorstellen*] in intuition an object that is *not itself present*" (*CPR*, B 151).[15] Such an activity may involve the representing of an object in accordance with laws of association, so that the images involved depend on what is, or was, given to the senses. Or, alternatively, the subject, apart from any particular experience, represents the object of intuition in accordance with the categories a priori. In the former case imagination is an effect determined empirically and is thus contingent in a way that renders it opaque to transcendental analysis. In Kant's words, this empirical manner of representing intuitions is "reproductive" and "contributes nothing to the explanation of the possibility of a priori knowledge" (*CPR*, B 152). This sort of imaginative activity, Kant says here, falls within the domain of psychology, but not transcendental (i.e., critical) philosophy.

In the latter case, where, in the process of intuitively presenting an object the mind is active, Kant calls the activity "productive." It is the "first application" of the understanding to objects of *possible* intuition. Here the mind is creative in that it spontaneously presents an object in intuition; that is, the mind presents the object independently of empirical conditions. Kant holds that the only avenue for this sort of spontaneous "production" (synthesis) is via the categories of the understanding. Hence this sort of imaginative production is seen as "an action [*Wirkung*] of the understanding on the sensibility" (*CPR*, B 152), and the "transcendental act of imagination" is identified with the "synthetic influence of the understanding upon inner sense" (*CPR*, B 154). Since Kant has already declared the understanding to be the sole source of all acts of combination ("synthesis") (B 130), the condition of all synthetic knowledge a priori can only be the understanding, one of whose *tasks* is to be productively imaginative. The imagination simply has no independent status here.

For Kant, as mentioned, all acts of synthesis are acts of the understanding. Moreover, he claims that all acts of the understanding are judgments (*CPR*, A 69/B 94) and labels the understanding the "faculty of judgment" (*CPR*, A 69/B 94), as if to suggest that no other judgment is possible except judgments synthesizing representations in accordance with categories of the understanding. But, strictly speaking, it does not follow that all acts of judgment are acts of the understanding, or of synthesis. All that follows from the claims mentioned (at A 69/B 94) is that all acts of synthesis are judgments.

True, Kant's claim in the B-Deduction is a strong one: "All possible perceptions, and therefore everything that can come to empirical consciousness, that is, all appearances of nature, must, so far as their connection is concerned, be subject to the categories" (B 164–65). But even this strong claim does not rule out that human beings have a further capacity for *non*-synthetic judgment involving the imagination. Obviously human beings are capable of analytic judgments, but apart from this, we may also *contemplate* our (already synthesized) experience. We are capable of making judgments *about* judgments of experience, that is, about already categorized experience. There is no need to suppose that such "higher-order" judgments themselves involve application of the categories just because they take synthetic judgments for their "material." If such judgments are possible, as it were, "upon" synthetic judgments of the understanding, it may be that imagination is required by this *other* sort of nonsynthetic judgment,[16] in which case imagination could not be assimilated to the understanding. If such judgments are taken to be of any importance in the analysis of human experience, then there may be a place, after all, for the imagination as an independent faculty in Kant's philosophy.

Of course, this is precisely what happens in Kant's account of *reflective* judgment. In the *First Introduction to the Critique of Judgment,* Kant allows that "judgment is not merely an ability to subsume the particular under the universal (whose concept is given), but also, the other way round, an ability to find the universal for the particular,"[17] and he goes on to argue that the principle for performing the latter task cannot come from the understanding. The task of finding universals for particulars is the task of "reflective judgment": "To *reflect* (or consider [*belegen*]) is to hold given presentations [*Vorstellungen*] up to, and compare them with, either other presentations or one's cognitive power [itself], in reference to a concept that this [comparison] makes possible" (*FI,* 400/211′). Imagination, "the faculty of presenting in intuition an object that is not itself present" (*CPR,* B 151), obviously will have a role to play here insofar as given presentations are to be compared to (but not *combined* with) "other presentations" not themselves present. What these "other" presentations might be will be discussed in what follows, but it is clear that whatever they are, the imagination, as the faculty of "presenting" what is not present, will have to be involved.

Moreover, the "object" of reflective judgment is not an object of experience but rather a "purposive arrangement of nature in a system" (*FI,* 402/214′), so that this purposiveness is not the result of the application of a category. In Kant's words, it has "no basis... in terms of the universal laws of the understanding" (*FI,* 404/216′). Whatever work Kant holds that the imagination performs in such judgments, he does not want to say that reflective imagination is merely a task of the understanding. For this reason, reflective judgment cannot be constitutive of knowledge. It does not determine cognition but deals with appearances in an entirely different manner:

> So when reflective judgment tries to bring given appearances under empirical concepts of determinate natural things, it deals with them *technically* rather than schematically. In other words, it does not deal with them mechanically, as it were, like an instrument, guided by the understanding and the senses; it deals with them *artistically,* in terms of a principle that is universal but also indeterminate: the principle of a purposive arrangement of nature in a system. (*FI,* 401–402/213–214′)

This sort of judging, for Kant, is more holistic than the "determining" judgments of the understanding, and at the same time more tentative. (Its principle is "only a necessary presupposition" while that of the understanding is "law" [*FI,* 403/215′]). To borrow Rudolf Makkreel's terminology in his recent book on this topic, reflective judgment may be called *interpretive.*[18] It involves *technique* and is an "art," while the synthesizing activity of cognitive judgment proceeds "schematically" and is thus more "mechanical" in nature.

In light of all this, it is reasonable to wonder if the Böhmes' claim that Kant's is a philosophy of suppressed imagination is not a bit too hasty. Their point can be made for the second edition of the *Critique of Pure Reason*, and also for the *Critique of Practical Reason*, for that matter,[19] but in writing about reflection in the third *Critique* Kant demonstrates a willingness to consider a far more "imaginative" sort of judgment.

Imagination and the Problem of Taste

The Böhmes are of course aware of this defense and do consider the importance of the imagination in one kind of reflection, namely, in aesthetic reflective judgments of taste. They argue that although in these judgments the imagination is given a more independent role, still, Kant in effect finds in taste a "safe," segregated arena for the imagination, where the creative work of this faculty is reduced to mere "play."

> But it can still be established, that also here, where the independence of the imagination is at least accepted as play, the joy taken in this play occurs precisely where it is well mannered, that is, where it conforms to the understanding. Classicism delights in the allegorized and domesticated figures of Greek mythology—figures that once were gripping and overwhelming powers. The imagination itself is turned from Eros into Cupid (Putto), into a child that one delights in because it does of its own accord what one would otherwise ask of it. (*Das Andere*, 238–239)

With respect to Kant's theory of taste, the Böhmes' assessment is apt, and indeed, they could have said a good deal more. Taste, for Kant, although he hints at a substantive connection with morality, is closely associated with culture, serves (at best) to tame and discipline people by cloaking them in the *appearance* of morality.[20] Kant's account of taste is heavily invested in eighteenth-century British accounts, and to the extent that Kant departs from these theories in an attempt to find an a priori grounding for judgments of taste, he does so by insisting that in these judgments the "harmonious" activity of imagination and understanding "belongs to cognition in general" ("*zu einem Erkenntnis überhaupt gehört*" [*CJ*, 63/219]). Imagination is not absolutely free, but rather is "freely lawful,"[21] with the understanding setting its limits: "And yet to say that the *imagination* is *free* and yet *lawful of itself*, i.e., that it carries autonomy with it, is a contradiction. The understanding alone gives the law" (*CJ*, 241).

At section 50, in the third *Critique*, Kant sets up a dichotomy between genius/spirit/imagination, on the one hand, and discipline/taste/understanding, on the other. In judgments of taste, although the understanding is not the only operative faculty, it clearly is the *defining* one.

> In order for a work to be beautiful, it is not necessary that it be rich and original in ideas, but it is necessary that the imagination in its freedom be commensurate with the lawfulness of the understanding. For if the imagination is left in lawless freedom, all its riches produce nothing but nonsense, and it is judgment that adapts the imagination to the understanding. (*CJ*, 188/319)

Here Kant disassociates imagination from judgment, implicitly defining the latter as the ability to subject the imaginative faculty to the understanding. "Judgment . . . will sooner permit the imagination's freedom and wealth to be impaired than that the understanding be impaired" (*CJ*, 189/320). Thus, Kant argues, fine art requires "imagination, understanding, spirit, and taste," and it is the fourth condition, namely, taste, that sees to it that the other three elements are so ordered that imagination never gets the upper hand (*CJ*, 189/320n.55). Thus it would appear that the Böhmes are correct in saying that "the freedom of the imagination in art is also only apparent."[22]

IMAGINATIVE EXCESS AND MORAL PROGRESS

To view these aspects of Kant's theory of taste as a sort of final critical blow to the imagination would, however, be to overlook the fact that if Kant wanted to confine the imagination to the harmless realm of taste, he also seemed willing to permit the imagination's enthusiastic overflow into realms of greater importance, namely, the moral and the social. Kant's aesthetic theory involves more than just a theory of taste and "fine art."[23] In section 17 of the *Critique of Judgment*, Kant also defends the view, albeit briefly, that "a very strong imagination" (later in the "Critique of Aesthetic Judgment" he speaks of "spirit" or "genius") may form a partnership of sorts with reason. In section 17, Kant argues for the possibility of exhibiting the rational idea of humanity "as an aesthetic idea fully *in concreto* in a model image" (*CJ*, 81/233). That is, he maintains that it is possible for the imagination to exhibit an idea of reason in a concrete image.

> Hence that archetype of taste, which does indeed rest on reason's indeterminate idea of a maximum, but which still can be presented not through concepts but only in an individual exhibition [*Darstellung*], may more appropriately be called the ideal of the beautiful.

The ideal of beauty is not a symbol but rather the concrete "model" of "that which has the purpose of its existence within itself," or in other words, of a self-determining being—a human being (*CJ*, 81/233). In the last paragraph of this section Kant argues unequivocally for the possibility of "the visible expression of moral ideas" through imagination, in a manner that, while "taken only from experience," nevertheless *transforms* that experience into a presentation of something new.

> These moral ideas must be connected, in the idea of the highest purposiveness, with everything that our reason links with the morally good: goodness of soul, or purity, fortitude, or serenity, etc.; and in order for this connection to be made visible, as it were, in bodily expression (as an effect of what is inward), pure ideas of reason must be united with a very strong imagination in someone who seeks so much as to judge, let alone exhibit, it. (*CJ*, 84/235)

In the case of the ideal of beauty, a single "object," the human being that for Kant is essentially dual-natured, is artistically presented or "modeled" as the physical embodiment of its own moral (nonphysical) character.

Moral considerations and a "mighty" (*mächtige*) imagination are also introduced into aesthetic experience in Kant's discussion of aesthetic ideas, that is, of intuitive presentations of the imagination that "prompt much thought, but to which no determinate thought whatsoever . . . can be adequate" (*CJ*, 182/314). Aesthetic ideas are said to complement rational ideas since the latter are "concepts to which no *intuition* (presentation of the imagination) can be adequate" (*CJ*, 182/314). Aesthetic ideas are imaginative "excesses" that

> prompt . . . so much thought as can never be comprehended within a determinate concept and thereby the presentation aesthetically expands the concept itself and sets the power of intellectual ideas (i.e., of reason) in motion: it makes reason think more . . . than what can be apprehended and made distinct in the presentation. (*CJ*, 183/315)

Thus aesthetic ideas can be said to express a rational idea in sensible form. In Makkreel's formulation, the imagination, through aesthetic ideas, complements reason by striving to complete reason's ideas in experience. "Thought, which is a function of reason, is here [in the presence of an aesthetic idea] occasioned by an excess of intuitive content that cannot be contained within the concepts of the understanding."[24] Kant says that such creative imaginative presentations "make us add to a concept the thoughts of much that is ineffable, but the feeling of which quickens our cognitive powers and connects language, which otherwise would be mere letters, with spirit" (*CJ*, 185/316). That such an expression is possible is an idea that is new to Kant in the third *Critique*, where he grants the imagination a "transformative" (*umbildende*) power.

> For the imagination ([in its role] as a productive cognitive power) is very mighty when it creates, as it were, another nature out of the material that actual nature gives it. We use it to entertain ourselves when experience strikes us as overly routine. We may even restructure [*umbilden*] experience; and though in doing so we continue to follow analogical laws, yet we also follow principles which reside higher up, namely, in reason (and which are just as natural to us as those which the understanding follows in apprehending em-

> pirical nature)...for although it is under that law [of association] that nature lends us material, yet we can process that material into something quite different, namely, into something that surpasses [*übertrifft*] nature. (*CJ* 182/314)

Here Kant is describing a kind of "judging"—in the case of ideas of reason, one might call it "moral daydreaming"—in which imagination constructs presentations that "surpass," without transcending, nature.[25] The result of such presentations is that the imagination "enlivens" the idea of reason by making it present in intuition; that is, imagination is capable of making the rational idea "feel real." When such presentations are expressed in concrete form, in a way that communicates itself to others, a "mixed mode" experience of the sort Kant mentions in the ideal of beauty occurs, an experience that permits the subject to *feel* what in the rational (moral) ideal alone could only be *thought.*

The elevated role of imagination in these cases suggests, if not a *unity* of sensibility and reason in the human subject, then at least a higher place for the latter in human moral experience. In the (mixed mode) aesthetic experiences that Kant allows for *beyond* taste, rationality and sensibility (via the imagination) are both involved. But, unlike in the judgment of taste, the imagination is not restrained and "disciplined." In fact, it may be said that it is precisely imaginative *excess*, in the "multiplicity of partial presentations" (*CJ*, 185/316), that meets a need on the side of reason, insofar as this profligate presentation prompts in the subject a "lively interest" in reason's ideas.

Enthusiasm

Judgments involving what might be called "idealistic" imagination connect intuitive presentation with a moral idea, giving rise to a concrete, sensible ideal and to a kind of moral liveliness or interest that does not result from the intellectual idea alone. I have argued elsewhere that such moral "imaginings" might even serve as a subjective basis of rational hope for moral progress; that is, they may enable belief in the *possibility* of realizing moral ideas.[26] In the exhibition of its object, imagination makes the realization of that object *subjectively* possible—"imaginable." Perfect human virtue, for instance, may, in fact, be an unattainable ideal. But "a very strong imagination" can give this intellectual notion a flesh and blood quality that it did not have before, bringing it down to earth, as it were, and enabling human beings to envision actually attaining that which moral reason requires them to strive for.

The potential value of imagination's capacity to enliven morality is especially apparent in the case of Kant's doctrine of the Highest Good, that is, of a moral world in which virtue and happiness are commensurate, or at least in which human beings make every effort to maximize the correspondence of happiness to virtue.[27] In the *Critique of Practical Reason*, Kant argues that the moral law requires that human beings strive to bring about such a moral world on earth but that in order for this command to be legitimate, it must be possible for human beings to believe that such a command could be fulfilled; that is, they must have some rational hope that the end commanded is possible. As is well known, at this point Kant argues that human beings have no reason to suppose that they *can* bring about a perfectly moral world in which happiness coincides with virtue, and so they must postulate the existence of God (and the immortality of the soul) to ground their hope, and to make action in accordance with the moral law rational.[28]

Given the difficulties attendant on what has been called the "theological" doctrine of the Highest Good in Kant, which requires postulation of the existence of God to ground such hope,[29] it is worth looking at the accounts of aesthetic moral experiences in Kant's third *Critique* as a possible alternative to the postulate of God in the second *Critique*. That is, if, as Kant argues in the third *Critique*, we have the capacity to literally "make sense" of rational ideas like the Highest Good, why could not this capacity *itself* serve to ground our *hope* (not our certainty) that we ourselves could bring it about?

In light of Kant's very strong claims for the imagination's creative and enlivening powers in the third *Critique*, the question seems reasonable, and yet Kant does not go so far, in either the discussion of the ideal of beauty or of aesthetic ideas, as to suggest that these are necessary ingredients in human efforts to moral improvement.[30]

In his last completed work, an essay entitled "An Old Question Raised Again: Is the Human Race Constantly Progressing?" and published in 1798 (but written four years earlier), Kant raises much the same question of the possibility of predicting the moral progress of the human race: "There must be some experience in the human race which, as an event, points to the disposition and capacity of the human race to be the cause of its own advance toward the better, and... toward the human race as being the author of this advance."[31] Kant uses the question of moral progress to take the opportunity to express his own support for the goals, if not the means, of the French Revolution. Yet the "event" that indicates the human capacity for moral progress is not the Revolution but rather "the mode of thinking [*Denkungsart*] of the spectators." That is, the event that indicates human ability to be the "author" of a more moral world is the publicly expressed, nonopportunistic (*uneigennützig*) sympathy for those who participate in struggles to end human oppression. The glimmer of hope that history holds out to those seeking reason to believe in moral progress is the spectators' "wishful participation that borders on enthusiasm" (*OQ*, 143–144/85), an enthusiasm that Kant identifies as a "passionate participation in the good" (*OQ*, 145/86).

Kant's reference to enthusiasm is a reference to a particular kind of imagination. In this same passage (*OQ*, 145/86) Kant makes a point about "anthropology" that he repeatedly made in his lectures on the subject: "Genuine enthusiasm always moves only toward what is ideal and, indeed, to what is purely moral, such as the concept of right." In student notes from his anthropology lectures[32] taken during the 1770s, Kant told his students that "an enthusiast is always a noble Fantast, *full of life and strength*, and so, in addition, inclined to virtue. Indeed, much that is good disappears from the land where they are purged."[33] Here Kant is cited as saying that enthusiasm originates in the ideal of perfection and hence is a *kind* of fanaticism. In the published anthropology lectures, he defines an enthusiast as a *visionary* or *fantast* and the latter as a person who "fails to collate his imaginings with laws of experience." In the same place he adds that, when accompanied by "passion" (*Affect*), fanatacism becomes enthusiasm (*Anthr.*, 74/202). That is, enthusiasm is the condition of passionate participation in moral "imaginings" that fail to "harmonize with concepts" (*Anthr.*, 48/172) but are rather bound up with rational ideals. Arguably, the spectators to the Revolution, whose sympathetic fervor "borders" on enthusiasm, are also similar to the "noble fantast" in their ability to visualize and desire the ideal. The excessively creative imagination of the third *Critique* seems to find its place, after all, in moral and social vision.

KANT'S MORAL ENTHUSIASM AND ITS LIMITS

Yet Kant was never univocal in his praise of moral enthusiasm. In connection with his comments from the anthropology lectures and the late comment from the "Old Question," it is interesting to note a similar position expressed during the height of the critical period, in the *Critique of Practical Reason.* Kant argues that the "typic" of pure practical judgment guards against "the mysticism of practical reason, which makes into a schema that which should serve only as a symbol, i.e., proposes to supply real yet nonsensuous intuitions (of an invisible kingdom of God) for the application of the moral law and thus plunges into the transcendent" (*CPrR*, 73/70–71). But he contrasts this plunge favorably with the "empiricism of practical reason."

> The protest against empiricism of practical reason is much more important and commendable, because mysticism is compatible with the purity and sublimity of the moral law; and as it is not natural to ordinary ways of thinking [*Denkungsart*] to stretch its imagination to supersensuous intuitions, the danger from this side is not so general.... [E]mpiricism [of practical reason] is far more dangerous than all mystical enthusiasm, which can never be a lasting condition for any great number of persons. (*CPrR*, 73–74/70–71)

Here Kant expresses a thoroughly ambivalent attitude to the imagination when used to present ideas of reason. Whereas he is quite clear that practical reason based on empirical principles is "degrading" because it is generally allied with (sensuous) inclination, he is not at all convinced that imagination "stretched" to the supersensuous is so bad. The "rationalism of practical reason" is a safer bet, if one had to choose. In one brief passage in the heart of his mature moral theory, Kant manages to both criticize and defend the enthusiast (say, Swedenborg) and, at the same time, his rationalist forefathers. So far as moral theory is concerned, passionate rationalist speculation about the good is *less* dangerous than dwelling on "empirical interest, with which inclinations generally are secretly in league" (*CPrR*, 74/71). Mystical enthusiasm will only ever be "a lasting condition" for a small number of persons, and even then is compatible with the purity and sublimity of the moral law because it involves imaginative transcendence of inclinations and sensibility. In conjunction with Kant's other claims about the positive moral value of enthusiasm, it appears that he always maintained a certain regard for visionaries that went beyond simply enlightened tolerance. His rejection of Swedenborg, and of metaphysics, was perhaps more nuanced than the Böhmes suggest.[34]

Yet Kant also held that attempts at imaginative transcendence by regular people are bound to fail, and in the third *Critique* he argues that this very *failure* of imagination may give rise to an appreciation of reason's superiority to imagination (and sensibility).[35] This subordination of the imagination may be traced to two quite different motivations, one of which is not obviously lamentable. Kant's aversion to what he took to be a kind of moral elitism in rationalism led him to reject the notion of any sort of intuitive access to the rational (moral), even if he did not totally reject those who claimed to have it. Kant was convinced that enlightenment proscribed taking oneself to be better equipped to grasp moral principles and hence to set oneself up as a moral authority over others. Moreover, Kant came to hold this view as a result of his "enthusiastic" reception of Rousseau's critique of reason and Kant's own (not atypical) enlightenment desire for a social order that would advance human dignity.[36]

Kant's own moral enthusiasm deserves to be counted among the important motivational forces behind critical philosophy, and if so counted, the force of the Böhmes' critique is somewhat weakened. Intuitive access to the moral may indeed be creative and important, but it is not unproblematic. Imagination may accompany all sorts of "undesirable" characteristics, just as may understanding. Enormously creative persons may also be perfectly self-centered, and genius can be evil. Certainly Kant was correct, for *these* reasons, to hold that the way in which imagination functioned in conjunction with other capacities was central to evaluating its significance.

But it is in answering the question of just how Kant characterizes the possible "conjunctions" of the imagination and other faculties that the Böhmes' critique cannot be ignored. Kant never seemed entirely willing to admit the possibility of a genuine cooperative relation between imagination and reason, even though in his critical aesthetic theory he had worked out an account of imaginative creativity compatible with such a relation. The question naturally arises, why didn't Kant push the notion of the ideal of beauty, or of aesthetic ideas, further? Why didn't he find a place for the imagination in the moral? The role enthusiasm plays in Kant's social theory, as a glimmer of hope in the human quest for moral progress, is a way of doing precisely this, but it is undeniable that Kant himself was never *fully* convinced.[37] It is therefore quite possible that part of the answer lies in the Böhmes' hypothesis. In laying out the motivation for Kant's theoretical development, it ought not be overlooked that, for subconscious reasons that are all too transparent two centuries later, Kant may simply have not been able to grant the imagination a status equal to that of the "law-governed" branches of human experience. It was, after all, a faculty associated on the transcendental level with "lawlessness" and, on the empirical level, with the contaminating influences of the body, its feelings, and desires. There may well have been a sense in which Heidegger was after all right about one thing: it was not the failure of Kant's imagination that prevented his finally embracing the "lower" faculty, but rather a failure of nerve.

NOTES

References to Kant's work are to standard translations (cited in the notes) with translation page numbers followed by the page number of the original German in the Akademie edition, *Kants Gesammelte Schriften* (Berlin, 1900–1), except for page references to the *Critique of Pure Reason,* where the standard A/B edition pagination employed by Kemp Smith's translation is used.

1. See *Critique of Pure Reason* (*CPR*), trans. Norman Kemp Smith (New York, 1929), Introduction, A 15/B 29: "there are two stems of human knowledge, namely, *sensibility* and *understanding,* which perhaps spring from a common, but to us unknown, root." And also Heidegger, *Kant and the Problem of Metaphysics* (*KPM*), trans. James S. Churchill (Bloomington, 1962), 41–42, 173.

2. Dieter Henrich, "Die Einheit der Subjektivität," *Philosophische Rundschau* 3 (1955): 28–69. Translated by Günter Zöller as "On the Unity of Subjectivity," in Henrich, *The Unity of Reason: Essays on Kant's Philosophy,* ed. Richard Velkley (Cambridge, Mass., 1994). Translations in this chapter are Zöller's.

3. Henrich, "Die Einheit der Subjektivität," 32–39.

4. If any faculty is to be viewed as most fundamental to the structure of human subjectivity, Henrich argues, it is "apperception and its categories" (p. 44). Henrich does admit that this renunciation of hope for grounding subjectivity did not come easily to Kant (p. 46).

5. Henrich, "Die Einheit der Subjektivität," 44–45. The search for a unifying principle is seen by Kant to be a necessary *subjective* condition of reason, and hence the notion of a fundamental faculty or power is a regulative idea.

6. Ibid., 46. The quotation from Kant is from the *Critique of Judgment* (*CJ*), trans. Werner Pluhar (Indianapolis, 1987), 214/341.

7. Ibid., 50.

8. Ibid., 54.

9. See, e.g., *CPR*, A 78/B 103: "Synthesis in general... is the mere result of the power of imagination, a blind but indispensable function of the soul, without which we should have no knowledge whatsoever, but of which we are scarcely ever conscious." And A 123: "That the affinity of appearances... and so experience itself, should only be possible by means of this transcendental function of imagination, is indeed strange, but is nonetheless an obvious consequence of the preceding argument."

10. Gernot Böhme and Hartmut Böhme, *Das Andere der Vernunft: Zur Entwicklung von Rationalitätsstrukturen am Beispiel Kants* (Frankfurt am Main, 1985).

11. Ibid., 231.

12. Robin Schott's book, *Cognition and Eros: A Critique of the Kantian Paradigm* (Boston, 1988), presents another recent statement of this position from a feminist perspective.

13. The three-way debate between the Böhmes, Henrichians, and Heideggerians must be waived for the sake of space here. It is hinted at, however, in the insert to the Böhmes' chapter on the imagination in *Das Andere der Vernunft*, "Heideggers Philosophische Rehabilitierung der Einbildungskraft," 243–245.

14. See Richard Velkley, *Freedom and the End of Reason: On the Moral Foundations of Kant's Critical Philosophy* (Chicago, 1989), and Frederick C. Beiser, "Kant's Intellectual Development: 1746–1781," chapter 1 of *The Cambridge Companion to Kant* (New York, 1992), 26–61.

15. I have departed from Kemp Smith's use of "represent" to translate *vorstellen*. This is to avoid any misleading literal reading of the English term, which would suggest that whatever the imagination is presenting in intuition must have been present before (literally, is being "re-presented"). The German word *vorstellen* when read also in literal fashion does not carry the same meaning (but means literally, to "place in front of"). See also, Pluhar, translator's note in *Critique of Judgment*, 14.

16. On Kant's definition, analytic judgments require no imagination since their "objects" are already there, as it were, in the concept being analyzed, and, in any case, intuition is not involved.

17. *First Introduction to the Critique of Judgment* (*FI*) (Ak XX), trans. Werner Pluhar, in *Critique of Judgment*, 398/210'.

18. Rudolf A. Makkreel, *Imagination and Interpretation in Kant: The Hermeneutical Import of the Critique of Judgment* (Chicago, 1990).

19. Cf. *Critique of Practical Reason* (*CPrR*) (Ak. V), trans. Lewis White Beck (New York, 1988), 71–72/69.

20. E.g., see *Anthropology from a Pragmatic Point of View* (*Anthr.*) (Ak VII), trans. Mary J. Gregor (The Hague, 1974), 11–12/244: "Ideal taste has a tendency to promote morality in an external way. Making a man (*Mensch*) *well-mannered* as a social

being falls short of forming a *morally good* man, but it still prepares him for it by the effort he makes, in society, to please others (to make them love or admire him)." And also *CJ*, 52–53/210: "To show taste in our conduct (or in judging other people's conduct) is very different from expressing our moral way of thinking. For this contains a command and gives rise to a need, whereas moral taste only plays with the objects of liking without committing itself to any of them." For a discussion of the parallels between Kant's views on taste and femininity, see J. Kneller, "Discipline and Silence: Women and Imagination in Kant's Theory of Taste," in *Aesthetics in Feminist Perspective*, ed. Hilde Hein and Carolyn Korsmeyer (Bloomington, 1993), 179–192.

21. Kant speaks of the "*freie Gesetzmäßigkeit der Einbildungskraft*" (free lawfulness of the imagination) (*CJ*, 91/240).

22. *Das Andere*, 239.

23. For the sake of conserving space here, I ignore Kant's theory of the sublime. Although in it the imagination is allowed to "run wild," the role assigned to imagination vis-à-vis reason is no less problematic than that assigned to it vis-à-vis the understanding in judgments of taste. In the end it must be "humiliated" by reason. Cf. *Das Andere*, 215–223. I have also given a critique along feminist lines in "Kant's Immature Imagination," in *Modern Engendering: Critical Feminist Readings in Modern Western Philosophy*, ed. Bat Ami Bar-on (Albany, 1994), 141–153.

24. Makkreel, *Imagination and Interpretation*, 118, 121.

25. Makkreel makes this point in his comment on this passage, p. 120: "Kant's use of the term 'surpass' points to a significant difference in the way rational and aesthetic ideas may be said to go 'beyond' the limits of experience. Rational ideas transcend nature, and aesthetic ideas surpass it by transforming and enriching experience."

26. See Jane Kneller, "Imaginative Freedom and the German Enlightenment," *Journal of the History of Ideas* 51 (1990): 217–232.

27. Recently, scholars have debated whether or not the notion of the highest good involves, in Harry van der Linden's words, "the union of universal virtue and universal happiness" or the far more modest "moral society in which human agents attempt to make one another happy, but do not necessarily succeed" (*Kantian Ethics and Socialism* [Indianapolis, 1988], 42, 42ff.). Also see Andrews Reath, "Two Conceptions of the Highest Good in Kant," *Journal of the History of Philosophy* 26, no. 4 (October 1988): 593–619. Van der Linden distinguishes between a teleological conception (the "highest good desirable") and a moral conception (the "highest moral good"). Reath makes a similar distinction between a "theological" and a "secular (or political)" conception of the highest good (p. 594ff.).

28. See *Critique of Practical Reason*, trans. Lewis White Beck (New York, 1988), 112–118/108–115; 124/119; 128–130/124–125.

29. The term is Andrews Reath's (see n. 23, above). Although I find both their accounts extremely useful in sorting out the different strands in Kant's thought, both Reath and van der Linden are inclined to dismiss the "spiritualized" account of the Highest Good in Kant. This, it seems to me, has the unfortunate effect of disconnecting Kant's notion from the *felt* response that is part of the happiness component of the Highest Good. In Kant's account, the postulate of God's existence on the

"theological" reading served to do more than ground rational belief in a future paradise. It also channeled *desire* for such a state of affairs into faith in God. The virtue of finding a role for the *imagination* in grounding efforts to bring about the "highest good desirable" is that it provides a this-worldly channel, and hence a justification, for the *desire* to do so. (For a critique of the Postulate as an answer to the question of how the Highest Good is to be realized, see also John Silber, "Kant's Conception of the Highest Good as Immanent and Transcendent," *Philosophical Review* 68 [1959]: 474–475, and my "Imaginative Freedom and the German Enlightenment," 225.)

30. Kant does suggest that beauty might serve as a symbol of morality and thus act as a sort of bridge to the moral from taste, because the beautiful arouses sensations that are "somehow analogous" to the feeling present when we make moral judgments (*CJ*, 230/354). But even apart from the vagueness of his arguments, the point here is that Kant fails to follow up on the much more intimate relationships between morality and aesthetic experience suggested in the "ideal" and in his account of aesthetic ideas. For a different reading of the connection between taste and morality, see Paul Guyer, "Feeling and Freedom: Kant on Aesthetics and Morality," *Journal of Aesthetics and Art Criticism* 48, no. 2 (Spring 1990): 137–146.

31. The essay, although complete in its own right, was included as the second part of the 1798 publication entitled *Streit der Fakultäten*. The translation here is from *Kant on History*, ed. Lewis White Beck (New York, 1986), 137–154. The citation is from p. 142/84.

32. Based on the notes taken by a student, Theodor Friederich Brauer, dated 1779, taken from transcripts now available at the Philips-Universität Marburg. I would like to thank Werner Stark for assistance in the use of these materials and for helpful information about the historical context in which they were written. Although these sources are from student transcriptions of Kant's lectures and are therefore not the final word on any disputed question in Kant interpretation, nothing that I rely on here is essentially new to Kant, but rather corroborates views expressed elsewhere on enthusiasm. I have relied only on passages from Brauer that also appear in notes taken down by other students during that time.

33. Brauer notes (see n. 32 above), MS p. 88.

34. For a defense of the view that Kant never fully rejected rationalist metaphysics, see Karl Ameriks, "The Critique of Metaphysics: Kant and Traditional Ontology," in *Cambridge Companion to Kant*, 249–279.

35. This appreciation is the feeling of the sublime: See *CJ*, sec. 29, "On the Modality of a Judgment about the Sublime in Nature": "The [sublime] is what genuinely characterizes man's morality, where reason must exert its dominance over sensibility, except that in an aesthetic judgment about the sublime we present this dominance as being exerted by the imagination itself, as an instrument of reason" (128/268–269). And also: "the [imagination], acting in accordance with principles of the schematism of judgment[,] ... is an instrument of reason and its ideas.... In this reflection of the aesthetic power of judgment [i.e., of imagination], by which it seeks to elevate itself to the point of being adequate to reason ... we present the object itself as subjectively purposive, precisely because objectively the imagination, [even] in its greatest expansion, is inadequate to reason (129–130/269).

36. See Velkley, *Freedom and the End of Reason*, 6–8, 32–43; and Beiser, "Kant's Intellectual Development," 43–46, and also Dieter Henrich, "Kant und Hegel," in *Selbstverhältnisse* (Stuttgart, 1982), 183–184, on Rousseau's influence on the "emotional and imaginative side" of Kant's thought.

37. Enthusiasm, for Kant, was "not to be wholly esteemed, since passion as such deserves censure" (*OQ*, 145/86). See also the passage at *CPR*, B 128, in which enthusiasm is seen as one of "two rocks" between which critical philosophy must navigate.

This cautious attitude was not shared by Kant's "enthusiastic" followers. The "System-Programme" fragment (attributed by various scholars to either Hegel or Hölderlin or Schelling, or to all three, or to some combination thereof) is a good example of an attempt to carry out in practice some of Kant's views on the modeling of the ideal in art: "I am now convinced that the highest act of Reason, the one through which it encompasses all Ideas, is an aesthetic act." Although its authorship is uncertain, the point here is simply that, seen in light of Kant's views on the ideal of beauty and aesthetic ideas, the early romantic period in Germany, for which this fragment is a kind of manifesto, may be seen as an extension of Kant's aesthetic theory. The Böhmes' claim that romanticism is an "intermezzo" thus is not entirely accurate. See "The 'Earliest System-Programme of German Idealism' (Berne, 1796): an Ethics," trans. H. S. Harris, in *Hegel's Development: Toward the Sunlight 1770–1801* (Oxford, 1972), 510–513. On p. 249ff., Harris also discusses the fragment's origin, proposing his own view that it was authored by Hegel.

The Gender of Enlightenment

Robin May Schott

Enlightenment is one of the most debated themes of contemporary intellectual discourse. The eighteenth-century claim that progress is possible through the use of reason and the advancement and spread of knowledge is summed up in Kant's dictum, "Have courage to use your own reason!"[1] This view has been reiterated and updated by contemporary defenders of enlightenment such as Jürgen Habermas. In Habermas's view, the Enlightenment tradition is the only possible source of rational judgment in the face of the irrationality, prejudice, blind obedience to authority, and violence that characterized the darkest days of German history under Hitler. It is only through enlightenment that rational criteria for the critique of domination and for the possibility of emancipation is possible.[2]

Criticism of Enlightenment commitments have abounded in many diverse quarters. Earlier members of the Frankfurt School of social theory, such as Max Horkheimer and Theodor Adorno, argued that enlightenment represents Western culture's attempt to dominate sensuous existence by means of a controlling rationality, which finds its fullest expression in the historical period of the eighteenth century. Far from ensuring the progress of reason and emancipation, enlightenment reason has resulted in the return of the repressed, in the eruption of barbarism in twentieth-century Germany.[3] Recent writers such as Berel Lang have reiterated this thesis, arguing that the Enlightenment claims for universal truths and its extreme notions of the individual, autonomous, ahistorical self contribute directly to genocide.[4] In his view, the Enlightenment's insistence on the universality of rational judgment makes it unable to deal with any claims of particularism and any judgments influenced by historical factors. The obvious exclusion of women, servants, and Jews from the call to enlightenment coexisted with its principle of tolerance.[5] Ultimately, according to Lang, the inability of Enlightenment rationality to provide controls for determining the status of groups excluded from its domain leads to the possibility of unbounded destruction of these groups.[6]

Criticism of the project of the Enlightenment from postmodernist quarters has been just as intense. Writers such as Jean-François Lyotard, Jacques Derrida, and Michel Foucault, loosely grouped by others (though not by themselves) under the umbrella of postmodernism, have attacked the hegemony of enlightenment rationality, its claim to grasp universal truth, and the concomitant rejection of any form of historicity or particularism. Enlightenment, it might be said, disenfranchises not only other possible interpretations but also the groups that initiate these interpretations. It thus readily can be wielded as an instrument of power in the service of its own vision of scientific truth.[7]

Feminist theorists have a particularly embattled relation to the question of enlightenment. Some feminists argue that the Enlightenment tradition of individual reason, progress, and freedom is a precondition for the discourse of women's liberation, and for the political gains that women have won. Even feminists who have a qualified relation to the Enlightenment (i.e., who argue that its fulfillment would advance the historical task of self-scrutiny) suggest that women have not yet had their enlightenment.[8] On this view, even though women have been viewed by Enlightenment thinkers as not fully rational, and even though women have been severely restricted in their educational opportunities, which form a prerequisite for achieving the free use of reason, nonetheless one should demand that the Enlightenment be completed by incorporating previously excluded groups. It is appealing for many to use the Enlightenment tools of rationality and objectivity to argue the case for women's emancipation.[9]

By contrast, many feminist theorists argue that the fundamental commitments of the Enlightenment are antithetical to feminist politics and theory and that feminists must throw their caps in the ring with postmodern critics. Not only have enlightenment thinkers excluded women from the province of autonomy but feminist notions of self, knowledge, and truth are contradictory to fundamental enlightenment commitments as well.[10] Feminists, like postmodernists, are skeptical of all transcendental, transhistorical claims for truth and argue that "universality" is itself a reflection of the experience of the dominant social group. On this view, feminists are committed to showing that reason is not divorced from "merely contingent" existence, that the self is embedded in social relations, that the self is embodied and is thus historically specific and partial. Jane Flax writes, "What Kant's self calls its 'own' reason and the methods by which reason's contents become present or self-evident, are no freer from empirical contingency than is the so-called phenomenal self."[11] Moreover, feminists argue that this desire to detach the self from contingency and embodiment is itself an effect of particular gender relations, itself an expression of the flight of masculinity from the temporal, embodied, uncertain realm of phenomenal existence.

Before evaluating the claims laid on the present by the philosophical project emerging from the Enlightenment, in particular its implications for feminism, I will make some brief historical comments about the situation of women during the Age of Enlightenment. Although this discussion is best left to historians, it is an important context for understanding Kant's discussion of enlightenment. I will then discuss Kant's notion of self-imposed tutelage and emancipation in his essay "What Is Enlightenment?" and re-pose the questions of autonomy and heteronomy from a feminist perspective.

Historians are divided about the historical implications of the Enlightenment for women. It was certainly not a period of unambivalent progress for women. The most positive reading of this period is that the Enlightenment legitimized safeguards in theory which were not secured in practice for nearly another century.[12] Looking at the Age of Enlightenment in France, Claire Moses argues that the eighteenth century ended in repression. The uniform legal system enshrined the Rousseauian concept of the difference of women from men. The Civil Code recognized the rights of all citizens but excluded women from citizenship. Therefore, women's status worsened in relation to men's status. Moreover, some women's status worsened absolutely. Whereas earlier some noble women could escape the full harshness of patriarchal laws, these opportunities were now erased.[13] Moses argues that the eighteenth-century views of women were contradictory, providing both encouragement for the emergence of feminism and the weapons to gun it down. For example, the Civil Code served as a rallying point for women in enshrining the Rousseauian concept of the difference between women and men, in which women remained subordinate to men. Not only did it incite feminist protest because it discriminated against women, but, in proclaiming the political significance of sex, it also intensified women's sense of sex identification.[14]

The Enlightenment's theoretical legitimization of the rights to organize, lecture publicly, and publish freely were not secured for women in France until 1879. In the years that followed, women won the right to secondary education, the gradual opening of the university to them, and the right to practice "public" professions (newspaper publishing, medicine, law). In 1907, women were granted equal authority with the father over children and the right to control their own earnings, but women in France had to wait until 1944 to gain the right to vote.[15]

In terms of women's education in the Age of Enlightenment, it is clear that women's literacy in France lagged far behind men's.[16] The feminist political activist Olympe de Gouges dictated all her works to a secretary because she was unable to write. And the four youngest daughters of Louis

XV, after several years at the convent, were still illiterate. Despite deficiencies in formal instruction, many women were able to complete their education independently.[17] Women's education in France varied significantly depending on their class and region. Upper-class girls and daughters of the bourgeoisie received their early education at home, and later were sent to a convent until they were to be married. Although there are idealized descriptions of the social life of convents, a more realistic picture includes harrowing practices such as girls being sent to pray alone, in the vaults where nuns were buried, as punishment.[18] The social function of the convents was most important; reading, writing, and catechism occupied a distant second place. Other "safe" subjects included the lives of the saints, needlework, and sewing, whereas novels, mythology, physical or natural sciences, ancient philosophy, and even history except in its most elementary form remained taboo.[19] Girls from impoverished families depended on charity schools for education, which provided training in manual skills and crafts. Although progress in the education of women in France was achieved in the eighteenth century (the level of literacy improved, the need for organized public education was recognized), women's exclusion from formal higher education and participation in the professions during this period continued to hamper their achievements.

Women were excluded from university education in Germany as well (including Königsberg University where Kant studied and taught) during the Age of Enlightenment.[20] And although universities were not centers of cultural innovation during the eighteenth century, they remained the locus in Germany for philosophical and scientific work.[21] Women's exclusion from university life was considered so natural that only the most recent scholars of German education make note of it. By 1914, women constituted 7 percent of the student body in Prussia—marking a dramatic increase in their enrollment since 1900.[22] Women's absence from the academies ensured their exclusion from training in medicine, law, and government positions in Germany until the late nineteenth and twentieth century.[23]

It is in this historical context that Kant's view of women is situated. Far from challenging women's exclusion from education on egalitarian grounds, Kant mocks women's attempts at serious philosophical and scientific work. Kant asserts that women's character, in contrast to men's, is wholly defined by natural needs. Women's lack of self-determination, in his view, is intrinsic to their nature. He writes, "Nature was concerned about the preservation of the embryo and implanted fear into the woman's character, a fear of physical injury and a timidity towards similar dangers. On the basis of this weakness, the woman legitimately asks for masculine protection."[24] Because of their natural fear and timidity, Kant views women as unsuited for scholarly work. He mockingly describes the scholarly women who "use their books somewhat like a watch, that is, they wear the watch so it can be noticed that they have one, although it is usually broken or does not show the correct time."[25] Kant's remarks on women in the *Anthropology* echo his sentiments in *Observations on the Feeling of the Beautiful and the Sublime.* In that early work, Kant notes, "A woman who has a head full of Greek, like Mme. Dacier, or carries on fundamental controversies about mechanics, like the Marquise du Châtelet, might as well even have a beard, for perhaps that would express more obviously the mien of profundity for which she strives."[26] In Kant's view, women's philosophy is "not to reason, but to sense." And he adds, "I hardly believe that the fair sex is capable of principles."[27] No wonder that under these conditions the woman "makes no secret in wishing that she might rather be a man, so that she could give larger and freer latitude to her inclinations; no man, however, would want to be a woman."[28]

In providing the Marquise du Châtelet with a beard, Kant suggests that there is a contradiction between women and scholarship that is rooted in a natural condition, not a social one. Some biographical remarks about the Marquise du Châtelet help in evaluating Kant's views. By the time of her death in 1749, Emilie du Châtelet was not only well known in French intellectual circles but also had been elected to the Bologna Academy of Sciences. She had published on the metaphysics of natural science, on the nature of fire and heat, and on the nature of force. In addition, she had completed a translation of Newton's *Principia Mathematica* and had anonymously coauthored with Voltaire a popularization of Newtonian physics.

Despite her scientific vocation, Emilie du Châtelet was hampered throughout her life by her inability to obtain the systematic learning provided to boys, to be educated in an institutional context as opposed to a private tutoring situation, and to travel freely and to work undisturbed by household obligations. Thus she was hindered in carrying out anything like a long-term research program.[29] Because her intellectual training was limited to her relationship with a small set of famous figures (e.g., Voltaire), it was difficult for her to take the step from tutelage to independence. Her responsibilities for family, household, friends, and social duties made it impossible for her to lead the life of a full-time scientist. She was able to achieve as much as she did by functioning on four or five hours of sleep a night. When necessary, she survived on even less, dipping her arms in ice water to stay awake.[30]

Although the discipline required for the Marquise du Châtelet to accomplish scientific work matches Kant's own stern discipline in life, it is clear that Kant had little sympathy for the frustrations of intelligent women like her. His views are further illustrated by his correspondence with Maria von Herbert, an intelligent young aristocratic woman who had studied Kant's writings together with a male friend. In a letter to Kant dated January 1793, Maria von Herbert writes to Kant of her own personal despair and frustration with her life. "Even when I am not frustrated by any external circumstances and have nothing to do all day, I'm tormented by a boredom that makes my life unbearable."[31] Although Kant had responded to an earlier letter of Maria's discussing her moral failings, he failed to respond to this letter. Instead, he sent it on to another young lady as an example of "mental derangement" that occurs when young ladies succumb to "the errors of a sublimated fantasy."[32] He failed to consider the possibility that this young woman's despair may have arisen in part from external circumstances that smothered her urge to do something in the world. In my view, the lives of these two women provide counterexamples to Kant's view concerning the inverse relationship between civil freedom and freedom of mind, expressed in "What Is Enlightenment?" The restrictions placed on these women's lives did not encourage the flourishing of their intellectual development but rather furthered the very form of intellectual tutelage that Kant ostensibly deplored.

It is important to bear in mind concrete historical features when evaluating the philosophical work of the period. Social practices are not "outside" the sphere of culture in which philosophy operates. Rather, philosophy can be viewed as a reflective appropriation of cultural and historical traditions.[33] Therefore, in turning to Kant's essay "What Is Enlightenment?" new perspectives are disclosed if one asks: What could this conception of enlightenment have meant to women of the period, and how would women's experiences have challenged Kant's formulations?

Kant has only one reference to women in particular in this short essay. He writes, "the step to competence is held to be very dangerous by the far greater portion of mankind (and by the entire fair sex)."[34] His general indifference to differentiating the possibilities of enlightenment for men and for women appears to arise from his view that the subject of enlightenment (humanity) that is called on to free itself from self-imposed tutelage is a universal one. He never qualifies his claim by saying it is for masters and not their servants, men and not women, Christians and not Jews. Therefore, any reference to particular kinds of groups or classes of individuals in society seems out of place. Although Kant says "Have courage to use your own reason!"[35] where this courage comes from, what conflicts within individuals' lives it encounters, and what factors interfere with its realization—none of these are his concerns. Rather, Kant's project is to address enlightenment as a demand for the individual to use reason; and reason, as Kant's critical writings attest, is viewed as a universal, ahistorical faculty.[36]

And yet for the contemporary reader, the question of inclusion and exclusion of particular groups in the domain of enlightened thought becomes pressing. As the critics of enlightenment mentioned above have argued, the universal subject of enlightened thought had particular unacknowledged qualifications. As already noted, Kant claims that all women are afraid of enlightenment (he did not, however, turn his attention to how this fear might be counteracted). Similarly, it is difficult to see how Kant might include servants or domestics in his call for enlightenment, since these latter are, in Kant's view, a legal possession of the master. In his letter to C. G. Schutz dated 10 July 1797, Kant writes of this relationship as follows: "The right to use a man for domestic purposes is analogous to a right to an object, for which the servant is not free to terminate his connections with the household and he may therefore be caught and returned by force."[37] In Kant's claim that the servant "belongs" to the master just as an object does, it is difficult to see how there would be any domain left to the servant in which reason could be exercised freely. Historically, women of all classes and men of the servant class could not share equally with bourgeois men in the "public" exercise of reason, which Kant defines as the "use which a person makes of it as a scholar before the reading public."[38]

Similarly, Kant's discussion of self-incurred tutelage is not formulated with reference to women's experience. Kant begins his essay with the claim that "enlightenment is man's release from his self-incurred tutelage. Tutelage is man's inability to make use of his understanding without direction from another. Self-incurred is this tutelage when its cause lies not in lack of reason but in lack of resolution and courage to use it without direction from another."[39] In this context, it is helpful to recall the little we know about the lives of women like Emilie du Châtelet and Maria von Herbert. These women did apparently experience their education as being a form of tutelage. Emilie du Châtelet's self-doubt, self-deprecation, and tendency to choose safe, "dependent" research projects such as translation, criticism, and commentary may have been a result of her personal indebtedness to friends such as Voltaire who were already famous, which made it difficult for her to take the step from pupil to colleague, from tutelage to independence.[40] And one can imagine from Kant's response to Maria von Herbert's letters that for him, the only conceivable relation a woman could have to philosophy is to be tutored by a mentor. In his letter to Elizabeth Motherby, Kant notes that Maria refers to his writings as being "difficult to understand without an explanation."[41] The implication is with a proper explanation, Maria may have been saved from the reefs of her "sublimated fantasy."

Thus the extent to which these women's tutelage was self-imposed arose from their very desire to gain knowledge and to resist being defined by what is "pleasant and pointless."[42] But their difficulties in escaping from it cannot be explained by "laziness and cowardice" (the reasons Kant gives for mankind's tutelage).[43] Nor is it likely that they were "fond" of this state.[44] Rather, their state of tutelage seems to be a result of social forces and restrictions stronger than their power to change them.[45]

Just as Kant's discussion of tutelage does not explain obstacles to enlightenment faced by "humanity," but at best explains the obstacles faced by certain groups of people (e.g., middle-class men with education and civil office who could become, for example, military officers and clergymen), so too Kant's conception of enlightenment also has to be understood as a particular historical construction. For Kant, rationality is possible only on the basis of excluding emotion. He does invoke "courage" in the use of reason, just as elsewhere he invokes "respect" for the moral law. But only this kind of feeling that is "self-wrought by a rational concept" and is not rooted in inclination or fear can be praiseworthy.[46] But concerning emotion in general, Kant expresses only disdain. In the *Anthropology from a Pragmatic Point of View*, he writes, "To be subject to emotions and passions is probably always an illness of mind because both emotion and passion exclude the sovereignty of reason."[47] Similarly, "Passion, on the other hand, no man wishes for himself. Who wants to have himself put in chains when he can be free?"[48] Since emotion and passion threaten the sovereignty of reason, they must be excluded from ordinary consciousness.

Kant's attempt to exclude emotion from rationality is premised on the assumption that his rational posture is itself wholly nonemotional. Yet the emotional currents of Kantian rationality are clearly expressed in his personal correspondence. Maria von Herbert wrote to Kant during a personal crisis, in which she had revealed to a friend that she had formerly loved another man and this friend now treated her with coldness. Kant responds to Maria in a didactic manner. Although Kant acknowledges that in men there is a limit on candor (in some men more than in others) that interferes with the ideal of friendship, he distinguishes this lack of candor from lack of sincerity, from dishonesty in expressing one's thoughts.[49] Kant adjudicates Maria of being guilty of this latter sin and for rightly feeling the pains of conscience: "For conscience must focus on every transgression, like a judge who does not dispose of the documents, when a crime has been sentenced, but records them in the archives in order to sharpen the judgment of justice in new cases of a similar or even dissimilar offense that may appear before him."[50] Kant admits that he is answering her in the form of sermon: "instruction, penalty, and solace, of which I beg you to devote yourself somewhat more to the first two."[51]

In this letter, Kant epitomizes the ascetic priest described by Nietzsche: the inventor of bad conscience, the upholder of self-punishment, the antagonist of the fulfillment of sensual pleasures. Nietzsche writes in the *Genealogy of Morals*, "Every suffering sheep says to himself, 'I suffer; it must be somebody's fault.' But his shepherd, the ascetic priest, says to him, 'You are quite right, my sheep, somebody must be at fault here, but that somebody is yourself. You alone are to blame—you alone are to blame for yourself.' "[52]

Kant's response to Maria gives support to the view that his moral philosophy is an existential choice, a manner of living "with our eyes fixed on abstract, impartial principles,"[53] and not merely a position to be held in debates about rational principles. Kant's philosophy is paradigmatic of what contemporary critics call the perspective of impartial reason. As Iris Young writes, "Impartial reason must judge from a point of view outside the particular perspectives of persons involved in interaction, able to totalize these perspectives into a whole or general will. This is the point of view of a solitary transcendent God."[54] But this perspective is built on the assumption that the impartial self is a disembodied, disembedded self. As Seyla Benhabib notes in reference to the impartial self in the theories of Rawls and Kohlberg, "this is a strange world: it is one in which individuals are grown up before they have been born; in which boys are men before they have been children; a world where neither mother, nor sister, nor wife exist."[55] It is a self that abstracts from concrete individuality and identity and thus ultimately makes the concept of the Other as different from oneself incoherent.[56]

One may object that an argument proving Kant's exclusion of emotion from morality does not argue for the role of emotions in ethics. This objection exemplifies the commitments of the Kantian paradigm, to which much contemporary academic discourse is heir. My claim, however, is that this rational detachment is already an emotional posture with consequences for human relations (witness Kant's letter to Maria von Herbert and his refusal to respond to her subsequent letters). But the failure to acknowledge the emotional content of detached impartiality precludes the possibility of evaluating how we are to use emotions, which emotions are positive and which are negative. As Young notes in reference to the exclusion of desire, affectivity, and need from deontological reason, "Since all desiring is equally suspect, we have no way of distinguishing which desires are good and which bad, which will expand the person's capacities and relations with others, and which stunt the person and foster violence. In being excluded from understanding, all desiring, feeling, and needs become unconscious, but certainly do not thereby cease to motivate action and behavior."[57] Nietzsche notes in the *Genealogy of Morals* that human beings have the capacity of oblivion, by which "what we experience and digest psychologically does not... emerge into consciousness.... The role of this active oblivion is that of a concierge: to shut temporarily the doors and windows of consciousness; to protect us from the noise and agitation with which our lower organs work for or against one another; to introduce a little quiet into our consciousness so as to make room for the nobler functions and functionaries of our organism which do the governing and planning. This concierge maintains order and etiquette in the household of the psyche."[58] But as Nietzsche and, following him, Freud, Horkheimer, and Adorno have argued, this edifice remains harnessed to the noise and agitation of the psyche. In refusing to acknowledge the existence of nonrational motivations, one forfeits the possibility of self-understanding.

Much contemporary debate in moral theory revolves around the paradigm of autonomy that Kant articulated. Autonomy, in Kant's view, is the moral equivalent of the Enlightenment motto "Have courage to use your own reason!" In the *Foundations of the Metaphysics of Morals*, Kant defines the principle of autonomy in which man is "subject only to his own, yet universal legislation, and that he is only bound to act in accordance with his own will, which is, however, designed by nature to be a will giving universal laws."[59] Just as enlightened reason must exclude the influence of emotions, so moral behavior "wholly excludes the influence of inclination" such as sympathy and sensual love.[60] Only then can rational judgments be universalizable and detachable from the concrete context in which they are made.

Many feminists have vociferously criticized this model of autonomy because of its presumption of detachment, universality, and disembeddedness. Writers such as Carol Gilligan, and those following in her wake, advocate the legitimacy of an alternative to this Kantian model of autonomy that they call the care perspective. The care perspective, evident in many women's responses to moral dilemmas, emphasizes the individual's connectedness with others. In this perspective, individuals make moral choices by concretely assessing who will be hurt and who will be helped by particular decisions.[61]

The viability of a care perspective has been heatedly debated both within feminist and nonfeminist circles. Feminists such as Claudia Card criticize this conception on the grounds that it presumes traditional gender dualism, itself the product of patriarchal history. They argue that the care perspective advocates traditional feminine virtues that may be survival strategies for women in forced relations of dependencies but are hardly an emancipated vision for the future. Many feminists, however, defend this posture as an alternative conception of moral autonomy, as a form of reasoning motivated by persons' sense of their own concrete identity that also acknowledges human connectedness.[62] Others, like Benhabib, seek to integrate Kantian moral autonomy with care, a position that "allows us to recognize the dignity of the generalized other through an acknowledgment of the moral identity of the concrete other."[63]

The attention given to the debate about impartiality versus care in academic journals as well as popular ones attests to the historical nerve that it has touched. To some extent, interest in this debate has been sparked by the problematizing of gender identity in contemporary culture. But its significance is also connected to a paradigm shift in contemporary intellectual discourse—across fields such as psychology, moral philosophy, and literary analysis—a shift that challenges the notion that there is individual, subjective identity that exists as a deep self, a unified whole, an isolated ego. Challenging the Kantian conception of the subject is certainly not unique to the present debate. It finds historical antecedents in Hegel's concept of reciprocal recognition and in Marx's concept of the fundamentally social character of human identity. But the question of intersubjectivity has achieved a certain historical urgency today, in light of the crisis of the philosophy of the subject.

The phrase "care perspective" may in fact be a misnomer for the analysis of human interrelatedness. "Care" seems too thin, mild, and one-dimensional to account for the dynamics of human connectedness. As experience of intimacy teaches, relations may include feelings of love and anger and resentment simultaneously. Relatedness might express the possible depth of harmony between two individuals, as well as the cruelty that individuals can exercise against each other; and these different dynamics can coexist within the same relationship. Therefore, "care" cannot be taken as descriptive of the range of emotions involved in human connectedness. Moreover, the care perspective cannot be formulated by the normative principle "Be compassionate" or "Take responsibility."[64] The care perspective is committed to concrete, individual decision making as opposed to abstract, universal rules, which cannot help in deciding between conflicts of responsibilities.

But I would suggest that the radical potential within "care" theories, which go beyond what many of these theorists themselves argue, is to challenge the primacy of the category of autonomy that has prevailed since Kant. In discussing the Kantian subject, Lucien Goldmann once wrote, "That it could never pass from the *I* to the *we*, that in spite of Kant's genius it always remained within the framework of bourgeois individualist thought, these are the ultimate limits of Kant's thought."[65] In our times we may need to perform another conceptual revolution, as Kant did with previous philosophers and as Marx did with Hegel, to reverse the moral weight given to autonomy and heteronomy and to argue for a concept of moral and political theory that is premised on the heteronomy, the interdependence of individuals.[66] Individuals who have close friends, lovers, children, or parents do need to make decisions on the basis of what is best for the "we" of which they form a part. Why shouldn't this acknowledgment of relations be a starting point for moral philosophy, as opposed to beginning with the model of the individual as cut off from intimacy, which Kant personified in his own life and which has become the paradigm of moral philosophy? The health and happiness of these collectivities depend, of course, on balancing to the greatest extent possible the conflicting needs of individuals involved in these relationships. From this perspective, heteronomy includes respect for individuals' integrity and desire to make their own decisions; but individual priorities cannot be absolute. Moreover, these groups do change:

children grow up, partners separate, individuals die, interests and needs change with personal development. However, to privilege the autonomy of the individual as the primary factor in moral thinking makes human separateness and detachment morally normative.

A number of objections may be raised to these suggestions. For example, one might argue that even recognizing the primacy of heteronomy in the moral domain does not undercut the need for a Kantian principle of rational autonomy in the political domain, in order to protect individuals' rights against violent encroachment. A principle that validates the group per se over the individual might pose an even greater danger of exclusion, harassment, and violence than has occurred under the inheritance of the Enlightenment. If radical Right, homophobic, antiabortion advocates achieved their "we" as the primary political agenda, imagine what would happen to individual women, lesbian and gay activists, and AIDS research and support groups.

A number of responses to this objection are in order. First of all, it is important to point out the discrepancy between Kant's moral theory and a political recognition of equal rights. For example, in the *Metaphysical Elements of Justice*, Kant argues "that one ought to obey the legislative authority that now exists, regardless of its origin" and adds that there can be "no legitimate resistance of the people to the legislative chief of the state."[67] Because Kant viewed legislative authority as grounded in the law-giving form of the will, the particular laws in society are viewed as morally binding. Thus Kant's moral theory offers no political protection for, for example, women, servants, or Jews, who might have been discriminated against in existing law. As Young argues, in modern normative political theory and practice, impartiality in the public realm is attained by the exclusion of those linked to particular interests, needs, and concrete identities. The notion of the impartial public domain assumes a "homogeneity of citizens. . . . It excludes from the public those individuals and groups that do not fit the model of the rational citizen who can transcend body and sentiment."[68]

If one were interested in developing the political implications of moral heteronomy, I think it would be fruitful to look at examples such as the Scandinavian welfare states, which have a basic commitment to providing fundamental conditions of human dignity, including money, housing, and health care, to all the members of the community.[69] One might also consider the political party for women in Iceland, a path the National Organization of Women is seeking to pursue. These political parties seek recognition for a particular group in society. Political conflicts between different groups obviously entail negotiation and compromise, to achieve a "rational consensus." But such a consensus can never be achieved, or considered fully rational, if it is cut off from concrete identities, needs, interests, and emotions of the individuals within these groups.

How then does one assess the significance of Kant's essay "What Is Enlightenment?" for the contemporary world? With many of the critics of the Enlightenment, I challenge its fundamental conception of rationality, autonomy, and freedom. This philosophical position has been the hallmark of a historical period in Western European and American society characterized by imperialism, the hegemony of dominant groups over other groups excluded from wealth, political power, and often basic human respect. And yet it would be naive to think that we can free ourselves of this heritage merely by intellectual critique. Even in reacting against Enlightenment assumptions, postmodern and feminist critics are determined by these assumptions, often using the very tools they seek to reject. We may be heir to a tradition that constrains our ability to think the unthought, but nonetheless we must respond to the demand to create a new future, shaped by the contributions of women and Third World people, whose history is the underside of Enlightenment tolerance. We must find a way of living the practical contradiction between the past from which we seek to free ourselves and the future that we desire to create.

NOTES

1. Immanuel Kant, "What is Enlightenment?" in *Kant on History*, trans. Lewis White Beck (New York, 1963), 3.

2. Habermas argues for "the way back" to enlightenment, in contrast to Horkheimer's and Adorno's efforts to show its self-destruction. *The Philosophical Discourses of Modernity*, trans. Frederick Lawrence (Cambridge, Mass., 1987), 128.

3. See Max Horkheimer and Theodor Adorno, *Dialectic of Enlightenment*, trans. John Cumming (New York, 1972), xi.

4. Berel Lang, *Act and Idea in the Nazi Genocide* (Chicago, 1990), 179ff.

5. I will discuss Kant's lack of egalitarianism regarding women and servants below. Lang also notes that few figures in the Enlightenment extended their tolerance to Jews. Kant did not view Judaism as having the status of a true religion but considered it rather a cult based on external rituals and therefore removed from the moral domain. Voltaire repeated many of the conventional slurs from the past (e.g., his reference to Jews as "the most contemptible of all nations . . . robbers, seditious") and clearly considered the Jews to be themselves intolerant (by maintaining their separateness), thereby exempting them from the privilege of being tolerated by others. (Lang, *Act and Idea*, 185).

6. Lang, *Act and Idea*, 188.

7. In Foucault's essay "Kant on Enlightenment and Revolution," trans. Colin Gordon, *Economy and Society* 15, no. 1 (1986), 88–96, he argues that Kant develops an "ontology of the present" in "What Is Enlightenment?" which should be distinguished from the "analytic of truth" that Kant develops in his critical philosophy. However, Foucault's critique of Kant does extend to this "analytic of truth."

8. See Christine di Stefano, "Dilemmas of Difference," in *Feminism/Postmodernism*, ed. Linda J. Nicholson (New York, 1990), 75. Di Stefano's suggestion that post-

modernism may be a theory whose time has come for men, but not for women, implies that women still need to carry out the Enlightenment tasks of developing a centered self and a coherent system of truth.

9. See Jane Flax's discussion of this position in "Postmodernism and Gender Relations," in *Feminism/Postmodernism*, 42.

10. Jane Flax, "Postmodernism and Gender Relations," in *Feminism/Postmodernism*, 42. Flax writes, "The way(s) to feminist future(s) cannot lie in reviving or appropriating Enlightenment concepts of the person or knowledge."

11. Ibid., 43.

12. Claire G. Moses, "The Legacy of the Eighteenth Century: A Look at the Future," in *French Women and the Age of Enlightenment*, ed. Samia I. Spencer (Bloomington, 1984), 413.

13. Ibid., 409–410.

14. Ibid. In terms of the view from Germany, one should note Kant's enthusiasm for the French Revolution and the political constitution that emerged from it. See Foucault, "Kant on Enlightenment and Revolution," 94.

15. Ibid., 413–414.

16. For example, between 1719 and 1730, a teacher in the Vosges region asked thirty-six couples to sign the marriage register. Although twenty-three men would write their names, thirty-two of the women were unable to write a cross, much less their names. Jean Larnac, *Histoire de la litterature feminine en France* (Paris, 1929), 132. Cited in Samia I. Spencer, "Women and Education," in *French Women and the Age of Enlightenment*, 95.

17. Spencer, "Women and Education," 83–84.

18. Ibid., 86.

19. Ibid., 84.

20. Some few aristocratic women in Prussia, such as Dorothea von Schlozer, were able to acquire a university education in the eighteenth century. However, they were also frustrated by their inability to use their education. But university education did not open up for women more generally until the twentieth century. As in France, the professions of medicine, teaching, and law began to open up gradually to women in the 1880s and 1890s. James C. Albisetti, "Women and the Professions in Imperial Germany," in *German Women in the Eighteenth and Nineteenth Centuries*, ed. Ruth-Ellen B. Joeres and Mary Jo Maynes (Bloomington, 1986), 96.

21. Wolff, Kant, Fichte, Schelling, Hegel, and Schleiermacher were all university professors. By contrast, in England scholars such as Darwin, Spencer, Mill, Bentham, Ricardo, Hume, Locke, Hobbes, and Bacon were not connected with university life. See Friedrich Paulsen, *The German Universities and University Study*, trans. Frank Thilly and William W. Elwant (New York, 1906), 4–5.

22. Charles E. McClelland, *State, Society, and University in Germany, 1700–1914* (Cambridge, 1980), 250.

23. The difficulty women have in gaining access to education and cultural authority remains an issue today. Michele Le Doeuff notes that although creative areas in philosophy today do not lie in the area of academic work, it is still crucial to note that since 1974 the number of women who pass selective examinations for teaching jobs has been very small ("Women and Philosophy," in *French Feminist* Thought, ed. Toril Moi [Oxford, 1987], 200–201). She explains this phenomenon

in part by differences between men's and women's philosophical writing: "Men treat the text familiarly and knock it about happily; women treat it with a politeness for which girls' education has its share of responsibility. If the timidity and the desire to flatter are not too strong, this form of reading can, I think, produce great successes, a distanced kind of reading which enables one to see what is implicit in the text or to pick out the 'gaps' in theorization. The question is whether it is because this kind of reading is not highly valued that the women fail, or whether it is not highly valued just because it is evidently feminine. I prefer the second hypothesis, and would add that the feminine is excluded because it is associated with the idea of lack of authority" (p. 205).

24. Kant, *Anthropology from a Pragmatic Point of View*, trans. Victor Lyle Dowdell (Carbondale and Edwardsville, 1978), 219.

25. Ibid., 221.

26. Kant, *Observations on the Feeling of the Beautiful and Sublime*, trans. John T. Goldthwait (Berkeley, Los Angeles, and London, 1960), sec. 3, p. 78.

27. Ibid., 132–133.

28. *Anthropology*, 222.

29. Linda Gardiner, "Women in Science," in *French Women and the Age of Enlightenment*, 184ff.

30. Ibid., 189.

31. Immanuel Kant, *Philosophical Correspondence 1759–99*, ed. and trans. Arnulf Zweig (Chicago, 1967), 201.

32. Letter to Elisabeth Motherby, 11 February, 1793, in *Philosophical Correspondence*, 204.

33. Hans-Georg Gadamer, *Philosophical Hermeneutics*, ed. and trans. David E. Linge (Berkeley, Los Angeles, and London, 1976), 28.

34. "What Is Enlightenment?" 3.

35. Ibid.

36. See my book *Cognition and Eros: A Critique of the Kantian Paradigm* (Boston, 1988), for a discussion of Kant's conception of rationality. In particular, see chap. 9.

37. *Philosophical Correspondence*, 236.

38. "What Is Enlightenment?" 5. Although Kant did not express particular interest in extending Enlightenment ideas to women, a few of his contemporaries did—notably Theodor Gottlieb von Hippel. Hippel called for improving women's education and giving women opportunities for meaningful activity. Ruth P. Dawson, "'And This Shield Is Called Self-Reliance': Emerging Feminist Consciousness in the Late 18th Century," in *German Women in the Eighteenth and Nineteenth Centuries*, 158. There were many women writers of the eighteenth and nineteenth centuries who have been "unjustly forgotten." However, these women had to struggle against enormous social forces that prescribed women's "proper" role in the home and family. Women writers were not taken seriously. They appeared in the shadows of men, and they often wrote pseudonymously or anonymously in order to get published. Moreover, they faced a certain "vacuum of experience" because of their exclusion from education, government, military office, and business. Patricia Herminghouse, "Women and the Literary Enterprise in Nineteenth-Century Germany," in *German Women in the Eighteenth and Nineteenth Centuries*, 79–90.

39. "What Is Enlightenment?" 3.

40. Gardiner, "Women in Science," 187.

41. *Philosophical Correspondence*, 204.

42. Maria's letter to Kant, January 1793, in *Philosophical Correspondence*, 201.

43. "What Is Enlightenment?" 3.

44. Ibid., 4.

45. Maria von Herbert did commit suicide, nine years after her last letter to Kant (*Philosophical Correspondence*, 26).

46. Immanuel Kant, *Foundations of the Metaphysics of Morals*, trans. Lewis White Beck (Indianapolis, 1959), 17.

47. *Anthropology*, par. 73, p. 155.

48. Ibid., par. 74, p. 157.

49. *Philosophical Correspondence*, 188–189.

50. Ibid., 189–190.

51. Ibid., 190.

52. Friedrich Nietzsche, *The Genealogy of Morals*, in *The Birth of Tragedy and the Genealogy of Morals*, trans. Francis Golffing (New York, 1956), 264.

53. Thomas E. Hill, Jr., "The Importance of Autonomy," in *Women and Moral Theory*, ed. Eva Feder Kittay and Diana T. Meyers (Totawa, N.J., 1987), 132. Although Hill is seeking to defend a view of Kantian autonomy as part of a debate about moral principles, not a way of living life, he acknowledges that Kant conflated the two and thus seems to undercut his own thesis.

54. Iris Young, "Impartiality and the Civic Public: Some Implications of Feminist Critiques of Moral and Political Theory," in *Throwing Like a Girl and Other Essays in Feminist Philosophy and Social Theory* (Bloomington, 1990), 96.

55. Seyla Benhabib, "The Generalized and the Concrete Other: The Kohlberg-Gilligan Controversy and Moral Theory," in *Women and Moral Theory*, 162.

56. Benhabib notes that "Rawls recapitulates a basic problem with the Kantian conception of the self, namely, that noumenal selves cannot be *individuated*. If all that belongs to them as embodied affective, suffering creatures, their memory and history, their ties and relations to others, are to be subsumed under the phenomenal realm, then what we are left with is an empty mask that is everyone and no one" (p. 166).

57. Young, "Impartiality and the Civic Public," 98.

58. Nietzsche, *Genealogy of Morals*, 189.

59. *Foundations*, 51.

60. *Foundations*, 17.

61. Carol Gilligan, *In a Different Voice: Psychological Theory and Women's Development* (Cambridge, Mass., 1982). See also articles debating Gilligan's work in *Women and Moral Theory*.

62. Diana T. Meyers, "The Socialized Individual and Individual Autonomy: An Intersection between Philosophy and Psychology," in *Women and Moral Theory*, 139, 152.

63. Benhabib, "Generalized and Concrete Other," 169.

64. Thomas Hill suggests that these rules are what attentiveness to a "caring" solution implies. "The Importance of Autonomy," 132.

65. Lucien Goldmann, *Immanuel Kant*, trans. Robert Black (London, 1971), 170.

66. The meaning of heteronomy has also to be redefined. In Kant's view, heteronomy refers to everything outside of the universal legislation of reason. All of these other factors were subsumed under the concept of nature (*Foundations*, 51). Kant's concept of heteronomy provides no tools for analyzing and distinguishing the nature of one's own emotions, the influence of other persons, or the impact of physical constraints on an individual. Therefore, he has no means of acknowledging the possibility of mutuality between persons, other than a shared abstract respect for the moral law.

67. Immanuel Kant, *The Metaphysical Elements of Justice*, trans. John Ladd (Indianapolis, 1959), 85–86.

68. Young, "Impartiality and the Civic Public," 98, 100.

69. Unfortunately, the commitments of the social welfare state in Scandinavia are now in jeopardy: witness recent significant cutbacks in social services in both Denmark and Sweden.

Autonomy, Individuality, and Self-Determination

Lewis Hinchman

The quest for autonomy has been a pervasive, though scarcely uncontested, motif in much of twentieth-century moral philosophy. And most of the philosophers who have defended some version of autonomy have acknowledged the affinities between their own inquiries and those of certain Enlightenment thinkers, above all Kant.[1] However, as one compares recent work on autonomy to Kant's remarks about it, important differences emerge. Kant had presumed, in his *Groundwork of the Metaphysics of Morals*, the literal meaning of autonomy: obedience to a self-imposed law. He treated it as a constraint, a rule of moral conduct that is "objective" in the sense that it is what all rational beings would agree ought to be done. A sampling of contemporary studies reveals a shift of attention from the objective content and "constraining" force of the rules chosen by autonomous agents to the character of those agents and the process by which they reach decisions. The autonomous individual has been described recently as having "moral convictions and principles... genuinely his own, rooted in his own character, and not merely inherited,"[2] as engaging in a continuing "process of criticism and re-evaluation,"[3] or as possessing the "higher order capacity... to choose his or her ends, whatever they are."[4] These remarks suggest that it no longer matters *what* rules one chooses to follow: the main requirement is that the choices be truly one's own, that one must not have been manipulated, gulled, brainwashed, or conditioned into making them. Given this disparity in what would be considered autonomous agency, one might conclude that contemporary philosophers are in fact writing about issues quite distinct from those that preoccupied Kant.

But, in my view, that would be a mistaken inference. In addition to his rigorous "metaphysical" theory of moral autonomy in the *Groundwork*, Kant sketched out a different, socially and politically oriented account in his

1784 essay, "What Is Enlightenment?"—one that has close affinities to contemporary conceptions of autonomy. In "What Is Enlightenment?" Kant used the word *Mündigkeit* (maturity) to characterize a critical, self-determining stance. Kant began the essay by observing that "enlightenment is man's emergence from his self-incurred immaturity. Immaturity is man's inability to make use of his understanding without the guidance of another."[5] Those who, in Kant's terms, achieve "maturity" by taking responsibility for their own thoughts, decisions, and actions would be good candidates for autonomy in the sense that contemporary philosophers use the word. In short, the filiations between modern autonomy and its Kantian equivalents lead back not only to Kant's formal ethics but also—and even more strikingly—to the Enlightenment project of disarming superstition and tradition, while encouraging the formation of an independent, reflective mentality. Indeed, one of the most influential contemporary defenders of autonomy, Jürgen Habermas, has consciously reappropriated Kant's understanding of maturity, particularly the connection spelled out in "What Is Enlightenment?" between self-guidance and public discussion.

Still, contemporary theories of autonomy cannot be viewed simply as elaborations of Kantian *Autonomie* or *Mündigkeit.* Between Kant and the twentieth century, two momentous intellectual events intervened which decisively altered the terms of the debate. First, alongside the rationalist tradition that Kant inherited and in some respects continued, there developed what Charles Taylor has called an "expressivist" movement,[6] exemplified in the writings of Goethe, Schiller, Humboldt, Hölderlin, and others. These writers insisted that a truly self-directed life would involve *individuality*: the noninterchangeable uniqueness of each person ought to pervade and guide all of his or her works and actions. We shall see in detail how individuality, as it were, has been absorbed into the modern notion of autonomy despite the dissimilarity of their respective intellectual origins.

Contemporary ideas about autonomy (especially on the "postmodern" side) have also been shaped by its historicization. In Kant, enlightenment, maturity, and moral autonomy were, to be sure, not entirely ahistorical categories. Kant did hypothesize that his own age might have reached a certain threshold beyond which people would become able to direct their own lives and dispense with blind obedience to authority. But Hegel initiated a transformation that has led to our seeing the autonomous individual as a peculiar kind of historical fiction, one that later became a vehicle of Western cultural imperialism. For those drawn to the historically mediated concept of autonomy, it is no longer a matter of theorizing from "within" the horizon of autonomy but of explaining why, in rather specific contexts, Europeans were ever misled into imagining that they could direct their own lives, set their own rules, and find a place to stand outside of all power/knowledge complexes. The challenge to defenders of autonomy in our time has therefore sharpened considerably. They cannot assume an audience that will take philosophical concepts on their own terms, as having a nonderivative, independent status. They must try instead to show that the impetus toward autonomy does derive simply from features—and distortions—specific to modern European history.

The ideal of an autonomous, mature, self-directed life, then, has not really been eclipsed. It has instead acquired a multidimensional, "reflected" quality as its exponents have tried to respond and to incorporate aspects of these countermovements into their theories. Liberals, postmodernists, and critical theorists all end up defending *some* notion of autonomy; yet those versions differ so profoundly that their affinities often pass unnoticed. I try to make some of those affinities explicit by illuminating their Enlightenment, and especially Kantian, elements and explaining how these became transformed under the pressure of romantic individuality and historicism.

I

Theories of autonomy present variations of a basic pattern. There is first a ruling, law-giving, controlling, or evaluating element (the *nomos*) situated *within* the individual (for, if it were outside, autonomy would not even get off the ground). The controlling or evaluating aspect of the self must relate itself to another internal element that, by definition, would vitiate personal autonomy if it were not directed, ruled, or evaluated critically. Finally, one or both of these internal elements must be seen as implicated in a larger transindividual context that may variously promote or thwart the project of being autonomous. Disagreement about the worth of autonomy as well as historical shifts in its definition often hinge on the way these elements are characterized and interlinked.

Enlightenment philosophers did not create the ideal of autonomous agency from scratch. They could draw on both the figure of the Stoic sage and on certain implications of the new natural sciences, especially in their Cartesian form, to arrive at a notion of human self-direction. Indeed, the originality of Enlightenment autonomy only emerges when one contrasts it to the images of self and world that preceded it.

Stoic autonomy, according to one scholar, had "little to do with being controlled by others, and everything to do with the active control one's will asserts over one's own urges and impulses."[7] In other words, it resulted from a successful encounter between a ruling element (will or, more accurately, reason) and an unruly internal factor, such as fear, anger, or grief, defined as beyond the pale of reason and arising spontaneously or naturally. Self-sufficiency, the Stoic precursor of autonomy, meant achieving a distance and detachment from one's impulses or passions, not allowing them to determine one's state of mind and actions.

The external environment of the Stoic sage affected this internal encounter in two ways. First, the sage recognized that other people might try to control or even enslave him and thus at least outwardly negate his autonomy. But the outcome of their endeavor depended solely on his internal decision whether to allow himself to be controlled. If he were indifferent to the external marks of control—for example, pain, humiliation, self-abnegation—he could maintain an inner tranquillity or imperturbability (*ataraxia*). At least for some Stoic writers, the key to attaining that inner composure lay in a vision of the order of nature. Attuned to the external goodness and necessity of things, the Stoic could overlook the trivial commotions and passions that preoccupied most people.[8] Thus the external world as harmonious totality could promote autonomy, counteracting the destabilizing influences of particular events.

Descartes, Locke, Shaftesbury, and other early modern philosophers shared this Stoic sense of a normative order in nature. But, as Taylor has shown, they subtly and gradually altered its significance by conceptualizing nature as a set of mechanical processes rather than as a text to be interpreted.[9] Nature could still be considered an artifice of the deity and thus purposive, but only in the sense that the cogs and gears of a machine display their purposes in performing the function for which they were designed. Stoic self-sufficiency would soon slide over into a quite different attitude, one that actually encouraged a person to rearrange the elements of the natural world (and his or her inner life) to make them serve more efficiently the Creator's intentions.[10] Self-mastery could yield to mastery of the world by means of scientific knowledge.

This demystification of nature altered the notion of self-mastery that the seventeenth century inherited from antiquity. The element of the self to be subordinated and controlled could no longer simply be encountered as an internal manifestation of chaos or slavery. Although from the point of view of the "ruling" element, these impulses might appear as nothing but tokens of disorder, they in fact belonged to the totality of a mechanically understood, thoroughly orderly universe. If that universe had purposes, then so, obviously, did passion and desires. Thus reason had less the task of neutralizing, ignoring, or suppressing passions, than of overseeing their correct, efficient operation: "reason rules the passions when it can hold them to their normal instrumental function. The beginning of reason for Descartes was a matter of instrumental control."[11]

These transformations in the definitions of the "ruled" element of the soul and the status of nature presaged an even more momentous shift in the definition of the actual self, the "ruling" element that would become the locus of autonomy in Kant. René Descartes's epistemology marked a stage in this shift. What I know of the world are only the *representations* of it that my mind assembles. But that process of assembling or constructing a picture of reality is influenced, usually for the worse, by "appetites and preceptors,"[12] both of which becloud the mind's natural operations by substituting opinion and prejudice for methodical reasoning. Descartes thus implicitly anticipated Kant's definition of enlightenment by challenging individuals to use their own intellects without the guidance of established authorities. The inwardly free self of the Stoic tradition now became an intellectually autonomous self practicing methodical doubt on all received opinion and determined to accept only clear and distinct ideas as true.

Even though John Locke's empiricism would seem to undercut the premise of an autonomous self detached from material processes, he actually developed many of these Cartesian themes in a different idiom. Taylor discovers in Locke's epistemology and psychology an "ideal of independence and self-responsibility" that uncompromisingly rejects all dependence on custom, authority, or the passions.[13] Its source is the "punctual self," that is, a self understood as able to objectify, reflect on, and reform the operations of the mind, but which is itself "extensionless" and no part of the psychological processes of which it takes notice. In Locke more clearly even than in Descartes, intellectual independence and moral responsibility fused with objectification, disengagement, and the potential, at least, for rational control of the inner life.

But Locke and Descartes still reasoned within a theocratic framework. They did not envision the self as legislating its own norms; rather, God as artificer had contrived the human soul to make it a fit instrument for its proper destiny. The Enlightenment would later debate what that destiny is and how exactly humans have been endowed with it (whether through intellect, moral sense, or in some other way). But early modern philosophy did unquestionably predispose succeeding generations to regard autonomy in light of certain *Bestimmungen* (destinies, vocations, definitions) that would give support and objective validity to the project of living a self-directed life.

II

Contrary to what we might expect, the literature of the *Aufklärung* (excepting Kant's writings, of course) rarely made autonomy an explicit issue. The notion that human beings should live by standards of moral rectitude that cannot be derived from nature but must be legislated by reason alone simply did not occur to most *Aufklärer* before Kant.[14] They saw no grounds to believe that human dignity would suffer a blow if one did what nature and/or nature's God intended. However, even though most Enlightenment writers rarely invoked autonomy by name as a moral ideal, they often advocated the outlook that Kant called "Mündigkeit": a zeal to liberate oneself from superstition, discover the truth by one's own efforts, and be guided by one's own light rather than by any authority. In fact, as Kant himself noted, there was a latent tension in the corpus of Enlightenment writings between the many calls to lead a moral, independent life, on the one hand, and, on the other, the rather passive, mechanical, and naturalistic image of human psychology that pervaded many treatises of the day.[15]

Moses Mendelssohn's 1784 essay "Über die Frage: Was heisst aufklären?" typified the pattern of thought about human agency that had begun to emerge in early modern philosophy.[16] Mendelssohn was deeply influenced by Shaftesbury, a self-professed Stoic, and by the rationalist, teleological metaphysics of Christian Wolff, who had attempted to demonstrate by deductive reasoning the essential harmony and order of the universe. Accordingly, he posed the problem of rational inquiry and reflection in terms of wider contexts of nature and human nature.

Enlightenment along with culture and education (*Bildung*) are aspects of "societal life." They are efforts to *improve* our social condition.[17] Thus the freedom to investigate, publish, or discuss delicate topics such as religion must finally depend on whether doing so will improve society and its members taken either as human beings *tout court* or as citizens of a specific state. On the whole, Mendelssohn was inclined to believe that free inquiry benefits society, at least in the long run.[18] However, he was careful to point out that unrestricted inquiry and communication could harm societal life under certain circumstances, for example, in a state that depended on the uncritical acceptance of "prejudice" for the maintenance of moral conduct.[19]

In short, Mendelssohn presumed a consequentialist, vaguely utilitarian ethics. The goal is social improvement, toward which reflection and unlimited free inquiry constitute only important means. No one can claim an absolute right to subject all traditional authority to critical examination, because the social order is grounded on cooperation to achieve the common good, not on the rights or dignity of the individual person.

But Mendelssohn did envision a convergence of social harmony, progress, and individual self-development. He remarked, "I set, at all times, the destiny of man [*Bestimmung des Menschen*] as the measure and goal of all our strivings and efforts, as a point on which we must set our eyes if we do not wish to lose ourselves."[20] The expression "destiny of man" is evidently borrowed from a book of that title written by Johann Joachim Spalding in 1748.[21] For Spalding, the moral impulse in human beings, the urge to bring about universal happiness, derives from their divine nature and can only be finally realized in the Kingdom of God. The Christian trappings of this theory would have appealed less to the Jewish Mendelssohn than the way it connected morality and hence enlightenment to a wider teleological context defined by divine purposes and made manifest in human nature (to wit, moral sentiments). Mendelssohn's whole approach to enlightenment thus presupposed a fairly clear schema: "social life" characterized by varying degrees of Bildung (education or "formation") but mainly still under the influence of superstition and ignorance; human nature understood teleologically as involving a moral-religious destiny; enlightenment as movement toward that destiny, the chief means for improving our social existence.

Mendelssohn's account of enlightenment seems to be fairly typical of a wide range of quasi-utilitarian theories and arguments advanced in Germany during the latter half of the eighteenth century. Christian Gotthilf Salzmann, for example, defined "true" enlightenment as acquisition of the "knowledge that is most necessary and useful to edify man's temperament, promote his efficiency and satisfaction, preserve his health, strengthen his bodily powers and improve his state of being."[22] Similarly, Joachim Heinrich Campe observed that the term "enlightenment" encompassed "every increase in useful knowledge as well as every stimulus to thinking for oneself about objects that have some relation to human well-being."[23] Yet another utilitarian definition was proferred by Andreas Riem: "enlightenment [is] nothing else but the effort of the human spirit to illuminate all objects of the world of ideas, all human opinions and their results and everything that influences humanity, according to a doctrine of pure reason, in order to promote the useful."[24] All of these definitions of enlightenment agree with Mendelssohn's in relating it to an understanding of human nature or "destiny" treated as the *telos* of human action. Enlightenment—and the development of our critical faculties that it stimulates—only has an instrumental value; it is useful in helping to bring about a certain objective state of affairs. It does not, as Horst Stuke points out, "aim at the autonomy of the thinking subject or of the critical-emancipatory function of thinking for oneself, at least in matters of religion."[25]

This image of human agency as dominated by natural or divine order was certainly not unique to the German Enlightenment. Even a "radical" philosophe such as Claude-Adrien Helvetius, determined to challenge the legitimacy of the existing order in France, did not value autonomy for its own sake. For example, he advocated freedom of the press,[26] but only because it would enable citizens to "perfect their laws."[27] The truth is good only because it is useful.[28] Ultimately, Helvetius's ethics envisioned a manipulative legislator cognizant of the axiom that "to guide the motions of the human puppet, it is necessary to know the wires by which he is moved."[29] Paradoxically, the "maturity" we achieve in casting aside superstition and metaphysics seems to imply acquiescence in a thoroughly determined, mechanistic order. The best we can do, on the "radical" Enlightenment view, is to replace irrational, counterproductive conditioning with laws and mores that maximize pleasure and minimize pain.

The reformist bent of someone such as Mendelssohn and Helvetius certainly implied the value of self-direction, critique, and "maturity" in the use of one's intellect, but their teleological and/or naturalistic horizons tended to draw their attention to the objects of reform rather than the process, the subjective or formal aspect, of enlightenment. But autonomy understood as an explicit, self-conscious aspiration, an indispensable expression of human dignity, first crystallizes in Kant. The outlines of Kant's "official" theory of moral autonomy are familiar and may be summarized briefly by reference to the scheme suggested earlier.

For Kant, autonomy involves, as with the Stoics, a contest between reason and certain spontaneous, unreflective reactions that must be mastered. But Kant defined both elements more precisely. Moral autonomy requires that agents give themselves the law by which they act. That law, of course, must be the categorical imperative. Autonomy requires that one interrupt the natural flow of inclinations, replacing the object's effect on the will with the motive of reason. The Stoic merely sought to stave off entrapping and unsettling influences by attaining inner tranquillity. By contrast, Kant's moral agent negated their power, overriding them by another kind of causality, derived from pure reason.

More important, the role of the external world has changed almost completely in Kant's version of moral autonomy. It has now been defined, following the new science, as a realm of physical motions and laws. But one must also assume the existence of other self-legislating (autonomous) beings toward whom the agent has moral duties. Taken together, these autonomous agents constituted a "kingdom of ends," a "systematic union of rational beings by common objective laws."[30] Autonomy essentially involved the kingdom of ends, since, when individuals submitted their maxims to the test of universalizability, they imagined them to be laws capable of being followed by all other "citizens" of that kingdom. Thus autonomous agents alone could claim an absolute right to be treated according to the moral law (as ends rather than as means only) because they were capable of self-legislation and were not simply (in Helvetius's word) "puppets": "Autonomy then is the basis of the dignity of human and of every rational nature."[31]

Earlier I suggested that Kant's metaphysical account of autonomy did not fully express the meaning of the term today and that his idea of Mündigkeit captures its contemporary sense more accurately. Yet I believe there is a connection between his notions of autonomy and maturity. Moral autonomy depends, Kant insisted, on the capacity to universalize one's maxims, to ask whether they could be adopted as laws by all rational beings. In the *Groundwork*, Kant took for granted the capacity to universalize, but in other writings he sketched in some of the factors that affect this faculty as well as the knack of applying rules to real-life situations. Kant's formal ethics, depending as it does on the notion of self-legislated moral rules, actually *required* these "psychological" additions. For if Kant could not show that—

and how—we universalize our maxims, then his whole notion of moral autonomy would have become uselessly counterfactual, something like writing an ethics for wolves or pigs.

In the *Critique of Judgment*, Kant pointed out that our judgments must rely in part on the *sensus communis*, the "power to judge that in reflecting takes account (*a priori*) in our thought, of everyone else's way of presenting [something], in order *as it were* to compare our own judgment with human reason in general and thus escape the illusion that arises from the ease of mistaking subjective and private conditions for objective ones."[32] The most formidable obstacles to universalizing one's judgments proved to be "prejudice" and "superstition." People whose thinking cannot advance beyond these impediments demonstrate thereby their need to be "guided by others." The proper remedy for prejudice and superstition, Kant remarked, is "enlightenment."[33] Although referring to aesthetic judgments in this context, Kant implied that these have a bearing on moral judgments too.[34] We must be able to learn how to escape the bias inherent in judging things in light of our own interest and ingrained prejudices. The "enlightened" mind in aesthetic *and* moral matters will learn to disengage itself from the patterns of seeing and responding that self-interest and habit have rendered almost automatic, and will consider a situation from the viewpoint of other (rational) beings. In both cases we "put ourselves in the position of everyone else, merely by abstracting from the limitations that (may) happen to attach to our own judging."[35]

The idea of a sensus communis in the *Critique of Judgment* has an analogue in Kant's essay on enlightenment. While it was difficult for individuals to escape from their self-incurred immaturity, Kant observed "that the public should enlighten itself is more possible; indeed, if only freedom is granted, enlightenment is almost sure to follow."[36] The public meant, for Kant, the *reading* public addressed by scholars and literati in journals like the *Berlinische Monatsschrift.* On one level, Kant's essay on enlightenment represented merely one more contribution to ongoing debates about freedom of the press and its limitations.[37] But from the viewpoint of political theory, this essay changed the terms in which the notion of autonomy had traditionally been posed. We have moved from the Stoic position, in which the autonomous sage wages a personal struggle against passions and desires, to "enlightened" autonomy, in which intellectually emancipated individuals participate in a continuous public, critical discussion, at least vicariously through books and journals. Such discussion enlivens and develops individuals' powers of universalization while dissolving the encrustations of prejudice and habit. Thus both moral autonomy and universality of aesthetic judgment presuppose the formative influence of public enlightenment.

If one places Kant's various accounts of autonomy and Mündigkeit in the context of the mainstream of the Enlightenment, they at first appear idiosyncratic and unorthodox. Most other Enlightenment figures emphasized the objective values and goals of their movement: utility, self-improvement, scientific progress, cultural development (Bildung), and (speaking anachronistically) the modernization of regime and society. Although Kant too treated the progress of humanity as the moral "final purpose" of the world, and hypothesized a civilizing telos of nature working through man's "unsociable sociability," he carefully avoided grounding his conceptions of moral worth and autonomy on these postulates.[38] Still, judging from the benefit of hindsight, one might suggest that Kant grasped the critical, self-liberating spirit of the Enlightenment better than most of his contemporaries did. At any rate, his invocation of moral autonomy, intellectual independence, and public debate marked a turning point in the Enlightenment. One current, represented by the utilitarian wing, emphasized its objectivizing, modernizing, and "scientific" side and downplayed the theme of autonomy. This wing has been transformed, after various complex theoretical shifts of emphasis, into modern utilitarianism and certain schools of social science but has also influenced Foucault via Nietzsche's "positivistic" writings. Meanwhile, Kantian ideas have entered into contemporary notions of autonomy directly, but also obliquely, through the media of romanticism and German idealism, which, of course, complained about the dualisms and disharmonies of Kant's critical philosophy and sought to overcome them in diverse syntheses of the allegedly sundered, alienated elements of the human self. It is difficult to understand the accretions of meaning that have grown up around "autonomy" without taking into account its assimilation by these post-Kantian movements. Moreover, they have affected even the twentieth-century currents of thought that still cling to Kant's program of emancipating the intellect from immaturity, especially the critical theory of Habermas, contemporary American liberalism after the manner of Rawls, Feinberg, Richards, and others, and even some postmodern writers like Foucault.

III

We will not be able to understand twentieth-century accounts of autonomy without acknowledging how deeply they have been influenced by a different, aesthetic-metaphysical tradition that variously has been called romanticism, expressivism, or in certain cases the "counter-Enlightenment."[39] Some of its luminaries, such as Goethe, Schiller, Herder, and Wilhelm von Humboldt, also contemn a life lived under the aegis of unexamined prejudice, sheer habit, and mental sloth. But their counterimage to such a life usually goes by the name of "individuality." It describes the way in which a person, or even a whole nation—drawing on traditions, language, culture, and natural environment—can fashion an inchoate, unformed identity into a many-sided, coherent, aesthetically pleasing totality. The idea is precisely not to adopt a universalizing stance toward one's own moral and emotional life, to "get outside" the self toward some more impartial, truer vantage point, but instead to externalize what has always lain within, albeit only dimly recognized, as the unique, noninterchangeble core of self. Humboldt remarked that "the ultimate object of all our moral strivings is solely to discover, nourish, and re-create what truly exists in ourselves and others."[40]

Notice that the elements of autonomy have changed their relative positions in these invocations of individuality. Natural impulses, passions, feelings, and inchoate strivings for coherence used to be classed as irrational obstacles to autonomy and thus as the element to be controlled, ruled, and mastered. Now they become the "law," the very nomos in autonomy. Reason, the formerly ordering, controlling element in the Kantian scheme, now must accommodate itself to the inner law of a person's unique individuality. In a sense, it becomes precisely the element to be directed and ruled so that it does not block off the channels of individual self-expression.

The external environment displays a twofold character. On one side, especially in Goethe and Schiller, nature is often portrayed as a demonic, demiurgic power that actually strives for expression in the individuality of the person (especially the artist). Echoing the Stoics, albeit in a very different context, Goethe, Schiller, and Schelling can treat nature as a meaning-laden macrocosm intensified and concentrated within the microcosmic individual. By contrast, especially in John Stuart Mill's *On Liberty*, society's rules, conventions, and pressures assume a repressive, stifling aspect. While the Aufklärer had denounced convention or prejudice for hampering a person's intellect (especially the ability to universalize judgments and adopt other points of view), the defenders of individuality indicted it for making people inauthentic automatons. What counts in this new image of self-direction is that my thoughts, ideas, actions, and social relationships should really be mine, expressing my individual nature rather than the internalized expectations of others. On this account, society—even a reading public such as Kant invoked—becomes potentially inimical to the project of self-determination.

Before tracing out the fate of the concept of autonomy in the twentieth century, we need to describe one other way in which it was challenged and transformed in the nineteenth century. Although Hegel did not directly criticize the notion of autonomy that Kant worked out, he undermined it by treating the Enlightenment generally as a "shape of consciousness" that belonged to a now-superseded context of spirit's self-development.[41] From the vantage point of Hegel's *Phenomenology* and *History of Philosophy*, the Enlightenment, including especially Kant's polemical essay, appears naive because it does not reflect on its own process of self-constitution.

In Hegel's view, Kant simply did not recognize the continuity between spirit's self-manifestation as Enlightenment and its previous "shapes," especially religious faith. A historically adequate notion of the Enlightenment would have to restore that continuity and read its dichotomizations of truth/error, enlightenment/superstition, and autonomy/heteronomy as ways to deny and suppress the myriad connections (even identities) between it and the religious, political, and cultural patterns that its champions scorned. In this sense, Hegelian "enlightenment" is far more latitudinarian, inclusive, and historicist than the Aufklärung itself.

Hegel's *Phenomenology* thus alters the context of the discussion of autonomy in two respects. On the one hand, the demand for autonomy can now be ascribed to a certain stage of European history; its critical, emancipatory thrust can be blunted by treating it as the symptom of an incomplete, naive self-understanding, a relic of a kind of culture now behind us. In a different direction, the notion of autonomy can be interpreted as the expression of what Taylor called the "punctual self" that emerged in early modern European philosophy. On this reading, which is consciously Hegelian, the question "Can and should a person aspire to be autonomous, mature, and self-determining?" resolves itself into a deeper question: "Doesn't it distort matters to treat the self as though it really *could*, out of its own resources, objectify and disengage from its social and cultural milieu, universalize its judgment, purge itself of prejudice?" On either reading, autonomy can no longer be taken on its own terms; it must be interrogated so as to yield up clues about the hidden contexts that allow it to surface as a political and philosophical issue in the first place (e.g., the formation of the modern self, the "normalization" of society, the interweaving of metaphysical with gender-specific categories).

IV

One factor that renders the twentieth-century political landscape so complex is the way in which ideals, theories, ideologies, and evaluations from earlier periods of history survive into the present. In the case of autonomy, we shall see that its liberal-Kantian variant persists in an almost pure form (e.g., in John Rawls), along with other hybrid shapes influenced by romantic individuality, Hegelianism, and existentialism. Then we will see how this tradition in all of its variants has been challenged by more historicist currents of thought that, following the road mapped by Hegel, want to question the very context in which the "autonomous self" could be constituted at all.

Adopting the standpoint of Kant's moral philosophy, Rawls accepts the equation of morality and autonomy and tries to make it more persuasive than Kant did. One objection to Kant's theory is that there is no compelling reason to assume that the person who chooses to lead a bad life has not acted autonomously. Why couldn't such a life represent that person's considered judgment about how to express his or her essential nature? Rawls replies: If a human being's essential nature is to be free, equal, and rational, then people can best express that nature by showing that they are free from "natural contingencies and social accident." Rawls's "original position" by definition satisfies these conditions, since it requires us not to "look at the social order from our situation but take up a point of view that everyone can adopt on an equal footing."[42] Therefore, to act on principles chosen in the original position means acting on the basis of reason alone, rather than having one's decisions dictated by inclinations to attain objects that are desirable because of one's particular station. Rawls concludes: "Following the Kantian interpretation of justice as fairness, we can say that by acting from these principles persons are acting autonomously: they are acting from principles that they would acknowledge under conditions that best express their nature as free and rational beings."[43]

Yet Rawlsian autonomy differs from its Kantian prototype in at least one important respect. Rawls feels compelled to defend it against what can be called the "brave new world syndrome": the suspicion that what might appear to be autonomous thoughts or decisions could have been manipulated by conditioning, genetic engineering, or social pressures so subtle that they would be difficult to detect. What if the rationality and universality that Kant regarded as the hallmark of autonomy was instead merely part of the circuitry of social control? Rawls dismisses such concerns rather condescendingly as appropriate to "times of social doubt and loss of faith in long-established values."[44] Since Rawls himself has *not* lost faith in such values (i.e., the Kantian ones), he sees no reason to worry much about the issue of whether our apparently rational, self-legislated moral standards are really our own.[45]

But other liberal theorists of autonomy have been much more concerned about what they sometimes call the "authenticity" of our choices and even our feelings. Unlike Rawls, they have incorporated into their work elements of the tradition of "individuality" referred to earlier. Indeed, many of the liberal theories we shall examine prove to be unstable amalgams of Kantian and romantic-individualist elements, running the gamut from predominantly rationalist theories to those that verge on pure individual self-expression. In my view, none has really succeeded in showing how these elements can be made to cohere.

At the "rationalist" end stands Richard Lindley's *Autonomy*. Partly in response to the brave new world syndrome, he advocates a notion of autonomy that stresses "active theoretical rationality," a "disposition to question received wisdom, or indeed any proposition one is inclined to accept... out of concern for truth itself."[46] Of course, the ideal of Kantian "maturity" underlies Lindley's position, but now it is deepened by a conviction that would-be autonomous individuals must ceaselessly struggle against the distortions and deceptions that elites want to impose on them. Moral autonomy in the sense of Kant and Rawls is not sufficient to escape a brave new world; autonomous individuals must also *in fact* "not be deluded about the nature of their goals and the consequences of their actions."[47]

In itself, such a conception of autonomy would be coherent, although it threatens to founder on our lack of an uncontested vision of moral, political, and religious truth. But Lindley, clearly impressed by the romantic-individualist tradition, also stipulates that "autonomy requires a person to reflect on the influences of her culture, to sort out those of her felt impulses which are really expressions of her unique nature from those which are merely the product of external impulses."[48] Active theoretical rationality seems to concern the intersubjectively verifiable or falsifiable *content* of a person's beliefs; the individuality criterion appears to interrogate their *origin* and thus their authenticity. What, if any, is the necessary connection between these criteria?

Still further toward the romantic-individualist end of the spectrum, we encounter a cluster of arguments worked out by some eminent analytic philosophers. John Christman's *The Inner Citadel* groups them under the rubric of the "Dworkin-Frankfurt (D-F) model,"[49] although his own theory and that of Joel Feinberg resemble this model enough that we may discuss all four together. All of these thinkers believe themselves to be working in the Kantian tradition, in the loose sense that they treat autonomous decisions (or an autonomous life) as self-legislated. But they abandon Kant's (and Rawls's) equation of autonomy with obedience to the moral law. As Gerald Dworkin bluntly puts it, "There is no specific content to the decisions an autonomous person may take.... [A] saint or a sinner, a rugged individualist or a conformist" would all qualify.[50]

The D-F model constructs a two-tier system of reflective choice. Every agent has "first-order" desires and preferences that correspond roughly to Kant's "inclinations." But most people also have the capacity to reflect on those preferences with an eye to deciding whether they really want to have them or not. Autonomy obtains in Dworkin's version when two conditions are satisfied: "(a) a person must *identify with* his desires, goals, and values; (b) such identification is not itself influenced in ways which make the process of identification... alien to the individual."[51] Feinberg's account differs mainly in emphasizing the "committed process of continually reconstructing the value system" one has inherited, which I take to satisfy condition (b).

Obviously, these accounts of autonomy, even though constructed by "liberal" philosophers otherwise in the Enlightenment tradition, have far more affinity to romantic-individualist quests for a true self. Moreover, Feinberg's comments betray how much the brave new world syndrome affects his thinking as well. "What liberals have always rightly deplored has been the effects on individual character of social manipulation, the condition in which individuality is swallowed up by the collective mass, and persons are interchangeable parts in a great organic machine."[52] Actually, Mill seems to have been the only bona fide liberal before the twentieth century who worried much about individuality. Enlightenment liberals such as Kant simply did not think of autonomy in those terms at all. Feinberg is inadvertently projecting onto the liberal tradition aspirations toward romantic individuality that were espoused by some writers of dubious liberal credentials.

Starting from very different assumptions, Ernst Tugendhat, a German analytic philosopher, approaches rather closely to the D-F model. Having rejected the paradigm of theoretical self-consciousness that prevailed in the writings of the German idealists, Tugendhat tries to rescue the notion of self-determination through a critical reading of Heidegger. Tugendhat finds in the latter the insight that human existence is unique in posing fundamental questions about its very meaning. People do not merely have wants and preferences; they may also ask whether the whole of their existence is meaningful or empty, resolute or adrift, and even whether it should be continued at all. Moreover, they may also evade such questions and "flee" from self-responsibility. What is decisive, though, is that this sort of existential self-interrogation cannot be universal à la Kant and Rawls. Only the individual can do it, and only in light of his or her own unique existence. The questions posed are thus eminently practical ones, because the way they are answered will determine who a person is going to be. We literally choose ourselves. Or, more exactly, we either make that choice in full awareness or we relinquish it to the inertia of everyday life and its internal agent, *das Man* (the collective and impersonal "they"), that always constitutes one dimension of individual identity. To exist "authentically"—to be an "individual," in the language of an older tradition—thus means, among other things, that I choose for myself rather than allow the impersonal "they" to make my choices for me.

Tugendhat accepts Heidegger's argument up to a point. He speaks of the irreducible existential, individual component in all choice: "there is an ultimate point in deliberation at which we simply can no longer justify the decision objectively; rather what is best for me at this point is itself only constituted in my wanting it."[53] If my decision making could be thoroughly rationalized (as for example in Kant and Rawls), then, Tugendhat claims, the decisions would no longer really be mine; the element of individual will would be lacking. However, Tugendhat cannot accept Heidegger's complete divorce of existential choice from moral reasoning. He therefore constructs an account of self-determination that supplements *Being and Time* by adding an account of rational justification in decision making as well as a more elaborate and "positive" way of taking into account the consensus of one's community. Tugendhat's "final" theory of self-determination thus ultimately comes to resemble the D-F model: a choice cannot be understood as self-determined (a) if one denies its irreducible volitional character, that is, if one claims to reduce it to rationality, or (b) if one denies that it must be able to rest on justification at all, casting it as a pure act of individuality.

Almost all these theories share the following complex of elements. There are first impulses, desires, and preferences, but these now have an ambiguous status. Either they can be authentically mine, or they may have been induced in me by an outside, alien source. The focus of autonomy must then be the second-order reflection and evaluation that lead me either to identify with these states, desires, and preferences or to reject them as infiltrations of das Man. The evaluation and decision making must be rational, even in Tugendhat, and oriented to objective truth, as in Lindley. But it can never become too rational. The external world is now viewed almost entirely negatively, as a threat to autonomy, except perhaps in Tugendhat, who still clings to the Kantian notion of a rational public opinion. There is no "nomos" left in autonomy, no sense of a law or rule that individuals give to themselves. Nor do these contemporary theories have any sense of a sustaining natural order (even a postulated one as in Kant) that might be favorable to self-determination. For liberal philosophers, autonomy has become a deeply problematic concept: its advocates are no longer really committed to the Enlightenment projects of reform and self-improvement, but they are unwilling to forgo the advantages of reason and reflective deliberation. It is not clear how autonomy can be both Kantian and romantic-individualist yet still remain a coherent idea. If one starts from the Heideggerian position but concedes that decisions ought to involve some rational deliberation, how does one know where to draw the line? At what point does a rationalized decision cease to embody the agent's will? But if one begins from Kantian and analytic premises while defining autonomy in terms of authenticity and individual self-expression, how can one distinguish clearly (as Kant and Rawls still can) between autonomy and heteronomy? Dworkin's answer would be that if a person's second-order identifications are "influenced overly by others," then his decisions lack procedural independence, that is, "his motivational structure is his but not his own."[54] But how much is "overly"? As critics have often objected, wouldn't we need a third-order reflection to check on whether second-order reflections were overly influenced? And wouldn't that generate an infinite regress?

V

One way postmodernist thinkers might interpret these predominantly liberal and analytic theories of autonomy would be to recognize that their advocates are seeking to defend something of great value: a certain spark of resistance, a refusal to be governed, at least in certain ways and at a certain price,[55] the right to struggle against vulnerability to manipulation and control. But their resistance must fail, because it depends on language that has become implicated in the very forms of social control they want to defy. Whatever may have been the liberating potential during the eighteenth century of notions such as "individuality," "objective truth," the "autonomous subject," or "public consensus," in the late twentieth they only serve to obscure patterns of social control and domination that require a different, subtler analysis.[56] In a nutshell, this is the kind of critique that "postmodern" thinkers such as Foucault have made of autonomy and related notions.

Difficulties in evaluating postmodern critiques arise when one questions whether they are rejecting only the discourse of autonomy or in some respects the "substance" of it as well, the political and ethical aspirations that Kant had in mind when he urged his readers, qua members of the enlightened public, to throw off the yoke of tutelage and use their own intellects.[57] To achieve some clarity on this question, I will try to piece together a Foucauldian "theory" of autonomy, recognizing that Foucault probably would have rejected the word *theory* to characterize his writings about the cluster of issues that bear on this theme.

Kant's accounts of autonomy, as we have noted, featured a superior element, practical reason (the noumenal self)—imposing rules on a set of phenomenal impulses and inclinations. The former was identified with the "true" self, the latter with alien (i.e., natural) causality. What allowed practical reason to work in the "real" world was the sensus communis, the consensus of an instructed public that encouraged and helped individuals make their exit from self-incurred immaturity, by getting them to transcend their narrow, particular, self-interested view of things and to move toward an unsituated, universal perspective. Insofar as Kant's autonomous self designates the subject of modern philosophy, Foucault would not accept it at face value. As he so often points out, the subject is *constituted* differently in a variety of historically distinct practices and relationships: "[The subject] is a form and this form is not above all or always identical to itself . . . and it is precisely the historical constitution of these different forms of subject relating to games of truth that interest me."[58] To Foucault, then, Kant's invocation of a transcendental self as the reference point of autonomy simply overlooks the process of constitution, an issue we considered in discussing Hegel earlier.

However, Foucault's process of constitution does not, like Hegel's, take place primarily in the realm of philosophical or religious self-interpretations (though these certainly do play some role); rather, the modern self is constituted by a series of disciplinary practices that become particularly visible in institutions designed to enforce regular, predictable behavior (e.g., prisons, schools, armies). The autonomous subject of philosophy and the juridical individual correspond to the controlled and manipulated subject of scientific experiments, medical knowledge, and political domination.[59] From Foucault's perspective, it becomes much easier to relate the "autonomy" side of the Enlightenment to its "social control" side, as expressed in Helvetius, Mendelssohn, and numerous obscure Aufklärer who toiled in the vineyards of the "popular" Enlightenment.[60]

If one attends to the language of the quest for autonomy as described by contemporary theorists, it bears a close resemblance to the techniques of "confession" that Foucault described in the *History of Sexuality.* To be autonomous for Dworkin, Young, or Tugendhat would mean being able to sort out those aspects of self that are truly one's own, from those that are alien or imposed. Foucault related this sort of self-inquisition to techniques of power.

> The obligation to confess is now relayed through so many different points, is so deeply ingrained in us that we no longer perceive it as the effect of a power that constrains us; on the contrary it seems to us that truth, lodged in our most secret nature, "demands" only to surface; that if it fails to do so, this is because a constraint holds it in place. . . . [I]t can finally be articulated only at the price of a kind of liberation.[61]

In other words, the lines of social control do not simply connect to our preferences and thoughts; they encircle the very process of self-reflection. In principle, there can be no "procedural independence" in second-order evaluation, as Feinberg had stipulated for an autonomous self-relation. Therefore, the only light one can shed on the self as presupposed by autonomy theory comes from a "genealogy of the subject as a subject of ethical actions"[62] that unearths, in very specific contexts, the forms of subjection, how they changed over time, and how they were resisted. In sum, conventional liberal-analytic theories of autonomy would only depict a simulacrum of self-determination, since the pattern of self-interrogation they prescribe simply continues, in a disguised shape, a venerable technique of discipline and normalization.

Some commentators have concluded that Foucault embraced a "scientistic concept of theory," a "functional model of discourse and practice" that would exclude, on methodological grounds, any notion of autonomy.[63] But scattered remarks, especially in his later writings and interviews, suggest a different conclusion. In a rare reflection on the genealogy of his own work, Foucault aligned himself not with Helvetius and Comte but with Hegel, Nietzsche, Weber, and the Frankfurt School. Like them, he tried to elaborate a "critical philosophy" that would also be an "ontology of the present, an ontology of ourselves."[64] And in his essay "What Is Enlightenment?" Foucault suggested that he had adopted at least the attitude of Kant's work of the same title, one that commits the critic to "analyzing and reflecting upon limits."[65] In practice, this would certainly mean opposing the sort of humanism of which Kant was a part, but "by the principle of a critique and a permanent creation of ourselves in our autonomy."[66]

Foucault, in short, did depart at least now and then from his customarily detached, "scientistic" viewpoint and engage himself as a partisan of autonomy, in some sense. Determining exactly what he meant by it is another matter. Perhaps the most tantalizing clue may be his remark that critique, reflecting on limits, now means almost the opposite of what it did in 1784:

> This critique will be genealogical in the sense that it will not deduce from the form of what we are what it is impossible for us to do and know; but it will separate out, from the contingency that has made us what we are, the possibility of no longer being, doing or thinking what we are, do, or think—seeking to give new impetus, as far and wide as possible, to the undefined work of freedom.[67]

We cannot treat autonomy in the Kantian manner as action or thought in accord with a self that is universal and rational. Rather, our autonomous impulses emanate from the corners and pockets of our being that have escaped being completely caught up in the meshes of universalizing, normalizing practices.

However, Foucault could not have meant by autonomy anything like the impetus toward individuality or authenticity as Mill and his liberal successors understood it. Criticizing Jean-Paul Sartre, who held one version of this view, Foucault observed, "I think that from the theoretical point of view, Sartre avoids the idea of the self as something which is given to us, but through the moral notion of authenticity, he turns back to the idea that we have to be ourselves—to be truly our true self." What Foucault objected to in the equation "autonomy = authenticity" was the assumption that, however inchoate it may be, we have a "true self" to be discovered. Following Nietzsche, he wanted to claim that the self must be created: "From the idea that the self is not given to us, I think that there is only one practical consequence: we have to create ourselves as a work of art."[68]

Foucault made these remarks while completing his study of the history of sexuality. Evidently he had become fascinated by the "technology" of the self practiced by the Stoics and Cynics. Thus, ironically, Foucauldian autonomy came full circle and resurrected a certain kind of Stoic autonomy,[69] albeit understood in a highly idiosyncratic, selective way. As Foucault read these ancient writers, they tended to see their desires, pleasures, social relationships—in short, their entire lives—as elements of an aesthetic whole to be created for their own satisfaction, but also for possible spectators. Their ascetic practices had nothing to do with hostility to desire per se, or fear of its corrupting influence, as would be the case for Christianity later. They simply wanted to achieve a harmony that would be impossible unless they knew how to govern themselves and keep unruly elements in their proper place. Aesthetic Stoicism appealed to Foucault because it contains a model for how the quest for autonomy can be kept separate from issues of scientific truth, moral correctness, and political authority, that is, exactly the "normalizations" to which it had been so closely tied by Kant, Mendelssohn, and the other Aufklärer.[70] Although Foucault never put it this way, he seemed to be suggesting that moral autonomy and the closely related idea of intellectual maturity in Kant involve orientation to universal standards. I am expected to shed my prejudices and think of myself as a participant in the Kingdom of Ends, the sensus communis or the reading public. I cannot "create" myself, since I am, as a rational being, irrevocably committed to an objective view of my situation. But in aesthetic Stoicism, I do not need to take account of any transindividual standard, any "we," except the very general requirements of beauty and harmony. Although my life may appear beautiful to others, I alone know how it got to be that way, since I created the blueprint of what I intended to be and labored to realize it against the recalcitrance of the flesh. Indeed, it is misleading to say that "I" created myself as a work of art, since that statement implies that I preceded the act of creation. But Foucault insisted that the opposite is true: "We should not have to refer the creative activity of somebody to the kind of relation he has to himself, but should relate the kind of relation one has to oneself to a creative activity."[71]

In terms of the framework adopted earlier for discussing different conceptions of autonomy, Foucault's "late" account now looks like this: the "ruled" elements, those subject to nomos, are bodily desires and especially pleasures but also our "relations to self," the stances we take toward our own existence, or what analytic philosophers call second-order preferences. The ruling element simply cannot be described (except in negative terms) since it has been boiled down to pure creative activity that cannot be traced back to any antecedent. The external elements that affect autonomy are above all the patterns of social control that have constituted us as the selves we now are, that have "normalized" us and formed the relations to selves that we have become. Thus autonomy for Foucault involved, first, the Herculean effort to carry out a "critique" of the constitution of the selves we now are and then, in whatever spaces of freedom we have managed to clear, the project of creating (or re-creating) "a beautiful life."[72] The only "external" aids we might have would be those traditions, such as aesthetic Stoicism, that have been half-forgotten or obscured by the dominant power/knowledge complex. Foucault's vision of autonomy was, in a way, what remained when one had stripped away the shells or layers of objective knowledge and rational orientation that still characterized earlier conceptions of a self-directed life. Once one dissolved such notions as a *Bestimmung des Menschen*, a moral law, the public, or even a true individuality, what could autonomy mean besides an activity in which certain forms of self-relation issue mysteriously from a hidden source?

It is not certain, however, that these elements of earlier versions of autonomy really deserve to be scrapped. There may be a way to preserve them in a less problematic, less metaphysical form.

VI

Postmodernists have not been the only recent social theorists to thematize the process of constitution of modern subjectivity. The Frankfurt School, especially Horkheimer and Adorno's *Dialectic of Enlightenment*, anticipated many of Foucault's arguments by a generation. These thinkers desublimated the Kantian conception of reason's "maturity" into its unspoken telos: the imperative of self-preservation.[73] The linchpin of all of Kant's critiques, they argued, is the subject, the "I think" of transcendental apperception. But the "I" does not conjure itself into existence ex nihilo. It emerges as a detached, punctual self-consciousness in the course of a millennia-long historical struggle to achieve distance from and domination over the forces of nature, both internal and external. The very power of reason to dissolve superstitions, discredit objectivist metaphysics, and arbitrate the boundaries of its own operations are (or at least have been predominately) instruments in humankind's collective effort to preserve itself. Thus, according to Horkheimer and Adorno, Kant's explicit appeal to "man" to use his own intellect without the tutelage of another carried the implicit message that "immaturity" means lack of self-discipline, relapse into primitive and obsolescent modes of thought, failure to keep up with the latest moves in the formalization of reason.

But autonomy and maturity understood as the assertion of humanity's collective effort at self-preservation recoil against themselves. For one thing, reason progressively disenchants the world by subjugating its "nonidentical" elements (including those aspects of individual existence not deployed in the service of survival) to the process of rationalization, that is, the principle of identity developed into formal logic and scientific reasoning. In short, humanity ends up instrumentalizing the autonomous self and whatever remains of the world that still charms, arrests, enchants, or frightens. Slavery to things, to matter, to religious belief is broken only by a deeper enslavement to the blind, "natural" drive for self-preservation.[74] Thus autonomy cancels itself; maturity degenerates into uncritical positivism.

The *Dialectic of Enlightenment* parallels many of Foucault's arguments about the regime of power/knowledge. In our context, the most crucial argument is the one that, at least in tendency, "unmasks" appeals to autonomous reason and maturity as contributions, albeit unintended, to the smoother and more efficient functioning of the process of social reproduction. Although Foucault would have rejected the premise of a single subject "behind" that process, he too would have underscored the instrumental, system-maintaining function of such appeals. Not surprisingly, Adorno and Horkheimer, like Foucault, painted themselves into a tight corner. By defining autonomy, maturity, universalizability, and the other key terms of Enlightenment rhetoric in so relentlessly instrumentalist a way, they left themselves few resources from which to fashion an alternative vision of a self-directed life. Horkheimer and Adorno could only glimpse rays of hope in the few nooks and crannies of our "enlightened" society that have not yet quite completely succumbed to the imperatives of functional, instrumental reason: the "negative" dialectic of critical theory itself and certain forms of modern art.

This is the point at which Habermas's work becomes important for anyone who aspires to preserve the continuity of autonomy as an ideal from the Enlightenment to the present. He is one of the few contemporary social theorists who takes seriously the sociohistorical process of constitution of the so-called autonomous individual and yet finds a way to defend the rational core of autonomy that Kant had stressed.

As far back as 1965, Habermas insisted on the differentiation of reason according to the "interests" that guide it. On the one hand, reason has been an instrument in the collective, historical struggle for self-preservation (as Adorno and Horkheimer claimed). On the other hand, reason is not simply equivalent to "claws and teeth" as a tool of adaptation. For one thing, it develops and is exercised in the "communication system of a social life-world"[75] that cannot be reduced without distortion to a system of survival. Moreover, participants in the life-world may reflect rationally on the practices, beliefs, and institutions of social life as well as the relationship between these and the ongoing process of social reproduction, in terms of issues that transcend simple survival, for example, justice.

Adapting Kant's argument about the transcendental constitution of the objects of knowledge under categories and intuitions, Habermas's theory of knowledge-constitutive "interests" captures the way in which such interests are already inscribed in what we apprehend empirically. Of these, the relevant one for our context is the "emancipatory interest" in self-reflection that may "release the subject from dependence on hypostatized powers"[76] and that finds expression in "sciences of action" like psychoanalysis and the Marxist critique of ideology.

Although Habermas's terminology and even some of his specific arguments have evolved, he has never abandoned the belief that reason plays an emancipatory role, that it is not simply an instrument of social and technical control. And he has been consistent in tracing this emancipatory role back to language, especially the model of dialogue.

> The human interest in autonomy and responsibility [these two words translate the German *Mündigkeit*] is not mere fancy, for it can be apprehended a priori. What raises us out of nature is the only thing whose nature we can know: *language*. Through its structure, autonomy and responsibility are posited for us. Our first sentence expresses unequivocally the intention of universal and unconstrained consensus.[77]

These lines have defined Habermas's research program for more than a quarter of a century. Only against the implicit background of an ideal speech situation, as he later would call it, can philosophy discover "the traces of violence that deform repeated attempts at dialogue and recurrently close off the path to unconstrained communication."[78] The claim that language contains an a priori element means only that, in the everyday context of speech, we assume a consensus about norms, which, however, we could always problematize and make into the object of a discourse. The latter would commit us to treating the other participant as a subject, someone who can give an account of what she does and why she does it. That account and the alternative one we might provide would then be measured against one another in such a way that we would recognize and submit to the persuasive power of the better argument.

In short, the way that Habermas unpacks the intention of language use reveals in it the tendency toward universalization that Kant made the touchstone of autonomy. But from Habermas's point of view, it would be unacceptable to call failure to achieve the ideal speech situation self-incurred immaturity; the point, rather, is to investigate the structural reasons why in actual practice we do not achieve it and why force and fraud so often determine which "argument" carries the day.

At the highest level of generality, then, truth must enter into the definition of autonomy, just as it did for the major Enlightenment figures considered earlier. And so too must the notion of a "public," as Kant suggested, since the "public" embodies the standard of rational speech moving toward consensus. But Kant's model of autonomy falls short of Habermas's criteria in at least two respects. First, Kant simply did not realize that the processes of modernization (the development of productive forces, the rationalization of beliefs, the growth of bureaucracy, etc.) then so closely linked to enlightenment could insinuate themselves into the human personality in ways that might (as Foucault would have it) "normalize" people and thereby impede autonomy. Thus, second, he did not realize that, in countering its absorption into the rationalization of the world, the self would have to develop the powers of resistance that have been associated, in this discussion, with individuality and authenticity.

Habermas's theory of autonomy takes these tendencies into account. On one side, he carefully distinguishes three different kinds of validity claims that, in principle, a participant in communicative action might have to redeem: (a) truth, (b) normative rightness, and (c) authenticity. All of these validity claims ultimately presuppose the possibility of discursive coming-to-agreement (*Verständigung*). Habermas's model of communicative action thus resembles Kant's enlightened public, in the sense that both philosophers distinguish discussions governed by the "better argument" from pseudocommunication distorted by force, ideology, and interest (a distinction, incidentally, that is not often made by postmodern writers). However, each of the three kinds of validity claims has its proper standards and can only be adjudicated on its own terms. The third, "authenticity," corresponds to the versions of autonomy defended by Tugendhat, Young, and other liberal writers. Like them, Habermas emphasizes that our actions and speech may embody an inner dimension of genuineness such that we put them forward as sincerely our own and not as feigned, mendacious, or reified. For Habermas, this dimension of individuality/authenticity has close affinity to the aesthetic autonomy adumbrated by Foucault.[79] However, as noted, it does implicitly require that one defend the choice of "who one wants to be."[80] This choice is not a pure creative act; it actually resembles the criterion of independence for second-order evaluations described by Dworkin. But for Habermas, it involves a complicated effort to achieve a narrative unity of one's own life by joining together the fragments of past and present into a coherent whole, to "build up new identities from shattered or superseded identities, and to integrate them with old identities in such a way that the fabric of one's interactions is organized into the unity of a life history that is both unmistakable and accountable."[81]

Clearly, individuality in this sense presupposes the ability to universalize, to think of one's identity in light of certain universal standards of what one could or should be. These, in turn, arise and persist in the life-world that both preserves and continually criticizes traditional norms. Accordingly, Habermas tries to link the Kantian "public-universal" notion of autonomy to the individualizing, romantic-expressive strain in the following way.

> The ideal communication community can be seen to contain two utopian projections. Each of them stylizes one of two moments still fused together in ritual practice: the moral-practical and the expressive.... Let us imagine individuals being socialized as members of an ideal communication community; they would in the same measure acquire an identity with two complementary aspects: one universalizing, one particularizing. On one hand, these persons raised under idealized conditions learn to orient themselves within a

> universalistic framework, that is, to act autonomously. On the other hand, they learn to use this autonomy, which makes them equal to every other morally acting subject, to develop themselves in their subjectivity and singularity.[82]

The perspective Habermas sketches out here (borrowed from G. H. Mead) suggests that the Kantian and the romantic-individualizing theories of autonomy actually belong together if one considers their historical process of constitution. The progress of enlightenment—of modernizing and rationalizing traditional beliefs and practices—extricated the reflective, universalizing subject from the web of relationships that had previously surrounded it, but at the same time objectivized that self as a "puppet" whose "strings" one needed to control more effectively. Individuality, authenticity, and aesthetic self-creation are all just so many ways to tag the inner tensions in the concept of autonomy and to redefine it as a process of liberating oneself from internal normalization. What Habermas adds is the observation that individual authenticity presupposes, at least implicitly, the existence of a life-world that has not become thoroughly instrumentalized, one in which a "public," rational discussion of traditional norms and values can continuously but critically reappropriate them. Even the most intensely individual self-reflection has a covert connection to the standards of public discourse and accountability. Because that is so, autonomy qua individuality has an inherent limitation. In Hegel's *Phenomenology*, the various shapes of *Individualität* that try to develop purely expressivist, self-referential norms eventually "experience" their inclusion in the common life of *Geist.* Habermas, in his own way, has re-created this dialectical movement by reaffirming the indispensability of Kantian/universalist autonomy to its romantic-individualistic critics.

NOTES

1. For a sample of such acknowledgments, see, e.g., Robert Young, *Personal Autonomy: Beyond Negative and Positive Liberty* (New York, 1986), 2; Richard Lindley, *Autonomy* (Atlantic Highlands, N.J., 1986), 13–27; and Joel Feinberg, "Autonomy," p. 34, Thomas Hill, "The Kantian Conception of Autonomy," Robert Young, "Autonomy and the Inner Self," and David A. J. Richards, "Rights and Autonomy," p. 207, all in *The Inner Citadel,* ed. John Christman (New York and Oxford, 1989).

2. Feinberg, "Autonomy," 36.

3. S. I. Benn, "Freedom, Autonomy and the Concept of a Person," *Proceedings of the Aristotelian Society* (January 1976): 124.

4. Richards, "Rights and Autonomy," 207.

5. Immanuel Kant, "An Answer to the Question: What Is Enlightenment?" in *Kant: Political Writings,* ed. Hans Reiss (Cambridge, 1991), 54. The word *Unmündigkeit* usually suggested legal nonage, i.e., the status of requiring a guardian (*Vormund*)

to handle one's affairs. See also Kant's *Anthropology from a Pragmatic Point of View*, trans. Mary J. Gregor (The Hague, 1974), 79–80.

6. See Charles Taylor, *Hegel* (Cambridge, 1975), 3–50.

7. Michael J. Meyer, "Stoics, Rights, and Autonomy," *American Philosophical Quarterly* 24, no. 7 (July 1987): 267–271.

8. See Charles Taylor, *Sources of the Self* (Cambridge, Mass., 1989), 126.

9. Ibid., 143–176.

10. Consider, for example, Locke's famous "biblical" justification of private property in par. 34 of the *Second Treatise.*

11. Taylor, *Sources of the Self,* 150.

12. René Descartes, *Discourse on Method* (Indianapolis, 1980), 14.

13. Taylor, *Sources of the Self,* 167.

14. See Horst Stuke, "Aufklärung," in *Geschichtliche Grundbegriffe: Historisches Lexikon zur politisch-sozialen Sprache in Deutschland,* ed. Otto Brunner, Werner Conze, and Reinhard Koselleck (Stuttgart, 1975), 265. On the unorthodoxy and originality of Kant's essay, see James Schmidt, "The Question of Enlightenment: Kant, Mendelssohn, and the *Mittwochgesellschaft,*" *Journal of the History of Ideas* 50, no. 2 (1989): 269–270. Let it be noted, however, that Rousseau's notion of the general will does present a principle of self-legislation that is analogous to and influential for Kant's own.

15. See Immanuel Kant, *Fundamental Principles of the Metaphysics of Morals,* trans. Thomas K. Abbot (Indianapolis, 1949), 49–50 (p. 62 in the Rosenkrantz-Schubert edition).

16. For a detailed and thorough comparison of the two articles, see James Schmidt, "What Enlightenment Was: How Moses Mendelssohn and Immanuel Kant Responded to the *Berlinische Monatsschrift,*" *Journal of the History of Philosophy* 30, no. 1 (1992): 77–102.

17. Moses Mendelssohn, "Über die Frage: Was heisst aufklären?" in *Gesammelte Schriften Jubilaeumsausgabe,* ed. A. Altmann et al. (Stuttgart–Bad Cannstadt, 1971), 6, no. 1: 115–119.

18. See Moses Mendelssohn, "Votum zu Moehsens Aufsatz über Aufklärung," in *Gesammelte Schriften* 6, no. 1: 110.

19. Mendelssohn, "Über die Frage," 117.

20. Ibid., 115.

21. See Schmidt, "What Enlightenment Was," 82–86.

22. Cited in Stuke, "Aufklärung," 256. All translations from Stuke are the author's.

23. Ibid., 263.

24. Ibid., 274.

25. Ibid., 272.

26. Claude-Adrien Helvetius, *A Treatise on Man* (New York, 1970), II:317.

27. Ibid., II:129.

28. Claude-Adrien Helvetius, *Essays on the Mind* (New York, 1970), 292.

29. Helvetius, *Treatise on Man,* I:4.

30. Kant, *Fundamental Principles,* 50 (p. 63, Rosencrantz-Schubert).

31. Ibid., 53 (p. 67, Rosencrantz-Schubert).

32. Kant, *Critique of Judgment*, trans. Werner J. Pluhar (Indianapolis, 1987), par. 40, p. 160.

33. Ibid., 161.

34. Ibid., 228.

35. Ibid., 160.

36. Kant, "What Is Enlightenment?" 4.

37. On the political context of Kant's writings and in particular the debate over liberty of the press, see Schmidt, "The Question of Enlightenment," 285–290, and Eckhardt Hellmuth, "Aufklärung und Pressefreiheit: Zur Debatte der Berliner Mittwochsgesellschaft während der Jahre 1783 und 1784," *Zeitschrift für historische Forschung* (1982): 315–345.

38. See, e.g., Kant's essays, "Über den Gemeinspruch: Das mag in der Theorie richtig sein, taugt aber nicht fur die Praxis" and "Idee zu einer allgemeinen Geschichte in weltbürgerlicher Absicht," both in Immanuel Kant, *Politische Schriften* (Koeln and Opladen, 1965), 9–24, 64–103.

39. For a useful discussion of the German resistance to the Enlightenment during the late eighteenth and early nineteenth century, consult Isaiah Berlin, "The Counter-Enlightenment," in *Against the Current*, ed. Henry Hardy (New York, 1980), 7–20.

40. The following sketch represents an abbreviated and selective account of the development of the individuality idea. For a fuller discussion, see the author's "The Idea of Individuality: Origins, Meaning, and Political Significance," *Journal of Politics* 52, no. 3 (August 1990): 759–781.

41. For a more complete and detailed version of the following comments, see the author's *Hegel's Critique of the Enlightenment* (Gainesville, 1984), 94–184.

42. John Rawls, *A Theory of Justice* (Cambridge, Mass., 1971), 516.

43. Ibid., 515.

44. Ibid., 518, 519.

45. Let it be noted, though, that Rawls lately has seemed to limit his theory of justice (and hence also his conception of full autonomy?) to "a democratic society under modern conditions." See, for example, John Rawls, "Kantian Constructivism in Moral Theory," *Journal of Philosophy* 77, no. 9 (September 1980): 518.

46. Lindley, *Autonomy*, 48.

47. Ibid., 50.

48. Ibid., 53.

49. For Christman's characterization of the model, see *The Inner Citadel*, 6–10.

50. Gerald Dworkin, "The Concept of Autonomy," in Christman, *The Inner Citadel*, 62.

51. Ibid., 61.

52. Feinberg, "Autonomy," 45.

53. Ernst Tugendhat, *Self-Consciousness and Self-Determination* (Cambridge, Mass., 1986), 213.

54. Dworkin, "The Concept of Autonomy," 61.

55. See Michel Foucault, "Qu'est-ce que la critique [Critique et *Aufklärung*]," *Bulletin de la Société française de Philosophie* 84 (1990): 35–63 [translated above, pp. 382–398].

56. For a spirited indictment of liberalism on these grounds, see David Gruber, "Foucault's Critique of the Liberal Individual," *Journal of Philosophy* (November 1989): 615–621.

57. Nancy Fraser's essay, "Foucault—A Young Conservative?" in her *Unruly Practices* (Minneapolis: University of Minnesota Press, 1989), 35–53, provides an excellent summary of the alternative readings of Foucault on the question of whether or not he is a humanist, an issue that has obvious relevance for this study.

58. "The Ethic of Care for the Self as a Practice of Freedom: An Interview with Michel Foucault conducted by Raul Fornet-Betancourt, Helmut Becker, and Alfredo Gomez-Mueller," *Philosophy and Social Criticism* 12, nos. 2–3 (1987): 121.

59. On the double meaning of "subject," see Michel Foucault, *The History of Sexuality*, Vol. I: *An Introduction* (New York, 1980), 60. For Foucault's critique of liberal individualism, see "Two Lectures," in *Power/Knowledge: Selected Interviews and Other Writings, 1972–1977, by Michel Foucault*, ed. Colin Gordon (New York, 1980), "Second Lecture," 98: "The individual is an effect of power . . . and . . . the element of its articulation."

60. For a valuable summary of the efforts of the "popular" Enlightenment and its contribution to modernization and normalization of a recalcitrant rural population, see Jonathan Knudsen, "On Enlightenment for the Common Man" (above, pp. 270–290).

61. Foucault, *History of Sexuality*, I:60.

62. Michel Foucault, "On the Genealogy of Ethics: An Overview of Work in Progress," in *The Foucault Reader*, ed. Paul Rabinow (New York, 1984), 356.

63. See Christoph Menke, "Zur Kritik der hermeneutischen Utopie," in *Ethos der Moderne: Foucault's Kritik der Aufklärung*, ed. Eva Erdmann, Rainer Forst, and Axel Honneth (Frankfurt and New York, 1990), 102.

64. Michel Foucault, "Kant on Enlightenment and Revolution," *Economy and Society* 15, no. 1 (February 1986): 96.

65. Foucault, "What Is Enlightenment?" in *The Foucault Reader*, 45.

66. Ibid., 49.

67. Ibid., 46.

68. Foucault, "On the Genealogy of Ethics," 351.

69. On the Stoic connection, see Foucault's references to Seneca and Plutarch and his comments about Stoic ethics in "On the Genealogy of Ethics," 341–342, and the interview "Ethic of Care," *Philosophy and Social Criticism*, 113.

70. Foucault, "On the Genealogy of Ethics," 341.

71. Ibid.

72. Ibid.

73. Max Horkheimer and Theodor Adorno, *Dialektik der Aufklärung* (Amsterdam, 1947), 102.

74. Ibid., 107.

75. See Jürgen Habermas, *Knowledge and Human Interests* (Boston, 1971), 313.

76. Ibid., 310.

77. Ibid., 314.

78. Ibid., 315.

79. On this affinity, consult either of two excellent articles: Steven White,

"Foucault's Challenge to Critical Theory," *American Political Science Review* 80, no. 2 (June 1986): 420–430, or Thomas McCarthy, "The Critique of Impure Reason: Foucault and the Frankfurt School," *Political Theory* 18, no. 3 (August 1990): 437–461.

80. Jürgen Habermas, *The Theory of Communicative Action* (Boston, 1987), 2:99.

81. Ibid., 92. The imperative of taking control of the narratives about oneself also figures prominently in certain feminist versions of autonomy theory. See, e.g., Diana T. Meyers, "Personal Autonomy and the Paradox of Feminine Socialization," *Journal of Philosophy* 84, no. 11 (November 1987): 619–628.

82. Ibid., 97.

Enlightened Cosmopolitanism: The Political Perspective of the Kantian "Sublime"

Kevin Paul Geiman

One of the aims of the Enlightenment was to introduce clarity into thought and morality into practice. In so doing, it also called for a *novus ordo sæculorum*, a "new world order" that would facilitate that aim. Now if enlightenment is the emergence of humankind from its self-incurred immaturity on the basis of the courage to use its own understanding, the implication is that this same humankind should have the courage to call for the political order that makes maturity and understanding possible. Already in Kant's essay on enlightenment one begins to make out a politics proper for the life of the mind. Legislative authority may in no way hinder citizens in the free, public use of their reason. As private persons, employed in particular tasks and professions, they may be kept from propounding views different from that of their employer, be it the state, the church, or any other authority. But that authority would overstep its bounds if it sought to keep them from participation in a larger, worldwide community of discourse and dissent. Kant saw that safeguarding the advent of this community of broadened thought, in which all took themselves as members of a cosmopolitan whole, would require not only rationalizing existing political associations to make room for a public sphere at the state level but also moving toward a universal form of political association. In another essay from 1784, "Idea for a Universal History with Cosmopolitan Intent," he went on to postulate that the achievement of such a well-ordered state was necessarily contingent on the gradual establishment of an international confederation of states. Because rational ability is something that can only be developed in the species as a whole, any standing condition of military activity between states would constitute a barrier to the eventual full growth of that rational ability by occupying human agents in destructive, rather than constructive, enterprises. A further implication would be that as long as any state was threatened from the outside by an opposing force or was itself threatening another state, it would have to take those measures often associated with state security, and in so doing would necessarily have to curtail the free expression of its citizens and limit the scope of civil liberties.

These thoughts found their fullest expression in *Toward Perpetual Peace: A Philosophical Sketch* (1795) in which Kant drew up definitive articles setting the parameters of a cosmopolitan politics that would allow for the full development of a human reason unhindered in its various concrete tasks by the debts, misery, and waste of belligerent confrontations. First, the constitution of every state should be republican, allowing the voice of the citizenry to determine what policies will be adopted. War would be less likely, because the citizenry would not be as swift to commit their money and their sons to an unnecessary military action as would a prince or a self-appointed cabinet. Second, Kant maintained that international right should be based on a federation of free states. One state would be less likely to meddle in the internal affairs of a second if the second was itself internally strong and not bound by some colonial tie. Third, all of the earth's inhabitants should enjoy the cosmopolitan right of hospitality in all lands of the planet. Because of the physical limitation imposed by the earth itself, humankind would have to learn to live together in such a way that they could encounter one another without immediately provoking the kind of hostilities colonial acquisition brought with it. Most important, Kant now linked respect for human rights to the ideal of a perpetual peace, speaking of the condition "where a violation of rights in one part of the world is felt *everywhere*" as being "a necessary complement to the unwritten code of political and international right, transforming it into a universal right of humanity." This universal feeling of respect for human rights is the ultimate guarantor of perpetual peace. Without it, the other provisions to be taken in that direction would be superfluous, for, as Kant continues, "only under this condition can we flatter ourselves that we are continually advancing towards a perpetual peace"[1] and, with it, toward the fulfillment of the highest purpose of nature,[2] and that we are, after all, living in an age of enlightenment.

The discussion surrounding the Kantian political tracts lasted for some twenty years.[3] One of the questions that emerged and persisted during the course of this discussion was whether cosmopolitanism was at all a defensible political perspective or whether some form of patriotism was the proper attitude to take. The proposals Kant made for an international confederation of republican states, and the expectation he held that humankind would one day be led—if not by rational choice, then certainly by inclination—to a peaceful coexistence in which human rights were respected, came at a time when lines were being drawn between those who welcomed the new order making its way into Europe and those who were retrenching against it. Between the writing of the essay on enlightenment and *Perpetual*

Peace, the French Revolution had sent a shock wave through the old political order, provoking dissent and minor revolutions throughout Europe.[4] And yet the Proclamation of the Rights of Man and the Citizen was never implemented, and the new regime in France showed itself to be less than the bastion of liberty, equality, and fraternity it had claimed to be. It is in some respects quite remarkable that Kant should not only have held to his prerevolutionary political perspective but have deepened it as well, particularly at a time when many, even those who had most advocated popular enlightenment and had been unafraid of its potentially revolutionary consequences, were reconsidering their positions.[5]

These texts also came at a time when it was not entirely clear that philosophical reflection could stand up to the task of addressing the difficulties that the recent political events posed for a theory of liberating politics, and beyond the immediate practical questions, problems with the theoretical underpinnings of a cosmopolitan perspective quickly came to the fore. The Enlightenment call to the use of reason had been under attack from the beginning, and by 1795 most of the fundamental claims Kant had made in *Critique of Pure Reason* had been severely criticized.[6] That he based this cosmopolitan perspective on certain assumptions about the nature and the power of reason (rather than on principles of empirical human nature) only served to diminish its plausibility in the eyes of some. If reason was necessarily culture-bound, language-dependent, and only locally advanced, as many of Kant's contemporaries were maintaining, then the possibility of basing a cosmopolitan perspective on it was suspect. Still some, otherwise reasonably sympathetic to the Kantian program, found Kant's defense of cosmopolitanism along quasi-"natural" lines to be curious and, ultimately, self-defeating. Friedrich Schlegel made precisely this point in his critique of *Perpetual Peace*, claiming that Kant's use of such natural prodding as the need for trade could in no way stand as a *proof* that humankind would reach such a goal, or even as a sufficient indication that one ought to try to work toward it.

> It is not enough that the means of the possibility of the *external promptings of fate* to effect a gradual bringing about of perpetual peace are shown. One expects an answer to the question *whether the internal development of humanity* would lead in that direction? . . . [O]nly the (actual) *necessary laws of experience* can guarantee a future success. *The laws of political history* and the *principles of political formation* are the only data out of which it can be shown that perpetual peace is no empty idea but rather a task.[7]

Of course, Kant had used an external prompting, the spread of commerce, as an indication that humankind would one day reach a state of peace, asserting that "the *spirit of commerce* sooner or later takes hold of every people, and it cannot exist side by side with war."[8] Otherwise bellicose states would eventually have to make some genuine gestures in the direction of respecting human rights and national sovereignty if they were to carry on trade. However, Kant elsewhere decried this same commercial spirit as one that serves to foster "base selfishness, cowardice, and softness, and to debase the way of thinking of [a] people."[9] Clearly, Kant would not have based his whole argument on a contingent fact of human nature.

Indeed, throughout the political tracts it becomes clear that for Kant the highest aim of politics, like the aim of enlightenment, is not to make *things* better but to make *us* better. A revolution that resulted only in a net gain in human welfare is not to be praised; praiseworthy is the change in the ways of thinking of the people that would allow them to sense a violation of right.[10] An international association of trading partners, like a band of thieves, might be forced into some kind of nonaggression pact with one another for their own mutual survival and thereby inaugurate a perpetual peace, but unless there was a widespread shared feeling among all the earth's inhabitants for one another's human rights, such an alliance would of itself signify no moral gain and, indeed, might actually signal a disastrous frame of mind. For, as Kant notes, "human rights have to do with more than order (and rest). Great order and rest can be brought about through universal oppression."[11] Of course, commercialism is not cosmopolitanism, but what cosmopolitanism was, was itself a nagging question, as the question of enlightenment had been ten years earlier. Following Kant, cosmopolitanism was at least a transnational perspective in which primacy was given to the maintenance and extension of human rights; at most it reflected the highest aspirations of humankind. In an article written by Drost von Müller entitled "Thoughts on Cosmopolitanism and Patriotism," the difference in the two perspectives was claimed to lie in the fact that while both the cosmopolitan and the patriot acted in political life out of love of humanity, the former understood by humanity the whole of humanity while the latter understood humanity in terms of national or local belonging. This whole of humanity, von Müller claimed,

> is an idea of our reason. In this idea all of the millions of rational beings on this earth are one, and this includes the past and the future. [. . .] It is this idea then that underlies the wishes and efforts of the cosmopolitan. In consideration of it, so many of the things held by men to be important disappear before its sublimity. Development and formation of all human powers and abilities, spreading of enlightenment, perfection and ennobling, and consequently advancement of the happiness of the human species: the duties of the cosmopolitan aim at this alone. On the other hand, fame and wealth, power and greatness of individual states lose their often so exalted value in the eyes of the cosmopolitan and disappear as being insignificant in his view. This view is not aimed at the individual, but rather at the whole; and where it is a question of the welfare of humanity, there even his fellow citizens appear to him only as a negligible part in the sublime whole.[12]

Here cosmopolitanism is cast in a necessary relation to enlightenment, a way of looking at things that issues forth in certain practical actions. The language is openly Kantian; it is the Kant of the third *Critique.* In effect, the kind of thinking Kant there calls sublime is, in its political application, enlightened cosmopolitanism.

It may at first appear misguided to turn to Kant's analysis of aesthetic judgment—and to the more recondite analysis of the sublime—for a grounding for a political perspective. This is so only if one takes the analysis of aesthetic judgment in the sense of a philosophy of art. But *Critique of Judgment* is a critique of reflective judgment, and although Kant does address matters pertaining to philosophy of art in it, reflective judgment is a broader power, and the sublime, far from being simply a somewhat curious category in Enlightenment philosophy of art,[13] is in many respects judgment's highest moment in Kant's formulation, with applications far beyond the merely artistic. Kant divides the analytic of the sublime in the third *Critique* into two parts, the first having to do with the mathematically sublime, the second with the dynamically sublime. I hope to show that, taken together, the mathematically and dynamically sublime provide the critical framework for the cosmopolitan political perspective Kant developed in his political tracts. The analytic of the mathematically sublime answers the question of how such a perspective is at all possible; the analytic of the dynamically sublime answers the question of how it emerges as a task rather than as a merely historical postulate.

Critique of Judgment is a critique of reflective judgment. Reflective judgments are those we make concerning particular cases for which there is no universal rule, principle, or law (Ak 179). They concern matters that are neither wholly under the domain of reason (freedom) nor wholly under the domain of the understanding (knowledge). It is the work of the understanding to determine the laws of nature and to order phenomenal appearances accordingly, and the work of reason to determine the laws of freedom (the moral law) and to order the actions of rational agents accordingly. Reflective judgments mediate between the understanding and reason. Since the moral law does not tell us how the world operates, and the laws of science do not give us a morality, reflective judgment bridges the "great gulf" (Ak 195) that lies between the two domains, marking out the degree to which states of affairs or objects reflect either a harmony or a discordance of the two domains on the basis of the feelings of pleasure and displeasure in the judging subject. Because of the mediating role it plays with respect to understanding and reason, reflective judgment provides a point of orientation for the mind.[14] Depending on the case, a judgment that a state of affairs does not harmonize with both the understanding and reason may refer the mind either toward the understanding (to carry out more scientific research to find out why nature does not harmonize and what the limits of its alterability might be) or toward reason (to determine which of other possible actions to take that may well harmonize).

According to Kant, only the understanding and reason can legislate, that is, determine laws for any possible natural appearance or moral action. Hence reflective judgments are always particular with respect to their object. This is perhaps most easily shown in the case of beauty. To say that a rose is beautiful (a reflective judgment of beauty) is not to say that every rose ought to be so, nor does it warrant the claim that the given flower is not a rose because it is not beautiful. The assertion "This rose is beautiful" is consistent with "That rose is not."

Although particular with respect to the object, reflective judgments are necessary and universal with respect to judging subjects. When I judge the rose to be beautiful, I am making a statement that reflects my subjective sensibility with regard to it. My sensibility is the determining factor here, and yet, in claiming that the rose is beautiful *to me*, I also hold out that *everyone else* will think so, too. This necessity, Kant writes,

> is of a special kind. It is not a theoretical objective necessity, allowing us to cognize a priori that everyone *will feel* this liking for the object I call beautiful. Nor is it a practical objective necessity where . . . this liking is a necessary consequence of an objective law and means nothing other than that one absolutely (without further intention) ought to act in a certain way. Rather, as a necessity that is thought in an aesthetic judgment, it can only be called *exemplary*, i.e., a necessity of the assent of *everyone* to a judgment that is regarded as an example of a universal rule that we are unable to state. (Ak 236–237)

Exemplary necessity is the kind of necessity that is reflected in the actual reflective judgments we do make and how we expect them to be received by others. When I point out a beautiful sunset to a friend I do not do so to inform her of my state of pleasure; I do it to offer her the opportunity to look upon it and enjoy its beauty herself. I am disappointed when she does not find it beautiful, too, and more disappointing perhaps is the fact that I cannot convince her to like it. There is nothing particular about the sunset I could mention that would count as conclusive proof that it is beautiful, and she is certainly not morally deficient for not seeing it in this way. As it stands, our divergent judgments reflect that we do not share a common form of sensibility, a common perspective, and have something less than a common life together. The point here is not to turn sunsets (or any other object) into the determining factor of human relationships but to turn human relationships into the determining factor of a common worldview. As Kant writes, "The aesthetic universality we attribute to a judgment must be of a special kind; for although it does not connect the predicate of beauty with the concept of the *object*, considered in its entire logical sphere, yet it extends that predicate over the entire sphere of *judging persons*" (Ak 215). The necessity of reflective judgments is provided by a kind of solidarity of sensibility that we always presuppose when we make such judgments. Indeed, as Kant continues, "nothing is postulated in a judgment of taste except such a universal voice about a liking unmediated by concepts" (Ak 216). And this *universal voice* is what makes reflective judgments possible in the first place (Ak 217).

Two points are worth noting here. First, the "appeal to humanity" made in reflective judgments is not the same thing as an appeal to the majority. The line of reasoning in matters of judgment is not "Because most persons find this painting beautiful, it is beautiful," but "Because I am like most persons, I can expect most persons to find this beautiful." We do not vote on matters of taste any more than we vote on matters of truth or morality. That there may be judges who do not find it beautiful does not invalidate the judgment made but sets those judges apart from the rest. Such folk are said to lack taste, and, as experience shows, like tends to associate with like; we do not try to convince these people, we dissociate ourselves from them. This leads to the second point, namely, that reflective judgments have pragmatic import, although they do not determine a determinate practical (moral) course of action. One can say that where there is reflective judgment there is a community of judges and, where such judgment is lacking, no such community emerges. But one cannot say what this community will look like, what particular judgments it would have to find itself in agreement over, or even when this community might come into being. The most one can claim is that no one is in principle excluded from it and that, indeed, the ideal situation is one in which all possible agents are participants with the proviso that none be forced into it (one cannot be forced to find something beautiful, or sublime for that matter).

Up to this point we have been following Kant's account of reflective judgments referring to judgments of beauty as examples. The universality and necessity that accompany these judgments accompany those on the sublime as well. Still there are differences between the two kinds of judgment. One is that judgments concerning the beautiful have to do with the *quality* of an object or state of affairs as a bounded entity; judgments concerning the sublime reflect something's unbounded *quantity* (Ak 244). In the beautiful, the liking of the subject that is reflected is one that arises from the sense of life's being furthered, whereas that reflected in a judgment on the sublime arises after a feeling of life's being hindered or threatened in the face of such unboundedness. Finally, and Kant takes this to be the major difference between the two, in judgments on the beautiful there appears to be a confirmation of the subject's powers almost as if the object being judged were made for the subject, whereas in those on the sublime, it appears as though the object were contrapurposive for our powers (Ak 245). All of these characteristics are reflected in Kant's claim that "while taste for the beautiful presupposes and sustains the mind in *restful* contemplation, the feeling for the sublime carries with it, as its character, a mental *agitation*" (Ak 247). According to Kant, the mind may be agitated in two ways, either with respect to the cognitive power or with respect to the power of desire. The first is what is called the mathematically sublime, the second the dynamically sublime.

The mathematically sublime is something of a misnomer, at least if one understands by mathematical something having to do with numbers. At issue is the determination of magnitude, and at the beginning of his analysis of this form of the sublime Kant distinguishes between a logical determination of magnitude and an aesthetic one (Ak 249). A logical determination is the ascription of a numerical standard to an object, for example, when I make the judgment that the distance from my home to the office is seventeen miles. An aesthetic determination is the judgment that it is a long distance from my home to the office. In the first case, disputes are settled with whatever device is handy that has mile markings on it, and one need only know how to count to make the correct determination of length. Given that a determinate standard is applied, the distance can be equated with other distances, for example, it is also seventeen miles from the office to the zoo. In the second case, dispute settlement is carried on in a rough way through an appeal to what passes as a long distance from home to office. Much can come into play here: what counts as a reasonable time to get to work, the cost of paying for the transportation relative to the money earned, the ways the time could be otherwise spent, and so forth. The judgment that the distance is indeed long is therefore made with reference to a variety of factors, all of which need to be taken into account and none of which is dispensable with respect to the others. Further, the fact that seventeen miles might be a long way to work does not mean that any seventeen-mile journey is long. Seventeen miles is not a long distance to travel when one goes on vacation, for example.

There are other judgments of magnitude that do not rely on empirical standards. Kant's two examples are "the magnitude [or degree] of a certain virtue, or of the civil liberty and justice in a country" and "the magnitude [or degree] of the correctness or incorrectness of some observation or measurement" (Ak 249). The first, Kant states, relies on an a priori practical standard, the second on an a priori theoretical standard. Both are a priori in that one does not have to wait to compare among empirical givens to make the assessment, in fact "one that is given a priori would be confined, because of the deficiencies of the judging subject, to subjective conditions of an exhibition *in concreto*" (Ak 249). The standard of estimation is "the infinite as a *whole*" (Ak 254), a standard that, for that reason, is "not only large, but large absolutely, in every respect (beyond all comparison), i.e., sublime" (Ak 250). Properly speaking, according to Kant, it is the "expansion of the mind itself" (Ak 249) that results from its inadequacy to the use of this standard that is most truly sublime. Kant does not develop his analysis of these two a priori standards in any great detail; his major concern in the "A" section of the Analytic of the Sublime is to address the point of the mental agitation that accompanies them. His examples, however, provide clues as to what they are and how they function.

The example of an a priori theoretical standard was the degree or magnitude of the correctness or incorrectness of some observation or measurement. All science aims at assembling a system of true observations on data. Whenever a claim that *X* is the case is brought forth, a subject is called on to make an assessment of that claim. Any such claim necessarily refers to a particular phenomenon, and yet the estimation of its truth requires the idea of the whole of nature construed as a complete system (a world) in which all phenomena are organized in relation to one another. For example, assessing the truth of a claim in chemistry would require not only that it be accurate with respect to the phenomenon in question but also that it be consistent with all other scientific claims. But it is not possible for any statement to be true given this standard. Our knowledge is based on the appearances of things, not things as they are in themselves. Because of this limitation, we are never in a position of knowing whether our knowledge accurately and completely reflects the world as it is. Thus there is a gap between our knowledge of the world and the world itself. This does not imply a fatalism of knowledge, the position that one should not even begin to find answers, but it does imply fallibility. Further, contemporary science or, better, the natural sciences together in no way present a complete, coherent system of nature. It is not yet known, for example, how to properly relate physics and chemistry and biology into an ordered whole. Thus on two counts, there will always be a remainder left by any knowledge claim, and hence no claim can ever be wholly correct.

The same holds true for practical matters, and the a priori practical standard, the magnitude or degree of a certain virtue or of the civil liberty and justice in a country, functions in much the same way. According to Kant, a moral action is one that an agent could legislate for a systematic unity of agents, a kingdom of universal respect. In everyday action, it is not known how to act with respect to this systematic unity, for it is an idea of the whole of humanity (without spatial and temporal limitation), and no agent can begin mentally to grasp the whole of humanity in a way that would be serviceable for the determination of an action. Further, it is not always known how to relate and decide on two courses of action, both of which may be in accordance with the moral law but which cannot be implemented at the same time or in the same respect. Thus there is a gap between the moral law and our ability to act on it. At the individual level, then, any act I have to judge as to its morality is bound to come up short; at the social level, any act or system of practical actions, like respect for human rights, is bound to come up short. And still, in the act of judging a given particular action, the subject finds itself aware of the practical moral law all the same and, in recognizing his own limitation, finds it sublime. For present purposes, we can leave the issue of personal actions aside; at stake in a cosmopolitan perspective are social-political actions and states of affairs.

It might be objected that a comparative analysis is sufficient for political matters. It may be thought that a political policy that aims at human rights can be based on a numerical standard and that the best way to achieve this is to reward reductions in human rights violations in hopes that reductions will continue, eventually leading to a state where they are nil. But if the only basis for an assessment of the extent of human rights in a given state is a comparative, numerical one, certain practical consequences can be expected. First, it effectively states that some standard other than human rights is more important in the determination of policy. The value is placed on the reward or the incentive rather than on the human rights violations proper. One could expect that aims at curtailing such violations would continue only as long as the incentive was there. Further, a government may feel itself warranted to begin meddling in the internal affairs of that state on the ground that this state has a (comparatively) bad human rights record, thereby violating those citizens' right of self-determination.

Second, the use of a comparative standard has negative results at home as well. A government seeking to suppress citizens at home may easily find an "enemy" abroad, thereby focusing the citizens' attention away from possible rights violations at home. Even if there is no direct governmental manipulation, citizens who know their lot to be better than that of others in the world can more easily be lulled into a general complacency about the plight of their immediate neighbors under the (comparative) pretext, "If you think it's bad here, you should be there." Finally, because a comparative standard is an empirical one, based on observable information, it cannot address the question of the rights of future generations. Because they do not exist empirically, they would be irrelevant to present judgment. It is only on the basis of the kind of a priori standard Kant discovers in judgments concerning the sublime that the issue of future generations can at all emerge as a problem.

To make a judgment concerning the magnitude of respect for human rights in aesthetic rather than numerical terms, then, is (contrary to general intuition) to make a stronger judgment. To begin with, sheer numbers do not make as much difference as do people's sensitivity. Amnesty International may compile statistic upon statistic, and they may even distribute the compilations to every household. But unless the recipients of this information feel something akin to outrage at the data, nothing will get done. The facts themselves will not directly prompt one to carry out any particular course of action, it is the discrepancy between the standard and the facts that does. *Aesthetically* one can never be satisfied as long as there are human rights violations, whereas one may be *numerically* satisfied that there are fewer, allowing one to see through the political game of making trading agreements with and giving diplomatic favors to a given state based on the reduction of human rights violations by *x* percent. To the cosmopolitan, national prestige, military strength, and domestic well-being (all of which are judged comparatively) are as naught in comparison to the universal rights of humankind, the (sublime) standard "in comparison to which everything else is small" (Ak 250). It is because of this that Kant can write that "the rights of man must be held sacred, however great a sacrifice the ruling power may have to make. There can be no half measures here.... For all politics must bend the knee before right, although politics may hope in return to arrive, however slowly, at a stage of lasting brilliance."[15]

Judgments of the mathematically sublime are aesthetic judgments and, like them, admit of universality and necessity; one who holds to the high standard of human rights Kant speaks of should be able to expect others to concur in the judgment that no state can be put in the position of superiority over another on that issue or on any other. This necessity, it will be recalled, was not logical or moral necessity but exemplary necessity. One cannot, therefore, provide a logical proof or a moral command to convince someone of the cosmopolitan perspective or oblige them to share it. The most one can do is provide examples that show that this is how agents such as we actually do judge and what kinds of interaction follow from not judging accordingly. Kant, of course, found his example in the enthusiasm of the onlookers for the effort exerted in the French Revolution in the direction of a constitutional state and the guarantee of human rights. One may easily find others. The Vietnamese government's denunciation of the breakdown of the USSR in 1991 reveals much about those making the judgment. It reveals at best a shortsighted, at worst a self-seeking, attitude, which to the sentiments of humanity at large appears petty and small. Now unless reference is made to humanity at large (rather than to some pet aim of the one judging), the judgment that the Vietnamese government's judgment is petty and small will itself appear petty and small and self-seeking. All Kant needs to do to make cosmopolitanism a defensible perspective is to make appeal to the structures that invariably show themselves in such rounds of judgments. That we make judgments of sublimity in magnitude at all is, on Kant's account, not a contingent fact of human nature but a necessary structure of (aesthetic) experience. At that point the burden of proof is on the adversary to show that there are no such structures or no such experience.

Up to this point we have been considering the cosmopolitan perspective in the Analytic of the Sublime from the standpoint of the mathematically sublime. There, the agitation that accompanied a reflective judgment was a cognitive one based on the inability of the mind to present the whole (of humanity) in a single intuition at the same time that it was relying on this idea for the judgment. In the case of the dynamically sublime, the agitation is one that concerns the power of desire (Ak 247). Dynamically sublime judgments present themselves in cases "when in an aesthetic judgment we consider nature as a might that has no dominance over us" (Ak 260). Human agents are natural agents and, as such, are subject to the demands of natural survival: food, shelter, clothing, companionship. In the best of ordinary circumstances we experience no conflict in the fulfillment of these demands; we are not tormented at the thought of securing the daily bread, and an evening of friendship is not a cause for concern. Even external nature appears to cooperate in our efforts here. The cycle of seasons brings forth the harvest, and others' desire for companionship complements our own. In other circumstances, however, the attempt to fulfill these natural demands is frustrated by nature itself. Drought and famine, earthquakes and hurricanes may threaten the ability to make it from one day to the next, and another's differences may make further interaction impossible. In such cases, according to Kant, we judge nature aesthetically as something that arouses fear.

Now not every natural phenomenon that arouses fear in a subject is one about which the judgment can be made that it is sublime. A natural phenomenon that arouses fear is also sublime, according to Kant, if it provokes in the subject a "magnitude of resistance" that demonstrates the subject's superiority over the phenomenon (Ak 260). The judgment of sublimity, properly speaking, is thus made not with respect to nature but to the second, supersensible, nature of the subject, to a point of reference in which the natural concerns of the subject diminish in importance as motives for action.

> If in judging nature aesthetically we call it sublime, we do so not because nature arouses fear, but because it calls forth our strength . . . to regard as small the [objects] of our [natural] concerns: property, health, and life, and because of this we regard nature's might (to which we are indeed subjected in these [natural] concerns) as yet not having such dominance over us, as persons, that we should have to bow to it if our highest principles were at stake and we had to choose between upholding or abandoning them. (Ak 262)

The kind of mental attunement that the dynamically sublime in nature brings forth in us is paid for in the coin of comfort, stability, and surety, for it occurs "only through sacrifice (which is a deprivation—though one that serves our inner freedom—in return for which it reveals in us an unfathomable depth of this supersensible power, whose consequences extend beyond what we can foresee)" (Ak 271). Effectively, the mind gets better (i.e., more attuned to sublimity) only to the degree that things get worse. It is in this sense that Kant can claim that

> even war has something of the sublime about it if it is carried on in an orderly way and with respect for the sanctity of citizens' rights. At the same time that it makes the way of thinking of a people that carries it on in this way all the more sublime in proportion to the number of dangers in the face of which it courageously stood its ground. (Ak 263)

This is not high praise for war. It is high praise for the moral resolve that shows itself when challenged with war. Kant appears to think that this is such a widely held feeling that he offers it as something of a justification for the very idea of the sublimity in nature.

> For what is it that is an object of the highest admiration even to the savage? It is a person who is not terrified, not afraid, and hence does not yield to danger but promptly sets to work with vigor and full deliberation. Even in a fully civilized society there remains this superior esteem for the warrior, except that we demand more of him: that he also demonstrate all the virtues of peace—gentleness, sympathy, and even appropriate care for his own person—precisely because they reveal to us that his mind cannot be subdued by danger. (Ak 262)

War is not a good. Neither are earthquakes, floods, famines, and all the other natural calamities that plague humanity. Kant is not making the mistake of saying that because such events prompt us to good, they must be good (and hence pursued, as in the case of war). Rather, the point is to note that with the occurrence of such natural events, human agents do in fact rise up and act so as to keep the "humanity in [their] person" and, by extension, humanity in others "from being degraded" (Ak 262). The difference is a subtle, but important, one and may help explain Kant's insistence on keeping to an aesthetic based on the judger rather than on the thing judged.

Again, as with all aesthetic judgments, judgments concerning the sublime in nature carry with them (exemplary) universality and necessity. And yet, in §29 of the Analytic of the Sublime, Kant makes a point of addressing the particularities of this universality and necessity as regards these judgments. Kant writes, "It is a fact that what is called sublime by us, having been prepared through culture, comes across as merely repellent to a person who is uncultured and lacking in the development of moral ideas" (Ak 265). Why should this be, and why should the sublime in nature be singled out? For Kant, culture "make[s] headway against the tyranny of man's propensity to the senses and prepare[s] him for a sovereignty in which reason alone is to dominate" (Ak 434) by challenging common, natural conceptions of what constitutes the height of human existence. Of course, the kind of culture will make a difference. Kant decries "romances and maudlin plays; insipid moral precepts that dally with (falsely) so-called noble attitudes but that in fact make the heart languid and insensitive to the stern precept of duty, and that hence make the heart incapable of any respect for the dignity of humanity in our own person and for human rights" (Ak 273). He also criticizes a certain kind of religion, one that places emphasis on "images and childish devices" rather than the pure command of morality, because it leaves the adherent in a state of effective stupor, and, as Kant notes, governments have no difficulty using this to their advantage (Ak 274–275). By extension, one could add the "images and childish devices" a government may promote among its citizens. What is common to all of these is the feeling of well-being they instill in those who hear or practice them by filling in the voids and gaps that otherwise agitate the mind and press the understanding or reason into service. When a symbol, a song, or a slogan replaces thinking, reflection, and criticism, the receptivity to the kind of challenge the sublime puts forth is likely to diminish.

According to Kant, simplicity, defined as artless purposiveness, is nature's style in the sublime (Ak 275). Could there be a culture of simplicity, and, if so, what would it look like? Regrettably, Kant does not provide much by way of an indication. His account of the sublime is, by his own admission, "abstract [...and] wholly negative as regards the sensible" (Ak 274). Indeed, earlier in *Critique of Judgment*, Kant claimed that reflective judgment does not give rise to a doctrine (as a determinate set of content-laden propositions or maxims) but only to critique (Ak 170, 194). Still, at this point he mentions the commandment against idolatry.

> Perhaps the most sublime passage in the Jewish Law is the commandment: Thou shalt not make unto thee any graven image, or any likeness of any thing that is in heaven or on earth, or under the earth, etc. This commandment alone can explain the enthusiasm that the Jewish people in its civilized era felt for its religion when it compared itself with other peoples, or can explain the pride that Islam inspires. (Ak 274)

A culture built along these lines, a culture that places more emphasis on the invisible than on the visible (without seeking to enclose the invisible in the visible), would seem to be the kind required to prepare minds to be receptive to sublimity in nature and, with it, to the moral law. As Kant continues,

> It is indeed a mistake to worry that depriving this presentation of whatever could commend it to the senses will result in its carrying with it no more than a cold and lifeless approval without any moving force or emotion. It is exactly the other way round. For once the senses no longer see anything before them, while yet the unmistakable and indelible idea... remains, one should sooner need to temper the momentum of an unbounded imagination so as to keep it from rising to the level of enthusiasm, than to seek to support these ideas with images and childlike devices. (Ak 274)

It is not that a new culture would have to be constructed as much as it is that the current culture (to the extent that it deals in symbolic trappings and images) would have to be destroyed.

The task of the sublime is, therefore, a negating one. But it is precisely in this that cosmopolitanism can be viewed as a sublime perspective, for cosmopolitanism, at least in Kant's version of it, requires the elimination of all political barriers on the free exercise of thought and moral action. Just as personal enlightenment involved dispensing with the book, the spiritual adviser, and the doctor, the conditions for the gradual enlightenment of the species involve dispensing with massive armaments and the superiority of one state over another (in terms of political power) and assuring that all inhabitants of the planet have an equal chance to make a living for themselves. Now Kant holds that there will be no lack of evils, and hence no lack of opportunities for human agents to recognize and demonstrate their freedom from external nature or their own natural inclinations. To this extent, one can make the reflective (teleological) judgment that nature will one day lead humankind to a state of perpetual peace in which human rights are respected. But one is equally warranted in the assertion that humans at present are capable of doing (and have the duty to do) what may take nature millennia to accomplish.

Does the Analytic of the Sublime provide a basis for a cosmopolitan political perspective? The answer is yes and no. No, because cosmopolitanism cannot provide "laws of political history and the principles of political formation" as Schlegel, for one, had requested; as a perspective, it can serve to orient action but not direct it. But if one gives up the desire for something like historical laws, the answer is yes, because the analysis of the sublime can allow one to "see" possibilities in experience that one without such a perspective would miss, without however falling into fanaticism, "which is the delusion of wanting to *see* something beyond all bounds of sensibility" (Ak 275). It can achieve this because the sublime is, on Kant's account, simply a form of aesthetic experience that all agents in principle share. To this degree it is a "necessary law of experience" that is always operative.

History shows that cosmopolitanism did not fare well. Under Hegel, it became the violent incarnation of Absolute Spirit in history. For Marx, the withering away of the state meant the international dictatorship of the proletariat. According to the practice of capitalism it meant the creation of a world market in which politics could play only a facilitating role. The reactions to these various positions and programs (in Nietzsche, in the anarchist strands of socialism, in certain forms of the ecological movement, for example) reveal something that neither Hegel, nor Marx, nor capital can account for. They reveal attempts to do away with structures of thought and governance that stifle the human spirit by denying the sensible and the profitable. To this extent they may be (and often are) considered to have their sublime elements about them.[16] What the kind of cosmopolitan perspective Kant develops suggests, however, is that without a concomitant emphasis on the gradual recognition of human rights, even such movements can quickly fall into new forms of domination. Simple negation is not liberation, and the drive to liberate must itself be tempered by the sober and patient task of establishing a state of respect for human rights. The only new world order worthy of the name would be one in which, as Kant imagined, the violation of rights in one part of the world would be felt everywhere.

Might ours be an age of enlightenment?

NOTES

1. Kant, *Perpetual Peace,* in *Kant's Political Writings,* 2d ed., ed. Hans Reiss (New York, 1989), 107–108.

2. Immanuel Kant, "Idea for a Universal History with Cosmopolitan Purpose," in *Kant's Political Writings,* 51.

3. The present volume reflects much of the earlier discussion until the mid-1790s; for developments after 1795, see Anita and Walter Dietze, eds., *Ewiger Friede? Dokumente einer deutschen Diskussion um 1800* (Munich, 1989).

4. For an overview of the Jacobin activities in central and eastern Europe, see Helmut Reinalter, *Die Französische Revolution und Mitteleuropa* (Frankfurt am Main, 1988).

5. Christoph Martin Wieland is an interesting case in point. Although rather flippant in his early enthusiasm for enlightenment, his writings after the Revolution reflect a more guarded stance.

6. For the details of this critique, see Frederick Beiser, *The Fate of Reason: German Philosophy from Kant to Fichte* (Cambridge, Mass., 1987).

7. Friedrich Schlegel, "Versuch über den Begriff des Republikanismus. Veranlaßt durch die Kantische Schrift zum ewigen Frieden," *Deutschland* 3.7, no. 2 (1796); reprinted in Zwi Batscha and Richard Saage, eds., *Friedensutopien* (Frankfurt am Main, 1979), 106.

8. Kant, *Perpetual Peace,* 114.

9. Immanuel Kant, *Critique of Judgment,* trans. Werner S. Pluhar (Indianapolis, 1987), Ak. 263. Future references to this work will be made according to the Akademie page numbering and included in the text.

10. "An Answer to the Question, 'What Is Enlightenment?' in *Kant's Political Writings,* 54–60.

11. Immanuel Kant, cited in *Materialien zu Kants Rechtsphilosophie,* ed. Zwi Batscha (Frankfurt am Main, 1976), 38.

12. Drost von Müller, "Gedanken über Kosmopolitismus und Patriotismus," *Der Kosmopolit, eine Monatsshrift zur Beförderung wahrer und allgemeiner Humanität* 5 (1797); reprinted in *Von der ständischen zur bürgerlichen Gesellschaft,* ed. Zwi Batscha and Jörn Garber (Frankfurt am Main, 1981), 261–262.

13. See, for example, Paul Crowther's charges against the category of the sublime in *The Kantian Sublime: From Morality to Art* (New York, 1989).

14. In some respects, *Critique of Judgment* is a fuller account of the position Kant took in "What Is Orientation in Thinking?" written four years earlier.

15. "Toward Perpetual Peace," 125.

16. See, for example, Jean-François Lyotard's recent attempts to describe presentations of "the fact that the unpresentable exists" which he takes to be indications of sublimity.

CONTRIBUTORS TO PARTS II AND III

Frederick C. Beiser is Professor of Philosophy at Indiana University. He is the author of *The Fate of Reason: German Philosophy from Kant to Fichte* (Cambridge: Harvard University Press, 1987) and *Enlightenment, Revolution, and Romanticism: The Genesis of Modern German Political Thought 1790–1800* (Cambridge: Harvard University Press, 1992) and the editor of *The Cambridge Companion to Hegel* (Cambridge: Cambridge University Press, 1993).

Günter Birtsch is Professor of Modern History at the University of Trier. He is the author of *Die Nation als sittliche Idee: Der Nationalstaatsbegriff in Geschichtsschreibung und politischer Gedankenwelt J. G. Droysens* (Cologne: Bohlau, 1964) and the editor of *Grund- und Freiheitsrechte im Wandel von Gesellschaft und Geschichte* (Göttingen: Vandenhoeck and Ruprecht, 1981) and *Grund- und Freiheitsrechte von der ständischen zur bürgerliche Gesellschaft* (Göttingen: Vandenhoeck and Ruprecht, 1987). He is an editor of the journal *Aufklärung.*

Rüdiger Bittner is Professor of Philosophy at the University of Bielefeld. He is the author of *What Reason Demands* (Cambridge: Cambridge University Press, 1989) and of articles on the theory of action, moral philosophy, and the history of philosophy. He is the co-editor of *Das Ästhetische Urteil* (Cologne: Kiepenheuer & Witsch, 1977) and *Materialien zu Kants* Kritik der praktischen Vernunft (Frankfurt am Main: Suhrkamp, 1975).

Gernot Böhme is Professor of Philosophy at the Technische Hochschule in Darmstadt. His books include *Alternativen der Wissenschaft* (Frankfurt: Suhrkamp, 1980), *Für eine ökologische Naturästhetik* (Frankfurt: Suhrkamp, 1989), *Natürlich Natur: Über Natur im Zeitalter ihrer technischen Reproduzierbarkeit* (Frankfurt: Suhrkamp, 1992), *Am Ende des Baconschen Zeitalters* (Frankfurt: Suhrkamp, 1993), and *Atmosphäre: Essays zur neuen Ästhetik* (Frankfurt: Suhrkamp, 1995).

Hartmut Böhme is Professor of Literature at the University of Hamburg. His books include *Anomie und Entfremdung* (Kronberg: Scriptor-Verlag, 1974), *Natur und Subjekt* (Frankfurt: Suhrkamp, 1988), *Albrecht Dürer: Melencolia I* (Frankfurt: Fischer, 1989), and *Hubert Fichte: Riten des Autors und Leben der Literatur* (Stuttgart: J. B. Metzler, 1992).

Michel Foucault (1926–1984) was Professor of History and Systems of Thought at the Collège de France. English translations of his works include *Madness and Civilization* (New York: Vintage, 1965), *The Order of Things* (New York: Vintage, 1970), *Discipline and Punish* (New York: Vintage, 1977), and three volumes of his *History of Sexuality* (New York: Pantheon, 1978, 1985, 1987).

Kevin Paul Geiman is Assistant Professor of Philosophy at Valparaiso University. He is the translator of Jean-François Lyotard's *Political Writings* (Minneapolis: University of Minnesota Press, 1993) and is currently at work on a book, *"No Empty Idea": Perpetual Peace in Germany, 1712–1815.*

Garrett Green is Professor and Chair of the Department of Religious Studies at Connecticut College. He is the author of *Imagining God: Theology and the Religious Imagination* (San Francisco: Harper and Row, 1989) and the translator of J. G. Fichte's *Attempt at a Critique of All Revelation* (Cambridge: Cambridge University Press, 1978).

Jürgen Habermas is Professor Emeritus of Philosophy and Sociology at the J. W. von Goethe University in Frankfurt. His best-known works include *Knowledge and Human Interests* (Boston: Beacon Press, 1971), *Theory of Communicative Action* (Boston: Beacon Press, 1984, 1987), and *The Philosophical Discourse of Modernity* (Cambridge: MIT Press, 1990). His most recent book is *Faktizität und Geltung. Beiträge zur Diskurstheorie des Rechts und des demokratischen Rechtsstaats* (Frankfurt: Suhrkamp, 1992).

Lewis Hinchman is Professor of Political Science at Clarkson University. He is the author of *Hegel's Critique of Enlightenment* (Gainesville: University of Florida Press, 1984) and co-editor of *Hannah Arendt: Critical Essays* (Albany: State University of New York Press, 1994).

Max Horkheimer (1895–1973) was Professor of Social Philosophy and Director of the Institute for Social Research at the University of Frankfurt. During the Second World War he and his colleagues emigrated to the United States, reestablishing the Institute at Columbia University. English translations of his works include *Eclipse of Reason* (New York: Oxford University Press, 1947), *Critical Theory* (New York: Herder and Herder, 1972), *Between Philosophy and Social Science: Selected Early Writings* (Cambridge: MIT Press, 1993), and *Dialectic of Enlightenment* (New York: Herder and Herder, 1972), which he wrote with Theodor Adorno.

Jane Kneller is Assistant Professor of Philosophy at Colorado State University. She has published work on Kant's aesthetic and moral theory as well as a number of papers reading Kant from a feminist perspective.

Jonathan B. Knudsen is Professor of History at Wellesley College and the author of *Justus Möser and the German Enlightenment* (Cambridge: Cambridge University Press, 1986). He is completing a cultural history of Berlin in the first half of the nineteenth century.

John Christian Laursen is Associate Professor of Political Science at the University of California, Riverside. He is the author of *The Politics of Skepticism in the Ancients, Montaigne, Hume, and Kant* (Leiden: Brill, 1992) and editor of *New Essays in the Political Thought of the Huguenots of the Refuge* (Leiden: Brill, 1995).

Georg Picht (1913–1982) was Professor of the Philosophy of Religion in the Protestant theological faculty at Heidelberg University. His works include *Wahrheit, Vernunft, Verantwortung* (Stuttgart: Klett, 1969), *Hier und Jetzt: Philosophieren nach Auschwitz und Hiroshima* (Stuttgart: Klett-Cotta, 1980), and *Philosophie der Verantwortung* (Stuttgart: Klett-Cotta, 1985).

Dale E. Snow is Associate Professor of Philosophy at Loyola College of Maryland. She is the author of *Schelling and the End of Idealism* (Albany: State University of New York Press, 1996).

James Schmidt is Chair of the Political Science Department at Boston University. He is the author of *Maurice Merleau-Ponty: Between Phenomenology and Structuralism* (New York: St. Martin's Press, 1985) as well as articles on the idea of enlightenment in the eighteenth and twentieth centuries.

Robin May Schott is affiliated with the Center for Feminist Studies at the University of Copenhagen. She is the author of *Cognition and Eros: A Critique of the Kantian Paradigm* (Boston: Beacon Press, 1988) and the editor of the forthcoming volume *Feminist Interpretations of Kant.*

Rudolph Vierhaus is Professor of History at the University of Göttingen and was Director of the Max Planck Institute for History in Göttingen. He is the author of *Germany in the Age of Absolutism* (Cambridge: Cambridge University Press, 1988) as well as numerous monographs and essays on eighteenth-century Germany, some of which have been collected in *Deutschland im 18. Jahrhundert. Politische Verfassung, soziales Gefüge, geistige Bewegungen* (Göttingen: Vandenhoeck and Ruprecht, 1987).

SELECT BIBLIOGRAPHY

This bibliography falls into three sections. The first part lists collections and reprints of eighteenth-century German discussions of the nature and consequences of enlightenment. The second focuses on some of the more important historical studies of the German Enlightenment with special attention to studies of the writers translated in the first part of this book and of the themes they addressed. The third concentrates on literature discussing or developing the issues raised in the last part of this book.

I. REPRINTS OF EIGHTEENTH-CENTURY TEXTS ON THE NATURE AND CONSEQUENCES OF ENLIGHTENMENT

Bahr, Ehrhard, ed. *Was ist Aufklärung? Thesen und Definitionen.* Stuttgart: Reclam, 1974.

Batscha, Zwi, ed. *Aufklärung und Gedankenfreiheit: 15 Anregungen, aus der Geschichte zu lernen.* Frankfurt am Main: Suhrkamp, 1977.

———. *"Despotismus von jeder Art reizt zur Widersetzlichkeit": Die Französische Revolution in der deutsche Popularphilosophie.* Frankfurt am Main: Suhrkamp, 1989.

Eberle, Friedrich, and Theo Stammen, eds. *Die Französische Revolution in Deutschland: Zeitgenössische Texte deutscher Autoren.* Stuttgart: Reclam, 1989.

Garber, Jörn, ed. *Kritik der Revolution. Theorie des deutschen Frühkonservatismus 1790–1810.* Kronberg/Ts.: Scriptor, 1976.

———, ed. *Revolutionäre Vernunft. Texte zur jakobischen und liberalen Revolutionsrezeption in Deutschland 1789–1810.* Kronberg/Ts.: Scriptor, 1974.

Geismar, Martin von [pseudonym for Edgar Bauer], ed. *Bibliothek der deutschen Aufklärer des achtzehnten Jahrhunderts.* [1846] Reprint. Darmstadt: Wissenschaftliche Buchgesellschaft, 1963.

Hinske, Norbert, and Michael Albrecht, eds. *Was ist Aufklärung? Beiträge aus der Berlinischen Monatsschrift.* 4th ed. Darmstadt: Wissenschaftliche Buchgesellschaft, 1990.

Reinhold, Karl Leonhard. *Schriften zur Religionskritik und Aufklärung 1782–1784.* Ed. Zwi Batscha. Bremen: Jacobi Verlag, 1977.

Weber, Peter, ed. *Berlinische Monatsschrift (1783–1796): Auswahl.* Leipzig: Reclam, 1986.

II. HISTORICAL AND CRITICAL STUDIES OF THE GERMAN ENLIGHTENMENT

Agethen, Manfred. *Geheimbund und Utopie: Illuminaten, Freimaurer und deutsche Spätaufklärung.* Munich: Oldenbourg, 1984.

Albrecht, Wolfgang. "Aufklärung, Reform, Revolution oder 'Bewirkt Aufklärung Revolutionen?' Über ein Zentralproblem der Aufklärungsdebatte in Deutschland." *Lessing Yearbook* 22 (1990): 1–75.

Alexander, W. M. "Johann Georg Hamann: Metacritic of Kant." *Journal of the History of Ideas* 27 (1966): 137–144.

Allison, Henry E. *Lessing and the Enlightenment.* Ann Arbor: University of Michigan Press, 1966.

Altmann, Alexander. *Moses Mendelssohn: A Biographical Study.* University, Alabama: University of Alabama Press, 1973.

———. *Die trostvolle Aufklärung: Studien zur Metaphysik und politische Theorie Moses Mendelssohns.* Stuttgart–Bad Cannstatt: Frommann-Holzboog, 1982.

Anchor, Robert. *The Enlightenment Tradition.* Berkeley and Los Angeles: University of California Press, 1979.

Aner, Karl. *Die Theologie der Lessingzeit.* Halle: Niemeyer, 1927.

Arkush, Allan. *Moses Mendelssohn and the Enlightenment.* Albany: State University of New York Press, 1994.

Axin, Sidney. "Kant, Authority, and the French Revolution." *Journal of the History of Ideas* 32 (1971): 423–432.

Bahr, Ehrhard. "Kant, Mendelssohnn, and the Problem of 'Enlightenment from Above.'" *Eighteenth-Century Life* 8 (1982): 1–12.

Bahr, Ehrhard, Edward P. Harris, and Laurence G. Lyon, eds. *Humanität und Dialog: Lessing und Mendelssohn in neuer Sicht: Beiträge zum Internationalen Lessing-Mendelssohn-Symposium anläßlich des 250. Geburtstages von Lessing und Mendelssohn.* Detroit: Wayne State University Press, 1982.

Bahr, Ehrhard, and Thomas P. Saine, eds. *The Internalized Revolution: German Reactions to the French Revolution, 1789–1989.* New York: Garland, 1992.

Bal, Karol. "Aufklärung und Religion beim Mendelssohn, Kant, und dem jungen Hegel." *Deutsche Zeitschrift für Philosophie* 27 (1979): 1248–1257.

Barnard, Frederick M. "'Aufklärung' and 'Mündigkeit': Thomasius, Kant, Herder." *Deutsche Vierteljahresschrift für Literaturwissenschaft und Geistesgeschichte* 57 (1983): 278–297.

Bayer, Oswald. "Hamanns Metakritik im ersten Entwurf." *Kantstudien* 81 (1990): 435–453.

———. "Selbstverschuldete Vormundschaft: Hamanns Kontroverse mit Kant um *wahre* Aufklärung." In *Der Wirklichkeitsanspruch von Theologie und Religion*, ed. Dieter Henke. Tübingen: J. C. B. Mohr, 1976.

———. *Zeitgenosse im Widerspruch: Johann Georg Hamann als radikaler Aufklärer.* Munich: Piper, 1988.

Beck, Lewis White. "Kant and the Right of Revolution." *Journal of the History of Ideas* 32 (1971): 411–422.

Begemann, Christoph. *Furcht und Angst im Prozess der Aufklärung. Zur Literatur- und Bewußtsein- geschichte des 18. Jahrhunderts.* Frankfurt am Main: Athenäum, 1987.

Behrens, C. B. A. *Society, Government, and the Enlightenment: The Experiences of Eighteenth-Century France and Prussia.* New York: Harper and Row, 1985.

Beiser, Frederick C. *Enlightenment, Revolution, and Romanticism.* Cambridge: Harvard University Press, 1992.

———. *The Fate of Reason: German Philosophy from Kant to Fichte.* Cambridge: Harvard University Press, 1987.

Belaval, Yvon. "L'Aufklaerung a Contre-Lumières." *Archives de Philosophie* 42 (1979): 631–634.

Blanke, Horst Walter. *Aufklärung und Historik: Aufsätze zur Entwicklung der Geschichtswissenschaft, Kirchengeschichte und Geschichtstheorie in der deutschen Aufklärung.* Waltrop: Spenner, 1991.

Blanning T. C. W. "The Enlightenment in Catholic Germany." In *The Enlightenment in National Context,* ed. Roy Porter and Mikulás Teich. Cambridge: Cambridge University Press, 1981.

———. "France during the French Revolution through German Eyes." In *The Impact of the French Revolution on European Consciousness,* ed. H. T. Mason and W. Doyle. Gloucester: Alan Sutton, 1989.

———. *Reform and Revolution in Mainz, 1743–1803.* New York: Cambridge University Press, 1974.

Bödeker, Hans Erich. "Aufklärung als Kommunikationsprozess." *Aufklärung 2* (1987): 89–111.

Bödeker, Hans Erich, and Ulrich Herrmann, eds. *Aufklärung als Politisierung, Politisierung der Aufklärung.* Hamburg: F. Meiner, 1987.

———. *Über den Prozess der Aufklärung in Deutschland im 18. Jahrhundert: Personen, Institutionen und Medien.* Göttingen: Vandenhoeck and Ruprecht, 1987.

Bödeker, Hans Erich, et al. *Aufklärung und Geschichte: Studien zur deutschen Geschichtswissenschaft im 18. Jahrhundert.* Göttingen: Vandenhoeck and Ruprecht, 1986.

Bödeker, Hans Erich, and Per Ohrgaard, eds. *Aufklärung als Problem und Aufgabe: Festschrift für Sven-Aage Jorgensen.* Munich: Fink, 1994.

Böning, Holger. *Volksaufklärung: Bibliographisches Handbuch zur Popularisierung aufklärerischen Denkens im deutschen Sprachraum von den Anfangen bis 1850.* Stuttgart–Bad Cannstadt: Frommann-Holzboog, 1990.

———, ed. *Französische Revolution und deutsche Öffentlichkeit: Wandlungen in Presse und Alltagskultur am Ende des achtzehnten Jahrhunderts.* Munich: K. G. Saur, 1992.

Bourel, Dominique. "Moses Mendelssohn et l'*Aufklärung.*" *Dix-huitième Siècle* 10 (1968): 13–21.

Bruch, J. L. "Kant et les Lumières." *Revue de Metaphysique et Morale* 79 (1974): 457–472.

Brüggemann, Fritz. *Das Weltbild der deutschen Aufklärung. Philosophische Grundlagen und Literarische Auswirkung: Leibniz, Wolff, Gottsched, Brockes, Haller.* Leipzig: P. Reclam, 1930.

Brunschwig, Henri. *Enlightenment and Romanticism in Eighteenth-Century Prussia.* Chicago: University of Chicago Press, 1974.

Büchsel, E. "Aufklärung und christliche Freiheit: J. G. Hamann contra I. Kant." *Neue Zeitschrift für systematische Theologie* 4 (1962): 133–157.

Burg, Peter. *Kant und die französische Revolution.* Berlin: Duncker and Humblot, 1974.

Butts, Robert E. "The Grammar of Reason: Hamann's Challenge to Kant." *Synthese* 75 (1988): 251–283.

Cassirer, Ernst. *The Philosophy of the Enlightenment.* Princeton: Princeton University Press, 1951.

Clark, Jonathan P. "Beyond Rhyme or Reason: Fanaticism and the Transference of Interpretive Paradigms from the Seventeenth-Century Orthodoxy to the Aesthetics of Enlightenment." *MLN* 105 (1990): 563–582.

Craig, Gordon A. "Frederick the Great and Moses Mendelssohn: Thoughts on Jewish Emancipation. *Leo Baeck Institute Year Book* 32 (1987): 3–10.

Dann, Otto, and Diethelm Klippel, eds. *Naturrecht, Spätaufklärung, Revolution.* Hamburg: F. Meiner, 1995.

Denker, Rolf. *Grenzen liberaler Aufklärung bei Kant und anderen.* Stuttgart: Kohlhammer, 1968.

Dülmen, Richard van. *Der Geheimbund der Illuminaten.* Stuttgart–Bad Cannstatt: Frommann-Holzboog, 1977.

———. *The Society of the Enlightenment.* New York: St. Martin's Press, 1992.

Epstein, Klaus. *The Genesis of German Conservatism.* Princeton: Princeton University Press, 1966.

Fischer, Michael W. *Die Aufklärung und ihr Gegenteil: Die Rolle der Geheimbunde in Wissenschaft und Politik.* Berlin: Duncker and Humblot, 1982.

Flygt, Sten Gunnar. *The Notorious Dr. Bahrdt.* Nashville: Vanderbilt University Press, 1963.

Frank, Luanne. "Herder and the Maturation of Hamann's Metacritical Thought: A Chapter in the Pre-History of the *Metakritik.*" In *Johann Gottfried Herder: Innovator Through the Ages,* ed. Wulf Koepke and Samson B. Knoll. Bonn: Bouvier, 1982.

Gajek, Bernhard, and Albert Meier, eds. *Johann Georg Hamann und die Krise der Aufklärung: Acta des fünften Internationalen Hamann-Kolloquiums (1988).* New York: Peter Lang, 1990.

Gay, Peter. *The Enlightenment: An Interpretation.* 2 vols. New York: Knopf, 1966–1969.

Ginzberg, Carlo. "High and Low: The Theme of Forbidden Knowledge in the Sixteenth and Seventeenth Centuries." *Past & Present* 73 (1976): 28–41.

Goetschel, Willi. "Publicizing Enlightenment: Kant's Concept of Enlightenment." In Goetschel, *Constituting Critique: Kant's Writings as Critical Praxis.* Durham: Duke University Press, 1994.

Hammacher, Klaus. "Ein bemerkenswerter Einfluß Französischen Denkens: Friedrich Heinrich Jacobis (1743–1819) Auseinandersetzung mit Voltaire und Rousseau." *Revue Internationale de Philosophie* 32 (1978): 327–347.

Hellmuth, Eckhart. "Aufklärung und Pressefreiheit: Zur Debatte der Berliner Mittwochsgesellschaft während der Jahre 1783 und 1784." *Zeitschrift für historisches Forschung* 9 (1982): 315–345.

———. "Ernst Ferdinand Klein." *Aufklärung* 2 (1987): 121–123.

———, ed. *The Transformation of Political Culture: England and Germany in the Late Eighteenth Century.* London: Oxford University Press, 1990.

Hinchman, Lewis. *Hegel's Critique of Enlightenment.* Gainesville: University of Florida Press, 1984.

Hinske, Norbert. "Zwischen Aufklärung und Vernunftkritik. Die philosophische Bedeutung des Kantschen Logikcorpus." *Aufklärung* 7 (1992): 57–71.

———, ed. *Ich handle mit Vernunft: Moses Mendelssohn und die europäische Aufklärung.* Hamburg: F. Meiner, 1981.

Hoffmeister, Gerhart, ed. *The French Revolution and the Age of Goethe.* New York: Georg Olms, 1989.

Hübner, Kurt. "Die Politische Philosophie Kants und Hegels: Zwei Repliken auf die französische Revolution." *Geschichte in Wissenschaft und Unterricht* 40 (1989): 404–419.

Hulme, Peter, and Ludmilla Jordanova, eds. *The Enlightenment and Its Shadows.* New York: Routledge, 1990.

Im Hof, Ulrich. *The Enlightenment: The Making of Europe.* Oxford: Blackwell, 1994.

———. *Das Gesellige Jahrhundert: Gesellschaft und Gesellschaften im Zeitalter der Aufklärung.* Munich: Beck, 1982.

Ingrao, Charles. "The Problem of 'Enlightened Absolutism' and the German States." *Journal of Modern History* 58, suppl. (1986): s161–s180.

Jacob, Margaret C. *Living the Enlightenment: Freemasonry and Politics in Eighteenth-Century Europe.* New York: Oxford University Press, 1991.

———. *The Radical Enlightenment: Pantheists, Freemasons, and Republicans.* Boston: Allen and Unwin, 1981.

Jamme, Christoph, and Gerhard Kurz, eds. *Idealismus und Aufklärung: Kontinuität und Kritik der Aufklärung in Philosophie und Poesie um 1800.* Stuttgart: Klett-Cotta, 1988.

Jüttner, Siegfried, and Jochen Schlobach, eds. *Europäische Aufklärung(en): Einheit und nationale Vielfalt.* Hamburg: F. Meiner, 1992.

Keller, Ludwig. "Die Berliner Mittwochs-gesellschaft." *Monatshefte der Comenius-Gesellschaft* V:3–4 (1896): 67–94.

Kempf, Thomas. *Aufklärung als Disziplinierung: Studien zum Diskurs des Wissens in Intelligenzblättern und gelehrten Beilagen der zweiten Hälfte des 18. Jahrhunderts.* Munich: Iudicium-Verlag, 1991.

Klippel, Diethelm. "Von der Aufklärung der Herrscher zur Herrschaft der Aufklärung." *Zeitschrift für historische Forschung* 17 (1990): 193–210.

Kneller, Jane. "Imaginative Freedom and the German Enlightenment." *Journal of the History of Ideas* 51 (1990): 217–232.

Knudsen, Jonathan B. "Friedrich Nicolai's 'wirkliche Welt': On Common Sense in the German Enlightenment." In *Mentalitäten und Lebensverhältnisse: Beispiele aus der Sozialgeschichte der Neuzeit. Rudolf Vierhaus zum 60. Geburtstag,* ed. "Mitarbeitern und Schülern." Göttingen: Vandenhoeck and Ruprecht, 1982.

———. *Justus Möser and the German Enlightenment.* Cambridge: Cambridge University Press, 1986.

Kopitzsch, Franklin. "Die deutsche Aufklärung. Leistungen, Grenzen, Wirkungen." *Archiv für Sozialgeschichte* 23 (1983): 1–21.

———, ed. *Aufklärung, Absolutismus und Bürgertum in Deutschland: Zwölf Aufsätze.* Munich: Nymphenburger Verlagshandlung, 1976.

Koselleck, Reinhart. *Critique and Crisis: Enlightenment and the Pathogenesis of Modern Society*. Cambridge: MIT Press, 1988.

Krause, Reinhard. *Die Predigt der späten deutschen Aufklärung (1770–1805)*. Stuttgart: Calwer Verlag, 1965.

Krauss, Werner. *Studien zur deutschen und französischen Aufklärung*. Berlin: Rutten and Loening, 1963.

Krieger, Leonard. *An Essay on the Theory of Enlightened Despotism*. Chicago: University of Chicago Press, 1975.

———. *Kings and Philosophers, 1689–1789*. New York: W. W. Norton, 1970.

Laursen, John Christian. "Kant and Schlözer on the French Revolution and the Rights of Man in the Context of Publicity." In *Revolution and Enlightenment in Europe*, ed. Timothy O'Hagen. Aberdeen: Aberdeen University Press, 1991.

———. "Publicity and Cosmopolitanism in Late Eighteenth-Century Germany." *History of European Ideas* 16 (1993): 117–122.

———. "Skepticism and Intellectual Freedom: The Philosophical Foundations of Kant's Politics of Publicity." *History of Political Thought* 10 (1989): 99–133.

La Vopa, Anthony J. "The Birth of Public Opinion." *Wilson Quarterly* 15 (1991): 46–55.

———. "Conceiving a Public: Ideas and Society in Eighteenth-Century Europe." *Journal of Modern History* 64 (1992): 79–116.

———. "The Politics of Enlightenment: Friedrich Gedike and German Professional Ideology." *Journal of Modern History* 6 (1990): 34–56.

———. "The Revelatory Moment: Fichte and the French Revolution." *Central European History* 22 (1989): 130–159.

Lauth, Reinhard. "Nouvelles recherches sur Reinhold et l'Aufklaerung." *Archives de Philosophie* 42 (1979): 593–629.

Leiss, Elisabeth. "'Die Vernunft ist ein Wetterhahn': Johann Georg Hamanns Sprachtheorie und die Dialektik der Aufklärung." *Zeitschrift für Germanistische Linguistik* 19 (1991): 259–273.

Lestition, Steven. "Kant and the End of the Enlightenment in Prussia." *Journal of Modern History* 65 (1993): 57–112.

Liebel, Helen P. "Enlightened Despotism and the Crisis of Society in Germany." *Enlightenment Essays* 1 (1970): 151–168.

Liepert, Anita. "Aufklärung und Religionskritik bei Kant." *Deutsche Zeitschrift für Philosophie* 22 (1974): 359–368.

Lorenzen, Max-Otto. *Metaphysik als Grenzgang: Die Idee der Aufklärung unter dem Primat der praktischen Vernunft in der Philosophie Immanuel Kants*. Hamburg: F. Meiner, 1991.

Lötzsch, Frieder. "Moses Mendelssohn und Immanuel Kant im Gespräch über Aufklärung." *Wolfenbüttelen Studien zur Aufklärung* 4 (1977): 163–186.

———. "Zur Genealogie der Frage: 'Was ist Aufklärung?'" *Theokratia* 2 (1970–1972): 307–322.

Lütkehaus, Ludger. "Karl Friedrich Bahrdt, Immanuel Kant und die Gegenaufklärung in Preussen (1788–1798)." *Jahrbuch des Instituts für Deutsche Geschichte* 9 (1980): 83–106.

Majetschak, Stefan. "Metakritik und Sprache: Zu Johann Georg Hamanns Kant-

Verständnis und seinen metakritischen Implikationen." *Kantstudien* 80 (1989): 447–471.

Manheim, Ernst. *Aufklärung und öffentliche Meinung: Studien zur Soziologie der Öffentlichkeit im 18. Jahrhunderts*. Stuttgart–Bad Cannstatt: Frommann-Holzboog, 1979.

Martens, Wolfgang. *Die Botschaft der Tugend. Die Aufklärung im Spiegel der deutschen moralischen Wochenschriften.* Stuttgart: Metzler, 1968.

McCarthy, John A. "The Art of Reading and the Goals of the German Enlightenment." *Lessing Yearbook* 16 (1984): 79–84.

———. *Crossing Boundaries: A Theory and History of Essay Writing in German 1680–1815*. Philadelphia: University of Pennsylvania Press, 1989.

———. "Die gefesselte Muse? Wieland und die Pressefreiheit." *MLN* 99 (1984): 437–460.

———. "Politics and Morality in Eighteenth-Century Germany." *Deutsche Vierteljahrsschrift für Literaturwissenschaft und Geistesgeschichte* 68 (1994): 77–98.

———. "'Das sicherste Kennzeichen einer gesunden, nervösen Staatsverfassung': Lessing und die Pressefreiheit." *Lessing Yearbook* 16 (1986): 225–244.

Mederer, Wolfgang. *Romantik als Aufklärung der Aufklärung? Ein Beitrag zur Rekonstruktion politischer Theorie in der deutschen Romantik.* New York: Lang, 1987.

Möller, Horst. *Aufklärung in Preussen: der Verleger, Publizist und Geschichtsschreiber Friedrich Nicolai.* Berlin: Colloquium Verlag, 1974.

———. *Vernunft und Kritik: Deutsche Aufklärung im 17. und 18. Jahrhundert.* Frankfurt am Main: Suhrkamp, 1986.

Mori, Massimo. "Aufklärung und Kritizismus in Kants Geschichtsphilosophie. *Aufklärung* 5 (1990): 81–102.

Mühlpfordt, Günter. "Bahrdts Weg zum revolutionären Demokratismus: Das Werden seiner Lehre von Staat des Volkswohls." *Zeitschrift für Geschichtswissenschaft* 29 (1981): 996–1017.

———. "Deutsche Präjakobiner. Karl Friedrich Bahrdt und die beiden Forster." *Zeitschrift für Geschichtswissenschaft* 28 (1980): 970–989.

———. "Lesengesellschaften und bürgerliche Umgestaltung: Ein Organisationsversuch des deutschen Aufklärers Bahrdt vor der französischen Revolution." *Zeitschrift für Geschichtswissenschaft* 28 (1980): 730–751.

Nehren, Birgit. "Selbstdenken und gesunde Vernunft. Über eine wiederentdeckte Quelle zur Mittwochsgesellschaft." *Aufklärung* 1 (1986): 87–101.

Niewöhner, Friedrich. "Mendelssohn als Philosoph, Aufklärer, Jude. Oder Aufklärung mit dem Talmud." *Zeitschrift für Religions- und Geistesgeschichte* 41(1989): 119–133.

Nisbet, H. B. "'Was ist Aufklärung?' The Concept of Enlightenment in Eighteenth-Century Germany." *Journal of European Studies* 12 (1982): 77–95.

O'Flaherty, James C. *Johann Georg Hamann.* Boston: Twayne, 1979.

———. *The Quarrel of Reason with Itself: Essays on Hamann, Michaelis, Lessing, Nietzsche.* Columbia, S.C.: Camden House, 1988.

O'Neill, Onora. "The Public Use of Reason." In O'Neill, *Constructions of Reason: Explorations of Kant's Practical Philosophy.* Cambridge: Cambridge University Press, 1989.

Oelmüller, Willi. *Die unbefriedigte Aufklärung: Beiträge zu einer Theorie der Moderne von Lessing, Kant und Hegel.* Frankfurt am Main: Suhrkamp, 1979.

Oz-Salzberger, Fania. *Translating the Enlightenment: Scottish Civic Discourse in Eighteenth-Century Germany*. New York: Oxford University Press, 1995.

Parry, Geraint. "Enlightened Government and Its Critics in Eighteenth-Century Germany." *Historical Journal* 6 (1963): 178–192.

Philipp, Wolfgang. *Das Werden der Aufklärung in theologiegeschichtlicher Sicht. Forschungen zur systematischen Theologie und Religionsphilosophie.* Göttingen: Vandenhoeck and Ruprecht, 1957.

Pott, Martin. *Aufklärung und Aberglaube: Die deutsche Frühaufklärung im Spiegel ihrer Aberglaubenskritik.* Tübingen: Niemeyer, 1992.

Pütz, Peter. *Die deutsche Aufklärung*. Darmstadt: Wissenschaftliche Buchgesellschaft, 1978.

———, ed. *Erforschung der deutschen Aufklärung*. Königstein/Ts.: Verlagsgruppe Athenäum, Hain, Scriptor, Hanstein, 1980.

Raabe, Paul. "Die Zeitschrift als Medium der Aufklärung." *Wolfenbütteler Studien zur Aufklärung* 1 (1974): 99–136.

Raabe, Paul, and Wilhelm Schmidt-Biggemann, eds. *Aufklärung in Deutschland*. Bonn: Hohwacht, 1979.

Raeff, Marc. "The Well-Ordered Police State and the Development of Modernity in Seventeenth- and Eighteenth-Century Europe: An Attempt at a Comparative Perspective." *American Historical Review* 80 (1975): 1221–1243.

Rau, Fritz. "Die Aufklärung im evangelischen Kirchengesangbuch." *Zeitschrift für Religions- und Geistesgeschichte* 36 (1984): 335–345.

Reill, Peter Hanns. *The German Enlightenment and the Rise of Historicism*. Berkeley and Los Angeles: University of California Press, 1975.

Rendtorff, Trutz, ed. *Religion als Problem der Aufklärung: Eine Bilanz aus der religionstheoretischen Forschung*. Göttingen: Vandenhoeck and Ruprecht, 1980.

Roehr, Sabine. *A Primer on German Enlightenment: With a translation of Karl Leonhard Reinhold's "The Fundamental Concepts and Principles of Ethics."* Columbia: University of Missouri Press, 1995.

Saine, Thomas P. *Black Bread—White Bread: German Intellectuals and the French Revolution*. Columbia, S.C.: Camden House, 1988.

———. "A Peculiar German View of the French Revolution: The Revolution as a German Reformation." In *Aufnahme—Weitergabe. Festschrift für Heinz Moenkemeyer zum 68. Geburtstag*, ed. John A. McCarthy and Albert R. Kipa. Hamburg: Helmut Buske, 1982.

———. *Von der Kopernikanischen bis zur Französischen Revolution: Die Auseinandersetzung der deutschen Frühaufklärung mit der neuen Zeit*. Berlin: E. Schmidt, 1987.

———. "Who's Afraid of Christian Wolff?" In *Anticipations of the Enlightenment in England, France, and Germany*, ed. Alan Charles Kors and Paul J. Korshin. Philadelphia: University of Pennsylvania Press, 1987.

Sauder, Gehard. "Aufklärung des Vorurteils—Vorurteile der Aufklärung." *Deutsche Vierteljahresschrift für Literaturwissenschaft und Geistesgeschichte* 57 (1983): 259–277.

Sauder, Gehard, and Christoph Weiss. *Carl Friedrich Bahrdt (1740–1792)*. St. Ingbert: Werner J. Rohrig, 1992.

Scheel, Heinrich. *Die Begegnung deutscher Aufklärer mit der Revolution*. Berlin: Akademie-Verlag, 1973.

Schlobach, Jochen. "Französische Aufklärung und deutschen Fürsten." *Zeitschrift für historische Forschung* 17 (1990): 327–349.

Schmidt, James. "The Question of Enlightenment: Kant, Mendelssohn, and the Mittwochsgesellschaft." *Journal of the History of Ideas* 50 (1989): 269–291.

———. "What Enlightenment Was: How Moses Mendelssohn and Immanuel Kant Answered the *Berlinische Monatsschrift*." *Journal of the History of Philosophy* 30 (1992): 77–101.

Schmidt-Biggemann, Wilhelm. *Theodizee und Tatsachen: Das philosophische Profil der deutschen Aufklärung*. Frankfurt am Main: Suhrkamp, 1988.

Schneiders, Werner. *Aufklärung und Vorurteilskritik: Studien zur Geschichte der Vorurteilstheorie*. Stuttgart–Bad Cannstatt: Frommann-Holzboog, 1983.

———. *Hoffnung auf Vernunft: Aufklärungsphilosophie in Deutschland*. Hamburg: F. Meiner, 1990.

———. *Die wahre Aufklärung*. Munich: Karl Alber, 1974.

———, ed. *Aufklärung als Mission: Akzeptanzprobleme und Kommunikationsdefizite*. Marburg: Hitzeroth Verlag, 1993.

———, ed. *Christian Wolff 1679–1754*. Hamburg: F. Meiner, 1983.

Schoenborn, Alexander von. "Kant's Philosophy of Religion Reconsidered: Reason, Religion, and the Unfinished Business of the Enlightenment." *Philosophy and Theology* 6 (1991): 101–116.

Schulz, Eberhard Günter. "Kant und die Berliner Aufklärung." In *Akten des 4. Internationalen Kant-Kongresses, Mainz 1974*. Teil II, 1: Sektionen, ed. Gerhard Funke. Berlin: de Gruyter, 1974: 60–80.

Schwartz, Paul. *Der erste Kulturkampf in Preussen um Kirche und Schule, 1778–1798*. Berlin: Weidmann, 1925.

Snow, Dale Evarts. "F. H. Jacobi and the Development of German Idealism." *Journal of the History of Philosophy* 25 (1987): 397–415.

Stuke, Horst. "Aufklärung." In *Geschichtliche Grundbegriffe*, ed. Otto Brunner, Werner Conze, and Reinhart Koselleck, 1:243–342. Stuttgart: Ernst Klett Verlag, 1972.

Timm, Eitel, ed. *Geist und Gesellschaft: Zur deutschen Rezeption der Französischen Revolution*. Munich: Fink, 1990.

Tortarolo, Edoardo. "Zensur, öffentliche Meinung und Politik in der Berliner Spätaufklärung." *Leipziger Beiträge zur Universalgeschichte und vergleichenden Gesellschaftsforschung* 3 (1991): 80–90.

Unger, Rudolf. *Hamann und die Aufklärung: Studien zur Vorgeschichte des romantischen Geistes im 18. Jahrhundert*. Halle: Max Niemeyer Verlag, 1925.

Venturi, Franco. *Utopia and Reform in the Enlightenment*. Cambridge: Cambridge University Press, 1971.

———. "Was ist Aufklärung? Sapere Aude!" In *Europe des lumières*, 39–42. Paris: Mouton, 1971.

Vierhaus, Rudolf. "Aufklärung als Emanzipationsprozess." *Aufklärung* 2 (1987): 9–18.

———. *Deutschland im 18. Jahrhundert. Politische Verfassung, soziales Gefüge, geistige Bewegungen*. Göttingen: Vandenhoeck and Ruprecht, 1987.

———. *Germany in the Age of Absolutism*. Cambridge: Cambridge University Press, 1988.

Voss, Jürgen. "Zur deutschen Aufklärungsdiskussion im späten 18. Jahrhundert." *Innsbrucker Historische Studien* 7–8 (1985): 263–283.

Weis, Eberhard. "Enlightenment and Absolutism in the Holy Roman Empire: Thoughts on Enlightened Absolutism in Germany." *Journal of Modern History* 58, suppl. (1986): s181–s197.

Wellek, Rene. "Between Kant and Fichte: Karl Leonhard Reinhold." *Journal of the History of Ideas* 45 (1984): 323–327.

Whaley, Joachim. "Enlightenment and History in Germany." *Historical Journal* 31 (1988): 195–199.

———. "The Protestant Enlightenment in Germany." In *The Enlightenment in National Context*, ed. Roy Porter and Mikulás Teich. Cambridge: Cambridge University Press, 1981.

Wilson, W. Daniel. "Shades of the Illuminati Conspiracy: Koselleck on Enlightenment and Revolution." In *The Enlightenment and Its Legacy: Studies in German Literature in Honor of Helga Slessarev*, ed. Sara Friedrichsmeyer and Barbara Becker-Cantarino. Bonn: Bouvier, 1991.

Wohlfart, Gunter. "Hamanns Kantkritik." *Kantstudien* 75 (1984): 398–419.

Wolff, Hans Matthias. *Die Weltanschauung der deutschen Aufklärung in geschichtlicher Entwicklung*. Bern: A. Francke, 1949.

III. TWENTIETH-CENTURY DISCUSSIONS OF THE IDEA OF ENLIGHTENMENT

Adorno, Theodor. *Aesthetic Theory*. London: Routledge and Kegan Paul, 1984.

———. "The Culture Industry Reconsidered." *New German Critique* 6 (1975): 12–19.

———. *Erziehung zur Mündigkeit*. Frankfurt am Main: Suhrkamp, 1970.

———. *Minima Moralia*. London: NLB, 1974.

———. *Negative Dialectics*. New York: Seabury, 1973.

———. *Philosophy of Modern Music*. New York: Seabury, 1973.

———. "Theses against Occultism." *Telos* 19 (1974): 7–12.

Albert, Hans. *Aufklärung und Steuerung*. Hamburg: Hoffmann und Campe, 1976.

Améry, Jean. "Enlightenment as Philosophi Perennis." In Améry, *Radical Humanism: Selected Essays*. Bloomington: Indiana University Press, 1984.

Apel, Karl Otto, et al. *Hermeneutik und Ideologiekritik*. Frankfurt am Main: Suhrkamp, 1971.

Barnouw, Dagmar. "Modernity and Enlightenment Thought." In *The Enlightenment and Its Legacy: Studies in German Literature in Honor of Helga Slessarev*, ed. Sara Friedrichsmeyer and Barbara Becker-Cantarino. Bonn: Bouvier, 1991.

Beck, Ulrich, and Wolfgang Bonss, eds. *Weder Sozialtechnologie noch Aufklärung? Analysen zur Verwendung sozialwissenschaftlichen Wissens*. Frankfurt am Main: Suhrkamp, 1989.

Becker-Cantarino, Barbara. "Foucault on Kant: Deconstructing the Enlightenment?" In *The Enlightenment and Its Legacy: Studies in German Literature in Honor of Helga Slessarev*, ed. Sara Friedrichsmeyer and Barbara Becker-Cantarino. Bonn: Bouvier, 1991.

Benhabib, Seyla. *Critique, Norm, and Utopia: A Study of the Foundations of Critical Theory*. New York: Columbia University Press, 1986.

———. "Epistemologies of Postmodernism: A Rejoinder to Jean-François Lyotard." In *Feminism/Postmodernism*, ed. Linda J. Nicholson. New York: Routledge, 1990.

Benhabib, Seyla, Wolfgang Bonss, and John McCole, eds. *On Max Horkheimer*. Cambridge: MIT Press, 1993.

Benhabib, Seyla, and Drucilla Cornell, eds. *Feminism as Critique*. Minneapolis: University of Minnesota Press, 1987.

Benjamin, Jessica. "The End of Internalization: Adorno's Social Psychology." *Telos* 32 (1977): 42–64.

Bennett, Jane. *Unthinking Faith and Enlightenment: Nature and the State in a Post-Hegelian Era*. New York: New York University Press, 1987.

Bernstein, Richard J. "The Rage Against Reason." *Philosophy and Literature* 10 (1986): 186–210.

———, ed. *Habermas and Modernity*. Cambridge: MIT Press, 1985.

Bittner, Rüdiger. *What Reason Demands*. Cambridge: Cambridge University Press, 1989.

Bleicher, Josef, ed. *Contemporary Hermeneutics: Hermeneutics as Method, Philosophy, and Critique*. London: Routledge and Kegan Paul, 1980.

Blumenberg, Hans. *The Legitimacy of the Modern Age*. Cambridge: MIT Press, 1983.

Böhme, Gernot, and Hartmut Böhme. *Das Andere der Vernunft: Zur Entwicklung von Rationalitätsstrukturen am Beispiel Kants*. Frankfurt am Main: Suhrkamp, 1985.

Braaten, Jane. *Habermas's Critical Theory of Society*. Albany: State University of New York Press, 1991.

Bubner, Rüdiger. "Theory and Practice in Light of the Hermeneutic-Criticist Controversy." *Cultural Hermeneutics* 2 (1975): 337–352.

Buhler, Axel, ed. *Unzeitgemässe Hermeneutik: Verstehen und Interpretation im Denken der Aufklärung*. Frankfurt am Main: Vittorio Klostermann, 1994.

Cochetti, Stefano. *Mythos und Dialektik der Aufklärung*. Königstein/Ts.: A. Hain, 1985.

Connerton, Paul. *The Tragedy of Enlightenment: An Essay on the Frankfurt School*. Cambridge: Cambridge University Press, 1980.

Cook, Deborah. "Remapping Modernity." *British Journal of Aesthetics* 30 (1990): 35–45.

Dallmayr, Fred. "The Discourse of Modernity: Hegel and Habermas." *Journal of Philosophy* 84 (1987): 682–692.

Dejung, Christoph. "Für Voltaire: Bemerkungen zum gleichnamigen Fragment im Anhang der *Dialektik der Aufklärung* von Horkheimer und Adorno." *Studia Philosophica* 51 (1992): 183–202.

Depew, David J. "The Habermas–Gadamer Debate in Hegelian Perspective." *Philosophy and Social Criticism* 8 (1981): 425–446.

Dews, Peter. *Logics of Disintegration: Post-Structuralist Thought and the Claims of Critical Theory*. New York: Verso, 1987.

DiStefano, Christine. "Dilemmas of Difference: Feminism, Modernity, Postmodernity." *Women & Politics* 8 (1988): 1–24.

Donougho, Martin. "The Cunning of Odysseus: A Theme in Hegel, Lukács, and Adorno." *Philosophy and Social Criticism* 8 (1981): 11–43.

Doody, John A. "MacIntyre and Habermas on Practical Reason." *American Catholic Philosophical Quarterly* 65 (1991): 143–158.

Dreyfus, Hubert L., and Paul Rabinow. "What is Maturity? Habermas and Foucault on 'What is Enlightenment?' " In *Foucault: A Critical Reader*, ed. David Couzens Hoy. Oxford: Basil Blackwell, 1986.

Dubiel, Helmut. *Theory and Politics: Studies in the Development of Critical Theory*. Cambridge: MIT Press, 1985.

Erdmann, Eva, Rainer Forst, and Axel Honneth, eds. *Ethos der Moderne: Foucaults Kritik der Aufklärung*. New York: Campus, 1990.

Figal, Gunter. "Selbsterhaltung und Selbstverzicht: Zur Kritik der Neuzeitlichen Subjektivität bei Max Horkheimer und Walter Benjamin." *Zeitschrift für philosophische Forschung* 37 (1983): 161–180.

Flax, Jane. *Thinking Fragments: Psychoanalysis, Feminism, and Postmodernism in the Contemporary West*. Berkeley and Los Angeles: University of California Press, 1989.

Foucault, Michel. "About the Beginnings of a Hermeneutics of the Self." *Political Theory* 21 (1993): 198–227.

———. *Discipline and Punish*. New York: Vintage Books, 1979.

———. "Kant on Enlightenment and Revolution." *Economy and Society* 15 (1986): 88–96.

———. *Madness and Civilization: A History of Insanity in the Age of Reason*. New York: Vintage Books, 1973.

———. *The Order of Things*. New York: Vintage, 1970.

———. "What Is Enlightenment?" In Paul Rabinow, ed., *The Foucault Reader*. New York: Pantheon Books, 1984.

Fraser, Nancy. *Unruly Practices*. Minneapolis: University of Minnesota Press, 1989.

Freundlieb, Dieter. "Rationalism v. Irrationalism? Habermas's Response to Foucault." *Inquiry* 31 (1988): 171–192.

Gadamer, Hans-Georg. *Philosophical Hermeneutics*. Berkeley and Los Angeles: University of California Press, 1976.

———. *Reason in the Age of Science*. Cambridge: MIT Press, 1981.

———. *Truth and Method*, 2d rev. ed. New York: Continuum, 1989.

Gall, Robert S. "Between Tradition and Critique." *Auslegung* 8 (1981): 5–18.

Gay, Peter. *The Bridge of Criticism; Dialogues among Lucian, Erasmus, and Voltaire on the Enlightenment—On History and Hope, Imagination and Reason, Constraint and Freedom—and On Its Meaning for Our Time*. New York: Harper and Row, 1970.

Geuss, Raymond. *The Idea of a Critical Theory: Habermas and the Frankfurt School*. Cambridge: Cambridge University Press, 1981.

Giurlanda, Paul. "Habermas' Critique of Gadamer: Does it Stand Up?" *International Philosophical Quarterly* 27 (1987): 33–41.

Gordon, Colin. "Question, Ethos, Event: Foucault on Kant and Enlightenment." *Economy and Society* 15 (1986): 71–87.

Grass, Gunter, et al. *Der Traum der Vernunft: Vom Elend der Aufklärung*. Darmstadt: Luchterhand, 1985.

Grimminger, Rolf. *Die Ordnung, das Chaos und die Kunst: Für eine neue Dialektik der Aufklärung*. Frankfurt am Main: Suhrkamp, 1986.

Guillemot, Jean-Louis. "L'Evolution de la critique de l'hermeneutique chez Habermas." *Eidos* 11 (1993): 55–75.

Gunter, Klaus. "Dialektik der Aufklärung in der Idee der Freiheit: Zur Kritik des

Freiheitsbegriffs bei Adorno." *Zeitschrift für philosophische Forschung* 39 (1985): 229–260.

Habermas, Jürgen. *Knowledge and Human Interests.* Boston: Beacon, 1971.

———. "Modernity versus Post-Modernity." *New German Critique* 22 (1981): 3–14.

———. *The New Conservatism.* Cambridge: MIT Press, 1989.

———. *The Philosophical Discourse of Modernity.* Cambridge: MIT Press, 1987.

———. *The Structural Transformation of the Public Sphere.* Cambridge: MIT Press, 1989.

———. "Taking Aim at the Heart of the Present: On Foucault's Lecture on Kant's *What is Enlightenment?*" In *Critique and Power: Recasting the Foucault-Habermas Debate,* ed. Michael Kelly. Cambridge: MIT Press, 1994.

———. *The Theory of Communicative Action.* 2 vols. Boston: Beacon, 1984, 1987.

Habermas, Jürgen, and Niklas Luhmann. *Theorie der Gesellschaft oder Sozial Technologie—Was leist die Systemforschung?* Frankfurt am Main: Suhrkamp, 1971.

Hampe, Johann Christoph. *Ehre und Elend der Aufklärung gestern wie heute: Ein engagierter Vergleich.* Munich: Kaiser, 1971.

Harding, Sandra. "Feminism, Science, and the Anti-Enlightenment Critiques." In *Feminism/Postmodernism,* ed. Linda J. Nicholson. New York: Routledge, 1990.

Harpham, Geoffrey Galt. "So . . . What 'Is' Enlightenment? An Inquisition into Modernity." *Critical Inquiry* 20 (1994): 524–556.

Hasenclever, Volker F. W., ed. *Denken als Widerspruch: Plädoyers gegen die Irrationalität oder ist Vernunft nicht mehr gefragt? Reden zum Lessing-Preis.* Frankfurt am Main: Eichborn Verlag, 1982.

Hastedt, Heiner. *Aufklärung und Technik: Grundprobleme einer Ethik der Technik.* Frankfurt am Main: Suhrkamp, 1991.

Held, David. *Introduction to Critical Theory: Horkheimer to Habermas.* Berkeley and Los Angeles: University of California Press, 1980.

Hiley, David R. "Foucault and the Question of Enlightenment." *Philosophy and Social Criticism* 11 (1985): 63–84.

Hjort, Anne Meete. "The Conditions of Dialogue: Approaches to the Habermas–Gadamer Debate." *Eidos* 4 (1985): 11–37.

Hodge, Joanna. "Habermas and Foucault: Contesting Rationality." *Irish Philosophical Journal* 7 (1990): 60–78.

Hohendahl, Peter Uwe. "The *Dialectic of Enlightenment* Revisited: Habermas's Critique of the Frankfurt School." *New German Critique* 35 (1985): 3–26.

Holub, Robert C. "The Enlightenment of Dialectic: Jürgen Habermas's Critique of the Frankfurt School." In *Impure Reason: Dialectic of Enlightenment in Germany,* ed. W. Daniel Wilson and Robert C. Holub. Detroit: Wayne State University Press, 1993.

———. *Jürgen Habermas: Critic in the Public Sphere.* London: Routledge, 1991.

Honneth, Axel. "Enlightenment and Rationality." *Journal of Philosophy* 84 (1987): 692–699.

Horkheimer, Max. *Between Philosophy and Social Science: Selected Early Writings.* Cambridge: MIT Press, 1993.

———. *Critical Theory.* New York: Herder and Herder, 1972.

———. *Dawn and Decline: Notes 1926–1931 and 1950–1969.* New York: Seabury, 1978.

———. "The End of Reason." In *The Essential Frankfurt School Reader*, ed. Andrew Arato and Eike Gebhardt. New York: Urizen Books, 1978.

———. "Kants Philosophie und die Aufklärung." In Horkheimer, *Zur Kritik der instrumentellen Vernunft*. Frankfurt am Main: Fischer, 1967.

Horkheimer, Max, and Theodor W. Adorno. *Dialectic of Enlightenment*. New York: Herder and Herder, 1972.

How, Alan R. "A Case of Creative Misreading: Habermas's Evolution of Gadamer's Hermeneutics." *Journal of the British Society for Phenomenology* 16 (1985): 132–144.

———. "Dialogue as Productive Limitation in Social Theory: The Habermas–Gadamer Debate." *Journal of the British Society for Phenomenology* 11 (1980): 131–143.

Huelsmann, Heinrich. "Hermeneutik und Dialektik: Kritische Betrachtungen zur Theologie und Aufklärung." *Zeitschrift für philosophische Forschung* 25 (1971): 98–108.

Ingram, David. *Habermas and the Dialectic of Reason*. New Haven: Yale University Press.

Jay, Martin. *The Dialectical Imagination: A History of the Frankfurt School and the Institute of Social Research, 1923–1950*. Boston: Little, Brown, 1973.

Johnson, Pauline. "Feminism and the Enlightenment." *Radical Philosophy* 63 (1993): 3–12.

Kaiser, Volker. "Poeticizing the Enlightenment: The Case of Richard Rorty and Kant's Question." In *Impure Reason: Dialectic of Enlightenment in Germany*, ed. W. Daniel Wilson and Robert C. Holub. Detroit: Wayne State University Press, 1993.

Kayser, Martina. "Walter Benjamin: Aberglaube, Aufklärung, und Theologie." *Tijdschrift voor de Studie van de Verlichting en van het Vrije Denken* 12 (1984): 129–136.

Kelly, Michael. "The Gadamer–Habermas Debate Revisited: The Question of Ethics." *Philosophy and Social Criticism* 14 (1988): 369–389.

———, ed. *Hermeneutics and Critical Theory in Ethics and Politics*. Cambridge: MIT Press, 1990.

Kneller, Jane. "Discipline and Silence: Women and Imagination in Kant's Theory of Taste." In *Aesthetics in Feminist Perspective*, ed. Hilde Hein and Carolyn Korsmeyer. Bloomington: Indiana University Press, 1993.

———. "Kant's Immature Imagination." In *Modern Engendering: Critical Feminist Readings in Modern Western Philosophy*, ed. Bat Ami Bar-on. Albany: State University of New York Press, 1994.

Kolakowski, Leszek. "The Idolatry of Politics." *Atlantic Community Quarterly* 24 (1986): 219–230.

Kortian, Garbis. *Metacritique: The Philosophical Argument of Jürgen Habermas*. Cambridge: Cambridge University Press, 1980.

Kulke, Christine, and Elvira Scheich, eds. *Zwielicht der Vernunft: Die Dialektik der Aufklärung aus der Sicht von Frauen*. Pfaffenweiler: Centaurus, 1992.

Kunneman, Harry, and Hent de Vries, eds. *Die Aktualität der Dialektik der Aufklärung zwischen Moderne und Postmoderne*. Frankfurt am Main: Campus-Verlag, 1989.

Landmann, Michael. "Critiques of Reason from Weber to Bloch." *Telos* 29 (1976): 187–198.

Lovenich, Friedhelm. *Paradigmenwechsel: Über die Dialektik der Aufklärung in der revidierten Kritischen Theorie.* Wurzburg: Koenigshausen, 1990.

Lowenthal, Leo. *Critical Theory and Frankfurt Theorists: Lectures, Correspondence, Conversations.* New Brunswick, N.J.: Transaction Books, 1989.

Luhmann, Niklas. *Soziologische Aufklärung.* 4 vols. Cologne: Westdeustscher Verlag, 1970–1987.

Lübbe, Hermann. *Philosophie nach der Aufklärung: von der Notwendigkeit pragmatischer Vernunft.* Dusseldorf: Econ Verlag, 1980.

Lyotard, Jean-François. *The Postmodern Condition.* Minneapolis: University of Minnesota Press, 1984.

MacIntyre, Alasdair. *After Virtue.* Notre Dame: University of Notre Dame Press, 1981.

———. *Three Rival Versions of Moral Inquiry: Encyclopedia, Genealogy, and Tradition.* Notre Dame: University of Notre Dame Press, 1990.

———. *Whose Justice? Which Rationality?* Notre Dame: University of Notre Dame Press, 1988.

Mahon, Michael. "Michel Foucault's Archaeology, Enlightenment, and Critique." *Human Studies* 16 (1993): 129–141.

Marcuse, Ludwig. "Einige Aufklärungen." *Club Voltaire* 2 (1965): 13–33.

McCarthy, John A. "*Verständigung* and *Dialektik*: On Consensus Theory and the Dialectic of Enlightenment." In *Impure Reason: Dialectic of Enlightenment in Germany*, ed. W. Daniel Wilson and Robert C. Holub. Detroit: Wayne State University Press, 1993.

McCarthy, Thomas. *The Critical Theory of Jürgen Habermas.* Cambridge: MIT Press, 1978.

———. *Ideals and Illusions: On Reconstruction and Deconstruction in Contemporary Critical Theory.* Cambridge: MIT Press, 1991.

Mendelson, Jack. "The Habermas–Gadamer Debate." *New German Critique* 18 (1979): 44–73.

Misgeld, Dieter. "Discourse and Conversation: The Theory of Communicative Competence and Hermeneutics in the Light of the Debate between Habermas and Gadamer." *Cultural Hermeneutics* 4 (1977): 321–344.

Mittelstrass, Jürgen. *Neuzeit und Aufklärung.* Berlin: de Gruyter, 1970.

Nägele, Rainer. "Public Voice and Private Voice: Freud, Habermas, and the Dialectic of Enlightenment." In Nägele, *Reading after Freud.* New York: Columbia University Press, 1989.

Norris, Christopher. "What Is Enlightenment? Kant and Foucault." In *The Cambridge Companion to Foucault*, ed. Gary Gutting. Cambridge: Cambridge University Press, 1994.

Nuyen, A. T. "Adorno and the French Post-Structuralists on the Other of Reason." *Journal of Speculative Philosophy* (1990): 310–322.

Owen, David. *Maturity and Modernity: Nietzsche, Weber, Foucault and the Ambivalence of Reason.* New York: Routledge, 1994.

Palmer, L. M. "Gadamer and the Enlightenment's Prejudice Against all Prejudices." *Clio* 22 (1993): 369–376.

Putnam, Hilary. *The Many Faces of Realism.* LaSalle, Ill.: Open Court, 1987.

Rabinbach, Anson. "Between Enlightenment and the Apocalypse: Benjamin, Bloch, and Modern German Jewish Messianism." *New German Critique* 34 (1985): 78–124.

Racevskis, Karlis. *Postmodernism and the Search for Enlightenment.* Charlottesville: University Press of Virginia, 1993.

———. "A Return to 'The Heavenly City': Carl Becker's Paradox in a Structuralist Perspective." *Clio* 8 (1979): 165–174.

Rajchman, John. "Habermas' Complaint." In *Philosophical Events: Essays of the '80s.* New York: Columbia University Press, 1991.

Reckermann, Alfons. "Die 'Schuld' der Form und Möglichkeiten ihrer Kompensation: Überlegungen zur Kritik der Rationalität bei Horkheimer und Adorno." *Zeitschrift für philosophische Forschung* 42 (1988): 417–432.

Reijen, Willem van, and Gunzelin Schmid Noerr, eds. *Vierzig Jahre Flaschenpost: "Dialektik der Aufklärung," 1947–1987.* Frankfurt am Main: Fischer, 1987.

Rocco, Christopher. "Between Modernity and Postmodernity: Reading *Dialectic of Enlightenment* Against the Grain." *Political Theory* 22 (1994): 71–97.

Rooney, Phyllis A. "Recent Work in Feminist Discussions of Reason." *American Philosophical Quarterly* 31 (1994): 1–21.

Rorty, Richard. *Consequences of Pragmatism: Essays, 1972–1980.* Minneapolis: University of Minnesota Press, 1982.

———. *Contingency, Irony, and Solidarity.* Cambridge: Cambridge University Press, 1989.

———. *Essays on Heidegger and Others.* Cambridge: Cambridge University Press, 1991.

———. *Objectivity, Relativism, and Truth.* Cambridge: Cambridge University Press, 1991.

———. *Philosophy and the Mirror of Nature.* Princeton: Princeton University Press, 1979.

Ruddick, Sara. "New Feminist Work on Knowledge, Reason and Objectivity." *Hypatia* 8 (1993): 140–149.

Rudolph, Werner. *Auf der Suche nach dem verlorenen Sinn: Die* Dialektik der Aufklärung *im System der Kritischen Theorie und ihr Verhältnis zur philosophischen Tradition.* Berlin: Schelzky and Jeep, 1992.

Rumble, Vanessa. "Sacrifice and Domination: Kantian and Kierkegaardian Paradigms of Self-Overcoming." *Philosophy and Social Criticism* 20 (1994): 19–35.

Rüsen, Jorn, Eberhard Lämmert, and Peter Glotz, eds. *Die Zukunft der Aufklärung.* Frankfurt am Main: Suhrkamp, 1988.

Schmid Noerr, Gunzelin. *Das Eingedenken der Natur im Subjekt: Zur Dialektik von Vernunft und Natur in der kritischen Theorie Horkheimers, Adornos und Marcuses.* Darmstadt: Wissenschaftliche Buchgesellschaft, 1990.

———, ed. *Metamorphosen der Aufklärung: Vernunftkritik heute.* Tübingen: Diskord, 1988.

Schmidt, Jochen, ed. *Aufklärung und Gegenaufklärung in der europäischen Literatur, Philosophie und Politik von der Antike bis zur Gegenwart.* Darmstadt: Wissenschaftliche Buchgesellschaft, 1989.

Schmidt, James. "Habermas on Foucault." In *Habermas and the Unfinished Project of Modernity: Critical Essays on* The Philosophical Discourse of Modernity, ed. Maurizio Passerin D'Entreves. Cambridge: Polity Press, 1996.

———. "Jürgen Habermas and the Difficulties of Enlightenment." *Social Research* 49 (1982): 181–208.

Schmidt, James, and Thomas E. Wartenberg. "Foucault's Enlightenment: Critique, Revolution, and the Fashioning of the Self. In *Critique and Power: Recasting the Foucault–Habermas Debate*, ed. Michael Kelly. Cambridge: MIT Press, 1994.

Schott, Robin May. *Cognition and Eros: A Critique of the Kantian Paradigm.* Boston: Beacon Press, 1988.

———. "Rereading the Canon: Kantian Purity and the Suppression of Eros." In *Modern Engendering: Critical Feminist Readings in Modern Western Philosophy*, ed. Bat Ami Bar-on. Albany: State University of New York Press, 1994.

Silverman, Hugh J., ed. *Gadamer and Hermeneutics.* New York: Routledge, 1991.

Sloterdijk, Peter. *Critique of Cynical Reason.* Minneapolis: University of Minnesota Press, 1987.

Strasser, Peter. *Die verspielte Aufklärung.* Frankfurt am Main: Suhrkamp, 1986.

Strickland, Susan. "Feminism, Postmodernism, and Difference." In *Knowing the Difference: Feminist Perspectives in Epistemology*, ed. Kathleen Lennon and Margaret Whitford. New York: Routledge, 1994.

Thompson, John B., and David Held. *Habermas: Critical Debates.* Cambridge: MIT Press, 1982.

Todorov, Tzvetan. "The Deflection of the Enlightenment." *Partisan Review* 56 (1989): 581–592.

Wacherhauser, Brice R. "Prejudice, Reason, and Force." *Philosophy* 63 (1988): 231–252.

Walravens, Else. "Confrontation du concept d'Aufklärung de Horkheimer et Adorno et de celui de l'Aufklärung allemande." *Tijdschrift voor de Studie van de Verlichting en van het Vrije Denken* 12 (1984): 49–68.

Warnke, Georgia. *Gadamer: Hermeneutics, Tradition, and Reason.* Stanford: Stanford University Press, 1987.

Wellmer, Albrecht. *The Persistence of Modernity: Essays on Aesthetics, Ethics, and Postmodernism.* Cambridge: MIT Press, 1991.

White, Stephen K. "Foucault's Challenge to Critical Theory." *American Political Science Review* 80 (1986): 419–432.

———. *The Recent Work of Jürgen Habermas: Reason, Justice, and Modernity.* Cambridge: Cambridge University Press, 1988.

Wiggershaus, Rolf. *The Frankfurt School: Its History, Theories, and Political Significance.* Cambridge: MIT Press, 1994.

Wilson, Neil. "Punching Out the Enlightenment: A Discussion of Peter Sloterdijk's *Kritik der zynischen Vernunft. New German Critique* 41 (1987): 53–70.

Wokler, Robert. "Projecting the Enlightenment." In *After MacIntyre*, ed. John Horton. Notre Dame: University of Notre Dame Press, 1994.

Wolin, Richard. "Critical Theory and the Dialectic of Rationalism." *New German Critique* 41 (1987): 23–53.

Zöller, Michael, ed. *Aufklärung heute: Bedingungen unserer Freiheit.* Zürich: Edition Interfrom, 1980.

INDEX

Abbt, Thomas, 56n
Absolutism: checks on, 96n; enlightened, 13, 322 (*see also* Despotism, enlightened); and reform, 243–244, 245, 247–248, 336
Adorno, Theodor W., 20–21, 23–24, 28–29, 271, 354, 403, 405, 410, 419, 471, 479, 483n, 508
Aesthetic(s): education, 322, 325; in German idealism, 375; judgment, 526–529; Kant's theory of, 460–463; and self-creation, 507, 512
Agreement: and certainty, 104; intersubjectivity of, 30, 415
Alembert, Jean Le Rond D', 434, 436
Allgemeine Deutsche Bibliothek, 9, 237, 256
Allison, Henry E., 7–8
Amalthea, 270
American Revolution, 14, 177, 338
Améry, Jean, 16
Apel, Karl Otto, 415
Appearances: Kant's treatment of, 165n, 407, 467n; in metaphysical thought, 402, 405, 420; vs. the thing in itself, 141n, 439
Appius, Fabius, 204–205
Aristotle, 12, 170; on dreams, 433, 438
Arnauld, Antoine, 449
Atalhuapa, 180
Athenäum, 319, 322
Aufklärung. *See* Enlightenment
Augustine, Saint, 409
Authenticity, 500–503, 512
Authority: and enlightenment, 19, 174, 181, 213, 295, 335; idea of critique and, 385; and judgment, 98–99, 104, 106, 347; and maturity, 369, 386, 492–493; obedience to, 106, 217, 309, 471, 482, 489; political, 15, 131, 197, 280, 517; and women, 473
Autonomy: and enlightenment, 225–226, 492–497; feminist discussions of, 472–473, 480–482; Foucault on, 503–508; Habermas' account of, 509–512; individuality and, 364–365, 376–378, 497–499, 500–502; Kantian conception of, 489–492, 495–496; as moral concept, 492, 499–501; rationality and, 375–376, 380, 500

Bachelard, Gaston, 390
Bacon, Sir Francis, 333, 364
Bahrdt, Carl Friedrich, 7–8, 10
Baudelaire, Charles, 27
Bauer, Edgar, 39n
Bayer, Ostwald, 299
Bayle, Pierre, 436
Beautiful: Kant's account of, 460–462, 466, 470n, 522–523; and the sublime, 523–524
Becker, Rudolf Zacharias, 51n, 271, 273, 277–278, 280
Beethoven, Ludwig van, 43n
Beneke, Friedrich Wilhelm von, 240
Benhabib, Seyla, 479–480
Bentham, Jeremy, 28
Bergk, Johann Adam, 14
Berkeley, George, 154
Berlinische Monatschrift, 2–6, 9, 12, 29, 239–240, 247, 256, 258, 263, 271, 336, 496
Bestimmung des Menschen, 56n, 508. *See also* Destiny of man
Biblical criticism, 7, 69

Biester, Johann Erich, 6, 239–241, 246, 263
Bildung: and aesthetic education, 321–322; vs. culture, 53; degrees of, 494; and enlightenment, 53, 67; Hegel on, 21; misuse of, 56; and morality, politics, and religion, 324; and radical criticism, 325; and social and political change, 322. *See also* Culture; Education
Bloch, Ernst, 405, 426
Borowski, L. E., 439, 449
Bourgeois(ie): vs. citizen, 22–23; "dark writers" of, 27; and enlightenment, 339, 450; petit, 274
Bourgignon, Antonia, 437
Boussuet, Jacques, 219
Brandes, Ernst, 338
Bräß, Hermann, 278
Bräker, Ulrich, 282
Burke, Edmund: on French Revolution, 16, 21–22, 27–28; on tradition and prejudice, 17–19, 28
Büchsel, Elfriede, 294
Bürger, meaning of, 257

Cagliostro, Alessandro, 435
Cajamarca, 180
Calderón de la Barca, Pedro, 432
Calvin, John, 180
Campe, Joachim Heinrich, 494
Canguilhem, Georges, 390
Castillon, Friederich von, 271, 277
Catholicism, 74, 89, 155, 274, 278
Censorship: under Frederick II, 91–92; by the Vatican, 72–73; Wednesday Society discussion of, 4–6, 243–244, 272–273; Woellner's edict on, 9–10. *See also* Freedom, of expression; of the press
Charles I [King of England], 180, 309
Charles IX [King of France], 173
Châtelet, Emilie du, 475, 477
Christianity: Enlightenment interpretations of, 7–8, 172, 179, 183–184; and metaphysics, 442; and Prussian state, 6
Christman, John, 501
Cicero, Marcus Tullius, 72, 254
Citizen(s): duties of, 60–61; as end in itself, 222, 495; enlightenment of, 2, 10–11, 14, 49, 55, 102; free agreement of, 372–373; in Hegel, 23
Civil liberties, 476, 518, 524
Civil servants, 178, 257
Civil society: establishment of, 125–126; in Hegel, 22; purpose of, 194, 198–199; romantic critique of, 320
Civilization: as art of dissimulation, 447; industrial, 376; as moral appearance, 460; scientific and technical, 359–360, 369
Clergy: in Berlin, 7, 9, 240; as civil servants, 257, 259, 278–279, 296; and enlightenment, 50, 59, 179–180, 296; and freedom of conscience, 60–62, 99–100, 106, 122; threats posed by ignorance of, 73–74, 171–175, 180–183, 219
Cognition: a priori and a posteriori, 439; faculties of, 404, 437, 439; and image, 427; powers of, 228, 458, 461; subject of, 374
College of Cardinals, 72
Common man: deception of, 50, 271; enlightenment of, 273–283; ideas of, 68–69, 116; improvement of, 117; religious beliefs of, 10; superstitions of, 242
Communication: education as, 128; right to, 104, 127
Communicative action, 417, 421
Community: consensus of and authenticity, 502–503; and free expression, 30; and happiness, 197; linguistic, 415; and virtue, 312
Comte, August, 505
Concept(s): empirical, 458; enlightenment as clarification of, 65–72, 81, 98; metaphysical, 404; primordial image and, 402; reason and, 155–158; and rights, 228; truth and, 129–131, 174, 362
Condorcet, Marie-Jean-Antoine-Nicolas, Marquis de, 334
Conscience: direction of, 383; moral, 182, 230–231; right of, 128–129, 175, 227, 372
Consciousness: enlightened, 378–380; historical, 409–411; and the sensible, 454; transcendental vs. empirical, 374, 456–458
Constitution: democratic vs. monarchical, 210n; enlightenment and improvement of, 121, 177, 222, 227–229; reform of Prussian, 245–247, 339; religious, 61; republican, 15, 336; of self, 504; and virtue, 314
Contracts, 125, 132, 246. *See also* Social contract
Cosmology, 402
Cosmopolitan(ism): chiliasm, 146–147, 295; duties of, 520–521; Kant's ideal of, 518–521; and universal rights, 527, 529–530, 531–532; society, 5, 60; and the sublime, 531
Cranz, August Friedrich, 120
Crell, Nikolaus, 180
Critique: age of, 16; attitude of, 382–387; and enlightenment, 371–373, 398; of ideology, 405; of metaphysics and materialism, 421; public, 59–61, 82, 262–266, 371, 497; romantic, 322–325
Crusius, Christian August, 438, 453
Culture: and civilization, 447; and enlightenment, 53–54, 56, 226, 366, 493, 497; in

Hegel, 21–22; intellectual, 229; and morality, 219; national, 54, 223; rational, 66–67, 70; and senses, 229, 529
Curtius, Marcus, 116

Deception: and dissimulation, 446–447; by elites, 501; and enlightenment, 174, 215; of judges, 179; of the people, 50, 184, 272; and religion, 181–183; by ruler, 175, 177–178
Delameau, Jean, 279–280
Derrida, Jacques, 404, 418, 472
Descartes, Rene, 75n, 333, 432–433, 491–492
Despotism: ecclesiastical, 6, 89, 155, 175; enlightened, 308–310, 313; forms of, 200, 311; vs. freedom, 200–202; and revolution, 13, 15, 59, 227
Destiny of man, 53–55, 57n, 61, 128, 218, 493–494
Deutsches Museum, 307–308
Dilthey, Wilhelm, 393
Dieterich, Johann Samuel, 36n, 238, 243
Dohm, Christian Wilhelm von, 237, 241, 244, 273
Dominican order, 171, 184n
Döderlein, Christian Albrecht, 181
Dreams, 432–434
Duty: aristocratic, 245; of citizens, 275; internal vs. external, 128; of mankind, 229; moral, 133, 182; and rights, 125, 136–137, 227–228; of subjects, 176; of writers, 230

Eberhard, Johann August, 8, 327n
Ecclesiastical Department (Prussia), 237, 239, 250n
Education: of peasantry, 276; popular, 238, 273 (*see also* Enlightenment, popular); reform of, 50, 276; of women, 474, 485n. *See also* Bildung
Ego: identity of, 402–403, 424n; isolated, 481; shrinkage of, 365; transcendental and empirical, 408
Eichhorn, Johann Gottfried, 181
Empedocles, 361
Emser, Hieronymus, 172
Encyclopédistes, 361
Engel, Johann Jacob, 237, 241
Enlighteners (*Aufklärer*): criticism of, 9; true and false, 172, 213
Enlightenment: age of, 16, 62, 335, 369, 371, 436; in Austria, 11, 74; and authority, 19, 335; and autonomy, 379, 492; Berlin, 3, 6, 12, 13, 239; and *Bildung*, 53, 67, 218–219; and censorship, 4–6, 10, 73, 243–244, 272–273; of citizen, 2, 10–11, 14, 49, 55, 103; consequences of, 4, 24, 54, 215, 340, 353, 366–367, 437, 443, 567; as courage to use one's own understanding, 58–59, 226, 348–349, 387–388, 471; criticisms of, 1–2, 6–7, 9, 16–20, 22–25, 26–29, 172, 176, 352–356, 436–437, 472–473; as critique, 322, 351–352, 371, 388, 392, 398; critique of prejudices, 4–5, 7–8, 49, 55, 59, 82, 174–176, 181, 236, 270, 325; and culture, 53–54, 56, 226, 366, 493, 497; dangers of, 21, 24, 56, 174, 183, 213, 273, 291, 310, 353; vs. darkness and obscurity, 79–82; as development of capacity for rationality, 65–66; and domination, 20, 25–27, 295, 338, 393; as exit from immaturity, 58, 291–294, 302–303, 340, 345–349, 368–370, 379–380, 386–387, 492–493; and faith, 2, 23, 73, 381; feminist critique of, 472–473, 480–483; and freedom, 21, 59, 82, 213, 314, 357; French, 360–362, 388–389, 473; German vs. English terms for, 349; Hamann's critique of, 291–303; and happiness, 215, 317, 494; as intellectual power, 212–213; Jacobi's critique of, 306–314; limits of, 4–6, 24, 80, 174, 270; material vs. formal, 225–229; and modernity, 331, 391, 497; as modification of social life, 53–54; and mythology, 23–24, 365–366; and politics, 12–13, 50–51, 62–63, 174–179, 192, 212–215, 218–220, 223–224, 227–229, 277–279, 313–314, 339–341; popular, 68–69, 270–283; and religion, 8–9, 60–63, 171–174, 179–184, 214–215, 302–303; as a requirement of human understanding, 169–174; as process, 66, 242, 345, 371; and progress, 20, 26, 61, 139, 183, 217–218, 296, 321, 512; and reason, 66, 219, 242, 373–374, 450, 471–472; and revolutions, 11–15, 21, 25–26, 59, 121–122, 177–178, 217–231, 330–331, 334–335, 337–338, 520; romantic critique of, 317–326, 351; as thinking for oneself, 97–98; "true" vs. "false," 14, 147, 213–215, 219–220, 270, 494; and truth, 81, 353, 374; and utility, 174, 494, 497; Wednesday Society's conception of, 241–244: women and, 58, 471–483
Enthusiasm, 282, 435, 440–441, 456, 462–466, 470n
Erhard, Christian Daniel, 270, 272
Error(s): causes of, 50, 70, 139, 183, 184; consequences of, 71, 115, 221, 243; and politics, 135, 177, 192, 260; removal of, 61, 130, 192; vs. truth, 129–130, 207, 236; "useful," 4
Ewald, Johann Ludwig, 116, 275

Fabius, Quintus, 206
Faith: and enlightenment, 2, 23, 73, 381; and reason, 12–13, 301–303, 310, 323, 336, 359–360
Fanaticism: and enthusiasm, 464; false enlightenment as, 215; in politics, 218–219, 365; struggle of enlightenment against, 7–9, 435–437
Fast, Patritius, 74–75, 76n, 77n
Febronius, Justinus, 191, 209n, 307
Feinberg, Joel, 501–502, 505
Fenelon, François, 219
Ferdinand, Karl Wilhelm, 278
Ferguson, Adam, 198, 310, 312, 314
Feuerbach, Ludwig, 374
Feyerabend, Paul, 413
Fichte, Johann Gottlieb, 10, 326, 347, 454
Fincklestein, Karl Wilhelm Finck von, 175
Fischer, Kuno, 437
Flax, Jane, 472
Flögel, Carl Friedrich, 148
Foucault, Michel: on autonomy, 503–508, 510–511; on enlightenment, 26–28, 472; on madness, 450; and Nietzsche, 26, 497, 506
Francis I [King of France], 51
Frankfurt School, 22–23, 388–389, 391, 471, 505, 508–512. *See also* Adorno; Habermas; Horkheimer
Frederick II [King of Prussia]: on censorship, 3–4, 59, 62–63, 87–93, 105–106, 268, 387; on German language, 50, 271–272; Hamann's view of, 294–298; Kant's view of, 295–296; policies of, 171, 178, 277; on religion, 50, 62, 272; Voltaire's view on, 294–295
Frederick William II [King of Prussia]: and censorship, 8–9, 105–106, 258; and Kant, 10, 259; religious faith of, 7, 10, 259; and Woellner, 6–7
Freedom: and enlightenment, 59–63, 176, 225–226; of expression, 4–6, 10, 29–30, 100–108, 126–139, 298, 518; as independence, 375–377; of individual, 22–23; political, 63, 93, 173–176, 192–209, 311–314; of the press, 87–93, 100–112, 114–117, 257–267 (*see also* Censorship); of thought, 63, 89–92, 99–100, 121–123, 146, 247, 263, 372
French Revolution: and enlightenment, 11–12, 15–16, 21, 218–219, 228, 330–331, 334–335, 337–338; German response to, 13–14, 263; Hegel on, 21–22; Kant's view of, 14–15, 371–372, 463–464, 518–520; romantic critique of, 320–322; and Terror, 11, 22, 330–332, 337–339
Freud, Sigmund, 26, 377, 403, 479
Friends of Enlightenment, Society of. *See* Wednesday Society

Gadamer, Hans-Georg, 18–20, 28–29, 416
Gaismair, Michael, 275
Galileo, 69, 170, 179
Garve, Christian, 237, 283
Gebhard, Johann Georg, 240
Gedike, Friedrich, 6, 8, 239, 242–245, 273
Genius, 429–430, 460, 465
Gentz, Friedrich, 338
Gilligan, Carol, 480
Ginzburg, Carlo, 282–283
God: clarifying the concept of, 68–70; death of, 26, 377–378; and human freedom, 123–125, 134–135, 201; kingdom of, 126, 464, 493; and knowledge, 377–378; and reason, 361–362, 374
Goethe, Johann Wolfgang von, 497–498
Goeze, Johann Melchoir, 180
Goldman, Lucien, 481
Gottsched, Johann Christoph, 255
Governing, art of, 383–387
Göckingk, Leopold Friedrich Günther von, 241
Gramsci, Antonio, 279
Grotius, Hugo, 255, 264–266
Guardians, 58–59, 61, 63, 90, 130, 134, 136, 146–148, 199, 244, 270–271, 291–298
Guys, Constantin, 27

Habermas, Jürgen: on autonomy, 471, 509–512; on the colonization of the lifeworld, 279–280; critique of Gadamer, 19–20; on language and enlightenment, 30
Hamann, Johann Georg: as critic of enlightenment, 20, 28, 291–298; on Kant's *Critique of Pure Reason,* 298–301; theological views of, 301–303
Hamburger Correspondenten, 306
Hannibal, 206
Happiness: and enlightenment, 66, 71, 97–98, 334; and politics, 15, 88–90, 135, 195–197, 203–204, 207–208, 247; and virtue, 462–463
Hauschild, Johann Leonhard, 282
Hegel, G. W. F.: critique of enlightenment, 21–22, 29, 373–377, 389, 498–499; on faith and reason, 23, 310; on French Revolution, 335; history and reason in, 379–380, 409–411; on Jacobi, 312
Heidegger, Martin, 404, 426–428, 453–454, 466, 502
Heinicke, Samuel, 156
Heinzmann, Johann Georg, 263
Hellmuth, Eckhart, 24
Helvétius, Claude-Adrien, 156, 494, 495, 505
Hemsterhuis, Franz, 198–199, 303
Henrich, Dieter, 453–455
Herbert, Maria von, 475–476, 478–479
Herder, Johann Gottfried, 301, 321, 409, 443

Hertzberg, Ewald Friedrich von, 13, 175
Herz, Henriette, 319
Hobbes, Thomas, 195, 207, 266, 311, 351–353
Horace, 27
Horkheimer, Max, 20–25, 28–29, 271, 354, 403, 405, 471, 479, 508
Hölderlin, Friedrich, 319, 321–323
Human nature: and cognition, 129; enlightenment view of, 1, 332, 355–356, 493; judgments about, 108; reason and passion in, 193–194
Human sciences, 412–413
Humboldt, Wilhelm von, 237, 321, 409, 421, 497–498
Hume, David, 154, 266, 350, 437, 351
Husserl, Edmund, 388–389, 390
Hutchinson, Francis, 146
Hutten, Ulrich von, 215

Idealism: German, 20, 375, 454, 497; in Kant's *Critique of Pure Reason*, 158–159; and metaphysics, 404–405
Ideas: clear and distinct, 492; general, 154, 404; moral, 461–462; of reason, 155, 408, 410, 413, 421, 460–465; world of, 276
Illuminati, 240, 272, 276
Images, 403–404, 432–433
Imagination: and fear, 353–355; Kant's treatment of the, 428–437, 453–466
Immaturity [*Unmündigkeit*]: of citizens, 309; meaning of the word, 292, 346; and religion, 62–63, 302–303; self-incurred, 58–59, 146–148, 291–298, 340, 346–349, 368–371, 379–380, 386, 517. *See also* Maturity
Impartiality, 479–482
Index of Prohibited Books [*Index librorum prohibitorum*], 72–73
Individual: decline of, 360, 364–365, 375–380; freedom of, 22–23, 312; governing of, 383–384; worth of, 59, 408–409
Individuality: and autonomy, 497–512; romantic emphasis on, 323
Inquisition, 72, 74, 180, 372
Intuition, 154–159, 431, 442, 456–457, 461–462, 464–465, 527–528
Irwing, Karl Franz von, 239, 241, 244

Jacobi, Friedrich Heinrich: on enlightenment, 13, 313, 326; and Hamann, 300, 302; and Kant, 306, 310, 323–324; and Pantheism Dispute, 13, 306, 310–311; political views of, 12–13, 306–314; and Spinoza, 310–311, 313; and Wieland, 310–311, 314
Jaspers, Karl, 332, 403
Jerusalem, Johann Friedrich Wilhelm, 181
Jesuit Order, 169, 171, 178–180, 272
Joseph II, 66, 67, 71, 74, 99, 106, 173, 221, 306–307
Judaism, 7, 159, 184, 238, 301, 471, 530
Judgment(s): aesthetic, 521–532; analytic, 155–156, 457; freedom to communicate, 101–105, 107–112; and imagination, 454–460; impartiality in, 480; of the public, 92, 111, 256; reflective, 458, 521–523, 527, 530–531; synthetic, 155; of taste, 459, 462, 523

Kant, Immanuel: aesthetic theory of, 460–463; autonomy in, 489–492, 495–496; on categories, 456–458; cosmopolitan ideal of, 518–521; definition of enlightenment, 5–6, 16–17, 27, 29–30, 58–63, 145–148, 291–298, 340–341, 345–349, 368–372, 386–387, 480; on Frederick II, 295–296; and Frederick William II, 10, 259; on French Revolution, 14–15, 371–372, 463–464, 518–520; and Hamann, 291–303; on the imagination, 428–437, 453–466; and Jacobi, 306, 310, 323–324; on judgment, 454–460, 521–531; on madness, 449–451; on maturity and immaturity, 146–148, 491–498, 504; moral philosophy of, 480–483; on moral progress, 463–466; political theory of, 12, 15–16, 261–267, 340–341, 517–520; public and private use of reason in, 5, 148, 253–267, 295–298; concept of reason in, 154–159, 298–301, 406–409, 449–451; and skepticism, 323–324; and Swedenborg, 438–439; views on women, 474–480
Kierkegaard, Soren, 300, 401, 411, 421
Kittsteiner, Heinz, 279
Klein, Ernst Ferdinand, 4, 235, 238, 240–241, 243, 246–247, 272–273
Knigge, Adolf Freiherr von, 263, 276
Komarnick, Jan, 433, 440, 449, 460
Kraus, Christian Jacob, 293, 295–296, 298–300
Kroner, Richard, 306
Kuhn, Thomas, 413
Kyau, Friedrich Wilhelm Freiherr von, 115

Lang, Berel, 471
Language: and autonomy, 510; enlightenment and the refinement of, 50, 54, 271; and reason, 155–158, 299–300, 417–423, 448–449
Lavater, Johann Kaspar, 435, 447
Law(s): moral, 61, 124–127, 132–133, 202, 229–230, 488, 525–526; natural, 87, 222, 264–265, 362, 373–374, 385; obedience to, 176–178, 181–182, 218–219, 482; political, 125–126, 192–197, 201–202, 206–207, 228, 245–248, 308–314

Leibniz, Gottfried Wilhelm, 88, 333, 362, 432, 436
Lessing, Gotthold Ephraim, 3, 4, 7, 13, 191, 255–256, 307–308, 323, 349, 448
Leuschsenring, Franz von, 240–241, 247
Levin, Rahel, 319
Liberalism, 12–13, 337
Lindley, Richard, 500–501, 503
Literacy, 274, 281
Locke, John, 179, 362, 436, 491, 492
Louis XIV [King of France], 51, 173
Louis XVI [King of France], 2, 11
Luther, Martin, 117, 171, 180
Lyotard, Jean François, 399, 472

McCarthy, Thomas, 416
Machiavelli, Niccolo, 206–207, 314
MacIntyre, Alasdair, 20
Maimon, Solomon, 323–324
Makkreel, Rudolf, 458, 461
Mandeville, Bernard, 24
Mangold, Bernhard, 282
Marees, Simon Ludwig Eberhard de, 171, 181
Marx, Karl, 374, 377, 401, 411, 481, 531
Maturity [*Mündigkeit*]: and autonomy, 488–490, 492–497; enlightenment as, 345–349; fear of, 58–59; Kant vs. Hamann on, 291–303; and responsibility, 369–370, 380; thwarting of, 199, 313. *See also* Immaturity
Maus, Isaak, 282
Mayer, Johann Christoph Andreas, 241
Mayer, Johann Siegfried, 241
Mead, George Herbert, 415, 421, 512
Meaning, 389–390, 412–413, 420
Meisner, Heinrich, 241
Memmi, Albert, 279
Mendelssohn, Moses: correspondence with Kant, 441, 443; criticism of Jacobi, 307; definition of enlightenment, 2, 5, 271, 389, 493–494; political theory of, 12; role in Wednesday Society, 4–5, 238, 241, 244, 273
Metaphysics: demise of, 362–364; Kant on "dreams" of, 438–444, 465; and language, 155–157; and unity of reason, 399–423
Mill, John Stuart, 498, 502
Mittwochsgesellschaft. See Wednesday Society
Modernity: crisis of, 332–333; and subjectivity, 409–410
Monarchy: enlightened, 174–179, 223–224; limits on legislative power of, 62, 192–193; Prussian, 13, 99, 175; rebellions against, 219–220
Monday Club, 235–236
Montesquieu, 92, 321
Montgolfier, Joseph Michael and Jacques Étienne, 244
Moral sentiments, 56, 106, 229–230
Morality: and authority, 104; culture and, 222–223; enlightenment as threat to, 4–5, 377; improvement of, 49; vs. legislation, 107–108, 112; and taste, 459
Moser, Friedrich Karl von, 8, 9–10, 295
Moses, Claire, 473
Motherby, Elizabeth, 477
Möhsen, Johann Karl Wilhelm, 3–4, 236, 238, 240–242, 271–272, 277, 279
Möser, Justus, 192, 275, 310
Muller, Johannes von, 192, 306–307
Müller, Drost von, 520
Mündigkeit. See Maturity
Mysticism, 6, 464
Mythology: art and, 431–432; enlightenment and, 23–24, 355, 361–362, 365–366; metaphysics and, 401–403; romanticism and, 325

National Assembly (French), 21, 238, 241, 247
Nature: rational mastery over, 23, 333–334, 361, 363, 372, 450–451; scientific understanding of, 411–412, 491–492
Neology, 7, 13, 241
Newton, Sir Isaac, 442
Nicolai, Friedrich, 9, 237, 239, 241, 244, 256, 435
Nietzsche, Friedrich, 16, 24–27, 375, 377–380, 402, 404, 478–479, 505, 531
Nobility, rights of, 245–247
Novalis [pseud. Friedrich von Hardenberg], 317, 319, 320–323

O'Flaherty, James C., 300
Oaths, religious, 61, 133
Oberdeutsche Allgemeine Literaturzeitung, 11
Oeder, Georg Christian, 275
Oestrich, Gerhard, 279

Panopticon, 27–28, 31
Pantheism Controversy, 306, 310, 312
Parmenides, 401, 403
Pascal, Blaise, 377
Passion(s): mastery of, 199, 204, 207, 490–492, 496; reason and, 193–195, 362, 464, 478–479, 491–492; and rebellion, 215, 219–220
Patriotism, 92–93, 116, 246
Peace, 518–520
Peasantry, 115, 274, 275, 277, 280
Peter I [Tsar of Russia], 66
Petrarch, 25, 27
Philip II [King of Spain], 173
Philosophers: as advisors to rulers, 261–262; and masses, 67–68, 72; public role of, 386

Philosophy: demise of reason in, 359–367; and enlightenment, 170–172, 174, 179, 213, 380; metaphysical thinking in, 399–423; role of faculty of, 260; social influence of, 75, 91
Pierce, Charles Sanders, 415
Pietism, 274, 310, 335
Pistorius, H. A., 323–324
Pius VI, 307
Platner, Ernst, 32, 34
Plato, 145–146, 148, 314, 320, 361–362, 374, 378, 404, 415, 427
Plotinus, 399, 401–404
Pluralism, 364, 400, 403, 412, 418
Positivism, 364, 401
Power: arbitrary, 199–201, 205; coercive, 192–193, 197, 309–311; intellectual, 212–213; and knowledge, 392–398, 472, 508–509; will to, 368
Prejudice(s): defenses of, 17–19, 28–29, 244, 493; enlightenment critique of, 4–5, 7–8, 49, 55, 59, 82, 174–176, 181, 236, 270, 325; Frederick II's attack on, 90, 92–93; political, 177–179; religious, 169–174, 180, 183–184; Wedneday Society discussion of, 243–244
Progress: criticisms of, 330–333; and enlightenment, 177–178, 337–341, 370–372; modern ideal of, 333–337; moral and spiritual, 121–122, 133, 222, 463–464; scientific and technical, 4, 244, 359–363
Property: protection of, 196–197; rights of, 245–246
Prussia: as enlightened state, 175–177, 181, 294–295; freedom of expression in, 3–4, 6–11, 92–93; limitations on monarch in, 13; legal reform in, 245–248
Public: criticism by, 59–61, 82, 262–266, 371, 497; enlightenment of, 50, 59, 334–336; good, 12, 243–244; meaning of the term, 253–256; opinion, 120, 247; vs. private uses of reason, 5, 59–61, 63, 148, 253–254, 257, 295–297, 477; reading, 60, 116, 220, 263, 296, 335, 477, 496, 507
Publicity, 114–117, 262–267, 336
Pufendorf, Samuel von, 264–265
Putnam, Hillary, 414, 416
Putter, Johann Samuel, 99

Ranke, Leopold von, 339
Rationalism, 301, 363, 434–435, 437, 489
Rationality: communicative, 419–423; instrumental, 362–364, 375–377; problem of criteria of, 413–417; and rationalization, 388–391. *See also* Reason
Rawls, John, 499–500
Raynal, Guillaume Thomas François, 91
Reason: aesthetic, 155–158, 298–301, 325–326, 460–463; and autonomy, 490–492, 495–497; capacity for, 65–66, 70–71; and concepts, 155–158; and enlightenment, 66, 219, 242, 373–374, 450, 471–472; and enthusiasm, 462–466; and faith, 6–11, 12–13, 301–303, 310, 323, 336, 359–360; and freedom, 132, 226, 260, 310–311, 333–334, 371, 376–377; vs. the imagination, 426–451, 456–459; and individuality, 499–503; instrumental, 23–24, 270, 360–363, 456; and language, 155–158, 299–300, 417–423, 448–449; and passions, 193–195, 362, 464, 478–479, 491–492; and politics, 218–221, 242–244, 311–312, 314, 332–334, 338–339, 370–374; practical, 218, 226, 407–408, 464–465; and prejudice, 17–18, 29, 325; public vs. private use of, 5, 59–61, 63, 148, 253–254, 257, 295–297, 477; pure, 154–159, 300–301, 372–373; and religion, 171–174, 274, 312, 363; scientific, 350–351, 359–360, 362, 379–380; self-destruction of, 359–367, 374–381; and social contract, 194–195; and tradition, 16–18, 20, 155; unity of, 399–423; and women, 474–478
Reflection, 19–20, 101–105, 132, 410
Reformation, 183, 389
Rehberg, August William, 323–324, 338
Reimarus, Hermann Samuel, 7
Reinecke, Friedrich Ludwig von, 214
Relativism, 412–419
Religion: criticism of, 16, 155, 371, 350–352; deception and, 181–183; and enlightenment, 8–9, 60–63, 171–174, 179–184, 214–215, 302–303; Frederick II's view of, 3–4, 50, 62, 272; Frederick William II's view of, 7, 10, 259; and immaturity, 62–63, 302–303; and metaphysics, 402–403; reason and, 6–11, 12–13, 171–174, 274, 301–303, 310, 312, 323, 336, 359–360, 363; and society, 198–199; Woellner's edict on, 2, 9, 131, 237, 247, 259
Renaissance, 333, 385
Revolution, 11–15, 25–26, 59, 121–122, 177–178, 217–231, 330–331, 334–335, 337–338, 520
Riedel, Just, 254, 256
Riem, Andreas, 9, 10, 13–14, 494
Right(s): of authors and writers, 105–112, 257–258 (*see also* Freedom, of the press); of conscience, 99–100, 128–129, 175, 227, 372; cosmopolitan, 518–520, 527, 529–530, 531–532; and duties, 125, 136–137, 227–228; inalienable, 125, 128–130, 132–133, 136, 227–228, 247; of man, 90–91, 99–100, 106, 169–170; to privacy, 108–

Right(s) (*cont.*)
112; of property, 196–197, 245–247; to revolt, 14–15, 258, 263, 265; of rulers, 123–126, 265–266, 308–310, 385; to speak, 100–105 (*see also* Freedom, of expression); of women, 473
Ritter, Joachim, 22, 412
Romanticism: critique of enlightenment, 29, 317–326, 353; and individualism, 323, 490, 500–501
Rorty, Richard, 20, 414–416
Roth, Friedrich, 308
Rothe Zeitung, 278
Rousseau, Jean Jacques, 22, 25, 121, 266, 321, 346, 408, 431, 448, 456, 465
Royal Academy of Sciences (Prussia), 50, 235, 239
Ruge, Arnold, 337

Sack, Friedrich Samuel Gottfried, 7, 9
Salzman, Christian Gotthilf, 349, 494
Sartre, Jean-Paul, 390, 506
Schelling, Friedrich Wilhelm Joseph, 319–321, 323, 406, 454, 498
Schenda, Rudolf, 276
Schiller, Johann Christoph Friedrich von, 321–322, 356, 497–498
Schings, Hans-Jürgen, 436
Schlegel, A. W., 319–320
Schlegel, Friedrich, 317, 319, 320–321, 322–323, 519, 531
Schleiermacher, Ernst David, 319–320, 322, 323, 409
Schlözer, August Ludwig von, 263, 266
Schmid, Gottlieb Ernst, 240
Schneider, Eulogius, 263
Schopenhauer, Arthur, 25, 313
Schulze, G. E., 323–324
Schütz, C. G., 254, 477
Science: criticism of, 331; and nature, 411–412, 491–492; philosophy of, 412–414; and politics, 370; and power, 392–393; and reason, 350–351, 359–360, 362, 379–380; and society, 359–360, 364, 369, 390
Scipio Calvus, Gnaeus Cornelius, 206
Scotus, John Duns, 404
Secret societies, 3, 51, 82, 235, 272
Self: -activity, 223; -critique, 409, 416; -determination, 193, 198, 310, 474, 494–495, 502, 505; -discipline, 274; -expression, 498, 503; feminist conception of, 472–473; -identity, 402; independence of, 471, 510–512; -interest, 200, 229, 231, 248, 258, 496; -knowledge, 408; -mastery, 491–492; -mediation, 410; noumenal, 504; -objectification, 419; "punctual," 499; sense of, 313; -verification, 103–104; -understanding, 480
Selle, Christian Gottlieb, 239, 241, 246–247
Sensation, 154, 158, 174, 324, 433–434
Senses: pleasures of, 228; vs. reason, 450
Sensibility: concepts and, 157–158; cultivation of, 324; and judgment, 522; and reason, 462, 465; and understanding, 453–454
Sensus communis, 154, 504
Servitus, Michael, 180
Shaftesbury, Anthony Ashley Cooper, 1st Earl of, 436, 491, 493
Siebman, H. C., 240
Social contract, 6, 125–126, 128, 136, 194–195, 218, 311–312
Society: civil (*see* Civil society); corporate, 245–246; cosmopolitan, 5, 60, 257; modern industrial, 339, 359, 362–363, 400, 412; ranks in, 5, 242, 246
Socrates, 72, 82, 206–207, 403
Spalding, Johann Joachim, 7, 9, 181, 241, 493
Spinoza, Benedict de: interpretation of the Bible, 351–352, 356; and Pantheism dispute, 13, 323; on the passions, 195, 204; political theory of, 309–314
Spirit, 460–461; absolute, 410–411
State: administration of, 206, 418–419; benefits of freedom of expression for, 106, 135; conceptions of, 12–13, 245–248, 312–313; corporate, 245; enlightenment and, 174–179, 181–182; interest of, 196; and morality, 202, 221–222; relations between, 517–518
Stoicism, 490–492, 495–496, 506–507
Stollberg-Wernigerode, Ernst zu, 214
Stözel, Adolf, 241
Struensee, Karl August von, 240–241
Stuke, Horst, 494
Subject: and history, 19; relativity and finitude of, 391; philosophy of, 399, 413, 419–420; transcendental, 374, 406–408
Sublime: and the beautiful, 440–441; and cosmopolitanism, 531; dynamically, 521, 528; Kant's definition of, 524–525; mathematically, 521, 524, 527; in nature, 529–530
Superstition: Christianity and, 7–8, 74–75, 89–90, 172–174, 219, 282; enlightenment critique of, 11, 20–21, 24, 55–56, 115, 242, 272–273, 276, 350–351, 357, 361–362, 372, 494; false enlightenment and, 215; and human nature, 355–356; and morality, 207; of philosophy, 156; of rulers, 123; and sciences, 226
Svarez, Carl Gottlieb, 4–5, 10, 240–241, 243–248, 273
Swedenborg, Emanuel, 430, 433, 435, 437–449, 465